Development and Disability

For Betty

Development and Disability
Second Edition

Vicky Lewis

Blackwell
Publishing

350 Main Street, Malden, MA 02148-5018, USA
108 Cowley Road, Oxford OX4 1JF, UK
54 University Street, Carlton, Victoria 3053, Australia
Kurfürstendamm 57, 10707 Berlin, Germany

First edition published 1987
Second edition published 2003 by Blackwell Publishers Ltd, a Blackwell Publishing company

Library of Congress Cataloging-in-Publication Data

Lewis, Vicky, 1948–
     Development and disability / Vicky Lewis. — 2nd ed.
       p.   cm.
     Previous ed. published as: Development and handicap, 1987.
     Includes bibliographical references and indexes.
     ISBN 0–631–23466–7 (hbk : alk. paper) — ISBN 0–631–19274–3 (pbk. : alk. paper)
     1. Handicapped children—Development.   I. Title.
     RJ137 .L49 2002
     649′.151—dc21

                                                    2002006263

A catalogue record for this title is available from the British Library.

Set in 10 on 12 pt Sabon
by Ace Filmsetting Ltd, Frome, Somerset
Printed and bound in the United Kingdom
by TJ International, Padstow, Cornwall

For further information on
Blackwell Publishers, visit our website:
http://www.blackwellpublishing.com

Contents

Preface to the first edition

The idea for this book arose out of an option course I have taught to third year psychology undergraduates for a number of years. Before taking this course all the students have taken courses that examine the development of the non-handicapped child. The third year option course aims to take their understanding of development a stage further and asks what can be learned about the process of development by studying the development of children who are handicapped in a variety of ways. The suggestion that it should form the basis of a book came from Cathy Urwin, who contributed to the course in its early days.

Throughout the book, and indeed in its title, I have used the term handicap, rather than a term such as children with special educational needs. There are several reasons for this. The idea for the book was initially discussed with publishers in the late 1970s, and the title Development and Handicap emerged without any intention of it being used as the published title. At this time the term handicap was fairly widely used, whereas now there is a strong preference for less stigmatized terms, a preference which I personally support. However the title Development and Handicap stuck. This was partly because the children, whose development is described in this book, are different from normal children and from many children with special educational needs. In most cases the ways in which they are different can be specified in non-educational terms as well as in educational terms; for example, they may be different in the extent of their visual or auditory abilities, in their chromosomes, or in terms of a motor restriction. In contrast, the difficulties facing many other children with special educational needs can only be specified in terms of their actual needs. Although most of the children described in this book will have special educational needs, it is the specificity of their difficulties which has led me to include them, and to retain the label handicap. However, it is important to realize and remember that for many of them, although their difficulty may be a handicap in the sense that it prevents them from following a normal course of development, their difficulty may not prevent them from reaching levels of development similar to those reached by normal children. Thus a handicap may affect development, but not necessarily preclude it.

In writing the book I have deliberately chosen to use 'she' rather than 'he', except where I refer to particular individuals who are male. The vast majority of non-fiction books refer to individuals as 'he', unless they are developmental texts and want to refer to parents when 'she' is commonly used. While many authors, especially those writing books since the late 1970s, acknowledge that their use of 'he' does not preclude the female members of the species, I have chosen to reverse the situation. Thus in this text, unless otherwise specified, 'she' should be taken to refer to both male and female.

There are a great many people who have contributed to this book in one way or another and I am grateful to them all. It is impossible to mention everyone. However, there are some to whom I am particularly indebted. My first thanks go to all the children and families that I have worked with over the years. Their interest in my work and willingness to talk with me and share their problems and achievements have fostered my interest in the development of children with special educational needs. Peter Bryant supported my particular interest in children with Down's Syndrome, both while I was a doctoral student and afterwards. I am grateful to Cathy Urwin who persuaded me to embark on writing the book. More recently, Graham Gibbs has made many suggestions about ways of clarifying what I am trying to say and, more than anyone else, has encouraged me throughout. The many students who have taken my course at Warwick have contributed an enormous amount; I have learned a great deal from organizing the course and by talking with them. Dennis Bancroft, Jill Boucher, Glyn Collis and Ann Lewis read and commented on drafts of each chapter. Their comments were invaluable and spurred me on to finish the book. My thanks also go to Grant MacIntyre and Adam Sisman for their encouragement. Finally, Philip Carpenter has been a helpful, patient and supportive editor. I am grateful to you all.

Preface to the second edition

The years since the first edition of this book was published have seen an explosion in research examining the development of children with disabilities. This is reflected in the publication of huge numbers of books and new journals focusing on the development of children with disabilities, and the inclusion of papers on developmental psychopathology within journals which were previously mainly confined to studies of typically developing children. This upsurge in interest is very welcome and much of the research effort has taken our understanding of how various disabilities may affect development far beyond what could have been envisaged 20 or 30 years ago. A great deal more is known about the development of children with disabilities than when the first edition of this book was published.

This growth in knowledge is well illustrated with respect to autism, one of the disabilities included in this book, by Rutter's 1998 Emanuel Miller Memorial Lecture (1999) in which he describes four phases of research. The first two phases take us from the 1950s to the mid-1980s. The next phase covers the late 1980s and early 1990s, and the fourth phase the late 1990s. Given that the first edition of this book, *Development and Handicap*, was published in 1987, and covered research up to the mid-1980s, a second edition was clearly needed.

In writing this second edition I have retained the overall structure of the first edition because, in general, that seemed to work well. I have also retained the same disabilities as in the first edition with the exception of children with thalidomide. Understandably, there is no new literature on the development of children with thalidomide and so this section could not be updated. It therefore seemed best to omit it. Nevertheless, the study of children with thalidomide is important and of particular significance theoretically, and readers interested in this area should refer to the first edition. In place of studies of children with thalidomide I have included children with developmental coordination disorder. This large group of children has attracted much research interest since I wrote the first edition and their inclusion seemed very appropriate.

One of the problems with the structure of the first and now this edition is that different aspects of development are examined in separate sections. It is becoming increasingly clear that examining different aspects of development in isolation from other aspects can be misleading. This presents a problem of where to locate each piece of research when it has something to say about a number of different aspects of development. My solution is not ideal. I have located research in the section where it seems to have the most to contribute. However, I would urge you to read around each section. For example, if you want to discover about the perceptual abilities of children with Down's syndrome, you will find relevant information in the section on perceptual development, but also in other sections, particularly those on cognitive development and on social and emotional development.

Many events and people have contributed to the production of this second edition in a variety of different ways. The enthusiasm of undergraduates taking the third year option I used to teach at Warwick University on the development of children with disabilities eventually convinced me that the first edition made a useful contribution. I never cease to be surprised by how many of my colleagues within developmental psychology nationally and internationally made use of the first edition both in their teaching and as a resource for research. It clearly filled a gap in the market and in recent years I have often been asked when the next edition would be available. The massive increase in publications focusing on the psychological development of children with disabilities has made it clear that a second edition was essential to keep pace with changes in our knowledge and understanding of children with disabilities. In addition, my own research with children with disabilities and that of research students I have supervised have kept alive my firm belief that understanding the development of such children has a vital role to play in progressing our understanding of developmental processes and in developing ways of supporting development particularly of children with disabilities.

The Open University provided me with the space and time to write this second edition and I am particularly grateful to Alan Bassindale, Will Swann, and Peter Barnes. They, together with Chris Golding and other colleagues in the Centre for Childhood, Development and Learning, made it possible for me to devote myself to what turned out to be an enormous task. Colleagues in computing resuscitated my computer on several occasions, research assistants identified and requested relevant research papers, and library staff obtained obscure publications. Sarah Bird and other members of the editorial team at Blackwell Publishers were both patient and encouraging. I thank you all.

A number of colleagues suggested ways of updating the chapters in the first edition and others read and commented on drafts of the revised chapters. Their comments were invaluable and I thank them all: Jill Boucher, Tony Charman, Cliff Cunningham, Sue Gregory, Margaret Harris, Charles Hulme, Helen McConachie, Sarah Norgate, Beverley Plester, Gunilla Preisler, John Wann, Jennifer Wishart, Ingram Wright. In addition, many researchers responded generously to my requests for papers, both published and unpublished.

My family, especially Betty, Graham, Emma, and Josie, have continually reassured me that I could complete this edition and their love and faith in me has been wonderful. Without their encouragement I would never have kept at it. Finally, although they will never know it, I don't think I could have completed this book without the distraction, anxiety, and pleasure provided by Ali, Molly, and Mia.

I am grateful to all I have specifically mentioned and to many others who have given me ideas, encouragement, and support over the years.

chapter one

Children with disabilities

Introduction

Why study children with disabilities?

This book is about disability. It is also about development. However, it does not just describe the development of children with disabilities, rather it examines their development as a way of furthering our understanding of the processes underlying development in general. Any account of development needs to be able to explain how individual children without any disability develop and how, when there is a disability, the developmental process is altered. An understanding of how a particular disability may change the course of development in individual children can also illuminate our understanding of what may be going on in typically developing (TD) children; for example, it may alter the emphasis any explanation places on particular experiences, may help to clarify the relationship between different areas of development, and may throw light on prerequisites for particular developments.

This is not a new approach. A number of others, both before and since the publication of the first edition of this book, have pointed to the value of studying the development of children with disabilities for elucidating the developmental process (e.g., Adamson & Romski, 1997; Bishop & Mogford, 1993; Burack, Charman, Yirmiya, & Zelazo, 2001; Cicchetti & Beeghly, 1990; Cicchetti & Pogge-Hesse, 1982; Cicchetti & Schneider-Rosen, 1983; Cicchetti & Stroufe, 1978; Pérez-Pereira & Conti-Ramsden,

1999; Wode, 1983). Language development in children with a range of disabilities has attracted particular attention as a way of extending our understanding of how language develops.

However, there is a problem with drawing implications about developmental processes from studies of children with disabilities which was pointed out by Urwin (1983). Urwin, writing about the development of communication in blind children, argued that it is important to consider the development of children with a disability with care. If their development is underestimated, the role of disability in development may be overestimated. In studies of children with disabilities it is important to be sure that what we are looking at is genuine development and neither an artifact of the situation nor of our expectations of how a disability may influence the course of development. We also need to be certain that any conclusions we reach as to the role of a disability in development cannot be attributed to some other problem or difficulty.

This book is not only about theory. It is also considers the practical implications of studies examining the development of children with disabilities. Although the book examines the theoretical and practical implications in separate chapters, it is not intended that they should be seen as separate. A theoretical account which can explain the development of both TD children and children with disabilities is crucial for deciding how children with disabilities may be helped and in indicating what the priorities for help should be. Theory is also valuable as a way of guiding further research. Conversely, practical suggestions which are tried, and prove successful, can be a useful way of testing any theory. The theory must be able to accommodate the results of any intervention. However, it does not follow that the theory underlying a successful intervention necessarily explains how that development usually comes about. For example, behavior modification, based on learning theory, may be used successfully to teach some aspects of language to children with learning difficulties (LDs), but this does not mean that learning theory explains the language acquisition of TD children.

Terminology

The first edition of this book had the title *Development and Handicap* and in the Preface to that edition I outlined my reasons for using the term handicap both in the title and throughout the text. I have given this second edition the title *Development and Disability*. The original motivation for this change was to distinguish "handicap," "disability," and "impairment" following the classification proposed by the World Health Organization (1980). In this classification impairment was defined as "any loss or abnormality of psychological, physiological or anatomical structure or function," disability as "any restriction or lack (resulting from an impairment) of ability to perform an activity in the manner or within the range considered normal for a human being," and handicap as "a disadvantage for a given individual, resulting from an impairment or disability, that limits or prevents the fulfillment of a role (depending on age, sex, social and cultural factors)." The children whose development is the focus for this book are, according to these definitions, disabled rather than handicapped and therefore early on in writing the second edition I decided to use disability rather than handicap both in the title and within the text.

However, during the 1990s the World Health Organization set about revising their earlier classification. The outcome of this process is a revised system in which handicap has been dropped and disability retained as an overall term reflecting the interaction between individuals and the social and physical environment (World Health Organization, 2001). Nevertheless, despite the broadening of this definition it still seemed appropriate to retain the term disability in this book.

However, terminology goes beyond the use of disability and handicap. Increasingly, professionals and academics, as well as parents and families, have emphasized the importance of seeing the child first and foremost, rather than the disability. This has led to a shift in how children with particular disabilities are referred to. The convention which has been adopted is to use the phrase "children with Down's syndrome" rather than "Down's syndrome children," "children with autism" rather than "autistic children," "children with spina bifida" rather than "spina bifida children," and so on and I have used this phrasing throughout. I have also used the term "children with learning difficulties" rather than "children with a problem in learning" as proposed in the 2001 World Health Organization classification.

I have used the term "children with Down's syndrome" rather than "children with Down syndrome" (e.g., Cicchetti & Beeghly, 1990) and I shall refer to these children as children with DS. The justification for using "children with Down syndrome" has been that "children with Down's syndrome" may lead to the children being seen as an extension of the syndrome, rather than as themselves. It seems to me that this concern is overcome by the term "children with Down's syndrome" and, given that Down first identified the constellation of clinical features characteristic of children with Down's syndrome, I feel that the term Down's syndrome is still appropriate.

Although the strategy of putting the child first is widely accepted, in many situations it is not always particularly straightforward. Consider blindness. Should we say "children who are blind," "children with visual impairments," or "blind children"? Most children, who for educational purposes are considered blind, can see something and for this reason the term visual impairment is often used in preference to blind since the latter implies that the children cannot see. However, within this group it is important to distinguish between those who cannot see anything or only shades of light and dark and those who have enough vision to make out the shape and form of objects in their environment. The former are often described as children with profound visual impairments; the latter as children with severe visual impairments. In this book I have decided to use the term blind children, where necessary distinguishing between those with profound and those with severe visual impairments.

Like blindness, hearing loss is rarely total but varies from mild to profound. In addition, about 10% of deaf children have at least one deaf parent and a significant proportion of these families will be part of a cultural minority with their own distinct language – a sign language. The preference of this group is to be described as Deaf, with a capital D, just as any other cultural group label. In addition, this group perceive their deafness as a significant aspect of their identity and therefore argue that it should be given prominence. Thus, children with hearing impairments born to Deaf parents would be most appropriately described as Deaf children. However, children with hearing impairments born to hearing parents are not born into Deaf culture, although they may become part of it as they get older. It is therefore more appropriate to describe these children as deaf children. In this book I have chosen to use the term deaf children to refer to all children with severe or profound deafness, regardless of the hearing status of their parents.

There is also an issue of how to refer to children who do not have any disabilities, particularly when their development is being compared to that of children with particular disabilities. Obviously such children can be described as children without any disability. Some authors refer to them as normal children. However, use of the term normal implies that children with disabilities are not normal whereas in reality many aspects of their development may be very similar to children without a disability. In this book I have chosen to use the term typically developing (TD) children to refer to children who do not have any disability and whose development is following a normal trajectory. For consistency, I shall refer to the development of these children as typical.

How the book is organized

The book considers five disabilities: blindness, deafness, motor difficulties, Down's syndrome (DS), and autism. The development of children with each disability is described separately in chapters 2–6. Chapter 7 considers the practical implications of the studies discussed in previous chapters, and chapter 8 examines the theoretical implications of the studies. The remainder of this first chapter describes each of the disabilities, and discusses their incidence and causes. The final section of this chapter outlines some of the difficulties in studying children with disabilities. Readers whose main interest is in the psychological consequences of disability should move to the final section of this chapter. The remaining sections of this first chapter can be used as a reference source for details of the disabilities as and when required.

Some facts about disability

Blindness

Approximately 80% of children who are blind can see something, even though their vision may be very limited or restricted to only a small portion of their visual field (Webster & Roe, 1998). The nature of the vision that a child has is important because of its implications for development. For example, a child who has peripheral vision but no central vision will not be able to see what is straight ahead, but will be able to see things off to the side, as if holding opaque disks a short distance from each eye and looking straight at them. Such a child will be unable to read print, but may be quite mobile and run around freely. In contrast, a child with only central vision, as if looking through long tubes held up to each eye, may be very cautious in her movements but be able to read print. Yet another child may have vision which is blurred at all distances and positions, while another may be extremely near sighted. Both of these children are likely to move about cautiously, although the near sighted child may be able to read print and inspect objects visually if she holds them right up to her eyes. The child with blurred vision at all distances is unlikely to be able to do either of these things. Some of these differences in the nature of the blindness are characteristic of certain eye conditions which will be examined later in this section.

The method most commonly used for assessing how much and how clearly a person can see, or visual acuity, is the Snellen chart, the chart of letters or digits of decreasing size seen in most opticians, premises. This measures distance vision under controlled conditions. For a person with typical sight the Snellen reading will be 6/6 in metric measurement, or 20/20 in imperial measurement. This means that the person can see at 6 meters, or 20 feet, the letters she should be able to see at 6 meters, or 20 feet. If you have 6/12 vision this means that something that a person with 6/6 vision can see at 12 meters needs to be brought to 6 meters for you to be able to see it clearly. If you have 3/60 vision something which the typical eye could see at 60 meters would have to be brought 57 meters nearer, to a distance of 3 meters for you to be able to see it clearly. Beyond 3/60 vision, sight is usually measured by the distance at which the person can accurately count the number of fingers held up. Some blind people may not be able to perceive even fingers, but they may have some light perception. Light perception is similar to what a sighted person would see with her eyes closed when something solid is passed between a light and her eyes. Other blind people may not even have light perception.

Obviously the Snellen chart cannot be used with children who are not yet able to identify letters, or who can see very little. The visual acuity of such children can be assessed in various ways, for example, getting the child to match a letter on the chart to the corresponding letter on a card she holds, examining a child's visual response to black and white gratings composed of lines of specific widths which are moved in front of her eyes, or by recording the electrical activity in the visual regions of her brain when a visual stimulus is presented (for fuller descriptions see Teplin, 1995; Webster & Roe, 1998).

Although children's visual acuity is important, what they can do with the vision they have is more important. For example, two children may have 6/60 vision, but one be very near sighted and the other not. As a child gets older her visual efficiency may improve, although her acuity remains much the same, because she gets better at using the vision she has. In fact, the use which a child with a severe visual impairment makes of her residual vision may be an indicator of her intelligence, and of the sort of support and learning opportunities she has had. There are various scales which can be used to assess the school child's residual use of her vision, for example, the Barraga Visual Efficiency Scale (Barraga, 1970) and the Look and Think Checklist (Tobin, Tooze, Chapman, & Moss, 1978). Neither of these just measures what the child can see, but assesses the sense that the child makes of what she can see.

Legal definitions of blindness vary. For example, in the UK a person is defined as blind either if she has a central visual acuity of 3/60 or less in her better eye with correcting glasses, or if her central visual acuity is better than 3/60 and she has a peripheral field defect such that the widest angle that the visual field subtends is no greater than 20 degrees, that is, less than a 16th of the peripheral field. In the USA the legal definition is central visual acuity of 20/200 or less in the better eye with correction, equivalent to 6/60 metric, or a visual field of 20 degrees or less. In the UK partially sighted people are those with visual acuities between 3/60 and 6/60 in the better eye after all necessary medical or surgical treatment has been given and compensating lenses provided, whereas in the USA the range is 20/200–20/70 with correction, or 6/60 to about 20/60. However, in terms of education, a crucial question is whether the child can make use of materials which involve sight, such as print, or whether alternative methods need to be used, such as braille (e.g. Tobin, 1994).

Blindness is fairly infrequent and its incidence depends on the age of the population examined as well as the definition used. Many sighted people have never met a blind person, and those who have most probably know an elderly blind person rather than a blind child. The incidence of blindness in childhood also varies with age, since some children become blind, while others are born blind. It also varies with the country in which the child is born. Blindness is much more common in developing countries than in developed countries because a number of diseases which are fairly common in developing countries are associated with blindness. Most of these could be prevented. In the UK, it is estimated that about 10–20 per 10,000 school children, or approximately 25,000 children, have a visual impairment which has educational implications (Walker, Tobin & McKennell, 1992; Webster & Roe, 1998), although Teplin (1995) suggests a range of 2–10 per 10,000 children. Tirosh, Schnitzer, Atar, and Jaffe (1992) reported an incidence of 10 per 10,000 preschool children, with the incidence of light perception or less being 3 per 10,000, of acuity of 6/60 or less 4 per 10,000, and 3 children per 10,000 having visual acuities enabling independent walking and avoidance of large obstacles.

Visual impairments have many different causes (for a detailed summary see, for example, Webster & Roe, 1998), although in possibly as many as half the cases of blindness present from birth, that is, congenital blindness, the exact cause is unknown. Most children who have some form of visual impairment have something wrong with their eye or eyes. For example, in anopthalmia the eyes are actually missing. In retinoblastoma, a malignant tumor develops on the retina, the light sensitive cells at the back of the eye, and, if untreated by removal of the eye (enucleation) and radiation therapies, the tumor can spread along the optic nerve to the brain. The age of onset of the tumor varies, and can be inherited. Some of these children may be more able in certain areas than children blind due to other causes (e.g., Williams, 1968; Witkin, Oltman, Chase, & Friedman, 1971), although the exact nature and explanation of any superiority is not clear (Warren, 1984).

A common cause of blindness is congenital cataract, in which the lens of the eye is cloudy. If the opacity of the lens is very dense the lens may be removed and glasses provided, although the person's vision is still likely to be poor. This condition is sometimes inherited.

Another inherited condition is albinism and is the result of a partial or total lack of pigment from the eyes, and also from the hair and the skin.

The irises, that part of the eyes which is normally coloured blue, green, or brown, are usually very pale and, because the eyes cannot screen out bright light, these children are very sensitive to light, or "photophobic." The functioning of the retina may also be affected. Individuals with albinism can usually read print. They may also show nystagmus, a condition in which the eyes shift rapidly from side to side.

Congenital glaucoma is a further condition which is usually inherited. The normal eye is filled with fluids which are being produced and reabsorbed all the time. In glaucoma the outflow of one of the fluids, vitreous humor, is impaired and, as more is produced, pressure builds up and constricts the blood vessels which nourish the retinal cells. Unless the pressure is relieved surgically the retinal cells die, those at the periphery first, resulting in reduced peripheral vision.

In a further condition the eyes are oval rather than round and, because the lens cannot accommodate sufficiently, the image falls short of the retina, resulting in myopia, or shortsightedness. The more elongated the eye ball the greater the myopia.

A condition which results in peripheral vision is macula degeneration, where the light receptor cells in the central portion of the retina have failed to develop or have been destroyed by disease. If the mother contracts rubella (German measles) in the first three months of pregnancy, the baby may be born with cataracts and other problems, notably deafness.

In retinopathy of prematurity, or retrolental fibroplasia, small portions of the retina may be left intact. It is caused by an excess of oxygen, which may be administered at birth to premature underweight babies to keep them alive and to try to prevent brain damage. The oxygen excess causes the retinal blood vessels to grow abnormally, leading to retinal damage, although small portions of the retina may remain healthy.

In retinal dysplasia the retina fails to develop properly, resulting in little or no vision. This condition can be inherited.

In some children the visual impairment is due to neural damage, for example, optic nerve hypoplasia, atrophy of the optic nerve, or cortical brain damage. In optic nerve hypoplasia the optic nerve fails to develop properly in utero whereas in optic nerve atrophy the fibers become damaged, the extent of the child's vision depending on the number and location of the undeveloped or damaged fibers. Optic nerve hypoplasia is congenital and not thought to be genetic and, similarly, optic nerve atrophy is usually congenital but seldom inherited. In cortical visual impairment, often resulting from lack of oxygen at birth, the eyes are usually unaffected and the blindness is secondary to some brain malfunction. These children often have additional severe disabilities.

Some children may become visually impaired later on in their lives through direct injury or as a result of an infection such as meningitis, where the membrane covering the brain and spinal chord becomes inflamed. These children are said to be adventitiously blinded, and the visual experiences they have had, particularly if extensive, are likely to have implications for their developmental progress.

Deafness

When I think of deafness I immediately imagine two groups of people: those whom I assume cannot hear at all and who probably use a sign language I cannot understand, and the hard-of-hearing, commonly people who have gradually become increasingly deaf as they have got older. It is clear that deafness varies, and in fact the variation is much greater than my first two groups suggest. Deafness is, however, rarely total.

Deafness can vary in several ways. It is not just a case of how deaf someone is, but also the nature of the deafness: for example, can they hear high notes as clearly as low notes? This is important information because it has implications for learning to speak, for whether or not a hearing aid would be useful, and for education. It is also important as a background for understanding deaf children's developmental difficulties.

Deafness is graded along two scales. One is intensity which is measured in decibels (dB) or units of sound. The normal threshold for hearing pure tones is 0 dB. The second scale is frequency, measured in Hertz (Hz). The frequency range for the normal ear is from about 20–20,000 Hz, and the frequencies which are important for speech fall between 250 and 4000 Hz.

On the intensity scale, a loss of about 20–25 dB is hardly significant. Even up to 40 dB a person could hear speech if she listened carefully but, compared to a hearing person, she would be slower to notice that someone was speaking. A person with a loss of up to 55 dB could hear sounds but would have difficulties interpreting them, although a hearing aid might help. These people are described as partially hearing. By using a hearing aid it is usually possible to gain about 30 dB, and in certain cases more. Hearing aids are not really useful unless the hearing loss is greater than 40 dB. With smaller losses the gains in intensity that are possible using an aid are counteracted by the distortion which occurs. Aids are of most use for losses of 40–55 dB.

Losses of over 55 dB present increasingly severe problems: someone with a loss of 95 dB or more perhaps being able to hear a very loud noise close by, such as a pneumatic drill, but more on the basis of the vibration produced than the noise itself. People with losses over 95 dB are said to have profound hearing impairments (Powers, 1998). Usually a hearing aid will not be of any use, although it may help some, particularly when the loss occurs after some language has been acquired. In certain cases amplification is actually painful and so cannot be used: this is called loudness recruitment.

When measuring hearing it is necessary to find out if tones of different frequencies as well as intensities can be heard, since the pattern of intensity loss can vary over the frequency range. The pattern of loss is important as it can tell us something about what aspects of speech will be heard. This is because, although vowels and consonants are complex sounds made up of many different frequency components, they can be distinguished on the basis of frequency. The frequency components of vowels are concentrated below 1000 Hz while the frequency components of consonants tend to fall above 1000 Hz. A person with a high frequency loss will tend only to hear the vowel sounds of speech, and this makes speech very difficult to interpret. Being able to hear consonants is much more useful. In addition, consonants are about 15 dB quieter than vowels. This means that someone with a 55 dB loss across the frequency range will hear more vowels than consonants.

Hearing aids can raise the intensity of certain frequencies or reduce the intensity of others. This will be particularly useful for those with a greater loss of the high frequencies than of the low frequencies. By selectively reducing the amplitude of the lower frequencies, the frequencies characteristic of consonants will be made more salient and this will aid speech perception.

Since the late 1980s cochlear implants for children have become available in the UK normally as part of oral programs, although for children to be considered for a cochlear implant in Sweden they and their families must already be using sign language (Preisler, Ahlström, & Tvingstedt, 1997). A cochlear implant involves sound being picked up by a microphone worn behind the ear and transmitted via a speech processor through a thin wire to electrodes implanted in the cochlear, which then stimulate the auditory nerve. Cochlear implants have become quite common among profoundly deaf children and Power and Hyde (1997) indicate that about 50% of profoundly deaf children born in Australia between 1990 and 1993 received cochlear implants. If children are fitted at a preschool age some benefits have been seen in speech perception (e.g., Brinton, 2001; Geers & Moog, 1994; Harrison et al., 2001; Miyamoto, Kirk, Svirsky, & Sehgal, 1999; Svirsky, Robbins, Kirk, Pisoni, & Miyamoto, 2000; Tomblin, Spencer, Flock, Tyler, & Gantz, 1999). However, in my view, cochlear implantation is not justified for three main reasons: any benefits observed are small, equivalent to no more than a 15 dB advantage; implanted children will still experience significant difficulties in communication, socialization, and cognition (e.g.,

Preisler et al., 1997); and because of the ethical issues it raises (e.g., Hindley, 1997; Lane & Bahan, 1998).

Four categories of hearing loss are used within the educational system in the UK: mild 21–40 dB; moderate 41–70 dB; severe 71–95 dB; profound 96+ dB (Eatough, 1995). However, as far as educational provision is concerned the crucial factor is whether or not the child is able to process language auditorily.

Like blindness, there is a tremendous variety in the nature and extent of deafness, and from a developmental point of view it is especially important to be able to assess what each child can hear. Unfortunately it is difficult to make accurate hearing assessments of very young children, although there are techniques which can be used, some of which will be described later. In general, children who have at least one deaf parent and children who have profound bilateral hearing losses, that is losses greater than 95 dB in both ears, are identified in the first year, but children with hearing parents who have a smaller loss may go undetected for much longer, particularly since hearing parents may interpret their infant's heightened visual sensitivity as a response to environmental sounds and voices (Koester, Papoušek, & Smith-Gray, 2000).

The problem is not just one of detection but also one of how to measure the sorts of sounds children with hearing losses can hear. In the UK babies are routinely screened at 6–12 months. At this age hearing babies will respond to sound-making objects which are out of sight and to one side by turning their heads towards the sound. Babies who cannot hear will not orient to the sound. If sounds of different frequencies are used this can provide some idea of the nature of any hearing loss. However, care needs to be taken to ensure that the sound is the only cue to turn. Of course, a baby may not turn towards the sound for other reasons. She may have an attentional problem or some physical disability which prevents her making the head turn. Also, a child with a small hearing loss may turn quite accurately to the correct side, and therefore her hearing loss will go unidentified.

Although the head turn test is routine, there are methods which enable earlier screening of hearing, even within the first few days (see, for example, Green, 1999). However, these require specialized equipment which is not routinely available. In one, the baby lies in a cradle and her movements and heart and respiration rates are monitored by computer (e.g., Simmons, 1977). Tones of various intensities and frequencies are presented and any physiological reactions are noted. This sort of equipment can be used to identify babies who show abnormal reactions to sounds and their development can then be monitored very carefully. Another technique is the otoacoustic emission test which can be carried out while the infant is asleep. It involves an instrument making a short audible click in the outer ear canal. If there is no abnormality between the outer ear and the cochlea, the cochlea will produce a small echo which is detected by the instrument. The absence of an echo suggests there may be a problem which then needs further investigation. An even more elaborate technique, evoked response testing, records brain activity when sounds of varying intensities are presented.

Measurement becomes easier as children get older. Between about 18 months and 3 years children can be asked to do certain things, and the consonant and vowel structure of the requests and their amplitudes varied. Also, children's language may give a good indication of what they can and cannot hear.

Above 3 years a pure tone audiogram can be obtained. This is done for each ear and shows the intensity loss over the frequency range. The procedure requires that children indicate when they hear a tone, and to achieve this with young children you have to build up to it gradually so that the task is clear. In the first instance children might be taught to respond to the sight of a drum being beaten, then the drum is moved out of sight and beaten. Eventually pure tones are presented.

The number of children who are identified as having a hearing impairment increases with increasing age. There are two reasons for this. The first is that as children get older it is easier to identify a hearing loss, particularly if it is mild or moderate. Second, some children are not deaf when they are born, but become deaf later on. Kyle and Allsop's (1982) interviews with deaf 16–65-year-olds revealed that 72.6% were deaf at birth, 13.1% became deaf in the first 2 years, 8.6% between 3 and 5, and 6.8% became deaf after the age of 5. In the UK it is estimated that there are between 50,000 and 70,000 people who were born deaf, but 7,700,000 people with a hearing loss (Gregory, Bishop, & Sheldon, 1995). Davis, Wood, Healy, Webb, and Rowe (1995) reported that each year about 12 out of 10,000 children are born with a hearing loss of 40 dB or more, with about 4 having losses of 95 dB or more. In the USA it has been estimated that between 500,000 and 700,000 children have impaired hearing (Green, 1981).

Deafness seems to affect slightly more boys than girls although the difference is small. However, more deaf boys have additional disabilities – about 35% compared to 30% of deaf girls.

Deafness can be caused by damage to different anatomical areas of the ear, and the characteristics of the resulting deafness and time of onset vary. However, in about a third to a half of deaf children the cause is unknown, although Kyle and Allsop (1982) report that 54.9% of the deaf 16–65-year-olds they interviewed did not know the cause of their deafness, which in 79% was profound. However, since this figure is not based on medical records, it may be an overestimate.

The ear can be divided into three parts, the external ear, the middle ear, and the inner ear. The two main types of loss are conductive and sensorineural which result from pathology of, or damage to, the middle ear and the inner ear respectively. Sensorineural deafness is the more common and the more drastic. It involves damage to the sensory hair cells of the cochlea or the auditory nerve and is usually irreversible. In comparison a conductive disorder is seldom total and is usually reversible. It involves an air bone gap somewhere in the cavity of the middle ear which is spanned by three bones. Mixed conductive and sensorineural losses also occur, and in a few cases there is some central malfunction of the auditory pathways within the central nervous system.

A sensorineural loss can occur prenatally, perinatally, or postnatally. By far the most common cause of sensorineural deafness is genetic, probably accounting for 40–60%. In most cases it is carried by a recessive gene such that if both parents are deaf the child is four times more likely to be deaf than if only one parent is deaf. In fact, one or both parents of about 10% of deaf children are themselves deaf.

Children who inherit their deafness seldom have additional disabilities. Unfortunately, the remaining causes of sensorineural deafness often result in other problems as well. About a third of deaf children have at least one additional disability.

In the prenatal period the second main cause of deafness is maternal rubella, or German measles, which can also cause visual problems, central nervous system damage, and congenital heart disease. Rubella results in deafness in about 22% of children whose mothers contract it in the first 2 months of pregnancy. This is probably the most susceptible period because it is when the inner ear completes its development. Damage from rubella contracted by the mother later in pregnancy is relatively unlikely. Rubella accounts for about 10% of deaf children, but following the rubella epidemic in the USA in 1964–6 the figure rose to around 40%.

At the time of birth there are two main hazards, incompatibility between the rhesus factors in maternal and fetal blood, and cerebral anoxia, a restriction of oxygen to the brain. Together, these account for 10–20% of cases and often leave the children with multiple disabilities. The anoxia may be associated with prematurity and, compared to full-term babies, such children are four times more likely to be deaf.

The final group of causes of sensorineural deafness occurs postnatally and is due to bacterial infections of the central nervous system. Such children commonly have multiple disabilities. The main infection is meningitis which results in inflammation of the meninges, the covering of the brain and spinal cord. Less than 5% of children who contract meningitis become deaf, accounting for about 10% of the deaf population. The other, but less common, infection leading to deafness is encephalitis.

The main cause of conductive deafness is otitis media or middle ear infection which occurs and can reoccur in childhood. It seldom results in total deafness but because it may reoccur it can lead to fluctuating levels of hearing.

Finally, deafness can result from damage to the auditory pathways within the central nervous system. This may result from the mother being exposed to a teratogen during pregnancy.

Motor disability

I am going to concentrate on three motor disabilities: spina bifida (SB), cerebral palsy (CP), and developmental coordination disorder (DCD). The first two often involve a degree of brain damage, whereas definitions of the latter specifically rule out neurological problems. None of the three disabilities presents straightforward motor problems, and this is a difficulty when interpreting the findings and examining their implications for theory.

Spina bifida

Spina bifida literally means a divided or split spine. In the embryo the spinal cord originates from a flat sheet of cells. A groove forms along the length of this sheet and normally the cells on either side of the groove grow over and eventually meet, forming a tube, the neural tube. This subsequently differentiates into the brain and spinal cord, covered by skull bones and spinal vertebrae respectively. SB occurs if, during the second and third months of pregnancy, the cells fail to close over at some point along the groove, leaving the cord exposed at that point.

There are several different sorts of spinal damage of this type. In SB occulta the vertebrae do not fuse right over but the cord itself is usually undamaged and often all that can be detected is a slight bump in the skin somewhere along the spinal column. Since this rarely has any adverse effects on development I shall not be concerned any more with it. The other main type is SB cystica, subdivided into myelomeningocele and meningocele. Both are characterized by a sac-like cyst on the skin's surface which contains membranes and fluid which have escaped through the gap left by the unfused vertebrae. In myelomeningocele part of the spinal cord and attached nervous tissue protrudes through the gap, whereas in meningocele the spinal cord remains in its correct position and only the cord's covering, the meninges, and the fluid surrounding the cord, the cerebrospinal fluid, protrude into the cyst. Not surprisingly, myelomeningocele is by far the most serious of the two conditions, and unfortunately it is also the most common, accounting for about 85% of all cases of SB cystica.

SB can occur anywhere along the spinal column, although it is most common in the lower back, the lumbar region, where the vertebrae close over last. The lesion site is important since in myelomeningocele nerves which originate below the lesion will usually fail to operate their respective muscles, thus preventing movement. Nerves to the hips, legs, and bladder originate in the lumbar region. Below this in the sacral region nerves innervating the spincter muscles of the urethra and rectum originate. Thus, the primary problems in SB, particularly myelomeningocele, are those of incontinence (e.g., Lie et al., 1991) and paralysis of the legs. In a longitudinal study into adulthood Hunt (1990) found that survival was lowest and disability highest among individuals with a lesion above the 11th thoracic vertebra, whereas those with lesions below the third lumbar vertebra were most likely to survive and had most disabilities.

Unfortunately in many cases of SB hydrocephalus is an additional problem. This is associated with myelomeningocele in 85% of cases and usually results from an abnormality of the brainstem and cerebellum called the Arnold-Ciari malformation. This blocks the outflow of cerebrospinal fluid from the ventricles within the brain and unless the obstruction is bypassed by the insertion of a shunt to drain off the excess fluid the accumulated fluid exerts pressure on the brain and skull, causing damage to brain cells and head enlargement. A consequence of hydrocephalus may be LDs, which makes it more difficult to ascertain the effects of the motor problems on development.

SB has been known about for a long time, with descriptions as far back as 2000 BC. However, until about the 1960s, the majority of babies born with SB died shortly after birth, particularly those with severe myelomeningocele and associated hydrocephalus. These babies died for a variety of reasons, notably some infection of the central nervous system which attacked the exposed portion of the spinal cord, or as a direct consequence of the hydrocephalus. The reduction in the mortality rate was brought about mainly by advances in medicine. In the 1940s the development of antibiotic treatment enabled previously fatal infections of the central nervous system to be controlled, and this together with improved surgical expertise prevented the deaths of many children with SB. Another advance was the development in 1956 of a shunt to control the circulation of cerebrospinal fluid. This could be inserted in cases of hydrocephalus to drain off the excess fluid and direct it back into the blood system.

The incidence of myelomeningocele ranges from 10 to 50 of every 10,000 live births (Shurtleff & Lemire, 1995). In Britain the incidence of SB is about 20 for every 10,000 births. Based on a 25-year follow-up Bowman, McLone, Grant, Tomita, and Ito (2001) report that three quarters of children with myelomeningocele reach early adulthood. Slightly more girls than boys are affected, the ratio being around 1.3:1. The prevalence of SB varies in different parts of the world. For example, it has been reported as very low, 1 or 2 per 10,000 births, in certain black communities, whereas the incidence in Ireland is as high as 40 or 50 per 10,000 births. Prevalence also varies with maternal age, mothers under 20 and those over 35 being most at risk for producing a baby with SB, and mothers over 40 being most at risk for bearing a child with hydrocephalus. Families in social classes IV and V run a slightly greater risk, particularly if the mother is over 30 or if she has three or more children. Another seemingly odd finding is that more babies with SB are conceived between the months of April and June than at other times of the year in England, although there is no peak time for hydrocephalus (Rogers & Weatherall, 1976).

All these factors point to the possibility of some environmental cause and the mother's diet has come under scrutiny. The argument is that the mother's diet is likely to be poor if she lives in an industrial area, has little money to spend on food and many mouths to feed. The relationship with the month of conception is interesting since it suggests that it is early on in pregnancy that diet is crucial, when the neural tube is formed. In England, in spring and early summer, food is often expensive and of poor quality because the new season's vegetables are not yet available. At this time the mother's diet may be deficient in certain respects. Various dietary culprits have been considered in the past, ranging from blighted potatoes to excessive tea drinking, but vitamins have attracted most attention. In 1981 Smithells et al. reported that the likelihood of a woman who had already given birth to a baby with a neural tube defect having another child with a similar disability was much reduced if the woman took additional vitamins for a month before conceiving and for two months after. This finding has support from other groups of workers (e.g., Holmes-Siedle, Lindenbaum, & Galliard, 1982), and has obvious practical implications.

Despite the attractiveness of this explanation it seems unlikely that it is the whole answer. First, by no means all women living in poor conditions, with large families to support on low incomes and who conceive when fresh food is in short supply, have children with neural tube defects. Second, some babies with SB are born to women in advantageous circumstances. Third, women who have already had a child damaged in this way run a much greater risk of having another child with similar problems than the rest of the population. Between 3% and 6% of parents with a child with SB conceive a second child with the same disability (e.g., Carter, 1974). It seems likely that there is some complex genetic explanation, such that certain mothers (or fathers) are predisposed to produce a child with neural tube damage given certain environmental conditions, in particular depleted vitamin supplies.

Unlike SB, which is always congenital, hydrocephalus can be either congenital or the result of some postnatal infection, notably meningitis, where the membrane covering the brain and spinal cord becomes inflamed.

Cerebral palsy

CP has been described as "a disorder of movement and posture resulting from a permanent, non-progressive defect or lesion of the immature brain" (Bax, 1964). As well as motor behavior problems, which can range from barely detectable to almost complete physical helplessness, there may be any or a combination of difficulties in vision, hearing, speech, and intellectual ability. Between a third and two thirds of children with CP may also have fits. So even though two children may both have CP the differences between them may be much greater than their similarities. This makes it particularly difficult to draw conclusions about the effects of these children's motor difficulties on development.

Nevertheless, it is the motor difficulties that define this group and several different types of motor problems have been identified. Three quarters of people with CP experience spastic movements due to a failure of the muscles to relax so that their movements seem stiff and rigid as a result of damage to the motor cortex. An arm may be held pressed against the body with the forearm bent at right angles to the upper arm and the hand bent against the forearm. The fist may be clenched tightly. The leg is often bent at the knee and rotates inwards from the hip. The person may walk on the outside of their foot, resulting in a scissored gait if both legs are involved. Balance may be poor because of the way that their weight is distributed. Not all limbs are necessarily affected, although they are in about a third of people with spastic CP. The equal involvement of all four limbs is known variously as quadraplegia, tetraplegia, or double plegia. About a quarter of people with spastic CP have hemiplegia involving a leg and arm on one side of the body. In diplegia, accounting for 20%, all the limbs are involved, but the legs are more affected than the arms. In 18% only the legs are affected, known as paraplegia. In a very small proportion, less than 2% in each case, the arms are more affected than the legs (bilateral hemiplegia), three limbs are affected, usually two legs and an arm (triplegia), or only one limb is affected, usually a leg (monoplegia).

The second largest group have athetoid CP. As a result of damage to the basal ganglia people with athetoid CP have an excess of uncontrollable movements which interfere with their normal body movements. Their movements seem to be of a writhing, lurching nature and their head is often drawn back. Uncontrolled facial grimacing and dribbling is common. Although the lack of motor control is usually generalized to the whole body, in a few people only certain limbs are affected. These are then described by the classification used for spastic CP.

A much smaller group have ataxic CP. This condition is due to cerebellar damage and results in poor coordination of movement and disturbed balance. The person may appear clumsy and unsteady and have difficulty locating themselves in space. They may rush downhill and fall over, but come to a standstill when walking uphill.

The remaining people with CP have a variety of motor problems ranging from rigidity of the muscles to complete floppiness or some mixture of the conditions described above.

CP is probably slightly more common than SB with estimates ranging from 15 to 25 babies per 10,000 babies born alive. Boyle, Decouflé, and Yeargin-Allsopp (1994) indicate a prevalence for children and adolescents with CP in the USA of 25 per 10,000. Marginally more boys than girls are born with CP.

Unlike SB which is always congenital, CP can develop after birth. Postnatal causes including meningitis account for about 10% of children with CP. Other postnatal causes of CP include encephalitis, and various sorts of trauma, such as fractures of the skull, brain tumors, and restrictions of the blood supply to parts of the brain. But the main causes of CP occur prenatally or perinatally. Rhesus incompatibility between the blood of the fetus and the blood of the mother and subsequent hemolytic disease of the newborn used to account for 10% of these children, especially those with athetoid CP, but this has now largely been prevented by giving the baby a blood transfusion shortly after birth. Maternal rubella is sometimes implicated, but lack of oxygen, or anoxia, at birth probably accounts for up to 10% of children with CP (e.g., Nelson & Ellenberg, 1986). This can occur for a variety of reasons which may be associated with prematurity, low birth weight, or a lengthy labor although it has been suggested that children experiencing asphyxia at birth already have a disability which causes the asphyxia (e.g., Miller, 1989). This has obvious practical implications for prevention.

There have been suggestions that certain mothers may be more likely than others to produce fetuses with disabilities. These come from reports of mothers of children with CP having had more miscarriages or still births than mothers of TD children. For example, Illingworth (1958) states that mothers of children with CP have a 35% greater loss than mothers of TD children. This has led to some suggestions, as yet unsubstantiated, of a genetic contribution. However, Hewett (1970) questions this raised incidence, reporting that 15% of the mothers in her study had a history of miscarriages and still births compared to a reported 22% among women who mostly gave birth to TD children (Newson & Newson, cited in Hewett, 1970). Also CP seldom reoccurs in the same family. In Hewett's own study, 14 children (8%) had a TD twin, an unlikely finding if there is a large genetic contribution.

Developmental coordination disorder

Children with DCD have difficulties carrying out daily activities requiring skilled movements and motor coordination such as tying shoelaces, fastening buttons, catching and throwing balls, using scissors and cutlery, riding a bicycle, playing sport, writing. These are greater than expected given their age and intelligence, affect academic achievement, cannot be explained by any neurological or medical condition, and persist into adolescence (e.g., Geuze, Jongmans, Schoemaker, & Smits-Englesman, 2001). However, the absence of any neurological impairment in all children with DCD is questioned by Jongmans, Mercuri, Dubowitz, and Henderson's longitudinal study (e.g., 1998) which found that significantly more 6-year-olds who had DCD and were premature had abnormal brain scans shortly after birth than children who were premature but did not present with DCD.

Children who have these difficulties have been assigned various labels over the years, including clumsy child syndrome, developmental dyspraxia, developmental apraxia and agnosia, perceptual-motor dysfunction, sensory integrative dysfunction. However, in 1994 it was agreed that the term children with DCD should be used (e.g., Polatajko, Fox, & Missiuna, 1995), although there is still debate about whether there are differences between children with DCD and children previously given some of the other labels (e.g., Henderson & Barnett, 1998; Missiuna & Polatajko, 1995). The motor problems found in children with DCD are also seen in children with a variety of other difficulties, particularly those with poor attention and hyperactivity (e.g., Kadesjö & Gillberg, 1999; Landgren, Kjellman, & Gillberg, 1998; Piek, Pitcher, & Hay, 1999), dyslexia (e.g., Kaplan, Wilson, Dewey, & Crawford, 1998), language impairments (e.g., Powell & Bishop, 1992), and LDs (e.g., Martini, Heath, & Missiuna, 1999). However, as far as it is possible, I shall restrict myself to children with DCD without other difficulties, other than those resulting from the motor problems.

It is generally agreed that children with DCD are heterogeneous with respect to the problems they have. Dewey and Kaplan (1994) have suggested that three main groups can be distinguished: problems with balance, coordination, and everyday activities such as combing their hair and writing; problems of planning and carrying out a sequence of motor actions; problems in all areas.

Given the nature of the difficulties children with DCD are seldom identified before the age of 4 or 5 years. The incidence varies between studies, primarily because there is no agreed criterion for DCD in terms of performance on a specific test of motor skill. Nevertheless, most studies identify an incidence of around 500–1,000 per 10,000 children. For example, Kadesjö and Gillberg (1999) examined over 400 children aged 6–8 years living in a particular area of Sweden and attending mainstream school. Twenty children (4.9%) were identified as having severe DCD based on a test of their gross and fine motor skills, and 18 of these were boys. A further 35 children (8.6%) were identified as having moderate DCD and 29 of these were boys. Almost half of these children showed evidence of severe to moderate symptoms of attention deficit hyperactivity disorder (ADHD). In another report of this study, Kadesjö and Gillberg (1998) indicated that when the children with ADHD were removed from the sample, 2.7% of the children had severe DCD, and 4.6% had moderate DCD, with an overall ratio for boys to girls of 5.3:1.

A much higher prevalence was reported by Piek and Edwards (1997) in Australia for 171 children aged 9–11 years in mainstream schools. Using the Movement Assessment Battery for Children (Henderson & Sugden, 1992) which assesses manual dexterity, ball skills, and balance, 14 children were identified with severe DCD (8%) and a further 18 (10%) had moderate DCD. Piek and Edwards reported that no children with behavioral problems were included, which implies that children with attention difficulties were excluded. It is therefore particularly surprising that they identified a much higher incidence than Kadesjö and Gillberg. A further difference between these two studies is that in Piek and Edwards' study only 17 (53%) children with DCD were boys.

These two studies indicate the difficulties which arise when different studies use different tests and when there is no agreed definition for what constitutes either severe or moderate DCD. Thus, neither the *Diagnostic and Statistical Manual of Mental Disorders*–IV (DSM-IV, American Psychiatric Association, 1994) nor the *International Classification of Diseases* 10 (ICD-10, World Health Organization, 1993) provides quantifiable definitions. Until definitions are agreed, the incidence of DCD will vary between studies. Nevertheless, these two rather different studies make it clear that the prevalence of children with DCD is fairly high, even when children with additional difficulties are excluded.

The cause of DCD is not known and it may be that DCD includes a number of discrete motor disorders, each with its own cause. Kaplan et al. (1998) argue that because DCD is often associated with either ADHD or reading difficulties or both, these difficulties reflect atypical brain development. They hypothesize that one or a number of factors adversely influence brain development and the effects of this on the development of motor and other skills depends on the timing, location, and extent of the disruption to brain development. Support for atypical brain development comes from Jongmans et al. (e.g., 1998).

Down's syndrome

The recognition of DS is usually attributed to J. Langdon H. Down (1866), although there are earlier reports of individuals who fit the category (e.g., Esquirol, 1838; Séguin, 1846). However, after Down's original paper there were many reports which confirmed his observations. These reports based their diagnosis on a number of distinct clinical features.

A well-known clinical feature of DS is the slant and shape of the eyes, which resemble those of people of oriental origin. The top of the head of people with DS is flatter than that of people without DS, and their heads are shorter from front to back. The nose is often small with a flattened bridge and the nostrils point forward. The tongue is usually furrowed and becomes increasingly so as individuals with DS get older, and their teeth, which often appear later than in TD children, are frequently irregular. The ears too may be different, often small, and in particular the lobes may be reduced in size or even absent.

The hands have attracted much attention. They are typically broad with short fingers, and the little finger is likely to be small and crooked and with only one crease. In many people with DS there is a characteristic fold across the palm called the four finger crease or simian line. It has been reported that the joints are hyperflexible. A further well-known characteristic is a wide space between the first and second toe.

A clinical diagnosis of DS is made if an individual has learning difficulties and four or more of the above characteristics. However, the physical appearance of children with DS, as rated by teachers, is not related to the children's mental age, academic achievements, self-sufficiency, number of behavior problems, or social life (Cunningham, Turner, Sloper, & Knussen, 1991).

It is no longer necessary to rely entirely on clinical features for a diagnosis. DS is associated with distinct chromosome patterns which can confirm a clinical diagnosis. The chromosome abnormality was not identified until 1959, although Mittwoch in 1952 concluded that people with DS have 24 pairs of chromosomes. At this time the normal complement of chromosomes was unknown, but a few years later it was reported to be 23 pairs (Tjio & Levan, 1956). These pairs are distinct and, with the exception of two chromosomes determining the individual's sex, they are assigned numbers in order of decreasing chromosome size from 1 to 22. Pairs of chromosomes are assigned to groups as follows: A, pairs 1–3; B,

pairs 4 and 5; C, pairs 6–12; D, pairs 13–15; E, pairs 16–18; F, pairs 19
and 20; G, pairs 21, 22, and the sex chromosomes. Mittwoch was later
shown to be correct in terms of DS being genetic in origin, but incorrect in
the actual number of chromosomes present.

The most common chromosomal aberration resulting in DS is an additional chromosome number 21 (e.g., Jacobs, Baikie, Court Brown, & Strong,
1959). This karyotype is variously labelled standard trisomy, trisomy 21,
or autosomal trisomy G, after the group label, and accounts for about 95%
of all people with DS. Gene mapping studies have indicated that 225 genes
are located on chromosome 21, the additional genetic material involved
amounting to around 1–1.5% of the total human genome (Hattori et al.,
2000). Identifying the functions of the different genes on chromosome 21 is
an important area for future research (e.g., Sinet, 1999).

Approximately 3% of people with DS have a translocation. Here, the
major part of an additional chromosome of the G group is fused onto the
major part of another chromosome of the same group or the D group.
These two karyotypes are usually referred to as G/G and D/G
translocations, respectively, and they each account for about 1.5% of people with DS. Since two chromosomes have been fused there are 46 chromosomes in each cell as opposed to 47 in the standard trisomy. In some
cases of a translocation, a parent carries the translocated chromosomes.
This parent will not have DS, but since two chromosomes are fused together they will only have 45 chromosomes. The remaining 2% of people
with DS have two or more different cell types, one of the cell types having
a DS karyotype and the remainder one or more other karyotypes. A combination of cells with different karyotypes is known as a mosaic.

The discovery that DS is chromosomal in origin led to the development
of prenatal screening tests, with mothers found to be carrying a fetus with
DS being offered terminations (e.g. Fortuny, 1999). The best known test
is the amniocentesis where a sample of fluid surrounding the fetus is removed and the chromosomes of the fetal and maternal cells in the amniotic fluid examined. Such prenatal testing is not routine but is usually
restricted to women who have an increased risk of having a child with
DS, for example, older women and women who have particular levels of
substances such as alphafet protein in their blood.

DS is often associated with medical problems. Cunningham (1986) reported that medical problems were diagnosed in the first year for 43% of
181 children with DS, especially cardiac malformations and hearing loss.
Sixteen percent of the children had mild cardiac problems and a further
16% had severe problems. Heart disorders are often a cause of death of
babies and young children with DS. Thus, Frid, Drott, Lundell, Rasmussen,
and Anneren (1999) reported that whereas 44% of children with DS and
a congenital heart defect died in the first 10 years, less than 5% of those

without a heart defect died in the same period. Hearing loss is also quite common, with as many as two thirds having a significant loss which may fluctuate over time (e.g. Cunningham & McArthur, 1981; Kehoe, 1978).

Many children with DS also have visual problems. Leonard, Bower, Petterson, and Leonard (1999) found that more than three quarters of a group of school-age children with DS had eye conditions and were five times more likely to wear glasses than other children. In an ongoing longitudinal study J. M. Woodhouse and colleagues have reported that children with DS differ from TD children with respect to visual accommodation, squints, visual acuity, and refractive errors (e.g., Woodhouse et al., 1997; J. M. Woodhouse et al., 1996). Thus, only 4 out of 49 children with DS aged between 3 months and 5 years showed normal accommodation, and about a quarter had squints. Although all the children under 2 years had visual acuity within the normal range, the improvement seen in TD children beyond this age was not observed (J. M. Woodhouse et al., 1996). This longitudinal study also demonstrated that whereas in the first year of life 25–30% of infants with DS and TD infants have refractive errors, from 1 year such problems are seen in less than 10% of TD children compared to over 50% of children with DS (Woodhouse et al., 1997). Clearly, it is important to take account of the auditory and visual problems when we examine the development of the child with DS, although Woodhouse et al. (unpublished) found no relationship between accommodation error and developmental level in 34 children with DS aged 1–7 years.

Estimates of the incidence of DS vary, but there is agreement that it is the most common form of learning difficulty, accounting for about one third of all children with severe learning difficulties (Wishart & Duffy, 1990), with an incidence of 12–13 in every 10,000 live births (e.g., Torfs & Christianson, 1998). Wishart (1988, 1993) estimated that each year about 100,000 babies with DS are born worldwide, with 7,000 being born in the United States and 1,000 in the UK. The incidence of DS has been explored in two ways: by surveying large populations, often relying on clinical rather than chromosomal diagnosis, or by carrying out chromosome studies of consecutive liveborn babies. A survey of 19 regions of 11 European countries between 1980 and 1986 reported that out of almost 1.5 million live and still births, almost 14 per 10,000 had DS, although the prevalence in different areas varied: the number of babies born with DS ranged from 5.8 per 10,000 in Odense, Denmark to 19.8 in Galway, Ireland (Dolk et al., 1990). It is very likely that the number of children with DS who are conceived is much higher, since it is estimated that somewhere between 60% and 70% of all trisomic 21 fetuses abort spontaneously early in pregnancy (e.g., Lindsten et al., 1981), and a number will be terminated following prenatal diagnosis.

DS occurs in all populations and social classes and it is often reported that more boys than girls have DS. Thus, Cunningham (1986) reported that 55% of 181 babies with DS were boys, 34% were in families in social classes I and II, 38% in III and 26% in IV and V. The sex difference in DS becomes more marked with age since girls with DS have a higher mortality rate in the first few years of life than boys (Scully, 1973).

The prevalence of DS in the population declines with age since individuals with DS have a greater risk of dying, especially in childhood, than TD individuals. Thus, Sadetzki et al. (1999) reported that infant mortality rates for DS in Israel were 24 times higher than in the general population in the 1980s. Among Cowie's (1970) sample of 81 babies with DS, 13 (16%) had died before the age of 2 years, 8 (10%) within the first 17 weeks. Cunningham (1986) reported that around 10% of 181 children with DS had died by the age of 2 years.

One reason for this high mortality is the prevalence of congenital heart disease. A second is that people with DS are more likely to get infectious diseases than TD people, and more likely to die as a result of some infectious respiratory disease (Øster, Mikkelsen, & Nielsen, 1975). A consequence of this is that, with the increasing availability of drugs to combat infection, people with DS are living longer now than in the past (e.g., Carr, 1994). Carr pointed out that in 1929 the life expectancy of people with DS was estimated as 9 years, in 1947 as 12 years, whereas reaching 60 years is no longer unusual. Nevertheless, despite improved medical care, people with DS are still more likely to die at a younger age than TD people.

The incidence of DS increases with maternal age. This relationship between maternal age and DS has been confirmed many times. Lindsten et al. (1981) report an incidence of 10 per 10,000 live births for women under 28; 10–20 per 10,000 for women aged 29–33; 20–30 per 10,000 for mothers aged 34–36. By 40 the incidence had jumped to 114.6 per 10,000 births, and at over 40 the incidence was 470.6 per 10,000.

For the majority of people with DS the factor(s) causing the chromosomal abnormality is obscure. As early as 1883 Shuttleworth argued that they were unfinished children whose development for some reason was incomplete. Sutherland in 1899 pointed to syphilis, and Down's son (R. L. Langdon-Down) in 1906 pointed to familial tuberculosis. None of these suggestions has had any support and all have been discarded. Other suggestions which have been similarly unsupported include maternal stress, parental alcoholism, thyroid deficiency, and a small amniotic sac.

The discovery that DS is genetic in origin led to an increasing search for the cause. Although Waardenburg as early as 1932 suggested that DS might be due to nondisjunction or failure of the chromosomes to separate during the formation of the ovum or sperm, which has since been confirmed, it is still unclear why this might occur (Epstein, 1999). In a very few people with DS, the cause will be the inheritance of a translocation, although the mechanism by which the parent acquires the translocation is unknown.

Autism

Autism is not new, although it has only been acknowledged as a condition since the early 1940s. One of the earliest accounts of a child who is now thought to have had autism was by Itard in 1801/7 (see 1964). Itard described a boy deemed to have been raised by wolves who has become known as the wild boy of Aveyron. This boy, Victor, was found at the age of about 10 or 11 living in a wood. Itard's description of Victor makes it quite clear that today he would have been diagnosed as having autism.

Kanner was the first person to attempt to classify systematically the behavior of children with autism in 1943. In this paper he provided detailed case studies of eight boys and three girls and extracted about 10 features, although in a later paper with Eisenberg (1956) five separate areas were identified: a profound lack of affective contact with other people; an obsessive desire for things to be kept the same; a fascination with objects; communication difficulties; good cognitive potential. Kanner also stressed that the symptoms must be present from early childhood.

Over the years, aspects of Kanner's characteristics have been challenged. There have been two main challenges, one concerning the intelligence of the children, and the other concerning the primary symptom. Kanner's conclusion that these children were of good cognitive potential was based on observing that they usually look normal and intelligent and often have intelligent professional parents. In addition, he observed that children with autism are often exceptionally good at something, like remembering all the items on a shopping list, or a nursery rhyme after only one hearing. He assumed that this must reflect an underlying intelligence. However, it is now realized that you do not have to be equally good or bad at everything, and that it is possible for children with learning difficulties to be good at some things. The current view of autism is that the majority have learning difficulties, which are often severe, and that in some children these difficulties coexist with isolated skills.

The second challenge to Kanner's original proposal has been to question which behaviors are most important, or primary, to the condition. Kanner held that the absence of any emotional response to people was of fundamental importance, together with an insistence on things staying the same. One of the problems with this position is that these behaviors cannot account for the other behaviors which go to make up the condition. As we shall see in chapter 6, others, notably Baron-Cohen (e.g., 1992), Hobson (e.g., 1993), Tager-Flusberg (e.g., 2001), Ozonoff and colleagues (e.g., Ozonoff, Pennington, & Rogers 1991a), Hughes and colleagues (e.g., Hughes, Russell, & Robbins 1994), and Frith and Happé (e.g., 1994) have made a number of very specific, although different, proposals concerning the basic impairment in autism. Hobson and Tager-Flusberg argue for the primacy of early social difficulties, whereas the other accounts emphasize different cognitive mechanisms.

Nevertheless, most of Kanner's clinical observations have stood the test of time. Thus, the criteria for autism in the *Diagnostic and Statistical Manual of Mental Disorders* (DSM-IV, American Psychiatric Association, 1994) and the *International Classification of Diseases* (ICD-10, World Health Organization, 1993) are based on impairments in reciprocal social interaction, impairments in verbal and nonverbal communication and imagination, and a restricted repertoire of activities and interests. In addition, autism is commonly associated with structural and functional brain abnormalities (e.g., Bailey et al., 1998a; Deb & Thompson, 1998; Rumsey & Ernst, 2000), with as many as a third of children with autism having particularly large heads (e.g., Fidler, Bailey, & Smalley, 2000; Miles, Hadden, Takahashi, & Hillman, 2000; W. Woodhouse et al., 1996) which may be most marked in infancy and early childhood (Courchesne et al., 2001), although Fombonne, Roge, Claverie, Courty, and Fremolle (1999) noted that some may have especially small heads.

Despite all this, reaching a diagnosis of autism is not straightforward. This is because the nature and extent of the behaviors that contribute to a diagnosis of autism vary considerably between children. In addition, unlike some developmental disabilities, such as DS, there is no single definitive characteristic of autism which is common to all children who are given this diagnosis, although recent advances in genetics (see page 33) indicate that genetic markers may be identified in the near future. Consequently it is inappropriate to refer to autism as a syndrome (e.g., Boucher, 1998). Autism has also been described as a constellation of behaviors which vary in severity from mild to severe (e.g., Wing, 1988). This continuum account accommodates the fact that although all children with autism have impairments in social interaction, communication, and creativity, they vary in the extent of their difficulties in each of the three areas. Thus, one child might present with severely impaired social and communicative behaviors but relatively few repetitive stereotyped mannerisms, whereas another might have extreme difficulties interacting socially and highly repetitive and stereotyped behavior, but her communication skills might be quite good.

In DSM-IV (1994) autism is one of five disorders included under the general heading of pervasive developmental disorders (PDD), although there has been controversy over the use of this term (e.g., Gillberg, 1991; Happé & Frith, 1991; Volkmar & Cohen, 1991). The other disorders included within PDD are Asperger syndrome (AS), disintegrative disorder, Rett disorder, and atypical autism or pervasive developmental disorder not otherwise specified (PDD-NOS).

In reality it is often difficult to assign children to one disorder rather than another with certainty. Thus, while Mahoney et al. (1998) found that diagnoses of PDD, autism, and AS were reliable, those of PDD-NOS were not. In an interesting study, Prior et al. (1998) interviewed parents and administered various tasks to 48 children and adolescents who had been clinically diagnosed with autism, 69 with AS, and 18 with PDD-NOS. Cluster analysis of the data revealed three groupings with individuals with each diagnosis evident in all three clusters, although children with one diagnosis dominated each cluster. Thus, almost half of those with a clinical diagnosis of autism were in cluster A with a quarter in each of the other two clusters. Fifty-eight percent of those with a diagnosis of AS were in cluster B, with 22% and 20% in clusters A and C respectively. The percentage of those with a diagnosis of PDD-NOS in clusters A, B, and C were 39, 5, and 56 respectively. These and other findings have led to the view that autism is not a distinct disorder but rather is part of a spectrum of disabilities varying in the severity of social, cognitive, and linguistic impairments. Interestingly, Wing (1997) proposed that groups can be identified within the spectrum in terms of social behavior. She distinguishes four groups: aloof; passive; active but odd; loners. Nevertheless, in this book I shall restrict myself primarily to studies of children who are reported to have been diagnosed clinically with autism, although in doing this it is important to acknowledge the likely heterogeneity of such groups.

Autism is usually diagnosed by a combination of methods, including direct observations of the child, information provided by caregivers, and the results of psychometric assessments of verbal and nonverbal skills. Observations of the child are often guided by scales and schedules such as the Autism Diagnostic Observation Schedule (ADOS, Lord et al., 1989; and ADOS-G, Lord et al., 2000) and the Childhood Autism Rating Scale (CARS, Schopler, Reichler, & Rocher-Renner, 1988). Interviews with caregivers about the child's developmental history and current behavior usually follow a structured format such as the Autism Diagnostic Interview (ADI-R, Le Couteur et al., 1989). A number of studies have demonstrated that diagnosis by experienced clinicians, DSM-IV criteria, observations of behavior, and structured interviews with parents are fairly reliable (e.g. Klin, Lang, Cicchetti, & Volkmar, 2000; Lord et al., 1997; Lord et al., 2000; Pilowsky, Yirmiya, Shulman, & Dover, 1998). Thus, Lord et al. (1997) reported that the ADI/ADI-R differentiated individuals with autism identified by experienced clinicians, from individuals with learning difficulties and language impairments. Further, Lord et al. (2000) reported good interrater and test-retest reliability for the ADOS-G, and Pilowsky et al. found 86% agreement between diagnoses based on ADI-R and CARS for 83 individuals with suspected autism aged 2–34 years.

Autism is seldom diagnosed before the age of 3 years and often much later. Thus, Howlin and Moore (1997), based on a questionnaire to over 1,000 families, reported 6 years as the mean age at diagnosis, although 93% of the parents had expressed concern by the child's third birthday and almost 10% by the age of 6 months. Similarly, Gilchrist et al. (2001) reported that 77% of parents of 13 children with autism reported concerns before the child was 3 years old. This concern is borne out by home videos of the early years of children subsequently diagnosed with autism. These have demonstrated that many children show characteristic behaviors from the age of about 1 year (e.g., Lösche, 1990; Osterling & Dawson, 1994; Werner, Dawson, Osterling, & Dinno, 2000). These early behaviors include the children failing to orient to their names or to look at other people's faces, and absence of behaviors involved in sharing interest with others such as pointing and showing. These behaviors raise the possibility that autism could be detected before the age of 3 years in at least some children.

A number of these behaviors have been included in The Checklist for Autism in Toddlers (CHAT, Baron-Cohen, Allen, & Gillberg, 1992). The CHAT examines joint attention, social interest, protodeclarative pointing, social play, and pretence through observing the child and questioning the parent. Baron-Cohen et al. administered the CHAT to 41 children aged 1½ years who had a sibling with autism and were therefore at greater risk of autism than in the general population (see page 30). Four children failed two or more of the five areas examined and these children, but none of the others, were diagnosed with autism according to DSM-III criteria at the age of 2½ years.

A more extensive population study of over 16,000 children indicates that the CHAT may be good at identifying some children under the age of 2 years who go on to obtain a diagnosis of autism but may miss others (Baird et al., 2000). The CHAT led to the correct identification of 19 children aged 1½ years who went on to obtain a diagnosis of autism by the age of 7 years. However, a further 31 children with autism were not picked up by the CHAT. Importantly, it is clear that the CHAT does identify some children early on who may be at risk of autism and who therefore should be followed up.

The data collected in this study were also used to examine the stability of early diagnosis of autism by clinicians and the ADI-R (Cox et al., 1999). From the initial CHAT screening three groups of children were identified:

children at high risk for autism because they did not demonstrate protodeclarative pointing, follow another person's line of gaze or engage in pretend play; children at medium risk for autism because they did not show protodeclarative pointing but did either monitor gaze or pretend; the remaining children at no risk for autism. Samples of children from the three groups were followed up at 20 and 42 months. On each occasion a parent was interviewed using the ADI-R, a clinician assessed the child, and verbal and nonverbal tests were administered. Clinical diagnosis was found to be both stable and sensitive across the two ages, whereas the ADI-R failed to identify a number of children at 20 months who received a diagnosis of autism at 42 months. In agreement with these clinical findings, a number of studies have reported good stability of clinical diagnosis between 2 and 3 years of age (e.g. Lord, 1995; Stone et al., 1999a). In addition, Sigman and Ruskin (1999) reported that of 51 children diagnosed with autism between 3 and 5 years, 45 obtained the same diagnosis 8–9 years later and those that did not continued to have significant difficulties.

Autism is relatively infrequent although recently its incidence has been reported to be higher than earlier reports suggested. In a review of 23 epidemiological studies published between 1966 and 1999, Fombonne (1999) reported estimates of between 0.7 and 21.08 per 10,000 of the population, with a median of 5.2 per 10,000 and with about four times as many males as females. Fombonne reported an incidence of over 7 per 10,000 for surveys published since 1989, and Powell et al. (2000) reported an annual increase in autism of 18% between 1991 and 1996. More recently, Baird et al. (2000) reported a prevalence of just over 30 per 10,000 based on a population of over 16,000 children aged 7 years who had been screened at 1½, 3, 5, and 7 years, and Chakrabarti and Fombonne (2001) reported a prevalence of 16.8 per 10,000 based on a population of over 15,000 children aged 2–7 years screened for developmental difficulties in 1998/9.

Several reasons have been proposed to explain this apparent increase. One which received much attention concerned the measles, mumps, and rubella (MMR) vaccine. However, several studies have reported that the increased incidence of autism has not been paralleled by a corresponding increase in the uptake of MMR vaccination (e.g., Kaye, Melero-Montes, & Jick, 2001; Taylor et al., 1999). Thus, Kaye et al. reported that although the incidence of autism increased between 1988 and 1993, the uptake of MMR vaccine remained constant at over 95%. Fombonne (2001) argues against an epidemic of autism, pointing out that the increased numbers can be accounted for by methodological problems, changes in diagnostic criteria and age of diagnosis, greater awareness of autism, and improved services.

Despite its infrequency, much research has focused on trying to discover the cause of autism. In the 1940s and 1950s the source of the problem was often placed with the parents. It was argued that the children do not have a disability at birth, and that the way in which they are brought up leads to their subsequent behavior. In support of this sort of view many early papers described the parents of children with autism as being highly intelligent, but unsociable, unable to show their emotions, cold, and detached. They were often professional people, and the impression created was that they were very distant from their children, showing them little affection or warmth. The role of upbringing as a causal factor has been challenged and discredited for many years (e.g., Rutter, Bartak, & Newman, 1971). However, as we shall see shortly, the observations concerning parental characteristics are consistent with a genetic explanation of autism.

More recent evidence points to autism having a genetic basis (e.g., Szatmari, Jones, Zwaigenbaum, & MacLean, 1998). Several different strands of evidence indicate this conclusion: the incidence of autism among siblings of children with autism; the different concordance rates for autism in identical and fraternal or non-identical twins; the psychological characteristics of the parents and siblings of children with autism; chromosomal abnormalities associated with autism. I shall consider each of these areas in turn (see also Bailey, Palferman, Heavey, & Le Couteur, 1998b).

The prevalence of autism among the brothers and sisters of individuals with autism is about 200–300 per 10,000 (e.g., Bolton et al., 1994), which is considerably higher than in the general population even when compared to the higher prevalence rates reported recently. Bolton et al. reported that of 99 individuals with autism aged 5–36 years, 4 of their 137 siblings met the criteria for autism (a prevalence of 292 per 10,000) and a further 4 siblings, while not meeting the criteria fully, had difficulties in social interaction and communication and showed repetitive behaviors. In comparison, none of the siblings of individuals with DS had autism.

If the raised incidence of autism among the siblings of individuals with autism is to be explained by genetic factors, different concordance rates for autism should be found among identical and fraternal twins. This is because identical or monozygotic twins have exactly the same genetic make-up, whereas fraternal or dizygotic twins have the same degree of genetic resemblance as siblings, on average 50%. Therefore, if autism is due solely to genetic factors, and if one monozygotic twin has autism, we would expect the other twin also to have autism. However, if the twins are dizygotic, and one has autism, the other twin is as likely as any other sibling to have autism. In other words, monozygotic twins should be concordant for autism, whereas the prevalence of autism among dizygotic twins should be similar to that found for siblings.

A number of studies have now demonstrated that the concordance for autism among monozygotic twins is about 78% on average, compared to three reports of 0% and one of 23% for dizygotic twins (Bailey et al., 1995; Folstein & Rutter, 1977; Ritvo, Freeman, Mason-Brothers, Mo, & Ritvo, 1985; Steffenburg et al., 1989). The two studies by Ritvo et al. and by Steffenburg et al. reported concordance rates for autism among the monozygotic twins of over 90%. Importantly, although the rates were lower in the other two studies, when the diagnosis was extended to include language and/or cognitive difficulties rather than just autism, the concordance rates among the monozygotic twins increased to over 80%, whereas extending the criteria for the dizygotic twins only increased the concordance to 10%. Similarly, Le Couteur et al. (1996) reported a concordance rate for autism among 28 monozygotic twin pairs of over 70% whereas the concordance rate for autism among 20 dizygotic twin pairs was 0%. However, of the 9 monozygotic twin pairs who were discordant for autism, 7 were concordant when communication and social difficulties were included whereas only 2 of the dizygotic twin pairs were concordant for this broader phenotype.

It is clear from the raised prevalence of autism and related difficulties among the siblings and co-twins of children with autism that genetic factors are involved. Also the fact that around four times as many boys as girls have autism is in line with a genetic explanation. Bailey et al. (1995) calculated the heritability for autism to be greater than 90%. However, it is also evident that the nature of the inheritance is not straightforward and more than one gene must be involved. It has been suggested that two to four genes are most likely to be involved, although it is acknowledged that as many as 10 or even more may be implicated (Folstein, Bisson, Santangelo, & Piven, 1998). It follows from this that while only those individuals who have most or all the genes responsible for autism will exhibit autism, their close relatives may have some of the genes. In this case we might expect to see an increased likelihood of mild forms of the behaviors characterizing autism among relatives

A number of studies have reported autistic behaviors in the first degree relatives of individuals with autism. For example, Bolton et al. (1994) found greater evidence of social and communicative difficulties and stereotypic behaviors among the parents and siblings of individuals with autism than among the first degree relatives of individuals with DS. Similarly, Murphy et al. (2000) reported more evidence of certain personality traits, including aloofness, shyness, over-sensitivity, among the relatives of individuals with autism compared to those of individuals with DS. The everyday activities and preferences of the brothers and parents of boys with autism or AS, boys with reading difficulties, and TD boys were examined via a questionnaire by Briskman, Happé, and Frith (2001). The activities and preferences of the brothers of the children in the different groups did not differ. However, the parents of children with autism and AS reported greater preference for solitary activities and less interest and skill in social interactions than the parents of the other children. There were also occupational differences, with 43% of the fathers of the children with autism and AS having occupations requiring a focus on detail, such as engineering, accountancy, and computing compared to less than 20% of the fathers of the other children.

If these findings are due to close relatives of individuals with autism possessing some but not all of the genes responsible for autism then where there are two children with autism in the same family the first degree relatives should show clearer evidence of such behaviors. Although a direct comparison has not been made between families with one and families with two or more children with autism, Piven and colleagues (Piven & Palmer, 1997; Piven et al., 1997) reported that parents who had two children with autism, in comparison to parents of children with DS, had lower nonverbal IQs, difficulty with planning how to move rings to create a tower of rings ordered by size (the Tower of Hanoi task) and certain reading tests, more rigid behavior, were more aloof, had more speech and pragmatic language difficulties, and 37% reported no friendships, compared to 4% for the parents of children with DS.

A number of studies have examined aspects of cognitive ability, such as IQ, reading and spelling among first degree relatives of individuals with autism, but have not demonstrated consistent differences in the cognitive abilities of parents and siblings of individuals with autism, compared to the relatives of individuals without autism (e.g., Folstein et al., 1999; Fombonne, Bolton, Prior, Jordan, & Rutter, 1997; Leboyer, Plumet, Goldblum, Perez-Diaz, & Marchaland, 1995). However, other studies have demonstrated that parents and siblings of children with autism are more likely than first degree relatives of children without autism to show evidence of specific difficulties which are characteristic of autism. These include difficulty understanding that other people have minds (e.g., Baron-Cohen & Hammer, 1997), limited goal-directed behavior (referred to as problems of executive function) (e.g., Hughes, Leboyer, & Bouvard, 1997; Hughes, Plumet, & Leboyer, 1999; Ozonoff, Rogers, Farnham, & Pennington, 1993), and weak central coherence (e.g., Happé, Briskman, and Frith, 2001). Interestingly, in some of the studies involving parents it is the fathers who show the most marked difficulties (e.g., Happé et al., 2001; Hughes et al., 1997), which is consistent with the higher incidence of autism among males. In addition, several studies have reported significant correlations between task performance and ratings of everyday behavior for parents of children with autism but not for parents of children without autism (Briskman et al., 2001; Hughes et al., 1997).

It is clear from these and other studies that certain difficulties which are characteristic of individuals with autism may be found in some of their parents and siblings, although not in all. In addition, it may be that some parents have greater difficulties in one area, and others have greater difficulties in another area (Happé et al, 2001; Hughes et al., 1997). Such findings further support the view that autism is due to the presence of a number of different genes, since the parents of individuals with autism may have different combinations of the genes and therefore exhibit different aspects of autistic-like behavior (e.g., Folstein et al., 1999). This leads to the prediction that the parents of children with autism may differ from one another in terms of the autistic-like characteristics they exhibit: thus, one parent may have difficulties in tasks requiring executive function, whereas the other parent may show weak central coherence. As far as I know this prediction has not been tested.

If specific genes contribute to the expression of the different behaviors seen in children with autism, then it should be possible to find evidence of chromosomal abnormalities associated with autism. Gillberg (1998) reviewed a number of studies and concluded that most chromosomes have been associated with autism. Nevertheless, several chromosomes, particularly 15 and also 5, 8, 13, 17, and 18, are likely candidates. Lauritsen, Mors, Mortensen, and Ewald (1999) also pointed to the probable involvement of chromosome 15, as well as finding that most of the other chromosomes have also been suggested. Philippe et al. (1999) identified 11 chromosomal regions linked to autism: chromosomes 2, 4, 5, 6, 7, 10, 15, 16, 18, 19, and the sex chromosome, and Palferman et al. (2001) identified significant regions on chromosomes 2, 7, and 16. Clearly a number of different strategies are necessary in the search for the contributory genes, including studying the genotypes of individuals with autism alongside those of their close relatives, particularly those relatives who demonstrate autistic-like behaviors (e.g., Folstein et al., 1998).

It is now clear that autism has a genetic basis and that a number of different genes are involved. In addition to the evidence cited above, further support for the conclusion that autism has a genetic origin comes from the fact that it is sometimes associated with medical conditions which are thought to be genetically transmitted, such as Tourette's syndrome and tuberous sclerosis. Thus, Baron-Cohen, Mortimore, Moriarty, Izaguirre, and Robertson (1999a) reported a minimum prevalence of Tourette's syndrome in individuals with autism of just over 8% and Rutter (1999) concluded that about a quarter of individuals with tuberous sclerosis have autism, with a further quarter showing autistic-like behaviors. Nevertheless, less than 5% of individuals with autism will have tuberous sclerosis which is believed to involve genes on chromosomes 9 and 16 (see Szatmari et al., 1998).

Difficulties in studying children with disabilities

The study of the development of children with disabilities is not straight-forward and in this section I want to discuss some of the problems which arise (see also Lewis & Collis, 1997).

The very fact that particular children are grouped together and labeled as blind, or deaf or as having DS suggests that the children in each group share certain characteristics. It is obviously true that they will have certain features in common, but earlier sections of this chapter have demonstrated that the nature of the disabilities of children who might be ascribed the same label may be very different. Indeed, the notion of autism as part of a spectrum of disabilities, rather than as a distinct disorder, points to the variability observed in individuals with autism. It is also important to remember that children who share a similar disability will be different from one another in other ways. Knowing the pathology of the disability is not enough, since each child will have been exposed to different experiences and this alone will influence the effect of the disability on that child's development. All children are individuals, and this applies as much to those who have a disability as to those who do not.

Another problem which arises when we begin to explore the consequences of a particular disability for development is the question of whether any different behaviors or developments we observe are primary or secondary to the disability. Has the disability caused the behavior directly or is the behavior the result of some secondary effect of the disability? For example, if a child with a disability lives away from her family in some form of residential care and her language development is delayed, the delay may not be a direct consequence of her disability: rather it may be due to some aspect of the residential environment.

In many studies of children with disabilities the development of two or more groups of children is compared. Often this is with the intention of finding out how the disability has affected development. A difficulty here is to select a group against whom to compare the development of the children with disabilities. For example, children with DS could be judged to be similar in some sense to all of the following: children with learning difficulties but not DS of the same chronological and mental ages; younger children with no disabilities at a similar stage of development; children of the same chronological age but with no disabilities; older children with DS; their siblings with no disabilities. Any or all of these comparisons could be justified and yet none of them is ideal.

A further problem occurs in studies of children with sensory or motor difficulties. Take blind children. Many studies of blind children have involved comparisons between the performance of blind children and the performance of sighted children who have been blindfolded. However, blindfolding sighted children may disadvantage them because they will have to carry out the task in a different way from how they would normally do it. This therefore raises questions about the value of such comparisons.

This problem of making comparisons is particularly apparent where some measure of intelligence is required, especially with those children who are deprived of a sense. Should a blind child be assessed just on the verbal items of an intelligence test which has been standardized with sighted children, or should test items be specially designed to take account of the fact that the blind child cannot see? Both of these approaches have been used with blind children, although there are drawbacks to them both. Specially designed tests such as the Williams Intelligence Test for Children with Defective Vision (Williams, 1956) or the Intelligence Test for Visually Impaired Children 6–15 years (ITVIC, Dekker, 1993), which have been constructed for, and standardized on, blind children, can only be used to make comparisons between blind children.

The alternative of using, for example, the verbal scale of the Wechsler Intelligence Scale for Children (WISC, Wechsler, 1974) is also not very satisfactory. Tests which have been standardized on a sighted population are not very reliable when they are used with a different population, and the tester is ignoring those aspects of intelligence which would be assessed by those parts of the test which are omitted. It has been suggested that these particular difficulties could be overcome by comparing the performances of blind children to the performances of blindfolded sighted children. However, this is not ideal, since even though blindfolded, the sighted children will be influenced by their experiences of sight. Also, as noted above, they will be carrying out the items in a very different way from how they would normally, and their performance could not be taken as representative of their real ability.

A similar problem arises when designing ways of studying children with disabilities, a problem which is exacerbated when comparison groups are included. Researchers interested in the development of children with disabilities are often interested in how a process or development observed in children without disabilities is affected by the disability. This very often leads to the use of methods which have been employed to study the phenomenon in typically developing children. Such methods may be inappropriate to study the phenomenon in children with particular disabilities. But conversely, it may be inappropriate to draw conclusions when a phenomenon has been studied in two groups of children using different methods.

Related to all this is the problem of how to interpret any differences, or for that matter similarities, in the behaviors of children with and without a particular disability. Does a difference indicate that a process which is presumed to underpin the behavior in a child without the disability is missing in the child with the disability? Or does it mean that the child with the disability is processing the information differently? Or what?

There are no satisfactory answers to these sorts of problems. The study of children with disabilities and the interpretation of what is observed are fraught with difficulties. Nevertheless, it is important to bear these issues in mind when examining the development of children who have disabilities.

chapter two

How do blind children develop?

Introduction

One of the most detailed and fascinating accounts of the development of blind children is given by Selma Fraiberg in her book *Insights from the Blind* (1977). She makes quite clear in this book that blind children who are thought not to have any other disability, develop differently, not just from sighted children, but from one another. She illustrates this by two case histories which she describes in some detail. One of the children, Toni, was first seen at 5 months.

> She was five months old . . . When her mother went over to her and called her name, Toni's face broke into a gorgeous smile, and she made agreeable responsive noises. I called her name and waited. There was no smile. . . . (A)t eight months . . . (s)oon after she heard our voices, strange voices, she became sober, almost frozen in her posture. Later, when I held Toni . . . she began to cry, squirmed in my arms, and strained away from my body . . . At ten months Toni demonstrated for the first time her ability to reach and attain an object on sound cue alone . . . Between eight and ten months . . . we would see Toni stretch out on the floor, prone on the rug, and for long periods of time lie quite still, smiling softly to herself. . . (A)t ten months . . . (s)he was still unable to creep, but the walker provided mobility, and Toni was cruising around the house with tremendous energy and making discoveries and rediscoveries at every port. . . . she absolutely refused to get into the prone position . . . (A)t thirteen months . . . she began walking with support – and now also creeping . . . she had a small and useful vocabulary,

she was using her hands for fine discriminations, and she was now expert in reaching and attaining objects on sound cue . . . (B)eginning in the second year . . . (w)hen Toni became anxious . . . she would fall into a stuporous sleep.

Fraiberg's second case history was of a child, Peter, who was almost 9 years old when she first saw him:

He walked uncertainly with support . . . paid no attention to me or to my voice and sat or lay on the picnic table absently mouthing a rubber toy. Occasionally he made an irrelevant statement. . . . After a while he came close to me and fingered me. Then, without any change of facial expression and without any show of feeling, he began to dig his fingernails into the skin of my arm, very hard, causing me to wince with pain. . . . When Peter lost an object he was mouthing, he showed no reaction to loss and did not search for it. . . . While his mother was with us, I observed that his reaction to her was in no discernible way different from his reaction to me, to the nurse, or to the dog. At no time . . . did he ask a direct question, express a need through gesture or language, or answer a question put to him. . . . Peter always referred to himself in the third person. . . . There were no toys to which Peter had any attachment. When he showed transitory interest in objects, he brought them to his mouth, sucked on them, and chewed them. He did not explore them with his hands; . . . He still preferred soft foods, . . . there were typically much echolalia and toneless repetition of stereotyped phrases.

These excerpts show clearly that blindness can have very different consequences for the development of individual children. Much of Toni's development parallels that of sighted children although even for her there are some obvious differences: her delay in reaching and crawling; her period of lying passively on the floor and her later retreat into sleep when anxious. Peter presents a marked contrast, and even though he is much older it seems extremely unlikely that Toni's early progress would lead to this.

Children like Toni who seem to be succeeding are of particular relevance to the question of how blindness affects development. However, children like Peter are also relevant since any account of why some blind children develop like Toni must also be capable of explaining Peter's less successful development. Given that the focus is on blindness I shall consider only studies of blind children thought not to have any other disabilities. However, it is often hard to be sure that blind children have no additional disabilities, especially if they are born blind. Peter may have had some brain damage which further restricted his development, although neurological tests were negative.

Motor development

Blind children are delayed, relative to sighted children, in achieving various motor milestones, such as reaching and walking, although a small amount of vision can have a marked effect (e.g., Hatton, Bailey, Burchinal, & Ferrell, 1997). Blind children are also less active and their fine motor skills are qualitatively different from those of their sighted peers. Thus, Reimer, Smits-Engelsman and Siemonsma-Boom (1999) found that 6–11-year-old blind children were slower than sighted children on various manual dexterity tasks such as putting rings on pegs and threading beads, although they were as able as the sighted children to make judgments based on how much they had moved their arm.

Hatton et al. examined the assessment and medical records of 113 children aged between 12 and 73 months with a range of visual impairments and no additional disabilities. On the motor scale of the Battelle Developmental Inventory the developmental age of those with light perception or less was calculated using hierarchical linear modeling to be 18 months at a chronological age of 30 months. However, the children with some form perception had an expected developmental age of 22 months at 30 months chronological age. Those with even more vision had a mean motor developmental age of 26 months at 30 months chronological age.

Three aspects of the motor development of blind children have attracted particular attention: delays in reaching for objects; delays in becoming mobile; stereotyped, repetitive behaviors.

When and how do blind babies reach for objects?

For children with little or no sight it seems obvious that they will learn a great deal about the environment by touching or feeling it, but blind babies are slower to reach out into the environment than sighted babies. This difference is interesting because it illustrates the role of vision in the development of reaching.

Babies with no effective vision may not reach out for a toy until they are 10–11 months old, or in some cases even later. Thus, Peter was not reaching at the age of 9 years. This contrasts with sighted babies who start to reach at around 4 to 5 months. Why is there this delay for blind babies? Obviously sighted babies can see the toy, and this acts as an incentive. Although blind babies may hear the noise of the rattle, the noise will usually be intermittent and therefore unlike the continuous experience of the toy that sighted babies have while looking at it. In the first 8 or 9 months sighted babies will not search for a toy that has been covered up, even if it is making a noise (Bigelow, 1983), so perhaps it is not surprising that blind babies do not reach for a noise that stops.

But it is probably more complicated than this. For blind babies to reach they have to know that there is something to reach for, that the sound they hear has a source which is within reaching distance. This discovery must be much easier for sighted babies who see objects while they emit noises, and when they turn towards a sound they will often see the toy or person who made the noise. Sighted babies will have many more opportunities than blind babies to discover that sounds have sources which can be located, and there is even some evidence to suggest that babies may be born with this ability. We do not know anything about this early ability in blind babies, and it seems fairly likely that even if blind babies are born with the ability to turn their eyes towards the source of a sound, this will disappear after their repeated failure to find the source. Alternatively, the behavior may appear to persist. For example, the baby may turn her head, not to locate the sound, but in order to equalize the time at which the sound reaches both her ears.

So how do blind children come to realize that sounds have locations and sources? They will probably only discover this through reaching. Interestingly, sighted infants will reach for a toy that makes a noise in the dark from about 4 months, similar to the age at which they begin to reach for objects they can see (e.g., Clifton, Muir, Ashmead, & Clarkson, 1993). By this age, sighted children have discovered that sounds have sources, an understanding that blind children of this age do not yet have.

In order to reach, blind babies have to venture out into a space they know nothing about. When sighted babies see a brightly colored toy they may move their arms and legs and even make contact with the toy by chance. When blind children hear the sound of a rattle they may go quiet and still, not because they are uninterested but because they are listening, attending to the noise. Before they will reach out blind babies have to know that there is something out there whose presence is signaled by the noise, although, even when they know that there is an object there, they may not reach for some other reason. However, until they do realize that they can reach out to grasp a toy, objects may just seem to emerge from time to time when they come into contact with their hands. When the hands of blind babies do make chance encounters with objects, these tend not to be repeated. By contrast, sighted babies repeat the contact, for example, clasping and reclasping one hand with the other. This clasping behavior, which occurs in sighted babies at about 16 weeks, has not been observed in blind babies (Fraiberg, 1968). However, Fraiberg, Siegel, and Gibson (1966) did observe that blind babies tend to make tentative finger movements in the direction of a toy just before they start to reach. They interpreted this as a sign that the babies were ready to start reaching.

Interestingly, research suggests that tactual information may be much more useful to blind babies than auditory information. For example, Gerhardt (1982) reported that a blind girl reached on touch and sound cues at 8 and 11 months respectively. In a more extensive study Bigelow (1986) examined the reaching behavior of five blind children from 11 months under various conditions. She found that the children reached at a younger age for an object placed somewhere on their body (either a limb or trunk), for an object they had been holding and either dropped or was removed, than for an object emitting a sound with which they had had no prior contact. However, sound did make reaching more likely if the child had previously held the object. The primacy of tactual cues in guiding reaching, at least early on, may also explain Fraiberg's observation of blind babies between 5 and 8 months feeling their parents' faces.

The problem for blind babies is that sound does not tell them that there is a tangible object out there in the same way that sight does, unless they have had some previous contact with the object. It is only from experience that we know that sounds usually come from something tangible. As Landau (1991a) has argued, sound information is inferior to visual information for indicating that an object is available. Sound can only convey information about relative position. A possible solution to this was suggested by Bower (1977) and involves children wearing a sonic device on a headband. The device emits sound waves which reflect back off objects, the nature of the echo varying depending on the distance and size of the object. Using this device Aitken and Bower (1982) reported that three blind children aged 5–8 months immediately made use of the additional information whereas five children aged 13–20 months did not, although two 13-month-old children did show some response with the device, whereas the older children showed no response. However, Sampaio (1989) found that blind children aged between 5 and 48 months all responded appropriately, often making scanning movements with their head when an object intercepted the sonic beam. Nevertheless, although there has been some criticism of the sonic device (e.g., Kay & Strelow, 1977) and failures to replicate (e.g., Harris, Humphrey, Muir, & Dodwell, 1989), its implications should not be denied.

What are the consequences of this delay in reaching? Does it actually matter? Fraiberg has commented that there may be wide-ranging implications of such a delay for babies who will depend on their hands for information later on. She goes further to argue that blind babies must be able to reach towards a sound before they will begin to crawl (Fraiberg, 1977). In support of this, Bigelow (1992a) found that a blind boy crawled and reached for a toy making a continuous noise which had been taken from him at 23 months; two other boys showed both behaviors the first time they were observed at 13 and 32 months. Bigelow also reported that the three boys reached for a silent toy which had been taken from them at 28, 17, and 35 months respectively and started to walk unsupported at 32, 17, and 36 months, i.e., at the same age or a few months later. In the next section I shall consider the effect of blindness on mobility in more detail.

How are posture and mobility affected by blindness?

Blind babies are delayed in many aspects of mobility. For example, Levtzion-Korach, Tennenbaum, Schnitzer, and Ornoy (2000) reported that 40 blind children were delayed in rolling over (8.2 months for the blind children compared to 4 months for sighted children on whom the tests were standardized), crawling (13.2 and 8 months), standing alone with support (14.4 and 8.1 months), sitting from a supine position (11.9 and 8.3 months), walking with help (16.6 and 9.6 months), walking alone (19.3 and 11.7 months), climbing stairs with help (28.8 and 16.1 months), standing on one foot (52.4 and 22.7 months), jumping with two feet (40 and 23.4 months), and climbing stairs alone (38.3 and 25 months). Nevertheless, some blind children will develop motor skills at similar ages to sighted children. For example, Preisler (1995) observed seven blind children to sit with support between 5 and 11 months, sit without support and stand with support between 8 and 14 months, walk with support between 10 and 18 months.

Although Levtzion-Korach et al.'s study points to delays in a wide range of motor behaviors, other authors (e.g., Adelson & Fraiberg, 1974) have argued that more marked delays are observed in motor behaviors which are self-initiated than in behaviors which just require the maintenance of a position which has already been achieved. It seems likely that vision is particularly important for self-initiated movements: for example, sighted babies roll over to get nearer to a toy, stand up to reach things on the table and walk to a parent on the other side of the room. Just as blind children do not have the visual enticement to reach, so they do not have the incentive to move around in the space beyond.

Most blind children become mobile, although the onset of mobility is likely to be delayed and we saw that Peter was not walking independently at 9 years. Sampaio, Bril, and Brenière (1989) studied the walking behavior of two blind infants aged 17 and 29 months and six sighted infants and found that although their gaits were similar to begin with, the gaits of the blind children did not develop in the same way. Blind children are likely to continue walking with feet slightly apart and arms outstretched for much longer and they may need to be told how sighted people walk. In addition, although they may become adept at moving around at home, they may find it extremely difficult to walk as confidently outside. In the absence of sight blind children make use of other cues, mainly auditory, and the sorts of auditory cues available indoors about spaces and obstacles will be very different from those outside.

The use of auditory cues by blind children when walking was explored by Ashmead et al. (1998a) and Millar (1999). Ashmead et al. found that when 7–18-year-old blind youngsters wore headphones eliminating auditory cues to one or both ears they walked more slowly down a hallway and made more contact with the walls. In addition, when the hallway suddenly widened on one side, the blind youngsters veered to that side if their hearing was not masked but veered less if their hearing on that side was masked. Ashmead et al. concluded that blind children make use of low-frequency sounds which build up as a wall is approached and compare the intensity of the sound at the two ears to guide the direction in which they walk.

In a rather different setup Millar (1999) asked 6–12-year-old blind children to walk in a straight line across an open space within a larger room. All the children walked in a straight line in a pre-test but when a sound was made to one side they veered towards the sound, whereas when they carried a 2 lb weight in one hand they compensated by veering towards the opposite side. Thus, without any other cues to help them orient themselves, the children were unable to ignore irrelevant sounds and weights.

It is clear that blind children are much slower to reach the main motor milestones than sighted children. Thus, as well as not being able to see things that are going on, blind children will have fewer opportunities for interacting with the environment by reaching and moving around. It is interesting that Toni lay passively on a rug for periods of time in the months before she began to reach and move around, and that as soon as she developed these behaviors she refused to lie on the rug. Blind babies are often observed to turn to their own bodies in this and other ways for stimulation. This may be the beginning of stereotyped, repetitive behaviors, previously called blindisms, which do not seem to be directed towards a recognizable goal and can persist into childhood and beyond.

Stereotyped, repetitive behaviors

The most prevalent stereotyped, repetitive behaviors in blind children reported by parents are eye poking, body rocking, repetitive hand and finger movements, and repetitive manipulation of objects (e.g., Fazzi et al., 1999; Tröster, Brambring, & Beelmann 1991a, 1991b). Many of these sorts of behaviors can also be observed in sighted children but they tend to disappear quite early on. Institutionalized children also tend to exhibit these sorts of behaviors persistently. Tröster et al. (1991a) reported that the parents of

85 blind children aged 1–7 years indicated that all the children showed at least one stereotyped behavior, and half of the children exhibited five or more different behaviors. Similarly, Fazzi et al, (1999) reported that 10 blind children aged 4 months to 5 years and without any neurological disabilities all showed at least one stereotyped behavior. Tröster et al. (1991b) further reported that 85 blind children between 5 months and 8 years exhibited on average five or more repetitive behaviors a week and three or more each day. They also observed that these behaviors seemed to increase over the first couple of years but decreased between the ages of 3 and 6 years.

The stability of these behaviors was examined by Brambring and Tröster (1992) who asked the parents of 52 infants and young blind children to complete two questionnaires between 11 and 20 months apart. The two most frequent behaviors reported were eye poking and body rocking and these were also the most stable over time. Perhaps not surprisingly, for individual children the most frequent behaviors were the most stable and the older the child, the more stable the behavior.

Tröster et al. (1991a) noted that although these behaviors were more likely to occur when the children were bored, they were also reported to occur when they were excited and when cognitive demands were placed on them. There also seem to be age differences in the situations in which these behaviors occur. Tröster et al. (1991b) reported that in the first year of life these behaviors were more likely to occur when the situation was either monotonous or very arousing. In older children they tended to occur when cognitive demands were made of them.

This suggests two possible explanations for the behaviors: to increase the general level of sensory stimulation in the absence of outside stimulation, and as a way of withdrawing from demanding situations. In a detailed study of four blind children aged 10–13 years who showed high levels of rocking behavior, McHugh and Pyfer (1999) found that they were all characterized by long periods of time in hospital, delayed motor development, a preference for sedentary activities, and limited peer relationships. However, all the children were blind due to retinopathy of prematurity and three were suspected of having learning difficulties. As a result, the findings may not be generalizable. Nevertheless, it is clear that all blind children show some stereotyped, repetitive behaviors although there are marked individual differences. It seems likely that such behaviors will interfere with learning opportunities and also may lead to stigmatization.

Perceptual development

It might be expected that blind children, deprived of the visual sense and therefore relying on information from other modalities, would become particularly sensitive to non-visual information. But is there any evidence for this? Does deprivation of the visual sense result in the intact modalities compensating by becoming more sensitive or does it lead to a deficit because the intact modalities are unable to develop to their full potential in the absence of vision? In the next three sections I shall consider the evidence from studies of the olfactory, auditory, and tactual abilities of blind children.

How good are blind children at perceiving olfactory information?

Rosenbluth, Grossman, and Kaitz (2000) examined the threshold at which an odor was judged to be present by blind and sighted 5–17-year-olds and found no evidence of any difference. However, when asked to name 25 different common odors the blind children and adolescents labeled more, although the two groups did not differ when they had to choose which of four odors they were smelling. These findings indicate that the olfactory sense of blind children is no more sensitive than that of sighted children. However, presumably because they cannot discriminate everyday substances and materials visually, they pay more attention to how they smell than sighted children and therefore are better able to name them.

How good are blind children at perceiving auditory information?

Studies of motor development show that blind children are able to make use of auditory information to find out about their environment. Thus, some very young blind children seem to use auditory information to find out about objects if they are provided with a sonicguide (e.g., Sampaio, 1989) and older blind children use auditory information to avoid walking into walls (e.g., Ashmead et al., 1998a). But are their auditory skills more efficient than those of sighted children? To answer this question it is necessary to compare the performance of blind and sighted children on auditory tasks, which was not done in these studies. However, such a comparison was made by Ashmead et al. (1998b).

Ashmead et al. compared the spatial hearing of 6–20-year-old blind individuals who had light perception or less and 12–15-year-old sighted adolescents. All the participants wore blindfolds while being tested. The blind participants were able to judge that one sound was to the left or right of, or above or below, another sound when a smaller angle separated them than were the sighted adolescents. The blind children were also able to tell which of two sounds was nearest to them when a smaller distance separated the two sounds compared to the sighted children. This shows clearly that the ability to spatially locate one sound relative to another is more finely tuned in blind children and adolescents than in sighted adolescents. Interestingly, there was no difference in the ability to reach accurately for sounds presented to the left, right, above, or below, but the blind participants were more accurate in judging the distance of a sound. These findings could be interpreted as evidence for compensation. However, Ashmead et al. point out that although the blind children performed better than the sighted children on some of the tasks, the differences were not great and because of this they argue that these findings do not provide evidence of one modality compensating for another, rather that the blind children made greater use of their spatial hearing ability.

There is some physiological support for this conclusion from a series of studies by Naveen and colleagues (e.g., Naveen, Srinivas, Nirmala, Nagendra, & Telles, 1997; Naveen et al., 1998). These researchers recorded auditory evoked potentials from blind and sighted 13–16-year-olds and found evidence of more efficient functioning of the auditory pathway of the blind. They further found no evidence that areas of the brain which normally respond to visual stimulation had taken over any auditory processing. Thus, it appears that in the absence of sight, blind children make more efficient use of auditory information.

Does blindness affect the perception of tactual information?

Studies of tactual perception in blind children have focused on two different questions: how do blind children use the tactual modality to explore objects and how does blind children's identification of objects tactually compare with that of sighted children?

A number of studies have examined how blind children explore objects and surfaces. For example, Landau (1991a) presented sighted children and three blind children aged 18–36 months with two objects in turn which differed in shape, texture, or size and reported that if the objects differed in shape, the children rotated them; if they differed in texture, the children rubbed the surfaces. Landau also reported that a 3-year-old blind child was very good at correctly identifying textures (rough, bumpy, and smooth) and shapes (triangle, square, and circle), although her performance on shape judgments depended on the size of the object and whether or not it was fixed. If the shape was large and fixed and either a square or a triangle she made more errors. Landau argues that with such objects the opportunities for useful tactual exploration were reduced. It is much easier to explore a small shape which you can rotate, than a large fixed object.

Younger blind children were studied by Schellingerhout, Smitsman, and van Galen as they explored textures (1997) and small objects (1998). The children were aged 8, 12, 15, and 20 months and felt a textured rubber surface on five visits with 2 weeks between visits. The surface had a regular pattern of bumps graded from large close to the child and small further away. Over the five visits the children increased the amount of rubbing with the whole hand, rubbing with just the fingers, and fingering, but there was no change in the amount of static contact with the surface, hitting, or mouthing. There was an increase with age in the amount of rubbing involving just the fingers. On a sixth visit three surfaces were presented in turn: the textured surface, a surface with regular bumps, and a flat surface. Only the oldest children showed different amounts of rubbing and fingering, most occurring with the graded surface, least with the flat surface. This study shows that blind children use a variety of different ways to explore surfaces but it is only as they approach 2 years that they begin to differentiate their use of these different strategies.

In the same study the children also had the opportunity to explore a toy car and a key ring linked to a ball which were attached to the graded surface (Schellingerhout et al., 1998). The 8-month-olds grasped and mouthed the objects and from 12 months the children began to finger and rotate the objects, and no mouthing was observed in the 20-month-old infants. Schellingerhout et al. conclude that different exploratory actions are afforded by surfaces and objects by 8 months in blind infants, although they point out that the blind children were slower to begin fingering the objects than sighted children who have been observed to do this from 5 months (Ruff, Saltarelli, Capozoli, & Dubiner, 1992). Nevertheless, given the different ages at which blind and sighted infants reach for objects, this finding is not particularly surprising.

The study by Schellingerhout et al. (1997) demonstrates that the oldest blind children were able to discriminate the different textures, although obviously the absence of differential behavior in the younger infants to the three surfaces does not prove that they did not notice the differences. But is there any evidence that younger blind children can discriminate between different textures? A study by Catherwood, Drew, Hein, and Grainger (1998) of two infants aged 6 and 10 months suggests that they can. The infants were familiarized for 30 seconds to an object which was one of two possible shapes and had one of two possible textures. They were then presented with the familiar object and three novel objects: same shape, different texture; different shape, same texture; and different shape, different texture. The novel objects were touched two to three times longer than the familiarized object, with most touch occurring to the objects with a different texture. Although these data were only collected from two infants and no statistical analysis was carried out, they do suggest that blind infants can discriminate objects on the basis of touch from at least 6 months. These preliminary findings warrant further study.

Several studies have examined the tactual abilities of older blind children (e.g. D'Angiulli, Kennedy, & Heller, 1998; Morrongiello, Humphrey, Timney, Choi, & Rocca, 1994). Morrongiello et al. examined the ability of 3–8-year-old blind children and sighted children to identify tactually everyday objects that could be manipulated easily (e.g., a shoe), miniature versions of relatively small objects (e.g., a rolling pin), miniature versions of large objects (e.g., a bicycle), and oversized versions of small objects (e.g., a key). The blind and sighted children did not differ in the number of objects they identified correctly, and both groups made more errors and were slower with miniaturized small and large objects. There was also consistency between the blind and sighted children in which part of an object they were touching when they identified it. These findings suggest that the ways in which blind and sighted children use touch to identify objects and their ability to name felt objects are similar.

However, D'Angiulli et al. (1998) reported that older blind children may develop superior strategies for gathering tactual information than sighted children. In this study blind children and blindfolded sighted children aged 8–13 years had to identify raised line drawings of everyday objects (e.g., a face, scissors). None of the blind children had experience of raised line drawings and they recognized more pictures than the sighted children. Interestingly, the sighted children recognized as many drawings as the blind children when the researcher guided their index finger around the drawing. It would be interesting to examine how the blind children explored the drawings.

Taken together, the findings on olfactory, auditory, and tactual perceptual abilities of blind children do not provide any evidence for these modalities compensating for the absence of vision. However, through using these modalities to gain information from the environment blind children seem to make more efficient use of auditory and tactual information and develop more effective ways of gathering information than sighted children who can rely on vision. This conclusion is supported by a study of blind adults who used braille (Grant, Thiagarajah, & Sathian, 2000). The blind adults were better than sighted adults on a discrimination task involving braille-type dots, although with practice the group difference disappeared. On a tactual discrimination task involving ridged gratings the two groups did not differ either before or after practice.

Cognitive development

More than 50 years ago, Lowenfeld (1948) pointed to three general restrictions associated with blindness, all of which could have effects for cognitive development. The first was the range and variety of experiences available to the blind child. These will be limited because the intact senses of a blind child are unable to bring her direct experience of the same sort that vision can. Second, her ability to get about is reduced. This will affect the opportunities that she has for experience and social contact. Finally, she does not have the same control of her environment and of herself as the sighted child, because she has little or no perception of the space beyond that which she occupies.

All these point strongly to some cognitive impairment in the blind child. However, there is a different way of looking at this. For example, Landau (1991b) argues that any differences in the early cognitive development of blind children are primarily due to differences in the nature of the information about the world which is available to them. Thus, whereas others (e.g., Bower & Wishart, 1979) have suggested that without vision it is not possible to develop concepts of space or vision, Landau argues that this is possible using non-visual information. This may result in differences in the understanding that blind children may have, not as a result of any cognitive impairment, but because the information they receive through channels other than vision is different. In addition, Landau has also pointed out that much of the knowledge that blind children have will be very similar to that of sighted children. We shall consider some of Landau's experimental findings supporting this position later. In the sections that follow I shall examine blind children's intelligence, understanding of objects and spatial relationships, understanding of people, understanding of quantity and number, and memory.

How intelligent are blind children?

Kolk (1977) reviewed a number of studies concerned with the intelligence of blind children and concluded that "in general, average IQ scores do not differ significantly" for blind children and sighted children. However, Hatton et al. (1997) calculated, using hierarchical linear modeling, that on the cognitive developmental scale of the Battelle Developmental Inventory the developmental age of 186 children aged between 12 and 73 months with a range of visual impairments and some with additional disabilities was 18 months at a chronological age of 30 months. The cognitive developmental age ranged from 17 months for children with light perception or less to 25 months for those with some useful vision.

Differences have also been reported later in childhood. An average intelligent quotient (IQ) of 92 on the Verbal Scale of the Wechsler Intelligence Scale for Children (WISC) was reported by Tillman (1967a, 1973) for 110 blind children aged 7–13 years, compared with 96.5 for a matched

group of sighted children. Tillman (1967b) broke down the scale and
found that the sighted children were superior to the blind children on
comprehension and tasks requiring the children to spot similarities. There
were no differences between the groups on information, arithmetic and
vocabulary scales. Others have reported that blind children may actually
be superior to sighted children on digit span tasks (see page 71). The
explanation proposed by Tillman is that blind children fail to integrate all
the different facts they learn, so that each item of information is kept
separate and has a separate frame of reference from every other item.
They are not impaired on items which just ask for information, like the
arithmetic and vocabulary items. They are impaired on items such as comprehension or judging similarities, which involve relating different items
of information. It is as though all the educational experiences of the blind
child are kept in separate compartments. If this is correct, then it may be
concluded that vision enables links to be made between different experiences, links which assist in making effective use of experiences.

    However, it may not be appropriate to assess blind children using ma-
terials and tasks designed for and standardized on sighted children, even
if adjustments are made to the materials and administration. Instead, assessment methods should be designed specifically for blind children and
standardized on populations of blind children. These can then be used to
identify blind children who are not performing at the level expected for
this population. Probably the best known assessments for young blind
children are the Reynell–Zinkin Scales (Reynell, 1979) which use materials suitable for blind children up to the age of 5 years. There are six
subscales: social adaptation, assessing understanding of the social environment, ability to adapt to it through self-help skills and responses to
people; sensorimotor understanding, examining object understanding;
exploration of the environment beyond immediate reach; response to sound
and verbal comprehension; structure of vocalizations and expressive language; content of expressive language and vocabulary. The Reynell–Zinkin
Scales have not been standardized, but for each scale approximate age
levels are provided for blind children, children who are partially sighted,
and sighted children.

    Reynell (1978) reported comparisons between sighted children and blind
children and at some point on all scales the sighted children were ahead.
On the social adaptation scale the children were similar initially but from
about 18 months large differences of up to 18 months occurred which
persisted until about 4 years when the blind children had usually caught
up. On the sensorimotor and exploration scales the children were similar
until about 12 months when large differences emerged, the blind children
having caught up by about 5 years. Differences were found in the first
year only for language comprehension, whereas for the structure of lan-

guage they are reported to be similar for about a year, and from about 18 months the sighted children moved ahead by about 6 months. On language content the sighted children were ahead by about 12 months throughout. Although these scales can be useful for identifying blind children who are falling behind other blind children, they are limited in that they do not examine different ways of interacting with the environment.

Interestingly, no relationship has been reported between socioeconomic status based on the occupational and educational levels of both parents and blind children's development assessed by the Reynell–Zinkin Scales for blind children with visual acuities ranging from no light perception to 20/200 both when the children were 20–36 months old (Dote-Kwan & Hughes, 1994) and 12–15 months later (Dote-Kwan, Hughes, & Taylor, 1997). However, as we shall see in a later section, the blind child's development is correlated with how her mother interacts with her (see pages 78–79).

A test for use with older blind children, the Intelligence Test for Visually Impaired Children, has been developed by Dekker (1993). This includes an assessment of the child's vision and their spatial, reasoning, and linguistic abilities. In a study of 155 blind children in Holland and Belgium, Dekker reports that those children with some useful vision did better on the spatial tasks, while those with no vision had better verbal memories. However, like the Reynell–Zinkin Scales, this test is of most use in identifying blind children who may be having specific problems in certain areas.

What do young blind children understand about objects?

Blind babies cannot look around and experience objects visually, and until they begin to explore objects with their hands and mouths their main contact with the world will be the sound of people talking and the feel of other people touching and playing with them. How does lack of vision affect their understanding of objects?

Blind children reach for objects later than sighted children, and they are slower to get mobile. These delays will restrict the contact the children have with near and further afield objects. Even when they do reach, and become mobile, most of their experience of objects will be through touch. Touch, unlike vision, cannot be used to glance at an object. Visual glances can be very useful to give a general impression, but, to use touch without vision, you have to touch parts of an object in turn. The experience that blind babies have of objects will be sequential and much less extensive than sighted children's visual experience. It will be much more difficult for blind babies to understand the total extent of many objects, and to relate one part of an object to another part. Imagine trying to make sense of a car, or a tree, or a house by touch without any prior visual experience. Similarly, fragile objects, such as soap bubbles, and very small objects, like ants, are less accessible through touch.

Auditory information is also very different from visual information. Unlike vision, which is continuous unless you decide to look elsewhere or the lights are turned off, sounds are seldom continuous. A sound may be heard one minute and absent the next. This will make it more difficult for blind children to understand that objects are permanent entities.

Given the differences in the nature of the information available to blind children it would perhaps be surprising if they had exactly the same understanding of objects and their environment as sighted children. Their understanding has been explored in a number of different ways. For example, Kephart, Kephart, and Schwarz (1974) asked blind and sighted 5–7-year-olds to verbally describe features of an imagined environment. When describing a house, the 5-year-old blind children were more likely to mention the front door, the sighted children the roof and walls. The blind children gave far less detail than the sighted children about what might be found in the garden, along the street, or in the town and gave more inappropriate suggestions. Interestingly, Murphy and Vogel (1985) describe a sighted boy of above average intelligence who, because of severe immune deficiency, had to live in a sterile isolator from birth and who did not think that houses had four walls until he had the opportunity to walk around one at the age of 6 years. Blind children may also believe things about their environment which are incorrect. For example, Gibbs (1981) described a blind 6-year-old who asked for increasingly long sticks to touch the ceiling. The only problem was that he was trying to feel the ceiling in the garden. He did not realize that the outside had no ceiling.

Another approach has been to look at when blind children understand that objects continue to exist when they are no longer in contact with them. Fraiberg (1968) reported that blind children do not have a mature understanding of the permanence of objects until about 3–5 years. However, it seems likely that blind children do have an object concept earlier than this. In the first place, they request objects from well before 3 years, indicating an awareness of the objects' existence. Second, Bigelow (1986) and Rogers and Puchalski (1988) report blind children showing earlier evidence of object permanence skills, even though both report some delay. In Roger and Puchalski's most difficult task, the child felt an object in the tester's hand and maintained contact with it while it was covered by a container and then a cloth was placed over the object, container, and hands; at this point the child's hand was removed and the tester removed her hand, leaving the object under the container, and cloth. The 10 children successfully retrieved the object at ages between 13 and 26 months, the average age being 20.8 months. This still represents a delay of about 8 months compared to sighted children, and the task is not equivalent to an invisible displacement which is used to test the full object concept. An invisible displacement task for a sighted child would be the child watching an object being hidden in one location (the tester's hand), the closed hand being moved under one cloth and then under a second cloth, and then the tester showing the child her empty hand. The child is then encouraged to find the object.

Thus, there is some delay in the object concept development of blind children, although it may be less marked than suggested by Fraiberg. Why is it delayed? Fraiberg believed that the delay stemmed from blind children giving up searching when things are not found. As a result of this children may deduce that objects cease to exist when they cannot be found. This belief in itself makes the further development of a mature object concept less likely, since there will be no point in children continuing to search.

However, Fraiberg (1977) pointed out that young blind children may have some concept of objects before they begin to reach towards them, but that they show this in more subtle ways than sighted children, and these signs may be overlooked. She observed a 6-month-old blind child called Robbie move his hands across the table top after he had dropped a toy. At 8 months Robbie's hands made grasping motions when he heard the sound of a favorite toy. These sorts of observations have practical implications for how parents can help their blind baby

Children's understanding of objects can also be studied through their play. Compared to sighted children, blind children engage in more manipulative play (e.g., Tait, 1972) and less constructive and spontaneous imaginative play (e.g., Dunlea, 1984; Fraiberg, 1977; Fraiberg & Adelson, 1975; Rogers & Puchalski, 1984). Based on parental responses to a questionnaire, Tröster and Brambring (1994) reported that blind children and sighted children who engaged in undifferentiated manipulation of objects were aged 16 and 8 months respectively, those relating objects were 26 and 13 months respectively, those manipulating objects appropriately were 40 and 24 months respectively, and those playing symbolically were 55 and 35 months respectively. In other words, the play of the blind children showed marked delays.

However, a small amount of vision can have a significant effect. Hughes, Dote-Kwan, and Dolendo (1998) observed 6 children with profound visual impairments (PVI) and 7 children with severe visual impairments (SVI) aged 32–52 months while playing alone with toys at home. The two groups of children had mean chronological and developmental ages of 41 months and 38 months (PVI) and 38 months and 52 months (SVI) respectively. The children with PVI spent about three quarters of the time exploring the toys, indiscriminately mouthing and manipulating them, compared to 44% for the children with SVI. The children with PVI spent almost no time playing with the toys appropriately, compared to 42% for the children with SVI. None of the children with PVI and only 2 of the children with SVI played symbolically. Hughes et al. indicate that the different play behaviors of the children with PVI were equivalent to 12-month-old sighted children (indiscriminate manipulation), 9-month-old sighted children (appropriate manipulation), and 7-month-old sighted children (symbolic play). Thus, the blind children showed extremely delayed play behaviors, especially symbolic play, and well below the levels expected on the basis of their developmental ages.

Tröster and Brambring (1994) also found differences in blind and sighted children's toy preferences: the blind children were reported to prefer noise-making objects, household objects, and naturally occurring objects, whereas the sighted children preferred symbolic and construction toys, picture-touch books, and painting and handicraft materials.

Despite the above evidence indicating that blind children seldom play symbolically, there is some evidence that in certain situations blind children will play symbolically. For example, Pérez-Pereira and Castro (1992) reported that twin 3-year-old girls, one of whom was blind, frequently engaged in imaginative play. Chen (1996) also reported symbolic play when blind children aged 20–30 months played with their parents. Lewis, Norgate, Collis and Reynolds (2000a) found no difference between 2–7-year-old blind children and sighted children on the Test of Pretend Play (Lewis & Boucher, 1997), a structured test of symbolic play assessing the ability to substitute one thing for another, to refer to an absent object, or to attribute a property to an object which it does not have. Together, these findings suggest that blind children can play symbolically provided that they have the support of a play partner or the situation is well structured.

A number of studies have examined whether or not the play of blind children is related to other areas of development, notably language. In their study of blind children under 3 years, Rogers and Puchalski (1984) reported that children who copied the tester playing imaginatively had higher sensorimotor scores and more advanced language skills on the Reynell–Zinkin Scales than the children who did not produce imaginative play. However, the children did not differ in chronological age, level of vision, or performance on object permanence tasks. Interestingly, Rogers and Puchalski also noted that the children producing imaginative play were using the word "No," whereas the other children were not. They suggest that this may indicate that the child realizes that she possesses a point of view and can imagine a situation which is different from the present one. They argue that for blind children the use of "No" may be a better indicator of cognitive ability in the sensorimotor period than performance on object permanence tasks.

Other studies have also reported a relationship between symbolic play and language. Ferguson and Buultjens (1995) reported significant correlations between symbolic play and both receptive and expressive language based on Reynell–Zinkin scores for blind children aged between 16 months and 6 years. However, given that both language and symbolic play increase with increasing age this relationship could be explained by age effects. In their study, Lewis et al. (2000a) covaried out chronological age and found that the relationship between symbolic play and both expressive and receptive language remained. In other words, language and symbolic play are related in blind children independently of chronological age, as is found in sighted children (e.g., Lewis, Boucher, Lupton, & Watson 2000b).

Another way of examining children's understanding of objects is to look at whether they classify objects in any systematic way. Gerhardt (1982) reported that a blind girl, aged 18 months, grouped together similar objects when given a selection of objects varying in shape and the noise they made. Interestingly, and in agreement with Bigelow's (1986) findings that reaching behavior is determine more by touch than by sound, shape rather than sound was more likely to govern her groupings. In contrast to this case study, Dunlea (1989) found no evidence of classification in young blind children who were just beginning to talk. Further support for the idea that blind children may find it difficult to classify objects comes from a study of 6–11-year-olds by Dimcovic and Tobin (1995). The children were presented with four objects and had to choose the odd one out which could be in terms of shape, size, area, or position. The blind children found this very difficult. Out of 30 blind children, only 2 of the oldest were totally successful on this task, compared with 13 blindfolded sighted children. In contrast, 18 of the blind children were 100% successful at identifying which of four words was the odd one out in terms of belonging to a different category than the others, although the sighted children still did better on this task, 29 of them performing at ceiling. This study suggests that the visual modality may help children discover how different objects can be grouped into categories in terms of shared features.

The understanding of objects that a blind child has will necessarily be different from that of the sighted child, and in many cases she may always have a different understanding even as an adult. Vision tends to be a unifying sense. The outcomes of events which can be observed can be anticipated and it is easier to extract the rules by which things happen when you can watch the event rather than having to rely on tactual and auditory information. For example, imagine the different experiences of a blind child and a sighted child when their parent hammers a nail into the wall. The sighted child can see all the preparations and can watch her parent line up the nail and raise the hammer to hit it. The sound of the hammer hitting the nail may be the first thing that the blind child experiences. In this sort of way vision can often provide a context for events which helps the child make sense of them.

What do young blind children understand about spatial relationships?

Given the nature of the information available in the absence of vision it has been suggested that blind children may not develop a spatial understanding of the world, rather their understanding may be in temporal or kinesthetic terms. Blind children's understanding of spatial relationships has been examined through their ability to recognize objects when rotated (Landau, 1991a), understand the relationship between different spatial terms referring to object parts (Landau, 1991a), recognize and reconstruct spatial relationships between objects (Ungar, Blades, & Spencer, 1995a) or people (Landau, 1991b), relate different locations (Bigelow, 1991a, 1996; Landau, Spelke, & Gleitman, 1984; Lewis, Collis, Shadlock, Potts, & Norgate, 2002; Morrongiello, Timney, Humphrey, Anderson, & Skory, 1995; Ochaita & Huertas, 1993), make kinesthetic judgments about distances (Millar & Ittyerah, 1991), use maps (e.g., Ungar et al., 1995b, 1996, 1997) and give verbal directions (Edwards, Ungar, & Blades, 1998; Iverson, 1999; Iverson & Goldin-Meadow, 1997).

The ability to recognize objects rotated through 180° was studied in one blind girl between 40 and 48 months and in sighted children aged 3–4 years by Landau (Experiment 3, 1991a). The children were first presented with a standard object consisting of a shape with two appendages and then presented with the standard and a distracter object which was of the same shape as the standard but the appendages were attached to different surfaces. Both objects were either presented in the same orientation as the standard object was initially or rotated through 180° either horizontally, vertically, or diagonally. The blind child identified the standard object at a level greater than expected by chance, as did the sighted children. Clearly this one blind child was able to encode the spatial characteristics of these objects and mentally rotate the object. The same child, when aged 45–48 months, could also correctly identify the spatial parts of unfamiliar objects (top, bottom, front, back, side) when given one label (Experiment 4, Landau, 1991a). In addition, she performed above chance level, but not as well as 4-year-old sighted children, when the object was not canonically presented (e.g., the bottom was labeled the top, or the side facing the child was labeled the back). This indicates that this 4-year-old blind child had a similar understanding as sighted children of spatial relationships within a single object. But do blind children also understand spatial relationships between objects?

This was explored by Ungar et al. (1995a). In this study 5–12-year-old children, some totally blind and some with residual vision, felt different shapes arranged in a circular shallow box and then reconstructed the array on the box lid. They did this under several conditions: with one, three or five objects; immediately or after 1 minute; in the same position or after moving 90° around the box. The delay had no effect on accuracy, but the children positioned the objects more accurately when there were fewer objects and when their relationship to the box did not change. In terms of accuracy there were no age differences or effects of any residual vision. However, there were effects of age and residual vision on how the children initially explored the objects. The children with some residual vision were most likely to look at the objects and not use their hands, particularly when under 8 years. The younger blind children were most likely to touch each object in turn, whereas the blind children of 8 years and older were more likely to use their hands to discover either how the objects related to each other or how the objects related to each other and to the edge of the box. Children using this latter strategy produced the most accurate reconstructions.

Ungar et al.'s study shows that by 8 years blind children have developed ways of exploring object arrangements which enable them to reproduce the array accurately. However, even at this age they have difficulties mentally rotating the arrangement of objects. In a rather different setup involving the position of people, Landau and Spelke (1985) reported in Landau, 1991b) found that a blind 2-year-old was unable to mentally rotate the relative positions of two people. The girl sat at a table opposite the researcher and reached towards person X to her left and person Y to her right. The two people, X and Y, were identified by name but were silent throughout and the child did not touch them. When she moved to the other side of the table she did not reverse the direction of her reaches to X and Y, and did not do so until she was 5 years old. In contrast, sighted 2-year-olds wearing goggles, which prevented them from seeing the layout, were more likely to reach correctly in both situations.

Landau (1991b) argues that reaching is likely to encourage young blind children to use their own bodies as a frame of reference. It is relevant to note that the younger blind children in Ungar et al.'s (1995a) study spontaneously used a pointing strategy when trying to memorize the locations of different shapes, as if trying to remember the objects' positions relative to themselves.

In support of the idea that reaching may encourage the use of an egocentric frame of reference, Landau et al. (1984) found that the same blind girl at 31 months showed an understanding of the relationships between different locations within a room when she had physically walked between some of them. The girl walked with the researcher from location A to three other locations B, C, and D in a room and at each location felt an object. She then walked alone from either B, C, or D to named locations, a task she managed quite successfully although many of the routes she took were curved. Landau (1991b) argues that in this situation the blind girl seemed to have constructed and be using some form of spatial map. This is in contrast to sighted children who seem to make use of spatial knowledge both when reaching and walking.

However, Landau et al.'s conclusions are based on one child and Morrongiello et al. (1995) failed to replicate their findings. In particular, no blind children under 4½ years cooperated with the procedure which immediately raises questions about the generalizability of Landau et al.'s findings. The 6 blind children who did take part were 4–9 years old and their ability to walk between different locations in a space measuring 12' by 16' was compared to that of 6 blindfolded sighted children matched for age and sex. Morrongiello et al. took various objective measures, some of which were the same as those taken by Landau et al.: the direction in which the child initially turned; the closest the child ever got to the named location; and the distance between the child's final position and the correct location. The children did not differ on the first two measures but the sighted children ended up closer to the location. Both groups were helped if a beating metronome was placed at the location they started from. However, without a metronome, the blind children ended up on average almost 6' from the correct location. With a metronome they ended up on average about 2' from the correct location, the same distance as the sighted children without the metronome. Morrongiello et al. (1995) argue that their findings indicate that blind children can build up spatial knowledge about locations in their environment, but that this is easier for a blindfolded sighted child who has experienced spatial relationships between locations visually.

Evidence from two studies by Bigelow (1991a, 1996) also suggests that blind children find it hard to build up a representation of space. Bigelow examined the understanding that 4 blind boys and sighted children had of the relationships between different rooms and spaces in their own homes, gardens, and neighborhoods. In the first study 2 boys with profound visual impairments aged 6 and 8 years, two boys with severe visual impairments aged 6 and 7, and 8 sighted children aged 4–6 years were visited in their own homes every 2 months for up to 15 months and asked to point to familiar places inside and outside the house. The boys with profound visual impairments tended to point to the route they would take to another room or location rather than directly at the room. The other children were much more likely to point along the straight line connecting their position to the named location. Like Morrongiello et al., Bigelow concluded that vision facilitates spatial knowledge. Nevertheless, the blind boys were able to point to familiar objects in the same room, indicating some spatial knowledge of their environment.

Bigelow carried out a second study with the same blind boys when they were 4 years older and additional sighted children aged 8–12 years. In this study the children had to choose the shortest of three imaginary ropes going from where they were sitting to different places around their homes. On some of the trials the ropes were described as magic because they could go in straight lines through walls, ceilings, and floors. On other trials the ropes were described as string which could be rolled along the floor between different places. The boys with profound visual impairments succeeded on these tasks at around the age of 13 years, whereas the boys with severe visual impairments succeeded mainly on the first visit and the sighted children when they were 9 or 10 years old.

Bigelow's findings suggest that in the absence of vision children find it much harder to build up a spatial representation of familiar spaces in Euclidean terms and tend to rely on routes to relate different places. However, while Bigelow's second study overcame the problem that blind children seldom point, it introduced further complications, in particular the need for the children to compare the imagined lengths of ropes which sometimes went through solid structures. Using more child-friendly tasks, such as the child orienting themselves or a teddy towards particular rooms and identifying which cube represented which room when cubes are used to model the child's house, Lewis et al. (2002) reported that a blind boy of 7 years showed clear evidence of understanding the spatial arrangement of rooms in his home in Euclidean terms.

Ochaita and Huertas (1993) found that 14–18-year-old blind adolescents, compared to 9–11-year-olds, produced more accurate models of a space with landmarks which they had previously walked around and were more accurate when estimating distances between landmarks. There were also differences between the 14-year-olds and the 17-year-olds, demonstrating that the ability to represent spatial relationships continues to improve throughout adolescence.

Millar and Ittyerah (1991) examined the ability of 9–18-year-old blind children and adolescents to reproduce the length of a line they had previously felt. The young people first made a 10 cm movement from left to right across their midline. This was followed by a 20-second delay in which they either did nothing, said "blah blah" repeatedly, rehearsed the 10 cm movement, made a 5 cm or 20 cm movement. They were then asked to make a 10 cm movement. Carrying out a 20 cm movement during the delay led to movements greater than 10 cm, whereas the 5 cm movement in the delay resulted in shorter movements. Saying "blah blah" had no effect. The same results were found with 7–9-year-old sighted children who were blindfolded, which led Millar and Ittyerah to argue that both the sighted and the blind children must have been able to code the spatial movements kinesthetically. Interestingly, similar results were obtained if during the delay they simply had to mentally practice making the movement.

I now want to consider blind children's use of maps to locate and guide themselves around space. Ungar et al. have carried out a series of studies exploring the map skills of 6–13-year-old blind children (1995b, 1996; 1997). In one study (Ungar et al., 1996) they examined the ability of 6–12-year-old blind children to locate themselves on a map. The visual abilities of the children varied from total blindness to good residual vision. Twenty-five tiles, of which 16 had unique markings and 9 were unmarked, were laid out in a five by five matrix. The children were given a map of the layout and then taken to a tile and asked to identify where they were on the map. They were then taken in a straight line to the next two tiles and asked where they were when they reached each tile and then, when between the third and fourth tile along the same line, to predict the next tile. The children were correct more than 75% of the time and performed best when the route began from a marked tile. There was no effect of age, visual ability, or whether the orientation of the map matched the tiles or differed by 90°. Clearly these children could use the map to locate themselves.

In a further study Ungar et al. (1995b) looked at how blind and sighted 6–13-year-olds went about learning maps. The sighted children produced more accurate reconstructions of a map than the blind children, which was accounted for by the difference in how the two groups tended to approach the task. The blind children were more likely to read out the names of buildings or describe features and trace routes, whereas the sighted children focused on the spatial relationships between different features and the edges of the map. However, despite the overall group difference there were large differences between children in the two groups. When 7 braille users who produced the most accurate maps were compared to 7 braille users who produced the least accurate maps, the former were found to be using strategies similar to the sighted children. Thus, blind children can make good use of the spatial relationships of objects located on a map but they are less likely to do so than sighted children.

In a third study, Ungar et al. (1997) gave a map to blind and sighted children which showed three objects positioned along a straight path. The children then walked along the actual path, saw or felt the first two objects which were already in place and then had to place the third object according to its position on the map, relative to the other objects. The blind children were worse at this task than the sighted children, although their accuracy improved with age. Interestingly, two 10-year-old blind children spontaneously used the most effective strategy to work out the position of the third object, calculating the ratio on the map between the first and second objects and the second and third objects and applying this to the path. However, the majority of the blind children used less effective strategies. In a second part of the study Ungar et al. trained all the blind children in the ratio strategy just described and found that this improved their accuracy.

Finally, I want to consider the ability of blind children to give directions. Edwards et al. (1998) reported that blind children aged 7–12 gave longer directions for a new pupil to get from one place to another in their school and made more references to following edges, avoiding specific hazards, and using tactual information than sighted children of a similar age. Iverson and Goldin-Meadow (1997) also found that 4 blind boys, aged 10–13 years, used more speech than sighted children and referred to more than six times as many landmarks along the route when asked to give a stranger directions for getting to different places in their school. The blind boys made little or no use of gesture. In contrast, sighted children of a similar age described as many steps in the routes using gesture as they did using speech. Iverson and Goldin-Meadow argue that these differences reflect the fact that in the absence of sight children cannot build up a representation of a route "at a glance," rather they have to construct it sequentially, piece by piece. They found some support for this suggestion in that the sighted children were less likely to gesture when they described the route in terms of a sequence of landmarks.

Further support for the idea of blind and sighted children constructing different representations of routes was provided in a later paper (Iverson, 1999). In this study, blind and sighted adolescents aged 9–19 years described a route to a location in their school to a stranger (as in the first study) and a route marked on a small-scale model measuring 35 cm by 35 cm. As predicted, the blind adolescents used more speech and less gesture than the sighted adolescents when describing routes in their schools, but in the model task both groups used more gestures and there were no group differences in the amount of speech or gesture used. Further, the adolescents seldom referred to landmarks in the model task whereas this was fairly common for school routes, especially among the blind. Finally, there was a significant negative correlation between segmenting the route and using gesture.

How can these different results be reconciled? It seems clear that there is variation in the understanding that blind children have of spatial relationships. Several case studies of blind children have demonstrated good spatial awareness in relatively young children. However, there is evidence from other studies that many blind children are delayed in developing an understanding of spatial relationships. Thus, blindness itself does not preclude an understanding of spatial relationships but it may make it more difficult. In addition, blind children and adolescents may represent spatial relationships differently from their sighted peers. This reminds me of an anecdote of a blind man who for years had been getting from shop A to shop B by turning left out of shop A and walking for 250 yards around several corners. When he was given a tactual map of the shopping area he was amazed to discover that shop B was actually next door to shop A, to the right. Clearly vision can facilitate spatial knowledge, but lack of vision does not preclude spatial knowledge of either the relationships between parts of an object or between objects.

What do young blind children understand about themselves and other people?

In this section I shall examine blind children's understanding of body parts, their appreciation of what sighted people can do and see, their ability to take different visual perspectives and to understand that other people have different thoughts and beliefs.

Blind children may be unaware of things we take for granted, for example, that people have two hands. They cannot perceive other people's bodies at a glance as sighted children can, nor can they look at themselves in a mirror. They can only feel one part at a time, and they may have real difficulties understanding how all the different parts relate to each other, even though many of their actions will be centered on their own bodies. Interestingly, Kephart et al. (1974) found that 5–7-year-old blind children, when asked to describe a child verbally, gave less information than sighted children, in particular fewer facial details and they often omitted fingers and ears. Problems in understanding how body parts are related may create real problems later on, particularly in societies where touching is taboo. The blind adolescent may be especially confused about differences between the sexes.

If blind children are constructing their understanding of other people through tactual and auditory experiences they are likely to be slower than sighted children to understand that people can do things for them. Blind babies will not be able to watch the actions of others on objects, nor anticipate the end result. They will not be able to observe any visual consequences of their own actions. In the first year of life sighted children will be discovering about cause and effect by manipulating toys and objects, and observing the actions of other people. Long before they can talk, sighted children will see a toy they want, gesture towards it, make noises, look at their parent, and generally make their request quite clear. This reflects an understanding that people can do things. But blind children will not gesture or make requesting noises towards out of reach objects until they realize that there are objects beyond their reach, that they have particular locations, and that others can get them. They do not have sight to prompt requests. They do not observe people bringing objects to them, objects just arrive in their hands. In fact, it may be sometime after blind children have begun to talk that they show an understanding of other people's ability to do things, and this may be marked by a rapid expansion of their language skills as they realize that they can use language to get people to do things.

Similarly, blind children may be slower to develop an appropriate understanding of other people's experience and knowledge. This has been explored in several ways: by examining what they do when asked to show someone else an object or hide themselves or something from someone else. Both showing an object to another or hiding something require children to take the perspective of another person, that is, to imagine how something would be seen from a different vantage point. This understanding has been examined in several studies, as has their ability to understand that other people may have different knowledge and beliefs from their own. I shall consider these studies in the rest of this section.

Landau and Gleitman (1985) reported that a 3½-year-old blind girl oriented herself appropriately when asked to show a sighted person different parts of her clothing. However, when asked to show something to an adult she often moved closer, although at 4½ years she didn't move closer when asked to let her mother see an object "with her eyes." This suggests that from quite young blind children understand some of the implications of vision. In a particularly interesting study of two blind brothers, aged 4 and 6 years, Bigelow (1988) reported that when they were asked to show an object to each other or to a sighted relation they would hand the object to their brother, but realized that those with sight could view the object from a distance. However, if the object was more than 5 feet away the children often moved it closer if it was portable or said that it could not be seen if it could not be moved. Thus, to be seen by sighted people, they believed that objects had to be within 5 feet. It seems as though the boys' understanding of what can and cannot be seen has been guided by their own experience: while it is relatively easy to reach and touch objects which are close it is more difficult when objects are at a distance. This explanation can also account for why the younger child, when asked to show a sighted person something which had been attached to his back, did not turn around. He could feel the object himself and so presumed it was visible to another person.

In a second study, Bigelow (1991b) examined longitudinally how 2 blind boys, 2 boys with some residual vision, and sighted children hid a part or all of a toy or themselves. The blind boys were 6 and 7 years old, the boys with some sight were 5 and 6 years old, and the sighted children were between 4 and 6 years old. The children with some residual vision behaved more like the sighted children than the two blind boys. Over the course of a year the boys with some residual vision developed the ability to hide themselves or a toy completely and to indicate whether or not they could be seen. However, like the youngest sighted children, the blind boys were more likely to cover the toy or the part of their body with their hands, which often meant the hiding was only partial. When asked to hide themselves their behavior was often inappropriate, just covering their face (particularly the mouth), or making themselves small and keeping still and quiet. They were still unable to completely hide themselves when they were more than 7 and 9 years old respectively. For these children, hiding appeared to mean covering, as opposed to being out of sight behind a large object, for example.

The findings from these two studies indicate that blind children have a concept of seeing which is informed by experience of the tactual system. This raises the question of whether or not blind children are able to take the perspective of another person. Can they imagine what something might look like to someone who is not sitting or standing where they are? Miletic (1995) examined the perspective-taking skills of blind children, children with some residual vision, and sighted children, of mean age just under 9 years, by presenting them with an object with distinctive sides and asking them what a doll could see if the doll sat in a different position from the child. The blind children could do the task if the doll was sitting where they were sitting, and were occasionally correct when the doll sat opposite them, whereas the children with residual vision responded correctly to most of the doll's positions and the sighted children performed almost at ceiling.

Interestingly, in a previous study with blind adolescents and adolescents with some residual vision who were older, mean chronological age 13½ years, Miletic (1994) found that those blind adolescents trained to use a device converting visual information into vibrotactual stimulation to their fingertip were as able as children with some residual vision to describe what a doll would see from different positions and better than blind children not using the device. Miletic argues that this means that the difficulties that blind children have with tasks of this sort result from the difficulties they have obtaining relevant information from the environment, rather than from any cognitive deficit.

Four further studies have examined blind children's ability to take the perspective of another person. Landau and Gleitman (1985) reported that a 4½-year-old blind girl would walk around barriers to show something to her mother. This could indicate that she understood that her mother couldn't see something if her line of sight was blocked. Alternatively, the child may simply have thought the object needed to be brought closer for her mother to see it. Certainly, Bigelow (1991c) indicates that blind children may have difficulties knowing when a sighted person can see something. She reports three tasks in which three blind boys, three children with some residual vision, and sighted children were asked if a researcher could see a toy the child was holding when the researcher was: (i) up to 6 meters in front of the child with nothing in between; (ii) up to 6 meters behind the child with nothing in between; (iii) more than 1½ meters in front of the child with either furniture or walls blocking her view of the toy. Thus, the researcher could see the toy in (i) but not in (ii) or (iii). The sighted children succeeded on these tasks between the ages of 3 and 6 years and the children with some residual vision were between 6 and 7 years old when they were successful, whereas the blind children were over 8 years. Both the blind children and the children with some residual vision were more likely to give a correct response when the researcher was less than 1 meter away in tasks (i) and (ii).

In another study Bigelow (1992b) asked 2 blind boys, aged 6 years 4 months and 7 years 11 months at the outset, to position a toy so the researcher could see one part better than another part. Rather than orienting the relevant part towards the researcher, they tended to touch the part or cover the rest of the toy. They did not orient the toy appropriately until they were 7 years 5 months and 8 years 8 months respectively. In contrast, 2 boys with some residual vision and younger sighted children were much more likely to orient the toy so that the relevant part faced the tester. Once again, the characteristics of the tactual system seem to have been used by the blind boys to guide their understanding of the visual system: in order to feel a part of a toy, the toy does not have to be oriented towards you. In the absence of any vision this belief persisted for some time.

All these findings, using various methodologies, suggest that blind children find it very difficult to take the perspective of another person. However, Peterson, Peterson, and Webb (2000) produced rather different results. The children were aged between 5 and 13 years. The child sat on one side of a square table, one researcher sat opposite the child, and a second researcher sat 90° to the child's left or right. The paradigm was similar to that used by Bigelow (1992b) in that the child had to orient an object so that one of the researchers had the best view of a particular part. Twenty out of the 23 children tested always oriented the objects correctly and only 1 of the 3 children who did not perform at ceiling seemed to have a genuine difficulty with this perspective-taking task. Importantly,

10 of the 23 children were totally blind or had light perception and the rest had some residual vision, which makes the findings particularly impressive. Peterson et al. point out that previous studies may have used objects with parts that were not particularly easy to discriminate tactually and this might account for the difficulties experienced by blind children in other studies. Nevertheless, this study does suggest that blind children may be able to take the perspective of another person from as young as 5 years 7 months, the age of the youngest child in this study.

I now want to consider whether or not blind children understand that other people have knowledge and beliefs which may be different from their own, often described as understanding other minds (McAlpine & Moore, 1995; Minter, Hobson, & Bishop, 1998; Peterson et al., 2000; Pring, Dewart, & Brockbank, 1998). These studies have all used theory of mind tasks in which the child is presented with a scenario and asked what another person or character knows or is thinking. McAlpine and Moore (1995) gave 4–12-year-old children with a range of visual impairments two theory of mind tasks involving the child discovering that two containers (a polystyrene food container and a milk carton) had unexpected contents (a sock and water respectively). The children were then asked what another person would think was in the containers when they first saw them. Ten children passed both tasks and 5 children failed both tasks. Within the group there were 4 totally blind children and 2 of these, both 5 years old, failed both tasks. The other 2 blind children passed both tasks but they were 9 and 11½ years, older than the other children. McAlpine and Moore conclude that children with visual impairments of 20/400 or less are delayed in understanding that other people may have different beliefs.

McAlpine and Moore did not include any sighted children. However, Minter et al. (1998) included sighted children and also a larger group of blind children with light perception or less. The children were 5–9 years old and there were 21 in each group. There were two tasks. In the first the children all felt a warm teapot and were asked what they thought was in it. Most responded that there was tea or some other drink in the pot. However, when the "tea" was poured out it was found to be sand. The children were then asked what they thought was in the teapot when they first felt it and what a friend would think was in the pot if they felt it. Less than 10% of the sighted children gave incorrect answers, compared with 42% (child's original belief) and 53% (friend's belief) for the blind children. The blind children who failed had mental ages of 5 years 7 months, compared with 7 years 11 months for the children who passed. The second task involved three containers and a pencil. One researcher put the pencil in one box and while she was out of the room the child and a different researcher moved the pencil to another box. The theory of mind question concerned where the first researcher would look for her pencil.

All the sighted children and 80% of the blind children passed. Thus, the blind children did better on the changed location task than on the misleading container task.

Commenting on Minter et al.'s (1998) findings, Peterson et al. (2000) point out that the blind children may have performed better in the changed location task because they may have had less experience of teapots and be more likely to judge the contents of a teapot by smell than by touch. They also point out that misleading container tasks require more sophisticated perspective-taking skills than changed location tasks and suggest that this could account for Minter et al.'s results. In the changed location task the child only has to appreciate that the other person has not seen the object being moved, whereas in the misleading container task the child has to appreciate that the other person will expect certain contents and will be unaware that the contents have been tampered with. Peterson et al. therefore gave 5–13-year-old children with a range of visual impairments, but including 10 who were totally blind, a series of tasks: two misleading container tasks; two changed location tasks; a visual perspective task. The misleading container and changed location tasks were passed by between 62% and 73% of the children, and 87% of the children passed the perspective-taking task. Clearly perspective-taking skills are not influencing theory of mind performance in these children. Peterson et al. found that visual ability did not influence the likelihood of success on the theory of mind tasks but that age did, with only 14% of the 5½ to 7½-year-old children passing all four theory of mind tasks compared with 70% of the 11–13-year-old children. Peterson et al. argue that the improved performance of the children on these tasks was largely due to the care with which they selected and piloted materials to ensure they were suitable for research with blind children.

One way to overcome the problem of selecting suitable materials is to present tasks verbally. One of the changed location tasks used by Peterson et al. was presented verbally, and interestingly, more children passed this task than the other tasks. Pring et al. (1998) also employed a verbal theory of mind task with 9–13-year-old children with a range of visual impairments and sighted children. The children were read 24 stories in which characters said or did things, such as told lies, said something sarcastic, or misunderstood another character's knowledge or belief. When the children were asked why the characters behaved in these ways, the sighted children were aware of the mental state of the characters in an average of 19.4 stories, compared to 16.3 for the children with visual impairments. The children who had light perception or less did as well as the children with some residual vision. Clearly, although the blind children did not do as well as the sighted children, they still demonstrated an understanding of the mental states of others.

From the studies reviewed in this section it is clear that blind children do not have the same understanding of people as sighted children of similar age. Nevertheless, many blind children will come to understand and appreciate the feelings and beliefs of others and be able to imagine how the world looks from their perspective. However, in the absence of vision these developments take longer.

What do blind children understand about quantity and number?

According to Piaget (e.g., 1983), it is not until the concrete operational stage of development, from about 6 years, that sighted children use concepts such as number, volume, weight, mass, classification, and seriation appropriately. For this development, Piaget held that it was necessary for the child to have manipulated and acted on the environment through experiences with, for example, water and sand, plasticine, or arranging toy animals in lines. Blind children have far fewer experiences of the environment and are much less likely to engage in this sort of play since much of it is heavily dependent on a visual component, although there are obvious tactual impressions. If this sort of opportunity is a necessary prerequisite for such concepts to develop, blind children should be delayed in their acquisition.

A number of studies have reported delays (e.g., Gottesman, 1973; Hatwell, 1966; Markoulis, 1988; Miller, 1969; Tobin, 1972). One of the best known is Hatwell's study of conservation. This is the ability to recognize a quantity, which has been changed perceptually, as still retaining, for example, the same mass, weight, and volume. Hatwell found that blind children showed conservation of mass at 10 years and weight at 12 years approximately, compared to 7 and 8 years respectively for sighted children. On tasks in which the children had to seriate items verbally, Hatwell reported that blind children performed as well as sighted children, but Piaget has argued that this verbal ability is insufficient to compensate for the delayed sensorimotor development of blind individuals (Cromer, 1974). These studies seem to support Piaget's emphasis on the importance of active experimentation for the development of concrete operational intelligence. When it is limited, as in blind children, delays result.

In contrast, there are several studies which suggest that blind children may achieve at least some of these abilities within the sighted age range (Cromer, 1973; Ittyerah & Samarapungavan, 1989; Iverson & Goldin-Meadow, 1997). Cromer (1973) criticized Hatwell's study on several grounds. For example, Hatwell compared blind children from a rural setting with urbanized sighted children, and the blind children did not start school until 2 years after the sighted children. Either or both of these differences could account for the observed delays. Cromer himself found that there were no differences between the performances of blind children and sighted children, half of whom were blindfolded, on conservation of mass and amount. Unfortunately, Cromer did not have any blind children aged between 7 and 7¾ and, as Warren (1977) points out, this may be the age at which any differences between the two groups are most marked. Notwithstanding this, Cromer's study certainly failed to confirm the large delays reported by Hatwell.

Similarly, Iverson and Goldin-Meadow (1997) found no difference between the performance of 4 blind boys and 20 sighted children, half of whom wore blindfolds, aged 10–13 years on eight conservation tasks, including continuous quantity, length, number, and mass. The study by Ittyerah and Samarapungavan (1989) was more extensive in that it examined a number of Piagetian tasks in blind children, blindfolded sighted children, and sighted children aged between 4 and 12 years. They reported no differences between the groups on conservation of number and transitivity, both verbal and using one stick to judge the relative sizes of two other sticks. In addition, compared to the blindfolded sighted children, the blind children were better at seriation but less good on conservation of mass (though all of the children did poorly on this), object classification, and object rotation tasks.

On balance, it seems that blind children may be slightly delayed in developing the ability to conserve, although the actual delay may not be as great as early reports suggested. However, what is more interesting than the question of delay versus no delay, or how much delay, is the question of the processes underlying the development. Are the conservation skills of blind children the end result of the same process as occurs in sighted children or not? Cromer's study throws some light on this issue. As well as reporting the children's responses, Cromer also reports the reasons they gave for their judgments of conservation or non-conservation. What was particularly striking here was that there were no significant differences between the reasons given by the three groups of children, blind, sighted, and blindfolded, for either conservation or non-conservation responses.

In comparison, there were marked differences between the reasons given by the non-conservers and the conservers. Most of the non-conservers gave reasons referring to the dimensions of the containers, and the conservers mostly gave reasons which acknowledged the transformation, for example, "because they were the same before," and "all you did was change it." Despite these similarities between the reasons given by the blind children and the sighted children, there is a suggestion that the process may be different. In one task ping-pong balls were transferred from one of two identical wire mesh cylinders into a taller, thinner cylinder. Four of the 6 non-conserving blind children said that there were fewer balls in the tall container; all the sighted children who failed to conserve, whether blind-folded or not, said that the tall cylinder contained more balls. This suggests that the tactual and visual impressions of the children are not equivalent, and may reflect different underlying processes. That the difference is in the process rather than merely in the modality of the task is supported by the fact that the blindfolded sighted non-conserving children gave the same sorts of reasons as the sighted non-conservers, rather than reasons similar to those of the non-conservers who were blind.

There is also evidence that the ways in which blind and sighted children solve simple addition and subtraction problems may differ, indicating that the process by which they come to understand the meaning of numbers differs. Ahlberg (2000) reported that sighted children aged 6–7 years and blind children aged 5–9 years (see also Ahlberg & Csocsán, 1999) used some of the same strategies but also some different strategies to solve numerical problems. The following strategies were used equally often by both groups: producing random numbers; repeating numbers used in the question; giving a number which followed in sequence from a number used in the question; estimating the answer. Clearly answers based on these strategies are likely to be incorrect. Both groups also frequently used a strategy involving counting up or down and listening to how many numbers they had said, and they both infrequently touched something such as a table in order to try to keep track of particular numbers.

In comparison, the groups differed in their likely use of several strategies. The blind children made much more use of a double counting strategy in which they counted and kept track of two number sequences in parallel. Thus, a 7-year-old blind girl, when asked how she added 5 coins to 13 coins, said "14, 1; 15, 2; 16, 3; 17, 4. So there are 18." In contrast, the sighted children often made use of their fingers, for example, using them to represent the numbers involved and then counting those fingers, or they simply looked at their fingers and realized the answer without actually counting individual fingers. None of the blind children used their fingers. Both groups of children used their knowledge about the relationships between numbers to help them solve problems; however, these strategies were common among the blind children and infrequent in the sighted children. Thus, a 7-year-old blind boy subtracted 7 from 15 by taking "2 from 15 then 2 and 2 and 1." Similarly, the blind children frequently just said that they knew certain answers, for example, that 6 minus 3 is 3. This use of known number facts was fairly infrequent in the sighted children. This study clearly shows that blind children find ways of solving simple arithmetic problems in the absence of vision, although Ahlberg gives no information about how well the two groups of children performed.

Thus, despite not being able to visually experience their environment, blind children seem to come to much the same understanding of quantity and number as sighted children, although there may be slight delays. However, the ways in which they go about solving problems suggest that in the absence of vision they adopt different strategies.

How do blind children remember things?

Blind children are often reported to have good memories. For example, Hull and Mason (1995) found that 314 blind children aged 5–18 years could recall more digits on the digit-span test of the WISC (Wechsler, 1974) than the sighted children on whom it was standardized. Thus, at the age of 8 years the sighted children could recall about 10 digits, the blind children between 12 and 13. However, Wyver and Markham (1998) failed to find superior digit spans for 19 blind children aged 4–12 years compared to sighted children of similar age. The visual acuities of the children in this study ranged from no light perception to 6/60 and the authors do not indicate what proportion had light perception or less. Interestingly, when the blind children in Hull and Mason's study were divided into those who had had light perception or less from birth and those whose vision was better than this, the former group recalled more even though they were younger. Thus, it may be that superior digit spans are only a characteristic of children with light perception or less.

Several studies indicate that blind children with light perception or less may be better than sighted children at recalling information which has not been processed semantically. For example, Pring (1988) compared the free recall of 14-year-old blind adolescents and sighted adolescents of two lists of words which were read to them: the adolescents either repeated each word as it was read, or generated a word closely associated semantically. Although there was no overall difference between the two groups, the blind adolescents recalled more of the repeated words than the self-generated words, whereas the reverse was found for the sighted adolescents. This "reverse generation" effect was also found in other experiments using different methods and the adolescents reading the materials in braille or print, despite the fact that the adolescents had been matched for digit span.

Using a rather different paradigm Pring and Mulkern (1992) found that 11–15-year-old blind adolescents recalled more nonsense words that they had read out loud than sighted adolescents of similar age. Thus, once again, blind adolescents seem better than sighted adolescents at recalling information with little or no semantic meaning. Wyver and Markham (1998) did not find any difference in recall of nonsense words by their

4–12-year-old blind and sighted children. However, as we have already noted, some of these children had some form of perception.

However, the converse of Pring's findings is that when semantic process- ing might help memory, blind children may be disadvantaged. Some sup- port for this comes from Pathak and Pring (1989). Blind adolescents and sighted adolescents who were blindfolded, aged 12–16 years, felt three raised line drawings of objects. Then, one of the objects was named and the task was to identify the corresponding picture. Although in previous studies blind adolescents were better than sighted adolescents at identify- ing which of three raised line drawings of objects they had felt before, when required to identify which picture matched an object name they did less well than sighted adolescents. Pathak and Pring suggest that the sighted adolescents may be generating the objects' names as they feel the pictures, whereas the blind adolescents focus on the perceptual features and do not label the objects. In the selection task the sighted adolescents simply have to identify the picture with the same name, whereas the blind adolescents cannot do this.

These findings suggest that the way in which blind children and adoles- cents code information is different from sighted children. They seem to focus more on the perceptual features of material, and less on the mean- ing of the material. This can sometimes be to their advantage. However, it can sometimes mean that they find it more difficult to remember informa- tion. Interestingly, this difference could also account for why some 1–2- year-old blind children have expressive language skills considerably in advance of their comprehension skills (McConachie, 1990).

Although blind children are delayed in certain aspects of their cognitive development, the delays that are experienced by many of them are small. Blind children appear to develop similar concepts to sighted children, al- though the process by which this occurs will often be different. Neverthe- less, they are deprived of many of the sensorimotor experiences typical of sighted children's first 2 years, and this raises further questions about the effect this will have on language development. Will their language reflect the limitations of their cognitive development, or provide them with a means of lifting themselves out of their restricting environment?

The development of communication

The onset of language in blind children is a very significant event for most parents. Language provides the opportunity for parents and children to share what is going on. But how does blindness affect communication? In the sections that follow I shall examine how parents and blind children communicate before the children have acquired any language, how parents talk to their blind children, and how blindness may affect the children's acquisition and use of language. Finally, I shall consider the consequences of blindness for reading and writing.

How do blind children and their parents communicate before the children can speak?

Unless it is obvious at birth that a child is blind as, for example, in anophthalmia when one or both eyes are missing, the parents may first become suspicious when they notice that their baby does not look at their faces, smile at them when they smile or follow them as they move around the room. The lack of eye contact may cause the parents to feel rebuffed and they may withdraw from the baby. If this happens and persists, parent–child interaction may suffer.

Some parents may find it hard to talk to blind babies, to know what to talk about, and may react either by not talking at all, or by talking nonstop. Why is it so difficult to communicate with blind babies? Most parents find it relatively easy to talk to sighted babies. They talk about what the babies are doing, what they are doing, about the objects and events that they and the babies can see. Interestingly, Preisler (1991, 1995, 1997) reported that the interactions between blind babies and their mothers in the first 6 months are comparable to the interactions occurring between sighted babies and their mothers. In the absence of vision, the babies interacted fairly successfully with their parents: they smiled and vocalized as their parents approached, they cooed and smiled appropriately and engaged in body touching games and songs. Thus, in the first 6 months, when the emphasis is on the relationship between parent and baby, the interaction does not seem to be greatly affected if the baby cannot see. It is when the interaction would normally begin to involve objects that differences emerge.

From the age of about 9 months sighted babies begin to involve objects in interactions with their parents. They may see something, point to it, look towards their parents, make a noise, initiating a preverbal vocal exchange. They begin to engage in give and take routines, offering an object to their parents and taking it when returned. The nature of the interaction has altered by the inclusion of objects into the exchange. According to Preisler (1991, 1995, 1997), this does not happen until much later with blind children. This secondary intersubjectivity was not observed until the blind children were about 21 months old and could use language to share their interest in the environment with their parents. Interestingly, even a little residual vision affected this, such children sharing objects with their parents at a similar age to sighted children.

Does this have any significance for later development? Norgate, Collis, and Lewis (1998) suggest that it might. Norgate et al. examined the relationship between the extent to which objects were involved in parent–child interaction for 4 blind children between the ages of 1 and 3 years and their cognitive and language development at 5 years. At 5 years, 2 of the children showed marked delays in these areas whereas the other 2 were developing well. The focus of interest between the ages of 1 and 3 years was the rhymes and routines in which the dyads engaged. The children who were doing well at 5 years engaged in rhymes and routines with their parents for about 22% of the observation time compared to 51% for the 2 who did less well at 5 years. However, and more importantly, the nature of these activities differed between the two pairs of children. For the children who did well at 5 years, objects were involved in the early routines relatively frequently (35% and 69% of the time compared to 8% and 5% for the children showing delays at 5 years), they spent less time engaged in traditional nursery rhymes (21% and 1% compared to 36% and 69%), and they were more likely to initiate these sorts of activities.

What might have caused these early differences? One possibility is that they reflect preexisting developmental differences between the children. An alternative is that the parents of the 2 children who involved objects in their routines early on were more sensitive to their children's behavior and found ways to bring objects into the interaction. At the moment we have no way of distinguishing between these alternatives. However, Moore and McConachie (1994) suggest that parents of blind children may find it difficult to tune into their children's behavior. They examined interactions between parents and their blind babies aged 1–2 years. Half of the children had light perception or less; half had some residual vision. The parents of the blind children talked less about objects to which the children were attending and more about potential objects than the parents of the children with some vision. The parents of the blind children also made fewer references to the properties of objects to which the children were attending. In comparison, they were more likely to request information from the children.

These findings suggest that parents may find it difficult to adjust their interaction to the interests of their blind children. However, Pérez-Pereira and Conti-Ramsden (1999) point out that Moore and McConachie based their findings on one 15-minute observation of each dyad. Pérez-Pereira and Conti-Ramsden's own research with slightly older blind children raises questions as to whether cross-sectional studies involving such short observation periods provide a true picture of what is going on. Also, other researchers report that some parents are good at tuning into their child's interests. For example, Tobin (1992) describes how a "dialogue" developed between a 12-month-old blind girl and her mother: the child scratched the rough fabric on the arm of a chair several times, with no apparent intention; in one of the gaps her mother scratched the fabric and paused; the child repeated the action, stopped, and a "dialogue" developed with faster and faster alternations of turns by the child and her mother.

Blind children will show their interest in different ways from sighted children. Preisler (1997) points out that from about 9 months blind babies show their intentions and desires through vocalizations and body movements. Fraiberg (1977) noticed that although the faces of blind children may give nothing away, their hands often reflect their interest in a particular toy, searching for a toy they have dropped, casting away a toy they are not interested in, recognizing their parent's face by touching it, their awareness of their parent's departure. Their hands, rather than their faces, are their means of expression. As part of her intervention work with parents of blind babies, Fraiberg directed their attention away from their baby's face and towards their baby's hands. She reports that once it is pointed out to parents that their babies are expressing themselves, they become aware of and receptive to their baby's hand language. They then find it much easier and more rewarding to interact with their baby. Clearly, more research is needed to identify the ways in which blind babies express their interest and how parents interact successfully with their blind children.

As well as parents needing to be responsive to their children's interests, it is also important that children can take account of their parent's behavior. For example, Walden and Ogan (1988) found that sighted children from about 14 months look towards their parent when presented with a strange toy or a stranger approaches for cues about how to respond. What happens when the child cannot see? Recchia (1997, 1998) examined social referencing behaviors in blind children between the ages of 1 and 4 years when something rather strange happened – either a stranger approached and interacted with the child or an air blower was turned in the child's direction – compared with the introduction of two novel noisy toys. The children were more likely to quiet when the toys were presented and move towards them. In the more threatening situation the children were more likely to turn away, cry, or ignore the stranger or air blower. The children referenced their parents very infrequently and those that did were at least 2 years old. Interestingly, Recchia identified different sorts of dyads. When the parent and child were similar in terms of how much they communicated, with both being either low or high communicators, the children were more likely to turn to their mothers before approaching. However, in dyads where the mothers communicated little and the children communicated a lot, the children were most likely to approach without any reference to their mothers, whereas low communicating children with high communicating mothers tended not to approach until their mothers had communicated with them.

Thus, although in the first 6 months blind children and their parents may interact in ways very similar to sighted children and their parents, differences emerge soon after and are associated with the difficulties that blind children have in understanding that there are objects in the environment and people with whom they can share information. However, as we saw in the studies by Preisler and Recchia, these differences seem to be most marked in the first 2 years of life and may be overcome once blind children begin to talk. Language will enable them to discover what is going on around them, to ask questions about the environment, and at last their parents will be able to communicate with them. Nevertheless, even with the onset of language, blind children and their parents will not experience the environment in the same way. They may feel, hear, smell, and taste the same things, but much of the parents' experience and language is based on what they see, and this experience is not available to their children. How does this affect the language that others use to blind children?

Do parents speak differently to blind children and sighted children?

The language used by parents to young blind children needs to be adjusted to the children's experience of the environment. It also seems obvious that the parents' language is a potential source of information for blind children, information which might otherwise not be available. Thus, we might expect that the language spoken to blind children would be rich and informative. For some children this may be the case. Thus, Peters (1994) describes how the father of a boy aged 20–30 months, with a small amount of poor quality peripheral vision, provided a running narrative on what was going on, both about what he was doing and what the child was doing. He also used language to coach his son's behavior. Interestingly, this father was a linguist and had clearly thought a great deal about how to stimulate his son's language. Even so, his language was still very situation specific, presumably to minimize confusing the child in the absence of vision. Preisler (1997) points to variation in how parents talk to their blind children, some being very directive, others using language to tell the children about their own thoughts, feelings and ideas.

Nevertheless, a number of studies report that the language heard by many young blind children may be somewhat impoverished. For example, Kekelis and Andersen (1984; also Andersen, Dunlea, & Kekelis, 1993) found that the language spoken to 4 blind children observed monthly between 16 and 33 months differed from that spoken to 2 sighted children in a number of ways. From 19 months the blind children received more imperatives, more Wh- questions, fewer declaratives, and more labels, many of which were repeated, and more requests for actions. The parents of the sighted children elaborated on what was going on and provided descriptions of objects and events. This seldom occurred with the blind children. The parents of the blind children initiated more topics, especially at the younger ages, and these topics were mainly centered on what the children were doing. By contrast, the parents of the sighted children initiated fewer topics, but when they did these were more likely to focus on the environment than on the children. Thus, these blind children were receiving a much more restricted language input in terms of information about the environment.

Kekelis and Prinz (1996) also reported that mothers of blind children spoke more to their children than mothers of sighted children. They observed the interactions between 2 blind children aged 27 and 31 months and their parents and 2 sighted children aged 27 and 32 months and their parents monthly for 7 months. The blind children and sighted children were matched for mean length of utterance (MLU) initially. The mothers of the blind children produced between two and three times more utterances than their children, whereas the sighted children and their mothers produced a similar number of utterances. The mothers asked their children a similar number of questions, accounting for 14% and 28% of their utterances, but the blind children were asked many more questions testing their knowledge, whereas the sighted children were asked more questions about their feelings, wishes, or interpretations of events. Kekelis and Prinz point out that this latter sort of question is more likely to promote conversation. However, unlike previous studies, Kekelis and Prinz did not find that the mothers of these blind children used more directives.

Behl, Akers, Boyce, and Taylor (1996) found that although the mothers of 1–5-year-old blind children spoke more to their children than mothers of sighted children, this difference was not significant. However, these researchers did find that the mothers of the blind children were more physically involved with their children and controlled the children's activities to a greater extent than the mothers of sighted children.

Conti-Ramsden and Pérez-Pereira (1999; also Pérez-Pereira & Conti-Ramsden, 2001) suggest that increased maternal directives may be more common with younger blind children than studied by Kekelis and Prinz. They observed three children at 22, 23, and 25 months playing with their mothers at home. One child was totally blind, one had residual vision, and one was sighted. In agreement with Kekelis and Prinz's findings, the mother of the blind child produced two to three times more utterances than her child, whereas for the other dyads the contributions of mother and child were similar and all three children produced a similar number of utterances. Unlike previous studies, the mothers did not differ in the number of descriptions they gave. However, the mother of the blind child did use more directives than the other mothers. Conti-Ramsden and Pérez-Pereira made two important observations about the nature of the directives of the mother of the blind child. The first was that about 50 % of her directives included descriptions, compared to less than 20% of the other mothers'. The second observation was that the mother of the blind child tended to repeat directives, with 15–25% of her directives being repeated compared with less than 15% of the other mothers'. Interestingly, if repetitions of directives were not counted, the mothers did not differ in the number of directives they produced. It seems likely that the mother of the blind child repeated directives and provided descriptions within her directives in order to try to help her child make sense of what was going on.

Clearly, there are a number of differences in how parents talk to blind children and to sighted children. However, a number of these differences may simply reflect parents trying to provide their children with an input which can help them make sense of the environment. An important question to ask is whether how parents talk to their blind children has any impact on the children's development, particularly language development. In a series of studies based on observations of up to 18 mother–child dyads, Dote-Kwan and colleagues examined the relationship between the development of 20–36-month-old blind children and maternal behavior (Dote-Kwan, 1995; Hughes, Dote-Kwan & Dolendo, 1999), and followed them up 12–15 months later (Dote-Kwan et al., 1997).

Dote-Kwan (1995) found positive relationships between the development of eighteen 20–36-month-old blind children and a number of maternal behaviors: complying with the children's requests, repeating or rephrasing the children's utterances, adding new information to the children's utterance. Development in the children was negatively correlated with the mothers trying to attract their attention by saying their name repeatedly and encouraging them to engage in mobility tasks.

In a further paper, Hughes et al. (1999) reported positive correlations between the children's receptive and expressive language on the Reynell–Zinkin Scales at 20–36 months and both how appropriate the mothers' directives were and the quality of the mothers' control over the children's activities. In contrast, the children's pragmatic language skills were negatively correlated with how much the mothers controlled the activities and the amount of directives they used. These correlations are interesting; however, nothing causal can be inferred from them. In addition, Hughes et al. did not distinguish between the different levels of visual impairment, and this is crucial given the well-established impact of some vision on the behavior of both children and parents.

In order to examine the nature of these correlations, Dote-Kwan et al. (1997) revisited 15 of these mother–child dyads 12–15 months later and

examined the children's development on the Reynell–Zinkin Scales in relation to both concurrent maternal behaviors and maternal behaviors at
the earlier time point. Significant correlations were found between the
children's current development and the following maternal behaviors a
year earlier: complying with the children's requests; repeating and rephrasing what the children said; the mother's pacing of rate of speech and length
of pauses between utterances. Interestingly, these maternal behaviors were
less likely to be correlated with the children's current development.

Clearly there are a number of differences between how parents talk to
blind children and to sighted children and some evidence that how others
respond influences the children's development. Nevertheless, the most significant effect on their language will be their inability to see and experience their environment visually. But how is their language affected?

Is the language of blind children different from that of sighted children?

Blind children babble in much the same way as sighted children and at a
similar age (see, for example, Mills, 1987) although they may babble less,
presumably because they rely more on listening, and it is harder to listen
if you are making a noise yourself. In contrast, a number of early reports
suggested that blind children were delayed in attaining various language
milestones. However, it now seems likely that some of these delays were
due to the inclusion of children with additional disabilities, often as a
result of prematurity, and to the reliance on psychological test item performance rather than on systematic recording of language (e.g., Andersen,
Dunlea, & Kekelis, 1984; Mulford, 1988). Thus, in Mulford's (1988)
review of a number of papers reporting the early language development
of 16 blind children with no other disabilities, the mean age across the
studies for the appearance of the first word was 14.7 months, for 10 words
15.1 months, for 50 words 20.1 months, and for 100 words 21.3 months.
These are very similar to the ages reported for sighted children.

However, a paper published since Mulford's reports that while 9 children with some residual vision, first seen between 11 and 20 months,
began to talk at much the same age as sighted children and the blind
children included in Mulford's paper, 9 children who showed no visually
directed reaching were delayed by several months (McConachie & Moore,
1994). Although these differences were soon made up, it is difficult to
reconcile these findings with Mulford's, particularly as McConachie and
Moore report that all the children were developing normally on the basis
of the Sensorimotor Understanding Scale of the Reynell–Zinkin. Of course,
it is possible that several children did have some undetected developmental

problems, particularly as most of the children with no residual vision had diagnoses involving neural elements of the visual system. This is supported by 2 children whose expressive language was particularly delayed and who had raw scores on the sensorimotor scale below the mean for blind children.

Notwithstanding this one study, there is now a substantial body of literature suggesting that blind children begin to talk at much the same age as sighted children and their early vocabularies expand at much the same rate, although, as is found in sighted children, there are considerable individual differences (Pérez-Pereira & Conti-Ramsden, 1999). Despite this overall similarity, however, there are differences in the composition of the earliest vocabularies of blind children and sighted children. For example, when Bigelow (1987) compared the first 50 words of three blind children (one of whom could reach on sight at 8 months) with those of sighted children, she found that although the majority of the children's words were general nominals, the blind children had fewer of these and more specific nominals than the sighted children. The blind children also had more action words referring to their own actions, fewer modifiers and personal-social words, and no function words such as "allgone," "there," "more," compared to the sighted children. Interestingly, Bigelow (1990) reported that the two blind children who could not reach on sight were delayed in developing a full understanding of the permanence of objects and this was not achieved until after they had acquired some words. In contrast, the child who could reach on sight was not delayed on object permanence tasks and, like sighted children, began to talk at about the same time as he developed this understanding.

Dunlea (1989) concluded from her observations of 4 blind children and 1 sighted child that the blind children, in contrast to the sighted child, tended not to use their early words in contexts other than those in which the words were first learned. She reports that 41% of the sighted child's first 100 words were overextensions, compared with 8–13% for the blind children. She draws parallels between this and the observation that the blind children did not impose any sort of organization on sets of objects such as three round plastic rattles and three plastic balls, suggesting that in both situations these children are not identifying any general referent classes. A lack of generalization also seemed to apply to their comprehension. Word meanings were not generalized from one situation to another. Dunlea argues, on the basis of this, that when blind children begin to talk, they do not perceive the symbolic nature of words. However, as Norgate (1998) points out, blind children may be able to generalize but they may have fewer opportunities to show this ability, and when they do it may be unclear to the observer because of difficulties in the absence of vision of knowing to what the children are attending.

Nevertheless, differences in the composition of the early vocabularies of blind and sighted children can be understood in terms of their different experiences. Sight provides access to a range of objects and events. Sighted children use language to refer to the environment, for example, saying "no ball here" when their ball is out of reach. In contrast, blind children use language to comment on the objects they are in contact with and the actions they are engaged in, for example, saying "up" as they get up. Blind children have far less access to what other people are doing or different examples of the same object group and as a result rarely overgeneralize the words they use. Thus, their vocabularies contain fewer general nominals, more specific nominals, and more action words referring to their own actions, compared to sighted children. The lower incidence of modifiers can be explained partly by the information available to blind children and also, as we saw in the last section, because parents of blind children seldom elaborate on what is going on and provide few descriptions of objects and events.

Many of these observations have been examined in detail in a longitudinal study of twin girls, one of whom was sighted, the other blind (Pérez-Pereira & Castro, 1992; 1997). These girls were observed monthly from the age of 2 years 5 months to 5 years 4 months. In terms of MLU the blind twin was ahead of her sister during most of the period covered, although by the end of the study there was no difference. However, in agreement with Dunlea (1989) and others, the language of the blind twin throughout much of the period focused on her own actions and intentions rather than on the environment around her; she involved others less, seldom offering or showing an object, but she imitated the utterances of others, repeated her own utterances, and reproduced verbal routines to a greater extent than her sister. Nevertheless, most of the observed differences between the twins declined over the course of the study and by the age of 5 years both children were using language to refer to their own actions and intentions to a similar extent. Some differences persisted, although they were smaller: the blind twin continued to call out more, used less speech to accompany offering something to another person or to draw another's attention to something, and used fewer descriptions and more repetitions and routines.

It has been suggested that this repetition of language already heard or spoken, termed echolalia, may have little meaning for blind children. However, when Pérez-Pereira (1994) and Pérez-Pereira and Castro (1997) explored the nature of these utterances they observed that the blind twin in particular seldom produced exactly the same utterances, but they were usually modified in some way and she did this to a greater extent as she got older. On the basis of this they suggest that she was actively processing the language and reproducing it as a way of developing her language skills further. They also observed that most of these utterances were used as speech acts, for example, to attract another's attention, to offer or request something, to express an intention. It was further noted that these utterances were used to maintain the conversation, as suggested by others (e.g., Urwin, 1981). Certainly, older blind children are reported to ask more questions than sighted children (e.g., Erin, 1986), probably as a way of entering into and maintaining a conversation. In a similar way young blind children may discover that if they repeat something their parents have said, their parents may be more likely to carry on talking. Also, such repetitions and routines may serve to introduce many of the basics of communication, for example, that you talk in turns and turns are normally contingent.

A number of studies have indicated that blind children have particular problems using personal pronouns, such as "I" and "you" correctly (e.g., Andersen et al., 1984; Dunlea, 1989; Fraiberg & Adelson, 1973). Thus, blind children may refer to themselves as "you" rather than "I" when responding to a question. For example, if asked "Would you like a biscuit?" blind children might reply "You would like a biscuit" rather than "I would like a biscuit." A number of explanations have been proposed. Fraiberg (1977) drew parallels between incorrect use of pronouns and the difficulty she observed blind children had representing themselves in pretend play, and suggested that without sight the child has difficulty realizing that she is an individual, an "I" in a world of individuals. Andersen et al. (1984) suggested that the problem reflects a more general difficulty with deictic terms whose meaning depends on the perspective of the speaker and that this is much harder to appreciate in the absence of vision. Hobson (e.g.. 1993) has argued that there are a number of similarities between blind children and children with autism, including misuse of pronouns, and that both groups of children, for different reasons, have difficulties constructing an understanding of themselves and others.

However, studies by Pérez-Pereira (1999, Pérez-Pereira & Castro, 1997) indicate that not all blind children reverse pronouns. In 1997, Pérez-Pereira and Castro report that a blind girl made less than 3% pronoun errors between the ages of 2½ and 3½ years and less than 1% over the next 2 years. Her sighted twin made about 1% errors over the 3 years. In 1999, data are reported from 10 to 13 hour-long monthly recordings from 5 children, including the twins reported in 1997. Three children were blind and were observed from 22, 28, and 30 months; 1 had some residual vision and was observed from 14 months; the sighted twin was observed from 30 months. The youngest blind child correctly used first and second person pronouns before he was 2 years old, as did the child with some residual vision. The oldest blind child (the twin) correctly used personal pronouns at the time she was first observed. The sighted child was first observed to produce personal pronouns at the second recording when she was 32 months old. The child with some residual vision and the sighted child made no pronoun reversals. Only the third blind child made a significant number of pronoun reversals, 41%. These detailed studies demonstrate that while some blind children may produce a large number of pronoun reversals, pronoun reversal is not a characteristic of the language of all blind children. Pérez-Pereira also noted that imitation of others' language cannot explain the occurrence of pronoun reversals since although the children producing few reversals tended to do so in imitation, the child producing many reversals only produced 30% as a result of imitation.

Interestingly, the absence of vision does not just affect what children talk about but also seems to affect how clearly they talk. Mills (1987) reported that 3 blind children aged between 1 and 2 years made almost twice as many articulation errors of initial consonants of words than 3 sighted children when the sound was associated with a visible movement of the mouth. The children did not differ on sounds with no visible movement. Although these children were not followed up, it seems likely that these early differences will eventually disappear.

So far I have just examined the expressive language skills of blind children. I now want to consider their comprehension of language. McConachie (1990) examined the case records of 20 children with light perception or less and reported that between the ages of 1 and 2 years, 13 children had expressive language skills based on the Reynell–Zinkin Scales in excess of their comprehension by up to 13 months. For 20 children with some residual vision, 10 showed better expressive than comprehension skills but the advantage was at most 3 months. Records were also available for some of the children between the ages of 2 and 3 years and these showed that about a third of the children with light perception or less still had better expressive than comprehension skills. Pérez-Pereira and Conti-Ramsden (1999) indicate that this discrepancy seems to disappear by about 3½ years. Why should there be this discrepancy for blind children but not for children with some residual vision? Clearly, if blind children are simply imitating utterances they hear rather than using language to refer to things they know, this could account for the difference.

Blind children may have a different understanding of certain words than sighted children, but an understanding which makes sense given how they experience the environment. For example, Landau and Gleitman (1985) report that, when asked to look up, a blind 3-year-old reached her arms above her head, whereas blindfolded sighted children tilted their heads back. This child understood "look" to mean explore or examine. This is not very surprising, if you think about the contexts in which the blind child will have heard the word look, for example, "look at this" as the parent hands her a new object. Interestingly, Mills (1988) points out that words which are very visually oriented, such as see and look, may not only be interpreted tactually by blind children. For example, she observed blind children using "see" as if it meant "hear" and commented that the interpretation of a particular word may depend upon the context and possibly on individual children's preferences for particular modalities.

There may be certain words that blind children can never really understand in the same way as sighted children. The often cited example is color. However, color words are often associated with experiences available to blind children, such as the red glow of the fire associated with warmth, and in this way blind children are likely to develop an understanding of certain color terms. Urwin (1981) writes about a blind 4½-year-old who did not want to go into the coal shed because, she said, "It's dark in there." She was asked what she meant by dark and said, "Sort of still. And cold. Like when it's raining." Surely this is as rich an understanding of darkness as a sighted person could have? Blind children may have a perfectly adequate understanding of particular words but one which is based on experience through a different modality, experience of which sighted people are less aware because of the dominance of the visual modality.

Most of the differences between the language of blind children and sighted children reflect the former's reliance on experience through modalities other than vision. However, despite the fact that all blind children are deprived of visual experience to a marked degree, there is a great deal of variation between individual blind children in their acquisition of language. Unraveling the factors influencing this variation is an important task for future research.

How do blind children read and write?

Most blind children can see something. About three quarters are estimated to have visual acuities of 2/60 or better on the Snellen chart. But for many this will be insufficient for them to read and write print. Over the years many other systems have been designed, the current one being braille. This is a punctiform code devised by Louis Braille and first published in a pamphlet in 1839, although it was not officially introduced as a teaching medium until 1850.

Braille differs from print in a number of ways. Millar (e.g., 1997a, 1997b) identifies three important differences: its physical format, how information is taken in, and its orthography. In terms of physical format, all braille characters are represented by different combinations of up to six raised dots arranged in two columns, 6.2 cm high, each containing up to three raised dots. Unlike print, there is no redundancy in braille since the presence or absence of each of the six dots changes the meaning of the character. This lack of redundancy means that it is much more likely that braille characters will be misread than printed letters and young braille readers have been found to confuse characters which differ in terms of the number, position, and spatial arrangements of the dots (Lorimer & Tobin, 1980).

The second difference is that braille is read by moving the fingertips across the characters, whereas with print information is taken in during fixations. In addition, whereas some familiar printed words may be recognized by their overall shape, in braille the characters have to be scanned sequentially before the word can be identified. Many blind children develop ways of using both hands systematically to take in information. Some may use one hand to read and the other for keeping the place on the page and finding the next line. Millar (e.g., 1997b) describes how fluent readers will use the left hand to read the first half of a line, at which point the right hand takes over while the left hand moves to the start of the next line. The final difference Millar identifies is that although there are braille characters corresponding to each letter of the alphabet, as in print, there are also characters, known as contractions, for frequently occurring letter combinations (e.g., "ch," "ed," "wh") and common words (e.g., "and," "the," "with"). All these differences have implications for learning to read.

However, there is a further important factor. When sighted children first start school they are usually able to recognize and name some letters and may even be able to read certain words and possibly write their own name. They will have experienced letters and words on a daily basis even if they haven't known their meaning, for example, in story books, on labels on food and other domestic products, on the television, in the street, and so on. Blind children with no residual vision will miss all these experiences. Their first experience of letters and words in braille is likely to be when they start school.

Braille letters are introduced in a set sequence and, as a result, there are a finite number of words which can be read early on. This severely limits the available reading material (e.g., Harris & Barlow-Brown, 1997). But a further difficulty is that reading is likely to be restricted to school, unless other family members are also blind and use braille. Thus, blind children are deprived of the many opportunities that sighted children have to practice their reading and writing skills both before and after being introduced to braille.

It takes blind children over a year to learn the braille alphabet (Pring, 1994). But how do they learn to read? Harris and Barlow-Brown (1997) suggest three possible strategies. Given the limited braille vocabulary available to young blind children some may simply identify a key letter and use this to generate the word, thereby basing their reading on learned rote spellings. Others may rely more on an alphabetic strategy, identifying each letter and from this the whole word. Later on, when contractions are introduced, blind children may use a third strategy akin to whole word reading.

Given the laborious processes involved in learning braille, it is not surprising to find that blind children have lower reading ages than sighted children (Greaney & Reason, 1999). Greaney and Reason examined the braille reading of 22 blind children, mean age 10 years, using the Neale Analysis of Reading Ability (Neale, 1989). On the braille version of this test (Greaney, Tobin, & Hill, 1999) which is standardized for blind children, the children had reading ages for accuracy which matched their chronological age. However, when their scores were converted using the norms for sighted children reading print, the mean reading age for the blind children was 8 years. In other words, compared to sighted children, these blind children were reading at the same level as sighted children 2 years younger. Greaney and Reason also showed that this difference could not be explained by inferior phonological processing since their phonological skills were superior to those of sighted children. However, some blind children have poor phonological skills which may account for them having additional difficulties learning to read (Greaney & Reason, 1999).

Even fairly experienced braille readers only read at about half the speed at which average sighted people read print. Williams (1971) found that 30 blind 16-year-olds had an average reading speed for braille of 103 words per minute. Three of these adolescents had speeds of over 150 words per minute. In comparison, 21 out of 30 similarly aged sighted individuals read print at speeds in excess of 250 words per minute. Forty percent of the 488 children seen by Williams aged 10–16 read braille at speeds below 40 words per minute.

Reading and writing braille involve very different processes, unlike reading and writing print, and this is likely to cause additional difficulties for blind children. Braille letters are produced using a brailling machine which has six keys arranged in a horizontal line in front of the child, each key corresponding to one of the six dot positions. In order to produce a braille character the correct combination of keys must be depressed. The difficulty for blind children is that the relationship between what they are doing in reading and in writing will not be immediately obvious since although braille characters consist of a vertical array of dots, the keys on the brailling machine are arranged horizontally. When blind children are learning to write, they are taught that each key has a number (1 to the left, 6 to the right), and they learn the number combinations for each braille character. Interestingly, Barlow-Brown (1996) observed that some young blind children used these number combinations to identify particular letters when they were reading. The relationship between learning to read and to write braille is an area in need of more research.

Social and emotional development

How is interaction with adults affected when a child is blind?

Many social exchanges between sighted people are regulated by looking towards and away from the other person's face and by facial expressions such as smiles, frowns, yawns, laughs. From such cues we can gauge aspects of the other person's attention, interest, and understanding. When we interact with a baby visual cues are extremely important. What will happen if the baby is blind?

Blind babies' lack of eye contact can be particularly distressing for parents. Blind babies do smile, but to the sound of their parents' voices and to their body play. Rogers and Puchalski (1986) studied five blind children and five children with some residual vision and reported that all the children smiled when first observed between 4 and 12 months corrected for prematurity, most of the smiles being elicited by a familiar sound, touch, or game. However, the smiles of blind babies tend to be more fleeting and harder to evoke than sighted babies'. The continuous sight of a smiling face and the eye contact which occurs between parents and sighted babies seem to be powerful elicitors and maintainers of sighted babies' smiles. The cues available to blind babies are more intermittent than the visual cues which bombard sighted babies, apart from fairly vigorous games involving tickling. It is interesting that it is these sorts of games that most easily elicit smiles in blind babies. It is generally much more difficult to maintain interaction with blind children.

However, by as early as the end of the first month blind babies are reported to smile selectively to their parents' voices (Fraiberg, 1977), and in the next months they will smile readily when their parents play in familiar ways with them but they will squirm when strangers handle them. Their hands become more active and between 5 and 8 months Fraiberg observed that the blind babies obviously enjoyed feeling their parents' faces, yet they only briefly explored the faces of strangers. By this age there is clear differentiation of familiar and unfamiliar people. Nine out of 10 of Fraiberg's blind babies were first observed to show negative reactions when held by a stranger, such as crying or struggling to get away, sometime between 7 and 15 months. Tröster and Brambring (1992) reported that blind children were more likely to show avoidance reactions to strangers at 12 months than at 9 months, the ages having been corrected for prematurity.

These ages of differential reactions to familiar and unfamiliar people are approximately the same as those for sighted babies, although there are some blind children for whom these developments take longer or may never occur, as seen in Fraiberg's account of Peter. However, differences emerge when the responses of blind and sighted babies to their parents are examined more closely. Consider the situation when the parent walks into the baby's bedroom and, talking to her, bends over the cot. Both blind and sighted babies of 5 months will smile, and sighted, but not blind, babies will probably reach out towards their parents. Fraiberg did not observe this sort of proximity-seeking behavior in her 10 blind babies until 10–16 months.

Another difference between blind and sighted babies emerges when we look at how they react to their parent's departure. Sighted babies between the ages of 6 and 9 months protest when a parent leaves. Fraiberg's children were aged 11–22 months when they first showed this behavior, with a median of just under 12 months. This is consistent with Tröster and Brambring's (1992) findings of 9-month-old blind children not showing any anxiety when separated from their parents, whereas about half of a group of 12-month-old blind children did show such behavior.

Why are there these marked differences in the ages at which sighted and blind children reach out to their parents and protest at their disappearance? One possibility is that this relates to blind children's delayed understanding of object permanence (see pages 52–53). If blind children are delayed in understanding that other people continue to exist when they are no longer in contact with them then we should not expect them to reach out as their parent approaches or protest when their parent leaves. Sound does not of itself convey the presence of an object or person. Sighted babies will track things visually as they move around, and will find objects that they had lost sight of. But this cannot be done as easily with sound because it is seldom continuous.

Although this explanation is attractive, other factors may be involved. This is indicated by Rogers and Puchalski (1988) who looked at separation anxiety, fear of strangers, and performance on object permanence tasks in 11 blind children and 9 children with sufficient residual vision to enable them to reach on the basis of vision. Fifteen of the children did not show the expected relationship between separation/stranger reactions and object permanence: 11 children failed the object permanence tasks but reacted to separation and to strangers; 4 children succeeded on the object permanence tasks but did not react to separation or to strangers. Unfortunately the results for the children with and without some residual vision are not distinguished. Also half the children were premature.

Nevertheless, these findings are interesting and point to the need for more research in order to unravel the factors that influence these developments.

Unless blind children are actually in physical contact with their parents or their parents are talking, they will not know whether their parents are still there. Because of this, when blind children begin to talk they may try hard to keep their parents engaged in conversation by, for example, asking persistently what they are doing. Unlike sighted children who can keep in touch with their parents visually, blind children keep in contact by sound or touch. Their parents' responses will tell them that they are still there and indicate their whereabouts. This may also happen with strangers, blind children inundating them with questions. This is perhaps equivalent to the stares of sighted children.

The faces of blind children are often blank and expressionless. Tröster and Brambring (1992) report that 9- and 12-month-old blind children showed fewer emotions than sighted children and only one blind 12-month-old attempted to initiate contact with a parent, compared with almost 50% and 80% of sighted 9- and 12-month-olds respectively. This blankness may also be mirrored on the faces of those with whom blind children are interacting (Fraiberg, 1977), unlike when the baby is sighted. If we saw this sort of immobility of the facial muscles and the vacancy of the eyes in sighted children, we would assume a lack of interest or boredom, or even that the children had a learning disability. However, Galati, Miceli, and Sini (2001) reported that when 6–50-month-old blind children experienced various situations designed to elicit particular facial expressions they produced similar expressions to sighted children of the same age, although the frequency and duration of each expression were not examined.

There is also evidence that older blind children are not as good as sighted children at recognizing different emotions (Minter, Hobson, & Pring, 1991). In this study 6–12-year-old blind children and sighted children, 18 months younger but equated for language comprehension, were played tapes of object sounds, emotionally expressive noises (eg., gasps of fear, happy humming), and a passage read to express different emotions. There were no differences overall, although the blind children were better at identifying the objects than the emotions. Thus, if the children had been equated on ability to identify object sounds, the blind children would appear to be less good at identifying the emotions than the sighted children. Minter et al. suggest that blind children lack information about the context in which particular emotions occur and that this could explain why they are less good at identifying emotions than object sounds.

Another difficulty for blind children is knowing that when their parents are angry with them they are the same parents who love them. Sighted children can see that their parents remain the same and that it is just their tone of voice and facial expressions that change. Blind children hear only the change of tone, and because of their reliance on auditory information, it is much harder for them to realize that their parents are still the same. Blind children have a much more piecemeal image of their parents than sighted children. This difficulty in reconciling the angry with the loving parent may go some way towards explaining blind children's compliance with the requests of people who are important to them (Nagera & Colonna, 1965). If they find it hard to cope with their parents' different emotions, then they minimize the chance of arousing their anger by complying. In a similar way school-aged blind children often have difficulty dealing with their own age-appropriate aggression (Wills, 1970).

How is interaction with other children affected when a child is blind?

There has been little research examining the nature of the relationship between siblings when either one or both are blind, although Pérez-Pereira and Castro (1992) report that the twin girls they studied, 1 of whom was blind, interacted well, their interactions frequently involving shared play, especially pretence. Dunlea (1989) also reports that 2 siblings, both of whom were blind, regularly played together, as did 2 siblings, the younger of whom was blind. Nevertheless, more research is needed in this area.

Blind children are less likely to play with peers and siblings. The parents in Tröster and Brambring's (1994) questionnaire study reported that 40% of the blind children played with peers or siblings, compared to 78% of the sighted children. Not surprisingly, it is difficult for young blind children to interact successfully with sighted peers, particularly when the situation is unstructured. Preisler (1993, 1997) studied 9 blind children aged between 2 and 7 years who were integrated into nurseries for sighted children. These children, particularly the youngest, were seldom involved in group activities, although from the age of 4, several of the children became aware that they could get a response from their sighted peers by talking or doing something. However, for much of the time the children interacted with the adults in the nurseries, rather than with other children. They seldom engaged in play with their sighted peers and relatively little conversation occurred between the children.

Clearly sight increases the likelihood that children will interact with one another and even a little vision can increase the likelihood of interaction with other children. Schneekloth (1989) reported that partially sighted preschoolers spent 33% of the time playing alone compared to 56% for blind children and 14% for sighted children. However, the amount of interaction may be affected by the abilities of the other children. This was demonstrated by Skellenger, Rosenblum, and Jager (1997) for 3–6-year-old children with a range of visual impairments attending preschools for children with different disabilities. The children with no more than light perception spent 80% of the time in solitary activities, compared to 50–60% for the children with some residual vision. The children with little or no sight interacted more with adults than with their peers, the reverse being the case for the children with some residual vision.

Interestingly, from a practical point of view, Workman (1986) reports that preschool blind children were more likely to interact with sighted peers if adults provided the blind children with information about what was going on, such as who was present and what they were doing. Roe (1997; see Webster & Roe, 1998) also argues that teachers can support and facilitate the interaction between blind children and their sighted peers. Roe studied 20 blind children aged between 3 and 9 years and integrated into a number of different mainstream schools. Eight of the children had no vision and the others had varying degrees of residual vision up to a maximum of 6/60 Some of the children also had additional disabilities. The children varied in the extent of their interactions with other children: some were fairly passive, doing what others suggested; some showed relatively little interest in either play materials or other children; some played mostly alone; whereas others sought out interaction and joint activities. The latter children tended to be among the oldest and were more likely to have some residual vision.

Roe examined the requests that the blind children made to peers and to adults and also the requests that peers and adults made to them. Interestingly, the blind children made almost five times as many requests to their peers as to the adults (247 compared to 59). Of the blind children's requests to their peers, most were about information (33%), an object (22%), the location of something or someone (14%), or for another to do something (11%). The figures for the children's requests to adults were 49%, 14%, 7%, and 10% respectively. The sighted children made fewer requests (92) to the blind children and these mainly involved questions about the child's actions, wishes, or feelings (47%). The adults made a similar number of requests to the blind children (87) and most of these were also about the children's actions, feelings, and wishes (52%) and for information about their play (39%). Interestingly, although the sighted peers sometimes asked the blind children to hand over an object (7%), to get an object (4%), about how they were doing something (2%) or about the location of something or someone (7%), the adults never made these sorts of requests. Webster and Roe point out that the behavior of the adults may have increased the blind children's social isolation, rather than facilitated their interaction with their sighted peers. Clearly, these observations have a number of implications for ways of encouraging interaction.

As part of her longitudinal study of blind children, Preisler (1997) further reports that at the age of 10 years, when eight children were interviewed, five were attending mainstream schools and, although they were able to take part in the educational aspects of school life, they still had many difficulties interacting with their sighted peers and described themselves as lonely. Similarly, Huurre and Aro (1998) found that 54 blind adolescents in mainstream education, mean age 14 years, had fewer friends than sighted adolescents and the blind girls reported more feelings of loneliness. In a subsequent study, Huurre, Komulainen, and Aro (1999) found that blind adolescents' relationships with their peers were the main predictor of self-esteem, whereas their relationship with their parents was not predictive: those who related easily with their peers and had many friends had higher self-esteem.

Some of the difficulties blind adolescents experience may become less marked with age. A survey of 316 adolescents and young adults with a range of visual impairments, including 19% who relied on braille, found similar levels of loneliness to sighted young people, although the blind young people had smaller social networks, and a higher frequency of small networks (Kef, Hox, & Habekothé, 2000).

Clearly some blind children and young people are more successful than others at interacting with peers and forming friendships, and some children may have extreme difficulties. Preisler (1997) reported that three of the eight children seen at 10 years had been diagnosed with behaviors reminiscent of autism. These and other findings indicate that a proportion of blind children exhibit quite severe behavioral difficulties.

How prevalent are behavioral problems among blind children?

Cruickshank (1964) put the proportion of blind children showing severe behavioral problems as high as one third and in fact Fraiberg began her research with blind babies because she was referred a number of blind children who presented with quite marked disturbed behavior which shared a number of similarities with the behaviors associated with autism. However, unlike sighted children with autism, the perception of these blind children tended to remain mouth-centered, and perception by touching was minimal. Fraiberg concluded that the disturbed behaviors of many of these blind children were a consequence of the blindness itself. If this is correct, then, given our greater awareness of the problems facing the blind child and her parents due to the work of pioneers such as Fraiberg, the number of children presenting such problems should be much lower today.

Studies by Cass, Sonksen, and McConachie (1994) and Tirosh, Schnitzer, Davidovitch, and Cohen (1998) suggest that the incidence may not have declined. Cass et al. report that of 32 blind children who were showing typical development in the first 1½ years, 10 (31%) either ceased to develop, regressed, and/or showed increasingly disordered social interaction and communication by the age of 2½. None of these children were blind as a result of a peripheral disorder; all their visual diagnoses involved neural aspects of the visual system. However, they had also experienced more adverse environmental factors than the children who did not demonstrate these difficulties. In their study of 182 blind children aged 6 months to 5 years, of whom a third were totally blind, Tirosh et al. reported that half the children exhibited at least one behavioral problem although only two of the children met the criteria for autism on DSM III-R (American Psychiatric Association, 1987). The groups of children with and without behavioral problems did not differ in terms of the extent of their visual impairment, etiology or neurodevelopmental disorder but the children with behavior problems were more likely to come from families of lower socioeconomic status.

It is hard to eliminate the possibility that those children with particularly deviant behaviors have some brain damage. Indeed, in the past it was held that emotional disturbance was more prevalent among blind children due to retinopathy of prematurity (retrolental fibroplasia) who, because they are often premature, have a greater chance of having brain damage. However, a number of reports have failed to support this claim (e.g., Keeler, 1958; Norris, Spaulding, & Brodie, 1957). Keeler's study suggests that what seems to be critical for deviant development is total or near total congenital blindness plus a history of poor emotional stimulation in the first few months. This could explain the apparently raised incidence among children with retinopathy of prematurity. These children commonly spend their first few days or weeks in incubators. This would further limit the amount of contact and interaction they have with their parents. Also the parents' knowledge in many cases that their child has been blinded by some medical intervention might influence their subsequent interactions.

Nevertheless, it is possible that certain diagnoses of blindness are associated with particular deviant behaviors as a result of certain brain damage. One of these is Leber's amaurosis which accounts for about 10–18% of blind infants and is associated with various neurological abnormalities. In Cass et al.'s (1994) study only 2 children displayed increasingly disordered communication associated with developing nonverbal skills. These were the only children exhibiting developmental setback to have a diagnosis of Leber's amaurosis. This is in line with Rogers and Newhart-Larson's more detailed report (1989) that 5 boys under 6 years blind due to Leber's amaurosis all met the DSM-III criteria for infantile autism, whereas although 5 boys blind as a result of other causes, including 3 with retinopathy of prematurity, showed some features of autism they did not fulfill the DSM-III criteria. There was no difference between these two groups of boys on the Reynell-Zinkin subscales. Rogers and Newhart-Larson suggest that children with Leber's amaurosis and sighted children with autism may share some neurological abnormality which causes the behaviors characteristic of autism.

In contrast to these findings, Brown, Hobson, Lee, and Stevenson (1997) reported that only 1 child out of 3 blind as a result of Leber's amaurosis showed behaviors characteristic of autism. In this study, 24 congenitally blind children with no more than light perception and aged 3–9 years were examined for evidence of autistic-like behaviors. Fifteen had IQs above 70 and these were group matched for age and IQ with 10 sighted children. The other 9 blind children had IQs below 70 and these were group matched for age and IQ with nine sighted children with autism. For the groups with IQs over 70, the blind children showed more autistic-like features than the sighted children, in particular more stereotyped body movements, limited imaginative play, difficulties making friends, impaired nonverbal communication and speech production. In contrast, the 9 blind children with IQs below 70 were indistinguishable from the 9 sighted children with autism in terms of autistic-like behavior. Ten of the blind children met the criteria for autism based on a checklist of behaviors. Seven of these children had IQs below 70 and their blindness was due to congenital optic atrophy (3 children), retinopathy of prematurity (2 children), Leber's amaurosis, and bilateral retinal dysplasia. The other 3 children had IQs above 70 and their blindness was due to congenital optic atrophy (1 child) and retinopathy of prematurity (2 children). Of the 14 children who did not meet the criteria for autism, 2 had IQs below 70 and their blindness was caused by retinopathy of prematurity. The remaining 12 children had IQs above 70 and their blindness was caused by optic nerve hypoplasia, retinopathy of prematurity (6 children), Norrie's disease (2 children), congenital optic atrophy, Leber's amaurosis (2 children).

In a subsequent paper, Hobson, Lee, and Brown (1999) identified a number of differences in the behaviour of 9 blind children who showed autistic-like behavior and 9 sighted children with autism. The blind children showed more abnormal use of their bodies and objects, whereas the sighted children with autism were more likely to show marked abnormalities relating to people, responding emotionally, responding to taste, smell and touch, and in terms of the overall impression of autism. Both groups showed repetitive, stereotyped play isolated from others, although the blind children were more likely to play symbolically. Further, when subgroups of 6 blind children and 6 sighted children with severe autistic-like behaviors were compared, the blind children showed more echolalia, but were more likely to have a developmentally appropriate form of communication and imitate social behaviour than the children with autism. Interestingly, only 2 blind children were identified clinically as showing Kanner-type autism. The authors conclude that the social-emotional responsiveness of blind children showing autistic-like behavior differs qualitatively from the behavior of sighted children with autism.

It is clear that although many blind children may exhibit problem behaviors at some time, relatively few blind children present with severe behavior problems and those that do are likely to have additional learning difficulties probably as a consequence of brain damage. Nevertheless, some blind children who appear to be developing well may also show odd behaviors. For example, Toni would lie prone on the floor smiling to herself, and later fell into a deep sleep when she was anxious. For these children, a more relevant question concerns their reaction to their blindness.

What do blind children feel about themselves?

The realization for the blind child that she is different seems to come at around 5 or 6 years when she will begin to use sighted people to do things that she cannot (Burlingham, 1979). This in itself may present problems since the blind child may want to do things for herself and yet cannot without the support of a sighted peer or adult. This dependence on others may account for the relative absence of aggressive behavior in blind children. It may be that blind children are less aggressive, but an alternative view is that they fear showing aggression towards those people upon whom they depend so much, fearing that they may lose their support. A corollary of this lack of aggression is an apparent compliance with what others want of them. Burlingham (1979) talks of this compliance as "a thin disguise which hides the revolt against dependency." This conveys the feeling held by others that the phase of conflict between dependence and independence can be particularly difficult for the blind child. This phase occurs in many sighted children, but is usually resolved easily and quickly.

For individual blind children there may be particular episodes in their lives which are especially disturbing. The child who loses her sight in childhood, particularly if this occurs fairly late on in childhood, may have specific problems and fears. These may range from a fear of not being able to read to despair at never seeing people again. However, with support and assurances these difficulties can be overcome, and the child will gradually learn how to experience the environment through her intact senses. If she is able to overcome the initial despair and adjust to her sightless life she will be able to benefit from the visual experiences she had, and her knowledge of people, objects, and space in particular.

Blind children often go to residential schools, many from the age of 5. This may be particularly disruptive, since up until this age the child may have experienced few separations from her parents, and separations can be especially traumatic for the blind child who is so reliant on familiarity. Wills (1981) talks about how blind children can be prepared for this major change.

Many sighted children talk about things they will be able to do when they are older. Blind children are no exception, and some think that one of the things they will be able to do when they are older is to see (Burlingham, 1979). This is not so far fetched when we remember that around the age of 5 years blind children come to realize that they are different and that other people can do things which they cannot. Most of these people will be older, their parents or older siblings, and the blind child may think that when she reaches their age she will be able to see to do all the things she is presently dependent on others to do for her. This belief is understandable, but the gradual realization that she is different, and will always be different, must be particularly distressing.

As the blind child approaches adolescence further problems may arise. Throughout childhood she will have come to realize that some people are male, and others are female, but she may have a very unclear idea about what it is that distinguishes them. Adolescence, with its growing awareness of sexuality, often accompanied by taboos on touching other people's bodies, may be a period of great confusion and anxiety about her own and other people's bodies, and about her feelings.

Some blind children seem to adjust more easily and successfully than others. Why should this be so? Keeler's (1958) study points to the role of the early environment and the time of onset and extent of the blindness. Many researchers emphasize this role of the environment of blind children and believe it to be far more important than the nature of the blindness. However, the two can be seen to be related. The child who has even minimal vision is more likely to show an interest in her environment, to make some visual contact with her parents, and may even reach and become mobile using visual cues. This may be of great encouragement to her parents, and make it easier for them to interact successfully with her. Some of the factors which seem to be predictive of how the blind child feels about her disability, and of her development in general, are her parents' acceptance of her disability, their awareness of her signals and ability to read them, and their confidence in their role as parents. Factors like the parents' intelligence or social status seem to be relatively unimportant.

chapter three

How do deaf children develop?

Introduction

I have chosen to look at deafness as the second disability because hearing is one of our main senses, and because it has been argued that deaf people provide an ideal opportunity to examine the role of sound in development. The argument goes like this: deaf people cannot hear; hearing people can hear; any differences in the development of deaf and hearing people are due to their different hearing status; from this we can infer the role of hearing in typical development. In practice, the situation is much more complex than this. As outlined in chapter 1, there is tremendous variation in the nature and extent of deafness within the deaf population. Also, deaf children are individuals subject to particular experiences and environments. All of this makes for a reality which is extremely complicated but fascinating from the point of view of attempting to elucidate how development occurs.

Motor development

Deaf children who do not have any other disabilities are likely to reach the early major motor milestones, for example, sitting up, crawling, standing unaided, and walking at about the same time as hearing children (e.g., Preisler, 1995), although Koester et al. (2000) note that deaf infants produce more repetitive physical actions, such as kicking and rhythmically extending and flexing their arms and hands, than hearing infants. Despite these similarities, several studies indicate that deaf children have difficulties on some tests of balance and general coordination (e.g., Ittyerah & Sharma, 1997; Wiegersma & Van der Velde, 1983) and in tasks requiring fast and/or complex movements (Savelsbergh, Netelenbos, & Davids, 1989; Savelsbergh, Netelenbos, & Whiting, 1991). Deaf 7–11-year-olds are also more likely to be left-handed than hearing children and those who are right-handed tend to be less strongly so than hearing children (Ittyerah & Sharma, 1997; Mandal, Asthana, Dwivedi, & Bryden, 1999).

Some of the tasks on which Wiegersma and Van der Velde found that 6–10-year-old deaf children were less competent than hearing children involved dynamic coordination, for example, walking backwards and forwards along a narrow board, skipping and jumping, and hopping to and fro over a line. The deaf children were also less competent than hearing children on some tests of visual–motor coordination such as lacing a shoe-lace through holes in a board. However, there were no differences between the performances of the deaf and hearing children on other visual–motor tasks. A further finding was that deaf 8–10-year-olds, when the task required a movement, executed this movement more slowly than hearing children.

One possible explanation of these findings suggested by Wiegersma and Van der Velde was that auditory cues may facilitate the responses of hearing children. Two studies by Savelsbergh et al. (1991) provide some support for this explanation. In one study, deaf 10–13-year-olds made more errors than hearing children catching balls thrown from positions 90° or more outside their visual field, despite being given a visual signal. However, when the ball was projected from the machine a microswitch produced a sound of 20 dB which was audible to the hearing children. Interestingly, when the ball was thrown from straight ahead, the hearing children caught more balls after a bounce than the deaf children, although there was no difference when the ball did not bounce. In a second study exploring whether the auditory cues (of the microswitch and the bounce of the ball) explained the better performance of the hearing children, the same children had to press a button with both hands in response to a visual stimulus which was accompanied by a 15 dB sound. The deaf children took longer to press the button. This suggests that lack of auditory information may contribute to some of the slower motor responses of deaf children.

Perceptual development

Is the acuity of the other senses heightened?

Blind children and deaf children provide an ideal opportunity for testing the so-called sensory-compensation hypothesis, the idea that the loss of one sense may be compensated for by an increase in the sensitivity of the remaining senses. In the last chapter we saw that although the intact senses of blind children may not be more acute, the children may use them more effectively. For deaf children the picture is less clear – there is some evidence for more efficient use of their intact senses, but there is also evidence that the development of some perceptual mechanisms are advantaged by being able to hear.

The study by Savelsbergh et al. (1991) described in the last section showed that, when visual and auditory cues are available, hearing children respond faster and more accurately than deaf children, presumably because the auditory signals provide additional useful information which is not available visually.

Further evidence that hearing may influence visual mechanisms comes from the work of Quittner and colleagues (e.g., Quittner, Smith, Osberger, Mitchell, & Katz, 1994). In one study they found that 9–13-year-old profoundly deaf children who had cochlear implants performed like hearing children on a visual attention task (pressing a button whenever the number 9 appeared on a computer screen after the number 1), whereas deaf children without cochlear implants made more errors. Six-to-eight-year-old deaf children, some of whom had cochlear implants though for less time than the older children, made more errors than similar-aged hearing children. A second study compared the performance on the same task of 6–14-year-old deaf children, some of whom had cochlear implants, on two occasions about 8 months apart. There was no difference in performance at the first test which occurred on average 10 months after the children's implants were fitted, but 8 months later the children with cochlear implants were making fewer errors than the children without implants. Quittner et al. argue that these findings demonstrate that after about a year's experience with a cochlear implant the additional access to sound that it brings can improve visual attention in deaf children.

Taken together, the findings of Savelsbergh and Quittner et al. indicate that access to sound may enhance a child's visual abilities. However, there is some evidence that indicates that other experiences can influence the perceptual abilities of deaf children.

In particular, there is evidence that deaf children who learn to sign may have enhanced visual abilities. Thus, Bellugi et al. (1990) found that deaf children who signed were better at discriminating faces under different lighting and spatial orientation conditions than children who did not sign and, using a memory for faces task, this type of visual superiority has been found to persist into adulthood (e.g., Arnold & Mills, 2001; Arnold & Murray, 1998). Arnold and colleagues suggest that two factors can account for these findings. First, deaf children from an early age will pay particular attention to faces to make sense of what is going on, whereas hearing children will not focus so closely on faces because they can obtain information through the auditory channel as well. The second factor is that learning a sign language from childhood enhances certain visual–spatial skills. In support of the latter, Emmorey, Kosslyn, and Bellugi (e.g., 1993) found that deaf adults who signed had better visual imagery abilities than non-signing hearing adults.

Learning to sign has also been found to affect a rather different perceptual ability – recognition of a letter traced on the forehead as the correctly oriented letter rather than as its mirror image (Masataka, 1995). Masataka found that deaf 5-year-olds, who had deaf parents and were learning Japanese Sign Language, correctly pointed to either a drawn "p" or "q" when one was traced with a brush on their forehead, downward-facing palm or outward-facing palm, whereas hearing 5- and 3-year-olds and deaf 3-year-olds were much more likely to point to "p" when "q" was traced on these body surfaces and vice versa.

Thus, as with blind children, there does not seem to be any support for the sensory-compensation hypothesis. However, there is evidence that deafness can affect perception, both as a consequence of not being able to hear and, for those deaf children acquiring a sign language, as a result of learning a visual–spatial language.

Cognitive development

A great deal of interest has centered on the ability of deaf children to think and understand. Much of this interest has stemmed from the controversy surrounding the role of language in cognitive development. For many years philosophers and psychologists have debated whether or not language and thought are related and, if they are, the nature of the relationship. Before examining the role of deaf children in this controversy, let us consider the main views concerning the relationship between language and thought, or cognition.

Two extreme positions have been held by Watson (1913) and Chomsky (1975). Watson proposed that "thought processes are really motor habits in the larynx." In this view, thought, particularly verbal thought, and spoken language are the same process. By contrast, Chomsky argued that language is separate from cognition and develops independently from it. He proposed that language structures exist in the brain at birth, and that, provided children experience language, language will develop.

Both these extreme viewpoints have attracted much criticism. Other theorists have proposed that thought and language are related, although there is disagreement about the nature of the relationship, specifically whether thought determines language (Piaget, 1967), or language determines thought (e.g., Sapir, 1912; reprinted in Mandelbaum, 1958). Between these two positions is the view of Vygotsky (1962), who proposed that language and thought can influence each other.

Piaget (1967) argued that intelligence is dependent on children acting on the environment and taking account of the consequences of their actions. Through this, children construct an understanding of the environment which is reflected in intelligence. The language of the child is dependent, in Piaget's view, on the structure of intelligence. Thus, as knowledge or cognition develops, children's language will develop to reflect changes in their understanding. In this view, language reflects thought, although Piaget acknowledged that the acquisition of language enables the separation of thought from action.

Sapir's view was developed by Whorf (1940; reprinted in Carroll, 1956) who argued that perception and understanding of the world are dependent upon the language to which one is exposed. If the language children acquire ascribes an attribute to a phenomenon, or expresses a concept, they will experience and have an understanding of that attribute or concept. If the attribute or concept is not expressed in the language, children will have no experience or understanding of that attribute or concept. This is the strong version of the hypothesis. A weaker form proposes that certain aspects of language predispose individuals to think in particular ways.

Vygotsky's view can be seen as embodying several aspects of these different accounts. He proposed that thought and language are initially separate and develop in parallel until about the age of 2 years. At this point language and thought begin to merge and influence one another, with the eventual result that language can be used to help thinking and thought can be reflected in language. In other words, the relationship between thought and language is in both directions. This view can account for much research carried out in this field.

The study of deaf children was considered to provide a way of examining the relationship between language and cognition. If deaf people have no language, and if language is a prerequisite of cognition, then their ability to reason and think should be impaired or even absent. Conversely, if language is dependent upon cognition, their knowledge and understanding should be equivalent to that of hearing people.

All this presupposes that deaf people have no language. However, none of the theoretical viewpoints requires that the language is spoken language. It is now accepted that sign languages, for example American Sign Language (ASL) and British Sign Language (BSL), are languages in their own right (e.g., Bellugi, 1980; Kyle & Woll, 1985; Wilbur, 1987). For example in ASL, the signs consist of symbolic gestures, many of which stand for whole concepts. The meaning of each gesture is dependent on the shape, the location, the movement, and to a lesser extent the orientation of one or both hands. These components which occur simultaneously are called cheremes and correspond to the phonemes or sounds which occur successively in the production of a word in spoken language.

Signs in ASL, British Sign Language (BSL), and other sign languages, differ in several crucial ways from pantomime gestures, and this is one factor that led linguists to consider them proper languages. A pantomime gesture is iconic and involves the action of the hands "as if" representing an action or object, whereas a sign requires a particular shape, location, movement, and orientation of the hand or hands, and no other. Variation in any of these changes the meaning of the sign. The form of a sign may help understand its meaning once the sign has been explained but few signs carry their meaning directly. Signs are much more sophisticated than pantomime gestures. Also, there are rules for combining cheremes, which would not be evident if it were just pantomime. For example, if the hands move independently they must be of the same shape and move in the same way, whereas if the hands are of different shapes one hand must be stationary. Finally, if ASL and other natural sign languages were based on pure pantomime they would be readily understood by "foreigners," but in fact a BSL signer is incomprehensible to an ASL signer and vice versa.

There are several other features of ASL which contribute to its language status. It is unique in that it is not derived from written or spoken American. It has its own lexicon which does not correspond to spoken American and it also has its own grammar. For example, the signs for "I see you" and "you see me" are only differentiated by the direction of hand movement. This shows how the visual–spatial nature of the system has been utilized, rather than attempting to copy the sequential nature of grammar in spoken language.

In other words, sign languages are naturally occurring languages, in the same sense that French and English are naturally occurring languages. As in spoken languages, there are regional variations in each sign language and each has its own distinct grammatical features. This is in contrast to sign systems such as Signed Exact English and Paget-Gorman, which follow the grammatical rules of English. These latter sign systems are therefore representations of English in much the same way as written English is a representation of spoken English and are not languages in their own right.

Thus, although deaf people may have unintelligible speech, they may use a sign language of comparable complexity and sophistication to any naturally occurring spoken language. In this very important sense, deaf people who can communicate by sign language cannot be said to be without language. For this reason, study of the cognitive development of deaf people has turned out to be an unsatisfactory way of examining the relationship between language and cognition.

How intelligent are deaf children?

We hear too much about deaf people through the media to continue to equate being deaf with being dumb in the sense of stupid. But the change in our attitude towards regarding deaf people as intelligent, able members of our society is fairly recent and certainly incomplete. Linguistic skills are still rated very highly and we may all be guilty of misjudging a person's intellectual capabilities because we have paid too much attention to their spoken language. Here deaf people are obviously at a severe disadvantage. Powers (1996) found that although over 75% of 334 deaf 16-year-olds in mainstream schools in England were reported by their teachers to communicate through speech fairly easily, more than 50% of those with a profound hearing loss – amounting to 46 children – communicated through speech with difficulty. Similarly, Hyde and Power (1996) found that teachers rated 80% of 15 profoundly deaf 10–17-year-olds as not understandable at all or very hard to understand. Interestingly, Gregory et al. (1995) interviewed families who had initially adopted an oral approach with their deaf children, and reported that by their late teens/early 20s only 2 of the 31 profoundly deaf young people used oral English as their preferred language.

The IQs of deaf children assessed, for example, on the Performance Scale of the WISC (Wechsler, 1974) are found typically to fall within the normal range, although mean scores may fall below hearing children's average (e.g. Maller & Braden, 1993; Vernon, 1967). However, this test may not allow deaf children to demonstrate their real intellectual level. The intelligence of hearing children is usually based on their scores on both the Verbal and Performance Scales of the WISC but, because of deaf children's limited language skills, their intelligence is based on the Performance Scale. This raises two problems: how do the Verbal and Performance IQs compare, and, more importantly, how nonverbal is the Performance Scale? Graham and Shapiro (1953) suggest that deaf children's actual intelligence may have been underrated. They showed that, when the Performance scale of the WISC was given to hearing and deaf children using pantomime instructions, all the children obtained lower scores than hearing children who were given verbal instructions. There were some differences between the hearing and deaf groups given pantomime instructions, with the deaf children being superior on one subtest. These findings point to at least one influence of language on intelligence:

it helps performance on intelligence tests! But it is also quite clear that spoken language is not a prerequisite for cognition.

Interestingly, it has been reported that children with hereditary deafness have an average nonverbal IQ of 100 compared to 95 for children deaf for other reasons. Not surprisingly, deaf children with additional disabilities have an average IQ about 10 points below this. Further, children with two deaf parents have higher IQs than those with hearing parents (e.g., Conrad, 1979; Sisco and Anderson, 1980). If we assume that the intellectual potential of these children is similar at birth, the explanation for this latter finding must lie in the environment. There are several possibilities, each of which will be dealt with in more detail later: deaf parents are likely to accept the birth of their deaf children more easily than hearing parents and this may influence their early attitude towards and interaction with their children; deaf parents may use a sign language and therefore be able to communicate effectively with their young children from an earlier age than hearing parents; because of their experience of deafness, deaf parents may interact differently with their deaf children and this may have an influence on the children's early understanding of their environment.

Another way of examining intellectual ability is to look at academic achievement given the well-established relationship between intelligence and academic success. However, most evidence indicates that deaf children are not as successful academically as would be expected if they are of average intelligence. For example, Powers (1996) reported that 14% of 344 deaf 16-year-olds being educated in ordinary schools achieved 5 or more A–C grades at GCSE compared with national figures of 44% for hearing children. A couple of years later he repeated the survey and found very similar results: 18% of 435 deaf children obtained five or more A–C grades at GCSE compared with 45% for hearing children (Powers, 1998). In the 1998 paper Powers reports that about 20% of the variance in achievement could be accounted for by the age at which the children became deaf, socioeconomic status, and additional disabilities. Children from middle class families who became deaf after the age of 3 years and had no additional disability achieved the best GCSE grades.

A similar picture comes from Gregory et al.'s (1995) interviews with young deaf adults whose parents had adopted an oral only approach when the children were young. Seven percent left school with one or more A levels, compared to 22% of the general population. More worryingly, 46% of the young deaf people left school with no external examination qualifications, compared to about 10% in the general population.

Success within the academic system does not just require memory for facts and figures but also requires that children understand what is required and develop strategies for tackling problems. Interestingly, there is evidence that deaf children are less likely than hearing children to develop appropriate strategies when trying to solve problems. Das and Ojile (1995) found that less than 10% of 51 deaf 9–15 year olds used relevant strategies to solve verbal and nonverbal planning tasks. Similarly, less than 10% of 9–11-year-old hearing children approached the tasks strategically, whereas over 70% of the 12–15-year-old hearing children did. Further evidence that deaf children may use less effective strategies when solving problems comes from Marschark and Everhart (1999). Thirty-five deaf children and 36 hearing children aged 7–14 years had to ask questions to discover which one of 42 pictures the tester was holding, up to a maximum of 20 – the so called "Twenty Questions Game." Six deaf children and 19 hearing children asked constraint questions which narrowed down the options (such as "Is it an animal?" as opposed to "Is it a dog?"). Interestingly, of the five 13–14-year-old deaf children who asked constraint questions, 4 had played the game before, whereas of the 10 hearing children of similar aged who asked constraint questions, only 4 had prior experience of the game. This suggests that deaf children may find it much harder to develop appropriate strategies in new situations than hearing children. However, given the verbal nature of this task, the differences could simply reflect the deaf children's limited experience of superordinate terms.

Taken together, the findings on intelligence and academic achievements are depressing because the picture which is emerging is of children who are of similar intelligence to hearing children, at least in terms of their performance on intelligence tests, and yet they are not succeeding at school. As we shall see later, deaf children have many problems in communication, including reading and writing, and it is likely that these difficulties, rather than inferior intellectual abilities, account for their difficulties within the educational system.

Support for the view that communication difficulties may largely account for the poor academic achievement of deaf children, particularly those in oral settings, comes from Preisler et al. (1997). The policy in Sweden since the mid-1970s has been to use sign language and written Swedish with deaf children. Preisler et al. cite a report showing that deaf Swedish children in the 1990s, who therefore have been brought up while this policy was operating, are reaching academic levels very similar to hearing children.

Further support for the view that deaf children who can communicate effectively with others from an early age may be more successful than those who cannot comes from a rather different study. Jamieson and Pedersen (1993) studied a small number of deaf children with deaf parents (dcDP) using ASL, deaf children with hearing parents (dcHP) using oral methods, and hearing children with hearing parents (hcHP) at the age of about 5 years. The parents were asked to help their child assemble a pyramid of 21 interlocking wooden pieces (Wood & Middleton, 1975). The children first attempted it alone, then the parents helped, and finally the children attempted it again alone.

The dcDP and hcHP children were much more likely to succeed when they attempted the puzzle on their own after doing it with their parents than the dcHP children. Why should this be the case? Jamieson and Pedersen point to several findings which suggest that as a result of their parents' behavior when they were helping, the dcDP children became more efficient problem solvers than the dcHP children. In particular, success by the children on their own correlated with a measure of the responsiveness of parents when helping the children earlier. Thus, the dcDP and hcHP parents tended not to intervene when the children were succeeding, whereas the dcHP parents were likely to intervene even when the children were successful. Related to this, the dcHP parents initiated actions on many more occasions than either of the other parents and the dcHP children initiated actions on correspondingly fewer occasions. Interventions by the dcHP parents continued throughout the instruction phase, whereas the dcDP and hcHP parents gradually let their children take over.

These differences in style were also reflected in how the parents viewed the activity. Thus, the dcHP parents seemed to be following a plan, the aim of which was to complete the pyramid, whereas the other parents commented about the importance of responding to what the children did. Interestingly, when the children were attempting the puzzle on their own, the dcHP children appealed to their parents for help more often than the other children, which the authors suggest may indicate that they have learned to rely on others for help, rather than trying to work out the problem themselves.

In this section I have looked at cognitive development from the point of view of intelligence test scores and academic achievements. In the next four sections I shall examine deaf children's understanding of objects and of people, ability to reason abstractly, and memory processes to see whether being able to hear and to acquire spoken language plays any part in the cognitive processes involved.

What do young deaf children understand about objects?

Given that deafness is not confirmed in the majority of deaf children until they are over 1 year, our knowledge of deaf children's understanding of objects in the first year is based on observations of very few children, often dcDP children. For example, Preisler (1995) observed 7 deaf infants aged 6–18 months interacting with a parent. All 3 deaf children observed in the first year had deaf parents. Only 1 child was observed at 6 months and, when he and his mother were interacting, objects were involved for just over half the time. Three children were observed at 12 months and, when they were interacting with their parents, objects were involved over 80% of the time. This increasing involvement of objects in interaction over the first year is very similar to that observed in hearing children and suggests that deaf children may have a similar understanding of objects at this stage.

Preisler's observations indicate that the deaf children were mainly manipulating objects up to and including the 12-month observation rather than engaging with them in any other way. However, Spencer and Meadow-Orlans (1996) indicate that by 12 months there may be differences in how deaf and hearing children play with toys. Spencer and Meadow-Orlans looked at how 13 dcDP children, 15 dcHP children and 15 hcHP children played with toys when the children were 9, 12, and 18 months. At 9 months there were no differences in the children's play with a set of toys including a tea set, a toolbox, dolls and accessories, most of the time being spent manipulating single toys. At 12 months all the hcHP children played appropriately with the toys at least some of the time, whereas 3 dcDP and 7 dcHP children were still only manipulating the toys. By 18 months, all the children played appropriately with the toys, but while all the hcHP and dcDP children showed evidence of planning their play and substituting one object for another, only 8 dcHP children exhibited this more sophisticated play.

This study demonstrates that dcDP and dcHP children under 2 years can produce play which is as sophisticated as that of hearing children. This suggests that their understanding of objects is equivalent, certainly as far as object understanding is reflected in play. But there are some differences which need to be explained. In particular, why should the hcHP and dcDP children show more sophisticated play at 18 months than some of the dcHP children? In hearing children there is strong evidence for a relationship between play and language (e.g., McCune, 1995), in particular symbolic play (Lewis et al., 2000b). Could it therefore be that the hcHP and dcDP children produced more sophisticated play because their language skills were more advanced than the dcHP children? Spencer and Meadow-Orlans (1996) found some evidence for a relationship between expressive language (words or signs) and play and Lyon (1997) reported significant correlations, independent of CA, between expressive oral language and symbolic play in deaf 1–5-year-olds. Interestingly, this last study included some deaf children with very poor language skills who engaged in symbolic play but there were no children with good language skills who did not play symbolically. Nevertheless, in Spencer and Meadow-Orlans' study the strongest predictor of play level at 18 months was the responsiveness of the mother. As we shall see later (pages 117–119), there is considerable evidence that the early interactions in dcDP dyads are more successful than those occurring in most dcHP dyads. It seems likely therefore that the nature of the interaction which the child experiences with her mother can influence her level of play.

However, even if differences in the nature of dcDP and dcHP interactions can account for the findings at 18 months, there must be some other explanation of the differences at 12 months since at this age some of the dcDP children were producing play which was no more sophisticated than that of many of the dcHP children. Spencer and Meadow-Orlans suggest that at 12 months the hcHP children have much greater access to language than the deaf children. While the hearing children are playing, their mothers are likely to be commenting on their play and this may influence the level at which they play. The dcHP children will have little access to such talk. However, the same is also true of dcDP children, since at this age their parents have been found to produce far fewer signed utterances compared to the spoken utterances of hearing parents. We'll consider this in more detail in a later section (see page 125). In addition, it could be that by 12 months hearing children are taking more notice of things going on around them than deaf children simply because their attention is drawn by the sounds associated with different activities. Young hearing children may therefore have more experience of how others interact with objects and this may influence their own interactions with objects.

Although Spencer and Meadow-Orlans (1996) did not find a strong relationship between play and language in deaf children up to 18 months, Spencer (1996), studying 10 dcHP, 10 dcDP, and 10 hcHP children aged 24–28 months, found that those children, regardless of group, who had more language (words or signs) produced more play involving planning and object substitution. Unfortunately, there were no dcHP children who had more than 200 words/signs (the third and highest language level which Spencer distinguished) and so the language/play relationship could not be explored separately in the three groups. Nevertheless, this finding indicates that language, whether spoken language or sign language, may support the development of symbolic representations of objects.

The evidence on play reviewed in this section indicates that young deaf and hearing children have a similar understanding of objects and how they can be used, although there may be some differences which relate to the nature of their interactions with their parents and their language abilities and may also be affected by not being able to hear sounds. In addition, there are some things which deaf children will not know, at least not in the same way as hearing children, for example, that hens cluck and balloons go bang.

What do young deaf children understand about themselves and other people?

In the previous section we saw that deaf children seem to have a similar understanding of objects as hearing children. But do they understand that they can share their interest in particular objects with others and that others can share their interests with them? In her longitudinal study Preisler (1995) noted that the 2 dcDP children observed at 9 months showed evidence of secondary intersubjectivity. That is, they coordinated their attention to their parent with their attention to an object. For example, 1 of the deaf boys would look at things his mother pointed at, and would look to his mother when he was playing with a toy. This child clearly understood other people as communicative partners.

However, understanding people as communicative partners by deaf children under 1 year may be restricted to dcDP children. Meadow-Orlans and Spencer (1996) observed 20 dcDP, 19 dcHP, 21 hcHP, as well as 20 hcDP playing at 9, 12, and 18 months and reported that only the dcDP children showed evidence of coordinated joint attention at 9 months. At 12 and 18 months children in all groups showed coordinated joint attention, but the children who had parents of the same hearing status (i.e., dcDP and hcHP) showed significantly more coordinated joint attention than children with parents of different hearing status (i.e., dcHP and hcDP), although Harris and Mohay (1997) point out that the mothers' sensitivity and communicative competence may be more important than her hearing status.

By the age of about 4 years, hearing children understand that other people have thoughts, beliefs, and feelings which are different from their own (e.g., Lewis & Mitchell, 1994). One explanation is that this development comes about through listening to and contributing to conversations about mental states primarily within the family (e.g., Lillard, 1997). If this is the case, and if deaf children have limited access to the conversations of other people, particularly conversations about mental states, then their understanding of minds should be impaired. However, if their parents are also deaf and the children have access to sign language from an early age, then these deaf children should develop an understanding of minds.

Several studies have demonstrated that deaf children with limited conversational experiences have problems with theory of mind tasks (Peterson and Siegal, 1995, 1998; Russell et al., 1998). Peterson and Siegal (1995) administered a version of the Sally–Anne false belief task to twenty-six 8–13-year-old deaf children of average intelligence. Twenty-four of these children had hearing parents and, although sign language as well as spoken language was used at school, they had relatively little early experience of sign. Eighty-three percent of the deaf children failed to indicate the correct location in response to the question "Where will Sally look for her marble?" and there was no difference in CA or IQ between those who passed and those who failed. Interestingly, 2 dcDP children who had been using Australian sign language (Auslan) from an early age passed.

In a further study using a wider age range, 5–17 years, Russell et al. (1998) did find a relationship between age and success on the Sally–Anne task. This suggests that deaf children may be delayed in developing an understanding of minds. However, a number of other findings are not consistent with this conclusion: 6- and 10-year-old deaf children can predict how story characters will feel in different situations and use mental state terms more often than hearing children to explain the emotions (Rieffe & Meerum Terwogt, 2000); stories written by profoundly deaf 9–15-year-olds refer to mental states (e.g., Marschark, Green, Hindmarsh, & Walker, 2000; Yoshinaga-Itano & Downey, 1996); and 4–13-year-old deaf children seem to have a similar understanding of different emotions as hearing children (e.g., Hosie, Gray, Russell, Scott, & Hunter, 1998). However, Hosie et al. (2000) suggest that understanding when and why it might be appropriate to hide feelings of anger and happiness in social situations may be delayed in deaf children.

These findings on deaf children's false belief understanding are very similar to those reported for children with autism (see pages 274–277) and Peterson and Siegal (1998) confirmed this by comparing the performance of 6–12-year-old deaf children, 6–16-year-old children with autism, and 3–5-year-old TD children on a version of the Sally-Ann false belief task and a false photograph task. In the false photograph task the children took a Polaroid photograph of a doll in a bath and, while the photograph was developing, the doll was put into a bed. The test question concerned the doll's location in the photograph. On the false belief task the pass rates were: children with autism 48%; deaf children 40%; 3–4-year-olds 21% and 4–5-year-olds 69%. Consistent with other studies, more children with autism and more 3–4-year-old TD children failed the false belief task than the false photograph task, and this was also true of the deaf children.

In a further study, Peterson and Siegal (1999) confirmed that if deaf children do have access to conversations, either signed or spoken, from an early age they are more successful on false belief tasks. They found that 5–13-year-old dcDP children who used Auslan were as likely as 4-year-old hearing children to pass false belief tasks. Interestingly, deaf children with moderate to severe hearing losses who were successfully using oral language did as well as the dcDP signing children and the 4-year-old hearing children. However, dcHP children with severe to profound hearing losses who were using both spoken and sign language were much less successful and no different from children with autism. All this points to the important role of access to conversations, either signed or spoken, from an early age, in developing an understanding that others have different beliefs.

One of the limitations of Peterson and Siegal's study is the wide age range, given the relationship noted between age and success on false belief (Russell et al., 1998). However, Courtin and Melot (1998) examined 5–6-year-old dcDP children and found that they all passed at least two out of three false belief tasks, compared with less than 70% of 5-year-old hearing children, 55% of 6–8-year-old dcHP children who were using signing and less than 25% of 6–8-year-old dcHP children who were using oral methods. Interestingly, these authors also report that a number of deaf children had to be excluded because they did not understand the instructions and all these had hearing parents. Thus the success rates of the dcHP children in this study are effectively overestimates. However, Courtin and Melot's study does suggest that deaf children may fail theory of mind tasks because they fail to understand what is required rather than because they do not have an understanding of minds.

A difficulty with Courtin and Melot's study is the poor performance of the hearing children. Jackson (2001) found no difference on theory of mind performance for 5–11-year-old deaf children with signing parents, 5–8-year-old signing dcHP children, 5–13-year-old dcHP children using both sign and spoken language, 5–11-year-old dcHP oral children, and 3–4-year-old hcHP and they all performed less well than hcHP 7-year-olds. However, when the deaf children with signing parents were matched with hearing children for both age and receptive language ability, the hearing children outperformed the deaf children. Nevertheless, it is important to note that less than half the deaf children with signing parents came from families with at least one other deaf member. Also, a number of the children, including over half the dcHP children using both sign and spoken language, failed some of the questions designed to check their understanding of the tasks and these children were included in the analyses of theory of mind performance. Interestingly, theory of mind performance was related to age, rather than receptive language ability, for the deaf children with signing parents and the hearing children, but to language for the other deaf children. Jackson concludes that her results indicate that early on deaf children, regardless of language modality, lag about 1 to 2 years behind hearing children in their understanding of minds. At older ages deaf children with signing parents do not differ from hearing children, but the understanding of deaf children with more limited language experiences is still more like that of younger hearing children.

But what about deaf children's understanding of themselves? Do they see themselves as deaf? Martinez and Silvestre (1995) asked 12–17-year-old deaf and hearing adolescents to provide 20 answers to the question "Who am I?" All the deaf adolescents were in mainstream education and using oral language. There were very few differences between the categories of answers for the two groups. In addition, while the deaf adolescents were more likely to refer to their physical appearance than the hearing adolescents, very few made reference to their deafness.

Interestingly, Gregory et al. (1995) in their interviews with young deaf adults found that about a third of them reported that as a child they thought that when they became adults they would be able to hear, and often the realization that this was not the case came when they met deaf adults. Just over two thirds of these young people reported that they understood their own deafness by the age of about 11 years.

This raises the question as to how younger deaf children think of their deafness. Gregory, Smith, and Wells (1997) interviewed 25 deaf children aged 7–11 years who were being educated using sign language and spoken and written language, described as a sign bilingual approach. Interestingly, not all the children were able to answer the question "What does deaf mean?" The answers of those who did included "signing," "not hearing," "me," "hearing aids." Answers to the question "What does hearing mean?" included "hearing," "speaking," "specific people," "can't sign." Although 1 child said that deafness and hearing were the same, the answers from most of the children indicate that they do have an understanding of deafness and how it differs from hearing.

Can deaf children reason abstractly?

Furth's position, following Piagetian theory, was that any developmental lag in deaf children's cognitive skills was not due to any lack of intelligence or linguistic skill, but rather to lack of experience and training. Working with deaf adolescents, Furth (1973) reported that although some of them showed that they were able to understand symbolic logic and permutations despite very poor language skills, about half of them could not. What should we make of this? Since some deaf adolescents can think and reason in this abstract way, deafness itself cannot preclude this capability. However, we still need to explain why it is that some adolescents have more difficulty than others.

Furth's position is that an appropriate environment is needed to foster this sort of development. If we look at cross-cultural studies of abstract thought, a very similar argument has been made (e.g., Cole & Scribner, 1974). Cole and Scribner report that adolescents and young adults who have received little formal education perform poorly on abstract reasoning tasks, whereas individuals from a similar background, but who have had some formal education, perform fairly well. Their argument is that development beyond the concrete operational stage is a function of formal education. Although deaf adolescents experience formal education and are of average intelligence, their educational achievement is often poor. So perhaps it is not so far fetched to draw a parallel between these deaf adolescents and Cole and Scribner's uneducated adolescents. Both have a relative lack of formal education, either because they do not attend school or because their disability seems to prevent them from benefiting from it.

Gregory et al. (1995), based on their interviews with young deaf people whose parents were all hearing and who had initially adopted an oral-only approach, reach a very similar conclusion. Although they found that 19 of the 71 young people interviewed could give complex answers and 11 could understand complex questions, there were 10 other young people whose responses could not be used. In addition, the interview was not even attempted with a further 4 young deaf people because their parents indicated that their communication skills were insufficient. Gregory et al.'s interviews demonstrate that these young deaf people are not just deprived of language. In particular, these authors point to three consequences of these young people's deafness: difficulties of accessing the formal school curriculum because of lack of a shared communication system; limited development of reading and writing skills and consequent lack of opportunity to foster thinking through these media; lack of access to information gained indirectly, such as through hearing the conversations of others, watching television, and so on.

How do deaf children encode and store information?

The fact that deaf children have limited access to spoken language has led to questions about how they encode information. In particular, it has been suggested that deaf children will be better at coding visual information than verbal information. One way of examining this is to look at how well different sorts of information are recalled. A number of studies have confirmed that when tasks involve visual processing deaf children recall more than or at least as much as hearing children, whereas when verbal processing is called for, deaf children recall less than hearing children. Further, because of the differences in the visual and auditory modalities, it has been argued that deaf children may be more likely to retain spatial information than temporal information (e.g., Arnold & Murray, 1998; Marschark, 1993).

The effect of temporal order on recall was examined by Todman and Seedhouse (1994) using a visual task; 7–16-year-old deaf and hearing children, matched for nonverbal intelligence, learned actions in response to simple visual stimuli. In the test phase, there were three conditions: two or more visual stimuli were presented as a compound stimulus and the actions associated with component stimuli could be produced in any order; individual stimuli were presented in a sequence and the actions had to be produced either in any order or following the same sequence. The deaf children outperformed the hearing children in the first condition involving simultaneous presentation and free recall. However, the hearing children did better with sequential presentation and ordered recall.

Some confirmation of these findings was provided by Das and Ojile (1995), albeit using very different tasks. They compared the performance of deaf and hearing 9–15-year-olds on four tasks: a verbal successive task; a verbal simultaneous task; a nonverbal successive task; and a nonverbal simultaneous task. Consistent with previous findings, the deaf children did less well than the hearing children on the verbal tasks, and this was regardless of whether successive or simultaneous processing was required. However, the 9–11-year-old deaf children did better than similar-aged hearing children on the nonverbal tasks, and this difference was most marked when simultaneous processing was required. At older ages, the hearing children appeared to be doing slightly better than the deaf children on these nonverbal tasks.

One problem with research of this sort is that often visual tasks can be solved verbally (e.g., Marschark & Mayer, 1998). Thus, in Das and Ojile's study, one nonverbal task required the reproduction of a sequence of colored blocks. Clearly this could be done nonverbally using imagery, but it seems very likely that many of the hearing children would have named the colors and remembered the sequence of names. Some deaf children may also use this strategy.

Despite this problem there is support for deaf children favoring visual–spatial coding over verbal coding. Successive or sequential coding puts extra demand on deaf children and this is explained by the fact that verbal information is necessarily sequential, whereas visual information is often spatial rather than sequential and so deaf and hearing children differ in their experience. However, some deaf children do acquire spoken language and some deaf children acquire sign language which, although spatial and visual, also provides experience of receiving information in sequence. This raises the interesting question of whether the use of verbal coding by deaf children is related to their language proficiency.

When we are first presented with new information to remember, it initially goes into a short-term memory store. In order for it to be maintained in this store it needs to be rehearsed, which has been demonstrated by the fact that rehearsal leads to better recall. It is obviously possible to rehearse information using verbal labels, signs or imagery. Hearing children, when required to remember and reproduce a sequence such as pictures of objects or colored blocks, have been found to rehearse spontane-ously from about the age of 7–8 years, whereas deaf children do not show evidence of rehearsing material spontaneously until 10–13 years (e.g., Bebko, 1984). This age difference was confirmed by Bebko and McKinnon (1990) who further showed that the longer deaf children had received language training, whether oral or sign, the more likely they were to re-hearse spontaneously.

These findings were followed up by Bebko, Bell, Metcalfe-Haggert, and McKinnon (1998) using more sensitive measures of language than length of oral or sign instruction. In this study they demonstrated that the likeli-hood of 7–13-year-old deaf children rehearsing picture sequences sponta-neously was predicted by expressive language proficiency and speed of naming an array of pictures, but not by CA. Interestingly, Bebko et al. noted that the youngest deaf child to rehearse the material spontaneously had deaf parents and was presumably fluent in ASL.

Although deaf children do not perform as well on verbal tasks as hear-ing children, they are able to code this information, albeit not as success-fully. This raises the question of whether they code verbal information in the same way as hearing children but less efficiently, or whether they are using different strategies. Baddeley (1986) and colleagues have proposed that when verbal information is being memorized, labels are stored in a phonological store and are maintained in this store by means of an articu-latory rehearsal loop. Campbell and Wright (1990) explored whether orally trained deaf children stored information phonologically by seeing if their ability to recall pairs of pictures was affected by whether or not the names of the pictures rhymed. If deaf children are storing the names phonologically then rhyming should help recall.

Two groups of deaf children, mean ages about 10 and 14½ years, and hearing children mean age almost 8 years were shown six pairs of pictures which matched either in sound and spelling (e.g., box/fox), in sound but not spelling (e.g., hair/bear), semantically (e.g., cup/saucer), or randomly (e.g., lamp/book). The children were then presented with one of each pair and had to select the picture which had been paired with it from the six target pictures and four foils. All the children performed at ceiling when the pictures were semantically related. However, although the hearing children did much better when the picture names sounded similar than when they were randomly paired, there was no difference for the deaf children. This is clear evidence that these deaf children were not using the sound of the picture names as a cue to recall, whereas the younger hearing children were.

Despite this evidence that deaf children were not storing the names of the pictures phonologically, Campbell and Wright (1990) went on to ex-plore whether deaf children use the articulatory rehearsal loop. This has a limited capacity of about 2 seconds, demonstrated by the fact that more names can be rehearsed and subsequently recalled if the words contain few syllables than if they contain many syllables because verbalizing longer words takes more time. Deaf adolescents aged 12–17 years and two groups of hearing children, aged 6–11 and 13–14 years, recalled sets of four or six pictures in order, either selecting from a pack of 10 pictures and ordering them in sequence from left to right or saying in order the pictures' names. The sets differed in the number of syllables in the names: one (e.g., chair); two (e.g., rabbit); three (e.g., ambulance). The recall of the deaf adolescents was similar to that of the 6–11-year-old hearing children and both groups recalled fewer pictures with longer names when the names had to be said, though not when the pictures had to be ordered.

The findings from these two experiments suggest that deaf children do use the articulatory loop when they are required to use language, as in Campbell and Wright's second study, but that otherwise they tend not to store information phonologically. This is not very surprising given that profoundly deaf children will have little or no access to word sounds. However, there is no need for this information to be auditory. Research with deaf signing adults has demonstrated a phonological store and articulatory rehearsal for sign language (e.g., Wilson & Emmorey, 1998).

Lipreading provides deaf children with some phonological information, albeit in a different modality from hearing children, although lipreading does not provide as much information as spoken words. However, cued speech can provide additional information. In this system hand signs near the mouth are used to differentiate phonemes which cannot be distinguished visually. Thus, cued speech provides phonological information not otherwise available to deaf children. In an interesting paper Leybaert and Charlier (1996) report a study designed to explore some of Campbell and Wright's (1990) findings using deaf children exposed to cued speech from 3 years. The children had to remember and reproduce sequences of drawings of objects, and the object names were either monosyllabic and did not rhyme, monosyllabic and rhymed, or polysyllabic and did not rhyme. The deaf children, mean age 8 years 8 months, and hearing children, mean age 9 years 4 months, were less accurate when the object names rhymed or were polysyllabic than when the words were monosyllabic and did not rhyme, providing evidence that both groups of children were utilizing the articulatory loop.

In this section I have considered the cognitive development of deaf children from a number of perspectives. While a number of studies have shown that the cognitive skills of deaf children as a group differ from those of hearing children, what is of most interest is that in almost every case it had been demonstrated that although some deaf children may demonstrate delays in their cognitive development, this is not true of all deaf children. And what is more interesting is that there is a consistency in the findings. Thus, we have seen in a variety of situations that if deaf children have access to environmental information as a result of a shared communication system they perform as well as hearing children. This has clear implications for the education of deaf children, in particular the provision of a language they can acquire and through which they can share knowledge and information with others.

The development of communication

The study of communication in deaf children is of particular significance given its role in development. We have already seen that the cognitive development of dcDP children is more like that of hearing children than dcHP children. This raises interesting questions about how communication develops in these two groups of deaf children.

How do deaf children and their parents establish joint attention?

One of the prerequisites for communication is that the individuals involved can attend to the same thing. Earlier we saw that dcDP children engage in joint attention within the first year, at a similar age to hcHP children, whereas this does not occur until the second year for dcHP children (Meadow-Orlans & Spencer, 1996; Preisler, 1995). We consider this difference in this section.

Like hearing infants, deaf infants begin to show an interest in objects from about 4–5 months. When this happens, deaf parents tend to keep still and watch their infants and wait until the children look towards them before signing anything. This strategy may partly explained why deaf mothers have been observed to produce very few signs to their 7-month-old deaf infants (Harris, Clibbens, Chasin, & Tibbitts, 1989). In contrast, hearing parents may interrupt their infants' inspection of an object, either to regain their children's attention or to make some comment on what the children are looking at. This difference persists and was observed in 12–13-month-old deaf children by Spencer, Bodner-Johnson, and Gutfreund (1992). In this study the children sat facing their parent, who was either deaf or hearing, in a room containing a number of objects. The deaf children looked around at the objects as much as similar-aged hearing children. When the deaf children looked towards an object the deaf parents sat quietly until the children turned back to look at them. In contrast, the hearing parents were likely either to try to redirect the children's attention or to say something about the object while the children were still looking at it.

Hearing parents talk to their hearing children about what the children are doing. This is obviously an effective strategy since the children can simultaneously look at an object and hear the object's name, thus enabling links to be made between objects and their names. For this to happen, hearing children do not need to shift attention back to the adult. However, if the child is deaf, anything the parent communicates about things that the child is looking at requires that the child shifts attention from whatever she is attending to and towards her parent to either see signs or watch lip movements. Thus, links between objects and their names are not simultaneous. As well as waiting for their children to turn back to them before signing, deaf parents also adopt other strategies (e.g., Mohay, 2000).

One is that they will often shift the location of signs so that they occur within the child's line of gaze, ensuring that the sign and its context can be seen simultaneously (Harris et al., 1989). Harris et al. report that 71–100% of the signed utterances by dcDP parents to their infants between 7 and 20 months had a salient context and of these, 49–96% were within the child's visual field. Deaf parents tend to continue to relocate signs within the child's visual field until the child begins to actively look back to her parent for comment, a behavior which is apparent towards the end of the second year (e.g., Harris et al., 1989; Jamieson, 1997). Harris et al. reported that the proportion of signs to the four deaf children they studied which occurred when the children were looking at their deaf signing mothers increased from 44% at 7 months to 88% at 20 months. This relocating strategy and the waiting strategy can also be seen when deaf parents are looking at a picture book with their young deaf children. The parent will either go through the book and then act out or sign the story at the end (the waiting strategy) or will sign on each picture (the relocating strategy) (e.g., Jamieson, 1997; Lartz & Lestina, 1995).

Another strategy used by deaf parents is "bracketing" when they either point to an object to which the child is attending, then sign the object's name and then point again to the object, or, alternatively, sign the name, point and then repeat the name. In this way deaf parents maximize the likelihood that the children will make the link between the object and the sign, in much the same way as hearing parents will say the name of objects to which their hearing children are attending.

Of course, parents will often need to gain their deaf child's attention and differences have been observed in how hearing and deaf parents go about doing this. Deaf parents often initially try to capture their children's attention by looking at them and perhaps leaning towards them. If this is unsuccessful they may wave within the children's visual field and only if this is unsuccessful will they resort to physical contact, perhaps briefly tapping the children's hands or arms. Hearing parents are less likely to use physical means and more likely to use vocal means to attract their deaf children's attention (e.g., Koester, Karkowski, & Traci, 1998a).

Deaf and hearing parents also differ in the frequency with which they try to attract their deaf children's attention and in their likelihood of success. Harris and Mohay (1997) observed 18-month-old dcDP and dcHP children playing with their mothers. The deaf mothers made more attempts to obtain their deaf children's attention than the hearing mothers during 10 minutes of free play. In addition, all 5 deaf mothers successfully gained their children's attention at least three times, whereas only 1 of the 5 hearing mothers who attempted was successful more than three times. However, there was variability within the groups, particularly among the hearing mothers. Thus, 1 hearing mother sought to attract her deaf child's attention more often than 2 deaf mothers and was successful each time. In contrast, 1 hearing mother did not try to gain her child's attention throughout the period of observation and of the 5 hearing mothers who did try, three failed every time.

Not surprisingly, some of the strategies adopted by deaf parents to establish and maintain joint attention are also evident later on. In a study of 5-year-old deaf children and their parents assembling pieces of a wooden pyramid, Jamieson (1994a, 1994b) observed that the deaf parents obtained their children's attention before giving any instructions whereas the hearing parents of both deaf and hearing children were likely to talk to their children at the same time as demonstrating how to put together parts of the puzzle, even though this talk would have been mostly inaccessible to the deaf children. The requirement by the deaf parents that their children attended to them when they were giving an instruction or to the puzzle when they were demonstrating some action had a number of consequences. One was that the dcDP children looked back and forth between their parent and the object much more often than the other children, since the deaf parents would get their attention, give a direction and then redirect their children's attention back to the puzzle. Another was that the deaf parents asked fewer questions than the other parents, perhaps because this would necessitate a shift in attention. Third, the deaf parents' comments were much more focused on the task and what the children had to do compared to the hearing parents, perhaps again because comments not directly relevant to the task would require unnecessary attention shifts.

It is clear that most deaf parents and hearing parents differ in how they establish joint attention with their deaf children and in how successful they are. These differences stem from the experiences that deaf parents have in communicating with other deaf people and often through their use of sign language. Obviously most hearing parents do not have such experiences and cannot provide their children with a readily accessible language. Nevertheless, we know that hearing children communicate before they can speak and this raises interesting questions about whether or not deaf children of hearing parents are able to communicate before they have acquired any spoken language. In the next section I shall consider deaf children's use of gesture.

Do *deaf children use gesture to communicate with their hearing parents?*

Deaf children of hearing parents who are exposed to spoken language but not sign language develop systems of gestures which they use to communicate with their parents, sometimes described as homesign (e.g., Goldin-Meadow, Butcher, Mylander, & Dodge, 1994; Goldin-Meadow, McNeill, & Singleton, 1996; Goldin-Meadow & Mylander, 1998; Goldin-Meadow, Mylander, & Butcher, 1995). Of course, hearing children also use gestures but these tend to decline as they begin to talk. In comparison, as dcHP children get older, rather than their gestures declining, they begin to combine gestures, and to devise new gestures. These gestures are used to convey meanings to others. But do these gestures have any language-like properties?

For over two decades Goldin-Meadow and colleagues have studied early videos of 10 American deaf children whose hearing parents were committed to using just spoken language (e.g., Goldin-Meadow et al., 1996). These children were first seen at home between 1½ and 4 years and were videoed on a number of occasions. The children produced three different types of gestures: deictic gestures, often points, used to indicate particular objects, people, or locations; iconic or characterizing gestures which bore some visual similarity to the meaning being conveyed, rather like pantomime gestures; and marker gestures, common within the hearing population, such as shaking or nodding the head to indicate disagreement or agreement, or holding up a finger to convey the need to wait. The gestures were communicative in the sense that they were directed to another person, occurred after eye contact had been established with that person, did not involve any direct manipulation of a person or object, and were not part of a ritual.

The gestures produced by the children tended to be fairly stable over time. Thus, one child, David, whose gestures were studied in great detail between the ages of 2 years 10 months and 4 years 10 months, produced 190 different gestures and 109 of these were used more than once. Of the latter, there was very little variability in the form that repeated gestures took, with 90% taking the same form (Goldin-Meadow et al., 1994).

The children produced sequences of gestures, the combinations following particular orders, for example, a point to an object might be followed by a characterizing gesture conveying an action or attribute. Interestingly, these combinations reflected the sorts of semantic relations evident in hearing children's two-word utterances, indicating that the gestural systems of these children had some syntactic structure equivalent to natural language (e.g., Goldin-Meadow & Mylander, 1983).

A further characteristic of natural languages is that the words or signs can be broken down into parts, or morphemes. Goldin-Meadow et al. (1995) analyzed the gestures of four children in considerable detail and found that, like words, their gestures reflected an underlying morphological structure, in that each gesture was made up of a number of elements. Although the component gestures differed between the children, each child combined each component gesture with a number of other components to produce gestures which meant different things.

David's homesign was examined for two further characteristics of language: grammatical categories and reference to absent objects. All natural languages distinguish nouns and verbs, and Goldin-Meadow et al. (1994) looked to see if they could identify gestures used like nouns, like verbs and like adjectives, based on the communicative contexts in which the gestures occurred. Noun-like gestures were those which focused on something being talked about, verb-like gestures depicted an action, and adjective-like gestures indicated an attribute. One hundred and thirty-eight of David's different gestures could be assigned to one of these categories, of which 53 were coded as verbs, 23 as adjectives, and 62 as nouns. Interestingly, gestures used as nouns were fairly infrequent initially, the majority of early gestures signifying actions (verbs) and attributes (adjectives). At these early stages David pointed to draw attention to a particular object, so that the point served in place of a noun-like gesture. Thirty-nine gestures fell into two categories, most commonly nouns and verbs. However, like hearing children, David initially used these gestures in only one category. At the age of 3 years 3 months, when he began to use gestures in two categories, he marked the category by altering the form of the gesture and its position in the sequence which, Goldin-Meadow et al. argue, shows he was also able to distinguish these categories grammatically.

David was also observed to communicate in a variety of ways about things which were not present and did so consistently from 3 years 3 months (Butcher, Mylander, & Goldin-Meadow, 1991). For example, he produced gestures either near or directed at perceptually similar objects and produced gestures characterizing some aspect of an absent object near where it should be.

These observations were followed up by Morford and Goldin-Meadow (1997) who studied 4 of the original 10 deaf children, including David, over 2 years, beginning when the children were aged between 2 and 3 years old. Eighteen hearing children aged 1–3½ years were also studied. Three different sorts of reference to the nonpresent were distinguished: reference to objects, actions, attributes, or locations; reference to proximal events which occurred within the session; reference to distal events occurring either before or after the session or fantasy. There was evidence of reference to these different events among the hearing children at 1 year 4 months, 1 year 9 months, and 2 years 7 months respectively, compared to 2 years 7 months, 3 years, and 3 years 5 months for the deaf children. By the age of 3 years 5 months the hearing children referred to nonpresent objects, actions, attributes, and locations in 11% of their communications, proximal events in 16%, and distal or fantasy events in 10%. The corresponding figures for the deaf children were 12%, 4%, and 1%. Thus, although the deaf children did develop ways of referring to the nonpresent in their gestural systems, they were delayed, relative to hearing children, and most of their references were to nonpresent objects, actions, attributes, or locations. Morford and Goldin-Meadow argue that the further the intended message is from the present, the more important a shared lexicon is.

Goldin-Meadow (1997) also noted that these deaf children used their gestures in other ways that are reminiscent of hearing children. For example, the deaf children sometimes gestured, not to communicate to another person, but for themselves. Thus, one child while assembling some bricks made a gesture to indicate the next brick he wanted. However, when the researcher handed him the relevant brick this was ignored, suggesting that the gesture was for the child's own benefit rather than a request. Goldin-Meadow also reported that one deaf child used gesture to refer to his own gestures. The child wanted a Donald Duck toy which the researcher held behind her back. The child pursed his lips, representing Donald Duck's beak, pointed at his own lips and pointed towards the toy. The researcher handed him a different toy. The child shook his head, pursed his lips and pointed at them again. This was interpreted as "I say 'Donald Duck beak'."

Taken together, the results of these studies of a small number of deaf children indicate that when communication can only happen through gestures, the gestures take on at least some roles seen within natural languages. While very detailed, one of the limitations of this research is that only 10 American children have been studied and of these only a few have been studied in detail. Fortunately there are two other sources of evidence which provide corroborating support.

The first is a further study by Goldin-Meadow and Mylander (1998) in which they compared the homesign of 4 of the original children with the homesign of 4 deaf children being brought up in Taiwan. All the children were observed twice between 3½ and 5 years and there was marked similarity between the homesign of the children in these two different cultures.

The second piece of evidence is perhaps more convincing because it comes from a very different source. Bonvillian (1999) reports that one consequence of the opening of schools for deaf children in Nicaragua in 1980 was that this brought together groups of deaf children who had not met previously. The schools adopted an oral approach but out of class the children adapted the homesigns they had used within their own families. When subsequent groups of younger deaf children entered the schools in the late 1980s/early 1990s they learned the sign system which had been developed by the older children and took it further. The signs became increasingly arbitrary and the signing more fluent. The children distinguished clearly between nouns and verbs, used pronouns, marked verb agreement, and so on. In effect, over the course of less than two decades Nicaraguan Sign Language emerged with all the features of a fully grammatical language and without any apparent input from signing adults.

Clearly dcHP children who do not have access to sign language develop quite sophisticated ways of communicating using gestures. Their gestures reflect a number of features of spoken language although these emerge at later ages than in hearing children. But where do these gestures come from? Do the children create these language-like systems or are they learned from their parents?

Goldin-Meadow and colleagues have looked at the gestures produced by the parents of the deaf children whose homesign they have studied (e.g. Butcher et al., 1991; Goldin-Meadow et al., 1994; Goldin-Meadow & Mylander, 1983; 1998; Goldin-Meadow et al., 1995; Morford & Goldin-Meadow, 1997). These hearing parents used gestures. However, their gestures were not as extensive or as language-like as the homesign of their deaf children, and, more importantly, developments in the parents' gestures mostly followed developments in their children's gestures rather than vice versa.

For example, the gestures produced more than once by David's mother were much more variable, with only 59% taking the same form, compared to 90% for David (Goldin-Meadow et al., 1994). The parents seldom produced sequences of gestures and, when they did, the gestures, unlike their children's gesture sequences, did not follow specific orders (Goldin-Meadow & Mylander, 1983). Like the children's homesigns, the mothers' gestures could be decomposed into separate parts, but the morphological structures of these gestures were not as extensive as their children's (Goldin-Meadow et al., 1995). Interestingly, David's mother did differentiate nouns, verbs, and adjectives, but to a much lesser extent than David, and David regularly began to use gestures as nouns about 6 months earlier than his mother (Goldin-Meadow et al., 1994). David's mother also used gestures in two categories and was observed to do this before her son. However, her means of distinguishing the grammatical categories of gestures were less extensive and less systematic than David's. Butcher et al. (1991) reported that David's mother seldom used gestures to refer to objects which were not present, and this was confirmed by Morford and Goldin-Meadow (1997) who also showed that the mothers of four deaf children seldom referred to recent or more distant events. In addition, Goldin-Meadow (1997) notes that the mothers never used gestures to refer to their own gestures.

The study by Goldin-Meadow and Mylander (1998) of American and Taiwanese deaf children is particularly relevant to the question of the origins of deaf children's homesign. The mothers of these deaf children produced less complex gesture combinations than their children. However, more interesting, was the fact that the homesign of the American children was structurally more similar to the Taiwanese children's homesign than to that of their own mothers. The gestures of the Taiwanese mothers were more similar to, though lagged behind, those of their children. Goldin-Meadow and Mylander argue that this is further confirmation that the gesture systems are created by the deaf children and that cultural differences are likely to explain why Taiwanese mothers are more likely to follow their children's lead than American mothers.

It seems clear that the children are responsible for the language-like characteristics of their gesture systems, or homesign. However, as Goldin-Meadow et al. (1996) have argued, it seems that gestures only become language-like when they are the only means available for communication. Thus, dcHP children develop homesign with many language-like properties provided they have something to communicate about and people to communicate with. In contrast, their parents, who can already communicate through spoken language, use gestures to accompany their language and consequently their gestures do not show language properties to the same extent as their children's.

As well as using gestures, dcHP parents will also talk to their children, and may learn and use some sign language. Similarly, dcDP parents will use sign language with their children. In the next section I shall consider the nature of the language input that deaf children receive from their deaf and hearing parents and the question of whether or not this affects the children's output.

What language input do deaf children receive?

As we have seen, deaf signing parents adopt a number of strategies in order to ensure that their young children can see both their signs and the context to which they are referring. Deaf parents also change the form of their signs (e.g., Spencer & Lederberg, 1997), changes which have parallels with the simplified language spoken by hearing parents to young hearing children. Thus, deaf parents tend to use larger, more exaggerated sign movements and produce these more slowly, often repeating them. In addition, if a sign can have different meanings depending on how it is signed (for example, in ASL, "walk quickly" is normally differentiated from "walk slowly" by the speed with which the sign for walk is produced), the parent will use different signs.

Deaf parents also produce short utterances, perhaps only one or two signs in length. They also sign less than hearing parents talk to their young children. Thus, Harris (1992) reports that 4 deaf mothers produced between 13 and 101 signed utterances to their deaf 16-month-old infants in 20 minutes, of which 86% were single signs. In comparison, Harris, Jones, Brookes, and Grant (1986), studying maternal speech to 16-month-old hearing infants, report that the mother who said the least produced 83 utterances over 10 minutes (equivalent to 166 utterances over 20 minutes), a total of 255 words.

Interestingly, deaf and hearing children also adjust how they communicate depending on the hearing status of the children they are interacting with (e.g., Preisler, 1981; Spencer, Koester, & Meadow-Orlans, 1994). Thus, Preisler observed that a 4-year-old deaf girl who began to sign at the age of 1 year, signed fluently with a deaf signing peer, but more slowly with her hearing parents using distinct hand movements and articulating each word, and with her 9-month-old deaf sister used even slower hand movements. The content of the communication between her and her signing peer was much more sophisticated than with her parents and there was no misunderstanding. Spencer et al. observed 4 deaf children and 4 hearing children aged 2½–3 years during free play in an integrated nursery. Two of the deaf children and 2 of the hearing children had deaf parents. The hearing children initiated interaction with hearing peers using vocalizations 48% of the time, but only 20% of the time with deaf peers. These differences were even more marked with hearing and deaf teachers.

When children get older and particularly in an instructional context, deaf parents may actually sign more to their children than hearing parents talk to either their hearing or deaf children. Thus, in her study of mothers helping their 5-year-old children assemble pieces into a pyramid, Jamieson (1994a) observed that in 5 minutes the 3 deaf mothers produced an average of about 150 signed utterances, compared with just under 100 and just over 60 spoken utterances by the dcHP and hcHP mothers respectively. In terms of the relative proportions of directives, closed questions, Wh-questions, comments, and phatics, the dcHP mothers were more similar to the hcHP mothers than to the dcDP mothers. About 50% of all the mothers' utterances were comments. For the dcHP and hcHP mothers directives and closed questions each accounted for about 15% of the utterances, followed by Wh-questions and phatics which were both around 10%. For the deaf mothers the proportions were: comments 54%; directives 35%; closed questions, Wh-questions and phatics all 5% or less.

It is worth noting, however, given Harris and Mohay's (1997) observation of variability among deaf and hearing parents, that 1 of the 3 dcHP mothers studied by Jamieson asked very few closed and Wh-questions and made many comments, and in both these respects was more similar to the deaf parents, although in other respects this parent was more similar to the hcHP parents.

It seems possible that both the age of the children and the instructional nature of the situation studied by Jamieson may have influenced the parents' talk. Power, Wood, Wood, and MacDougall (1990) observed 2–3-year-old and 5–6-year-old dcHP children playing with their mothers at home and some of the children were observed again 3 years later. Power et al. were particularly interested in how much the mothers controlled the conversation by, for example, requiring the children to repeat something or answer a question. There were no differences in how much the mothers of the two groups of deaf children controlled the conversations and, further, these mothers did not differ from mothers of 2–2½-year-old and 5–5½-year-old hearing children. However, the mothers of the 5–6-year-old deaf children were more likely to request the child to repair an utterance, either by seeking clarification or getting the child to correct something they had said, than the mothers of the 5-year-old hearing children (unfortunately these data were not available for the 2–3-year-old hearing children). Three years later the hearing mothers were still getting the deaf children to repair their utterances. However, the amount of repair requested by these mothers was less than that observed in teachers.

Do these different patterns have any consequence for the children's contribution? In Jamieson's (1994a) study the dcDP children and the hcHP children initiated conversational turns more than twice as often as the dcHP children. However, because of the differences in how much their parents contributed, the hcHP children initiated 25–43% of the conversation, compared with 13–23% for the dcDP children and 10–15% for the dcHP children.

Power et al. (1990) also examined how much the children took the initiative in the conversation, such as asking questions or giving information not specifically requested by their parents. The deaf children initiated far less than the hearing children of similar age and their contributions were considerably shorter. However, when the 5–6-year-old deaf children were compared to the 2–2½-year-old hearing children, whose MLU was similar, most of the differences disappeared.

Interestingly, Power et al. report a similar relationship between the mothers' behavior and the children's behavior for the older hearing and deaf children. Thus, if the mothers controlled the conversation or requested repairs, the children tended to initiate less and say less and misunderstand more than children with mothers who controlled less and requested fewer repairs. However, it was also found that younger deaf children who had mothers who took more control of the conversation initiated more. This suggests that adult control may be beneficial early on, but that as the child's linguistic ability increases it has negative effects.

So far in this section I have focused on communication between deaf children and their parents and we have seen that if the child's parents are also deaf communication proceeds much more smoothly and more like that between hearing children and their parents, than if the child is deaf and her parents can hear. The reason for this is that deaf parents are likely to be native signers and have ways of communicating that are appropriate for children who cannot hear.

A further advantage for dcDP children who use sign language is that they will also have access to sign conversations between other people. Access to such conversations is much more difficult for deaf children being brought up in hearing families, particularly if the children have poor oral skills. Thus, Gregory et al. (1995) report that many of the young deaf adults they interviewed, whose hearing parents had adopted an oral approach, tended to communicate with only one member of the family and often failed to find out about important family events at the same time as everyone else, such as a grandparent dying. Also, deaf children will be deprived of information available through the television and so on.

Deafness may present particular difficulties in educational settings. This is illustrated well by a study of an 8-year-old deaf boy with hearing parents being educated in an ordinary school assisted by an interpreter (Shaw & Jamieson, 1997). Most of the child's communication in class was with the interpreter and the focus of this communication was academic. It was very difficult for him to participate in class because there was often a lag between what the teacher was saying to the hearing children and the interpreter imparting this information to him. In addition, he did not have access to additional things which the teacher might say to individual children, or to things which the children said to one another. Such information can be very important for helping to clarify understanding and for becoming part of a social group. This deaf child was unable to share in this aspect of classroom culture.

Clearly growing up deaf in a hearing culture presents many problems and challenges. In contrast, deaf children who grow up with deaf signing parents experience fewer difficulties, certainly as far as communication is concerned, and in many ways are similar to hearing children growing up with hearing parents.

Is learning to sign like learning to speak?

The acceptance of sign languages as languages in their own right, each with its own distinct phonology, morphology, syntax, and semantics, has led to the important question of whether acquisition of a visual–manual language differs in any way from acquisition of an aural–oral language. In this section I shall consider a number of different characteristics of language, including babbling, age of language onset, vocabulary development, use of pronouns and negation, and private speech.

Babbling is characterized by the production of phonetic elements of the adult language systematically combined together as syllables and used without meaning or reference. As we shall see later, deaf children are delayed in vocal babbling. However, Petitto and Marentette (1991) report that dcDP infants may babble manually in the first year. Two dcDP infants and 3 hcHP infants were videoed at 10, 12, and 14 months. The deaf children produced nine times as many instances of manual babbling as the hearing children, although all the children produced a similar number of communicative gestures such as raising their arms to be picked up. In contrast, Meier and Willerman (1995) reported that the proportion of gestures produced by 3 dcDP and 2 hcHP children aged 7–15 months which met the criteria for manual babbling were similar. Interestingly, while Pettito and Marentette argue that their data point to an amodal language capacity underlying both signed and spoken language acquisition, Meier and Willerman suggest that manual and vocal babbling may reflect rhythmically organized motor developments.

Hearing children produce their first word at 11–14 months, have 10 and 50 words at 15 and 19 months respectively, and begin to combine words at 18–22 months. Petitto and Marentette reported that the two deaf children in their study began to produce signs at around 11 months, similar to the age at which the hearing children produced their first words. Schlesinger and Meadow (1972) followed the development of a deaf girl, Ann, from 8 to 22 months. Ann's parents were also deaf and used ASL. Ann first attempted to produce a recognizable sign at the age of 10 months. Her first combination (bye sleep) appeared at 14 months. By 19½ months she had a vocabulary of 142 signs and 14 manual letters of the alphabet. These observations of Ann suggest that her sign language development was ahead of hearing children's spoken language.

Bonvillian and colleagues also report evidence which supports this (e.g. Bonvillian, 1999; Bonvillian, Orlansky, & Novak, 1983; Bonvillian,

Richards, & Dooley, 1997). A longitudinal study of 22 children with deaf signing parents demonstrated that the children produced their first signs at an average age of 8.5 months, had 10 signs by 13.3 months on average and began to combine signs at a mean age of 16.7 months. However, there was marked variation in the ages at which the children reached these milestones: first sign – 5½–11 months; 10 different signs – 11–17 months; combining signs – 12½–22 months. Thus, although the milestones were reached earlier in terms of mean ages by the signing children, the age ranges overlap. In addition, the signing children in these studies were mainly hearing children with deaf parents. Nevertheless, given the overlap in age ranges for children using spoken and sign language, clearly the small number of deaf children included were not delayed in reaching these language milestones, relative to the ages at which hearing children reach the equivalent spoken language milestones.

In comparison, a study by Harris (1992) of 4 dcDP children suggests that some deaf children may be much slower to acquire sign language than suggested by the studies cited so far. In particular, Harris found marked differences between the children in the age of onset of signing and the size of early signed vocabularies. For example, she notes that at 2 years, only 1 of the 4 deaf children was reported by her mother to be using a large number of different signs. The mother of another child reported a few signs whereas the mothers of the other two children thought that they were not yet signing. In 20 minutes of observation these children produced 16, 7, 1, and 0 different signs respectively. In comparison, Harris observed hearing children of similar age for half the length of time and found that the most talkative child produced 77 different words and the least talkative 9 different words. In other words, none of the deaf children signed more words in the same length of time than the least talkative hearing child spoke.

Interestingly, Harris' study provides some evidence to explain the variations in age of onset of signing and size of early sign vocabulary. We have already seen that deaf infants receive less input, in terms of both quantity and complexity, than hearing infants. However, Harris' data indicate that amount of input is not the whole story. Thus one mother produced 101 signed utterances when her son was 16 months old but he only produced one sign at 24 months. Interestingly, this boy's mother brought objects and activities into her own signing space rather than relocating her signs into her son's visual field as the other mothers did. Harris argues that this mother's strategy may be a less effective way of enabling the child to make links between signs and the things for which they stand.

It seems clear from these studies that the early sign language development of deaf children, including the variation seen between them, is similar to the early spoken language development of hearing children. Also, on balance, there is no conclusive evidence that deaf children in general are either ahead of or behind hearing children with respect to early stages of language development.

A number of other similarities have also been demonstrated between the signing of deaf children and the spoken language of hearing children. For example, early signs seem to have some equivalence to whole phrases. At 15 months, Ann, in Schlesinger and Meadow's study, used the sign for smell to mean a number of different things: "I want to go to the bathroom"; "I'm soiled, please change me"; "I want the pretty smelling flower."

Schlesinger and Meadow also report that some of Ann's signs were variants on the adult form, rather like the baby talk of young hearing children. Other reports (e.g., Bellugi & Klima, 1972) provide evidence of further similarities in learning to sign and learning to speak. The concept and semantic relations which were expressed by one of their deaf children, Pola, matched those of hearing children. Linguistic rules tended to be overgeneralized initially and only later were they applied appropriately. The increase in the number of combinations of signs seemed to parallel that found for hearing children combining words.

Two aspects of American Sign Language which are particularly interesting in terms of comparing sign and spoken language are pronouns and negation. The reason for this is that pronouns and negation can be communicated non-linguistically in ways which are similar to how they are conveyed linguistically in ASL, whereas the same is not true for spoken language. In the previous section we saw that deaf children who have not been exposed to sign language will point to people. In ASL pronouns take the form of a point. Similarly, children who have not yet acquired any spoken or sign language will shake their head to reject something and the same headshake is also used linguistically within ASL. In comparison, the spoken linguistic form of both pronouns and negation are completely different from the non-linguistic point and headshake. This leads to the question of whether the similarity between the non-linguistic and linguistic forms within sign language will advantage the signing child.

Petitto (1987) studied the acquisition of pronouns in 2 deaf girls and reported that at 10 and 12 months they pointed to indicate another person. However, from 12 and 15 months respectively the deaf children stopped using points and were more likely to sign the person's name. Pronouns, the linguistic form of point, were produced for the first time at 22 and 21 months respectively. Also, when the deaf children started to use pronouns they made reversal errors similar to hearing children, signing "you" when they meant "me" and so on. They used pronouns correctly from the age of 27 and 25 months respectively, again similar ages to those observed in hearing children. The reversal errors seen in these deaf children's use of pronouns are particularly interesting because they occur despite the fact that earlier they pointed correctly to the person they in-tended to communicate something about. This is interpreted as evidence that the two systems, communicative points and linguistic points, are in-dependent.

The same picture emerged when the use of a headshake to indicate rejection was studied by Anderson and Reilly (1997). Based on observa-tions of 51 deaf children aged 1–5 years playing with their deaf signing parent, they report that rejection of a request was responded to by a headshake at 12 months, the same age as hearing children. At around 18 months the first sign indicating rejection was observed but this was not accompanied by a headshake. The first occurrence of a negative sign with a headshake was observed at 20 months. Thus, as with pronoun develop-ment, it seems that the use of the headshake within ASL develops inde-pendently of the earlier non-linguistic form. In other words, the sign language development of deaf children is not advantaged by the fact that early communicative gestures and later manual signing occur in the same modality.

Earlier we saw that dcHP children sometimes gesture to themselves, equivalent to the private speech of hearing children (Goldin-Meadow, 1997). Deaf signing children also sign to themselves. Jamieson (1995) observed two 6-year-old deaf children, who had deaf signing parents, at school while they were working independently during math lessons. Both children signed frequently to themselves, producing 117 and 172 instances of signed private speech over four 20-minute observation periods, and over 80% of these signs were task relevant. Jamieson argues that these deaf children are using sign to help them solve problems. She further notes that dcDP children have been observed to produce 80% more private speech than dcHP children, and argues that private speech is facilitated by exposure to sign language from early on.

Thus, the development of signing in deaf children being brought up by deaf signing parents seems to have many parallels with the development of spoken language in hearing children. This, along with the evidence that deaf children not exposed to sign language develop gestures which show a number of language-like characteristics, supports the idea of a general language capacity which is reflected in both oral–aural and manual–visual language of young children. Further evidence for this comes from two other sources: the hand preferences of deaf and hearing children; the ef-fect of age of acquisition on subsequent language ability, or critical period hypothesis.

By 3 years hearing children usually demonstrate a clear prefer-ence for using one hand rather than the other (e.g., McManus et al., 1988). Similarly, deaf signing children and hearing children living with deaf signing parents do not demonstrate a clear hand preference for non-sign motor actions until around the same age. However, they do develop a clear hand preference for signing which coincides with their production of signs around the age of 1 year (Bonvillian et al., 1997). Bonvillian et al. argue that the early hand preference shown in sign language reflects left cerebral specialization for language and parallels the specialization seen in hearing infants in response to speech (e.g., Molfese, Freeman, & Palermo, 1975). Interestingly, Leybaert (1998) has suggested that if orally educated deaf children under 3 years experience cued speech, a visual system which distinguishes sounds not visible on the lips, they may be more likely to show left hemisphere specialization for language compared to deaf children first experiencing cued speech when they are older.

Although there is evidence for a critical period for language acquisition in hearing children, much of the evidence comes from children who have been brought up in severely deprived situations and therefore the conclusions are questionable (Skuse, 1993). Deaf children provide an opportunity to examine the critical period hypothesis because, although the majority of deaf children will be brought up in supportive environments, only 10% of them will be exposed in infancy to a readily accessible language, i.e., those children with deaf signing parents.

In support of the critical period hypothesis Grimshaw, Adelstein, Bryden, and MacKinnon (1998) describe a deaf 19-year-old man brought up in rural Mexico with minimal education who used homesign. At the age of 15 years he was fitted with hearing aids. Despite the fact that with aids his hearing loss was only 35 dB over the next four years he developed very limited spoken language and his comprehension was poor. These authors conclude that it is very difficult to acquire spoken language after the age of 15 years.

Similarly, Mayberry and Eichen (1991) have demonstrated that the later deaf children begin to learn sign language, the poorer their subsequent sign language skills, even if they have extensive signing experience. Interestingly, some of the deaf people who learned to sign in adolescence had acquired spoken language skills during childhood. The sign language skills of these individuals were superior to those of others who had also learned sign language in adolescence but had not acquired any other language skills previously. This supports the idea that there is a critical period for language acquisition which is independent of modality.

The deaf children I have focused on in this section represent only a small proportion of deaf children. By far the largest group of deaf children are those who are initially exposed to spoken language only. These are mainly children whose parents can hear and the majority of these parents will hope that their child will eventually be able to communicate using spoken language. A crucial question to be answered for those children initially only exposed to spoken language concerns the quantity and quality of spoken language that they will be able to acquire.

How much spoken language can deaf children acquire?

The amount of spoken language that deaf children can acquire depends on many factors. For example, how much they can hear; whether what they hear is clear and not distorted; how much use they make of any residual hearing; whether the adults around them talk clearly.

Deaf children can usually make some use of residual hearing if their hearing loss is less than 60 dB. With such losses they may be able to distinguish speech sounds even though this ability may be based on different acoustic cues from those used by hearing people. However, as we have seen, the parents of deaf children may not be as helpful as they could be; much of their talk may occur when their children are not attending to them, and they are inclined to provide facts and answers rather than ask questions, for obvious reasons. This also seems to happen at school with teachers (Wood, 1981), although Wood, Wood, Griffiths, and Howarth (1986) have shown that, at least over short periods of time, teachers can change how they talk to 11-year-old deaf children. When the teachers asked fewer questions and focused more on what the children were trying to communicate, the children made longer and more frequent contributions. In addition to being exposed to rather different conversations from children who can hear, the majority of deaf children will also be denied access to conversations between other people, an experience which may be important for the hearing child's acquisition of language.

Deaf babies usually start to make vocalizations just like hearing babies but differences begin to emerge towards the end of the first year. From about 7 months hearing infants begin to babble, producing repetitions of consonant-vowel syllables such as "dadada." However, the production of these language-like vocalizations is delayed in deaf children (e.g., Oller and Eilers, 1988; Spencer, 1993a; Spencer & Lederberg, 1997), although they do gradually appear over the next year or so. Thus, Oller and Eilers (1988) reported that nine deaf children began producing syllabic babbling at 11–25 months compared to 6–10 months in hearing children. In a longitudinal study of 94 hearing infants and 37 deaf infants Eilers and Oller (1994) reported age ranges for syllabic babbling of 3–10 and 11–49 months respectively. Interestingly, Spencer reports an association between frequency of babbling at 12 months and spoken language production six months later in deaf children which, although not as strong as for hearing infants, was positive.

For deaf children the acquisition of words is a laborious business and only unusually bright deaf children will have as many as 200 words by the time they are 4–5 years old. By this age hearing children have vocabularies of around 2,000 words. Thus, Dodd, McIntosh, and Woodhouse (1998) assessed over several years the language skills of 16 deaf children aged 30–57 months at the outset. At the first assessment the group had a mean age of 50 months and their expressive language age based on MLU was 20 months. By the fifth assessment their mean CA was about 75 months and their language age about 35 months. In other words, the gap between CA and expressive language age increased as the children got older. However, their ability to name objects and events lagged behind their CA by about 18 months.

It is also clear that their understanding of spoken language is limited. Dodd et al. report that the children's language comprehension was 22–24 months below their CA across the assessment period. Further, Bishop (1983) reports 8–12-year-old deaf children as having less understanding of spoken language than 4-year-old hearing children. They may also have difficulties interpreting the meaning of what they hear. For example, the instruction "give the doll a bath" may be interpreted literally, and a bath passed to the doll. Hyde and Power (1996) found that 15 severely deaf teenagers, compared to 15 profoundly deaf teenagers, comprehended more spoken language, had better lip-reading skills, and understood finger-spelling better, but that there was no difference when Signed English was used.

A study by Gregory and Mogford (1981) is a useful source of information about the early words of young deaf children. They report that the average age at which 6 of the 8 deaf children studied said their first word was 16 months, compared to reports of hearing children saying their first words at about 11 months. Not surprisingly, it was found that the more deaf the child, the later the appearance of the first word. In fact the 2 most profoundly deaf children were saying fewer than 10 words by the time they were 4 years old. The other 6 children reached the 10 word stage at an average age of 23 months, compared to 12 months for hearing children. The rate at which words were acquired also differed for the deaf and hearing children. Hearing children took one month to get from 1 word to 10 words, but the deaf children took seven months. However, the rate of acquisition between 10 and 50 words was similar at about 6 to 7 words per month. But a difference shows up again when we look at the rate at which the next 50 words are acquired. For the deaf children the acquisition rate increases to around 10 words a month, but hearing children take only one month to acquire their second 50 words.

Both deaf and hearing children begin to combine words when their vocabularies have reached about 50 words, at about 30 and 18 months respectively. This is followed by a rapid increase in vocabulary size for hearing children, which is not seen in deaf children. Further study of the two-word stage is needed. It seems quite possible that the nature of the two-word stage will be different for deaf children. Gregory and Mogford cite the example of a deaf boy who was producing several two-word utterances at 30 months, including "not hot" and "hot tea." Two months later he said "not hot hot tea" meaning cold tea. This may reflect different processes underlying the way in which deaf children and hearing children combine words.

What sorts of words do deaf children acquire first? Gregory and Mogford report that at vocabulary sizes of both 50 and 100 words the deaf children, compared to hearing children, had fewer words naming objects and events, and more words used within a social relationship like "thank-you," or describing affective states like "ouch." At the 50-word stage the deaf children had more words to describe or demand an action and at the 100-word stage they had more words to describe the attributes of objects.

These differences are interesting. Deaf children are not just being taught the names of objects, although these form the largest group of words for both hearing and deaf children at this stage. In their early vocabularies deaf children have more words enabling them to control what is happening than hearing children. However, as Gregory and Mogford point out, these deaf children are older than the hearing children when they reach each of these stages. This may be the reason why they are saying different things. It would be interesting to compare the proportions of the different categories of words for deaf and hearing children of similar CA to see if they are saying more similar things than deaf and hearing children who are matched for vocabulary size.

The speech of deaf children, particularly those who are profoundly deaf, is often unintelligible to strangers and any proficiency that they gain in spoken language will soon disappear without constant spoken language tuition. Thus, Meline (1997) found that, despite quite large individual differences, articulation errors were significantly related to hearing loss in 5–12-year-old deaf children and reflected the sorts of errors commonly found in younger hearing children. Kyle (1981) reports that teacher ratings of the speech of 6–11-year-old deaf children showed no significant improvements over 3 years.

It is clear that many deaf children whose parents adopt an oral-only approach, at least in the early years, will fail to develop good oral skills. Thus, Gregory et al. (1995) found that the preferred language of the 82 young deaf adults whose parents only used spoken language when they were 6 years old, was BSL (31), Signed Supported English (13), spoken English (30), and 8 had very limited language skills. Preferred language use was related to hearing loss. For example, of those with a profound hearing loss, over 50% preferred BSL and less than 10% preferred spoken English. Interestingly, despite initially only using oral language, the parents in 32 families learned to sign, the majority after the children reached 12 years.

Clearly most profoundly deaf children face considerable difficulties in acquiring spoken language. However, there is some evidence that the spoken language skills of deaf children can benefit from early exposure to sign. Notoya, Suzuki, and Furukawa (1994) studied two dcHP Japanese children enrolled in a multisensory training program involving sign based on spoken Japanese, auditory training, lipreading and written language from 2 and 14 months respectively. Their parents also learned sign based on spoken Japanese. The children produced about 50 different signs by 18 months and spoke 50 different words by 30 months. However, by 42 months they had 550 different signs and words. Thus, by 3½ years their oral language had caught up with their sign language. In addition, both children produced two- and three-word sentences only a few months later than hearing children. These findings, admittedly on only 2 deaf children, suggest that early exposure to sign based on a spoken language can facilitate deaf children's acquisition of spoken language. This is further evidence in support of the critical period hypothesis discussed in the last section.

At the age of 5 years both these Japanese children had reading levels in advance of their hearing peers. This is interestingly since deaf children often experience considerable difficulties in reading.

Do deaf children have problems reading and writing?

Many deaf children have difficulties reading. In a classic study Conrad (1979) found that only 5 out of 202 profoundly deaf 15–16½-year-old deaf school leavers in England studied over a 2 year period had a reading age of 15 years, compared to about 50% of hearing children of similar age. More than 50% of the deaf school leavers had reading ages below 7 years 10 months and, not surprisingly, reading age was related to hearing loss and intelligence.

Most of these deaf children would have been educated using methods emphasizing spoken language and there is some evidence that since Conrad's study deaf school leavers educated orally are reading better, with average reading ages of around 13 years (e.g., Lynas, 1994). However, Kelly (1995) reports that, on average, deaf 18-year-olds read with the comprehension of a 10-year-old, with only 3% of them reading at a level appropriate for their age. Similarly, Gregory et al. (1995) report that although 32% of the 82 young deaf adults they studied could read with understanding, a quarter were functionally illiterate, either being able to read only single words or headlines or nothing at all. Why should reading be so difficult for deaf children?

Longitudinal studies of hearing children have found a strong relationship between awareness of the different sounds of spoken language independent of any meaning, or phonological awareness, before the children are able to read and subsequent reading ability (e.g., Goswami & Bryant, 1990). Given that deaf children, particularly those with a profound hearing loss, cannot hear the sounds of spoken language, it seems highly likely that they will have poor phonological awareness and that this might account for some of their reading difficulties.

Phonological awareness was examined in 4–6-year-old deaf children and 5-year-old hearing children, all of whom were just beginning to read, by Harris and Beech (1998). The children were shown a picture of an object (e.g., "doll") which the tester named and, if appropriate, signed, and then asked which of two further pictures (e.g., "cot" and " dog"), which were also named/signed, had a name like the first picture. In this example the correct response would be "dog" because it has the same initial sound as "doll"; other correct pairings shared the same middle sound (e.g., "hat" and "cat" but not "net") or the same final sound (e.g., "snake" and "cake" but not "rain"). The deaf children were correct 60% of the time, compared to 81% for the hearing children, a difference which was significant although the range of scores for the two groups overlapped considerably. In addition, phonological awareness was significantly correlated with the extent of improvement in reading ability over a year for both groups of children.

Obviously, correct responses on Harris and Beech's task could be based on how the words were spelled. However, at the time of testing the deaf and hearing children could read relatively few words, although the hearing children's reading scores show they could read more than the deaf children. Nevertheless, it seems clear that young deaf children can make judgments based on the similarity of the sounds of words, and therefore do have one of the skills thought to be a prerequisite of reading. But how do they do this if they cannot hear? One possibility is that they use lip-reading, a sort of visual phonological awareness. This receives some support from the fact that phonological awareness was correlated with the deaf children's oral ability and presumably those with good oral skills were also good at lip-reading, although this was not tested directly.

It is also supported by the evidence that rhyming judgments in deaf children benefit from early experience of cued speech which provides a way of distinguishing phonemes which cannot be differentiated on the lips (Charlier & Leybaert, 2000; Leybaert & Charlier, 1996). Leybaert and Charlier found that 4–6-year-old deaf children with experience of cued speech since the age of 30 months but who were not yet reading were as good as 5–6 year old hearing children at judging whether or not the names of objects shown in pictures rhymed, regardless of whether or not the spelling of the objects suggested rhyming. Interestingly, a number of deaf pre-readers had to be excluded from this last study because they did not understand the notion of rhyme: all the excluded children were either being educated orally and without cued speech or used sign language. In addition, deaf children, mean age 10 years, who had been exposed to cued speech at home from 3 years were as good as hearing children at making rhyming judgments. The accuracy of these children's judgments were well over 90%, regardless of spelling similarity. In contrast, 7–17-year-old deaf children with less experience of cued speech, 6–13-year-olds with experience of sign language and 9–18-year-olds orally educated made accurate judgments about 80–90% of the time with object pairs whose names were spelled similarly, but only 60–70% of the time when the spelling of the names did not indicate rhyming. These results are clear evidence that deaf children can code phonological information and can make judgments based on it. However, this only occurs if phonological information is available to them through the visual modality.

Harris and Beech suggest that phonological processing may not be the only route to reading. As evidence for this they describe 2 deaf children who performed poorly on the phonological awareness task but were among the best readers in the group, reading at levels equivalent to their hearing peers 2 years after the study started. What was interesting about these 2 children was that their parents were deaf and so presumably they were proficient signers. Clearly these children must have been using some other route into reading. Perhaps what is crucial is the ability to communicate, regardless of whether spoken or sign language is involved. However, Harris and Beech report that signing ability did not correlate with improvement in reading over 1 or 2 years which is counter to this explanation.

There is further evidence from other studies that deaf children who sign may become good readers. Thus, Notoya et al. (1994) reported this for the 2 children they studied and Lynas (1999) notes that Swedish and Danish deaf children, who are educated bilingually in sign and spoken language, have average or above average reading and writing skills. Further, Kelly (1995), looking at 16-year-old deaf adolescents who were reading at the expected level in comparison to those 16-year-olds reading at a 10-year-old level, noted that 3 of the 9 skilled readers had deaf parents, whereas all the parents of the average readers were hearing. Beech and Harris (1997) also note that out of 36 deaf children, 4 had deaf parents and used sign, and 3 of these had reading quotients among the top seven. Interestingly, Wilson and Hyde (1997) report improvements in the reading comprehension of 8–13-year-old deaf children when signed English pictures were associated with the text, particularly for children with reading ages below 7 years 2 months.

While Harris and Beech's and Leybaert and Charlier's studies have looked at phonological awareness in deaf children who are just beginning to read, other studies have looked at the ability of older deaf children to use phonological information. Thus, Sterne and Goswami (2000) examined the syllabic, rhyme, and phoneme awareness of 7–14-year-old deaf children who had reading ages of between 6 and 11 years. The deaf children were as able as hearing children of either the same CA or reading age at judging which of two pictures had the longest name on the basis of the number of syllables rather than number of letters. On tasks assessing rhyme awareness and phoneme awareness the deaf children performed above chance, although on both they did less well than reading age matched hearing children. The rhyming task required the children to identify which of three pictures had names which rhymed and the deaf children did better when the rhyming names shared orthography (e.g. sock, clock, bed) than when they did not (e.g., four, saw, car). The phoneme awareness task required the children to select a nonsense homophone from four possibilities to name a picture (e.g., boiz for a picture of two boys, rather than boin, roiz, or beiz). On this task the deaf children were 63% accurate, whereas the younger reading aged matched hearing children performed at ceiling.

Other studies have capitalized on English being an orthographically irregular language in that letters in different words are not always pronounced the same. For example, some words, like "cloud" and "break," are regular and follow grapheme-to-phoneme correspondence rules, whereas others are exceptions and do not, such as "cough" and "beast." It is therefore possible to construct lists of words and non-words which differ in the extent to which they follow grapheme–phoneme correspondence rules and ask children to identify or sort the words. If visual strategies are being used there should be no difference in speed and accuracy of identifying regular and exception words. But if phonological strategies are being used, regular words should be identified faster and more accurately than exception words, since with exception words the phonological strategy will not produce a word match and the word will have to be checked against known spellings, lengthening the decision time. This is known as the regularity effect. In addition, letter strings which are not words will rely on a phonological strategy and if they are pronounceable the decision should take longer than if they are unpronounceable.

Merrills, Underwood, and Wood (1994) found that deaf 11–16-year-olds who had reading ages of 7–8 years relied more on visual information than phonological information when making such judgments, although their visual word recognition skills were slower and less accurate than hearing children of similar age. However, like the hearing children, the deaf children took longer to identify pronounceable nonwords than unpronounceable ones, which the authors interpret as indicating that they are able to use phonological information.

In a second experiment Merrills et al. used capital letters to encourage the use of phonological strategies. However, whether or not the regular and exception words were in capitals or lower case, the deaf children took longer to identify regular words than exception words. The opposite was found for the hearing children. This is further evidence that the deaf children primarily rely on a visual strategy.

More evidence that deaf children use visual rather than phonological strategies when reading comes from Burden and Campbell (1994) and Beech and Harris (1997). Like Merrills et al., Burden and Campbell report that deaf children, mean CA 14 years 6 months and mean reading age 10 years 1 month, who were being educated orally, did not show the regularity effect, that is, they took as long to identify regular and exception words. In fact in this study the deaf children performed with similar speed and accuracy as hearing children of the same CA and faster and more accurately than hearing children of the same reading age.

Beech and Harris studied 6–12-year-old deaf children and 7–8-year-old hearing children, matched for reading age. In their first study the children had to sort cards on which were written regular and exception words from cards with non-words which were similar to the real words except one letter was changed. Overall the deaf children were more accurate than the hearing children. However, whereas the hearing children showed the regularity effect, in that they were more likely to be correct with regular words than exception words, the deaf children did not show this effect. In their second task they used exception words and nonwords which were either homophonic to the corresponding real word, that is, when pronounced sounded the same (e.g., "werd" corresponding to "word") or non-homophonic (e.g., "somo" corresponding to "some"). The hearing children, but not the deaf children, made more errors with the homophonic nonwords, which is consistent with the hearing children, but not the deaf children, using a phonological strategy. Interestingly, Beech and Harris report that this pattern of results was seen in the deaf children regardless of their reading ability or whether or not they relied primarily on spoken language or a sign system.

While these studies indicate that deaf children do not use phonological strategies to the same extent as hearing children, they do not demonstrate that deaf children cannot use phonological strategies. Evidence that deaf children can and do code written words phonologically comes from a study of the Stroop effect by Leybaert and Alegria (e.g., 1993). In the Stroop color-word test the names of colours (e.g., "red") are written in different colors (e.g., blue) and the color in which the word is written has to be named (i.e., blue). Leybaert and Alegria reported that 10–16-year-old orally educated deaf adolescents, like 8–9-year-old hearing children, responded more slowly when color names were used compared with when meaningless letter strings were used, and this effect was more marked when the children had to name the color in which the word was written than when they had to press a button of the same color. This is evidence that deaf children, like hearing children, process the written color names. Further, Leybaert and Alegria also found that nonword homophones, which when read sounded like real words (e.g., "rauze" which sounds like "rose," the French for pink), also slowed down response time when the color in which the letters had been written had to be spoken. This last finding is good evidence that deaf children can access phonological information and that this probably is involuntary given that in the Stroop test it is not necessary and actually interferes with performance. However, given that Beech and Harris did not report any effect for their non-word homophones for 6–12-year-old deaf children it may be that this effect develops with age.

I now want to consider deaf children's writing skills. Gregory et al. (1995) reported that 22% of the 82 young deaf adults they studied could write a letter to a friend without any help. However, 30% needed a great deal of help and a further 6% could not write at all. In an interesting study, Marschark, Mouradian, and Halas (1994) found that although the signed/spoken stories of 9–16-year-old deaf and hearing children were of similar length and discourse structure, the written stories of the deaf children were shorter than those of the hearing children. In addition, whereas the hearing children's written stories developed with age in terms of increased sentence length, readability, novelty, and complexity, the only age effect for the deaf children was the use of longer words. It is not clear why writing should be so difficult for deaf children.

A number of studies have examined deaf children's spelling. Overall, deaf children spell as well as children of similar reading age but not as well as children of the same CA (e.g., Burden & Campbell, 1994). But what is more interesting is whether they use a visual or phonological strategy for spelling. Burden and Campbell used pictures corresponding to specific words and asked deaf and hearing children to write down the names. Deaf school leavers, like hearing children of the same reading age, spelled more regular than exception words correctly, whereas for children of the same CA there was no difference. The regularity effect was interpreted as evidence that the deaf children were making use of phonological information in spelling the words. Their errors also indicated the use of phonological information. For example, "skwrl" was written for squirrel, "sponch" for sponge.

However, deaf children's use of a phonological strategy for spelling may depend on their oral skills. Using a similar methodology to Burden and Campbell but in French, Leybaert and Alegria (1995) also found evidence of the regularity effect for both 8–17-year-old deaf children and 6–9-year-old hearing children. Leybaert and Alegria assigned the deaf children to a younger and older age group, mean ages 10 years 9 months and 13 years 3 months, although, because the assignment was based on which class they were in at school, the two age groups overlapped. In addition, the deaf children's teachers rated the intelligibility of their spoken language. Particularly interesting were the misspellings of the different groups of children. About 90% of the hearing children's misspellings were phonological, compared to about 22% and 38% for the younger and older deaf children. However, when the profoundly deaf children's phonological errors were examined alongside the intelligibility of their speech, it was found that 18% and 15% of the intelligible and unintelligible young deaf children's errors respectively were phonological. For the older deaf children the corresponding figures were 43% and 19%. All but 2 of the 27 severely deaf children had intelligible speech and 31% and 46% of errors were phonological at the two ages respectively. These findings indicate that use of phonological information seems to develop with age provided that speech is intelligible.

Further support for the influence of speech intelligibility comes from Aaron, Keetay, Boyd, Palmatier, and Wacks (1998) who studied 9–18-year-old deaf children with a mean reading age of about 9 years who either did not communicate with spoken language or whose speech was ineffective for communication. Overall the deaf children could spell as well as children of similar reading age. However, the deaf children, unlike 8–12-year-old hearing children, produced fewer phonologically acceptable spelling errors and could generate fewer pairs of words which sound the same but are spelled differently (for example, "meat" and "meet"). In addition, the deaf children missed out fewer silent letters (for example, "sno" for "snow") than the hearing children when they misspelled a word, and when they had to write down from memory words previously seen the deaf children made more transpositions (e.g., "ture" for "true") and visual errors ("worb" for "word") than the hearing children and very few phonological errors. Further, when nonwords, some of which were pronounceable (e.g., "etak") some unpronounceable (e.g., "tkae"), had to be remembered, the deaf children correctly wrote down more pronounceable than unpronounceable nonwords and in this were similar to hearing children of the same reading age. Aaron et al. conclude that these deaf children were not relying on phonological information but rather on a visual strategy. In particular, they suggest that the deaf children may be utilizing knowledge, gained through reading, of likely letter sequences, rather than visually remembering whole words.

A study by Charlier and Leybaert (2000) once again demonstrates that cued speech can provide additional phonological information for deaf children. Deaf 7–18-year-olds educated with cued speech from 39 months on average, deaf 10–21-year-olds educated with cued speech from 85 months, and 8–12 year old hearing children matched with the deaf children for reading ability were presented with pictures or the written names of objects and had to write down two rhyming words for each target. The hearing children produced over 90% correct responses, the deaf children with early exposure to cued speech over 80% and the children exposed later to cued speech less than 60%. However, more interesting was the finding that 51%, 41% and 24% of the responses of the three groups respectively were correct and orthographically different from the spellings of the targets.

Leybaert (2000) has also demonstrated that early experience of cued speech affects deaf children's spelling mistakes. Two groups of 6–14-year-old deaf children with experience of cued speech from 18 and 38 months on average respectively were matched for general spelling level with 7–11-year-old hearing children. The children had to write down the words indicated by a picture or a sentence context. Given the matching procedure, the groups did not differ in terms of the proportion of words spelled correctly. However, the percentage of misspellings which were phonologically correct for the hearing children, the deaf children with early experience of cued speech, and the deaf children with later experience were 84%, 67%, and 36% respectively.

Cued speech can also help deaf children spell pseudowords, that is non-words which follow the structural characteristics of real words (Alegria, Charlier, & Mattys, 1999). Eight- to twelve-year-old deaf children who had experienced cued speech before the age of 2 years and 11–20-year-old deaf adolescents who had experienced cued speech after the age of 5 years watched a video of an adult pronouncing words and pseudowords with and without cued speech and wrote down the words/pseudowords. There was no difference between the two groups in terms of the number of responses which were phonologically appropriate. Cued speech helped both groups, although the group with early experience was helped more and this group also produced more responses which were phonologically appropriate for the pseudowords.

It is interesting that within this section, as well as in the other sections examining the development of communication in deaf children, a number of studies have indicated that deaf children born to deaf parents and with access to a sign language from early on, are more like hearing children than deaf children born to hearing parents. This has profound implications for practice which I shall consider in chapter 7. I now want to consider how deafness affects social development.

Social and emotional development

Successful interaction with other people is dependent on the individuals involved sharing a communication system. Much of the evidence considered so far has demonstrated that a major factor influencing the effectiveness of communication between deaf children and their parents is the hearing status of the parents. Deaf children with deaf signing parents communicate as effectively with their parents and other deaf signing people as hearing children communicate with hearing people. In contrast, many dcHP children experience difficulties and some never acquire an effective means of communication with other hearing people. In addition, while deaf parents make adjustments when they communicate with their young deaf children, equivalent to adjustments made by hearing parents communicating with hearing children, many dcHP parents communicate with their deaf children in ways which may not be particularly beneficial. This suggests that social interaction will present few, if any, problems to dcDP children but major difficulties for dcHP children.

How is interaction with other children affected by deafness?

Young deaf children engage in more solitary play and less pretend play than hearing children of similar age (e.g., Spencer & Deyo, 1993). Both these observations reflect the fact that interaction and play with others, particularly pretend/fantasy play, benefit from effective communication. Pretence, in particular, involves children making up stories, sharing ideas about imaginary environments and roles, and such activities will be extremely difficult for deaf children if they have limited language skills. Thus, Lederberg (1991) observed that deaf preschoolers with good language skills were more likely to play and communicate with more than one other child than those with less good language. Further, Lederberg, Ryan, and Robbins (1986) found significant correlations between the language competence of 4–7-year-old deaf children and several measures of their interaction with other deaf children, including total interaction time, total number of turns, and frequency of pretend play episodes. Rather surprisingly, Lederberg et al. did not find any correlations between the nature of interaction and language use during the interaction. They suggest that what may be crucial is not how much language is actually used during interaction, but the children's overall understanding of what communication involves.

Marvin and Kasal (1996) found that 4–6-year-olds in a preschool for deaf children communicated with their peers mostly about what was going on at the time, predominantly making comments about objects rather than people, and made fewer references than hearing children to past and imaginary events. However, the hearing status of the children with whom deaf children play may be influential. Thus, Levine and Antia (1997) observed 3–6-year-old deaf children who were integrated with hearing children for 2–24 hours each week and found that at 3–5 years the deaf children were more likely to play together, whereas at 5–6 years the deaf children were as likely to play together as for several of them to play together with hearing children. But what was more interesting was that the play differed depending on the hearing status of the group. When deaf children played together the play was mainly manipulative and constructive, whereas when two or more deaf children played with hearing children they engaged mainly in constructive and dramatic play, with dramatic play being most prevalent in these mixed groups when the children were 5–6 years old. Levine and Antia argue that these findings indicate that deaf children need other deaf children with whom to communicate, but also need hearing children to initiate and model more sophisticated play.

In settings where there are both deaf and hearing children, although children of different hearing status do interact with one another some of the time, deaf children are more likely to interact with deaf children, and hearing children with hearing children (e.g., Minnett, Clark, & Wilson, 1994; Spencer et al., 1994). This is probably due to communication with other children of the same hearing status being easier than with children of different hearing status and because hearing children are more likely to choose children with whom they can communicate easily, that is, children who can hear, as preferred play partners. Certainly, Rodriguez and Lana (1996) found that both familiarity and hearing status influenced the nature of the social interaction between 2–5-year-old deaf children and their deaf and hearing peers. Interactions of three or more turns were more frequent when two familiar deaf peers were interacting, next most frequent when unfamiliar deaf peers interacted, then deaf and familiar hearing peers, and least frequent when the deaf children interacted with an unfamiliar hearing child. Even deaf and hearing children who are very familiar with one another may not interact a great deal. Thus, Gaines and Halpern-Felsher (1995) also note that 1–3-year-old twins, one of whom was deaf, rarely interacted with one another, although they did both interact with adults.

The more effective the deaf children's communication is, the more similar their interaction is to that of hearing children (e.g., Preisler, 1983;

Preisler & Ahlström, 1997). Thus, Preisler (1983) observed 3–7-year-old deaf children who attended a nursery for deaf children. The children all had hearing parents and five children had started to learn to sign at 1–3 years; 10 started to learn at 3–6 years. The early sign language learners had more effective communication strategies and greater understanding of rules underlying communication with others than the children who began signing later. The early signers were very attentive to their play partners, and obtained their attention before communicating. They dealt with the past and future as easily as the present and communicated about fantasy.

If deaf children can sign and mix with other deaf signing children, their interaction will be very similar to that of hearing children. But dcHP children will not have easy access to other deaf children and teachers of 16-year-old deaf pupils have reported that 24% of them did not know any other deaf peers (Powers, 1996), let alone have any deaf friends. What happens to deaf children without access to deaf peers? Shaw and Jamieson (1995) observed that an 8-year-old deaf boy in a hearing school interacted out of lessons with his hearing peers only 25% of the time. These interactions were often very brief and broke down through misunderstandings.

Clearly deafness can be very isolating and can affect the nature of interaction with other children, particularly if there is no opportunity to mix with other deaf children. This may result in most interaction being with adults. How does deafness affect this?

How is interaction with adults affected by deafness?

A number of studies have shown that deaf and hearing parents differ in how they interact with their young deaf children, although there is much variation between parents (Harris & Mohay, 1997). Jamieson (1997) noted that when infants are less than 4 months old deaf mothers look at their deaf children more frequently and for longer than hearing mothers look at their hearing children, and generally their faces are very animated and expressive and they engage in much physical contact. In contrast, although hearing mothers engage in more vocal games and talk more to their 9-month-old deaf infants than deaf mothers with their deaf infants they do not do this any more than hearing mothers with hearing infants (Koester, Brooks, & Karkowski, 1998b).

One situation which has been used to explore the nature of early interaction is the still face paradigm. In this the parents interact normally with their infants for 3 minutes, followed by 2 minutes in which the parents keep still and look at their infant without showing any expression. There is then a further 2 minutes of normal interaction. Koester (1995) reports that overall, compared to 9-month-old hearing children, 9-month-old deaf infants with hearing mothers spent more time engaged in rhythmical motor activity and reached less towards their mothers. Although the deaf and hearing infants did not differ in how long they looked at their mothers, the deaf infants looked to and from their mothers less frequently. When their mothers adopted a still face, the hearing infants made more attempts to get their mothers to interact by leaning or reaching towards them whereas the deaf infants spent more time in self-comfort activities such as thumb sucking or rocking. During the first period of normal interaction, there were several differences in the co-occurrence of behaviors of the mothers and infants. Thus, the hearing infants showed more social behavior towards their mothers, smiling and reaching towards them, to which the mothers responded. The deaf infants looked more at their mothers and their mothers followed this with more activities which could be seen by their infants, for example finger play. These differences suggest that by the age of 9 months dcHP children are less actively engaged socially with their mothers than hcHP infants are with theirs. Is this also the case if the mother is also deaf?

Koester et al. (2000) noted that 9-month-old dcDP infants also engage in more rhythmical motor activity than hearing infants, although interestingly the deaf mothers responded more positively to this activity, interpreting it as a precursor of signing. The hearing mothers, on the other hand, tended to perceive this activity in their deaf children as hyperactivity. There was a difference in the still face episode with the dcDP infants showing more distress than the dcHP infants. Why should this happen? One possible explanation is that most deaf parents will be native signers and sign languages do not just involve particular hand shapes and movements, they also rely on facial expressions and body movements. The greater distress of dcDP infants may therefore arise because their parent's face is generally more animated than the faces of hearing parents.

However, evidence from a study of deaf parents by Reilly and Bellugi (1996) goes against this explanation. They found that when the deaf children were less than 2 years old their deaf signing parents often omitted facial expressions which normally accompany particular grammatical structures in ASL because of the confusion that these expressions might cause. For example, Wh- questions in ASL are accompanied by the signer making eye contact, furrowing their eyebrows and tilting their head. However, this facial expression, when not accompanying ASL, could signify anger, puzzlement or ending of the interaction. Thus, the greater distress of dcDP infants in the still face paradigm may simply indicate that by 9 months deaf parents usually demonstrate more positive facial affect to their infants, perhaps as a substitute for the positive vocal expressions of affect observed in hearing parents.

A study of dcHP and hcHP 18–25-month-olds by Lederberg and Mobley (1990) found that although the deaf children and their mothers experienced communication difficulties, this did not affect how securely attached the children were. Thus, based on the children's behavior during the Strange Situation procedure, 56% of the deaf children were found to be securely attached, compared to 61% of the hearing children. Further, no differences were observed in the quality of the interaction between these children and their mothers. For example, the mothers did not differ in how directive or intrusive they were, how positive or negative they were, and the children did not differ in how responsive they were, or in their engagement in the interaction. However, the deaf children interacted less with their mothers than the hearing children. This was despite the fact that the mothers of the deaf children initiated more and can probably be explained by the deaf children being more likely to terminate an interaction through not seeing or hearing a comment from their parents.

Rather different findings were reported by Meadow-Orlans and Steinberg (1993) who found that hearing mothers of 18-month-old deaf children were less sensitive, less flexible, less warm, and showed less consistency in their interactions than mothers of hearing children. Interestingly, Meadow-Orlans (1997) reports that interactions between dcDP mothers and their infants are qualitatively similar to those between hcHP mothers and their infants.

Lederberg and Prezbindowski (2000) suggest that the different results from Lederberg and Mobley's study and Meadow-Orlans and Steinberg's study are probably due to the use of different definitions of sensitivity and because Lederberg and Mobley's study included both college educated and non-college educated parents whereas Meadow-Orlans and Steinberg's parents were college educated. In a re-analysis of Lederberg and Mobley's findings, Lederberg and Prezbindowski found that the college educated mothers of hearing children were more sensitive than the college educated hearing mothers of the deaf children. There was no difference in the sensitivity of the mothers who had not been to college. However, whereas all the college educated mothers of hearing infants were judged to be sensitive, there was much more variability among the mothers of the deaf infants. In other words, deafness in a child does not have a consistent effect on how they and their parents interact. Other factors may be more important, including the parents' level of education.

All these studies have involved parents interacting with their children. However, many interactions are with people we do not know particularly well. Lederberg (1984) found that hearing women, who themselves had 4-year-old hearing girls, made more attempts to interact with unfamiliar

5-year-old deaf signing girls, selected as having better oral and sign communication skills than their classmates, than with unfamiliar hearing girls when either instructing or playing with them. However, even though the women modified their behavior towards the deaf girls, using fewer and simpler verbalizations, more gestures, and touching the children more often, their interaction attempts with them were less successful than with the hearing children and lasted for less time. Once again we see that having the same communication system greatly benefits social interaction.

As children get older the ability to communicate becomes increasingly important for successful interaction, and the majority of deaf children who do not have early access to sign language will experience increasing difficulties. Thus, Gregory (1976), based on interviews with dcHP parents, found that the amount of interaction between these deaf children and their hearing parents decreased after the age of 2 years, whereas the amount increases if children can hear. She further reported that the deaf children had more temper tantrums than hearing children. Many of the parents found bringing up their children frustrating and felt that strangers did not understand them. In several cases comments from strangers implied that they thought that the deaf children had learning difficulties.

In general agreement with Gregory, Denmark et al. (1979) note that more than 85% of parents of 75 deaf adolescents reported having had behavior problems with their children when they were of preschool age which were attributed to the deafness. At school age, over 60% of the parents reported difficulties with the children's behavior, and more than 70% had difficulties with behavior problems after the children left school.

Parents may also reprimand deaf and hearing children differently. Thus, Schlesinger and Meadow (1972), based on interviews with parents of deaf preschool children, report that the parents were less permissive than parents of hearing children, and were much more likely to use physical punishment for disciplining the children. Not only did these parents spank their children more than parents spank hearing children, but almost three-quarters of the parents of the deaf children felt comfortable with this method of discipline, whereas only a quarter of parents of hearing children did. Meadow (1980) found that whereas 69% of parents of hearing 4-year-olds would deprive the children of sweets or television as a punishment, only 5% of the parents of deaf 4-year-olds used this sort of punishment.

Clearly interaction with deaf children can be difficult and frustrating. How does it affect them?

What do deaf children feel about themselves?

Deaf children born to deaf parents who use sign language as their main means of communication are likely to grow up to be members of the community of deaf people, able to communicate easily among themselves and with positive views of themselves as deaf people. In contrast, dcHP children often do not achieve effective communication and as they grow up they may feel that they do not belong to a community of either hearing people or deaf people. It seems likely therefore that the hearing status of the parents of deaf children may play a crucial role in how the children adjust to their hearing impairment. However, dcHP parents will vary in terms of the ease with which they can communicate with their deaf children and in the attitudes that they hold towards deafness, and these factors may be very important in determining how well these deaf children adjust to their hearing loss.

In their interviews with young deaf adults whose parents had adopted an oral-only approach when they were children, Gregory et al. (1995) asked a series of questions about how they viewed themselves: as happy or sad; as confident or not very confident; whether they liked themselves, were proud of themselves, felt sorry for themselves, and whether they wanted to change in any way. Of the 61 adults interviewed, 31% answered all the questions positively. However, 46%, 11%, 7%, 3%, and 2% answered one, two, three, four, or five questions negatively respectively. Although there are no comparison data, these responses indicate that a number of young deaf people feel very negative about themselves. Such findings are also reflected in prevalence rates of psychiatric problems in deaf children and adolescents.

Hindley, Hill, McGuigan, and Kitson (1994) found that 11–16-year-old deaf children in London showed higher rates of psychiatric problems, mainly anxiety disorders and phobias, than inner city hearing children. Parents and teachers of 81 children completed screening questionnaires specially developed for use with deaf children and the children identified as likely to have psychiatric problems were then interviewed. A prevalence rate of 50%, adjusted for the likelihood of some cases having been missed, was found compared to prevalence rates of around 25% for hearing children. Interestingly, the prevalence rate was 61% among the 35 children attending hearing impaired units, where most used spoken language, compared to 42% for the 46 children attending schools for the deaf, where sign and spoken language were both used. It is interesting to note that hearing loss among the children in the hearing impaired units ranged from 40–96+ dB, whereas for the children attending deaf schools the range was 71–96+ db. It therefore seems unlikely that severity of deafness can account for the different prevalence rates in the two types of school. Hindley et al. suggest that schools for deaf pupils may provide the children with a more positive self-image than units attached to mainstream schools, as well as providing a more effective language for communication.

The importance of a shared communication system receives support from a prevalence study of psychiatric disorder in 6–21-year-old deaf individuals living in Finland by Sinkkonen (1994), cited by Hindley (1997). All the hearing mothers of these deaf children and young people had some signing skills, as did 94% of the fathers. A prevalence rate for psychiatric disorder of 19% was found which was similar to the 16% reported for hearing children and young people. Hindley suggests that more effective communication within these families allowed by signing, plus more positive attitudes to deafness, may explain this low rate.

There is also evidence that sign language opportunities may reduce the prevalence of psychiatric problems from a study of 2–11-year-old deaf children attending a deaf nursery and primary school (Vostanis, Hayes, & Du Feu, 1997a). All the teaching staff used a bilingual approach, involving both BSL and English. Thirty-five percent of the 46 children used sign language only, 63% used sign and speech, and just 1 child used speech only. Of the parents, 72% used the same method of communication as their children but 28% used a different method. Vostanis et al. report that two questionnaires, the Parent's Checklist and the Child Behavior Checklist, completed by parents identified 30% and 70% of the children as having psychiatric problems, whereas the equivalent questionnaires, the Teacher's Checklist and the Teacher's Report Form, filled in by teachers, identified 11% and 50% respectively as having problems. Vostanis et al. speculate that the lower prevalence of problems identified by teachers may be because the school's bilingual philosophy provided the deaf children with more communication opportunities than their home environments. Nevertheless, all the questionnaires showed a raised prevalence of problems compared to hearing children. Using the parental questionnaires, similar prevalences of 40% and 77% were also reported for a sample extended to include adolescents up to the age of 18 years (Vostanis, Hayes, Du Feu, & Warren, 1997b).

The studies by Vostanis and colleagues indicates that psychiatric problems are apparent in deaf children across a wide age range. But is there continuity within individuals? There is some evidence of continuity from Gregory et al.'s (1995) follow-up as young adults of 82 dcHP children whose parents initially adopted an oral-only approach. Gregory at al. report that 31 young adults were described by their parents as unhappy or a mixture of unhappy and happy. Interestingly, 87% of these had had many temper tantrums as young children, whereas of the 51 young adults who were described as happy, just over half, 53%, had had many temper tantrums. Further, of the 43 young adults who were described as easily bored, 81% had many childhood tantrums, compared to 49% of the 39 described as not easily bored or varying between easily and not easily bored. These data suggest that there is continuity between difficulties in childhood and certain negative characteristics in adulthood, although it is by no means inevitable. It would be interesting to know whether there was any relationship between the language competence of the young adults and their personality characteristics, but these data are not reported.

Once again in this section we have seen that the ability of deaf children to communicate easily and effectively with others affects their development, this time in the area of social interaction and adjustment. The practical implications of this will be considered in chapter 7.

chapter four

How do children with motor disabilities develop?

Introduction

In this chapter I shall consider children with spina bifida (SB), children with cerebral palsy (CP), and children with developmental coordination disorder (DCD). This covers a vast area in terms of the nature and extent of the motor difficulties and other problems that children with these disabilities experience. As a result it has been necessary to be selective, concentrating on studies which have particular implications for our understanding of developmental processes.

Motor development

There is a great deal of variation in the sort of motor skills that children with motor disabilities can develop, depending on the nature and severity of their disability. I shall consider the three types of motor disability in turn.

Usually the main motor problem facing children with SB is paralysis of the legs. We might therefore expect their motor difficulties to be in areas which require the use of their legs. Not surprisingly, these children are often delayed in standing and walking and some never manage to do either, although this depends on the level of the unfused vertebrae: the higher the lesion, the greater the motor disability (e.g. Holmbeck & Faier-Routman, 1995). Morrow and Wachs (1992) reported that of 22 children with SB under the age of 2 years, only 3 had normal locomotor abilities for their age. Anderson and Spain (1977) found that by the age of 3 years, 40% of children with SB could not walk or could only walk a few steps and by 6 years just under half were able to get around the house easily. Hetherington and Dennis (1999) reported that of 17 children with SB aged between 5 and 15 years, 11 could walk but the others had severe difficulties moving around. However, even those who could walk had great difficulty with tasks involving their lower limbs such as jumping and standing on one foot. Mobility is also affected by the presence of hydrocephalus. Thus, Scott et al. (1998) reported that 13% of children with SB and shunted hydrocephalus of mean age 9 years could walk without support, compared to 43% for children with SB and arrested hydrocephalus not requiring shunts and 100% of children with SB and no hydrocephalus.

But what is perhaps surprising is that children with SB often have problems using their hands. A much higher proportion are left-handed than found among TD children (e.g., Hetherington & Dennis, 1999; Loss, Yeates, & Enrile, 1998) and they are less skilled than TD children at tasks requiring fine motor control like picking up small objects, putting pegs into holes in a peg board, or tracing a picture. In their study, Hetherington and Dennis (1999) found that the children with SB performed at least one standard deviation below TD children on a range of neuromuscular tests of dexterity including placing beads on a rod and threading together a nut and bolt. Interestingly, this difficulty has been related to their paraplegia, in that they find it harder to keep their balance when they are sitting down and tend to support themselves with one hand. Thus, it will be difficult for them to gain experience in fine motor tasks and they will have fewer opportunities of using both hands together.

In children with CP all motor milestones seem to be delayed. Denhoff and Holden (1951) reported considerable delays in the development of early motor milestones: the average age at which 74 children with CP held up their heads was 12.4 months, and 86% of 28 children started to reach much later than the usual age of 5 months. Hewett (1970) found that by the age of 5 years or more, 38% of 125 children with CP could not sit unsupported, 10% had some balance when they sat but were unable to stand without support, and a further 10.4% could sit and stand but not walk. This means that less than half of these children could walk by 5 years. In addition, when children with CP do walk, the nature of their disability may led to very odd gaits (e.g., Holt, Fonseca, & LaFiandra, 2000) and poor balance (e.g., Liao, Jeng, Lai, Cheng, & Hu, 1997).

Children with CP experience a number of difficulties reaching for and grasping objects. They are often slow to reach and flex their fingers as their hand approaches an object, overextend their fingers, have a weak grasp, and the strength of their grip varies. Sugden and Utley (1995a, 1995b) and Utley and Sugden (1998) have carried out a series of studies with children and adolescents with hemiplegic CP aged between 3 and 18 years. They confirmed that reaching with the less affected hand was faster, more fluent, and showed greater accuracy than reaching with the more affected hand. However, when the task required the use of both hands, the two hands tended to work in unison, with the more affected hand moving at a similar speed to the less affected hand towards the object to be grasped, especially at the beginning of the reach.

The strength of grip has been examined by Eliasson, Gordon, and Forssberg (1991, 1992, 1995) who measured the force that children with CP aged between 6 and 8 years exerted as they grasped and lifted objects. In comparison to TD children of similar age, most of the children with CP gripped the object more firmly than was necessary and their ability to adjust the strength of their grip by the force they exerted as they lifted the object up was poor. In a subsequent study, Eliasson and Gordon (2000) reported that 7–13-year-olds with CP placed an object they had lifted more abruptly on the table and released their grip on the object more slowly and in a less coordinated manner than TD children of similar age. Interestingly, Kuhtz-Buschbeck, Sundholm, Eliasson, and Forssberg (2000) reported that when 6–18-year-olds with CP and TD individuals of similar age had to lift and hold an object with one hand at the same time as squeezing a rubber ball rhythmically in their other hand, the squeezing action was mirrored in the hand holding the object and this effect was 15 times stronger in the individuals with CP.

How can the motor problems of children with CP be explained? Van Mier, Hulstijn, and Meulenbroek (1994) suggested that they may result from the children having difficulty planning the motor movement. In their study, children with CP aged 8–10 years, and TD children and adults had to copy geometric shapes either immediately or after looking at the shapes for a second. The children with CP took longer to start copying than the TD children, but they benefited more from previewing the shapes than the TD children. Two other findings also led to the conclusion that the children with CP experienced planning difficulties. First, they made more movements above the paper before starting to copy than the other children. Second, the children with CP made more form errors in terms of omitting or adding elements of each shape or relating the elements incorrectly, but these errors decreased when they previewed the shapes.

Children with DCD have difficulties carrying out a range of motor behaviors and it is the presence of these difficulties combined with normal intelligence and the presumed absence of neurological or sensory impairment that leads to a diagnosis of DCD. For example, Henderson, Knight, Losse, and Jongmans (1991) describe a girl who was delayed in sitting, standing and walking and at 5 years could not fasten buttons, ride a tricycle or use a knife and fork but had a verbal IQ of 121, a reading age of 9½ years, and excellent understanding of number.

There are a number of tests available for assessing motor skill. One of the best known is the Movement Assessment Battery for Children, or Movement ABC (Henderson & Sugden, 1992), which was first published in 1972 as the Test of Motor Impairment (TOMI). This standardized test provides age norms for children between 4 and 12 years and comprises three tests of manual dexterity, two of ball skills, and three of dynamic and static balance, with different tests being used at different ages.

Studies vary in how the Movement ABC and other tests are used to identify children with DCD, with some only including children who score below the 5th centile point whereas others include children whose scores fall below the 10th, 15th, or even 20th centile point (e.g., Piek & Skinner, 1999; Smyth & Mason, 1997; van der Meulen, Denier van der Gon, Gielen, Gooskens, & Willemse, 1991a). Wann, Mon-Williams, and Carson (1998a) have argued that all studies of children with DCD should use the Movement ABC and that there needs to be some agreed criteria for inclusion within the group.

A further characteristic of DCD is that the motor difficulties tend to persist into adolescence, although some children do overcome their difficulties (e.g. Cantell, Smyth, & Ahonen, 1994; Christiansen, 2000; Losse et al., 1991; Visser, Geuze & Kalverboer, 1998). In 1982 Henderson and Hall described 34 6-year-olds, half of whom were identified with DCD on the TOMI. These children were tested again 10 years later by Losse et al. (1991) and the difference in TOMI scores between the two groups was still significant. However, the motor skills of some of the children on the TOMI did improve, with 4 of the 17 children originally identified with DCD achieving average TOMI scores 10 years later. Cantell et al. (1994) reported that over 50% of children initially diagnosed with DCD showed motor skills similar to TD children 10 years later: of 81 children identified with DCD at 5 years, 28 did not differ from TD children at 11 years on a variety of movement tasks, including the Movement ABC, and 44 did not differ at 15 years. More recently, Visser et al. (1998) administered the Movement ABC to two groups of boys every 6 months between 11½ and 14 years. One group had scores below the 10th percentile, the other scores above the 15th percentile at the outset. The difference in scores between the two groups decreased over time with the boys with scores initially below the 10th percentile showing improved skills. Nevertheless, at 14 years only a third of these boys achieved average scores.

One problem with both these studies is that the Movement ABC is standardized for children up to 12 years and the children taking part in these studies were older. Interestingly, when Christiansen (2000) re-examined

10 boys who, between 5 and 8 years, were diagnosed with deficits in attention, motor control, and perception (DAMP), a diagnosis commonly used in Scandinavia and which overlaps with attention deficit hyperactivity disorder (ADHD) and DCD, they all scored below the 5th percentile on the Movement ABC when aged 11–12 years. Further evidence of the problems these children faced was that none were involved in team sports at school, compared to over half of TD children.

Since the early 1990s many different aspects of the motor abilities of children with DCD have been researched. One finding is that children with DCD have slow reaction times and movement times (e.g., Geuze & van Dellen, 1990; Henderson, Rose & Henderson, 1992; Smyth, 1991; van der Meulen et al., 1991a; van der Meulen, Denier van der Gon, Gielen, Gooskens, & Willemse, 1991b). Thus, Henderson et al. reported that children with DCD aged 7–12 years were slower to stop pressing one key when prompted and took longer to move their hand to press a second key than TD children.

Children with DCD are also less good at anticipating when to make a movement (e.g. Geuze and van Dellen, 1990; Henderson et al., 1992; Hill & Wing, 1999; Williams, Woollacott, & Ivry, 1992). For example, Henderson et al. found that the children with DCD were much less accurate than children without DCD when they had to press a key to coincide with the last of five regular auditory beeps. Williams et al. observed that 6–7-year-old and 9–10-year-old children with DCD were less good than TD children of similar ages at maintaining a tapping rate on a keyboard and in judging whether the interval between two tones was longer or shorter than the interval between two tones heard previously. Similarly, Hill and Wing report that a 12-year-old boy with DCD was less able than a 9½ year old TD girl at maintaining an even rate of tapping set by a metronome. However, not all children with DCD demonstrate these difficulties. For example, Geuze and Van Dellen report that the ability to predict when to make a movement varied among 7–13-year-old children with DCD, with two 8-year-olds showing similar levels of anticipation to older TD children, whereas some older children with DCD showed little or no anticipation.

This variation in motor skill among children with DCD has been noted in other areas. For example, Wann, Mon-Williams, and Rushton (1998b) found individual differences in postural balance among six 10–12-year-old children with DCD when they stood with their eyes closed or open or when they stood in an artificial room whose walls could swing around them. Two of the children showed similar balance to TD children of similar age, whereas three of them had balance more characteristic of nursery-aged children. Not surprisingly, the children with DCD who did well on the balance tasks also did relatively well on the balance tests of the Movement ABC.

Children with DCD are also less dextrous (e.g., Barnett & Henderson, 1992; Maeland, 1992). Maeland administered the TOMI to 360 10-year-olds and 19 (5.5%) were identified with DCD. These children performed less well than TD children of similar age on several dexterity tasks, including fitting pegs into holes, copying geometric figures and tracing, and more than half the children had poor handwriting. Barnett and Henderson found that the human figure drawings of 5–13-year-old children with DCD were inferior to those of TD children matched for verbal IQ, and the drawing scores of the children with DCD correlated with their TOMI scores. Interestingly, when further drawings were collected from some of the children with DCD 18 months later, improvements were observed for the depiction of proportions, features, and detail but not in terms of motor control.

Coordinating two hands also presents difficulties for children with DCD (e.g. Sigmundsson, 1999). He reported that a sub-group of 7–9-year-old children with DCD with severe hand–eye coordination problems (HECP) were slower than TD children of similar age at threading beads onto a string and screwing nuts onto a bolt when holding the nut in their right hand. All the children were right-handed and the children with HECP were as fast as the TD children when they held the nut in their left hand. On the basis of these and other findings Sigmundsson suggests that these children may have a dysfunctional corpus callosum.

However, children with DCD do not have motor difficulties in all areas. For example, Maeland (1992) reported that 10-year-old children with DCD could tap as fast with their index finger as TD children. Hill (1998), found that children with DCD, mean age 9 years, were as accurate as TD children at copying unfamiliar hand postures or sequences of hand postures, although they were less accurate and made more errors (Hill, Bishop & Nimmo-Smith, 1998) when the hand movements were familiar and particularly when they involved an object, such as combing hair with a comb. Interestingly, the children with DCD were as accurate at copying familiar hand movements as 5–6-year-old TD children, which led Hill to suggest that their difficulties may reflect poor maturation of the kinesthetic system. She argues that they are able to copy unfamiliar hand movements because these depend less on the kinesthetic system and more on visual monitoring.

A maturational argument was also offered by Hill and Bishop (1998) who examined hand preference for picking up a card to the right or left of the midline in right-handed 7–11-year-old children with DCD and 5–6-year-old and 7–11-year-old TD children. The 7–11-year-old TD children were more likely to reach across to their left with their right hand than either the younger TD children or the children with DCD. Clearly this maturational explanation could be tested by studying children with DCD longitudinally, although it must be noted that it is not consistent with the findings discussed earlier showing that most children with DCD do not grow out of their difficulties.

Various other explanations have been offered to account for difficulties experienced by children with DCD. Some researchers (e.g., Williams et al., 1992) have suggested that their difficulties judging time intervals reflect a central timing problem. However, Piek and Skinner (1999) suggest that the difficulty may reflect problems in peripheral motor control. They presented 8–10-year-old children with a sequence of 3 to 5 stimuli visually and auditorily and the children then tapped the sequence on a key. Compared to TD children, the children with DCD took longer to respond, kept their finger on the key for longer, and the spacing of their taps was more variable. Piek and Skinner suggest that these differences may arise because the children with DCD have difficulty coordinating the contraction of the different muscle groups involved.

Support for this suggestion comes from a study of 7- and 10-year-old children with and without DCD by Huh, Williams, and Burke (1998). Huh et al. measured the neuromuscular characteristics of the children as they released one key and depressed a second key. In line with previous findings, the children with DCD took longer to make the movements, but what was interesting was that the onset latency of the antagonist muscle contraction was delayed and the duration of the agonist muscle contraction was increased in these children, relative to the TD children.

Further support for the suggestion that children with DCD may have difficulties controlling muscle action comes from two case studies reported by Hill and Wing (1998, 1999). These researchers examined the force and timing with which two boys, aged 9 and 11 years, gripped and held an object they picked up. Both boys, compared with two TD boys, showed an earlier increase in the force between their thumb and finger when moving the object downwards, and the 11-year-old boy also showed an earlier increase in force when moving the object up. Pereira, Landgren, Gillberg, and Forssberg (2001) also reported that children with DCD exerted greater force when lifting an object compared to children without DCD. Hill and Wing suggest that the differences they observed point towards the children with DCD having problems planning motor movement.

Van Mier et al. (1994) also argue that the problems experienced by children with DCD are due to difficulties programming and controlling motor movements. In this study, which I described earlier when discussing the motor difficulties associated with CP, 8–10-year-old children with DCD and TD children copied geometric shapes either immediately or after inspecting them for 1 second. Two findings led the authors to their conclusion that children with DCD experience problems of motor control: they did not benefit as much as the children with CP from previewing the shapes to be copied; they were more likely than the children with CP to include all the elements of the shapes but the elements often varied in size.

However, children with DCD can plan motor movements at some level. For example, Smyth and Mason (1997) report that 4–8-year-old children with and without DCD showed similar adjustments to how they grasped an object depending on how it had to be moved. Thus, it may be fine muscular adjustments that they find more difficult.

In addition to the explanations outlined above, other researchers have suggested that the motor problems experienced by children with DCD can be accounted for by perceptual difficulties. I shall consider these in the next section.

Perceptual development

If action is important for perception (e.g., Piaget & Inhelder, 1969) then children with motor disabilities should have perceptual difficulties. Some children do have problems, especially in areas involving awareness of spatial relationships. I shall consider the nature of the perceptual difficulties associated with each motor disability in turn.

Many children with SB, especially those with associated hydrocephalus, find the following sorts of tasks difficult: geometry; science subjects; geography; copying designs and letters (e.g., Anderson & Spain, 1977; Holler, Fennell, Crosson, Boggs, & Mickle, 1995). This could be due to their limited motor control, but this seems unlikely since they are just as poor at copying designs by arranging matches appropriately. Their writing of individual letters is reasonable, but the spatial qualities of what they write is poor: the letters within each word tend not to be spaced evenly, nor to lie on a straight line, and the same goes for the words within a sentence. A similar proportion to TD children of similar age and intelligence make reversal errors when they write, but the errors are different. Whereas TD children might write a "d" for a "b," or a "p" for a "g," children with SB and hydrocephalus are more likely to confuse letters involving a diagonal, for example writing "z" instead of "s."

Interestingly, Dennis, Lazenby, and Lockyer (2001) reported that 6–16-year-olds with SB, who all had shunts to control hydrocephalus, were as likely as children and adolescents of similar age and attending the same schools to perceive visual illusions such as the Müller-Lyer. However, the children and adolescents with SB were less likely to perceive multiple perceptions in figures such as in figure–ground reversing stimuli where two different objects can be seen to alternate with one another depending on which part of the figure is taken as the background.

Children with spastic CP also have visuo-perceptual problems which are related to neurological damage (e.g., Ito et al., 1996). A problem with mirror images or reversals is common, with as many as one in six having difficulties: they may write letters upside down or back to front. They seem to find it particularly difficult to copy designs, tending to orient sloping lines incorrectly, and to make mistakes at points where two lines make an angle. This is especially clear in their attempts to copy a diamond, their end product often bearing no relationship to the original (Abercrombie, 1964). Like children with SB, children with spastic CP have spatial problems so that they tend to relate parts of a figure incorrectly. This particular difficulty is apparent in their drawings of people. They also have difficulties drawing maps of a familiar space, adding landmarks to a map and pointing in the direction of a known landmark (Foreman, Orencas, Nicholas, Morton, & Gell, 1989).

Children with CP may also have problems judging distances and directions. They may find getting dressed difficult, for example, not knowing which sleeve to put an arm into. They may also have some tactual perceptual difficulties. For instance, although Eliasson et al. (1995) reported that 12 children with CP aged 6–8 years were as able as TD children to discriminate sandpaper from silk, they had more difficulties detecting differences in a two-point discrimination test: all the TD children but only six children with CP detected two points when they were 2–3 mm apart; three further children with CP identified two points at 5–7 mm; three children with CP required the distance to be greater than 7 mm.

The visual and auditory skills of children with CP are also impaired. Smith (1989) reported that 10 children with CP aged 7–10 years who were unable to speak but were of average intelligence were poor at visual and auditory discrimination. Interestingly, Wann (1991) found that individuals with CP may have particular difficulties with cross-modal tasks. He studied 8 adolescents with CP and learning difficulties aged 10–15 years, only 1 of whom could speak. The task involved moving a toy car on a track so its position matched that of a fixed car on a parallel track. In one condition both cars could be seen and felt (VP:VP, where V stands for vision, P for proprioception); in a second condition the fixed car could be seen and felt, but the moved car only felt (VP:P); in the third condition the fixed car could be seen and the moved car felt (V:P); in the final condition both cars could only be felt (P:P). The children with CP were much less accurate than TD adults and they had most difficulties with condition V:P when information had to be passed between modalities, whereas the adults made most errors in condition P:P.

One of the many labels which has been used to describe children with

DCD in the past is perceptual–motor dysfunction and so it is not surprising that DCD is associated with perceptual difficulties. The two main senses to have been explored are vision and perception of both the position and movement of the body and limbs, referred to as proprioception (static positional judgments) or kinesthesia (perception of movement) respectively, although in the literature these two terms are often not distinguished clearly.

A meta-analysis of 50 papers on DCD published between 1963 and 1996 by Wilson and McKenzie (1998) indicated that children with and without DCD could be discriminated in terms of visual–spatial ability, kinesthetic perception, and cross-modal skills, although impaired processing of visual information produced the most marked difference between the two groups.

Hulme, Biggerstaff, Moran, and McKinlay (1982) reported that children with DCD were poor, relative to TD children of similar age, at making length judgments visually, kinesthetically (based on the feel of an arm movement), and cross-modally, either visual to kinesthetic or vice versa. However, in this and subsequent papers exploring other motor skills, for example reproducing and tracing drawings of triangles (Lord & Hulme, 1988a), only performance in the visual modality correlated with motor ability, leading them to conclude that the main perceptual problem in DCD was visual–spatial, although obviously a correlation does not indicate anything about causality. The same relationship was reported by Fletcher-Flinn, Elmes, and Strugnell (1997) and others (e.g., Lefebvre & Reid, 1998; Parush, Yochman, Cohen, & Gershon, 1998) have also argued that visual–spatial problems may explain the motor difficulties experienced by children with DCD. This is despite children with DCD not appearing to have any problems of visual acuity or sensitivity (e.g., Lord & Hulme, 1987; Mon-Williams, Wann, & Pascal, 1994), although they are less good at visually tracking an oscillating dot of light, suggesting that their oculomotor control may be poor (Langaas, Mon-Williams, Wann, Pascal, & Thompson, 1998).

However, doubt was cast on Lord and Hulme's conclusion by Henderson, Barnett, and Henderson (1994) who, although they demonstrated poor visual–spatial skills in children with DCD aged 7–12 years using many of the same tasks, failed to find any relationship between these and motor ability. It has also been suggested that a particular visual–spatial problem for children with DCD may be disengaging attention (e.g., Wilson & Maruff, 1999; Wilson, Maruff, & McKenzie, 1997). However, given that around half of children with DCD also have attention deficit hyperactivity disorder which is characterized by a difficulty in disengaging from stimuli, this finding may simply reflect that association, rather than say anything specifically about DCD.

Although Hulme and colleagues did not find any relationship between motor ability in children with DCD and either their poor kinesthetic or cross-modal judgments involving both vision and kinesthesia, other researchers have argued that kinaesthesia and/or proprioception are particular areas of difficulty in DCD. For example, T. R. Smyth (1994) found that when 8½ year old children with DCD had to respond when their dominant arm was moved but not if their non-dominant arm was moved, their reaction time increased more than was observed in TD children, leading to the suggestion that children with DCD find it more difficult to tell which arm was moved. Interestingly, M. M. Smyth and Mason (1997) found no difference in the ability of 5–8-year-old children with DCD and TD children to indicate which of their arms had been raised higher when relying only on information from the felt position of their arms, although they were less good than TD children at raising one arm to match the height of the other arm when they had their eyes closed. In a subsequent paper, T. R. Smyth (1996) backtracked on his earlier suggestion of a specific kinesthetic difficulty. As before, he reported longer reaction times to kinesthetic stimuli for children with DCD relative to TD children, but found that the increase in reaction times when two kinesthetic stimuli had to be discriminated was similar in the two groups. In this paper he pointed to the possibility of a problem in the translation of information from one modality to another.

Within- and cross-modal difficulties involving proprioception (P) have been examined using a setup in which the children sit in front of a table and a mark is made on the top of the table, or a pin is stuck in it, and they have to stick a pin in the undersurface of the table to correspond to the position of the pin on the top while either viewing (V:P), viewing and touching (VP:P), or just touching (P:P) the mark or pin on the top. Using this paradigm M. M. Smyth and Mason (1997) reported that 5–8-year-old children with DCD positioned the pin less accurately than TD children of similar age and were much less accurate in condition P:P. The children with DCD also differed from the TD children in terms of the direction of their errors in the different conditions, i.e., whether they tend to stick the pin to the left or right of the correct position, or towards or away from their body (Smyth & Mason, 1998).

Sigmundsson, Ingvaldsen, and Whiting (1997a, 1997b) demonstrated that a sub-group of 7–9-years-old children with DCD with severe hand–eye coordination problems (HECP) performed less well than 5–6 and 7–9-year-old TD children in conditions V:P and VP:P. In condition P:P children with HECP performed less well than TD children of similar age, but similarly to the younger TD children. However, the children with HECP, but neither group of TD children, were less accurate in conditions VP:P and P:P when placing the pin with their non-preferred hand, a finding consistent with Sigmundsson's earlier suggestion that children with HECP may have a dysfunctional corpus callosum affecting the transfer of proprioceptive information from right hand to left hand.

To examine this further, Sigmundsson, Whiting, and Ingvaldsen (1999) devised a new task to enable condition P:P to be carried out using limbs on the same side of the body and therefore not requiring information to be transferred between hemispheres via the corpus callosum. The children wore dark glasses to remove any visual information and located a target on the undersurface of a low table with either their right or left big toe and then marked this position on the top of the table using either their right or left hand, producing two ipsilateral conditions $R_{toe}R_{hand}$, $L_{toe}L_{hand}$, and two contralateral conditions $R_{toe}L_{hand}$ and $L_{toe}R_{hand}$. The children with HECP were less accurate than the TD children in all conditions except $R_{toe}R_{hand}$, leading these researchers to argue that children with HECP have a right hemisphere deficit for processing proprioceptive information, possibly associated with a dysfunctional corpus callosum.

One of the problems with the table-top paradigm used by Sigmundsson and colleagues is that the proprioceptive information from the two limbs differs because one limb feels a pin on the top of the table, the other a pin underneath, and therefore the two limbs are oriented differently. This problem was partly overcome by Mon-Williams, Wann, and Pascal (1999) using a similar table arrangement, but the children had to position their dominant hand above the table so it matched how the researcher had oriented their non-dominant hand below the table, either with or without sight of their dominant hand. The 5–8-year-old children with DCD were much less accurate when they could see their dominant hand, whereas the reverse was found for TD children. This provides further support for children with DCD having particular difficulties relating visual and proprioceptive information. Interestingly, Newnham and McKenzie (1993) reported that 9–14-year-olds with DCD made more errors than TD children when they saw one shape and had to identify the same shape from two shapes on the basis of touch, and their performance correlated with the degree of motor disability. However, the groups did not differ when the task was carried out within the same modality (either visually or tactually) or when the target shape was presented tactually and the choice was made visually.

Clearly, children with DCD experience a number of perceptual difficulties and tasks involving the transfer of information across modalities seem to be particularly affected. However, whether or not any of these difficulties cause the motor problems associated with DCD is not clear. It is also quite likely that there are several different causes of the difficulties which manifest as DCD.

Cognitive development

It is clear from the findings examined in the first two sections of this chapter that children with SB, children with CP, and children with DCD differ from one another in many different ways. In the following sections I shall consider their intellectual abilities, understanding of objects and people, ability to attend, plan, and remember, and, finally, reading, spelling and arithmetic skills.

How intelligent are children with motor disabilities?

CP, SB, and DCD present different problems for examining whether or not motor disability affects intelligence. Many children with CP have brain damage which may affect their cognitive functioning, independently of any effect of their motor problems. Similarly, children with SB who also have hydrocephalus are very likely to have brain damage leading to some cognitive impairment. In contrast, children with SB but no hydrocephalus are unlikely to have brain damage. Children with DCD, on the other hand, are different again because two of the criteria for a diagnosis of DCD are that the children have no neurological impairments and are of normal intelligence, suggesting that normal intellectual ability can exist alongside the sorts of motor problems that characterize DCD.

Most children with CP have below average intelligence with only about 20% achieving normal levels. However, it is difficult to separate the relative contributions of motor disability and brain damage. If those children with spastic CP are examined, it is found that in general the more limbs that are affected the greater the likelihood of below average intelligence. This suggests that the motor disability does affect intelligence. Yet this is obviously not necessarily true since children with athetoid CP are often of average or above average intelligence. Also, since it is particularly difficult to assess the intelligence of children who have relatively little control over their movements and whose speech may be difficult to understand (e.g., Hur & Cochrane, 1995), it seems likely that these children's intelligence may have been underestimated.

The mean IQ of children with SB is below average, although around a quarter have average or above average IQs (e.g., Appleton et al., 1994). Appleton et al. reported a mean IQ of 79 for 78 young people with SB aged 7–19 years. Twenty-two had IQs below 70, 16 had IQs between 70 and 79, 21 between 80 and 89, 15 between 90 and 109, 3 between 110 and 119 and 1 had an IQ over 120. Almost three quarters of these young people had had a shunt inserted to control hydrocephalus and although

Appleton et al. did not examine the relationship between IQ and the presence of hydrocephalus, other studies have, and this provides a way of exploring the relationship between IQ and motor disability in children with SB who differ in terms of the extent of any brain damage.

Four groups of children with SB can be identified based on the presence or absence of hydrocephalus – I: no hydrocephalus; II: arrested or non-progressive hydrocephalus; III: hydrocephalus and a shunt; and IV: hydrocephalus and no shunt. Group I are least likely to have any brain damage. If group II children have any brain damage it is probably slight. Children in group III are likely to have some brain damage because of severe hydrocephalus, although the shunt may have prevented extensive damage. Finally, children in group IV are extremely likely to have severe brain damage.

Children in group I generally obtain IQs about 10–20 points higher than children in group III, and children in group III have IQs about 10 points higher than children in group IV (e.g., Wills, 1993). In line with this, Casari and Fantino (1998) reviewed assessments carried out on 178 children with SB aged 1–14 years and reported mean IQs of 98, 88, and 76 for groups I, II, and III respectively. Clearly, children with SB, especially those without hydrocephalus, can achieve IQs in the average range despite their motor disability. Further support for this comes from Scott et al. (1998) who identified 57 children with SB of mean age 8½ years and with either verbal or nonverbal IQs above 70. Of these children, 11 did not have hydrocephalus (I) and their mean verbal and nonverbal IQs were 108 and 110 respectively; 7 had arrested hydrocephalus (II) and IQs of 115 and 109 respectively, whereas 39 had hydrocephalus and shunts (III) and their mean IQs were 89 and 84 respectively.

Children with SB resulting from lesions high up the spinal column tend to have lower IQs than those with low lesions (e.g. Snow et al., 1994; Wills, Holmbeck, Dillon, & McLone, 1990), which might indicate a relationship between intelligence and motor difficulties. Snow et al. examined various cognitive and neuropsychological characteristics of 37 young people with SB aged 14–23 years and identified three groups. One group of 9 showed relatively mild deficits across the tasks. This group had a mean IQ of 92, 5 had shunts (56%), and 7 had fairly low lesions (78% at lumbar 4 or below). The two other groups exhibited moderate to severe problems. Twelve with moderate problems had a mean IQ of 80, 7 had shunts (58%), and 8 had fairly low lesions (67% at lumbar 4 or below). The final group of 16 with severe problems had a mean IQ of 71, 14 had shunts (88%), and 6 had fairly low lesions (38% at lumbar 4 or below).

However, Snow's results indicate that children with high lesions do not just have lower IQs but are also more likely to have hydrocephalus, and this could account for their low IQs. An earlier study by Wills et al.

(1990) provides some confirmation of this. They examined the IQs of 89 children with SB aged 4–14 years in terms of both lesion level and hydrocephalus. Eighteen children without hydrocephalus had a mean IQ of 96 regardless of lesion level. In contrast, the 71 children who had a shunt for hydrocephalus had a mean IQ of 89. When this last group was divided by lesion level, the children with a lesion in the thoracic region had a mean IQ of 81, compared to a mean IQ of over 90 for children with lower lesions. Thus, Wills (1993) suggests that the relationship between IQ and lesion level in SB appears to be due to hydrocephalus being more common in children with high lesions. In other words, the extent of the motor difficulties experienced by children with SB have fewer consequences for their intelligence than whether or not they have hydrocephalus.

Children with SB and hydrocephalus generally have higher verbal IQs than nonverbal IQs (e.g., Fletcher et al., 1992; Hetherington & Dennis, 1999; Holler et al., 1995; Ito et al., 1997). For example, Fletcher et al. reported that 20 children with SB and shunts aged 5–7 years had mean verbal and nonverbal IQs of 85 and 78 respectively, whereas the corresponding IQs for 13 children with SB but no hydrocephalus were 102 and 106. Ito et al. also reported mean verbal and nonverbal IQs of 93 and 76 respectively for 12 children with SB and hydrocephalus aged 6–13 years who were selected to have verbal IQs greater than 80. In this study all but one child had higher verbal than nonverbal IQs and for seven children the discrepancy exceeded 15 points. Interestingly, the size of the discrepancy correlated with a measure of the width of the lateral ventricles, suggesting that there may be a physiological explanation of this difference.

In contrast to both children with CP and children with SB, children with DCD generally have IQs within the normal range, although they may be below those of TD children of similar age (e.g., Cantell et al., 1994). Cantell et al. reported that children with DCD aged 7 years had verbal and nonverbal scores on subtests of the WISC below those of TD children of similar age, and the differences remained when they were retested 8 years later. However, this pattern is not reported in all studies. Some studies have found that children with DCD have lower nonverbal IQs than verbal IQs (e.g., Johnstone & Garcia, 1994; Lord & Hulme, 1988b), whereas others have reported the reverse (e.g., Henderson & Hall, 1982). Thus, Lord and Hulme reported a mean verbal IQ of 106 and performance IQ of 83 for 19 children with DCD of mean age 10 years. In agreement with this, Johnstone and Garcia describe a boy of 8 years with DCD who had a verbal IQ of 99 and a performance IQ of 68. However, Losse et al. (1991) reported that when children with DCD who at 6 years had verbal and nonverbal IQs of 103 and 100 respectively were retested 10 years later, their IQs were 88 and 98 respectively. In other words, their

verbal but not their nonverbal IQs had fallen. There is no clear explanation for these different patterns of results.

Although the three motor disabilities discussed in this chapter vary considerably in terms of the nature and extent of the motor problems, it nevertheless seems that a motor disability alone is not sufficient to cause
cognitive impairment. This raises the question of why some children with
motor disabilities are of below average intelligence. Brain damage may be
one factor. Another may be that although a motor disability itself may
not be particularly restricting intellectually, it may have environmental
consequences which are. The motor disability may seriously limit children's experience, and it may be that it is the extent of this limitation that
is crucial, rather than the severity of the disability that brought it about.
Whatever the reason, and it is likely to be different for individual children, the fact that intellectual development is not solely dependent on
motor action has important theoretical and practical implications.

What do children with motor disabilities understand about objects and people?

According to Piaget (1953), an important cognitive development during
the first 2 years is the growing understanding that objects and people
exist as independent entities and that they continue to exist even when
out of sight. He termed this the sensorimotor stage of development, and
the development of this understanding object/person permanence. For
Piaget, full comprehension of object/person permanence is a necessary
prerequisite for, and marks the beginning of, the next period of development: the pre-operational stage. Piaget argued that this development depends upon children actively manipulating the environment. Through this
activity children construct increasingly appropriate beliefs about objects
and people.

Given that some children with CP, some children with SB, and the majority of children with DCD are of average intelligence, it is unlikely that
their motor difficulties have prevented them from developing an understanding of the permanence of people and objects. Some confirmation of
this comes from a study of 15 children with SB aged 9–21 months by
Morrow and Wachs (1992). The children with SB did not differ from TD
children of similar age in their understanding of object permanence, how
they played with objects, or their understanding of object relations in
space such as appreciating the effect of gravity on objects. However, 4
children with SB could not be tested because their upper limbs were affected. It is therefore possible that had these children with more severe
motor problems been included, the performance of the two groups might

have differed. Nevertheless, Morrow and Wachs reported that the children with SB's understanding of objects did not correlate with any medical characteristics of the children, including hydrocephalus, lesion level, or locomotor ability, but did correlate with the nature of the home environment such as the availability of books and toys.

Further evidence that difficulties manipulating the environment do not necessarily lead to impaired understanding of people and objects comes from studies of children with other motor difficulties, for example, children damaged by the drug thalidomide (Gouin Décarie, 1969). However, it is important to note that most children with motor disabilities are able to manipulate objects in some way. Some may substitute the use of their mouth or feet for their hands, and others may have some use of their hands. Others may use their head or trunk, as in the case of a boy born without any arms and legs (Kopp & Shaperman, 1973, extended report).

Children's understanding of objects can also be explored through their play. Kennedy, Sheridan, Radlinski, and Beeghly (1991) examined the play of two 3-year-old children with CP monthly over 6 months as they played with a set of toys in the presence of a familiar teacher. Both children engaged in pretend play with the toys some of the time. However, in line with their overall developmental delay, the children tended to produce fairly simple play such as feeding the doll, and over the 6 months there was no evidence of their play becoming more sophisticated. Interestingly, Martlew (1989) observed no pretend play in a 3½-year-old girl with CP when she was at nursery, but she did engage in this sort of play at home. At nursery she spent over 50% of the time not involved with any materials, whereas at home she was involved in different activities most of the time.

Landry, Copeland, Lee, and Robinson (1990) observed 15 TD children and 15 children with SB and shunted hydrocephalus aged 6–12 years when they played alone with three different sets of materials. All the children had average to low-average IQs. The children played with the materials for a similar length of time, engaged in a similar number of different play activities, and initiated interaction with the researchers to the same extent. However, the children with SB spent more time manipulating the materials with no apparent goal and less time playing appropriately with the materials. Even though there were these differences, the children with SB still spent almost half the time on average playing appropriately with the material. The TD children spent about three quarters of the time playing in this way. Landry et al. suggest that children with SB may have difficulties sustaining appropriate play activity as a result of perceptual difficulties or reduced exploratory opportunities.

Children's understanding of people can be explored by examining how they relate to others and I shall examine this later (see pages 181–184).

Another way is to look at how they represent people. There is some evidence that children with SB and children with CP have difficulties in correctly relating the different parts of the human body in their drawings, and this difficulty has also been seen when children with CP are asked to assemble the cut-out parts of a human figure or face (Abercrombie, 1964). There are also reports of these children representing aspects of their own disability in their drawings. An 18-year-old boy with mild athetosis drew a man with his hands in his pockets saying, "I can't draw hands. Anyway, his probably aren't any better than mine, and mine certainly are a hurdle to me" (Cruickshank, 1976). However, we should not conclude from these sorts of observations that children with motor disabilities have a different understanding of people than TD children. Both children with CP and children with SB also have difficulties in correctly relating the parts of non-human figures in their drawings, so the problem is not specific to drawings of people.

Children with DCD aged 5–13 years produce human figure drawings which are 2 years behind that expected for their age on average (Barnett & Henderson, 1992). However, there is great variability: some of the children with DCD produced drawings of the standard expected for their age, whereas the drawings of several were equivalent to those of children 5 years younger. Nevertheless, overall and compared with drawings of TD children of similar age, the children with DCD were less good at correctly representing proportions and less likely to include particular features and details. It seems unlikely that these differences indicate that children with DCD have a different understanding of people than TD children. It may simply be that because of the difficulties they have controlling a pencil they find it difficult to draw and consequently spend less time discovering how to represent human beings.

In conclusion, there is relatively little evidence to suggest that the understanding of objects and people that children with motor disabilities have is any different from that of TD children.

Do children with motor disabilities have problems with attention, planning and remembering?

Ammerman et al. (1998) reported that 18 out of 54 children and adolescents with SB received scores on the Child Symptom Inventory (Gadow & Sprafkin, 1987), which is completed by a parent, suggesting ADHD. Thus, a third of these 6–18-year-olds, of whom 95% had hydrocephalus, had attention difficulties, compared to 10% in the normative sample. In support of these parental reports, several studies have demonstrated that children with SB and hydrocephalus find it difficult to attend to relevant information and ignore irrelevant information (Fletcher et al., 1996; Horn, Lorch, Lorch, & Culatta, 1985; Loss et al., 1998; Snow, 1999). Horn et al. found that 5–10-year-old children with SB and hydrocephalus and younger TD children matched for nonverbal mental age (NVMA) took longer to sort a pack of cards when the cards had relevant and irrelevant information than when the cards only contained relevant information. However, the presence of irrelevant information slowed the sorting speeds of the children with SB more than those of the TD children and, unlike for the TD children, the effect did not diminish over trials for the children with SB. In a second study, the children with SB made more errors than the TD children when identifying which of three drawings illustrated a verbal concept (such as top, medium) if the drawings also contained irrelevant information.

These findings were followed up by Fletcher et al. (1996) with 46 children with SB of mean age of 10 years. Thirty-two had shunted hydrocephalus, 5 non-progressive hydrocephalus and 9 did not have hydrocephalus. The mean IQs of the children in these three groups were 84, 108, and 111 respectively. A number of problem-solving tasks involving planning and attention were administered to these children, children with hydrocephalus but not SB, and TD children. The children with SB and shunted hydrocephalus did less well than the other children with SB and the TD children on the Tower of London task which involves planning a series of moves, the Wisconsin Card Sorting Task assessing the ability to shift attention from one dimension to another, Stroop Color and Word tests, and tasks requiring the cancellation of specific letters or shapes both assessing the ability to attend to relevant information and ignore irrelevant information. However, the nature of their performance on these tasks led Fletcher et al. to conclude that the children with SB and shunted hydrocephalus performed poorly not because of inferior executive planning skills, rather because of difficulties maintaining attention.

However, Snow (1999) argues that children with SB do have impaired planning ability. He reported that 8–12-year-old children with SB with IQs above 80, of whom two thirds had shunts, did less well than similarly aged children with attention deficit hyperactivity disorder (ADHD), children with LD, and TD children on two tasks: the Trail Making Test in which circles have to be connected on the basis of consecutive numbers or a mixture of letters and numbers, and the Wisconsin Card Sorting Test. These differences remained when IQ was covaried out. Snow concluded that children with SB have problems with visual planning and sequencing and show response perseveration. Snow suggested that these difficulties could account for Landry et al.'s (1990) finding that 6–12-year-old children with SB engaged in less goal-directed play behavior than TD children (see page 169).

Nevertheless, children with SB and hydrocephalus do seem to have attention problems. Loss et al. (1998) studied 46 children and adolescents aged 8–15 years with SB and IQs above 70, of whom 38 had shunts. The children with SB and shunted hydrocephalus did less well than their TD siblings of similar age on a number of tasks assessing the ability to encode information, to maintain attention, to select relevant information, and to shift attention. Interestingly, aspects of attention in the children with SB were related to several medical variables, including lesion level and number of shunt operations. So, once again, it seems that the attentional problems are more a consequence of brain damage due to hydrocephalus rather than because of the motor problems resulting from SB.

Children with SB and shunted hydrocephalus also have difficulties on certain memory tasks which Wills (1993) suggests may reflect their attention and planning difficulties. However, Scott et al. (1998) concluded that they have problems both encoding and retrieving information. Scott et al. compared children with and without SB who either had shunted hydrocephalus, arrested hydrocephalus, or no hydrocephalus on a range of memory tasks. The main aim of the study was to examine the effect of hydrocephalus on performance and the results are reported by hydrocephalus grouping, rather than distinguishing the different etiologies. Thus, the children with shunted hydrocephalus, of whom 56% had SB, did poorly on memory tasks requiring long-term storage and retrieval of both auditory and visual information, although they did as well as the children in the other groups when immediate recall of a spoken story was required. Interestingly, performance on the memory tasks did not correlate with fine motor skills. Thus, it seems that these memory difficulties are a consequence of the effects of hydrocephalus rather than any motor difficulties.

Further evidence that children with SB and hydrocephalus have impaired visual memories is suggested by a study of 3–12-month infants with SB, most of whom had hydrocephalus (Morrow & Wachs, 1992). Whereas 15 out of 19 TD infants looked more at a novel pattern, only 10 out of 20 infants with SB did. This difference just failed to reach significance. Interestingly, given the problems already noted for children with SB and hydrocephalus in attending and switching attention, Morrow and Wachs reported that at 3 months, 3 infants with SB appeared unable to shift attention from one pattern to the other.

Children with CP have also been shown to have impaired memories for both visual and auditory material (Smith, 1989). Smith reported that of 10 children with CP aged 7–10 years who were unable to speak but had average IQs, 8 performed more than two standard deviations below the population mean on visual memory, and 9 on an auditory memory test.

Thus, both children with SB and shunted hydrocephalus and children with CP have difficulties remembering information. However, these children are likely to have some brain damage and this could account for their poor memories, rather than their motor problems. However, one area that motor difficulties might be expected to influence is memory for spatial locations. McComas Dulberg, and Latter (1997) explored this possibility with children with SB and children with CP, mean age 7 years, who all used wheelchairs regularly. Unfortunately no information is provided about whether or not the children with SB also had hydrocephalus. However, given the relationship reported in other papers between walking without support and hydrocephalus (e.g., Scott et al., 1998), it seems likely that most of the children with SB would have had hydrocephalus.

In McComas et al.'s study the children had to collect 10 pieces of a jigsaw puzzle from 10 different locations around a room. The children were assigned to one of four training conditions on the basis of whether or not they chose which location to visit and whether or not they or a helper moved them. The children who moved themselves during training did better on the test trial when they had to choose and move themselves than those who were moved by a helper during training, indicating that active movement helped the development of spatial memory. Therefore, there may be aspects of memory which are influenced by motor disability.

Finally in this section I shall examine memory in children with DCD. Given the perceptual problems which have been reported for children with DCD it is not surprising that memory difficulties have been found. I have already mentioned a study by Newnham and McKenzie (1993) who found that 9–14-year-old children with DCD made more errors than TD children when they saw one shape and had to identify the same shape from two shapes on the basis of touch. These authors explain these findings as due to children with DCD having problems remembering visual information, and refer to several reports of poor visual memory in children with DCD. For example, Dewey (1991) found that children with DCD were poor at deferred imitation, and Dwyer and McKenzie (1994) reported that children with DCD were poor at reproducing a geometric pattern if there was a delay of 15 seconds filled with an articulation task, but not if reproduction was immediate.

Given that children with DCD have difficulties producing motor actions it is interesting to consider whether their memory for motor movements is impaired. This was explored by Skorji and McKenzie (1997) with children with DCD and TD children aged 8–12 years and matched for nonverbal IQ. The children had to repeat short sequences of motor movements either immediately or after a 15-second delay filled with various visual and kinesthetic activities. The groups did not differ in terms of repeating the movements regardless of order when there was no delay or if the delay was filled with a kinesthetic activity or non-spatial visual activity. However, if the delay was filled with a visual task which also had a spatial aspect, the children with DCD produced fewer complete movements. However, when order was also taken into account the children with DCD produced fewer correct sequences than the TD children when there was no delay and when the delay was filled with a visual spatial activity. Clearly the children with DCD could encode the movements but they had difficulties retaining information about sequences. In addition, their memories of the movements were adversely affected by visual–spatial activities indicating, once again, that they have difficulties retaining visual information.

Thus, it is clear that children with a range of motor problems, some of which are associated with brain damage, do experience memory difficulties. Nevertheless, it seems unlikely that the motor problems cause the memory impairments, rather that the memory difficulties result from the brain damage or other difficulties associated with the motor problems, such as perceptual difficulties.

Do children with motor disabilities have difficulties learning to read, spell and do arithmetic?

As we have already seen, many children with SB, especially those with hydrocephalus severe enough to need a shunt, are of below average intelligence and, not surprisingly, these children have problems at school (e.g., Casari & Fantino, 1998). Casari and Fantino reported that of 93 children with SB of school age, 24 (26%) were demonstrating good progress and 34 (37%) were more than one year behind for their age. Of the 34 who were behind, 29 (85%) had shunted hydrocephalus, whereas of the 24 who were doing well, 8 (33%) had shunted hydrocephalus.

Reading and arithmetic present children with SB with particular problems and this is evident both in the children's own reports (e.g., Appleton et al., 1994) and in test scores (e.g., Wills et al., 1990). Appleton et al. found that 79 young people with SB aged 7–19 years reported that they were less competent than TD young people in terms of general intellectual ability and reading, writing, and math, although they reported feeling as competent at spelling. In agreement with this, Wills et al. (1990) reported that children with SB, many of whom had shunts, had verbal and nonverbal IQs, and standardized reading and arithmetic scores which were significantly below the corresponding population means. However, the spelling score, although below the population score, was not significantly different from it. For those children for whom verbal IQs and scores on the tests of academic ability were available, no differences were found between verbal IQ and either standardized reading, spelling, or arithmetic scores. In other words, as a group, these children were demonstrating achievements in reading, spelling, and arithmetic appropriate for their IQ. However, more children had greater problems with arithmetic than with reading, rather than the reverse pattern which may reflect their visual–spatial and sequencing difficulties as well as absences from school for hospital treatment. Reading and spelling improved with age, but arithmetic skills declined.

Interestingly, the reading test used in this study involved the pronunciation of single words, and Wills (1993) indicates that although children with SB may not be impaired on this test relative to their IQ, their ability to comprehend text is impaired more than would be expected given their IQ. She suggests that this may be due to poor attention and problem solving. However, there is also evidence from Brookshire et al. (1995) that 5–7-year-old children with SB and hydrocephalus may have poorer phonological awareness than children with SB but not hydrocephalus, and this is likely to influence their reading.

Almost half of all children with CP over 8 years who took part in a survey between 1957 and 1966 were found to be behind in reading by 2 years or more for their mental age (Wilson, 1970), and Smith (1989) reported that only one out of ten 7–10-year-old children with CP who could not speak but had average IQs was reading at the level expected. Interestingly, the reading ability of these 10 children correlated with their ability to match visual stimuli but did not correlate with visual or auditory memory or the ability to blend sounds, suggesting that their reading difficulties are visually based, which fits with the perceptual problems they have with letter reversals and mirror images.

However, a study of 8–20-year-olds with CP, most of whom did not have any intelligible speech, indicated that phonological skills may also be important (Dahlgren Sandberg & Hjelmquist, 1997). Dahlgren Sandberg and Hjelmquist reported that 27 young people with CP were less good than young people with LD matched for chronological age (CA) and NVMA at identifying pictures corresponding to single words, although the groups did not differ on three other reading tests: separating printed words from nonwords; identifying incorrectly spelled irregular words which sounded correct (i.e., homophones); identifying the words completing sentences they read. Ten young people with CP scored on at least two of these reading tests and were labeled "readers." When compared with the 17 "nonreaders," the 10 "readers" were of similar age and IQ but had higher mental ages and did better on tests of visual and auditory memory, phonological awareness, and comprehension of a story read to them. Interestingly, the two groups did not differ in terms of motor or speech disability. However, the "readers" received more literacy training and were more likely to be integrated into mainstream schools. Clearly these educational differences may account for the group differences; alternatively the two groups may receive different educational opportunities because of their different levels of literacy.

Dahlgren Sandberg and Hjelmquist also examined the spelling abilities of the young people with CP and reported that a number of different measures indicated that their spelling was inferior to that of young people with LD and younger TD children matched for mental age.

Despite having average IQs, children with DCD have been reported to experience difficulties with reading, spelling, and arithmetic (e.g., Dewey & Kaplan, 1994; Kadesjö & Gillberg, 1999; Smyth, 1992). Dewey and Kaplan distinguished three groups of children with DCD aged 6–10 years: those with problems in all areas of balance, coordination, gesture, and sequencing (I); those with problems with balance, coordination, and gesture (II); those with problems of sequencing (III). All three groups did less well than children without motor problems on arithmetic, whereas for reading and spelling only group I did significantly worse than the children without motor difficulties. Kadesjö and Gillberg reported that children with DCD aged 6–8 years read aloud less well than TD children, and 2 and 3 years later their reading comprehension was found to be poor. However, some children with DCD do not experience these difficulties, particularly early on (e.g., Henderson et al., 1991; Johnstone & Garcia, 1994). For example, Johnstone and Garcia described an 8-year-old boy with DCD who had reading, spelling and arithmetic standardized scores of 111, 110, and 93 respectively.

The literacy skills, including reading and spelling, of 28 children with DCD aged 7–10 years with nonverbal IQs above 80 were explored by Fletcher-Flinn et al. (1997). Their average reading age was between 7 and 7½ years. Only 9 children were reading at or above the level for their age and 7 had reading ages 2 years below their CAs. The average spelling age was under 7 years. Only 2 children had spelling scores at or above the median normative score for their age and the spelling scores of 8 children were 2 years behind. In other words, 25% of these children had severe reading difficulties and almost 30% had severe spelling difficulties.

Fletcher-Flinn et al. also examined the relationships between reading and spelling and a variety of other abilities. Reading correlated with spelling but neither was correlated with either verbal or nonverbal ability or motor difficulties. Both correlated with a measure of phonological awareness involving tapping out the number of sounds in pseudowords. However, reading did not correlate with measures of visual perception, whereas spelling correlated with one measure of visual perception involving judging whether two triangles were identical or not.

Clearly many children with SB, CP, and DCD experience considerable problems with reading, spelling, and arithmetic. In some cases this results from general learning difficulties. However, the difficulties experienced by other children seem to relate to visual and/or auditory perceptual difficulties. Given these difficulties, it is not surprising that many experience problems at school.

The development of communication

Children with SB and children with CP often experience severe language difficulties, whereas children with DCD seem to have language skills similar to TD children of the same age. In the rest of this section I shall consider the language and communication skills of children with SB and children with CP.

As we have already seen, children with SB, especially those with hydrocephalus, often have higher verbal than nonverbal IQs (e.g., Fletcher et al., 1992). This suggests that their linguistic skills may be relatively spared. In line with this, Wills (1993) indicated that speech development in children with SB follows the same course as TD children, and their intonation, fluency, rate of speaking, and articulation are similar. However, much of what children with SB say may be inappropriate and irrelevant, albeit said using appropriate syntax (e.g., Tew, 1979) and parents of 5–13-year-old children with SB and hydrocephalus have reported more communication difficulties with their children than found with TD children (Holler et al., 1995).

Thus, while the language of children with SB may be articulate, fluent, and syntactically correct, it may not relate to the context or content of what others are saying. They may use social phrases and familiar language excessively and inappropriately, as well as tending to imitate what has been said rather than answer questions, and produce semantically anomalous or bizarre sentences. Tew and Laurence (1972) found these sorts of language difficulties in 28% of the population they studied, while Anderson and Spain (1977) found that around 40% of 6-year-olds showed this hyperverbal behavior, sometimes described as the "cocktail party syndrome." This behavior was more common in girls with SB who had shunts and who were more physically disabled than in other children. Interestingly, Morrow and Wachs (1992) reported that 9–21-month-old infants with SB verbally imitated more vocalizations and speech than TD infants, which may indicate that differences are evident early on.

Syntax was explored by Byrne, Abbeduto, and Brooks (1990) who recorded the spontaneous language of seven children with SB and hydrocephalus and seven TD children as they played with a researcher. Both groups of children had mean ages of 5½ years and average nonverbal IQs. No significant differences were found between the groups on various measures of syntax, including MLU, although the MLUs and lengths of clauses produced by the children with SB tended to be shorter.

Byrne et al. also examined the appropriateness of the children's language by administering the Preschool Language Assessment Instrument (PLAI). The PLAI examines concrete language, such as talking about objects which can be seen, and abstract language, such as talking about possible outcomes of a particular event. No significant differences between the groups were found, although, as with the syntax measures, the children with SB tended to do less well. The proportion of irrelevant responses was very low in both groups. Thus, this study provided no support for the observations that much of the language of children with SB is irrelevant. It further indicated that children with SB do not have particular problems with abstract language. The authors concluded that the semantic and pragmatic difficulties reported to be associated with SB may occur only in children with SB of below average IQ.

The PLAI was also administered by Culatta and Young (1992) to larger groups of children with SB and hydrocephalus and TD children than studied by Byrne et al. The children with SB had a mean CA of 6 years and mean verbal age based on concrete receptive vocabulary of 4¾ years. They were matched for verbal mental age with TD children who had a mean CA of 4¼ years. Once again the groups did not differ on the PLAI although the children with SB produced more irrelevant responses, especially when the tasks required abstract language. Thus, this study provides some support for the observation that the language of children with SB and hydrocephalus can be irrelevant.

However, neither of these studies provides much empirical support for the observations of Tew and others noted earlier. One reason for this may be because of the test that was used. It may be that differences are apparent in conversations rather than in a test format requiring answers to questions. Dennis and colleagues (e.g., Dennis & Barnes, 1993; Dennis, Jacennik, & Barnes, 1994) examined this possibility with 6–15-year-old TD children and children with hydrocephalus, about half of whom also had SB. The children all had verbal or nonverbal IQs of 70 or above. Dennis and Barnes reported that the children with hydrocephalus were inferior to the TD children on a range of tasks exploring their ability to use and understand oral discourse. In particular, the children with hydrocephalus were less good than the TD children at understanding that some sentences can have more than one meaning, understanding metaphors, making inferences in order to explain how an event came about, and generating a sentence given a picture and two or three key words.

In a further study involving most of the same children, Dennis et al. (1994) read a story to each child who then retold the story to the researcher. The narratives of the children with hydrocephalus, relative to those of the TD children, contained fewer clauses, were less concise, included fewer key points, and conveyed the story less clearly by, for example, including more content which was implausible, incomprehensible, or ambiguous. In other words, the narratives of the children with hydrocephalus were less cohesive and coherent than those of the TD children.

Dennis and her colleagues did not report the results of the children with SB and hydrocephalus separately from the children with hydrocephalus due to other causes. Thus, although about half the children with hydrocephalus had SB we cannot be sure that the characteristics of the narratives reported for the group as a whole would be evident if only the children with SB and hydrocephalus were considered. In particular, it would be useful to compare children with SB and hydrocephalus with children with SB and no hydrocephalus.

Such a comparison was made by Brookshire et al. (1995) who compared 20 children with SB and hydrocephalus with 13 children with SB and either no hydrocephalus or mild hydrocephalus, as well as other children with hydrocephalus due to different causes. The children were aged 5–7 years and had either verbal or nonverbal IQs of 70 or above. The children with SB and hydrocephalus did less well than the children with SB but no hydrocephalus on tasks assessing a variety of abilities: phonology; semantics including receptive vocabulary, word knowledge, generating words within a category, completing analogies; fluency; finding words to match targets semantically, rhythmically or visually. Thus, although Brookshire et al. did not explore conversational or discourse skills specifically, it seems likely that the language problems seen in children with SB are a consequence of hydrocephalus rather than SB. Interestingly, it has been suggested that the difficulties that children with SB and hydrocephalus have with language may reflect the difficulties they have in distinguishing relevant from irrelevant information and in attending to relevant material (see pages 170–172).

In contrast to the relatively good articulatory skills of children with SB, many children with CP have difficulties speaking, and some are unable to communicate orally because of an inability to control the muscles involved in speaking, a problem termed dysarthria. Smith (1989) noted that 50–75% of children with CP have speech and language difficulties. However, their receptive language skills may be relatively spared in relation to their expressive language abilities. Thus, Jones, Horn, and Warren (1999) reported that 4 children with CP aged 18–39 months had receptive language skills equivalent to TD children aged 7–16 months, whereas their expressive language skills were equivalent to those of TD children aged 3–7 months. Rather better language skills were reported by Kennedy et al. (1991) for 2 children with CP aged 3½ years. They had language comprehension ages of 2 years 9 months and 3 years, and expressive language ages of 1 year 7 months and 1 year 10 months. Although these children produced 14 and 64 different words over a 30-minute observation period, neither of them combined words and, interestingly, this single word usage paralleled their symbolic play which consisted of single symbolic acts.

Some children with CP may have relatively good language skills. Feldman, Janoski, Scher, and Wareham (1994) studied 6 children with CP who had been born prematurely but whose language was fairly intelligible. Their CAs, taking into account their prematurity, were 28–36 months and their IQs were 85–127. A spontaneous language sample was collected while the children interacted with their parent. As a group, the children with CP did not differ from TD children who were also premature in terms of either the number of words used or the syntactic complexity of their utterances, although the children with CP tended to produce slightly shorter utterances.

It seems very likely that if children with CP have difficulty talking this will affect their interaction with others. Pennington and McConachie (1999) studied 20 children with CP aged 2–10 years interacting with their mothers. IQs were not obtained for the 2 youngest children, but the nonverbal IQs of the remaining 18 children were above 77 and 6 of the children had IQs between 100 and 120. The children's language comprehension was within two standard deviations of the average. However, all had severe expressive language difficulties and were unintelligible to most people. Although no TD children were included as a comparison group, it was nevertheless clear that these mothers and their children interacted differently from TD children and their mothers. The mothers initiated many more of the topics than the children (65% compared with 8% of utterances) and, not surprisingly given the difference in initiations, the children responded more than their mothers (74% compared to 2%). In terms of what was communicated, the mothers requested information 32% of the time, asked the children to do something or pass an object (15%), provided information (15%), or confirmed or denied something (23%). When responding, the children confirmed or denied something 38% of the time, acknowledged something (15%) and provided information (13%).

In this study the children used a range of ways to communicate, including symbolic gestures 31% of the time, non-symbolic gestures (25%), vocalizations (21%), spoken language (6%) or a combination of symbolic gestures with either vocalizations (6%) or spoken language (7%). Only three children used a communication system when interacting with their mother. The children seldom asked for something to be done or for an object and made few requests for information. However, when the children were in a structured situation designed to elicit different types of communication, they demonstrated the ability to request information, actions, and objects. It seems likely that the control that their mothers took of the interaction did not provide openings for the children to communicate in these ways.

Interestingly, when Pennington and McConachie (2001a) compared these children with a group of children with CP whose speech was intelligible, the latter children were found to initiate more topics and express more functions than the children whose speech was unintelligible. However, very few differences between the mothers of the two groups of children were observed. Further, Pennington and McConachie (2001b) reported that speech intelligibility was the best predictor of how much the children contributed when interacting with their mothers, whereas motor function did not predict communication patterns. There were no relationships between the children's intelligibility or motor ability and how much their mothers initiated topics or were directive. Importantly, Pennington and McConachie point out that none of these children could move independently. Clearly more research is needed to examine the effect of increased motor skills on communication patterns.

Social and emotional development

How is social interaction with others affected by a motor disability?

There are many factors which have the potential to affect the interaction between children with motor disabilities and adults and other children. As Mulderij (1997) and Nassau and Drotar (1997) have pointed out, social interaction, particularly between peers, is affected by mobility, communication, the ability to join in activities, as well as attractiveness and cognitive ability. In addition, because of medical appointments and involvement in therapeutic programs, children with motor disabilities may have fewer opportunities to play and develop relationships with their peers. They may also attend schools some distance from their homes, making it difficult to foster peer relationships outside of school. All these factors suggest that social interaction between children with motor disabilities and others will differ from that between TD children.

There has been very little research examining social interaction between children with SB and other people. Seefeldt et al. (1997) compared interactions between parents and their 8–9-year-old children with SB and TD children while they made up rules for a board game. The parents of the two groups of children were similar in how much they listened to the children, requested input from the children, and encouraged conversation and collaboration. However, the mothers of children with SB of higher social status, based on occupation, education, gender, and marital status, were more receptive to things their children said than the mothers of children with SB of lower social status and the mothers of TD children of higher social status. The mothers of children with SB who were of lower social status were judged to be more authoritarian and less democratic than the other mothers.

The focus in Seefeldt et al.'s study was on the behavior of the parents and more research is needed looking at the children's behavior both when interacting with adults and with their peers. Children with SB, especially those with hydrocephalus, may appear friendly and socially responsive because of their verbosity. However, because the content of their language is often inappropriate this may create problems. In addition, Wills et al. (1990) pointed out that children with SB often behave inappropriately, being overly familiar, impulsive, and distractible. Nevertheless, mothers of 8–16-year-olds with SB rated their attachment to their children as fairly good, especially when the children had thoracic-level lesions (Holmbeck & Faier-Routman, 1995). In addition, it was noted in this study that mothers of children with high lesions were willing to give their children more control over decisions such as what the children watched on TV than those with children with lower lesions.

Several studies have reported that children and adolescents with SB often report feeling isolated from their peers (e.g., Appleton et al., 1994; Börjeson & Lagergren, 1990; Lord, Varzos, Behrman, Wicks & Wicks, 1990). Thus, Börjeson and Lagergren reported that out of 26 adolescents with SB aged 15–18 years, none reported that they were popular and 9 felt that they had no affinity with their classmates. In terms of contact with peers outside of school, 8 of the 21 adolescents who still lived at home either visited or were visited by a peer once a month or less. Fourteen of the adolescents felt that they could share their problems with friends. Lord et al. (1990) reported that 12–20-year-old adolescents with SB varied in how lonely they felt depending on their educational placement. Although they all reported greater feelings of loneliness than TD adolescents, those who attended a mixture of mainstream and special classes were less lonely than those either in mainstream classes or in special classes.

In contrast to SB where the main motor problem is paralysis, CP is often associated with unusual facial expressions and motor movements. These are likely to disrupt the formation of attachments between children and their parents, although this has not been studied. However, several studies have examined the interactions between children with CP and both their mothers and siblings.

Earlier I described a study by Pennington and McConachie (1999) which showed mothers of children with CP to be very directive. A couple of studies have examined children with CP and their siblings (Dallas,

Stevenson, & McGurk, 1993a, 1993b; Martlew, 1989). Martlew observed 3½-year-old twin girls, one of whom, Jane, had CP. Jane had a mental age of 30 months, whereas her motor development was equivalent to that of a 4–8-month-old and she could not move independently. Her receptive language age was 32 months, compared to an expressive language age of 4 months. The twins both attended the same nursery and were observed there and at home. In the nursery Jane spent about 80% of the observation periods on her own. She was never observed interacting with a group of children and seldom with another child, whereas her TD sister interacted with one or more children for over 40% of the time. The twins did not play together at the nursery.

Two- to thirteen-year-old children with CP and TD children were studied as they interacted with their TD siblings at home by Dallas et al. (1993a, 1993b). Twenty-seven of the 64 children with CP were independently mobile and only 10 of the children were totally immobile. The children and their siblings were observed as they drew pictures, completed puzzles, and played with toys. Regardless of the relative ages of the children, the children with CP were very passive and their siblings tended to control the interaction even if younger. The children with CP seldom initiated or directed the interaction. As a result the interaction between the siblings was much less reciprocal when one of them had CP. In addition, more aggression occurred between the siblings when neither had CP, which made the interaction more challenging and consequently provided more opportunities for the children to develop their social skills.

Although children with DCD have greater mobility than many children with either SB or CP, their motor difficulties may still make it difficult for them to join in many physical activities enjoyed by their TD peers. Smyth (1992) pointed out that because of their poor motor skills, children with DCD are less likely than TD children to be chosen to play physical games and as a result they may not be very popular. In line with this, Losse et al. (1991) noted that half the children who had been identified with DCD at the age of 6 years reported problems making friends at the age of 16 years. Difficulties with making friends and social isolation seem to emerge fairly early on. For example, Schoemaker and Kalverboer (1994) reported that 6–9-year-old children with DCD were less likely to be asked to play and had fewer playmates than their TD peers. Similarly, Henderson et al. (1991) described a girl who was initially popular when she started school but had become socially isolated by the age of 9 years.

These findings were confirmed by Smyth and Anderson (2000) who observed children with DCD aged 6–10 years in the school playground over several weeks. The children with DCD spent more time alone and were more often onlookers than the TD children. When they were with others the children with DCD were more likely to be with just one other child than in large groups and this was particularly true of boys. Thus, these observations provide further evidence that children with DCD are often excluded from peer interaction.

Clearly, motor difficulties affect social interaction in a number of different ways. In addition, the difficulties result in these children being more isolated and lonely than TD children. It seems likely that these difficulties will affect how children with motor disabilities behave and feel about themselves.

How do children with motor disabilities behave?

Children with SB have been reported to exhibit more behavior problems than TD children (e.g., Wallander, Feldman, & Varni, 1989a). Rather than directly observing the children, most studies have used rating scales such as the Child Behavior Checklist (e.g. Achenbach, 1991). This checklist is completed by parents and provides ratings of internalized behavior problems (such as anxiety, withdrawal, depression), externalized behavior problems (e.g., aggression, delinquency, hyperactivity), and social competence (in social activities, peer relations, and academic achievement).

Using this scale, Wallander et al. (1989a) reported that 4–16-year-olds with SB had significantly more internalized and externalized behavior problems and lower social competence than the group of TD children and adolescents on whom the scale was standardized. Nevertheless, the majority of the young people with SB did not have sufficiently high ratings to warrant a clinical diagnosis of maladjustment. Within the general population 10% would be expected to reach this level; among the young people with SB, 16% and 19% were judged maladjusted on the basis of their internalized and externalized behavior problems respectively, and 23% on the basis of social competence. Importantly, no relationships were found between the parents' ratings and the severity of the young people's disability.

Using a similar scale, the Social Skills Rating System (Gresham & Elliott, 1990), Lemanek, Jones, and Lieberman (2000) reported that 3–16-year-olds with SB had lower ratings of social competence, although the mean score was still within the average range, but did not differ from the normative group in terms of internalized or externalized behavior problems. However, there was some suggestion of a relationship between behavior problems and severity of SB, based on lesion level, presence or absence of a shunt, and mobility. Thus, fewer problems were reported for children with mild SB than for children with moderate SB, although children with severe SB had an intermediate number of problems and did not differ from the other two groups.

How can these different findings concerning behavior problems be explained? Obviously the use of different scales may account for the difference. However, there may be another explanation. Lemanek et al. specifically excluded individuals with learning difficulties, whereas Wallander et al. did not appear to. It may therefore be that the participants in Wallander et al.'s study included more with learning difficulties. Against this are the numbers in the two studies with shunts: 75% in Lemanek et al.'s study and 41% in Wallander et al.'s study, suggesting that fewer participants in Wallander et al.'s study had hydrocephalus. Further, Wallander et al. reported no effect of the number of operations for shunts on behavior problems or social competence.

Nevertheless, a relationship between hydrocephalus and behavior problems was demonstrated by Fletcher et al. (1995). Using the Child Behavior Checklist, Fletcher et al. reported that 26% of 23 children with SB and hydrocephalus aged 5–7 years were identified as maladjusted on the basis of their externalized and/or internalized behavior problems, compared to 11% of 9 children with SB but no hydrocephalus. Thus, if children have SB and hydrocephalus they seem to be at greater risk of developing behavior problems than if they have SB without hydrocephalus. Further support for this comes from Holmbeck and Faier-Routman (1995) who found that maternal reports of behavior problems in 8–16-year-olds with SB using the Child Behavior Checklist were not related to lesion level but were related to the presence or absence of a shunt.

The findings described so far provide mixed results in terms of whether or not there is any relationship between the severity of the children's disabilities and the children's behavior as reported by the parents. In order to look at this question more closely Hommeyer, Holmbeck, Wills, and Coers (1999) distinguished between behaviors which are likely to be directly affected by the motor and cognitive problems associated with SB, such as physical and academic competence, and behaviors which are less likely to be affected directly by the disability, such as internalized and externalized behavior problems and social competence. In their study of 8–9-years-olds with SB they found that children who were rated as less competent physically and academically by parents and/or teachers were more likely to have higher lesions, the myelomeningocele form of SB, shunts, and limited mobility. However, no direct relationships were found between the various measures of severity and either behavior problems or social competence. Nevertheless, several measures of behavior were indirectly related to shunt status and Hommeyer et al. suggest that children with SB who do less well at school may have more difficulties with peer relationships than those who are succeeding and that their poor peer relationships may lead to social and behavior problems.

If this is the case, then we might expect to see more behavior problems in older than in young children with SB and there is some support for this. The children in Fletcher et al.'s (1995) study were 5–7 years, whereas

Wallander et al. (1989a) and Lemanek et al. (2000) studied children and adolescents up to 16 years. Holler et al. (1995) noted that more socialization difficulties and conduct problems were reported by parents of 9–13-year-old children with SB and hydrocephalus than of 5–7-year-olds. Further, although Zurmöhle et al. (1998) reported no overall difference in the behavior problems reported by parents of 6–16-year-olds with SB and TD children and adolescents, more problems were evident in the 12–16-year-olds with SB than among the 6–11-year-olds. Thus, older children with SB and hydrocephalus are more likely to have behavior problems than younger children with SB and no hydrocephalus.

If there is an indirect association between motor disability and behavior problems, then children with CP should also show behavior problems. This has been confirmed in several studies (e.g., McDermott et al., 1996; Wallander et al., 1989b). Wallander et al. studied 6–11-year-olds, of whom 23 had SB and 27 had CP. The children with SB were rated by their parents on the Child Behavior Checklist to have higher social competence than the children with CP, but the combined group showed significantly more internalized and externalized behavior problems and lower social competence than the group on whom the scale was standardized. However, no relationship was found between the extent of the children's motor disabilities and behavior problems, and the children who were more severely disabled physically were more competent socially. Interestingly, Wallander, Hubert, and Varni (1988) found relatively few relationships between the children's behavior and maternal ratings of their own and their children's temperament. The only significant relationships were between increased internalized behavior problems and both high child activity and high maternal rhythmicity; increased externalized behavior problems and high child reactivity; greater social competence in children with good attention and mothers showing low rhythmicity.

A different scale was used by McDermott et al. for parents to rate the behavior problems of 4–17-year-olds with CP as part of a population study of more than 23,000 children in the USA. Over 25% of the parents of children with CP reported that they had behavior problems compared with 5% of parents of TD children. Thirty-nine percent of the young people with CP were reported to show dependency, 26% hyperactivity, 23% were headstrong, 13% conflicted with peers, 13% were anxious, and 11% showed antisocial behavior. Each of these behaviors was reported in 5% or less of the TD children. Interestingly, McDermott et al. cited a number of earlier studies reporting rates of behavior problems in children with CP ranging from 30–80% and suggested that the relatively low rate in their study may be because theirs was a population sample rather than based on children attending a clinic who might be expected to be more selected because of having problems.

Although the motor problems facing children with DCD are much less severe than those of many children with either SB or CP, we have already seen that they experience considerable difficulties interacting with peers and often feel very isolated. We might therefore expect children with DCD to exhibit emotional and behavior problems. In line with this, Fletcher-Flinn et al. (1997) reported that 43% of parents of 7–10-year-old children with DCD indicated that the children had some behavioral or emotional disorder. In a study of 6–9-year-old children with DCD by Schoemaker and Kalverboer (1994), teachers and parents reported that half the children with DCD were introverted compared to 6% of the TD children. However, neither teachers nor parents reported any differences between the children in terms of socially negative behavior or negative or positive task orientation.

A longitudinal study carried out in Sweden by Gillberg and colleagues suggested that children with DCD may not exhibit emotional and behavior problems until their mid teens. Gillberg et al. (e.g., Gillberg, Rasmussen, Carlström, Svenson, & Waldenström, 1982) identified seven 6-year-olds with DCD. At the age of 10 years, parents and/or teachers identified 33% of these children as having emotional or behavioral problems, compared with 20% for TD children. At 13 years the incidences of behavior problems were 20% and 25% respectively (Gillberg & Gillberg, 1989). However, when the same groups were interviewed at 16 and 17 years, of six adolescents with DCD, four (67%) were diagnosed with depression and anxiety disorders, three (30%) with substance abuse disorder, and one (17%) had attempted suicide (Hellgren, Gillberg, Bågenholm & Gillberg, 1994), whereas the corresponding figures for 45 TD adolescents were 11%, 2%, and 0% per cent. In agreement with this, when Losse et al. (1991) examined the school records of 16-year-olds who had been identified with and without DCD at 6 years, they found five times more instances of emotional and behavior problems among the adolescents with DCD than the TD adolescents. Over 80% of the adolescents with DCD had emotional and/or behavioral problems, compared with less than 50% of the TD adolescents.

Clearly, motor disabilities can lead to emotional and behavior problems, especially during adolescence, although this is not inevitable. This suggests that some young people with motor disabilities may have difficulty accepting their problems.

What do children with motor disabilities feel about themselves?

A number of studies have examined how children with SB perceive themselves by asking them to evaluate their competence in a range of areas using instruments such as the Self-Perception Profile for Children (Harter, 1985). Using a pictorial version of this scale, Fletcher et al. (1995) found no difference between the academic and social competence reported by 5–7-year-old children with and without SB. However, children with SB and hydrocephalus reported less physical competence than children with SB but no hydrocephalus and the latter did not differ from the TD children. Landry, Robinson, Copeland, and Garner (1993) also reported no difference in how 15 children with SB and 15 TD children aged 6–12 years rated their social and academic competence, although they found no difference in the children's ratings of their physical competence. This is slightly surprising since all the children in Landry et al.'s study had shunts for hydrocephalus. However, the children with SB and hydrocephalus in Fletcher et al.'s study had a mean IQ of 85, compared to 91 for the children in Landry et al.'s study. It is therefore possible that on average the children in Fletcher et al's study were less able.

Edwards-Beckett (1995), using a slightly different scale, also reported no differences in perceived competence between 6–12-year-old children with SB and TD children. These findings give some support to the suggestion that more able children with SB may not differ from TD children in terms of how they perceive their competence. Although no information was provided about whether or not the children with SB also had hydrocephalus and no measures of intelligence were reported, it was stated that all the children were in the appropriate school grade for their age, suggesting they were of average intelligence.

Adolescents as well as children were included in a study by Appleton et al. (1994) and these researchers did find differences in all three areas of competence. This suggests that as children with SB get older they may be more likely to rate their competence less highly than TD children. Thus, 79 children and adolescents with SB aged 7–19 years rated themselves as less competent socially, physically, and academically than TD young people, but no different in terms of behavior, appearance, or global self-worth/self-esteem. However, older females with SB had the lowest mean self-worth scores and females with SB felt that their appearance was more important than did the TD participants.

When Appleton et al. (1997) restricted the group to 9 years and above, the children and adolescents rated themselves as having less self-worth than the TD participants, and again the females with SB had the lowest mean score. The young people with SB also rated themselves as more depressed, with less energy and more suicidal thoughts than the TD young people. The view the young people with SB had of their appearance was strongly related to their reports of depression, self-worth and suicidal thoughts.

However, it is important to put these findings in perspective. Börjeson and Lagergren (1990) pointed out that although 40% of 15–18-year-olds with SB reported that they had occasionally wanted to cry because they felt so depressed, this figure is almost identical to the proportion of TD 14-year-olds reported to feel this way (Rutter, Graham, Chadwick, & Yule, 1976). In addition, Börjeson and Lagergren reported that most of the young people with SB generally felt positive. Further, although Wolman and Basco (1994) found that 45% of 12–22-year-olds with SB had low self-esteem, 55% had high self-esteem. In yet another study Zurmöhle et al. (1998) found no difference in reports of anxiety for 6–16-year-olds with SB compared to TD children and adolescents. Nevertheless, the parents of the 12–16-year-old females with SB reported that their children showed more depressed withdrawal than the parents reported for TD children, which probably relates to the lower self-esteem and concern with appearance reported for female adolescents with SB (e.g., Appleton et al., 1994).

A number of researchers have examined the relationship between how young people with SB view themselves and a variety of other factors, including parental behavior (e.g., Appleton et al., 1997; Edwards-Beckett, 1995; Wolman & Basco, 1994) and severity of the disability (e.g., Holmbeck & Faier-Routman, 1995; Hommeyer et al., 1999; Minchom et al., 1995). Thus, Appleton et al. reported that the children's perception of their parents' support, but not their perception of teacher, peer, or close friend support, was related to global self-worth and depression in the 7–19-year-olds they studied. Those who felt supported by their parents felt more positive about themselves. Edwards-Beckett examined the relationship with the expectations that the parents had for their children's development. Although the parents of the 6–12-year-olds with SB expected more of their children than the parents of TD children, there was no relationship between the parents' expectations and how their children perceived themselves. However, Wolman and Basco reported that higher self-esteem in 12–22-year-old young people with SB was associated with their parents treating them appropriately for their age or older and allowing them to do things. In addition, higher self-esteem was also associated with fewer problems at school, with feeling that others did not consider them disabled but, perhaps surprisingly, with feeling themselves to be disabled.

The relationship between severity of disability and self-concept was examined by Minchom et al. (1995) in the 79 children and adolescents studied by Appleton et al. (1994). None of the correlations between severity of disability and perceived social, physical, or academic competence were significant. However, there was a significant relationship between self-esteem and disability, with those with more severe disabilities having greater self-esteem. In addition, perception of appearance was also related to self-esteem.

Similarly, Holmbeck and Faier-Routman (1995), in their study of 8–16-year-olds with SB, found no relationship between severity of disability, in terms of either presence/absence of a shunt or lesion level, and the children's self-reports of physical, social, and academic competence, behavior, appearance or self-esteem. However, the parents rated the children with shunts as less competent and to have lower self-esteem.

In contrast to a relatively large number of studies examining what children and adolescents with SB think of themselves, there has been little study of this in children with CP. Nevertheless, some quotes from Cruickshank (1976) indicate that some may feel quite positive about themselves: "Now I am going to tell you how CPs feel. They feel like you, but they can't walk like you. If they aren't CPs, they grow up like nothing, but if they are CPs they have to work like mad. I am a CP and I like being a CP." This was said by a 13-year-old with CP. However, a 16-year-old adolescent with quadriplegic athetoid CP who could not walk and needed help with eating did not feel very positive: "When I can't succeed in something and when I know I could succeed if I weren't a CP, I get more than discouraged because I'm so helpless. You're stuck and you hate yourself for being stuck . . . why (did) the doctors let me live when I was born. I am no use to anyone the way I am."

In the last section I noted that several studies have reported increased emotional and behavioral problems in children with DCD, especially in adolescence. But how do they feel about themselves? T. R. Smyth (1992) argued that many children with DCD will experience feelings of incompetence, frustration, and depression as a result of their motor difficulties and social isolation. A longitudinal study of a girl with DCD described by Henderson et al. (1991) provided some support for this view. At the age of 15 years she completed the Harter scale. Her perception of her physical competence was very low, although she was more positive about her academic and social competence, except for items concerned with relationships with peers. However, she had very low self-esteem and appeared to be depressed much of the time.

Feelings of incompetence at physical activities and more anxiety were also reported by Schoemaker and Kalverboer (1994) for 6–9-year-old children with DCD, compared to TD children. Piek, Dworcan, Barrett, and Coleman (2000) also found that 8–13-year-old children with DCD reported lower physical competence on the Harter scale than TD children. However, the two groups of children did not differ in their reports of academic or social competence or global self-worth. Nevertheless, it is possible that differences may become apparent as the children move into adolescence.

The research examined in this section demonstrates that there is no simple relationship between motor disability and social and emotional development. Children with relatively minor motor limitations may experience many social and emotional problems, whereas others with severe motor difficulties may function well socially. Many factors are likely to contribute to these differences, including the behavior and expectations of the family, the motor and psychological characteristics of the child, the nature of her environment and her educational experiences. More research is needed before we can begin to explain the differences between individuals with motor disabilities.

chapter five

How do children with Down's syndrome develop?

Introduction

Children with Down's syndrome (DS) form the largest group of children with learning difficulties (LDs) and are usually identified at birth. As a result, they have been the focus of much research. Many aspects of their development have been studied, often with the aim of answering the question of whether the development of children with DS is quantitatively or qualitatively different from that of typically developing (TD) children. In other words, do children with DS follow the same pattern of development as TD children but go through each stage more slowly, or do different processes underlie their development? This idea of delay as opposed to difference in the development of people with LDs was first articulated by Zigler in 1967.

Zigler argued that children with LDs who had evidence of organic damage, as in DS, should be distinguished from those with no damage. He suggested that the latter group was characterized by delayed development, proposing that in these children the structures underlying intellectual processes were similar to those of TD children, producing a similar but slowed-down sequence to development and correspondingly similar responses. In children with organic damage it was presumed there were different structures, a different sequence of development and different responses. More recently, a number of researchers (e.g., Cicchetti & Beeghly, 1990), while acknowledging that the development of children with DS does differ in some ways from that of TD children, have concluded that the underlying structures and sequence of development are similar. This view contrasts to that of others (e.g., Hodapp & Zigler, 1990) who argue that although the sequence of development in children with DS and TD children may be similar, the structures underlying development in DS are different.

It is not clear whether either of these two positions is correct. Indeed, some have argued that attempting to answer the question of delay versus difference is pointless. For example, Wishart and Duffy (1990) have suggested that the answer depends on the level of analysis; the more detailed the level of analysis, the more likely it is that the difference position will be supported. Kamhi and Masterson (1989) argue that the delay/difference controversy has outlived any usefulness it may have had. They point out that the question of delay versus difference with respect to language and cognition is based on a number of incorrect assumptions, for example that cognitive ability can be inferred from mental age (MA) and can be assessed independently of language ability. They suggest that a more profitable way forward, and one which has far greater implications for both theory and practice, is for research to focus on unraveling the interrelationships between different developments in order to better understand how psychological development comes about.

Anderson's theory of the Minimal Cognitive Architecture (1992) provides a new way of looking at the notions of delay versus difference (e.g., Anderson, 2001). Anderson proposes that intelligence has two independent components. The first is speed of information processing, which is hypothesized to be fixed in any one individual and not open to developmental change. The second involves the development and acquisition of modules, such as modules for language, face perception, and so on. Intellectual disability can result from organic damage affecting either of these components. If speed of processing is affected then children's development will be delayed. However, if specific modules are affected, children's development will be different. Anderson proposes that children with DS have organic damage which causes a slow speed of processing, whereas children with some other disabilities, for example some children with autism, may have intact speed of processing but damage to particular modules.

In this chapter I shall consider various aspects of the development of children with DS by examining studies which have compared their development to that of TD children and those comparing their development to that of children with other LDs but not DS. Comparisons with the development of TD children can indicate how typical their development is; com-parisons with the development of children with LDs but not DS can indicate how unique the developments are to DS. A number of writers (e.g., Wagner, Ganiban, & Cicchetti, 1990) have pointed out that asking such questions about children with DS is different from the delay/difference approach since it enables a specific examination of the effect of DS on development, whereas the primary motivation behind the delay/difference approach is the role of organic damage as opposed to familial or cultural effects on development.

Motor development

Two different approaches to the study of motor development in children with DS can be distinguished. The first has been to document the ages at which particular motor skills are achieved and these demonstrate that children with DS attain the main motor landmarks at later ages on average than TD children and the gap seems to widen with increasing age (e.g., Henderson, 1986), although their motor skills continue to develop, albeit slowly, throughout the teenage years (e.g., Jobling, 1999; Jobling & Mon-Williams, 2000). However, these studies do not provide any indication as to why these developments are delayed. Possible explanations are emerging from the second approach in which closer attention is paid to specific mechanisms underlying particular motor skills. Studies reflecting both approaches will be discussed.

At birth most babies with DS show marked hypotonia and a different timescale for the emergence and disappearance of certain reflexes. For example, Cowie (1970) examined children with DS, some of whom were in institutions, at 2 weeks of term-related age, that is, CA after adjustment for gestation lengths other than 40 weeks. She reported poor muscle tone and the absence of normal traction (pulling to a sitting position) and placing responses (stepping up onto a surface when held upright and the top of the foot brushes the edge of the surface). They all had poor posture when suspended horizontally in space face downwards (ventral suspension) and, although they showed a typical response when held on their backs and the head and upper part of the body was dropped a couple of inches (Moro reflex) and a typical palmar (hand) grasp, these took longer to disappear than reported for TD babies.

It is not clear whether these early behaviors simply reflect problems in motor development or whether they are related to development in other areas. In support of the first view, Kokubun, Haishi, Okuzumi, and Hosobuchi (1995) found no relationship between the age when 27 children with DS started to walk and their IQs at 7 years or older. However, Cicchetti and Stroufe (1976) found that of 14 children with DS, the 4 most floppy or hypotonic were the slowest to laugh or smile, the last to show any fear, and had the lowest MAs in their second year of life.

Following the tradition of the first approach, Cunningham (1982) reports delays in the average age at which children with DS achieved particular motor milestones. For example, children with DS held their heads steady and balanced at an average age of 5 months, range 3–9 compared with 3 months, range 1–4 in TD children. The corresponding ages for sitting without support were 9 months, range 6–16 (DS) and 7 months, range 5–9 (TD) and for walking alone 19 months, range 13–48 (DS) and 12 months, range 9–17 (TD). Fine motor activities also emerged later, Cunningham reporting that children with DS grasped a dangling ring at an average age of 6 months, range 4–11 compared with 4 months, range 2–6 in TD children. The children with DS built a tower of 2-inch cubes by 20 months on average, range 14–32, compared with 14 months, range 10–19 for the TD children. Although these developments are delayed on average, it is important to note that there is a great deal of variation in the age at which individual children with DS achieve these developments, with some children reaching particular landmarks within the range found for TD children.

Interestingly, there is some evidence that the observed delays are not an inevitable consequence of DS. Thus, Kučera (1969) found that children with DS born before 1954 walked by an average age of 30 months, while those born between 1955 and 1966 walked by 22 months on average. This compares with 19 months in Cunningham's 1982 study. Cunningham points to a number of reasons for the earlier age of achievement, including improved health care and changes in attitudes, particularly in terms of increased expectations of what children with DS can achieve. We shall return to this latter explanation later in this chapter.

In the past, a number of papers have suggested that the motor development of children with DS in the first 6 months may be similar to that of TD children. However, more recently researchers (e.g., Block, 1991) have pointed out that these reports were often based on the results of developmental scales and these may not be sensitive to the sorts of differences which are apparent in the early months. Also, in such studies overall scores are usually compared and these mask any differences in the range of items passed and failed. Whereas TD children usually have only a few items between the first item failed and the last item passed, children with DS characteristically have many more. This means that, even when overall scores are similar, the profiles are very different. Again, we shall return to this point later.

Turning to the second approach to the study of motor development, a particular development which has received attention concerns the ability to maintain an upright posture. Kokubun and Koike (1995) suggest that poor muscle tone may explain the finding that children and adolescents with DS find it more difficult than individuals with LDs but not DS to balance on one foot and to walk along a narrow beam. In a further study, Kokubun et al. (1997) reported that when adolescents with DS stood looking straight ahead at a fixation point, the center of their foot pressure shifted from side to side and from back to front more frequently than that of adolescents with LDs due to other causes and they related this to the poor postural control and balance observed in individuals with DS. Interestingly, Kokubun (1999) found that, despite poorer balance, when adolescents with DS had to carry a glass full of water on a tray, they spilt no more water than individuals with other LDs. However, the adolescents with DS took more steps, suggesting that they were adopting a different strategy to compensate for their motor difficulties.

Butterworth and Cicchetti (1978) examined the role of vision in sitting and standing using an artificial room in which the walls and ceiling could be moved independently of the floor. Young children with DS were matched with TD children for the length of time they had been able to sit or stand unsupported. When standing, all the children made postural adjustments when the walls moved, but the children with DS were more likely to fall over, although falling over was rare after standing was well established. However, establishing standing took the children with DS longer, 7–12 months compared to 3 months in the TD children. There was no equivalent effect on sitting in younger children matched for how long they had been able to sit unsupported. The authors suggest that it takes longer for sensory information about balance to be calibrated against visual information in children with DS. Interestingly, Shumway-Cook and Woollacott (1985) report that six children with DS aged 15 months to 6 years responded similarly to TD children when the floor moved, but were slower to respond and the response was more variable. This was most marked in the youngest children, who were also more likely to fall over. Wade, Van Emmerik, and Kernozek (2000) also found that older children with DS, mean age around 10½ years, showed greater postural responses when the room moved than TD children of similar age. However, since none of these studies included children with LDs but not DS, the findings may be a characteristic of children with LDs rather than DS specifically.

Further evidence that children with DS have particular problems with postural and balance control comes from a longitudinal study of infants with DS and TD infants by Cobo-Lewis, Oller, Lynch, and Levine (1996). Using rotated principal components analysis, group, age of sitting unsupported, crawling, pulling to stand, and taking first steps all loaded highly on the first factor. In contrast, reaching and rolling contributed much less to this factor. These authors suggest that postural behaviors may have a common neuromuscular basis which is affected in DS.

As well as postural reactions, children with DS differ from TD children in how they perform certain motor tasks. While they acquire many basic motor skills, they often perform them more slowly. Thus, Charlton et al. (e.g., Charlton, Ihsen, & Lavelle 2000; Charlton, Ihsen, & Oxley 1996) report that children with DS, mean age 9 years, reached more slowly towards an object they had to pick up than TD children of either similar CA or MA. In a detailed analysis of the initial reaching action, they found that the children with DS took longer to slow down as they neared the object, their movements were more jerky, and the velocity profiles of their reaches varied much more over trials than those of the TD children. On the basis of these findings, Charlton et al. argue that the reaching actions of children with DS are different both quantitatively and qualitatively from those of TD children.

Similarly, Hogg and Moss (1983) reported that 15–44-month-old children with DS, compared to TD children matched for developmental level, were slower to pick up rods and insert them into holes, although there was no difference in how they held the rods. However, although of similar developmental level overall, the children differed with respect to items passed on the developmental scale used. In particular, the children with DS passed fewer items concerned with fine motor coordination than the TD children. So, perhaps it is not surprising that they differed on the experimental task. This illustrates the importance of matching children appropriately for the skill under investigation.

Interestingly, Moss and Hogg (1987) reported that older children with DS carried out a complex motor task involving three different movements in the same amount of time as TD children matched for MA. The children with DS, mean age about 7 years, had MAs between just under 2 to 5 years. Moss and Hogg were interested in whether, over a number of trials, the children would show evidence of integrating different movements and carrying them out in parallel rather than in series. They found some evidence of greater integration of movements in the TD children than in the children with DS but only for two movements. However, in contrast to their earlier study, the children with DS actually passed more performance items relative to language items than the TD children matched with them for MA.

Rather than matching children on overall MA, Frith and Frith (1974) matched children on their initial performance on a tracking task which was one of the tasks investigated. The other skill studied was tapping rate. Young people with DS aged 9–27 years were matched with young people with autism aged 5–18 years and TD children aged 4–8 years for initial performance on the tracking task. The young people with DS and with autism had MAs of 2–6 years. The young people with autism and the TD children showed improvement in their ability to track a moving target with their finger over time, whereas the young people with DS did not. In addition, the young people with DS tapped at a much slower rate than either the TD children or the young people with autism. Frith and Frith suggest that individuals with DS may fail, or take longer, to develop motor programs for such behaviors, continuing to rely on feedback, although Henderson (1985) argues that this cannot account for the slowness apparent at every level of motor control in people with DS. She suggests that individuals with DS are particularly delayed in initiating a response to a stimulus, rather than in the actual motor response once begun. This could be due to a number of reasons. They could have difficulties perceiving the information in the stimulus; they could have difficulties processing the information; they could have difficulties selecting the appropriate response or they could have difficulties activating the motor response. More research is necessary to distinguish these alternatives.

Another way to overcome the matching difficulty is to look in detail at the emergence of the same motor skill in children with DS and TD children. Such a study was carried out by Cunningham (1979; cited in Henderson, 1986) who observed the development of reaching in 12 children with DS and 10 TD children fortnightly from 4 weeks. Initially they were presented with a ball on a stick and, when they reached and touched this, a cube was presented on a table in front of them. In line with the first approach, the children with DS reached for the objects at a later age than the TD children, being 7 weeks behind on the first task and 18 weeks slower on the second task. However, what was more interesting, and relevant to the second approach, was the behavior of the children before and after success on the first task. Whereas the TD children made body movements and fairly accurate reaches towards the ball from early on, the early reaches of the children with DS were less accurate and decreased in frequency, and it was not until about 20 weeks that they began making similar movements towards the ball as the TD children. Also, when the TD children had reached for the ball and were presented with the cube they reached immediately, whereas the children with DS did not immediately transfer their skill, some not reaching for the cube for a further 6 weeks.

These observations are intriguing, suggesting that children with DS may not progress through the same stages as TD children when beginning to reach and do not transfer this skill from one situation to another as easily as TD children.

In conclusion, children with DS attain various motor milestones later than TD children. There are also a number of indications that their motor development may follow a different route from that seen in children without DS.

Perceptual development

Much early research on perception examined adults with DS rather than children. Adults with DS are often reported to be functioning intellectually at the level of 4–6-year-old TD children. If adults with DS behave in a different way from TD children then this has implications for the processes underlying the development of individuals with DS. However, there is a problem. Adults with DS and TD children, even if of similar developmental level, are of very different CAs and with very different experiences. TD children may process the environment in a particular way because of their level of development; adults with DS may process the environment differently because of their additional years of experience.

Nevertheless, evidence indicating that the brains of individuals with DS differ from those of people without DS both in terms of overall structure and neuronal organization (e.g., Courchesne, 1988; Uecker, Mangan, Obrzut, & Nadel, 1993) would be consistent with differences in psychological processing. Although processing differences are not inevitable if structure differs, the evidence of less elaborate neuronal development in individuals with DS may be related to the association between DS and reduced ability to synthesis information (Ganiban, Wagner, & Cicchetti, 1990).

In the sections which follow I shall restrict my discussion to research focusing on specific perceptual abilities. Other research relevant to perceptual ability, especially visual perception, can also be found in the sections on cognitive, communicative, and social and emotional development.

Are the visual abilities of children with DS different?

It is well established that children with DS under 1 year look at objects and people for longer than TD children of similar developmental level before responding (e.g., MacTurk, Vietze, McCarthy, McQuiston, & Yarrow, 1985; Vietze, McCarthy, McQuiston, MacTurk, & Yarrow, 1983). This suggests that they take longer to process information although their eventual responses may be similar. On the other hand, when the comparison is between children with DS and TD children of similar CA, differences in visual ability, other than just looking time, have been found (e.g., Fantz, Fagan, & Miranda, 1975; Miranda & Fantz, 1973, 1974).

The differences which have been reported between TD children and children with DS of similar CA are interesting. Miranda and Fantz (1973), using a visual preference technique, found that 8-month-old babies with DS looked at patterns for longer and showed fewer preferences between patterns than TD babies. However, a further study by the same researchers found that babies with DS develop the same preferences as TD babies when the patterns differ in form (e.g., straight versus curved lines) but at a later age (Fantz et al., 1975). Few differences in the ages at which the TD children and the children with DS developed preferences were found when the form of the pattern (squares) was kept constant but the number and size of the elements varied. Fantz et al. (1975) interpreted these findings as indicating that the emergence of preferences for patterns with more, smaller elements is probably related to the development of elementary visual and neural mechanisms involved in pattern perception, and these they consider to be developing normally in young babies with DS. However, the fact that the visual preferences of children with DS lag behind those of TD children when the patterns differ in form was taken by the researchers as evidence that these involve higher processes, which they argued are slower to develop in children with DS. In particular, it may be that infants with DS have impaired memory processes, relative to TD infants of similar age. As we shall see later, there is growing evidence of different memory processes in DS (see pages 216–219).

Although these findings suggest that the visual perceptual abilities of children with DS may be similar to TD children of similar developmental level but different from children of similar CA, three things should be borne in mind: the tasks are only examining a minute portion of the visual abilities of individuals with DS; similar end points can be reached by different routes; children with DS have a number of visual difficulties which may affect the clarity with which they see visual stimuli.

Are the tactual abilities of children with DS different?

The tactual abilities of children with DS are less good than those of TD children (e.g., Brandt, 1996; Lewis & Bryant, 1982). The ability of children with DS aged 12–46 months to recognize objects visually they had previously either seen (visual–visual tasks) or touched (tactual–visual tasks) was compared by Lewis and Bryant to TD children of similar developmental level. None of the children with DS performed above chance level on any of the tasks involving touch, whereas the TD children were successful on at least one task involving touch. For the TD children, but not the children with DS, performance on the tactual–visual tasks improved with increasing age. The performance of the children with DS on the visual–visual tasks was also inferior to that of the TD children. This study suggests that children with DS have a difficulty perceiving tactual information, discriminating objects tactually, remembering tactual information, or relating tactual and visual information. Of course, if children with DS just take longer to process tactual information, they should succeed on this task with longer tactual familiarization times (e.g., Wagner et al., 1990).

Lewis and Bryant also reported that if children with DS touched patterns or objects while looking at them, this had much the same effect on how they looked at them as touching patterns and objects had on the looking behavior of TD children. In particular, when touching was allowed, the children looked at the patterns and objects less often, but each look was longer, on average, than when touching was not allowed. This suggests that touching may serve the purpose for both groups of focusing their attention on the pattern. Interestingly, Krakow and Koop (1982) found that toddlers with DS were as likely as TD toddlers to touch and handle objects.

Tactual difficulties were also demonstrated in 7–11-year-old children with DS by Brandt (1996). Almost all the children with DS tested performed more than 3 standard deviations below 7-year-old TD children on three tactual tasks: identifying a shape traced on the palm of their hand; identifying which finger had been touched; identifying the relevant hole in a form board for a shape felt in a bag.

Interestingly, physiological evidence indicates that the tactual difficulties result from impaired peripheral function, rather than any central processing difficulty. Brandt and Rosén (1995) measured the speed of sensory nerve conduction and cortical activity when the thumb and middle finger of 11–16-year-old children with DS and TD children were stimulated. Although sensory nerve conduction was slower in the children with DS, there were no clear differences in cortical activity.

Taken together, these results indicate that the peripheral tactual abilities of children with DS, may be different rather than just slower to develop.

Are children with DS musical?

It has been suggested that people with DS are particularly musical. Probably the earliest reference to this ability was that of Fraser and Mitchell in 1876. Since then frequent reference has been made to this. Shuttleworth (1900) wrote of individuals with DS "their love of music great; their idea of time as well as tune remarkable." A few years later, in 1908, Tredgold described them as being very fond of music and of having a "marked sense of rhythm." Similar descriptions abound. But is there any evidence to support these claims? Are people with DS more musical than people with LDs but not DS, or TD children of similar MA or CA?

The evidence is sparse, and what there is either can be criticized methodologically or shows that although their sense of rhythm may be superior to that of people with LDs but not DS, when compared to TD people they are not especially musical.

One of the earliest studies was by Rollin (1946) who studied 8–48-year-olds with DS. The majority had been institutionalized for most of their lives and over half had recorded IQs of below 20. The wide age range, low IQ, and the extent of institutionalization are limiting enough factors, but the method itself leaves even more to be desired. They were all seated in a semi-circle in a hall while dance music was played. Their facial expressions were observed to see how much they were enjoying the music. This "experiment" provided no support for a marked sense of rhythm and fondness of music by people with DS. In addition, it was reported that none danced spontaneously, and only two danced when they were invited to.

More rigorously designed research has been reported since 1946. In 1959, Cantor and Girardeau reported that TD preschoolers were better than children with DS of similar MA at saying at which of two possible rates a metronome was beating and at tapping in time with the beat. However, there are several problems with this study. As Stratford and Ching (1983) point out, one task required a verbal response which may have been more difficult for the children with DS than for the TD children. Stratford and Ching also ask whether a response to a metronome beat can be taken as an indication of musical ability. In their own study, they found that children with DS were as good as TD children, all with MAs of 3½– 4 years, at tapping in time to three rhythms varying in complexity. Children with LDs but not DS did not do so well. Both the children with DS and the TD children anticipated the rhythms once they had heard them.

However, Stratford and Ching (1989) reported little difference between 7–19-year-olds with DS and other young people with LDs but not DS when their movements to four contrasting rhythms were rated. However, there were no TD children for comparison and the rating was made after a period of training. This study therefore confounds response to rhythm with ability to learn specific movements and so it is difficult to conclude much about perception of rhythm.

Two further studies have used more realistic stimuli. Glenn, Cunningham, and Joyce (1981) found that TD babies and babies with DS aged 5–14 months showed a preference for listening to a sung nursery rhyme over listening to a repeated tone. In addition, over half the babies in both groups more often selected the rhyme sung by a woman than the same rhyme played on an instrument. Although very different in design from the studies by Stratford and Ching, this study again suggests that individuals with DS may not be especially musical. However, Glenn et al. did report some differences. In particular, the babies with DS had a significantly longer response duration: when they were listening to either of the two alternative patterns they listened to them on average for longer than the TD babies. This raises the possibility that the way in which the two groups are processing the material may be different.

An extension of this research was reported in 1982 by Glenn and Cunningham. In this study babies with DS were matched with TD babies for MA, range 7½–13 months. All the babies had mothers who regularly sang them particular nursery rhymes. The babies were presented with a familiar rhyme and a nonsense rhyme in which the words in the familiar rhyme were replaced by nonsense words containing the same number of syllables. The authors took various measures of the babies' preferences: how long they listened to each; how often they listened; and the average duration of each period of listening. On the first two measures, but not on the third, both groups showed a preference for the familiar rhyme. As in the earlier study, the babies with DS listened for longer, both in total and on average, than the TD babies. As the babies got older in terms of MA they showed an increasing preference for the familiar rhyme.

This study is interesting because it reiterates the similarity between babies with DS and TD babies in what they like to listen to (out of the choices supplied) and it also says something about the nature of what the babies are responding to. It is not just intonation and stress patterns, although these are important and will be used if there is nothing else. Glenn and Cunningham's study shows that they appear to listen to the characteristics of single words which are familiar. The words probably do not have any meaning for the babies at this stage, but nevertheless they are recognized at some level.

Thus, despite the often reported observation that people with DS are musical, there is really no evidence to suggest that they are any more musical than TD people, although they may have a better sense of rhythm than other people with LDs. There is some evidence that they may take longer to process musical information, which may link with the memory limitations mentioned earlier and which will be discussed in more detail later.

Cognitive development

Cognitive development is particularly pertinent to the question of how DS affects development. Do children with DS pass through the same stages of cognitive development in the same way as TD children but take longer, or is their cognitive development different? Do they have a different understanding of their environment from TD children and those who also have LDs due to other causes?

How intelligent are children with DS?

There is general agreement that children with DS may attain IQs above 70 in the first year. Thus, Cunningham and Sloper (1976) report average mental quotients of between 80 and 90 at 6, 12, and 18 weeks for children with DS. Although the mean quotients fell below 100, they were within two standard deviations of the norm for TD children, and some babies had quotients between 90 and 110.

However, the IQs of children with DS decline with age (e.g., Carr, 1988, 1994; Hodapp, Evans & Gray, 1999; Rynders, 1999; Shepperdson, 1995; Sigman & Ruskin, 1999). Based on a longitudinal study of 54 children, not all of whom were seen at all ages, Carr reports mean ratio IQs of 73, 80, and 64 at 1½, 6, and 10 months. By 15 and 24 months these had fallen to 60 and 54 respectively and continued to fall, reaching a mean of 37 at 11 years. By 21 years the mean had increased slightly to 42, although this increase may be because a nonverbal scale, the Leiter, was used at 21 years, whereas the Merrill-Palmer scale used at 11 years includes some verbal items and, as we shall see later, the verbal abilities of individuals with DS are often more impaired than their nonverbal abilities (e.g., Klein & Mervis, 1999).

It is important to note that the fall in IQ with increasing age does not necessarily mean that individuals with DS are not developing, just that their rate of development is not keeping pace with their CA. For example, Sigman and Ruskin report that MAs of children aged 1–6 years ranged from 9–46 months and at 10–12 years the range was 20–89 months. Shepperdson (1995) reports that of 31 individuals with DS born in the mid-1960s and assessed for language and social competence when infants, teenagers and young adults, 22 showed progress, with most progress occurring between infancy and the teenage years. Nevertheless, 9 individuals did show very little development, scoring much the same in infancy and adulthood. In Carr's study the range in MA at 21 years was 1–8 years.

Unfortunately, early scores may not tell us very much about intelligence since items in developmental scales, particularly items at the lower end of the scale, are relatively insensitive indicators of intellectual ability. The behaviors which can be assessed in very young babies are extremely limited and few, if any, bear a clear relationship to later intellectual ability. Indeed, it has been argued that speed of habituation in infancy may be a much more accurate indicator of later intelligence in TD children than performance on developmental scales and, as we shall see later, although children with DS do show habituation, they take longer. In support of the poor predictive value of early test results, Carr (1992) reports no significant correlations between MA in the first 6 months and later, whereas MAs from 10 months onwards were correlated with subsequent test results.

In addition to the problem of what early scores may indicate, there is growing evidence that the performance of children with DS on developmental scales is rather different from that of children without DS (e.g., Wishart & Duffy, 1990). Wishart and Duffy administered the Bayley Scale of Mental Development to children with DS aged 6, 12, 18, 24, 36, and 48 months (3 children at each age) on two occasions separated by 1 or 2 weeks. The MAs obtained were 4½, 7, 11, 13, 19, and 22 months respectively, on both test sessions. However, although there was no difference between the overall scores obtained by the children on the two occasions, the passed items which made up the scores varied much more than expected. There were 74 examples of items which were failed on the first occasion and passed on the second, and 91 items initially passed and later failed. Wishart and Duffy argue that the variability is largely explained by fluctuations in the children's engagement with the task. These differences are important and raise the question of whether or not it is meaningful to match children with DS with other children without DS on the basis of overall performance on developmental scales. Similarities in overall performance clearly mask differences in actual performance on individual items.

In support of this, Wishart (1993) presents data on two children with DS who were administered the Bayley every 3 or 6 months over 18 months, with the Bayley being given twice at each test point. MAs are presented for one child tested between 2½ and 4 years, developmental quotients (DQs) for another child tested between 3½ and 5 years. When development was based on performance on the first administration of the Bayley at each time point, the MA of the first child plateaued from 3 years and the DQ of the second child decreased with age. However, when assessment was based on all items the children had ever passed up to each test point, the MA of the first child increased steadily over time and the DQ of the second child showed no decline with age. Wishart notes that avoiding test items was quite common which indicates that there may be some motivational or attentional explanation for the increasingly poor performance of children with DS on intelligence tests.

Nevertheless, when IQ is based on items passed on one occasion, the IQs of children with DS decline with increasing age. However, the range of IQs in any age group of children with DS is large. For example, Sigman and Ruskin (1999) report IQs of 66 children with DS aged 1–6 years ranging from 36 to 107. The IQs of the same children when aged 10–12 years ranged from 18 to 65. Only six of the children had a higher IQ at the older age and then only by four points. Similarly, Carr (1988) reports a range of about 60 points at each age she studied, with an upper level in early adulthood of about 70.

Another observation is that females with DS are more able than males. For example, in Carr's longitudinal study the females had mean IQs above the males at all ages, and by 21 years this difference was significant (1992).

At 21, the majority of males had IQs between 41 and 50, while the IQs of the majority of the females were between 51 and 60. No males had IQs over 60, whereas 10% of the females did. Conversely, while 18% of males had IQs of 20 and below, only 11% of females did. The reason for this superiority is unclear. A further observation is that individuals with a mosaic form of DS have, on average, higher IQs than those with the more frequent trisomy form. Fishler and Koch (1991) reported a mean IQ of 64, range 43–92 for 30 young people aged 2–18 years with mosaic DS compared with a mean of 52, range 18–78 for 30 individuals with trisomy DS matched for age, sex and socioeconomic status. Again, the reason for this superiority is unclear.

These two differences in intellectual level within the population of individuals with DS seem to be the most reliable. Carr (1992) reports no relationship between IQ and either socioeconomic status or parents' educational level, although she did find a relationship between academic achievements in reading, writing, and arithmetic at 21 years and socioeconomic status and IQ from 2 years. Nevertheless, it is important to note that many of the young adults with DS failed to score on the tests of academic skills.

Since most children with DS have below average IQs from early on, and their IQs are likely to decline with increasing age, a great deal of research has focused on trying to optimize their intellectual development. Unfortunately, although early reports were encouraging, more recent reports indicate that while intervention programs may produce short-term gains in development, these gains are not maintained (e.g., Cunningham, 1986; Pitcairn & Wishart, 2000).

Early intervention programs were motivated by several observations concerning the development of children with DS. One was that children with DS who lived at home for the first couple of years and were then institutionalized maintained their superior cognitive development for at least 3 or 4 years over those children with DS institutionalized from birth (e.g., Shipe & Shotwell, 1965). Similarly others (e.g., Carr, 1970) found that children with DS reared in institutions were cognitively behind those brought up at home. In addition, children in institutions given additional stimulation showed increased development (e.g., Bayley, Rhodes, & Gooch, 1966; Lyle, 1960; Tizard, 1960).

Early studies of children with DS living at home and involved in intervention programs reported that their development exceeded that expected of children with DS (e.g., Brinkworth, 1975; Buckley, 1985; Cunningham & Sloper, 1976; Rynders, Spiker, & Horrobin, 1978). These studies were interesting, because they indicated that children with DS may require a different environment from TD children if they are to develop maximally. For example, some of the 181 children who took part in Cunningham and Sloper's study were visited every 6 weeks from birth, and when they were 1-year-old they were ahead of children who were referred to the study when they were 6–12 months old and therefore received fewer visits. The early referrals were also ahead, at 1 year, compared with the children in Carr's (1975) study who were only visited three times in the first year. Carr's children and the late referrals in Cunningham and Sloper's study were of similar mental ability at 1 year. The late referrals gradually caught up with the early referrals as they received more visits. Cunningham and Sloper suggested that these children may have benefited from the frequent visits through their parents getting ideas about how to play with them as a result of watching the assessments that were being carried out. Obviously these parents were also getting a lot of support.

Despite the initial optimism caused by these and other studies, there is increasing evidence showing that early intervention does not result in any substantial long-term cognitive benefit (e.g., Cunningham, 1987; Gibson & Harris, 1988). Indeed Carr (1992) reports that children brought up at home, who were ahead of those in institutions at 4 years, were no longer ahead at 11 and 21 years. However, Cunningham (1986) points out there may be other gains from intervention, such as more advanced self-help skills.

Nevertheless, it is still important to consider why children involved in intervention studies show short-term gains. Cunningham (1986) suggests that the expectations of their parents are raised and this reduces the effect of what he terms a hidden deprivation resulting from low expectations. Others have pointed to general improvements in health care and educational opportunities as well as changes in attitudes (e.g., Wishart, 1990).

However, perhaps more important is the question of why intervention programs are not producing long-term cognitive gains in children with DS. Lupton and Lewis (1997) point to two possible explanations. The first is that intervention changes the nature of parent–child interaction and these changes restrict development in some way. In their study with TD children they provide some preliminary support for this suggestion. The second explanation, articulated by Wishart (e.g., 1991), is that our understanding of the way in which DS affects learning is inadequate and that therefore appropriate intervention programs cannot be designed. She argues that more research is needed to elucidate how children with DS do learn. She points to the need for more research charting the developmental progress of individual children with DS (e.g., Wishart, 1993), rather than cross-sectional studies of groups of children with DS. Longitudinal research is much more likely to throw light on the process of learning than cross-sectional studies. However, if progress is to be made in this venture it is necessary to look at specific developments.

What do children with DS understand about objects?

Over the first 2 years TD babies learn a great deal about objects. Given that most children with DS show delays in development over this period, it seems likely that they will take longer to reach each stage of object understanding compared with TD babies. But will there be any qualitative differences in what they understand about objects?

One of the first detailed studies on object understanding was by Morss (1983; 1985). He followed eight babies with DS and TD babies longitudinally. At the beginning of the study they were aged 8–22 months. Morss assessed their developing understanding of objects on a variety of Piagetian object permanence tasks (Piaget, 1953). These tasks involve hiding toys in a variety of different ways and observing the children's searching behavior. Not surprisingly, Morss found that the children with DS were delayed compared to TD children in succeeding at each of the tasks. In addition, the pattern of results was different. Once the TD children had succeeded on a particular task, they would continue to be successful on this task on later occasions. The children with DS were more varied and showed fewer examples of the characteristic errors observed on these tasks. Morss argued that babies with DS are developing in a different way from TD babies. While TD babies seem to follow the sequence of developments predicted by Piagetian theory, babies with DS do not. In particular, they do not show the same pattern of errors, and an understanding at one level does not seem to be consolidated and built on to the same extent as is observed in TD babies.

These findings have been confirmed and extended by Wishart (e.g., 1987, 1990, 1993). Wishart and Duffy (1990) tested 18 children with DS, aged 6–48 months, on four object permanence tasks: searching for an object hidden in one place, searching for the object when it was hidden in a second place, searching when the object was not found where expected, and searching for an object which was moved out of sight to a second place. The tasks were given to the children twice, with 1 or 2 weeks between the tests The performances of 12 children differed on at least one task between the two sessions: 8 showed improvement but 4 passed fewer tests on the second occasion. Also, for 6 of the 16 children who passed at least one test, the items they passed did not reflect the order of difficulty found in TD children. Interestingly, some of the children failed not because they searched incorrectly but because either they would not attend or they would not search, suggestive of a lack of motivation.

This motivational explanation is favored by Hasan and Messer (1997) to account for their failure to replicate Wishart and Duffy's findings with 10 children with DS aged 15–45 months at the outset of their study. These children were tested once a month for up to 10 months on a series of tasks. On object permanence all the children succeeded on the same or more advanced tasks on successive visits, with none showing any regression. On tasks requiring children to remember the locations of different objects, sort objects into groups on the basis of shared characteristics, and reproduce arrangements of blocks, performance was maintained on about two thirds of the visits, and only regressed on about 10% of visits. Hasan and Messer point to several differences between their study and that of Wishart and Duffy which might explain the findings. In particular, Hasan and Messer tested the children in their own homes and varied the administration of the tasks according to the children's level of interest. They argue that these differences may have motivated the children to respond.

The motivational argument is also consistent with Ruskin, Mundy, Kasari, and Sigman's (1994a) study in which the researcher demonstrated what could be done with different toys to children with DS and TD children, both of 17 months mean MA and matched for language. Although both groups of children explored the toys to the same extent and in similar ways, the children with DS produced shorter sequences of behavior with the toys, rejected the toys more often, and showed much less pleasure when playing with them. These findings are consistent with children with DS being less motivated to play. Clearly findings supporting a motivational explanation are in need of replication. If a lack of motivation can account for the apparent lack of consolidation of learning seen in Wishart and colleagues' studies then utilizing assessment techniques and teaching strategies adopted from our understanding of TD children may be completely inappropriate for children with DS.

Two further studies of the object permanence skills of children with DS nevertheless indicate that the processes underlying their development may differ from those in TD children or, alternatively, that Piaget's account of sensorimotor development is incorrect. Rast and Meltzoff (1995) examined the ability of 1½–3½-year-old children with DS to find objects which had been hidden in various ways (object permanence) alongside their ability to copy an action performed 5 minutes previously by the researcher (deferred imitation). According to Piagetian theory, the ability to find an object following invisible displacements should emerge at the same time as deferred imitation, as both are argued to require the ability to remember and represent an absent object/action. However, Rast and Meltzoff observed deferred imitation in children with DS who could not yet find an object following an invisible displacement. In other words, for these children, the emergence of deferred imitation was independent of, and preceded, being able to find an object following an invisible displacement.

Interestingly, Wright (1998), in a series of studies examining the ability of children with DS, mean age 2 years, to imitate the actions associated with hiding an object alongside their ability to search for hidden objects, demonstrated that in object permanence tasks children with DS may be relying on a representation of the action of hiding the object rather than a representation of the hidden object. Thus, Wright observed that if children with DS had to imitate the action of the researcher in order to find an object they were successful, but if they had to carry out a different action in order to retrieve the object they did less well than 1-year-old TD children of similar developmental level.

Children with DS of around 4 years old have been found to be as good at posting different shapes through appropriate holes in a box as 2-year-old TD children matched for MA but slower than TD children of similar CA (Pitcairn & Wishart, 1994). However, what was more interesting in this study was the behavior of the children with two "impossible" shapes for which there were no corresponding holes. The TD children quickly learned that these shapes could not be posted whereas the children with DS persisted in trying to post the shapes for much longer. In addition, the children with DS were much more likely than the TD children to avoid the impossible shape trials by some irrelevant distracting behavior such as making eye contact with the researcher and shouting or engaging in some sort of party piece, for example banging the table.

Interestingly, Linn, Goodman, and Lender (2000) also reported that when left to play alone with toys without the adults in the room intervening, children with DS, mean CA 4½ years, initiated twice as many episodes of interaction with the adults than TD children matched for MA over a 30-minute period. Further, the children with DS were passive for up to 10 minutes, for example staring into space or wandering around the room aimlessly, whereas the TD children were passive for 10 seconds or less. On average the children with DS spent increasing amounts of time in these sorts of passive behaviors over time. However, there was a great deal of variation in the behaviors of the children with DS which led to the group differences being non-significant. Nevertheless, Linn et al. argue that for some children with DS passive behavior may be a way of dealing with stimulating situations.

Object understanding can also be explored through play. Of particular interest is the development of symbolic play which can be observed to start in the second year in TD children. In symbolic play children pretend something other than reality, imagining that one object is another, has a characteristic it does not have, or is present when it is not. A number of studies have investigated the play of children with DS and generally report few differences between their play and the play of TD children of similar developmental level (e.g., Beeghly, 1998; Beeghly, Weiss-Perry, & Cicchetti, 1990; Libby, Powell, Messer & Jordan, 1998; Sigman & Ruskin, 1999), although, like TD children, children with DS produce higher quality play when playing with a parent than when playing alone (e.g., Cielinski, Vaughn, Seifer, & Contreras, 1995).

Libby et al. (1998) found no differences in the play of 5–6-year-old children with DS and TD children matched for language age when given conventional toys and non-representational materials and observed three times over 6–8 months. All 9 children with DS produced symbolic play, as did 8 of the 9 TD children. Similar findings were reported by Beeghly et al. (1990) who examined various behaviors, including play, of 35 children with DS aged 27–93 months matched for MA with TD children. Over a 30-minute play episode with their mothers, no differences were found between the two groups of children with respect to the amount of symbolic play, functional play, relational play, no play, and structured social play, although the children with DS under 56 months engaged in slightly more manipulative play than TD children of similar developmental level. Similar developments were seen with increasing age in both groups, with older children engaging in more symbolic and structured social play and less manipulative play than younger children.

However, although the symbolic play of the children with DS under 56 months did not differ from that of TD children, some differences were observed between children with DS over 68 months and TD children with whom they were matched. For example, although the two older groups were similar in terms of their best play, the play of the children with DS was less advanced overall, and this was particularly the case when their ability to substitute one object for another was considered. Beeghly et al. suggest that these findings can be accounted for by an increasing dissociation of linguistic, particularly syntactic, development and symbolic development generally in children with DS as they get older. In support of this, they report that whereas the play of the younger and older children in both groups was correlated with MA and, at the younger age with MLU in morphemes, the play of the older TD children was more highly correlated with MLU than was found in the children with DS. A significant correlation between play and MLU in morphemes was confirmed by Fewell, Ogura, Notari-Syverson, and Wheeden (1997) in their study of 15–54-month-old children with DS. In addition, although Sigman and Ruskin (1999) also found that the play skills of 1–6-year-old children with DS correlated with their language abilities, their play was not predictive of their language one year later.

Beeghly et al. (1990) also examined the relationships between play, affect, and cognition and report significant correlations between measures of these three areas. They found no difference between the children with and without DS matched for developmental level in terms of their affective responsiveness to play situations. On the basis of these findings, Beeghly et al. argue that affective, social, and cognitive aspects of symbolic functioning are similarly organized in children with DS and TD children matched for developmental level. However, more detailed longitudinal study of the symbolic play of children with DS seems warranted. It seems especially important to examine whether or not developments in symbolic play are maintained over time and consolidated and to explore further relationships with linguistic development as children with DS get older.

Another way to look at understanding of objects is to examine how children represent objects in their drawings. Drawing ability has been linked to intelligence (e.g., Harris, 1963) and so we would expect children with DS to produce less mature drawings than TD children of similar CA. Clements and Barrett (1994) found that 5–18-year-olds with DS produced less mature drawings of partial occlusions, such as a man standing behind a solid wall, than TD children matched for verbal ability. Interestingly, performance correlated with language ability in the TD children, but did not for the youngsters with DS, suggesting that the drawing skills of individuals with DS are different, rather than simply delayed, relative to TD children of similar verbal ability. However, Barrett and Eames (1996) argued that despite differences, children with DS progress through a similar sequence of drawing development to TD children.

Laws and Lawrence (2001), studying how 7–14-year-old children with DS and 3–8-year-old TD children matched for expressive vocabulary drew a teddy placed beside, inside, or behind either a transparent or opaque pot, concluded that the drawing development of children with DS follows a different pathway. The children with DS produced more detailed drawings of the bear but the maturity of their drawings was not related to expressive or receptive language, CA, or fine motor skills whereas this was the case for the TD children. Very few of the drawings showed partial occlusion and many drawings by the children with DS did not fit stages reported for TD children.

Similar conclusions were reached by Eames and Cox (1994) for adolescents with DS, mean age 16 years, matched for nonverbal ability with TD children, mean age 7 years: the drawings of the group with DS on 11 different drawing tasks, including occlusions, were inferior to those of the TD children and the correlation between drawing skill and nonverbal ability was not significant for the DS group but significant for the TD group.

Thus, there is clear evidence using a variety of different approaches that children with DS have a different understanding of objects from TD children.

What do children with DS understand about themselves and other people?

The understanding that children with DS have of themselves and others has been explored using a variety of methods: differential behavior towards people and objects; imitation of facial gestures of others; response to reflection in a mirror; drawings of human figures; ability to talk about feelings and awareness of others' beliefs and thoughts.

Carvajal and Iglesias (2000) found that when 3–14-month-old babies with DS and TD babies of similar age smiled they were more likely to be looking at their parent than a toy, indicating that at this age they understand something about the different significance of people and objects. Young babies with DS have also been found to imitate other people. Thus, Heimann and colleagues (Heimann & Ullstadius, 1999; Heimann, Ullstadius, & Swerlander, 1998) explored the ability of infants with DS at 1, 3, and 4 months to imitate facial gestures. Like TD infants, all five infants with DS observed at 1 month imitated tongue protrusion and, also like TD infants, fewer did so at 3 and 4 months. There were less marked effects of age for imitation of mouth opening, which also parallels observations of TD infants, with 3 out of 5 infants with DS imitating at 1 month, 6 out of 7 at 3 months, and 3 out of 7 at 4 months. Thus, overall, the ability to imitate facial gestures of another person seems similar in infants with DS and TD infants, which may indicate a similar understanding of others at this early age. But what of older children with DS?

Mans, Ciccetti, and Sroufe (1978) examined the reaction of children with DS, aged 1½–4 years, when they saw their reflection in a mirror and when, without them realizing, a smudge of rouge was put on their noses. The most obvious indication that children realize that what they see in the mirror is their own reflection, is if they touch the rouge on their nose. TD children begin to respond in this situation by around 15 months and the response is well established by 22 months (e.g., Bertenthal & Fischer, 1978). In Mans et al.'s study, only a quarter of the children with DS of 22 months or younger touched their noses, and these were the most developmentally able. Among the older children, a greater proportion responded in this way. The authors argue that this development follows the same process as in TD children, since its emergence is dependent more on MA than on CA. Other behaviors were also recorded, and about three quarters of the children showed some sort of change in their behavior when their noses had been colored. The most common reaction among the youngest children was a change from a positive response to one of puzzlement or sobriety, while the older children were more likely to show some sign of surprise or an increased positive response.

These findings were confirmed by Loveland (1987) who compared the reactions of children with DS aged 1½–5 years to those of TD children matched for developmental age in four situations in front of a mirror: free play, after some rouge had been put on their cheek, being asked "where's Mummy" as the mother appeared in the mirror behind them, and being asked "look, get Teddy" as teddy appeared behind them in the mirror.

Although more of the TD children responded appropriately in the three experimental conditions, none of the differences were significant. However, Loveland also noted that the children with DS seemed less focused on the tasks and, with their mother and with teddy, switched attention between the reflection and the object less frequently than the TD children. Thus, although there is a similarity in the behavior of children with DS and TD children of similar developmental level, there are indications that this apparent similarity may hide underlying differences in how the situations are being processed and responded to.

How children draw the human figure may also tell us something about their understanding of people. Cox and Maynard (1998) studied the human figure drawings of 8–11-year-olds with DS and two groups of TD children matched with the children with DS for CA and VMA. The drawings of the children with DS, whether from memory or drawing a picture of a doll, were similar to those of the TD children matched for VMA, but whereas the correlation between MA and drawing was significant for the TD children it was not for the children with DS, once again pointing to differences between the two groups.

Another way of exploring children's understanding of people is to examine whether they understand that other people may have different beliefs, thoughts, and feelings from themselves. Beeghly and Cicchetti (1997) looked for references to the feelings and internal states of others in the talk of young children. Children with DS aged 2–8 years were divided into two groups on the basis of MA, 1½–2½ years, and 2½–5 years and matched with TD children for developmental level. The children were videoed playing with their mothers and reading a picture book. Although the children with DS showed similar conversational skills in terms of number of turns and length of talk on a topic, they used fewer internal state words at both ages and their use of such words was more context bound relative to the TD children. In both groups internal state word use was correlated with language and, given that the language skills of children with DS are often more impaired than their nonverbal abilities, it could be that their language difficulties, rather than their understanding of others, limited their use of internal state words.

Some evidence for this comes from a study of adolescents with DS by Hesketh and Chapman (1998). Many of the examples of internal state words given by Beeghly and Cicchetti were verbs, such as "I think it's a cat." Hesketh and Chapman report that adolescents with DS produced fewer verbs per utterance overall than younger TD children matched for MLU. In addition, verbs such as know, think, remember, promise, were even less frequently used than other types of verbs. Thus, at least in part, Beeghly and Cicchetti's findings could simply reflect children with DS producing more sentences without verbs than TD children. There is also evidence that mothers of 3–8-year-old children with DS use fewer internal state words to their children than mothers of 2–5-year-old TD children, even when account is taken of differences in the children's MLU (Tingley, Gleason, & Hooshyar, 1994).

Further support for the suggestion that language differences, rather than lack of understanding of other people's thoughts and feelings, may explain the reduced use of internal state words by children with DS comes from their performance on theory of mind tasks. In theory of mind tasks characters are portrayed as having a belief or knowledge which differs from reality. If children understand that others can have different beliefs and thoughts, then they will respond on the basis of a character's belief even if it differs from reality. Baron-Cohen, Leslie, and Frith (1985) found that over three quarters of 6–17-year-olds with DS passed such a task, a proportion which was similar to that of 4-year-old TD children. Mitchell, Saltmarsh, and Russell (1997) found similar results for 8–16-year-olds with DS who had VMAs of 2½–7 years using a rather different task in which children had to select an object on the basis of a character's misbelief about its current location. For example, character 1 initially put one bowl on a table and a second bowl on a cupboard and then left the room; character 2 swapped the two bowls; character 1 then requested the bowl she put on the table, which was now on the cupboard. If children appreciate which bowl character 1 desires, they will ignore the reality of the character's request and get the bowl which is now on the cupboard. Again, about three quarters of the youngsters with DS succeeded on this task.

Interestingly, Swettenham (1996) has demonstrated that 6–16-year-old individuals with DS who failed a false belief task could learn to respond appropriately following training with the task on a computer. The children with DS took longer to learn the appropriate response than TD children of similar VMA, but following training, like TD children, also demonstrated an understanding of other people's minds on different tasks. Even so, whereas 3 months later the performance of the TD children had improved further, the children with DS had not progressed any further in their understanding.

However, it is worth noting that other researchers have reported that older, less able adolescents and adults with DS have not done as well as TD children of similar VMA on a variety of these sorts of tasks (Yirmiya, Solomonica-Levi, Shulman, & Pilowski, 1996; Zelazo, Burack, Benedetto, & Frye, 1996). This suggests that although DS does not preclude an understanding of other people's beliefs and desires, individuals with DS and severe LDs may have less understanding.

Thus, although there are some differences in the responses of children with DS on the various tasks described in this section, their understanding of people seems to be fairly similar to that of TD children of similar level of development.

Do children with DS encode and store information differently?

There is evidence of memory impairments associated with DS from a very young age. For example, Miranda and Fantz's (1974) study of recognition memory in TD children and children with DS at 8–16 weeks, 17–29 weeks, and 30–40 weeks demonstrated that the TD children showed recognition memory of abstract patterns at all ages, the children with DS only at the two older ages. Recognition of one of two photographs, and of a circular or checkerboard arrangement of squares, was demonstrated in the two older TD groups, but only the oldest group with DS showed recognition of a photograph, and no group with DS showed recognition for the arrangement of squares. Finally, the eldest TD children, but none of the groups with DS, showed recognition memory for colors. These results show that children with DS lag behind TD children for recognition memory of these four stimulus variations by at least 2 months. This lag was confirmed in a longitudinal study in which significant recognition memory was shown first by the TD children at 9 weeks and by the children with DS at 17 weeks.

The particular problem facing babies with DS seems to be one of remembering what they have seen rather than an inability to make the discrimination in the first place. This was shown by Miranda (1976) who found that although pairs of abstract patterns could be discriminated by babies with DS at 7 weeks using the preference method, they failed to show any sign of remembering these same patterns until they were about 17 weeks old. In comparison, the TD children remembered the patterns at 9 weeks.

A difficulty with this sort of study is that inferences about visual processing are based on looking behavior. Thus, if children with DS show a different pattern of visual preference from TD children it is argued that they are processing the information differently. However, if the looking behaviors of the two groups of children are similar they might still be processing the information differently but we cannot conclude this. An interesting study by Karrer, Karrer, Bloom, Chaney, and Davis (1998) provides psychophysiological evidence of processing differences in children with DS, even though their looking behavior was similar to that of TD children. Karrer et al. recorded event-related brain potentials (ERPs) from electrodes attached to the heads of children with DS and TD children, mean age 6 months, while they saw 160 brief presentations of two female faces, one presented on 20% of the trials, and the other on the remaining trials. No differences were observed in the infants' visual behavior, with both groups looking more at the less familiar face. Nevertheless, there were a number of differences in the ERPs of the two groups which the authors interpret as reflecting differences in underlying brain activity and therefore processing.

Of course, when differences are found between children with DS and TD children in terms of visual recognition memory, this could be due to a general memory impairment, rather than a specific difficulty with remembering visual information. Against this, Ohr and Fagen (1991) report no difference between children with and without DS aged 13–18 weeks in their ability to learn and remember a contingency. In this study, the babies initially learned an association between kicking and the movement of a mobile. No differences were found between the groups in their speed of acquisition or retention of this contingency 7 days later. However, the task used by Ohr and Fagen was very simple and evidence from Wishart suggests that differences in learning a contingency may emerge at older ages (e.g., 1991).

In her study, Wishart used a similar contingency task with 16 children with DS aged 6, 12, 18, and 24 months, each of whom was matched with two TD children, one on the basis of CA, one on MA. Interestingly, whereas the children with DS cooperated with the task, most of the older TD children did not. Once the TD children had detected the contingency they refused to cooperate, whereas the children with DS continued to respond. However, this study did show that overall the children with DS took longer to detect the contingency. Unfortunately, Wishart did not test the children's retention of the learned contingency, except within the test session. Nevertheless, her study does indicate that at least from 6 months children with DS may learn less quickly than TD children of similar CA and MA.

As children get older, memory becomes increasingly important. Information needs to be taken in, coded, organized, stored, sometimes for short periods of time, sometimes for long periods of time. Subsequently, information needs to be retrieved when required. Obviously if children's memory for information is limited this will affect their ability to learn and may manifest itself as LDs. Several researchers have studied the short-term and long-term memory abilities of children and adolescents with DS. It has been shown that their short-term memory for verbal material, but not for visual–spatial material, is impaired, relative to children with LDs but not DS (e.g., Jarrold, Baddeley, & Hewes, 1999a; 2000; Jarrold, Baddeley, & Phillips, 1999b; Laws, 1998). These findings suggest that the phonological loop component, but not the visual–spatial component, of working memory is impaired in DS. Further studies have indicated that long-term memory for verbal and visual–spatial information is inferior in individuals with DS relative to individuals with LDs but not DS and TD children of similar MA (e.g., Carlesimo, Marotta, & Vicari, 1997; Vicari, Bellucci, & Carlesimo, 2000a).

One explanation of the poor verbal short-term memories of children with DS has been that they rehearse verbal material more slowly than other children because of slower articulation rates. However, Jarrold and colleagues have argued that the impairment is not in the rehearsal process (e.g., 2000a). As evidence for this they found no relationship between articulation speed and short-term memory for long and short words for adolescents with DS of mean age 14 years. As they point out, this is not surprising given that TD children do not use rehearsal as a strategy until about 7 years (e.g., Gathercole, 1998) and all the adolescents with DS had VMAs below 7 years. Jarrold et al. suggest that the short-term memory problems that children with DS have for verbal material are likely to be due to either how the information is encoded or how it is stored.

The long-term memory abilities of individuals with DS of mean age 17 years have been explored by Carlesimo et al. (1997). They found long-term memory impairments in individuals with DS for both verbal and visual–spatial material. Thus, the individuals with DS were impaired, relative to individuals with LDs but not DS and TD children of similar MA, on immediate and delayed recall of lists of words and of a short story and on copying a figure and reproducing it again immediately and after a delay. Further findings led these authors to argue that impaired long-term memory in DS results from poor encoding and retrieval. For example, when the word lists consisted of words from three semantic categories, rather than unrelated words, this did not improve their recall.

Interestingly, individuals with DS seem to have fewer memory difficulties when implicit memory, rather than explicit memory is involved, for both verbal and visual–spatial material (e.g., Carlesimo et al., 1997; Nadel, 1999; Vicari et al., 2000a). Implicit or procedural memory tasks require individuals to draw on information provided within the task itself, whereas during explicit memory tasks individuals must draw on information gained in previous experiences. Individuals with DS are as able as others with LDs but not DS and TD children of similar MA at learning particular visual-spatial procedures presented within a task and completing words given the stem provided they have seen the whole word earlier. However, individuals with DS are impaired, relative to the others, when they have to learn lists of words or recognize which pictures they had previously seen when these pictures were presented alongside new pictures.

Taken together, these findings suggest that although some memory abilities of children and adolescents with DS may be similar to those of TD children of similar MA, overall individuals with DS have considerable memory difficulties. It seems very likely that this will affect their academic achievements.

What level of academic achievement can children with DS attain?

In the past it has been generally assumed that children and young people with DS will attain only very limited academic skills. However, a number of case studies have indicated that some individuals with DS can learn to read and write to a level which is useful for them (e.g., Butterfield, 1961; Duffen, 1976). Buckley (1985) suggests that as many as 40% of children with DS may be able to learn to read independently. Such a proportion is in agreement with Carr's (1988) finding that 16 (39%) of 41 young people with DS aged 21 years had reading ages of 6–12 years on the Neale reading test. The others failed to score on the test, although a further 15 could name some letters.

What distinguishes those children with DS who learn to read from those who do not? Carr identified a number of differences. Among those who could read, 75% were female, 87.5% had been brought up at home rather than in an institution, and 64% came from families in social classes I, II, and III non-manual based on the father's occupation. These latter two observations indicate that the nature of the environment may be important.

The effect of the environment is also evident in a study of much younger children with DS (Sloper, Cunningham, Turner, & Knussen, 1990a). Sloper et al. collected various information on 118 children with DS aged 6–14 years and found that teachers' ratings of the children's skills in reading, writing, and number were related to the type of school attended even when MA was taken into account. The greatest achievements were shown by children in mainstream schools and the least by those in schools for children with severe LDs. Given that this difference was found even when MA differences had been allowed for, Sloper et al. suggest that the effect of school may be due to the different importance placed on academic achievements in the different environments. In agreement with Carr's findings, they also report that girls were achieving more than boys overall, as were the older children and those children whose fathers felt that events in their lives were under their control.

The importance of age is also evident when the number of children attaining reading test scores in Sloper et al.'s study is considered. Only 20 (17%) of the children attained reading ages in comparison with Carr's 39%. This suggests that young people with DS continue to acquire academic skills well into adolescence. Indeed, Kay-Raining Bird, Cleave, and

McConnell (2000) report that the word recognition skills of 12 children with DS aged 6–12 years and attending mainstream schools improved over the next four and a half years.

The reading skills of TD children are related to their phonological awareness which indicates that learning to read in TD children involves the auditory system. Given that DS is associated with impaired verbal short- and long-term memory it is perhaps not surprising that children with DS have impaired phonological awareness. For example, Kay-Raining Bird et al. (2000) in their longitudinal study report that the phonological awareness skills of children with DS were poor at all ages and showed little or no improvement over four and a half years, despite improvements in reading. And consistent with poor phonological awareness, Kay-Raining Bird et al. report that the children were poor at reading nonsense words, a task requiring phonological skills.

Cossu, Rossini, and Marshall (1993) also examined the phonological awareness of 8–16-year-old young people with DS who were matched on ability to read regular and irregular words and non-words with 7–8-year-old TD children. The young people with DS did much less well than the TD children when required to identify the number of phonemes in a word, say a word but leave out the first two phonemes, blend letter sounds into a word, and spell words out loud. Between 75% and 96% of the TD children were successful on these different tasks, compared with 8–32% of the young people with DS.

These findings indicate that reading ability can develop in the absence of good phonological skills and that children with DS learn to read in a different way from TD children. For TD children the route to reading is primarily phonological and therefore phonological awareness is related to their reading ability. Perhaps the route taken by children with DS does not require phonological skills. Some support for this comes from the work of Buckley (e.g., 1985, 1993). She has observed that most children with DS can learn to read single words by 3–4 years, and some as young as 2 years, and that their reading ability may be in advance of their spoken language. Buckley argues that children with DS may be learning to read via a route involving a direct link between print and meaning, rather than between print and sound. She supports this with the observation that whereas most of the early reading errors of TD children are phonological, those of children with DS are usually either visual (confusing words that look similar, e.g., hair/rain) or semantic (confusing words with similar meanings, e.g., closed/shut). Because of this different route to reading, Buckley argues that reading may actually help the language and memory skills of children with DS and should be introduced early (e.g., 1999).

Much less research has been carried out on the mathematical achievements of children with DS, although Buckley (1985) suggests that number skills may be much more difficult for children with DS to acquire than reading skills because they are often abstract. Carr (1988) reports that on a test of mathematical ability 34 (83%) of the 21-year-olds with DS scored with ability ages of 4–7 years. An experimental study of number understanding was carried out by Caycho, Gunn and Siegal (1991) who found no difference between children with DS, mean CA of 9 years 7 months, and children without DS, mean age 4 years 6 months, matched for vocabulary level in counting up to eight objects and in pointing out when a puppet made mistakes counting objects. In the latter task the puppet made a variety of mistakes, sometimes missing out an object, sometimes counting one object twice, sometimes saying numbers in a random order, sometimes giving the wrong total. Over all the tasks, between one-third and two-thirds of the children answered correctly.

Support for Buckley's suggestion that number skills may be particularly difficult for children with DS because of the abstract nature of number comes from Stith and Fishbein (1996). In this study, adolescents with DS, adolescents with LDs but not DS, and 6–8-year-old TD children had to total the value of coins (pennies, nickels, and dimes) and make comparisons between sets of coins, total and compare the value of pieces of colored paper with the numbers 1, 5, or 10 written on them, or total and compare values when the information was just given verbally. All the participants had basic number skills although the TD children, who made very few errors on the tasks, scored higher on a mathematics test. The adolescents with DS and with LDs but not DS made more errors than the TD children, and the adolescents with DS had particular difficulties when coins were used.

The available evidence indicates that many children with DS can learn to read and acquire basic numeracy skills, although they may have difficulties applying their numeracy skills to real-life situations. However, there has been little systematic study of the writing skills of children with DS. Given the importance of literacy and numeracy for everyday living and given the suggestion that children with DS may learn to read in a different way from TD children, and have difficulties understanding the value of coins, it is clear that more research is needed into the development of these skills in children with DS.

The development of communication

How does DS influence early communication between these children and their parents?

DS has obvious physical signs which mean that a diagnosis is usually made within a few days of birth. Therefore, parents are likely to be aware, from very early on, that their baby is different, and they will probably hear things about the characteristic abilities and disabilities of children with DS from a variety of sources. They may also have their own expectations, correct or incorrect, of the implications of DS. All these sorts of factors are likely to influence how they approach their baby and communicate with her. In addition, babies with DS develop more slowly than TD babies, and there may be ways in which their development is actually different. How will all this influence the way in which babies with DS and their parents communicate with each other? I shall examine first the behaviors of babies and young children with DS, and then consider some of the evidence concerning the way in which parents characteristically behave towards these children. Finally, I shall examine the nature of the communication between children with DS and their parents.

Crying is one of the earliest signals and several studies have found that the cries of babies with DS in the first year are different from those of TD babies, both in quality and quantity. For example, they cry less frequently when in pain, their cries show more variation in intensity and are lower in pitch than the cries of TD babies (Fisichelli & Karelitz, 1966). They take longer to cry, make more whimpers and fewer gasps, fewer bursts of vocalizations, and fewer sounds than TD babies (Fisichelli, Haber, Davis, & Karelitz, 1966). Their pain cries are longer with a monotonous flat melody form and the pitch is lower (Lind, Vuorenkoski, Rosberg, Partanen, & Wasz-Höckert, 1970). The cries of babies with DS are perceived as a much weaker signal than the cries of TD babies (Freudenberg, Driscoll, & Stern, 1978).

There are also differences in the vocalization patterns of children with DS from early on. Berger and Cunningham (1981) observed TD babies and babies with DS once a fortnight until they were 6 months old. The number of vocalizations made by the TD babies increased over the first 3–4 months, and then declined. The babies with DS began much more slowly and made fewer vocalizations than the TD babies up to 4 months. However, the babies with DS showed no decline, and by the 20th week they were making significantly more vocalizations than the TD babies. Berger and Cunningham (1983) suggest that the decline in the TD babies' vocalizations after 4 months is because they are taking more notice of what other people are saying, and are spending an increasing amount of time listening. Babies with DS do not show this decline, although they may later, and so are neither listening nor taking so much notice of the fact that another person is speaking. These differences may be due to or exacerbated by the hearing difficulties often associated with DS (see page 23).

In addition, Berger and Cunningham noted differences in looking behavior. The babies with DS made eye contact with their mother at an average age of almost 7 weeks, about 2½ weeks after the TD babies did. The two groups also differed in how much they looked at their mothers over the six months. The TD children increased the duration of eye contact with their mothers up to 6–7 weeks, and kept at this level until 14–16 weeks, after which the time they spent in eye contact diminished rapidly. The babies with DS made very little eye contact up to about 3 months, when the duration gradually began to increase, and continued increasing throughout the study, so that by 6 months they were spending more time in eye contact with their mothers than the TD babies. More eye contact with the mother at 6 and 9 months by babies with DS compared to TD babies was also reported by Gunn, Berry, and Andrews (1982) and at 3–14 months by Carvajal and Iglesias (2000). These findings of greater eye contact by the babies with DS may be related to the longer looking times reported by Miranda and Fantz (1973) in their visual preference studies (see pages 199–200).

Thus, from the earliest months, babies with DS behave differently towards people than TD babies. Further differences emerge as they get older. There are several reports that from the end of the first year children with DS vocalize less (e.g., Buckhalt, Rutherford, & Goldberg, 1978; Greenwald & Leonard, 1979). Greenwald and Leonard observed that TD children, who were matched with children with DS for MA, were more likely to use words. None of the children with DS used words, rather they tended to rely more on gestures. In agreement with this, Franco and Wishart (1995) found that 2–4-year-olds with DS produced almost twice as many pointing gestures as TD children matched for expressive language, although a similar number of reaching gestures.

Young children with DS also seem to pay less attention than TD children to the talk of others. Glenn and Cunningham (1983) gave TD children and children with DS the opportunity of listening to recordings of their mother talking to either another adult or a baby. The children were seen twice: the children with DS at about 12 and 24 months and the TD children at about 9 and 17 months. All the children preferred to listen to baby talk on both occasions. However, by the second visit the TD children were listening for significantly longer, both in total and on average per listen, than they were during the first visit. For the children with DS there was a significant decline in listening time to baby talk by the second visit, although they still preferred this. Also, whereas on the first testing the TD children and the children with DS both listened less to an adult talking than to a rhyme, by the second testing the TD children spent much longer listening to the adult talking. There was no such change for the children with DS. Thus, somewhere between the end of the first year and the end of the second year, children with DS become less interested in listening to adults talking, whereas TD children become more interested.

Differences are also apparent in the interest shown by children with DS in what is going on around them. Gunn et al. (1982) reported that the 6- and 9-month-old babies with DS spent much less time than the TD babies looking around the room. However, Carvajal and Iglesias (2000) found that at 10–14 months both TD babies and babies with DS looked more at toys than at their mothers, whereas at younger ages the reverse was true. Interestingly, when Ruskin, Kasari, Mundy, and Sigman (1994b) compared the behaviors of children with DS and TD children, both of mean MA 17 months and matched for language, when presented with toys, some of which could be acted on to produce interesting effects, and when the researcher interacted with them, singing songs and gesturing, the children with DS paid much more attention in the social situation than in the toy situation. In the social situation, the children with DS looked at the researcher more frequently, joined in singing the song much more often, and were less off-task than the TD children. With the toys, the children with DS paid as much attention as the TD children but they rejected the toys more often.

Attending to people and objects or activities in a coordinated way is necessary for communication and differences have been found in the extent to which children with DS and TD children do this, even when matched for MA. For example, Legerstee and Weintraub (1997) observed 1–2- year-old children with DS and younger TD children matched for MA playing at home with their mothers on four occasions once every 2 months. The TD children spent a greater proportion of time in coordinated attention, that is, looking back and forth between toys and their mother, than the children with DS. However, children with DS with MAs greater than 12 months showed more coordinated attention than both children with DS and TD children with MAs of less than 12 months. Mundy, Kasari, Sigman, and Ruskin (1995) reported that 1–3-year-olds with DS made fewer requests for objects or help and were less likely to look in the appropriate direction when the researcher pointed to something than younger TD children of similar MA and language age, although there were no differences in behaviors such as looking back and forth between the researcher and a toy and showing toys to the researcher. Interestingly, Franco and Wishart (1995) also found that when toys were placed out of reach, a situation usually eliciting requests, children with DS under 3 years produced relatively few gestures. However, 3–4-year-old children with DS did gesture in this situation. Franco and Wishart further report that when with their mothers 2–4-year-old children with DS, like 1–2-year-old TD children, pointed to animated dolls more than 2 metres away and, again like TD children, the children with DS either looked at their mother before pointing or while they were pointing.

Thus, there are many ways in which babies and young children with DS react differently from TD children when they are with an adult. Do adults behave differently? If there are differences, are they due to adults responding to differences in the children's behavior, or because the adults know the children have DS?

A number of studies have reported that mothers of babies with DS talk more and more as the babies get older (e.g., Berger & Cunningham, 1983), especially when they are teaching their children how to play with something new (Buckhalt et al., 1978), whereas mothers of TD babies vocalize less and less as the babies get older. Although the lengths of mothers' utterances to babies with DS and TD babies are similar up to about 17 months (Buckhalt et al., 1978), at later ages the utterances of mothers to their children with DS are shorter (Buium, Rynders, & Turnure, 1974), more often incomplete and consisting of single words than the utterances spoken to TD children. These are characteristics of how adults talk to young children and probably reflect the mothers of both children adjusting their utterances in line with their own children's language skills. Thus, when 1–2-year-old children with DS are matched with TD children for MA there are no differences in the speed or length of utterances made by their mothers when speaking to them (Glenn & Cunningham, 1983).

Further evidence that mothers adjust their language to that of their children comes from Yoder, Hooshyar, Klee, and Schaffer (1996). They compared children with DS, mean age 7 years, with children with other LDs but not DS, mean age 4 years and matched with the children with DS for MLU. While playing with their mothers the children with DS produced more multi-word partially intelligible utterances than the children with LDs but not DS. Although the mothers of both groups of children expanded their children's utterances to a similar extent, the mothers of the children with DS expanded more of the partially intelligible sentences, the mothers of the other children more of the intelligible utterances.

The parents of children with DS may talk more to them because they are trying to help. Certainly mothers of 1–2-year-old children with DS give more verbal directions than mothers of TD children of similar MA (Jones, 1977), and Corter, Pepler, Stanhope, and Abramovitch (1992) found that mothers who had two children aged between 1 and 11, of whom one had DS, were more positive and gave more directions to the child with DS than to their other child. Interestingly, Landry, Garner, Pirie, and Swank (1994) found that mothers of 2½–6-year-old children with DS and mothers of 2–3-year-old TD children matched for receptive language used a similar number of directives when teaching their children how to do a puzzle, but the mothers of the children with DS used more directives when pretending to have a tea party. Landry et al. suggest that in the tea party situation the children's role is less clear and this may lead the mothers of the children with DS to give more guidance. Certainly, within the tea party scenario, although the children with DS were less likely than the TD children to comply with their mothers' requests, they were more likely to comply following a directive than following a suggestion. Vettel and Windsor (1997) further report that mothers of 3–5-year-old children with DS wait less time for their children to answer a question than mothers of TD children matched for MLU, although interestingly this seemed to be because when the children with DS did answer questions, they answered faster than the TD children. Thus, the mothers of the children with DS may have adjusted their wait time to their children's usual response times.

The suggestion that mothers give directions in order to try to help their children is supported by Mahoney, Fors, and Wood (1990). They compared children with DS, average age 30 months, to younger TD children matched for developmental and linguistic age. The mothers of the children with DS used more directives although the children were no less involved in the interaction than the TD children, suggesting that the mothers were trying to alter the children's behavior. This study also found that the mothers of the children with DS often requested actions which were relatively difficult and, rather than commenting on things that the children were attending to, were likely to require the children to change their focus of attention. Unfortunately, despite the intentions behind these actions, neither may be very helpful for the children. Support for this comes from Mahoney and Neville-Smith (1996) who found that 2–3-year-olds with DS were more likely to respond to a request from their parent if the request was related to what they were already doing and was within their current level of functioning.

In comparison, Landry and Chapieski (1989) did not find mothers of 12-month-old children with DS more directive than mothers of premature babies of similar mental and motor development. There were no differences in how often the mothers tried to direct their children's attention and mothers of both groups of children were more likely to act to maintain rather than redirect attention, although the mothers of children with DS were more likely to introduce a toy to the interaction when the children were not involved with anything. Differences were observed in the nonverbal strategies used, the mothers of the children with DS being more likely to physically orient their children and to offer toys less often. However, there were no differences in the verbal strategies used by the mothers. Although appearing to contradict the findings of other studies, it seems likely that the mothers of the premature children were also trying to support their children's development and this may account for the absence of any group difference in maternal directiveness in this study.

Roach, Barratt, Miller, and Leavitt (1998), studying 16–30-month-old children with DS and two groups of TD children, one of similar CA, one of similar MA, also report that the mothers of the children with DS were more directive than the mothers of the TD children. However, the mothers of children with DS also supported their children's object play to a greater extent and gave more vocal praise. Interestingly, for the children with DS there was no relationship between maternal directiveness and either the children's object play or their vocalizations. But there were significant correlations between maternal support for object play and the children's play and vocalizations. These authors conclude that maternal directive behavior may not have an adverse effect on the play of young children with DS.

There is also evidence that communication between children with DS and their parents may not proceed very smoothly. Several studies have demonstrated that when children have DS, many more clashes or overlaps occur between the children's vocalizations and the parents' vocalizations (e.g., Buckhalt et al., 1978; Jones, 1977). This lack of synchrony seems to be there from the earliest months in the baby with DS, and the frequency of overlaps greater than 1 second increases over the first 6 months (Berger, 1990; Berger & Cunningham, 1981; 1983). A number of factors may contribute to this. For example, that as they get older, children with DS seem to pay less and less attention to what other people are saying, and at the same time their parents are talking to them more than they would to TD children.

Children with DS will also communicate with other family members. Summers, Hahs, and Summers (1997) examined the conversations of 8–9-year-old TD children with a sibling of about 4 years while they played together. Twenty-six of the younger siblings were TD and 37 had disabilities, including 14 with DS. Interestingly, although the children with DS produced shorter MLUs and fewer words and utterances than the TD preschoolers, the siblings of the children with DS talked much more than the siblings of TD preschoolers. In addition, there was no relationship between the MLUs of the children with DS and their siblings, whereas there was a significant correlation when both siblings were TD. Nevertheless, the siblings of children with DS engaged in more joint activity than the siblings of TD children. However, they were also more likely to change the topic of conversation, although they were no more directive than the older siblings of TD children.

It is clear that early communication between children with DS and their mothers and older siblings is different from that which occurs between TD children and their mothers and siblings. But does this matter? Is it important for the subsequent development of babies with DS? If our present understanding of the relevance of early interaction for the development of TD babies is correct, then it seems that these delays and differences must have effects. It may be impossible to disentangle these likely effects from effects directly to do with the fact that the children have DS. Nevertheless, such possibilities should be considered, particularly since they may have implications for how these children's development could be aided.

Harris, Kasari, and Sigman (1996) found no relationship between mothers' verbal and nonverbal behavior when playing with their 1–3½-year-old children with DS and the children's gain in expressive language 13 months later. However, children whose mothers maintained their children's attention on an object selected by the children and did not try to redirect their children's attention made greater gains in receptive language 13 months later. A similar pattern of results was also observed for TD children of similar MA, although the relationships with receptive language were not significant.

A study from the same laboratory (Kasari, Freeman, Mundy, & Sigman, 1995) observed 1–3½-year-old children with DS and TD children matched for language age when a remotely controlled robot moved towards the child, and the parent and researcher expressed either fear or joy. For the TD children, the amount they looked from the robot to the parent was correlated with both their receptive and expressive language at the time of the experiment and also 13 months later; for the children with DS, the only significant correlation, which was small, was with their expressive language 13 months later. In addition, how quickly the TD children made their first shift in attention from parent to robot, or vice versa, was correlated with both their receptive and expressive language 13 months later; these correlations were not significant for the children with DS. For the children with DS, but not the TD children, their receptive and expressive language 13 months later were correlated with how much they looked at the robot. These results indicate that language development in TD children appears to be related to the extent to which they relate objects and people, whereas for children with DS the relationship appears to be with their interest in objects. These findings point to rather different processes underlying the development of language in children with DS.

An interesting study by Berger and Cunningham (1981) suggested that it might be possible to change certain aspects of the interaction between babies with DS and their parents. Berger and Cunningham noted that the increase in eye contact, which the babies with DS made with their mothers from 3 months onwards, seemed to be associated with the mothers becoming much more positive and involved with their babies. They additionally found that if the mothers of children with DS of around 23 weeks were asked to imitate their babies' facial and vocal behaviors and not to initiate anything themselves, their babies smiled more than when their mothers interacted with them normally. The babies with DS also made more noises when their mothers imitated them than when they interacted normally. This suggests that the behavior of the mothers may be inhibiting the babies with DS and that if the parents of babies with DS fit their behavior to the babies' then the babies respond more.

Unfortunately, these potentially exciting findings have not been replicated (Berger, 1990). Berger reports that seven children with DS who were visited at home on an average of four occasions between 14–43 weeks did not show any clear and consistent evidence of smiling and vocalizing more when their mothers imitated them compared to when they interacted normally. In the same study Berger also videoed the mothers playing with toys with their children in two conditions: with no intervention and when the mothers were asked to present the toys more slowly. Berger reports that some, but not all, of the children showed greater interest and manipulation of the toys when they were presented more slowly. This is clearly an area which needs more research before we are in a position to make suggestions about how to intervene most effectively.

It is clear from the evidence discussed in this section that the behaviors and early communicative interactions of young children with DS and their family members differ in many ways from those of TD children and their families. Young children with DS seem to pay less attention to what is going on around them, and take less notice of the vocalizations of other people. This may partly explain the delay in, and sometimes complete absence of, the development of meaningful vocalizations by some children with DS.

What are the characteristics of the language of children with DS?

The expressive language skills of children with DS are not as good as would be expected on the basis of their MA, although there are large individual differences. In particular, it is the syntactic skills which are most affected, with the majority of children with DS having lexical and pragmatic skills in line with their MA. A further problem is that these children often have poor articulation. Nevertheless, their comprehension of language is usually considerably better than their expressive language. In this section I shall consider the nature of the language of children with DS and also the relationship between their language and other areas of development.

Perhaps surprisingly, given the differences which appear later, the early vocalizations and babbling sounds of babies with DS seem to be quite similar and to follow the same developmental sequence as TD babies (e.g., Lynch, Oller, Steffens, & Buder, 1995a; Smith & Stoel-Gammon, 1996), although babies with DS begin to produce canonical babbles (e.g., "baba") several months later than TD babies and their production of these are less stable (Lynch et al., 1995b).

Children with DS are delayed in when they begin to produce words, although there is considerable variability between children which may be due in part to variations in hearing loss. For example, of 41 children with DS aged 20–82 months, most of whom were involved in an intervention project, Beeghly et al. (1990) report that 4 children aged 20–30 months had no spoken language, 7 aged 24–66 months had single words, 19 aged 26–74 months were beginning to combine words, 8 aged 60–82 months were combining words fairly consistently, and 3 aged 61–76 months were consistently combining words.

Their vocabularies do increase with age, although more slowly than TD children. Hart (1996) followed nine children with DS monthly from when the children were 1–3 years until they were 5 years old. The age at which they had acquired 50 words listed on the MacArthur Communicative Development Inventory (CDI: Fenson et al., 1991) varied between 2 and 4 years. Interestingly, whereas TD children's vocabularies typically increase very rapidly after 50 words have been acquired, this occurred to a much lesser extent, if at all, in the children with DS. In addition, while the TD children's MLU increased from 1 at 1 year to 3.5 at 3 years, by 5 years none of the children with DS had a MLU in excess of 3, and four of the children had MLUs of less than 2. A clear relationship is found between MLU and CA in TD children, but this relationship was not evident for 10 children with DS aged 6–15 years (Fabbretti, Pizzuto, Vicari, & Volterra, 1997), although Chapman, Seung, Schwartz, and Kay-Raining Bird (1998) did find a relationship between age and MLU for 47 children and adolescents aged 5–21 years.

The vocabularies of children with DS are generally in line with their MAs particular if both signs and spoken words are included (cited in Buckley, 1993; Miller, Seeley, Miolo, Rosin, & Murray-Branch, 1992). Caselli et al. (1998), also using the MacArthur CDI, found that 1–4-year-old Italian children with DS, matched with 8–17 month old TD children for word comprehension, produced a similar number of words although the children with DS were producing more gestures, especially as their comprehension of words improved. Harris, Bellugi, Bates, Jones, and Rossen (1997) also found that 1–6-year-old children with DS with fewer than 300 words were reported by their parents to use more gestures than similarly aged children with Williams syndrome (WS), a rare genetic disorder also associated with LDs, although the children did not differ on word comprehension or production. It seems likely that the relatively greater use of gestures in children with DS may reflect their good visual–spatial short-term memory and poor auditory short-term memory.

In contrast to their relatively preserved lexical skills, the grammatical constructions produced by children with DS are noticeably limited. Unlike TD children who usually begin to combine words when their vocabularies contain about 50 words, word combinations are not produced by children with DS until they have about 100 words (Buckley, 1993). And even though their vocabularies may continue to increase in size, the spoken language of children with DS is characterized by short telegraphic sentences. For example, Jenkins (1993) compared the expressive language skills of children with DS aged 6½–13½ matched for verbal comprehension with TD children and children with other LDs but not DS, and reported that the children with DS produced less mature language and in particular used fewer auxiliary verbs than the TD children and fewer pronouns than children in both comparison groups. However, the syntactic skills of individuals with DS do appear to continue to develop throughout adolescence and into early adulthood (Chapman et al., 1998).

Several studies using parental reports based on the MacArthur CDI have confirmed that poor syntactic skills are the main feature of the language of children with DS. For example, Harris et al. (1997) found that even though the children with DS and with WS, matched for word comprehension, were reported by their parents to be similarly delayed with respect to expressive word production, the children with DS produced sentences which were grammatically much simpler. Similarly, Vicari, Caselli, and Tonucci (2000b), using parental reports based on the MacArthur CDI and other assessments, found that 4–7-year-old children with DS matched with TD children for NVMA did not differ in lexical development but did differ in a number of other respects. In particular, the children with DS used simpler and more telegraphic sentences, understood less, and were able to repeat fewer phrases and made more errors. Nevertheless, a relationship was still found between the children's vocabulary and grammatical ability.

Many of the studies examining the language skills of children with DS have studied children acquiring English. English is characterized by relatively complex syntax and simple morphology. In other words, the ways in which morphemes are built up into words is relatively simple, whereas the ways in which words are combined into sentences is fairly complex. Italian, in comparison, has more straightforward syntax but more extensive morphological structures. Despite these differences in language structure, Fabbretti et al. (1997) found that when describing pictures 6–15-year-old Italian children with DS, compared to 2–6-year-old TD children matched for MLU, used similar vocabulary, produced a larger number of simple sentences, a similar number of complex utterances, made some morphological errors and left out more function words, such as articles, prepositions, pronouns, auxiliary verbs, and sometimes produced words and sentences which were semantically inconsistent with the pictures they were describing. From these findings, Fabbretti et al. argue that it is the morphosyntactic components of language which are most impaired in children with DS.

Fabbretti et al. only examined sentences which contained a verb in their analyses and it is noteworthy that Hesketh and Chapman (1998) found that adolescents with DS, average age 15½ years, produced fewer verbs per utterance than TD children, mean age 3½ years and matched for MLU, when talking about personal events or stories. Interestingly, the adolescents with DS produced a greater number of different verbs, presumably because they were chronologically older and had been exposed to language for much longer, and the number of verbs per utterance did increase with increases in MLU.

Fowler (1990) suggests that the syntactic problems observed in the language of children with DS may reflect problems in retaining long sentences in memory in order to process them. Given that phonological working memory has been found to be limited in children with DS (Hulme & MacKenzie, 1992), it seems likely that this is related to the suggestion that children with DS may learn to read not by using a phonological route but by relating the written word directly to its meaning (see page 220). However, it is likely that it is phonological long-term memory that is impaired since phonological short-term memory has been implicated in the acquisition of vocabulary (e.g., Gathercole & Badderley, 1989) which, as we have seen, is often well in advance of syntactic development in children with DS. Also, Vallar and Papagno (1993) report a case of a 23-year-old Italian woman with DS who had excellent vocabulary skills in more than one language and who had evidence of normal phonological short-term memory skills but impaired verbal long-term memory.

Despite the relatively poor syntactic skills, the pragmatic skills of children with DS are fairly good when compared to TD children of similar language ability. Thus, Johnston and Stansfield (1997) found that parents, interviewed using the Pragmatics Profile of Early Communication Skills (Dewart & Summers, 1988), reported very similar pragmatic skills for their 2½–4½-year-old children with DS and 1–2-year-old TD children matched for language comprehension age, with the children with DS being ahead of the TD children in several areas. Leifer and Lewis (1984) matched children with DS aged 3½–4½ with 1½–2-year-old TD children on the basis of MLU and found that when interacting with their mother for 30 minutes, the children with DS demonstrated better conversational skills than the TD children, the children with DS being more likely to answer questions appropriately and to take their turn in the conversation. Beeghly et al. (1990) report similar findings for children with DS aged 2½–7¾ compared to TD children matched for MLU. The children with

DS were better than the TD children at maintaining conversations and taking turns appropriately, although there were no differences when the children with DS were compared to TD children of similar MA.

In addition to differences in the structure of the language produced by children with DS, the pitch, or fundamental frequency, of their speech is higher than that of TD children (e.g., Weinberg & Zlatin, 1970). However, as they get older, the difference may diminish (e.g., Montague, Brown, & Hollien, 1974), until by adolescence it is actually lower (e.g., Goueffic, Vallencien, & Leroy-Boisivon, 1967).

The spoken language of children with DS is also characterized by poor articulation which often makes it difficult for others to understand what they are saying (e.g., Kumin, 1994; Stoel-Gammon, 1997). Thus, Kumin found that 59% of parents of over 700 children and adolescents with DS who had some spoken language reported frequent problems with intelligibility, 38% problems some of the time and only 3% few or no problems. Further, Brown-Sweeney and Smith (1997) report that 7–8-year-old and 12–13-year-old children with DS produced more articulation errors than TD children of similar CAs. Similarly, So and Dodd (1994) found that 4–9-year-old Cantonese-speaking children with DS made more articulation errors than children with LDs but not DS of similar CAs and MAs. Given that Cantonese has a simpler phonological structure than English, So and Dodd suggest that children with DS have impaired phonological planning.

However, some evidence suggests that children with DS eventually do acquire the repertoire of speech sounds, albeit in a different way. Thus, when Kumin, Councill, and Goodman (1994) examined 3 monthly-speech records of 60 children with DS between the ages of 9 months and 9 years, they found great variation in the age at which different speech sounds were produced and the order of emergence did not parallel that seen in TD children. Van Borsel (1996) found more similarities than differences in articulation of adolescents and young adults with DS compared to 2–4-year-old TD children. Interestingly, Dodd (1976) found that children with DS aged 10½ tended to pronounce words differently each time they said them. Based on this finding, Dodd and Leahy (1989) set up an intervention study with four young children with DS. The intervention involved the parents accepting only one pronunciation of selected words from their child. Encouragingly, considerable improvements in pronunciation were reported over a 13-week period.

Despite the poor expressive language skills of children with DS, their comprehension of language is usually reported to be much better. Thus, Hasan and Messer (1997) found that the comprehension skills of 10 children with DS aged 1–4 years exceeded their expressive language by 4–13 months. Parents of 1–4-year-old children with DS also report that their children's comprehension skills are better than their expressive language skills (Caselli et al., 1998), and Chapman and colleagues (e.g., 1998; Chapman, Schwartz, & Kay-Raining Bird, 1991) found no difference between the vocabulary and syntactic comprehension of 47 children and adolescents with DS aged 5–21 years and 2–6-year-old TD children matched for MA, although their comprehension of vocabulary was better than their comprehension of syntax and this difference increased with age.

Finally in this section I want to consider the relationship between language and other areas of development in children with DS, in particular early vocalizations, pre-linguistic communication, and cognitive development. Lynch et al. (1995b) reported a relationship between parental reports of the age at which their babies with DS began to babble and their social and communicative behaviors at 27 months. This is intriguing since a relationship has also been reported between nonverbal requesting and social interaction in children with DS aged 1–3 years and their expressive language a year later, a relationship which was not found in TD children who were initially of similar mental and language ages (Mundy et al., 1995). However, when initial language skills and CA were taken into account, there was no relationship between the ability of the children with DS to share attention with the researcher at time 1 and their subsequent expressive language. Given that, relative to TD children, the children with DS produced fewer nonverbal requests at time 1 and had poorer expressive language a year later, Mundy et al. suggest that requesting may be a particular area of difficulty for children with DS, both nonverbally and verbally. Interestingly, no relationships were found in the children with DS between MA and either expressive or receptive language a year later, or between various measures of nonverbal communication and receptive language a year later.

The relationship between language and specific measures of cognitive development in children with DS have also been explored. Moore, Clark, Mael, Rajotte, and Stoel-Gammon (1977) found a relationship between the MLU of 3½–5½-year-old children with DS and their understanding of objects, and of the ways in which objects relate to one another and to people, rather than to their CA or MA. However, when Messer and Hasan (1994) examine the use of particular types of words and object understanding in 1½–3-year-old children with DS, they found no clear relationships. Thus, there was no systematic association between the children using words to signify disappearance and their ability to find an object following an invisible displacement, between words signifying success and failure and understanding of means–ends, or between the vocabulary expansion and the ability to group related objects. However, they did find that most children did not start to produce two-word utterances until they showed evidence of being able to process two pieces of information, such as finding two objects hidden in different places.

Earlier in this chapter we saw that play, in particular symbolic play, has been found to be related to language development in children with DS, although the relationship is not as strong as for TD children (Beeghly et al., 1990) and does not predict language a year later (Sigman & Ruskin, 1999). When Beeghly et al. examined the symbolic play skills and linguistic abilities of 41 children with DS, the two areas seemed related, in that the children who had no language showed no symbolic play and children at the one-word stage showed evidence of simple symbolic schemes. However, when 28 of the children were matched with TD children for MLU, the symbolic play of the children with DS was ahead of that of the TD children in terms of complexity and awareness of social roles. Interestingly however, the two groups did not differ in their ability to substitute one object for another. When the children with DS were compared to TD children matched for MA, only the object substitution skills differed, with those of the children with DS being less mature. Following Bates, Bretherton, and Snyder (1988), Beeghly et al. suggest that the inferior object substitution skills of the children with DS may relate to their later syntactic difficulties.

It is quite clear from the evidence reviewed in this section that children with DS have particular difficulties with language. Their receptive language skills are much better than their expressive language abilities and, although they may have quite extensive vocabularies, their expressive language is characterized by poorly articulated short utterances. It seems very likely that these linguistic difficulties will lead to differences in how other people perceive them and interact with them.

Social and emotional development

Are children with DS particularly sociable?

In his account of DS, Down wrote: "they have considerable power of imitation, even bordering on being mimics. They are humorous, and a lively sense of the ridiculous often colours their mimicry" (1866). This view of people with DS as sociable, friendly, outgoing, and amusing has become almost as accepted a part of the syndrome as their LDs. However, it may simply reflect the fact that they show more interest in people than objects (e.g., Ruskin et al., 1994b).

An alternative explanation proposed by Fidler and Hodapp (1999) is that individuals with DS may be perceived as sociable because they tend to have more babylike facial features than other children. In order to examine this, they took objective measurements of the facial characteristics of photographs of twelve 10-year-old boys with DS and calculated an overall babyfaceness score. Undergraduates then rated the photographs for physical appearance, personality traits, and behavior. The babyfaceness scores correlated with perceived babyfaceness and the six photographs of children with the highest babyfaceness scores were judge to be more naive, warmer, more honest, kinder, more likely to cuddle with their mother, comply with friends, believe a far-fetched story, in other words more immature, than the children with lower babyfaceness scores. Given that photographs of children with DS are judged to be more babylike than photographs of TD children and children with other chromosomal abnormalities of similar age, this could account for children with DS being perceived as especially affectionate and easy to get on with.

Notwithstanding these findings, it is important to consider the social behaviors of children with DS and in this section I shall examine studies of temperament and personality, everyday social and living skills, behavior problems, and appreciation and expression of emotion. Unfortunately, with the exception of studies of emotion, most studies in this area have been based on ratings of the children's behavior, rather than on direct observation. Given Fidler and Hodapp's findings, it is possible that raters judge the children with DS to be more sociable than they actually are because the raters perceive them as more babylike. Alternatively, raters may have low expectations of individuals with DS and, as a result, any sociable behavior is overemphasized simply because it is not expected. Both of these would inflate the sociability ratings given to children with DS.

Babies with DS are often perceived as not particularly demanding, seldom crying for attention. However, this view that babies with DS are "good" babies is not supported by the literature on children with DS aged over 6 months, although Beeghly (1999), reviewing studies of temperament in children with DS based on parent rating scales, points out that methodological differences between studies make it difficult to reach clear conclusions. Nevertheless, she does conclude that although children with DS vary a great deal in their temperamental characteristics, many are characterized as less persistent, more sociable, and more positive in mood than TD children. As they get older, they are perceived as temperamentally easier than TD children of similar age, although this latter finding may simply reflect adaptation on the part of the family. In contrast, the results of studies examining the behavior of children with DS do not provide much support for the view of children with DS being especially sociable (e.g., Huntington & Simeonsson, 1993; Serafica, 1990), although there is some evidence that children with DS may be more sociable at younger ages than when older and that females with DS may be more sociable than males with DS.

A number of studies have examined the everyday social and living skills, or adaptive behavior, of children with DS. For example, Dykens, Hodapp, and Evans (1994) interviewed the parents of 1–12-year-old children with DS, using the Vineland Adaptive Behavior Scales which assess personal and social sufficiency in terms of communication, daily living skills, and socialization. The children, whose mean age was just over 6 years, were functioning at the level of 3-year-olds in each skill area on average, although their communicative skills were less good than their other skills. The skills developed with CA, particularly at the younger ages. Thus, the correlation between age and overall adaptive behavior was significant for children under 7 years old, although not for children aged 7 or older. Thus, the older children seemed to have reached a plateau in their adaptive behaviors.

A longitudinal study of adaptive behavior was carried out by Hauser-Cram et al. (1999) using the Vineland Adaptive Behavior Scales and following 54 children with DS from 3 months to 5 years. Although they do not report correlations with CA, the findings do indicate development with increasing age. However, they did not find any relationship between the mental development of the children and their adaptive behavior. They did report that the children's adaptive behaviors were best predicted by their mothers' assessment of how supportive and cohesive the family was.

Children and young people with DS are more dependent than TD young people, which is not surprising given the LDs commonly associated with DS. For example, Turner, Sloper, Knussen, and Cunningham (1991) examined self-sufficiency in 111 children with DS aged 6–14 and found that the most self-sufficient were characterized by, among other things, being older, more able intellectually and academically, showing fewer behavior problems, being less distractible, and more likely to be in an integrated school setting. Carr (1988) reported that at 21, when most TD young adults would be independent, just over 40% of 41 young people with DS were independent with feeding, bathing, dressing, and going to the toilet. These were among the most able intellectually. The others needed help in one or more of the areas. In addition, only 26% could be left alone for more than 1½ hours.

Thus, children and young people with DS show adaptive behaviors characteristic of younger TD children. Differences have also been found when children with DS have been compared to children with other LDs. For example, again using the Vineland Adaptive Behavior Scales, Loveland and Kelley (1991) report no differences in communication and daily living skills for children with DS and children with autism under 7 years, but the children with DS had more advanced socialization skills. Nevertheless, both groups of children were behaving like much younger TD children. Rodrigue, Morgan, and Geffken (1991) reported similar findings with young people with either autism or DS aged 2–19 years, and also found no difference in the socialization skills of the young people with DS and 1–9-year-old TD children, with both showing more sophisticated socialization skills than the young people with autism.

This comparison with children with autism may be somewhat misleading since one of the characteristics of autism is a lack of social skills (see chapter 6). However, a study by Gibbs and Thorpe (1983) suggests that children with DS may be more sociable than children with other LDs. They asked non-professional aides in schools for children with LDs to say which of over 100 adjectives characterized individual children with and without DS of about 11 years old. Although the raters were very familiar with children, some of the raters, even with repeated questioning, failed to show any awareness of their diagnoses. These latter raters were called the naive group. A number of adjectives were found to be consistently associated with DS and distinguished them from the other children. These fitted in quite well with the stereotype of children with DS as being outgoing and sociable. When the naive and non-naive raters were compared, it was found that the non-naive raters perceived the children with DS as fitting the stereotype more closely than the naive raters, although the stereotype still emerged from the naive raters. This supports the idea that adults' interpretation of children's behavior depends to some extent on what they expect. However, there was a marked difference between the naive raters' ratings of the children with and without DS, which suggests that children with DS of about 11 are perceived as more sociable than other children with LDs.

The prevalence of behavior problems associated with DS has attracted interest. Coe et al. (1999) compared parent and teacher reports of both adaptive behavior and behavior problems for 44 children with DS and 44 TD children, aged 6–15 years. Consistent with other reports, the children with DS had adaptive behavior scores characteristic of younger TD children. In terms of behavior problems, 32% of the mothers of the children with DS and 59% of their teachers reported severe behavior problems. The corresponding figures for the TD children were 14% and 19%. The parents of the children with DS reported more attention problems than the parents of TD children, whereas the teachers of the children with DS reported more conduct disorders, more attention problems, more psychotic behaviors, and more social withdrawal than the teachers of TD children.

Other studies also indicate that behavior problems are reported quite frequently for children with DS. For example, Gath and Gumley (1986) found that although 31% of 193 children with DS were judged to be well adjusted, 38% had significant behavior problems. In a study by Turner and Sloper (1996), parents of 91 children with DS aged 7–14 years reported an average of 15 behavior problems out of a possible 53, a prevalence of 28%. Three years later the same parents reported 11.8 behaviors on average, a prevalence of 22%. Dykens and Kasari (1997) reported that about two-thirds of a group of 35 children with DS, mean age 11 years, were described as stubborn, argumentative, inattentive, disobedient, and prone to withdrawal.

In comparison to these findings, Pueschel, Bernier, and Pezzullo (1991) found relatively few differences in behavior between 40 children and adolescents with DS aged 4–16 years and their nearest aged TD sibling. In this study parents completed behavior checklists for both children, and no differences were found for 102 of the 118 behaviors. The differences which did occur included the young people with DS preferring to play with younger children and acting too young for their age, concentrating less well, being more dependent, impulsive, irritable, and disobedient, demanding more attention, and having more problems sleeping than their siblings. Stores (1993) also found sleep problems to be more frequent in 36 children with DS aged 4½–13 than for 50 TD children aged 5½–11. Interestingly, Stores found a relationship between the frequency of sleep problems and irritability, hyperactivity, and number of stereotyped behaviors shown during the day. These preliminary findings warrant further study.

There is also evidence of continuity in behavior problems. Thus, although Turner and Sloper (1996) found a decline in the number of behavior problems reported by parents of children with DS over a 3-year period, continuity for the different behaviors ranged from 79% for telling deliberate lies to 13% for poor appetite. Carr (1992) also reported some continuity in behavior problems, with around 50% of children with DS at 11 who were either aggressive, had tantrums, pestered for attention, or were rebellious, showing similar behaviors at 21. Interestingly, the parents' approach to discipline did not seem to be related to whether the behavior persisted over the 10 years.

I now want to turn to a rather different aspect of social behavior, that of understanding emotions. How good are children with DS at understanding emotion? Knieps, Walden, and Baxter (1994) suggest that 1–3½-year-old children with DS may not perceive the affective nature of a situation in the same way as 1–2-year-old TD children, matched for developmental age. In this study parents reacted positively or fearfully to a mechanical toy. The affective responses of the TD infants corresponded with those of their parents. In comparison, the responses of the children with DS were not consistent with those of their parents, the children expressing more positive than negative affect in the fearful situation and more negative affect following positive reactions.

Children with DS also have difficulty recognizing that two different people are expressing the same emotion. Pitcairn and Wishart (2000) matched 8–14-year-old children with DS for the ability to recognize faces with similar aged children with LDs and 3–5-year-old TD children. The children with DS were less good than either of the other groups at identifying which of two photographs was of a person expressing the same emotion as a person in a third photograph, although the performance of the children with DS was above chance level. In comparison, the three groups of children did not differ when they had to identify which photograph was of the same person as the target photograph, or identify which of three photographs of the same person was expressing how a person in a story would be feeling. Interestingly, the overall performance of the children with LDs and the TD children correlated significantly with CA, whereas this was not the case for the children with DS.

Support for this latter finding comes from Kasari, Freeman, and Hughes (2001). The CA of children with DS, mean 7 years, was not correlated with three measures of emotion understanding: naming the emotions of happy, sad, anger, and fear drawn on faces made of felt; recognizing emotion terms by selecting the correct face when different emotions were named; identifying the appropriate face for a puppet involved in various scenarios. For TD children of similar MA, CA was correlated with naming and identifying emotions. In addition, whereas children with DS, mean CA 7 years MA 3 years, performed as well as TD children of similar MA on the tasks, older children with DS, mean MA 4 years, were less good at naming and identifying appropriate faces than TD children of similar MA. Further, over two years, when their MAs increased from 3 to 4 years, children with DS showed improved emotion-naming ability, but no change in their ability to recognize emotions or identify appropriate emotions.

Several studies have shown that children with DS may have better understanding of emotion and express more emotion than children with autism. For example, Loveland et al. (1994) found that 6–23-year-old individuals with DS and VMAs of 3–9 years were able to imitate facial expressions of happiness, anger, sadness, and surprise and produce the labeled emotion at above chance level and better than children with autism. In a further study, Loveland et al. (1995) played a script which verbally expressed an emotion and participants had to choose which of two actors on video were saying the script which was played out of synchrony with the video. Individuals with DS of similar ages to the previous study correctly identified the actor expressing the same affect on about 65% of trials, and again did better than children with autism even though the children with autism had higher verbal and NVMAs.

Children with DS also show more positive emotion when playing with their mothers than children with autism. St. James and Tager-Flusberg (1994) examined how much 3–8-year-old children with DS and children with autism, matched for MLU, laughed when playing with their mothers over the course of a year. The children with DS laughed more than the children with autism and for both groups the amount of laughter correlated with CA but not with nonverbal IQ or MLU. Bieberich and Morgan (1998) examined the quality of emotional expression while 5–12-year-old children, matched for receptive vocabulary, were playing with their mothers. The children with DS showed more positive affect and less negative affect than the children with autism.

As noted earlier, it is not surprising to find that children with DS show greater affective understanding and expression than children with autism, given that problems in social understanding are a characteristic of autism. This is further supported by Sigman and Ruskin (1999) who reported that 10–12-year-old children with DS showed as much helpful behavior and concern when the experimenter pretended to be distressed as children with LDs and more of these behaviors than children with autism.

Thus, children with DS may be no more sociable than TD children, and possibly less so, although they may be more sociable than children with certain other LDs, notably autism. As Gibbs and Thorpe (1983) and Pitcairn and Wishart (2000) point out, the stereotype of sociability often associated with DS is not supported by evidence.

How is interaction with adults affected by DS?

A number of studies discussed earlier indicate that the nature of early communication between young children with DS and their parents is rather different from that which occurs between TD children and their parents. There are differences in gaze behavior and vocalizations and children with DS are less likely to divide attention between their parent and objects than TD children. There are also differences in how parents behave towards their young children with DS. Overall, the early communications between young children with DS and their parents seem to be less well synchronized than when the children do not have DS. Thus, it is quite clear that interaction with adults is affected when the child has DS. In the present section I shall focus on the nature of the social interaction between adults and young children with DS.

A number of studies have examined the development of particular social behaviors in young children with DS. Berger and Cunningham (1981) reported that babies with DS smiled first on average at 7 weeks, 3 weeks after TD babies. For the TD children, the amount of smiling increased and peaked during the fourth month, after which it declined. The babies with DS, as well as starting to smile later, never attained the same levels as the TD babies. The amount they smiled increased more slowly, reaching a peak at around the beginning of the fifth month, after which it declined. It was also more difficult to elicit smiles from the babies with DS than from the TD babies. Carvajal and Iglesias (1997) also reported that 3–14-month-old babies with DS smiled less when interacting with their mother than TD babies of similar age. Nevertheless, both groups of babies smiled less when their parent adopted a still face, although for the babies with DS the difference between how much they smiled when their mothers interacted with them normally and when their face was immobile was not significant. In other words, the babies with DS seemed less sensitive than the TD babies to changes in their mothers' facial behavior.

Cicchetti and Stroufe (1976) looked at the development of smiling and laughing over the first 2 years of life. The children were observed in their own homes and their mothers played with them in a variety of ways designed to elicit smiles and laughter. The median age for the children first laughing was 10 months compared with 3–4 months for TD children. One child in the study never laughed. Just like TD children, the children with DS were more likely to laugh earlier at auditory and tactual events than at visual or social events. However, the children with DS were more likely to smile when the TD children would laugh, and they took longer to respond. This again supports the idea that children with DS may take longer to process information. Even by early in the second year, the children with DS still did not laugh at sights which cause TD children to laugh, such as their mother pretending to suck on a bottle.

In their study Cicchetti and Stroufe found a clear relationship between the children's cognitive ability and their responses to their mothers. When the group was divided into those who first laughed before 10 months and those who laughed later, there was no overlap between the developmental scores on the Bayley Scales (1969) for the two groups. The four most floppy children did not laugh until they were more than 13 months old. Cicchetti and Stroufe argue that these data support a delay in the development of smiling and laughing in children with DS and that the sequence is similar to that in TD children.

A number of studies have examined the responses of children with DS to being separated from their mothers. All these studies used some version of the classic Ainsworth and Wittig (1969) paradigm, in which the child is initially in a strange room with her mother, followed by a number of brief episodes, in various orders, in which the child is left in the room alone, with a stranger, or with a stranger and her mother. Serafica and Cicchetti (1976) observed the behaviors of children with DS and TD children at around 3 years. Overall, the children with DS reacted less than the TD children. For example, when the parent left, most of the TD children cried, but only one child with DS cried. When their mothers returned, the children with DS spent less time in physical contact with them than the TD children. Similar differences were also reported by Vaughn et al. (1994)

for over 100 children with DS aged 1–4½ years, relative to TD children of about 1 year. These findings suggest that children with DS are less perturbed by separation, and less concerned about getting close to their mother upon her return. This sort of explanation is backed up by what happened when they were alone in Serafica and Cicchetti's study: the TD children looked more towards the door and tended to move around the room, while the children with DS looked more around the room generally and kept fairly still. There was, however, no difference in the amount of smiling and movement towards the mother when she returned.

Cicchetti and Stroufe (1976) interpret these results as indicating a delay or lag in the development of fear reactions in children with DS. However, Thompson, Cicchetti, Lamb, and Malkin (1985) suggest that there may well be differences. They studied 19-month-old children with DS and report that, relative to TD children of similar developmental level and to children of similar CA, the children with DS were less distressed when separated from their parent and also took longer to respond. The children with DS also showed fewer emotional behaviors when separated.

A similar conclusion to Cicchetti and Stroufe was drawn by Berry, Gunn, and Andrews (1980) from their study of children with DS of around 2 years. They argue that children with DS and TD children show qualitatively similar sensitivities to strange situations in which they find themselves separated from their parent and in the presence of a stranger. However, in contrast to the previous studies, most of the children with DS cried when they were separated from their mothers, especially when they were left alone. As in other areas, it difficult to reach any firm conclusions as to the nature of the development of children with DS because of methodological differences between the studies. Not only did the children in these studies differ in age, but the experimental procedures varied. For example, the children were left alone for 3 minutes in the studies by Thompson et al. and Berry et al., but for less time in Serafica and Cicchetti's study.

In Berry et al.'s study, the children with DS seemed to be more aware of the strangeness of the situation and, in particular, of the exits and entrances of their mother and the stranger, than were the children in Serafica and Cicchetti's study. For example, the children with DS tended to watch the door most when they were alone, and least when they were first in the room with their mother. They kept in closer contact with their mother, and looked at her more after her return than before her departure. Unfortunately, as Berry et al. did not include any TD children, it is difficult to compare the two studies.

A further study by Cicchetti and Serafica (1981) with children with DS aged around 3 years led them to argue that although there may be quantitative differences between how TD children and children with DS react in strange settings, their patterns of responding are similar. However, they do point out that such conclusions are tentative. The children with DS showed a slight wariness towards the stranger, but generally responded quite positively, looking, smiling, approaching, and even touching the stranger if the mother was there as well, although they did vocalize less in the stranger's presence. This suggests that children with DS are less distressed than TD children on being left alone with a stranger. When the stranger became increasingly intrusive, the children's reactions became more negative, and their reaction on being reunited with their mother was much more positive than their reunion with the stranger.

These studies show that young children with DS may have a slightly reduced repertoire of behaviors towards people compared to TD children, and they seem to be rather less intense in their responses. Cicchetti and Serafica suggest that they may show less fear because they are less easily aroused. However, none of the studies discussed has really examined the mechanism involved and so the possibility remains that the processes underlying attachment behaviors are different in children with DS and TD children.

Cognitive ability of 2–3-year-old children with DS has also been found to be related to how securely attached they are about a year and a half later, as shown by their behavior in the Strange Situation paradigm (Atkinson et al., 1999), with those with the highest MAs early on being the most securely attached later. Interestingly, 47.5% of the 53 children studied by Atkinson et al. were judged to be securely attached, 20% were classified as insecure, and 32.5% could not be classified. Other studies have reported even higher percentages of children with DS producing patterns of behavior in the Strange Situation which cannot be classified (e.g., Vaughn et al., 1994). This is in contrast to 1-year-old TD children where Vaughn et al. found that 60% were securely attached, 37% insecurely attached, and only 3% unclassifiable. Atkinson et al. also found that those children with DS who were securely attached had more sensitive mothers than the insecure and unclassifiable children. Thus, security of attachment in children with DS is related to both maternal sensitivity and the children's cognitive ability.

In an interesting study also focusing on individual differences rather than group differences, Crawley and Spiker (1983) looked at relationships between various aspects of the children's behavior, and the mother's behavior, while 2-year-old children with DS and their mothers played at home. They found significant relationships between how sensitive the mothers were, the elaborateness of their play, how much stimulation they provided, and how much positive affect they showed to their children. They found no correlation between how sensitive the mothers were and how much they directed what went on. For the children, social initiative, play maturity, and social responsibility were all positively intercorrelated, and correlated with the children's developmental level. They found no relationship between how much the mothers directed the situation and any of the measures to do with the children's competence. If the mothers were directive, then the children were likely to be less interested and seldom to initiate play with objects. The more competent children were more likely to be those who played in harmony with their mothers. These mothers combined sensitivity and directness in ways that provided their children with appropriate stimulation. This study demonstrates clearly the individuality of both the children with DS and the adults with whom they are interacting.

One factor which may influence parents' attitudes to their children and their interaction with them is the impact of the birth on the family. Much has been written about the effects of the knowledge that a child has a disability on those around her, but I shall mention just a few studies. Both Gath (e.g., 1985) and Carr (e.g., 1988) have examined, in some detail, the consequences of the birth of a child with DS for the rest of the family. The initial response of the parents is, not surprisingly, usually one of shock and grief at the knowledge that they have a child with a lasting disability. The parents can often be seen to go through characteristic stages (e.g., Drotar, Baskiewicz, Irvin, Kennell, & Klaus 1975), although the effect will be different for each family. The relationship between the parents may be jeopardized although, if they had a good relationship before the birth, they may be drawn closer together afterwards.

Any disability in a child is going to have effects on the family, but there are likely to be particular effects of DS because it is one of the few disabilities associated with LDs which is diagnosed when the baby is only a few days old. From the beginning, the parents will have been told that their child will probably be unable to do certain things when she is older, and yet initially the parents may be unable to see any difference between their baby and other babies. Cunningham and Sloper (1976) point out that parents may not really notice any difference until their baby is about 7–8 months old, when she fails to start to do things that TD babies of this age are doing, like sitting up on their own, crawling, and standing with help. However, it seems likely that how parents are told initially that their child has DS will influence how they feel about the child. Cunningham, Morgan, and McGucken (1984) reported that those who were most satisfied with how the news was broken were positive and confident about the support services which were available. It seems very likely that such attitudes will make it easier for the parents to accept the child which in turn is likely to contribute to how parents interact with her.

How is interaction with other children affected by DS?

Three quarters of the mothers in Carr's (1988) study, interviewed when their children were 11 and 21, reported that having a child with DS had had either positive or a mixture of positive and negative consequences for other children in the family. Only 17% of mothers reported only negative consequences and this was when the children were 11. In general agreement, Crnic (1990) reports that mothers of children with DS under 8 years old were fairly positive about the effect of their children on the family. He also suggests that children with DS may cause less stress than children with different disabilities, perhaps because more information and help are available about DS than about other disabilities and there is a clearly identifiable peer group.

However, the effect on a child of having a brother or sister with DS is likely to be variable. Gath (1974), for example, reported that problems may arise for older girls in the family, although in 1985 she reported that better facilities had reduced the burden previously put on older daughters. In agreement with this, Carr (1988) found no obvious differences between the siblings of children and young people with and without DS at the ages of 5 and 21 years. Some siblings seem to benefit whereas others do not. It also seems likely that how siblings relate to one another will affect their relationships with their parents and vice versa. Some support for this comes from Corter et al.'s (1992) study of mothers with two children, one of whom had DS. They found that if the child with DS behaved in a negative way towards the sibling, the mother was more likely to show negative behavior towards the child with DS and the TD child showed less positive behavior to the mother.

Rather surprisingly, there has been relatively little research examining the nature of the interaction between siblings when one has DS. Abramovitch, Stanhope, Pepler, and Corter (1987), studying the same families as Corter et al., observed relatively few differences in sibling behavior when one sibling had DS compared with when both were TD, although when one had DS the TD sibling was more likely to assume the role of the "older" sibling, even if actually younger. Knott, Lewis, and Williams (1995), using the same observational methods, compared children with DS and children with autism interacting with a younger or older TD sibling. The children with DS spent more time interacting with their sibling than the children with autism, the TD children initiated more interactions than their sibling regardless of disability, and the children with DS responded more positively and imitated their sibling more often than the children with autism. This suggests that TD siblings are likely to control the interaction more when their sibling has a disability, including DS.

However, as we saw in an earlier section, TD children do not use more directives when their siblings have DS, although they do engage in more joint activity (Summers et al., 1997). Interestingly, Berger (1990) reported observing that TD children were often much better at getting their sibling with DS to play than the parents. He suggested that this may be because the siblings were less anxious about DS than the parents.

Children also interact with peers, both in and out of school. Out of school the level of involvement with other children seems to be lower for children with DS than found among TD children. For example, McConkey (1985) reports that most children with DS under 5 years had few opportunities to play regularly with other children although, compared with children of similar age who had LDs but not DS, they had more opportunities to play with siblings and with peers. Sloper, Turner, Knussen, and Cunningham (1990b) interviewed 123 families with children with DS aged 6–14, and reported that more than half the children took part in organized activities involving other children and over three-quarters played with children other than their siblings, although only half the children had playmates who could be thought of as their own friends. The children with the most contacts were among the most able and likely to come from families with a manual social class background who were not particularly achievement oriented. Nevertheless, 9% of the children only played with their siblings and 4% of families reported that their children had no informal play contact with other children. Even for those children who did play with peers, the frequency of play contacts was fairly low, with 80% of the contacts being weekly or less often, and the majority of the contacts were with younger children, with only 15% of the contacts being with children of similar age.

But what is the nature of the interaction between peers when one of the children has DS? This is becoming an increasingly important question as more and more children with DS are integrated into mainstream settings. Serafica (1990) reviewed a number of studies which have examined the nature of peer interaction when one of the children has DS. She reports studies by Sinson and Wetherick (1981, 1982) showing that TD preschool children interact very little with children with DS, tending to observe them from a distance and playing separately, although there is some evidence that children with DS interact more with peers as they get older (e.g., Knox, 1983). Interestingly, children with DS seem to engage in more peer interaction when the other children also have LDs (e.g., Rogers-Warren, 1980; cited in Serafica, 1990). However, as Serafica concludes, this is an area where more research is required.

chapter six

How do children with autism develop?

Introduction

Since Kanner's original article in 1943, autism has attracted a great deal of attention, particularly since the late 1980s (e.g., Rutter, 1999). Much of the relatively recent research activity stemmed from a landmark paper in 1985 demonstrating that over three quarters of children with autism have difficulties understanding that the beliefs they hold may differ from those of others (Baron-Cohen et al., 1985). This finding has been confirmed in many different studies, using a variety of different, and often ingenious, paradigms and focusing on a wide range of behaviors which are thought to depend on an understanding of minds (e.g., Baron-Cohen, 2000). It led to the proposal that a difficulty with understanding minds is the primary cognitive deficit in autism and can account for many of the difficulties which people with autism have in making sense of the world.

As we shall see shortly, this account of a very specific cognitive deficit has not gone unchallenged. However, what is clear and has stood the test of time is that people with autism exhibit a set of clinical behaviors, characterized by Wing's triad of impairments (1976). These are impairments in social behavior, impairments in communication, and the presence of stereotyped, repetitive behaviors. It has been argued that any theory which is to account for this triad of behaviors must meet three criteria (e.g., Happé, 1994a; Ozonoff et al., 1991a). It must specify a deficit which is universal in all people with autism; the deficit must be specific to autism; the deficit must causally precede the onset of behaviors characterizing autism and be present throughout development. The explanation in terms of a difficulty of understanding minds can account for many of the social and communicative problems associated with autism. However, the fact that some people with autism do demonstrate an understanding of minds in experimental tasks, albeit at older ages than TD children, the fact that a difficulty with understanding of minds cannot account for the stereotyped, repetitive behaviors, and the fact that children with autism behave differently prior to the age at which TD children show an understanding of minds have prompted other explanations of the underlying difficulty.

Two different types of explanation have been proposed (e.g., Charman, 1997). The first is that the theory of mind difficulties result from earlier social difficulties (e.g., Hobson, 1993; Tager-Flusberg, 2001). Thus, Hobson has argued that difficulties with affective aspects of interpersonal social relationships at an earlier stage of development are at the core of autism, and the difficulty with understanding minds is just one consequence of this. Tager-Flusberg and others (e.g., Baron-Cohen, 1993; Mundy, Sigman, & Kasari, 1993) have proposed that difficulties in understanding minds grows out of earlier difficulties in particular aspects of social perception, such as interpreting what another person is attending to from the direction of their eye gaze.

The second type of explanation is that autism results from rather different cognitive problems. One proposal is that the difficulties are due to a deficit in executive function (e.g., Ozonoff et al., 1991a; Russell, 1997). The argument in this account is that people with autism are poor at planning their behavior in order to achieve a particular goal. It is proposed that part of this problem stems from an inability to disengage from salient objects and a failure to inhibit responses which are inappropriate to achieving a specified goal. Similarly, Courchesne et al. (1994) have proposed that attention-shifting difficulties are at the core of autism. Another cognitive explanation is that people with autism have weak central coherence (e.g., Frith, 1989; Frith & Happé, 1994). In this account it is argued that although people with autism can process information, the information is not strongly linked together centrally, and thus the child's perception and understanding of the whole is weak, relative to her perception of the separate parts. In other words, children with autism see the individual trees but fail to see the forest.

These accounts are very different from one another although they are all seeking to explain the same condition. Because of their differences it is not surprising that each of them is better at explaining certain characteristics of autism than other characteristics. The evidence for and against some of these accounts will be discussed throughout this chapter. Interestingly, most of these accounts have emerged from considering the impairments evident in the behavior of individuals with autism. However, Happé (1999) has pointed out that we have learned more about the nature of autism by examining things that they can do alongside areas in which they have difficulties. Clearly it is crucial that any account can explain both strengths and weaknesses.

The focus in the present chapter will be on psychological evidence. However, in order to identify the underlying causes of autism it is important to look beyond psychological evidence. Bailey, Phillips, and Rutter (1996) argued that we need to move towards an account which draws together clinical, genetic, psychological, and physiological evidence. In chapter 1 I considered some of the clinical and genetic evidence. Physiological evidence is likely to make increasingly significant contributions to our understanding of autism in the future as a result of advances in brain imaging techniques (e.g., Deb & Thompson, 1998; Eliez & Reiss, 2000; Filipek, 1999). Of particular significance are functional neuro-imaging studies in which activity in different areas of the brain is measured while individuals engage in different tasks. Such studies can indicate whether problems associated with autism are linked to impairments in particular areas of the brain. While studies using these techniques are not discussed in any detail in this chapter, some will be mentioned at relevant points.

The lack of certainty as to the exact nature of the problem underlying autism makes this chapter rather different from the previous chapters. A further difference is that much of the literature on autism, though not all, has been concerned with describing and explaining the behaviors of these children. It has been less concerned with their development. Indeed the main comment which is often made about their development is that many of the symptoms become less severe as the children get older.

Like other disabilities discussed in this book, there is tremendous variability in the sorts of behaviors and abilities exhibited by children diagnosed as having autism. I shall focus on extreme forms of the behaviors, although the behaviors will not be present to the same degree, nor manifested in the same way, in all children given the label of autism.

Motor development

Children with autism reach the main motor milestones at much the same age as TD children, although there may be a slight delay. However, certain aspects of motor behavior are different (Smith & Bryson, 1994). For example, children with autism have a characteristic way of standing. They can very often be seen standing with their heads bowed as though they were gazing at the floor in front of them and their arms flexed at the elbow with their hands flopping down from their wrists as if they were extremely heavy. The balance of 4–7-year-olds with autism has been reported to be less stable than that of TD children when standing with either eyes closed or open (Gepner, Mestre, Masson, & de Schonen, 1995). Interestingly, Gepner et al. reported that none of the children had any gross motor problems, although they showed some clumsiness. This is in agreement with other studies reporting clumsiness among children with autism (e.g., Manjiviona & Prior, 1995).

When they walk, many of them go along on tip-toe without swinging their arms at all. Very often children with autism can be seen to repeat a particular movement over and over again. For example, they may rock backwards and forwards from one foot to the other; they may wave their arms and legs about and they may pull the same face again and again. These repetitive behaviors seem to be associated with times when they are excited or are absorbed in some sensory experience like watching a light flash on and off. At other times children with autism seem to provide stimulation for themselves. For example, they may twist their hands around in front of their eyes, or they may spin round and round for long periods without apparently becoming dizzy. Some children with autism who are severely disabled may even injure themselves: the ultimate in self-stimulation.

In a review of research on repetitive behaviors in individuals with autism, including repetitive motor behaviors, Turner (1999a) points out that the prevalence of these behaviors in people with autism is not related to IQ whereas this is the case in individuals with LDs but not autism. She summarizes a number of possible explanations for these repetitive behaviors associated with autism. One is that children with autism are highly aroused and that engaging in stereotyped, repetitive behaviors can act to decrease their arousal. Another is that these behaviors, or their consequences, are reinforcing and are therefore maintained. However, neither of these accounts is specific to autism since they also explain the existence of these behaviors in children with LDs but not autism. Nevertheless, as Turner shows, three explanations associated with autism also provide an account of the repetitive behaviors. Thus, proponents of the theory of mind account suggest that repetitive behaviors may be some sort of compensatory mechanism for the difficulties individuals with autism experience in social situations. Weak central coherence can account for children with autism focusing on particular aspects of the environment without regard to how they relate to other aspects, whereas the executive function account suggests that because of planning difficulties children with autism cannot shift from what they are involved in with the result that behaviors are repeated over and over again. Turner concludes that on current evidence none of these accounts can be ruled out.

Perceptual development

How do children with autism respond to sensory stimuli?

The way children with autism react to sensory experiences is often bizarre. At times they may act as though they do not experience the surrounding noises, sights and smells, nor feel things which touch them. They may show no response to a loud noise. They may show no recognition of a well-known person. They may be indifferent to pain or cold. They may not react to a visual stimulus. Thus, Gepner et al. (1995) reported that whereas TD children aged 4–7 wobbled when they stood in the dark and moving stimuli were projected onto a screen in front of them, children with autism did not show any postural reaction to the visual motion. However, at other times children with autism will show that their senses are intact. They will turn to the rustle of a piece of paper. They will gaze intently at a lighted lamp, a spinning top, or a portion of a patterned wallpaper. They will scratch or tap a surface for hours. Even more bizarre is the observation that some children with autism have an intense fear of certain everyday objects, a fear that can only be quelled by removing the object. On the other hand, they may seem oblivious to events that might be quite frightening to TD children, such as the rattle and roar of a large lorry.

This selectivity in the attention that children with autism pay to their environment has been confirmed experimentally. For example, Koegel and Wilhelm (1973) trained children with autism who had profound LDs and TD children to select one of two cards. On each card were drawings of two everyday objects. When the children had learned this discrimination, the extent to which their selection was based on both drawings was examined by presenting cards with drawings of the single objects. The children with autism tended to respond to only one of the trained drawings, while the TD children responded to both trained drawings. Differences can also be seen in the features that children with autism focus on when recognizing faces, relative to TD children. These findings will be discussed later. There is also some evidence that the sensations experienced by children with autism are not as distinct as the TD child's. For example, they may cover their eyes when they hear a sound which they find distressing.

How can these behaviors be explained? Many of the experiences which seem to be attractive to children with autism are repetitive: gazing at moving fingers; listening to bells chiming; tapping or scratching on a surface. Three of the accounts mentioned in the introduction to this chapter can account for these behaviors: executive function, attention-shifting difficulties, and central coherence. A characteristic of an executive function deficit is difficulty disengaging from the present (e.g., Hughes et al., 1994; Ozonoff et al., 1991a). The idea behind the executive function is that it enables a person to plan in order to achieve a goal, and part of planning requires that current activity can be put to one side and replaced by new activity. If children with autism lack executive control, then their attention may be captured by an object, or some aspect of an object or an action, and they will be unable to shift from this. Hence their behavior appears repetitive.

The account in terms of attention-shifting difficulties proposed by Courchesne and colleagues can also explain these behaviors. Interestingly, Harris, Courchesne, Townsend, Carper, and Lord (1999) reported that children with autism, aged 5–10 years, were slower than TD children to respond to a visual target following a visual cue, and the larger the orienting deficit the smaller the vermian lobules VI–VII of the cerebellum which were assessed 3 years earlier. Similarly, Pierce and Courchesne (2001) have reported an association between the size of this area of the cerebellum in children with autism and both extent of exploration and repetitive behaviors, whereas no such association was found in TD children.

The theory of central coherence is very different but can also provide an adequate account of the behaviors. This theory, articulated by Frith (1989) and later by Happé (1994b), proposes that the person with autism has difficulty making sense of situations because of difficulty in drawing together different aspects of the situation in order to create the whole. Thus children with autism will focus on the parts without showing awareness of the overall situation. If children with autism have difficulty in going beyond the sensory impressions because the separate impressions are not brought together into a whole, then this could explain why they engage in repetitive, apparently meaningless, behaviors.

It is important to note, however, that on many occasions children with autism, including those of low ability, recognize everyday objects as whole objects. For example, they respond appropriately to cups, spoons, chairs, and doors. They can also learn about places, for example, where the biscuits are kept, where to hang up their coat, how to get from one place to another. It is also quite evident that they come to recognize people they know well.

Are children with autism good at recognizing people?

Consistent with the idea of weak central coherence is evidence that although people with autism do recognize familiar people, the way in which they go about this may be different from TD children. For example, Langdell (1978) compared the ability of children and adolescents with autism to that of TD children of the same MA, TD children of the same

CAs, and children with LDs of similar CAs and MAs to recognize photographs of their peers. The children with autism were relatively able, having mean IQs above 60, with sufficient language to understand and respond to the task. The photographs were displayed in a variety of ways: upside down; nose only; eyes only; mouth and chin; nose, mouth, and chin; eyes, nose, mouth, and chin; eyebrows and above; eyes and above; and finally the full photograph was shown in the correct orientation. In line with previous research, the TD children were more accurate when they were shown features in the upper part of the face than when they were shown the lower part of the face. The children with LDs but not autism were similar, but the younger children with autism were better when shown the lower features than the upper features. The older children with autism were as good as the younger ones on the lower features, but as good as the TD children of the same CA with the upper features. Another result was that the older children with autism were more accurate than the comparison children at identifying the photographs when they were presented upside down. The younger children with autism were no different from the comparison children with this presentation.

This study shows that more able children with autism are able to recognize familiar people from photographs. However, the findings suggest that children with autism go about this process of identification in a rather different way from children who do not have autism. Children who do not have autism seem to be particularly responsive to features which can be thought of as essentially social, the eyes and the orientation of the face. In contrast, the children with autism do not give these characteristics any particular priority in their recognition of faces.

Recognition of familiar people by children with autism and children with LDs of similar age and language ability was also tested by Boucher, Lewis, and Collis (1998) using photographs of adults and children in their school and the children with autism were found to be impaired. This paper also looked at recognition of familiar voices and the ability of the children to match voices to photographs of familiar people. On both of these tasks the children with autism did less well than children of similar age and verbal ability, and there was some evidence that recognition of voices presented particular difficulties, although this was not replicated in a more carefully designed study (Boucher, Lewis, & Collis 2000).

The ability of children with autism to recognize recently seen photographs of unfamiliar people was examined by Boucher and Lewis (1992). In one experiment the children were familiarized with one set of photographs by finding each target photo from among a large display which included the target. This ensured that all the children attended to the materials. The children with autism were just as good at finding the target photos as children with LDs of similar verbal ability, although the children with autism subsequently recognized fewer of the photographs as familiar. Interestingly, there was no difference when photographs of buildings were used. Very similar findings were reported by de Gelder, Vroomen, and van der Heide (1991) and Celani, Battacchi, and Arcidiacono (1999).

Davies, Bishop, Manstead and Tantam (1994) demonstrated that IQ level affects performance. Children with autism and IQs above 75 were impaired, relative to verbal and nonverbal ability matched controls, on selecting photographs of the same person when different photographs showed the face either from different angles or expressing different emotions, whereas children with autism and lower IQs performed less well but no different from that of matched controls. The same results were obtained when the children had to select photographs in which the same emotion was being expressed, albeit by different people. The fact that differences were apparent in the higher ability children with autism, but not in the lower ability children, points to these difficulties being autism specific, rather than a result of general LDs. A similar pattern of results was also reported with non-facial pictures which lends support to the idea of weak central coherence.

In the Davies et al. study, the children with autism were matched for verbal and nonverbal ability. Many other studies of the ability of children with autism to recognize emotion have matched for either verbal or nonverbal ability. In general, differences have been found when children and adolescents are matched for nonverbal ability (e.g., Bormann-Kischkel, Vilsmeier, & Baude, 1995; Ozonoff, Pennington, & Rogers, 1990; Tantam, Monaghan, Nicholson, & Stirling, 1989) but not when the match is based on verbal ability (e.g., Braverman, Fein, Lucci, & Waterhouse, 1989; Hobson, Ouston, & Lee, 1988, 1989). However, Baron-Cohen, Spitz, and Cross (1993) have demonstrated that similarities in the recognition of emotion between children with autism and children of similar verbal ability may depend on the emotion involved. They reported that there was no difference in sorting emotions caused either by a particular situation or desire, but that the children with autism were inferior to children of similar verbal ability at sorting emotions such as surprise which tend to result from a belief. Awareness of beliefs depends upon an understanding of minds which these authors argue is specifically impaired in autism. This explanation may also account for the greater difficulty which children with autism have with complex emotions having an external locus of control such as pride and embarrassment (e.g., Capps, Yirmiya, & Sigman, 1992) and astonishment (e.g., Bormann-Kischkel et al., 1995).

Nevertheless, although children with autism may be as good as children of similar verbal ability at recognizing at least some emotions, this does not mean that they go about this in the same way. A number of studies suggest that children with autism may be using strategies which do not rely on understanding emotions. For example, inverting photographs has less effect on the performance of children with autism on emotion recognition tasks than on that of controls (e.g., Hobson et al., 1988). Support for this also comes from Davies et al. (1994) who noted that when selecting photos of the same person the children with autism might comment "he has got the same hair as that one," whereas the control children might comment "that's the same man." Such observations are consistent with the idea of weak central coherence in children with autism.

Most of the studies described above have used photographs. A rather different methodology was employed by Gepner, Deruelle, and Grynfeltt (2001). Four–to seven-year-old children with autism and 2–5-year-old TD children matched for developmental age watched a video in which an adult depicted the facial expressions of joy, surprise, sadness, and disgust. Regardless of whether the adult was shown maintaining the expression for 2 seconds or changing from a neutral expression to the emotion over 2 seconds, the children with autism were as able as the TD children to select the photograph showing the adult depicting the relevant emotion. These findings suggest that motion may facilitate the recognition of at least certain emotions in young children with autism.

Interestingly, Moore, Hobson and Lee (1997) also examined whether or not individuals with autism can infer emotion from movement, albeit using a different paradigm. In this study reflective patches were attached to the limbs and body of a person who was filmed carrying out various actions in the dark while a light shone on them. All that could be seen on the resulting film was the reflection of the light on the patches. Using this technique Moore et al. found that 10–19-year-old adolescents with autism were as good as adolescents with LDs matched for verbal ability at recognizing moving point-light displays of a person walking as distinct from point-light displays of various objects such as a ball bouncing. However, most adolescents with autism failed to refer to emotional states when the point-light displays were of people depicting different emotions, whereas most adolescents with LDs and younger TD children did. Further, the adolescents with autism were as able as adolescents with LDs to correctly name actions such as lifting, pushing, digging, shown in the point-light displays but were less good at correctly naming states such as itchy, tired, hurt.

Of relevance here is a further finding reported by Gepner et al. They found that when the children with autism and TD children were divided into two age groups, the younger groups did not differ in their ability to select the correct photograph but the older TD children performed better than the older children with autism. Given that the participants in Moore et al.'s study were all over 10 years old, it may be that differences in emotion recognition emerge with age.

Further support for face and emotion recognition difficulties in children with autism comes from a number of neuropsychological studies. Elgar and Campbell (2001) propose that face and emotion processing involves several cortical pathways linking various brain structures including the right fusiform gyrus and the amygdala. Interestingly, the right fusiform gyrus of individuals with autism is less activated by faces than by objects (Schultz et al., 2000). Further, Howard et al. (2000) reported that adolescents and adults with autism, compared to individuals of similar verbal IQ, were impaired at recognizing facially expressed fear and had poorer facial recognition memories, and these difficulties were associated with enlarged amygdalae which they suggest may indicate functional abnormalities. Critchley et al. (2000) have also demonstrated that the left amygdala and left cerebellum regions of the brains of adults with autism are not activated when they process facial expressions of emotion, whereas these areas are activated when TD adults process facial emotion.

It seems clear that although children and adolescents with autism can recognize people and emotions, they are not as good at either of these as those without autism. Further, even when their performance is as good as that of other children, it seems that they achieve this by attending to features rather than to the overall picture or photograph, although the study by Moore et al. suggests that they can integrate information into a whole. Nevertheless, attention to parts rather than the whole has been used as an explanation for one area at which children with autism excel, visual–spatial skills.

Do children with autism possess special visual–spatial skills?

When Kanner (1943) reported his original observations, he noticed that very often there was something at which the children were particularly good, at least in comparison to the rest of their behavior. A number of these areas of ability involve visual–spatial skills. For example, Kanner reported that all the children did well on the Seguin form board. Certainly their performance on items in intelligence tests which require such skills is superior to their performance on items requiring other sorts of skills (e.g., Lockyer & Rutter, 1969). An experiment by Shah and Frith (1983) supported this. Children and adolescents with autism were matched with children with LDs and TD children for MA, and their ability to locate a shape embedded in a drawing of an object was examined. The children with autism were more accurate and quicker than either of the other two groups. Their accuracy was commensurate with that expected of TD children of the same average CA.

Frith (1989) argued that an account in terms of central coherence can explain these findings since, if children with autism have weak central coherence, the pictures in which the shapes were hidden would not dominate over the separate components of the picture, with the result that they could find the so-called embedded figures more easily. Similarly, the performance of children with autism on form boards is good because they focus on the details of each shape, and the shapes are not linked together as a whole in their heads. A study by Ring et al. (1999) provides some physiological support for this in that different areas of the brain were activated when individuals with and without autism completed the Embedded Figures Test.

One of the criticisms of Shah and Frith's study has been that the materials confounded meaning with wholeness. This was overcome in a subsequent study by Shah and Frith (1993) in which meaningless block designs were used. The children's task was to reproduce abstract patterns using patterned blocks. This study also introduced a comparison between performance with whole patterns and performance with patterns which had been divided up into segments corresponding to the patterns on the blocks. When the whole patterns were used, the performance of the children with autism was superior to that of TD children and children with LDs. Segmenting the patterns eliminated this superiority. Once again these findings are consistent with the suggestion of weak central coherence associated with autism.

A study in 1996 compared the effect of using meaningful and meaningless materials on the ability of children with autism to perceive parts within a whole and failed to confirmed the previously reported superiority of children with autism (Brian & Bryson, 1996). However, the participants in this study were older than those in Shah and Frith's studies and generally more able, which raises the question of whether weak central coherence is only a difficulty during certain phases of development. Interestingly, when Jolliffe and Baron-Cohen (1997) repeated Shah and Frith's original study with older, more able people with autism, they too found no superiority but they did demonstrate that the adults with autism were faster than the TD adults, which Brian and Bryson had not.

Using a rather different paradigm but still relevant to visual–spatial skills, Happé (1996) has provided further evidence in support of weak central coherence. She argued that if children with autism perceive parts of a figure and are less aware of the wholeness of the figure, they should be less susceptible to visual illusions than either TD children or children with LDs. This was confirmed in her study. Thus, for example, children and adolescents with autism were more likely than the other participants to say that the two lines in the Muller–Lyer illusion were of the same length. However, Ropar and Mitchell (1999) questioned whether or not the use of a verbal judgment of same or different could account for this result. In their study, children and adolescents with autism had to adjust the length of the lines in the Muller–Lyer and Hat illusions and the diameter of circles in the Tichener and Ponzo illusions. Using this method, three-quarters of the individuals with autism were found to be susceptible to the illusions, which was similar to the proportion of individuals with LDs, individuals with AS, and TD children of similar VMA. This susceptibility to illusions by individuals with autism was confirmed in a subsequent study with different participants (Ropar & Mitchell, 2001).

In their second study, Ropar and Mitchell examined the possibility that cohort differences could explain the different findings in theirs and Happé's study, in particular whether the children in Happé's study had weaker central coherence than those in their own studies. To examine this, Ropar and Mitchell also gave the children and adolescents a series of visual–spatial tasks, including embedded figures and block design tests. In agreement with previous findings, the children and adolescents with autism performed well on these tasks. However, susceptibility to illusions did not correlate with performance on these visual–spatial tasks, suggesting that different mechanisms may underlie these two areas.

However, other observations of superior visual–spatial skill can be explained by children with autism having weaker central coherence than children who do not have autism. For example, children with autism will often notice a tiny object on a patterned carpet, whereas TD children might miss the object. This may be because the children with autism are not dominated by the overall pattern of the carpet.

An alternative to weak central coherence has been suggested by Mottron and colleagues (e.g., Mottron & Belleville, 1993). They propose that individuals with autism are good at processing both local and global information but, unlike individuals without autism, they fail to show a preference for processing at the global level, and hence have a hierarchization deficit. As a consequence they may show a local bias when others show a global bias as in tasks such as the Embedded Figures Test. However, unlike the weak central coherence account, the hierarchization account argues for intact global processing in autism, such as we saw in Moore et al.'s study of point-light displays.

Several further studies provide support for the intact global processing of individuals with autism (e.g., Mottron, Burack, Stauder, & Robaey, 1999a; Plaisted, O'Riordan, & Baron-Cohen, 1998; Rinehart, Bradshaw, Moss, Brereton, & Tonge, 2000). For example, Plaisted et al. examined the ability of 7–10-year-old children with autism and TD children matched for CA and VMA to detect a target letter of a particular color within arrays of distracter letters. In one condition the target letter (e.g., a red X) matched half the distracters in color but not form (e.g., red T's) and the other distracters in form but not color (e.g., green X's). Therefore to respond correctly the children had to take into account both form and color. In support of intact global processing in autism, the children with autism were faster at detecting the presence of these target letters than the TD children.

Further support for intact global processing in autism comes from studies by Mottron et al. and Rinehart et al. who used stimuli consisting of either letters or numbers composed of smaller letters or numbers respectively (Navon, 1977). Thus, a letter H might be made up of small H's or a different letter, such as S's. In the former the stimulus is the same at both the global and local levels, whereas in the latter, the global and local levels differ. The task was to respond by pressing one key for one target letter, a second key for another target letter. Only one target letter was present on any one trial and could be either large or small. The hierarchization deficit account predicts no effect of target size on speed of responding, whereas the weak central coherence account would predict that individuals with autism would perform faster than individuals without autism when the target letter was small. In fact, Mottron et al. found that 7–20-year-old individuals with autism with nonverbal IQs above 80 responded faster when the target was large than when it was small, whereas TD adolescents matched for age and IQ did not show this difference, although overall the TD adolescents responded faster. Despite not supporting either theory this result does suggest that global processing may be intact in individuals with autism.

Interestingly, and against the hierarchization deficit theory which proposes that processing of local information is independent of global processing, Mottron et al. reported that both groups responded faster when the target was small (i.e. local processing) if the large letter was morphologically similar to the small letter (e.g., large H made up of small A's) than if the letters were less morphologically similar (e.g., large H made up of small E's). Rinehart et al. (2000) also found a global advantage with Navon figures for both TD children and adolescents and individuals with autism, as well as finding that the responses of the individuals with autism to local stimuli were slower when the global stimulus required a different response. In other words, both these studies have demonstrated that individuals with autism can process information at a global level but that information at one level can interfere with processing of information at another level.

Further difficulties for both the weak central coherence and the hierarchization accounts come from two studies by Plaisted, Swettenham, and Rees (1999). Once again Navon figures were used. In one task 6–17-

year-olds with autism and TD individuals of similar age and nonverbal ability were not told whether the target would be a large or small letter (divided attention task) whereas in the other they were (selective attention task). Both theories would predict no difference between the two tasks. However, this was not the case. Both groups were faster to respond to the global target in the selective attention task. In the divided attention task the individuals with autism made more errors when the target appeared at the global level whereas the TD individuals made more errors with local targets. On the basis of these findings Plaisted et al. suggest that individuals with autism cannot inhibit responding at a local level unless they are instructed otherwise.

The evidence included in this section supports the view that children with autism pay particular attention to the details of patterns or objects and less attention to the overall figure. However, whether this is because of a difficulty incorporating separate pieces of information into an overall view (weak central coherence) or due to an absence of preference for the overall view (hierarchization deficit) is not resolved, although clearly in some situations individuals with autism are able to respond at the overall level, even though at other times they do not. The attention to detail shown by children with autism has also been examined in the context of the exceptional drawing ability of some of these children.

Do children with autism have exceptional drawing ability?

A small number of children with autism are exceptionally gifted artistically (e.g., Selfe, 1977, 1983). The children studied by Selfe produced pictures far superior in terms of their photographic likeness to reality than those of TD children of a similar age, in some cases equivalent to those of trained artists. The same is true of the buildings and objects drawn by Stephen Wiltshire (1987) and others studied by Hermelin and colleagues (e.g., Hermelin & Pring, with Buhler, Wolff, & Heaton, 1999). What seems to characterize the drawings produced by these children is the attention to and memory for detail. They reproduce on paper the lines and details which they see in front of them or which they remember. In this way they produce a far more accurate representation than average TD children whose focus is much more on the wholeness of what is being represented. For example, TD children's drawing of a cat lying in its basket may show all four legs of the cat, even if some are tucked out of sight, because they know that cats have four legs; children with autism may draw only one leg if that is all that can be seen. Children with autism draw what is seen, they are not influenced by knowledge of the whole object.

While the exceptional drawing ability fits with Frith's idea of weak central coherence, there is the problem that only a small number of children with autism show exceptional artistic talent. If the weak central coherence argument applied to all children with autism, we might expect all children with autism to produce more accurate or realistic drawings than younger TD children or children with LDs and not autism. This has not been shown to be the case when the children are matched for verbal ability (e.g., Charman & Baron-Cohen, 1993; Lewis & Boucher, 1991) or nonverbal ability (e.g., Eames & Cox, 1994). However, Pring, Hermelin, and Heavey (1995) pointed out that it could be that all children with autism have weak central coherence but that it is even weaker in those who are artistic. In support of this, Pring et al. demonstrated that TD child artists and artistic adults with autism were faster on a block design task than adults with autism who did not have any special artistic ability.

A further study by Mottron, Belleville, and Ménard (1999b) found evidence of a local bias when adolescents and young adults with autism copied lines drawings of objects and meaningless shapes made up of the same lines as the objects. The individuals with autism, who were 12 years and older and had nonverbal IQs greater than 90, copied more local than global features initially compared to TD participants matched for age and nonverbal ability. Further, when copying possible and impossible figures, the individuals with autism were less affected by the fact that some of the figures were impossible. While these findings could be seen to be consistent with the weak central coherence account, Mottron et al. argue on the basis of these and other findings that the results can be explained by the individuals with autism having difficulty maintaining several different spatial patterns in working memory. In comparison, Ropar and Mitchell (2001) failed to find evidence of a local bias when 9–18-year-olds with autism copied complex figures. Sixty-seven per cent of them used a local strategy, compared to 63% of 9–15-year-olds with LDs. However, in this study these participants were matched for VMA. Interestingly, around 50% of 7–12-year-old TD children used a local strategy, which suggests that differences might have occurred if the individuals with autism and LDs had been matched nonverbally, given that children with autism generally have higher nonverbal than verbal IQs (see pages 266–267).

If the exceptional drawing ability of some individuals with autism are a particular characteristic of these individuals then we might expect their artistic skills to be unaffected by outside influences. The question of whether formal teaching can influence the artistic person with autism was explored in a case study of Stephen Wiltshire by Pring and Hermelin, with Buhler and Walker (1997). Stephen was studied while he attended Art School and interestingly Pring et al. reported that the scope of Stephen's art developed in terms of the techniques he used. They illustrated this by his use of differences in tone, something which was absent in his previous drawings. However, they also reported that Stephen's art was still limited in terms of content and the absence of any indication that he was attempting to communicate anything to the viewer beyond the objects portrayed, despite teaching aimed at developing these aspects. Pring et al. viewed these limitations as reflecting the social and communicative impairments which are so characteristic of autism.

Studies of the drawings of children with autism who are not artistic have also demonstrated that certain characteristics of autism are evident in their drawings, in much the same way as has been observed in artistic children with autism. For example, the range of content of the drawings of children with autism, relative to children with LDs but not autism, is more restricted and repetitive (Lewis & Boucher, 1991) and Scott and Baron-Cohen (1996a) reported that children with autism were unable to draw pictures of unreal things which were imagined, such as a two-headed figure, although they could produce drawings of imagined real things. The latter finding was not confirmed by Leevers and Harris (1998) who, rather than asking the children to draw a complete object, simply asked the children to complete a partly drawn picture. Thus, the children were given a picture of a person without a head and asked to make the picture into an impossible person. The children with autism could do this as well as children with LDs and younger TD children. Leevers and Harris argued that their picture completion task demonstrated that children with autism can conceptualize impossible entities and that their task, compared to Scott and Baron-Cohen's, removed the need for the children to plan a whole picture. They argue that if children with autism have a problem with executive function and if, as in Scott and Baron-Cohen's study, they have to draw the whole figure, they may find it difficult to disengage from drawing a real figure in order to make it unreal.

In addition to some children with autism displaying exceptional drawing ability, other children with autism have been reported to show exceptional skills in different areas, particularly calculating calendar dates and playing musical instruments (for an account of a number of individuals with such skills see Hermelin, 2001). For example, O'Connor and Hermelin (1992) report the case of a boy with autism who, within a few seconds, could say what day of the week a particular date would fall up to 28 years ahead. If these exceptional skills reflect these children paying close attention to detail then we might expect children with autism who do not have these exceptional skills to show greater attention to detail in modalities other than the visual modality. Some evidence suggests that children with autism who do not have exceptional musical ability nevertheless may be particularly good at identifying and recognizing musical tones.

Do children with autism possess special musical skills?

A series of studies by Heaton and colleagues (e.g., Heaton, Hermelin, & Pring, 1998; Heaton, Pring, & Hermelin, 1999a) have reported that children with autism who do not have exceptional musical skills perform better than children without autism on a series of tasks assessing recognition and memory of tones and melodies. One task involved presenting four animal pictures, each accompanied by a different tone. The tones were presented again one at a time both immediately and a week later and the children had to identify the associated animal. In one study 64% of 7–15-year-olds with autism assigned 75% of the tones to the correct animal, compared to 7% of children and adolescents without autism of similar age, half of whom were matched with the individuals with autism for verbal IQ and half for nonverbal IQ. Three children with autism, but none of the others, performed at ceiling. In another study half the children with autism correctly indicated 75% of the time which one of the four tones used in the first study was missing when played chords containing three of the tones, compared to 6% of the other children.

On some other tasks the children with autism, as a group, did not show superior musical skills although individual children did. Thus, half the children with and without autism performed at chance level when they had to indicate, when they heard a tone, if it had been included in a previously heard chord of three tones. Nevertheless, almost a third of the children with autism responded correctly 80% of the time, and one boy responded correctly on over 90% of the trials. Intriguingly, this particular boy performed at or close to ceiling on many of these musical tasks and yet he was not particularly good at the Block Design subtest of the WISC. A further interesting finding was that the children and adolescents with autism were as able as individuals without autism to ascribe happy and sad emotions to melodies in the major and minor mode respectively (Heaton, Hermelin, & Pring, 1999b). This suggests that the difficulties that children with autism have recognizing emotion in people is confined to social stimuli.

Some of the tasks on which Heaton et al. (1999a) did not find differences between the children with and without autism involved melodies rather than single tones or chords. Thus, in one study the children were presented with two melodies and had to indicate if they were the same or different. The melodies could differ in two ways, both of which involved a changed note. However, in one the note change did not alter the overall contour of the melody, whereas in the other the contour was altered. If the children with autism are focusing on the individual tones, rather than the overall melody, then they would be expected to notice both sorts of changes. However, this was not confirmed, and both groups performed at chance level when the overall contour of the melody was maintained. Interestingly, one boy with autism identified all the differences.

This last finding suggests that individuals with autism may process melodies in terms of their global characteristics, which is counter to an explanation in terms of weak central coherence. Further confirmation that individuals with autism may process melodies globally comes from Mottron, Peretz, and Ménard (2000). Adolescents with autism and TD adolescents, all over 10 years old and with nonverbal IQs above 80, had to judge if two melodies were the same or different, regardless of any differences in pitch. The melodies could either be in the same key or one was transposed into a near key. Further, the pitch of one note in one of the melodies was changed such that the contour of the melody was either altered or remained the same. Overall, the two groups performed very similarly. Both did better in the untransformed condition than when one melody was transformed and when the note change altered the contour of the melody than when the contour was maintained. This indicates that both the TD adolescents and the adolescents with autism showed intact global processing.

Nevertheless, further analyses did demonstrate that in the untransformed condition the adolescents with autism were better than the TD adolescents at identifying a note difference when the melody contour was maintained. In other words, as well as showing no impairment of global processing, the adolescents with autism demonstrated better local processing. The absence of this group difference when the melody was transposed is further evidence that individuals with autism are making the judgment on the basis of the particular pitch of the individual note. Thus, in the auditory modality, as well as in the visual modality, Mottron and colleagues have provided evidence that both local and global processing are intact in individuals with autism, which is consistent with their theory that although individuals with autism have intact global and local processing skills, they fail to show a preference for global processing, the so-called hierarchization deficit hypothesis (Mottron & Belleville, 1993).

Whether or not these and other findings are accounted for in terms of weak central coherence, hierarchization deficit or something else will await further testing. However, what is clear is that up to 10% of children with autism demonstrate a so-called savant skill (e.g., Happé, 1994b). These islets of ability, along with the superior performance of children with autism on visual–spatial tasks generally, led Kanner (1943) to conclude that they were of normal cognitive potential. However, as we shall see in the next section, this view has not been supported by subsequent research.

Cognitive development

How intelligent are children with autism?

The majority of children with autism have LDs. Thus, Fombonne (1999) reviewed 12 epidemiological studies reporting IQ levels published between 1966 and 1999. Out of almost 2 million individuals aged between birth and 27 years studied, just over 4% were diagnosed with autism. Although there was variability in reported IQ levels across the studies, Fombonne concluded that around a quarter of individuals with autism have IQs above 70, just under a quarter have IQs between 50 and 69, and just over half have IQs below 50.

Non-epidemiological studies of children with autism are in general agreement with these figures, although again there is variation between studies. Thus, Folstein et al. (1999) reported that of 90 individuals with autism aged between 3 and 32 years, 21% had IQs below 30, 24% had IQs between 30 and 49, 17% between 50 and 69, and 38% had IQs above 70. Volkmar, Szatmari, and Sparrow (1993) reported somewhat lower IQs for 199 children and adults with autism: 48% had IQs below 35, 38% between 35 and 69, and 14% had IQs greater than 70. Interestingly, whereas 17% of the males had IQs above 70, this was only true of 2% of the females. There was also a difference at the lower end of the IQ scale, with 58% of the females having IQs below 35, compared to 46% of the males. Sigman and Ruskin's (1999) longitudinal study suggests that the number of children with autism with IQs above 70 may decline with age. They reported that the mean IQ of 43 children with autism assessed between 3 and 5 years was 51 and over 90% had IQs below 70. Eight to nine years later, the mean IQ of the same children was very similar at 49, but just under 70% now had IQs below 70.

Not surprisingly given the visual–spatial abilities associated with autism, their nonverbal IQs are generally higher than their verbal IQs, although this pattern is most marked in those with lower IQs (e.g., Siegel, Minshew, & Goldstein, 1996). Interestingly, Mawhood, Howlin, & Rutter (2000) followed up 19 boys with autism who at 4–9 years had nonverbal IQs of 70 and above. At 21–27 years these young men had a mean nonverbal IQ of 83 compared to a mean of 94 when they were children, and a mean verbal IQ of 82 compared to an earlier mean of 67. In other words, although the mean nonverbal IQ of these relatively able individuals with autism was greater than their verbal IQ in childhood, this difference had disappeared by adulthood.

Nevertheless, the intellectual profile of children with autism is quite distinct. They do much better on nonverbal items than on verbal items (e.g., Happé, 1994c), their visual–spatial skills stand out as being particularly good, and their rote memories are often exceptional. In addition, their reasoning abilities appear to be intact when compared to children with LDs and younger TD children matched for VMA (Scott & Baron-Cohen, 1996b), even when the task requires counterfactual reasoning (e.g., the syllogism "all cats bark; Rex is a cat; does Rex bark?") (Scott, Baron-Cohan, & Leslie, 1999).

Perhaps not surprisingly, given the range of behaviors which are in need of explanation, the search for a specific cognitive deficit has been fraught with controversy. However, Anderson's theory of the Minimal Cognitive Architecture (1992) provides a way of conceptualizing the intellectual abilities of children with autism. As outlined in chapter 5 (page 193), it is proposed that intelligence consists of two independent components: speed of information processing, and individual modules. The uneven profile which characterizes autism would be consistent with intact speed of processing but damage to certain modules. Some evidence in support of this proposal comes from a study of processing speed in children with autism by Scheuffgen, Happé, Anderson, and Frith (2000). Despite having below average IQs, the children with autism showed the same processing speed as TD children of similar age but above average IQ. Further, the children with autism showed faster processing speeds than children with LDs but not autism, matched for age and IQ. However, it is important to note that processing speed was based on inspection time in a visual discrimination task. Given that visual discrimination is relatively preserved in individuals with autism, this measure may not be tapping speed of processing generally.

Nevertheless, consistent with an account of certain modules being damaged in autism, a number of specific explanations have been proposed for aspects of the cognitive development of children with autism. I shall consider these in the following sections as I examine the findings.

Do children with autism have the same understanding of objects as other children?

Since the majority of children with autism are not diagnosed until they are at least 2 or 3 years old, relatively little is known about their behavior and understanding before this age, although the development of instruments identifying children at high risk of autism in the second year of life, such as the CHAT, is changing this. Thus, Swettenham et al. (1998) reported that 20-month-olds with autism, identified through CHAT, spent almost three-quarters of the time looking at objects in a free play setting whereas children with developmental delays but not autism looked at the objects for just over 50% of the time. In addition, the average duration of each look at an object by the children with autism was 11.1 seconds, over twice as long as that of both children with developmental delays and TD children of similar age. Clearly children with autism are interested in objects, but what do they understand?

Over the first couple of years TD children's understanding of objects develops rapidly and one way this period has been examined in children with autism has been by studying home movies (e.g., Lösche, 1990; Rosenthal, Massie, & Wulff 1980). Rosenthal et al. examined movies of nine children with autism, three of whom had been filmed until they were 3 years old, using Piaget's sensorimotor period as a framework (Piaget, 1953). One of the main achievements of this period is the realization by the child that objects exist independently of and separate from herself. According to Piaget, TD children reach this understanding between 18 and 24 months. Only one child in Rosenthal et al.'s study showed behaviors characteristic of the end of the sensorimotor period, and this was when the child was 29 months old. The behaviors of the majority were characteristic of developments reached earlier in the sensorimotor period, for example, finding an object which the child has watched being hidden, and which has not been hidden anywhere else immediately before. This behavior is characteristic of stage 4 of Piaget's sensorimotor period.

Similar findings were reported by Lösche. She examined home film material of eight TD children and eight children with autism between the ages of 4 and 42 months and analyzed episodes in which the children were attending to either an object or person. For six of the children with autism and all the TD children material was available in each of four periods across this age range: 4–12 months, 13–21 months, 22–30 months, and 31–42 months. In the period 4–12 months the majority of the children's behavior, both TD and those with autism, was representative of stage 3 of Piaget's sensorimotor period characterized by the children engaging in repetitive actions on objects. However, whereas with increasing age the TD children's behavior progressed through the sensorimotor stages, this was much less evident in the children with autism. Thus, at 31–42 months, over 40% of the behavior of the children with autism was characteristic of stage 4, compared to less than 10% of the TD children. Further, over 30% of the behavior of the TD children in this period was characteristic of behavior beyond the sensorimotor period, compared to less than 1% of the behavior of the children with autism.

Lösche also reported that behaviors leading to effects that were either immediate (e.g., banging two bricks together) or continuous (e.g., pulling a toy along) amounted to over 80% of the behavior of both groups of children when they were under 1 year. However, whereas by 31–42 months these had dropped to less than 40% for the TD children, they accounted for nearly 70% of the behavior of the children with autism. In contrast, at this age over 60% of the behavior of the TD children was directed at particular goals compared to 31% for the children with autism.

One interpretation of these observations is that the development of object understanding in children with autism is delayed, rather than different, and they reach the various stages later than TD children, although, from these studies, it is unclear whether or not children with autism reach these stages of object understanding at similar MAs to TD children. However, there are numerous accounts of older children with autism behaving in a bizarre way towards objects.

They often seem to be fascinated with regular patterns of objects. They will collect and arrange objects which they have found in an extremely systematic and repetitive way. They will make collections of things like stones and leaves, and get very upset if their arrangements are disturbed. They do not seem to collect objects for any apparent reason. They are likely to handle objects carefully, looking closely at them, turning them around, sniffing them and licking them, as though what are crucial are the sensations they get from the objects, rather than either what the objects are or what they could be used for. They may appear only to be interested in part of a toy or object. Children with autism may hold a toy car and just watch the wheels as they spin them around endlessly. Again, this would be consistent with their apparent interest in the parts rather than wholes which the idea of weak central coherence seeks to explain. Children with autism are not interested in the car wheels as that part of the car which enables it to be pushed across the floor. They are only interested in the effect of spinning the wheels around and around. Interestingly, Williams, Reddy, and Costall (2001) reported that although 3–5-year-old children with autism spent as much time as 1–2-year-old TD children and 1–5-year-old children with DS playing appropriately with toys representing everyday objects, their play was much less elaborate, less varied, and less integrated than that of the other children.

An alternative explanation of these behaviors is that children with autism have difficulties disengaging from objects. Thus, once their attention is captured by an object or by part of an object, they have difficulties shifting their attention elsewhere. Such an explanation forms part of the executive function account that argues that children with autism have specific difficulties with those mental operations which enable disengagement from current activity in order to pursue a goal which requires different actions. However, one of the difficulties with the executive function account is that deficits in this area are not confined to autism but can also be observed in children with other disorders (e.g., Pennington & Ozonoff, 1996). Also, Leekam, López, and Moore (2000) have demonstrated that 2–6-year-old children with autism are as able as children with LDs but not autism matched for nonverbal ability at shifting their attention from a target presented in front of them to a second target appearing to the left or right, regardless of whether the central target remains or disappears. In fact, not only were the children with autism as accurate at the other children, they responded faster.

Nevertheless, a difficulty disengaging from objects has been demonstrated in several studies. For example, Russell, Mauthner, Sharpe, and Tidswell (1991) used two boxes with windows so that the child could see into the boxes but an opponent could not. A chocolate was put in one of the boxes and the child had to indicate which box the opponent should look in. If the child pointed at the empty box, that was where the opponent looked and the child had the chocolate. Four-year-old TD children and children with LDs were good at deceiving their opponents, whereas 3-year-olds and children with autism typically failed to deceive their opponents and consequently lost the chocolate. Hughes and Russell (1993) found that removing the opponent, and therefore the need for deception, had no effect on the outcome. In one task, children with autism still pointed to the baited box even though they only got the sweet if they pointed to the empty box. In a second task children with autism were much more likely than children with LDs or younger TD children to persist in trying to retrieve a marble using an unsuccessful direct route rather than a known successful indirect route.

An interesting study by McEvoy, Rogers, and Pennington (1993) explored problems of inhibiting or deferring responses to objects in children with autism between 3 and 7 years, using a series of hiding tasks. The children with autism were as able as children with LDs and TD children to find an object they had seen hidden in one location, even if this location was different from the hiding place on a previous trial (the classic Piagetian A not B task), and even if there was a delay between hiding and searching. However, if a screen prevented the children from seeing where the object had been hidden, the children with autism perseverated to a greater extent than the others in searching at the location where they had previously found the object rather than trying a second location.

A problem with disengaging from the immediate context has also been suggested to account for another often reported characteristic of autism, namely that children with autism seldom engage in pretence, that is, they do not substitute one object for something else, or attribute a property to an object which it does not have, or act as if something is present when it is not. In order to engage in this type of play the child has to put reality to one side and play *as if* reality was different from how it is. Baron-Cohen (1987) found that, compared to TD 3–5-year-olds and 2–13-year-old children with DS, 4–13-year-old children with autism seldom used non-realistic objects in spontaneous pretend play.

In other words the children with autism did not use objects to stand for something else.

This finding has been confirmed in many studies (e.g., Charman et al., 1997; Libby et al., 1998; Sigman & Ruskin, 1999). Thus, Charman et al. reported that of 10 children who had been identified at high risk for autism on the basis of CHAT at 18 months and for whom a diagnosis was confirmed at 20 months, only one produced any spontaneous symbolic play at 20 months, compared to over 60% of TD children. However, given that the children in this study were all aged 20 months, developmental differences could explain these findings. In support of this, only two out of nine children with LDs but not autism of similar age produced any spontaneous symbolic play and both this group of children and the children with autism had significantly lower verbal and nonverbal abilities than the TD children.

Libby et al. matched 5–16-year-old children and adolescents with autism, 3–6-year-old children with DS, and 2-year-old TD children for receptive and expressive language. Although the children engaged in similar amounts of exploratory, relational, and functional play, the children with autism engaged in more sensorimotor play and less symbolic play than the others. Interestingly, 5 out of 9 children with autism did produce some symbolic play, compared to all 9 children with DS and 8 of the 9 TD children. However, further analyses of the symbolic play showed that although the children in the three groups produced similar amounts of object substitution, only 1 child with autism attributed a false property compared to all the children with DS and 7 TD children, and none of the children with autism referred to an absent object compared to 7 children with DS and 5 TD children.

Although a lack of symbolic play could be explained by executive function difficulties, the finding that some children with autism do produce symbolic play does not fit with this explanation. A further difficulty for this account is that children with autism have been shown to produce pretence in certain situations (e.g., Boucher & Lewis, 1990; Jarrold Boucher, & Smith, 1996; Lewis & Boucher, 1988; Libby, Powell, Messer & Jordan, 1997) and can use one object which has a particular function, such as a pencil, as if it was a different object with a different function, such as a toothbrush (Jarrold, Boucher, & Smith., 1994a).

In Lewis and Boucher's study, the children were given non-representational material, for example, a paper napkin or a short piece of drinking straw, along with a toy car or doll and asked what the doll/car could do with the material. All the children with autism produced some examples of pretence in this situation. Jarrold et al. (1996) also confirmed that children with autism can produce pretend play under certain conditions but argued that they have a difficulty in generating ideas for pretence. Jarrold,

Smith, Boucher, and Harris (1994b) have also shown that children with autism can understand pretend acts carried out by another person. Libby et al. reported that around 90% of children and adolescents with autism copied symbolic actions using either non-representational material (e.g., using a brick for a cup), counterfunctional objects (e.g., using a ball for a cup), or no object. Interestingly, when a sequence of pretend actions was modeled, such as going to bed, but the actions were modeled in a scrambled order, the children with autism were more likely than children with DS and TD children matched for verbal ability to repeat the actions in the scrambled order. However, Charman et al. (1997) reported that 20-month-old children with autism did not produce pretence in a structured task, whereas children with developmental delays of comparable age, non-verbal and verbal ability did.

The findings that children with autism can pretend creates difficulties for the executive function account of autism, since they indicate that children with autism can disengage and pretend. The findings are a problem for the theory of mind account of autism which also has been invoked to account for the findings of impaired pretence. Specifically, Leslie (1987) proposed that both pretend play and theory of mind are meta-representational in the sense that they both involve representations, of a pretended object and the mind of another respectively. If this is the case and if children with autism can pretend, they cannot have a general meta-representational deficit and therefore this raises doubt about a specific deficit in terms of impaired theory of mind. While Hobson (1990a) has criticized Leslie's view specifically with respect to pretend play, the finding that children with autism can produce symbolic play also creates difficulties for Hobson's own account that the ability to pretend is dependent on children understanding the different perspectives of others as a result of interacting with people and objects.

Three main explanations have been proposed to account for how children with autism behave towards objects – weak central coherence, executive function, meta-representation – and they all have limitations. We shall now consider what children with autism understand about other people to see if evidence in this area favors one theory more than another.

Do children with autism have the same understanding of people as other children?

From an early age children with autism show less interest in people than other children (Swettenham et al., 1998). Swettenham et al. reported that in a free play situation 20-month-old children with autism looked at their parent or the researchers for less than 5% of the time whereas children with developmental delays and TD children spent over 25% of the time looking at the adults. In addition, the mean length of look at the adults by the children with autism was 1.5 seconds, compared to 2.5 seconds in the other children. Interestingly, in a structured situation in which the children were prevented from carrying out an action by the researcher, Charman et al. (1997) reported that the 20-month-old children with autism looked less at the researcher than either children with developmental delays or TD children. Thus, from early on children with autism seem to show less interest in people and less understanding of their agency.

In agreement with the finding that children with autism are not particularly interested in people, both Dawson, Meltzoff, Osterling, Rinaldi, and Brown (1998a) and Leekam et al. (2000) reported difficulties establishing eye contact with them. Further, the children with autism in Dawson et al.'s study, who had a mean age of just over 5 years, were less likely than children with DS and TD children matched for verbal ability to follow the researcher's line of gaze or point to a stimulus. Similarly, Leekam et al. reported that only four out of twenty 2–6-year-old children with autism followed the researcher's line of gaze when she turned her head, compared to 13 out of 20 children with LDs of similar nonverbal ability. However, when the children were divided on the basis of nonverbal ability, the difference between the children with autism and the children with LDs was most evident in the children with MAs below 30 months and IQs below 70. Leekam, Hunnisett, and Moore (1998) also reported that half of a group of children with autism aged 5–13 years followed another person's gaze in laboratory settings and this ability was shown by all the children with VMAs of 48 months and above. Interestingly, only one child with autism was reported by their parent to follow a head turn when there were no other cues.

Despite a lack of interest in people, children with autism can recognize people although they may not be as good at this as children of similar nonverbal ability and may go about the process of recognition in a different way from other children (see pages 253–255). There is inconsistent evidence on the ability of children with autism to imitate (Smith and Bryson, 1994). Thus, Loveland et al. (1994) found that 8–26-year-olds with autism did not differ from individuals with DS in their ability to copy facial expressions, and Charman and Baron-Cohen (1994) reported that 5–18-year-olds with autism did not differ from individuals with LDs but similar VMAs in imitating another person's actions on objects and gestures. In contrast, Charman et al. (1997) found that 20-month-olds with autism were less likely to imitate actions on objects than either TD children of similar age or children with developmental delays of similar verbal and nonverbal ability.

There is also some evidence that certain aspects of imitation may be impaired in older individuals with autism. For example, Boucher and Lewis (1989) found 11–15-year-olds with autism produced more errors when required to copy a sequence of several actions with or without a delay than individuals with LDs but not autism matched for verbal and nonverbal ability. Further, Hobson and Lee (1999), while confirming that young people with autism can imitate single actions both immediately and after a short delay, found that they were less likely than individuals with LDs to imitate the style with which the other person carried out the action.

But what sense do children with autism make of themselves and other people? It is clear that children with autism do develop an understanding of self as indicated by their ability to recognize another person's visual point of view (e.g., Hobson, 1984) and recognize themselves in a mirror (e.g., Ferrari & Matthews, 1983; Spiker & Ricks, 1984), although it is interesting to note that Mitchell (1993) reported that children with autism show relatively little interest in their reflection. However, Lee and Hobson (1998) reported that when 9–19-year-old adolescents were interviewed about their understanding of themselves they were less likely, compared to adolescents with LDs of similar CA and receptive language ages, to describe themselves in terms of their social relationships with others and more likely to talk about physical than psychological attributes.

Other evidence suggests that children with autism have a difficulty understanding another person's mental point of view, or understanding that other people have minds. In this account it is argued that children with autism cannot comprehend that other people may have different beliefs about the world than they do, or that they themselves had a different belief about the world at a previous point in time. This account has a number of attractions, primarily because it can explain many of the social and communicative difficulties characteristic of children with autism, although the cause of the problem is unclear. However, although it is argued that understanding other minds is a core cognitive deficit in autism (e.g., Baron-Cohen, 2000), it is likely that it is a reflection of earlier difficulties. For example, it has been proposed that earlier impairments in social development lead to difficulties in understanding of other minds as a result of either deficits in imitation and emotion sharing (e.g., Rogers & Pennington, 1991), difficulties with affective aspects of social interaction (e.g., Hobson, 1993), or difficulties with joint attention (e.g., Baron-Cohen, 1993; Mundy et al., 1993; Tager-Flusberg, 2001). Other researchers have suggested that difficulties in understanding of minds may result from other cognitive impairments (e.g., Ozonoff et al., 1991a). However, what is not in doubt is that many children with autism have difficulties in tasks assessing understanding of other minds which are more severe than found in other children with LDs but not autism (e.g., Yirmiya, Erel, Shaked, & Solomonica-Levi, 1998).

The theory of mind account originated from a study by Baron-Cohen, Leslie, and Frith (1985). A scene was acted out between two dolls who were introduced to the child as Sally and Anne. The child first watched Sally put a marble in a basket, and then Sally left, leaving the basket behind. Anne then transferred the marble to a box. Sally returned and the children were asked where Sally would look for the marble. Over 85% of 3–6-year-old TD children and a similar proportion of 6–17-year-old young people with DS answered this question correctly. In contrast, 80% of 6–17-year-old young people with autism gave the wrong answer, although they could remember where Sally had put the marble originally and knew where it actually was. The authors interpreted this finding as an inability by the children with autism to impute beliefs to others. In other words, children with autism have a problem with first-order mental states, that is, understanding that another person believes something, and instead base their answers on current reality.

Since this paper numerous studies using the Sally–Anne and other paradigms have explored the so-called theory of mind deficit in autism, demonstrating that autism is associated with difficulties in attributing propositional mental states such as beliefs, knowledge, thoughts and intentions to themselves and other people (e.g., Baron-Cohen, 2000), although Russell and Hill (2001) failed to replicate previous findings that children and adolescents with autism have problems understanding intentions.

However, some children with autism do succeed on tasks involving mental states, with as many as 90% of the children and adolescents with autism succeeding at first-order tasks in one study (Dahlgren & Trillingsgaard, 1996). Importantly, the children and adolescents with autism in Dahlgren and Trillingsgaard's study had IQs between 70 and 130 and VMAs between 5 and 20 years. It is clear from a number of studies that those children who pass have higher VMAs than those who fail and also considerably higher than the VMA of 4 years which is when TD children succeed (e.g., Happé, 1995; Kazak, Collis, & Lewis, 1997; Yirmiya et al., 1996). This has led Happé to suggest that children with autism who succeed at theory of mind tasks have developed a strategy involving verbal mediation. This suggestion receives some support from several studies which have demonstrated that changing the nature of the language used in the task increases the likelihood that children with autism will be successful (e.g., Eisenmajer & Prior, 1991), as does reducing the complexity of the task (e.g., Tager-Flusberg & Sullivan, 1994).

It has also been reported that the performance of children with autism can be improved on certain false belief paradigms in various ways, including providing a photographic cue to the initial belief. Photographic cues have been used with the deceptive container paradigm. In this, children are shown a familiar container (such as a Smarties tube, a milk carton, a cereal packet) and asked what it contains. They are then shown that the actual contents differ from what was expected and asked what they originally thought was in the container. Charman and Lynggaard (1998) reported that 7–15-year-olds with autism did poorly on the standard deceptive container task but that their performance improved if, after they had labeled the presumed contents, they posted a picture of these contents in a box. Similar results were reported by Bowler and Briskman (2000) for the deceptive container paradigm, but not for the classic Sally–Anne paradigm. Further, a variety of techniques have shown that children with autism can be taught to pass theory of mind tasks. However, their learning does not generalize to other tasks and situations thought to involve theory of mind understanding (Swettenham, 2000). This lack of generalization further supports the view that children with autism who pass theory of mind tasks, whether as a result of teaching or not, have developed specific strategies, rather than their understanding of minds having advanced.

Most children with autism who understand first order mental states have difficulties with second-order mental states – that one person thinks that another person thinks something (e.g., Baron-Cohen, 1989a; Ozonoff et al., 1991a). However, Dahlgren and Trillingsgaard (1996) reported that of young people with autism aged 6–16 and with VMAs of 5–19, 60% passed second-order belief tasks. These authors argue that it is not just VMA which determines whether or not children with autism will pass a theory of mind task but also how close their VMA and CA are. Certainly a high proportion of people with AS, who have better language skills than people with autism, have been found to succeed at tasks involving second-order mental states (e.g., Bowler, 1992; Dahlgren & Trillingsgaard, 1996; Ozonoff, Rogers, & Pennington, 1991b). Interestingly, Bowler observed that they seldom justified their answers by reference to mental states, again suggesting the use of some other strategy.

Young people with autism and relatively high VMAs were studied by Leekam and Prior (1994) and just under 40% successfully attributed second-order mental states. However, these authors report that whereas young TD children who passed the mental state tasks could also distinguish between someone lying and joking, the young people with autism who passed the mental state task often did not distinguish lying and joking. This again suggests that individuals with autism who solve tasks involving mental states are doing so in a different way from individuals without autism. A similar conclusion was reached by Happé (1994d) who found that children and adolescents with autism, regardless of whether they passed second-order theory of mind tasks, first order tasks or failed, did not understand why certain characters in stories had said something that was not true when the reason involved a mental state. Interestingly, the young people with autism used as many mental state terms as children without autism, but they used them inappropriately.

The relationship between theory of mind ability and the ability to attribute social meaning was explored in an intriguing study by Klin (2000) using a setup which did not involve people. The adolescents and young adults with autism in this study had average IQs and all passed a second-order theory of mind task. Nevertheless, when asked what was going on when shown a video of simple geometric shapes moving in synchrony around the screen they were much less likely than TD adolescents and young adults to refer to cognitive or affective mental states or to attribute the shapes with social characteristics. This is particular clearly demonstrated by the narratives. Thus, an adolescent with autism commented, "The big triangle went into the rectangle. There was a small triangle and a circle. The big triangle went out. The shapes bounced off each other. . .". In comparison, a TD adolescent with a similar verbal IQ said, "What happened was that the larger triangle – which was like a bigger kid or a bully – and he had isolated himself from everything else until two new kids come along and the little one was a bit more shy, scared, and the smaller triangle more like stood up for himself and protected the little one. The big triangle got jealous of them, came out and started to pick on the smaller triangle. . .".

Physiological evidence also points to individuals with autism having difficulties with theory of mind. Stone (2000) reviews evidence indicating that areas of the frontal cortex, notably the dorsolateral frontal cortex, the orbitofrontal cortex, and the medial frontal cortex, as well as the amygdala located in the medial temporal lobes, are all involved in understanding minds. Part of this evidence comes from studies of individuals with AS. Thus, Happé et al. (1996) reported that five adults with AS did not show activity in the medial frontal cortex when reading stories requiring mental state inference. Further, Baron-Cohen et al. (1999b) reported that when TD individuals made judgments about what another person was thinking from their direction of gaze the amygdala was activated, but that this was not the case when individuals with AS engaged in this task.

On balance, therefore, it does seem as though many people with autism do have problems with theory of mind tasks and that if they solve them it seems to be because they are using some strategy other than understanding what is going on in the minds of others. Certainly, if a child does not understand what another person might be thinking or feeling, we would expect her to behave inappropriately towards other people and, as we shall see when we consider social and communicative behaviors in later sections, this is the case. Interestingly there is some physiological support for this from a study of 2–13-year-old children with autism by Ohnishi et al. (2000). They reported a relationship between decreased cerebral blood flow in the left medial prefrontal cortex and impairments in communication and social interaction.

However, despite the attraction of the theory of mind account, it has been criticized. One criticism has been that it cannot account for the repetitive and stereotyped behaviors which are also characteristic of autism. Happé and Frith (e.g., Frith & Happé, 1994; Happé, 1994b) circumvented this criticism by proposing that children with autism have both weak central coherence and a difficulty in understanding minds, and that these two difficulties are independent of each other. In support of this independence between theory of mind and weak central coherence, Happé (1994c) found that children with autism did particularly well on the block design task of the WISC, regardless of whether they passed or failed theory of mind tasks. Happé (1997) has also demonstrated this using a very different task involving homographs. She compared young TD children with children with autism with varying degrees of success on theory of mind tasks when reading homographs in which the correct pronunciation depended on the context of the sentence (e.g., "There was a big tear in her eye," "Molly was very happy, but in Lilian's eye there was a big tear"). If the target word occurred after the context had been set, the TD children did better than the children with autism and performance on theory of mind tasks did not relate to success on the task.

In contrast to these findings, Jarrold, Butler, Cottington, and Jimenez (2000b) reported that the ability of both children with autism aged 7–13 years and TD children aged 5–6 years to understand beliefs was related to their performance on both embedded figures and block design tasks when verbal mental age was taken into account, such that those with poor theory of mind ability showed weaker central coherence and vice versa. Interestingly, Jarrold et al. propose that weak central coherence is likely to precede theory of mind difficulties and even contribute to them. Happé (2000) makes a similar point when she suggests that although central coherence may be independent of a basic ability to represent mental states, it may influence children's social understanding, since social understanding, while dependent on the ability to represent mental states, is also influenced by other factors, including being able to integrate different sorts of information. Such an account could explain why some individuals with autism can pass second-order theory of mind tasks and yet still have weak central coherence and limited social skills in everyday situations.

Other researchers have proposed that the difficulty that children with autism have with theory of mind tasks stems from an underlying inability to disengage from the immediate environment. This is the executive function deficit (e.g., Hughes et al., 1994; Ozonoff et al., 1991a). This account proposes that the reason why so many children with autism fail theory of mind tasks is that they respond on the basis of current reality, for example, in the Sally and Anne task pointing to where Sally's marble actually is, rather than inhibiting this knowledge, and have difficulties holding relevant information in working memory. Two studies by Russell, Saltmarsh, and Hill (1999) support this suggestion. In both studies, children and adolescents with autism were matched for VMA with children and adolescents with LDs. In the first study, the individuals with autism performed less well on both a false belief task and a conflicting desire task which required them to ignore their own desire and to use information provided earlier in order to say what a puppet would desire. In comparison, the individuals with LDs did well on both tasks.

The second study ruled out the possibility that the individuals with autism had problems with these tasks because they both involve mental states, namely beliefs and desires. In this study, false belief performance was compared to a task involving a photograph of a scene which was altered while the photograph was developing, the so-called false photograph task. Previous studies of the false photograph task involved taking a Polaroid photograph of, for example, a doll and then changing the color of the doll's dress while the photograph was developing (Leekam & Perner, 1991; Leslie & Thaiss, 1992; Peterson & Siegal, 1998). These studies reported that children with autism had no difficulty indicating the color of the doll's dress in the photograph before seeing it even though it was now different. In their second study, Russell et al. administered a similar false photograph task in which a second character replaced the one photographed, as well as a modified version in which no character was present when the photograph was taken. They argued that the executive demands of this modified task more closely matched those of false belief tasks. Individuals with autism did less well than individuals with LDs on both the false belief task and the modified false photograph task but similarly on the standard false photograph task. This finding supports the proposal that individuals with autism have executive difficulties and these account for their problems in theory of mind tasks. However, as Russell et al. acknowledge, it could be that children with autism have both theory of mind and executive difficulties, although this is not a position they favor.

If limited executive skills contribute to the problems that most individuals with autism have with theory of mind tasks then we should expect to see such difficulties in other areas. I shall consider two of these in the next two sections examining the planning and memorizing abilities respectively.

Are children with autism able to plan?

In order to achieve a specified goal, it is necessary to be able to disengage from the present, ignore irrelevant information, inhibit any behavior which would interfere with attaining the goal, and carry through the required actions in a prescribed order, guided by some internal representation of a plan. Such behaviors are often described as being under the control of executive function and difficulties with these behaviors characteristically occur in individuals whose frontal lobes have been damaged. Individuals with frontal lobe damage may present with behavior which is rigid and inflexible, show a dislike of change, a preference for routines, perseveration and inability to inhibit responses, plus appearing to have knowledge which they cannot use in a meaningful way, often focusing on details rather than the whole picture. These characteristics are very reminiscent of autism and so it is not surprising to find evidence which suggests that people with autism have difficulties in tasks which require cognitive flexibility and forward planning.

However, it is not being argued that people with autism simply have frontal lobe damage, since otherwise children who experience frontal lobe lesions early on should develop autism, which they do not. Indeed, as I pointed out in the last section, some researchers have suggested that impairments in executive function may underpin the difficulties that people with autism have with theory of mind tasks. However, it might also be that executive function deficits are independent of theory of mind deficits but both share the same or similar biological substrate in the prefrontal cortex. In this section I shall consider the evidence that people with autism show inflexibility in cognitive tasks and have difficulties planning. However, a prior question is whether children with autism can generate ideas and behavior since if they have difficulties thinking up things to do this may give the appearance of planning difficulties.

The generative ability of children with autism has been investigated in a number of areas, including play (e.g., Jarrold et al., 1996; Lewis & Boucher, 1995), word fluency (e.g., Boucher, 1988), object use (e.g., Scott & Baron-Cohen, 1996a), and drawings (e.g., Lewis & Boucher, 1991). Although the results of these and other studies are not entirely consistent there is support for the view that children with autism have difficulties generating ideas. In a more recent paper, Turner (1999b) attempted to explore some of the inconsistencies in previous papers by administering a battery of tasks examining generative ability to two groups of children, adolescents, and adults with autism, one with verbal IQs above 75, the other with verbal IQs below 75, although all the participants had VMAs of at least 4 years. The individuals with autism of both ability levels, relative to individuals of similar age and verbal and nonverbal ability, were impaired at generating words with the same initial letter or from the same category, at suggesting different and imaginative uses for everyday objects and objects without a clear function, at thinking of different and imaginative things that meaningless line drawings might represent, at drawing novel but meaningless designs. Interestingly, on the latter task the individuals with autism produced as many designs as the comparison groups but more of their designs were disallowed because they involved repetition of all or part of a previous design, were of nameable objects, or simply scribbles. Turner suggested that this task is different from the other tasks because it is not necessary to have a particular design in mind at the outset since the design can be constructed gradually, whereas in the other tasks each idea is given as it is thought of. She argues that the design task, as well as reflecting generative difficulties, may also reflect difficulties in inhibiting behavior and planning. I shall now consider further evidence that children with autism have planning difficulties.

The first researchers to look for executive function deficits in children with autism were Prior and Hoffman (1990), although such difficulties had already been demonstrated in adults with autism (Rumsey, 1985; Rumsey & Hamburger, 1988, 1990). Prior and Hoffman compared the performance of relatively able children with autism with children matched for MA and CA on three tasks. They reported that the children with autism took longer and made more errors when learning a maze, made more errors when the rule for sorting cards was changed (the Wisconsin Card Sorting Task), and showed less evidence of planning when copying a complex figure (the Rey Osterrieth Complex Figure Test).

At the outset of this chapter I pointed out that it has been argued that any account of autism must satisfy three criteria: the deficit must be universal in all people with autism, regardless of ability; it must be specific to autism; and it must causally precede the onset of autism and be present throughout development. Although there is evidence that the proposed impairment in executive functioning goes some way to meeting these criteria, there are several reports which suggest that it does not.

Examining the universality criterion, Hughes et al. (1994) studied the performance of children and adolescents with autism across the ability range, children and adolescents with LDs of similar ability, and TD children, on tests which required either cognitive flexibility or forward planning. Two thirds of the children with autism failed both types of task, three-quarters failed the planning task, and over 90% failed the task requiring flexibility, whereas the children with LDs and the TD children were much more successful. Also relevant to the universality criterion is evidence that relatively able children with autism are more impaired on executive function tasks than on theory of mind tasks, compared to children of similar CA and verbal ability (Ozonoff et al., 1991a) and children with AS, who are impaired on tasks assessing executive function but not on theory of mind tasks (Ozonoff et al., 1991b).

Several researchers have attempted to identify specific aspects of executive function deficits associated with autism, as distinct from other disorders. Ozonoff, Strayer, McMahon and Filloux (1994) identified a lack of cognitive flexibility as being a characteristic of the deficit in children with autism and suggest that this may underpin their poor performance on a number of executive function tasks. In a subsequent study, Ozonoff and Jensen (1999) compared the performance of children and adolescents with autism, with Tourette's syndrome, with attention deficit hyperactivity disorder (ADHD), and without any disorders on tasks tapping different executive functions. Compared with the other groups, the individuals with autism showed more perseveration on the Wisconsin Card Sorting Task, confirming limited cognitive flexibility, and less planning on the Tower of Hanoi, whereas those with ADHD showed less inhibition than all the others on the Stroop word color test. Thus, Ozonoff and Jensen point to autism being associated with cognitive inflexibility and poor planning but adequate inhibition. They also observed that the executive impairments were less evident at older ages.

If impairments in executive function underlie the difficulties experienced by people with autism, then there should be a relationship between executive skills and those behaviors which characterize autism. This was examined by Dawson, Meltzoff, Osterling, and Rinaldi (1998b) using two tasks, one involving learning rules and visual recognition memory and thought to be under the control of the medial temporal lobe, and the other requiring working memory and inhibition for which the dorsolateral prefrontal cortex is thought to be responsible. The mean age of the children with autism was 5½ years and they performed less well on both tasks than either children with DS or TD children all with similar receptive language ages. However, whereas the temporal lobe task was correlated with a number of behaviors characterizing autism, this was not the case for the prefrontal task. This argues against the suggestion that impairments in skills mediated by the frontal lobe explain the difficulties characterizing autism. However, given Ozonoff and Jensen's finding that inhibitory control seems to be relatively unimpaired in autism and the fact that the frontal task used by Dawson et al. involved inhibition, the lack of relationship reported is perhaps not surprising.

Similarly, if executive impairments explain the difficulties which characterize autism then they should precede these behaviors. However, Griffith, Pennington, Wehner, and Rogers (1999) suggest that this is not the case. They gave a series of executive tasks to 3–5-year-old children with autism and children with developmental delays. Although the children with autism differed from the other children in terms of social and communicative skills and repetitive behaviors there were few differences between the groups on the executive tasks. And in fact when there were differences the children with autism performed better. This indicates that executive impairments do not precede the behaviors associated with autism. However, when Griffith et al. compared their data to Diamond, Prevor, Callender, and Druin's (1997) data from younger TD children, both the children with autism and the children with developmental delays were performing less well than expected for their MA. In other words, both groups were impaired on the executive tasks. It is therefore possible that executive impairments do precede the onset of behaviors characterizing autism, although the similar performance of the two groups raises questions about the specificity of the impairment.

In order to examine whether an executive deficit is present throughout development, Ozonoff and McEvoy (1994) administered executive function tasks to children with autism and children with LDs but not autism on two occasions 3 years apart. The executive function tasks examined both planning (the Tower of Hanoi) and flexibility (the Wisconsin Card Sorting Task). The children with LDs improved over time and on both occasions performed at a higher level than the children with autism whose performance remained much the same over time. The performance of the children with autism on theory of mind tasks were also fairly static on both occasions, whereas the children with LDs were at ceiling at the first test. The authors argue that impairments in both theory of mind and executive function appear to be fairly stable characteristics of autism.

One of the difficulties with the studies cited so far is that they have each only examined one of the criteria which need to be met in order to conclude that autism is associated with executive difficulties. In order to rectify this, Liss et al. (2001a) administered a range of executive tasks and assessments of behaviors associated with autism to high functioning children with autism and children with language disorders who all had nonverbal IQs of 80 or above. The only group difference on the executive tasks was that the children with autism showed more perseveration on the Wisconsin Card Sorting Task, a finding which agrees with the results of other researchers. However, when verbal IQ was covaried out, this difference disappeared. In addition, Liss et al. found considerable overlap in the performance of the two groups on the tasks, indicating that executive difficulties are not universal in or specific to autism.

Further, although performance on some of the tasks did correlate with behaviors characteristic of autism, most of these disappeared when verbal IQ was covaried out. On the basis of these results, Liss et al. argue that rather than executive difficulties causing autistic behaviors it is more likely that early difficulties, such as problems in joint attention, lead to the executive difficulties which some children with autism experience. However, contrary to this, Griffith et al. (1999) reported that executive function in 3–5-year-old children with autism correlated with a measure of joint attention a year later, but that joint attention at the first age point was not correlated with later executive ability.

Thus, although many children with autism show evidence of cognitive inflexibility and poor planning, it does not seem as though these are primary deficits. It also seems unlikely that these difficulties can account for the other problems which children with autism experience.

How good are children with autism at remembering things?

Kanner noticed that children with autism are often exceptionally good at remembering certain things. They may remember entire passages of conversations they have heard or recite nursery rhymes and poems without making an error. Many are particularly good at recognizing a piece of music on the basis of a few bars. They may notice when the slightest change is made to a room, such as the order of books on a shelf or the position of an ashtray on a table. Their memories seem to be very exact, with experiences appearing to be stored precisely as they occurred. Another feature is that the things that they do remember do not appear to be of any great importance; they do not seem to have selected particularly useful things to remember. These observations have been supported by research findings which show that children with autism may have good immediate and cued recall of words (e.g., Boucher, 1981; Boucher & Warrington, 1976) and cued recalled of activities (Boucher & Lewis, 1989). However, other research indicates that aspects of the memories of children with autism may be impaired.

We have already seen that children with autism are impaired at remembering which photographs of people they have seen previously (Boucher & Lewis, 1992), which suggests that delayed recall is impaired. This is supported by other findings which show that if there is a delay between the presentation of the material to be remembered and recall of the material, children with autism are impaired (e.g., Boucher, 1981; Boucher & Lewis, 1989; Boucher & Warrington, 1976). Thus, Boucher and Lewis found that 11–15-year-old adolescents with autism were impaired at producing a sequence of actions following either a demonstration or spoken instructions compared to adolescents with LDs of similar CA, nonverbal ability, and verbal ability. These adolescents with autism also had poorer recall of the various research tasks they had been involved in over a year than those with LDs, although cueing increased the number of activities recalled by both groups.

An interesting extension of this latter study was carried out by Millward, Powell, Messer, and Jordan (2000). Adolescents with autism were taken on a walk either alone or with a peer and along the way they (and their peer) engaged in various different activities. Following the walk without a peer the adolescents with autism recalled fewer activities than younger TD children of similar verbal ability and although cueing improved the recall of both groups, the difference remained. However, when they went with a peer there was no difference between the groups in the recall of the activities engaged in by the peer, whether cued or not. This suggests that it is personally experienced events that individuals with autism find hard to recall. Nevertheless, individuals with autism may be as good as younger TD children and children with LDs at recognizing whether they have heard a word before and whether they or another person said the word (Farrant, Blades, & Boucher, 1998).

The studies cited so far in this section have all involved children and adolescents with autism who also have LDs. It is therefore possible that LDs can explain the reported memory impairments rather than any specific consequence of autism. In order to address this question, Russell, Jarrold and Henry (1996) explored specifically whether it was those aspects of memory which depend upon some central processing capacity which are impaired. Children with autism, children with LDs, and TD children of similar verbal ability were given memory tasks which varied in the demands they made on central memory processes. When the task made little demand on central processes (immediate recall of a word list), there was little difference between the three groups. However, when the task required that the children carried out a cognitive task (e.g., counting dots on a card) while holding in memory other information (the number of dots on cards already counted), the children with autism did not differ from the children with LDs, but they did not perform as well as the TD children. This study therefore suggests that although the working memories of children with autism may be limited in capacity, this may simply reflect LDs rather than autism.

Another way of addressing the question of the role of LDs in any memory impairments is to study individuals with autism who do not have LDs. Bowler and colleagues have explored the memory abilities of adults with AS who all had verbal IQs of 70 or above (e.g., Bowler, Gardiner, & Grice, 2000; Bowler, Matthews, & Gardiner, 1997) and reported that they showed some of the same sorts of memory impairments as observed among less able individuals with autism. For example, adults with AS, like children with autism, recalled similar numbers of unrelated and related words whereas TD adults matched for ability recalled more related words. In comparison, several studies have reported that children and adolescents with autism with IQs above 70 may have intact memories (e.g., Mottron, Morasse, & Belleville, 2001; Renner, Klinger, & Klinger, 2000). Thus, Mottron et al. reported no differences in either free or cued recall of word lists for adolescents and adults with autism and IQs over 80 and TD individuals of similar age and ability. Similarly, Renner et al. found no differences between children and adolescents with autism and IQs over 70 and TD individuals of similar age and IQ on several memory tasks all involving delays filled with various activities: naming a line drawing of an object displayed for 50 msec or less which they have seen before; recognizing as familiar a previously seen drawing; recalling the names of drawn objects.

However, in both these latter studies, there are indications that the memory processes of the individuals with autism differed from those of TD individuals. Mottron et al. found that during cued recall the TD adolescents and adults were helped more by semantic clues (e.g., ". . . the name of a vegetable") than by syllabic clues (e.g., ". . . the word starting with NA"), whereas the adolescents and adults with autism recalled similar numbers of words with both types of clue. Renner et al. reported an effect which replicated an earlier finding by Boucher (1978). In both studies, the children without autism demonstrated primacy and recency effects of free recall in that they recalled more items from both the beginning and end of the list and fewest from the middle portion of the list. In contrast, the children with autism showed a gradual improvement in recall from the beginning to the end of the list. In other words, they showed the recency but not the primacy effect.

The development of communication

The absence of any intention to communicate meaningfully with other people was one of the characteristics of autism which Kanner originally identified. Disorders of communication have continued to be seen as central to autism as evidenced by them being part of the triad of impairments identified by Wing (1976). About half of all children with autism never acquire any useful speech (e.g., Lockyer & Rutter, 1969) and even in those children who do learn to speak, what they say and how they say it is very different from the language of TD children and even from the language of children with other severe language problems (e.g., Rutter, 1978). Further, the language achievements of children with autism are good predictors of their subsequent development. The more limited their language in childhood, the poorer the prognosis for their future development (Howlin, Mawhood, & Rutter, 2000; Lotter, 1974; Rutter, Greenfeld, & Lockyer, 1967).

Do children with autism communicate nonverbally?

TD children are able to let other people know what they are interested in before they can talk. For example, they may look at or point to a desired object and then look back and forth between the object and an adult. In comparison, children with autism tend not to communicate in this way (e.g., Charman et al., 1997; Swettenham et al., 1998). Both these studies reported data from 20-month-old children with autism. Swettenham et al. reported that in a free play situation the children with autism shifted their attention between different objects as often as children with developmental delays and TD children, but that the children with autism looked between an object and an adult and from one adult to another much less often. Similar findings were reported by Charman et al. when the children were presented with mechanical toys designed to interest them but also to cause some uncertainty. The children with autism looked between the toy and the adult less often than both children with developmental delays and TD children.

The children in these studies were all 20 months old. However, the finding of differences between the children with developmental delays and the children with autism is important because these children did not differ significantly in terms of their verbal and nonverbal abilities, although they both had lower abilities than the TD children. Stone, Ousley, Yoder, Hogan, and Hepburn (1997) also examined nonverbal communicative behaviors in 14 children with autism aged 2–3 years. Compared to 14 children with developmental delays and/or language impairments of similar CA, MA, and vocabulary size, the children with autism communicated less often with an adult during various activities designed to produce communication. In particular, although the children with autism made proportionately more requests, and all of them made at least one request, they were much less likely to draw the adult's attention to an interesting event or object. In fact, half the children with autism never directed the adult's attention, whereas all but 1 of the other children did. Similarly, Sigman and Ruskin (1999), in their longitudinal study of large numbers of children with autism, children with DS, and children with developmental delays, also reported that the children with autism initiated joint attention and responded to joint attention bids from others less than the other children both when first assessed between the ages of 2 and 6 years and at follow-up about 8 years later.

The faces of children with autism show little expression and they do not use their direction of gaze, hands, and bodies in the ways that TD children do. Children with autism do not use gestures spontaneously to compensate for any of the difficulties they have with speech. However, children with autism do use some form of nonverbal behavior. As babies and toddlers these children are often reported as crying and screaming to indicate that they want something. Apart from this screaming, they may not give any clues as to what they want, and it will be up to their parent to guess. This is rather like the way in which very young TD babies behave. But there is an important difference here. Ricks (1975) has demonstrated that parents of 3–5-year-old nonverbal children with autism can recognize the message of their own children's cries and those of nonverbal children with LDs but not autism of similar age, but that they cannot identify the message behind the cries of other nonverbal children with autism. Interestingly, Sheinkopf, Mundy, Oller, and Steffens (2000) reported that children with autism and children with developmental delays with mean ages between 3 and 4 years who had 5 words or fewer produced a similar proportion of syllables that were well formed, but the children with autism produced a far greater proportion of syllables with atypical vocal characteristics such as squeals, growls, and yells.

In their study, Stone et al. (1997) examined how the children communicated with the adult and reported that only two children with autism pointed towards an object, compared to nine of the other children. In addition, none of the children with autism showed the adult an object, whereas six of the other children did. However, nine of the children with autism manipulated the adult's hand in order to indicate a desired action. This behavior was only seen in three of the other children.

Two different forms of nonverbal communicative behaviors have been identified in TD children and both emerge around the end of the first year (Bates, Camaioni, & Volterra, 1975). The protoimperative form has the function of the child getting another person to do something, for example, to give the child an object she is pointing at. The protodeclarative form has the function of drawing another person's attention to something which you are looking at in order to share your interest with them, rather than as a request for them to give you anything. Children with autism have been found to understand and produce protoimperative points to the same extent as children with DS and younger TD children, but to be impaired in understanding and producing protodeclarative points (Baron-Cohen, 1989b). This difficulty with protodeclarative points has been linked to the theory of mind impairments found in autism, the argument being that the intention behind a protodeclarative point is to alter the mental state of another, whereas protoimperative forms are seeking to change the physical state of the environment. If children with autism do not understand that other people may have different thoughts, they will fail to interpret protodeclarative gestures appropriately.

A specific difficulty with protodeclarative gestures as opposed to protoimperative gestures was confirmed by Leekam, Baron-Cohen, Perrett, Milders, and Brown (1997). They found that children with autism could identify what another person was looking at solely from eye direction and that this was related to MA, but that they had difficulties sharing another person's visual interest and this was unrelated to MA.

However, Phillips, Gómez, Baron-Cohen, Laá, and Rivière (1995) questioned whether the imperative function in children with autism takes the same form as in TD children and children with LDs. In this study children with autism, aged 3–7 years, were more likely to use another object to obtain an out of reach object, whereas the other children were more likely to use a person. Although the children with autism did use an adult, perhaps leading the adult to the object, or pushing the adult's hand towards the toy, they were much less likely to look between the adult and the object. The authors interpret their findings as further support for the theory of mind impairment, in the sense that attention is a mental state. However, they also point out that the findings could be interpreted within the executive function account since looking from an object to an adult requires a shift of attention from one object to another, which, as we have already seen, is something children with autism find difficult.

A further study by Baron-Cohen, Campbell, Karmiloff-Smith, Grant, and Walker (1995) showed that in children with autism, understanding that eye direction indicates something about a person's mental state is related to the ability to pass theory of mind tasks. Children with autism could tell which of two cartoon figures was looking at them, but tended to identify the wrapper of a sweet they preferred rather than the wrapper a cartoon figure was looking at, and could not indicate which photograph showed someone thinking. Interestingly, Yirmiya, Pilowsky, Solomonica-Levi, and Shulman (1999) found that adolescents and adults with autism who passed theory of mind tasks made more eye contact with the adult who took part in the tasks than those who failed and this difference was not evident in individuals with DS, individuals with LDs, or TD children.

It seems clear from this and other evidence (e.g., Attwood, Frith, & Hermelin, 1988; Landry & Loveland, 1988; Mundy, Sigman, & Kasari, 1994) that children with autism have difficulties establishing joint attention with other people and understanding that behavior indicates something about mental states. Given that joint attention is seen as a prerequisite for normal language development, it is therefore not surprising that Mundy, Sigman, and Kasari (1990) have found that a measure of gestural nonverbal joint attention in children with autism, rather than language ability or IQ, predicted language ability 1 year later. Sigman and Ruskin (1999) further reported a significant correlation between rate of responding to bids for joint attention between 2 and 6 years and gain in expressive language age 8 years later. If these problems with joint attention affect early and subsequent language development, the question arises as to whether this influences the nature of the language that is acquired.

What are the characteristics of the spoken language of children with autism?

Most children with autism have severe language learning difficulties. Lotter (1966, 1967a, 1967b) found that 6 out of 32 children with autism aged 8–10 years were mute, and all these children had IQs below 55. A further 10 children had very limited language, just a few words, which they used neither for communication nor conversation. Thus about half of all children with autism acquire little or no language. Mawhood et al. (2000) tracked down 19 young men aged 21–27 years whose language and cognitive abilities had been assessed 18 years earlier. At the initial assessment they all had nonverbal IQs of 70 and above (Bartak, Rutter, & Cox, 1975). Verbal IQs were available for 9 individuals at both ages, and of these, 8 showed an increase in verbal IQ over time. For these 9, the mean increased from 66 to 82 despite a decrease in nonverbal IQ for 18 of the group from 94 to 83 over the same period. Nevertheless, observation of the men's linguistic abilities indicated that less than half produced good sentences. Of the others, 5 had immature speech, 4 produced at most a few single words, and 2 mainly repeated heard utterances.

As well as being delayed, the language of those who do speak is very different from TD children and children with LDs, both in content and usage. When children with autism do begin to talk they show none of the delight and enthusiasm seen in many TD children. But what is most striking about the language of children with autism is that although they may have reasonable vocabularies and adequate syntax (e.g., Tager-Flusberg, 1993), what they say may bear little relationship to what others are saying or doing. In other words, they do not adjust what they say to the social situation (e.g., Loveland & Tunali, 1991). These pragmatic difficulties manifest themselves as stilted and pedantic speech, abnormal prosody, turn-taking difficulties, inappropriate interruptions, and so on and have been explained within the theory of mind account (Tager-Flusberg, 2000). The argument is that if children with autism have no understanding of what might be going on in the minds of others they will fail to adjust their language appropriately (e.g., Baron-Cohen, 1988).

Much of what children with autism say may consist of apparently meaningless echoing of things they have heard, a phenomenon described as echolalia. They may repeat odd words, or whole sentences, or even entire conversations. Rydell and Mirenda (1991) observed three young children with autism interacting with a familiar adult and reported that between a third and three quarters of the children's utterances were echolalic. Interestingly, when the adult exerted control over the conversation, for example by using many directives and determining the topic of conversation, the children produced more utterances, though of similar length to when the adult did not exert control, and more immediate echolalia.

In a subsequent paper, Rydell and Mirenda (1994) confirmed these results with four further children and also reported for these and the three children in the earlier study that more delayed echolalic utterances followed adult utterances which were less controlling and more facilitative. There was also evidence that the children had some understanding of the meaning of their echolalic utterances. In addition, echolalia produced immediately was likely to be used by the children to provide information, to maintain the flow of conversation, to rehearse some aspect of language, or to help the children regulate their behavior. Echolalia produced after several intervening turns was more likely to involve requests for information, to provide information, to rehearse language, or regulate behavior. Thus, this study suggests that echolalic utterances may have greater linguistic purpose than was previously thought.

As well as reproducing verbatim what someone else has said, children with autism may also copy the way they talk, imitating their accent and intonation. This echolalia does not necessarily occur immediately. It may be delayed for days, weeks, or even years. It may occur repeatedly or just once. Often the echoed utterances are irrelevant to what the children are currently doing, or what others are doing, although this is not always the case.

For a number of children with autism, this echoing of heard words or phrases is as far as their language goes. But some do move on and speak spontaneously and it is then that the pragmatic difficulties become increasingly evident. Tager-Flusberg and Anderson (1991) examined the language of children with autism and children with DS over the course of a year while playing with a parent and compared this to existing data on TD children. Although the children's speech samples were fairly similar when they were using short utterances, differences appeared as they began to speak in longer utterances. Whereas the children with DS and TD children increasingly contributed to maintaining the topic by introducing new, relevant information and so on, this was not a characteristic of the utterances of the children with autism.

There are other ways in which the spontaneous speech of children with autism develops differently from TD children. They often show the sorts of immaturities seen in young TD children, but these characteristics may persist (Wing, 1969). One of the most common immaturities is the misuse of personal pronouns which Hobson (1990b) suggests may result from children with autism not understanding the distinction between self and other. For example, rather that saying, "I would like a drink," they are much more likely to say, "Do you want a drink?" Lee, Hobson, and Chiat (1994) comment that over-two thirds of a group of children and young people with autism between 8 and 23 years were reported to use pronouns incorrectly, whereas all of a group of young people with LDs used them correctly. However, there were few differences between the groups in indicating whether they or the researcher could see something, or who was in a photo (themselves, the researcher, or a peer). Lee et al. suggest that some people with autism may learn a strategy for using pronouns correctly rather than really understanding their use and, interestingly, they describe a young man with autism who had used pronouns appropriately in the experimental tasks but, as he left, said "Thank you for seeing you, Tony (the researcher's name)."

Children with autism also include relatively few cognitive mental state terms, such as remember, believe, and know, in their spontaneous speech whereas they will include terms referring to perception, desire, and emotion (Tager-Flusberg, 1992). Further, Ziatas, Durkin, and Pratt (1998) reported that children with autism with a mean CA of 8 years and mean VMA of 6 years were more likely than children with specific language impairment and TD children matched for VMA to fail a false belief task and show poor understanding and production of the belief terms know, think, and guess. These findings are consistent with the view that the language difficulties observed in children with autism are related to problems in comprehending minds, although they do not indicate anything about the nature of the relationship. However, if all the children studied by Ziatas et al. are considered, including a group with AS, it is seen that of the 38 who failed the false belief task only 1 demonstrated understanding of the belief terms and 5 showed the ability to express these terms correctly. These findings point to theory of mind difficulties causing the difficulties with understanding and using belief terms, rather than the reverse. Nevertheless, Hadwin, Baron-Cohen, Howlin, and Hill (1997) reported that when 4–13-year-old children with autism were taught how to pass mental state tasks this did not lead to an increase in their use of mental state terms when talking with a familiar adult about a story book, although this could be due to the children developing specific strategies for responding correctly in theory of mind tasks.

However, consistent with the view that theory of mind difficulties lead to differences in language is evidence that the language of children with autism is very literal, and the absence of idiom, metaphor, and allusion is noticeable. They talk about concrete things, rather than about anything abstract or things in the future. They may talk non-stop, and apparently quite knowledgeably, about something which interests them, but as soon as anything new is introduced they seem unable to include it. For example, a child with autism may be able to talk at length about a particular piece of music, but be unable to make any sort of comparison with another piece, or to say why she prefers a recording by one orchestra to another's. She may say she enjoys one and not the other, but be quite incapable of saying why. In other words, children with autism may have a reasonably good vocabulary but be unable to use the words to engage in any meaningful discourse.

The language abilities of children with autism have also been explored through their story telling abilities. As Loveland, McEvoy, Tunali, and Kelley (1990) pointed out telling a story requires taking account of what the listener needs to know and so if children with autism have difficulties understanding minds, story telling should reflect these difficulties. This has been confirmed in a number of studies (e.g., Loveland et al., 1990; Tager-Flusberg, 1995). In Loveland et al.'s study, the children watched a puppet show or video and had to tell an adult who had not been present what had happened. There were no differences in the narratives of the children with autism and children with DS of similar VMA in terms of narrative length or number of events recalled. However, there were qualitative differences. For example, the children with autism did not narrate the story as if it was fictional, and did not treat the puppet as a character. The children with autism also included more utterances which were bizarre or irrelevant.

Some of the examples given in Loveland et al.'s paper indicate that the children with autism did not use causal explanations whereas the children with DS did (one adolescent with DS said ". . . she looked at the papers. She was tired and she went for a walk . . ."). Tager-Flusberg (1995) confirmed this in her study in which children with autism, children with LDs, and TD children told a story from pictures. Although there were many similarities in the narratives of the children, the children with autism used no causal statements to link events, whereas the other children did. Interestingly, Tager-Flusberg reported no differences between the groups of children in their use of mental state language, although few children actually used such language.

Before concluding that these problems have their origins in autism, it is important to rule out the possibility that they are due to, or aggravated by, the parents of children with autism talking to their children in a different way. A number of studies have reported that the language learning environments of TD children and children with autism are very similar (e.g., Watson, 1998; Wolchik, 1983). In her study, Wolchik compared the way in which the mothers and fathers of 10 children with autism interacted, with the way parents and TD children interacted. The children in the two groups were of similar language ability and their average ages were almost 4 and almost 1 respectively. Some differences were found:

for example, parents of children with autism used less language which was related to the children's own verbal behavior and tended to ask more questions and provide more labels. This difference may account for the over-representation of nouns and names in the vocabularies of those children with autism who acquire some spoken language. However, there were no differences in terms of the parents giving the children directions about what they should or could say or in how much praise they gave their children's attempts. The similarities far outweighed the differences, and it would be impossible to account for the idiosyncratic language of children with autism by any of the observed differences. Most of the differences can be accounted for by the fact that the children with autism were much older when they began to speak.

Similarly, Watson reported few differences. She examined the focus of mothers' utterances to their 2–6-year-old children with autism compared to mothers with their 1–3-year-old TD children while they played together. The children were matched individually for receptive language age. Two thirds of the mothers' utterances to their children with autism were related to their child's focus of interest and this was similar to the mothers with TD children. However, the mothers of the children with autism produced more utterances than the mothers of the TD children which were related to what was happening although not to their child's focus of interest, such as asking the child to come and see what the mother was doing. Not surprisingly, as the receptive language age of the children with autism increased, they produced more utterances and their mothers talked more about the things the children were attending to.

If the pragmatic difficulties of children with autism result from them being unable to take account of what other people are thinking, then we should expect them to have difficulties understanding what other people say, if this understanding is dependent on an understanding of minds.

Do children with autism understand what is said to them?

Some children with autism appear to have no understanding of what is said to them, while others seem to understand quite a lot. However, their understanding is limited to concrete things and events, and breaks down if the conversation becomes abstract. They interpret things that are said to them literally. One of Kanner's original cases, Alfred, was asked, "What is this picture about?," to which he replied, "People are about." Another boy, when asked to put something down, put it on the floor. Often the understanding that children with autism have of a word is the meaning it had when first learned. Once again we see that children with autism are rigid in their behavior, cannot modify something already learned, and fail to use the context of the situation to help interpret what is said. Because of this inflexibility they cannot understand, except literally, idiomatic expressions such as: "Have you lost your tongue?" This inflexibility of meaning is not just confined to understanding what others say, but also to what they say themselves. Another of Kanner's cases learned to say "yes" when his father told him he would put him on his shoulders if he said "yes." For a long time afterwards "yes" was used by the boy to mean "I want to go on your shoulders."

If understanding of other minds is a problem for people with autism, then they should have difficulty understanding non-literal speech, such as irony, jokes, and metaphor, whereas they should understand similes since these can be interpreted literally. Happé (1993) found that young people with autism who failed first-order theory of mind tasks were worse at identifying which word completed a metaphor than young people who passed first- and second-order theory of mind tasks, although the groups did not differ on completing synonyms or similes. Happé also found that only young people with autism who passed second-order theory of mind tasks showed an understanding of irony.

A similar pattern of results was reported in a further paper by Happé (1994d). Adolescents and young people with autism, people with LDs, and TD children and adults had to say why a character in a story said something which was untrue – sometimes the character was being ironic, telling a white lie, telling a lie, using a figure of speech, etc. Interestingly, the young people with autism used as many mental state terms as the other groups, but often used them inappropriately whereas this was never the case with the other groups. The people with LDs and the TD adults correctly explained many of the reasons behind the character's behavior whereas those with autism made many mistakes and the number of mistakes made related to whether or not they had passed theory of mind tasks. Happé also observed that some of the most able people with autism found very ingenious ways of answering the questions which did not involve any reference to a mental state.

Similar findings have been reported by Dennis, Rogers, and Barnes (2001) for children with autism and children with AS of mean age 9 years and with verbal IQs above 70. They reported that although these children were as good as TD children of similar age at defining words and identifying different contexts for ambiguous sentences, they were less good at inferring what mental state verbs implied when heard in context, at drawing inferences from social scripts, and at understanding metaphor.

Comprehension of messages, where the interpretation of what the speaker actually means depends on an understanding of what the speaker actually wants, rather than on what the speaker actually says, has been explored by Mitchell and colleagues (Mitchell & Isaacs, 1994; Mitchell et al., 1997). The paradigm involved one character putting two objects (A and B) in two different locations (X and Y) and going out of the room; unbeknownst to the first character, a second character swaps the objects around; the first character, still out of the room, asks for the object in location X (which is now actually in location Y). In the 1994 study, over three-quarters of the children with autism judged literally, that is, chose the object in location X, as did a similar number of 3–4-year-olds. Less than half of a group of 4–5-year-old children chose the object in location X. In the 1997 study, the performance of children with autism was worse than that of children with DS, despite the fact that the children with DS were less able verbally.

Clearly children with autism do have difficulties understanding what is said to them, particularly when what is said depends upon an understanding of other minds. As well as providing a useful framework for understanding many of the language characteristics of children with autism, the theory of mind account can also explain many of the social impairments which are also associated with autism.

Social and emotional development

How does autism affect interaction with others?

Difficulties with social interaction are a major impairment in autism. Several studies have interviewed parents using the Survey form of the Vineland Adaptive Behavior Scales (VABS) to assess communication, daily living skills, socialization, and motor skills (Sparrow, Balla, & Cicchetti, 1984), and these confirm poor socialization skills (see Kraijer, 2000). Thus, Stone, Ousley, Hepburn, Hogan and Brown (1999b) reported poorer socialization and communication skills for children with autism aged 2–3 years compared with children with developmental delays, many of whom also had language impairments, of similar CA and MA. Similarly, mothers of 28–75-month-old children with autism reported that the children had fewer socialization skills than mothers of children with DS individually matched for CA and MA reported (Loveland & Kelley, 1991), although the two groups did not differ in reported communication and daily living skills. Rodrigue et al. (1991) also used the VABS with mothers of 2–19-year-olds with autism and with children with DS and TD children aged 1–9 years and again poorer socialization skills were reported for the individuals with autism. Interestingly, change in socialization skills with age are not a function of IQ level, whereas communication and daily living skills are (Freeman, Del'Homme, Guthrie, & Zhang, 1999) Further, Liss et al. (2001b) reported that 9-year-olds with autism had poorer socialization skills than children matched for IQ, regardless of whether their nonverbal IQs were above or below 80. However, the difference in socialization scores was greatest for the children with higher IQs and whereas IQ predicted social skills in the children with autism with IQs below 80, this was not found for children with autism and nonverbal IQs above 80.

In agreement with these findings, Howlin et al. (2000) reported that three-quarters of a group of young men with autism, aged 21–27 years and with nonverbal IQs greater than 70, had severe social problems. Over half had no or very limited social contacts and only three had close friends of a similar age with whom they shared interests and activities. There was a significant relationship between overall social competence and language ability. Interestingly, these young men with autism were reported to show few greeting behaviors. This is in line with Hobson and Lee's (1998) finding that 8–21-year-olds with autism were less likely than individuals with LDs of similar CA and VMA to respond verbally or nonverbally when either introduced to an unfamiliar person or someone left the room.

Kanner proposed that social aloofness was the primary problem in autism although, as we have seen, cognitive accounts offer a more parsimonious explanation of many characteristics, including social difficulties. However, Hobson (e.g., 1990b, 1993) has suggested that a basic impairment in the biological capacity to engage in social interaction may be the primary difficulty, proposing that if interaction with others is impaired from early on, children with autism will have fewer opportunities to develop an understanding that other people have minds. We have already seen that joint attention behaviors are impaired in children with autism and that proponents of the theory of mind account have argued that such behaviors are premised on an understanding that the other person has an intention to share an interest. Nevertheless, it is possible, following Hobson, that engaging in social interaction facilitates the development of an understanding of what is going on in other people's minds. These two positions are difficult to resolve since there is no disagreement about the behaviors which are observed, rather the disagreement is about whether the primary impairment is in the child's cognitive makeup or stems from their social impairments. However, Leslie and Frith (1990) have argued that a difficulty for Hobson's position is that autism is not usually associated with severe social difficulties from birth. It may be, as Klin, Volkmar, and Sparrow (1992) suggested, that social impairments are primary for some children with autism, and theory of mind deficits primary for others.

Interestingly, there is some neuropsychological evidence which supports the suggestion that the social and communicative difficulties associated with autism arise from difficulties with joint attention, which involves judging the direction of another person's gaze. Judging gaze direction has been reported to activate a region in the left amygdala in TD adults (e.g., Kawashima et al., 1999). We have already seen that the amygdala is not activated when individuals with AS make inferences from eye direction (Baron-Cohen et al., 1999b). In addition, Howard et al. (2000) reported that adolescents and adults with autism, compared to individuals of similar verbal IQ but without autism, were impaired at judging eye direction and also had enlarged amygdalae suggestive of functional abnormalities.

I shall now examine the social behaviors of children with autism. Given the usual age of diagnosis, there are few data on the very early social behaviors of children with autism although, as described in earlier sections, both Swettenham et al. (1998) and Charman et al. (1997) have reported that 20-month-old children with autism behave differently to children with developmental delays and TD children of similar age. Parental reports also indicate differences. Thus, Wimpory, Hobson, Williams, and Nash (2000) interviewed parents of children with autism and children with LDs aged between 2½ and 4 years about their children's behavior in the first 2 years. Importantly, the parents were not aware of their children's diagnoses at the time of the interviews. Fewer children with autism were reported to have engaged in person–person communicative behaviors such as greeting others, making eye contact, turn taking, communicating using noises. In addition, the parents of the children with autism reported that many did not engage in person–person–object interactions such as using eye contact to draw another person's attention to something, offering and giving objects, pointing at objects, and following the points of others. All of these behaviors are part of normal social interaction.

Several studies have examined children with autism at even earlier ages by looking at parental video recordings of the children. Of particular interest are two studies which looked at the videos of children subsequently diagnosed with autism and TD children taken in the first year of life (Osterling & Dawson, 1994; Werner et al., 2000). Osterling and Dawson focused on the children's first birthday parties and reported that the children with autism were less likely to look at faces, show things to others, point, or orient to their name appropriately. Videos of the same children plus videos of some additional children were studied by Werner et al. when the children were 8–10 months old. No differences were found between the two groups until 3 of the 15 children with autism who were reported to have had late onset autism were omitted from the analyses. The remaining children were less likely than the TD children to orient to their names but other social, communicative, or repetitive behaviors did not distinguish the two groups, although looking at the face of another person approached significance.

Despite this evidence of early differences in aspects of social behavior, several studies suggest that children with autism show similar attachment behaviors as other children. Dissanayake and Crossley (1996, 1997) compared the behaviors of children with autism, children with DS, and TD children aged 2½–6 years when a stranger entered a room where they were playing with their mother. The children with autism looked and smiled at their mothers less, rarely showed them toys, and engaged in less joint play. However, when the stranger entered the room all the children approached their mothers, sat on her lap, and engaged in physical contact, and there were no differences in how they responded, most behavior being directed at the mother. They also responded in very similar ways to separation and reunion with their mothers. These findings are consistent with earlier observations that children with autism, like TD children, respond differentially to their mothers and to strangers when separated and reunited (e.g., Sigman & Mundy, 1989). Dissanayake and Crossley also commented that the behaviors which did differentiate between the children in the different groups had more to do with how the children interacted socially with their parent, than with the proximity-seeking behaviors which are taken as evidence of attachment.

A very similar account was given by Kasari, Sigman, and Yirmiya (1993a) who reported that children with autism were more socially responsive to their parent than to a stranger in a play situation, but that the children with autism, compared to TD children and children with LDs, paid less attention to the toys provided, looked less at the adult, and made fewer attempts to engage the adults in joint activity. It was also found that the higher their MA and language ability, the more social behaviors the children with autism showed. Interestingly, when the adult initiated interaction there were very few differences between the children.

This last observation supports findings from earlier studies. Clark and Rutter (1981) found that, as the demands for a social response increased, children with autism were more likely to respond. This ties in with the findings of McHale, Simeonsson, Marcus, and Olley (1980) who found almost no social behavior between a group of children with autism when left alone, but when a teacher was with them the level of social behavior increased. However, this social behavior occurred towards the teacher rather than towards other children and most of it was initiated by the adult. Encouragingly, this study also reported that over an 8-month period the amount of social behavior exhibited by the children increased, while there was a decrease in their asocial behavior. Nevertheless, their social behavior with other people was still very different from that of TD children.

In a year-long longitudinal study, St. James and Tager-Flusberg (1994) noted that less humour occurred when young children with autism interacted with their mothers than between young children with DS and their mothers. Interestingly, the children with DS were much more likely to understand when their parent intentionally behaved in an unexpected way than were the children with autism.

Children, adolescents, and young adults with autism can produce recognizable facial emotions either when copying another person or when asked to show a particular emotion (Loveland et al., 1994). However, 5–13-year-olds with autism show less positive affect and more negative affect than children with DS when playing with toys with their parent (Bieberich & Morgan, 1998). Their response to another person's emotion also differs from that of other children. For example, Kasari, Sigman, Baumgartner, and Stipek (1993b) reported that children with autism, mean age 42 months, paid less attention to positive emotions expressed by others, such as praise on completing a puzzle, than children with LDs and younger TD children. The response of these children to a researcher showing distress after hitting her finger with a toy hammer was also examined by Sigman, Kasari, Kwon, and Yirmiya (1992). Compared with the other children, the children with autism showed less concern. In addition, when the adult expressed fear towards an approaching mechanical toy the children with autism showed more interest in the toy and approached it more readily, and when the adult pretended to be unwell fewer children with autism took any notice. Interestingly, when the reactions of these children to another's distress was reexamined about 1½ and 5 years later (Dissanayake, Sigman, & Kasari, 1996), it was found that the children's early reactions predicted how they responded later, indicating stability in response over time, although there was a relationship between amount of concern and MA.

A further study by Dissanayake, Sigman, and colleagues examined the behavioral and physiological reactions of 3–5-year-old children with autism and children with developmental delays to distress (Corona, Dissanayake, Arbelle, Wellington, & Sigman, 1998). The children had MAs and language ages of around 2 years. When the experimenter showed distress facially and vocally after pretending to hit her knee on a table, all the children showed more interest and concern than when she showed no distress. However, the children with developmental delays withdrew more from the experimenter when she was distressed and their heart rates decreased. These differences were not observed in the children with autism. In other words, the children with autism were able to distinguish between distress and neutral affect but they oriented less to the experimenter's distress than the children with developmental delays.

The responses of 20-month-old children with autism to distress was explored by Charman et al. (1997). When the researcher hit his thumb with a toy hammer less than half the children with autism looked at his face, whereas all the children with developmental delays and TD children did. In addition, none of the children with autism but 44% of the children with developmental delays and 68% of the TD children showed facial concern.

It is clear that many children with autism have difficulties understanding emotions. This seems to persist, even among those who are relatively able. Bemporad (1979) reported that one of Kanner's original cases was unable, at 31, to comprehend other people's feelings and could not predict how they might behave, despite average intelligence. Rutter (1983) also describes a young man who sought help because he was forever offending and upsetting people. He seemed unable to react appropriately towards others.

It is also quite clear that children with autism do not interact with others normally. They do not share their interests with others and seldom show any interest in what another person is doing. In line with this Dawson et al. (1998a) report that, compared to children with DS, children with autism oriented less to social stimuli such as hand clapping or calling the child's name, and more to non-social stimuli such as a jack-in-the-box.

Much of the evidence for the impaired social interaction of children with autism has been based on their interactions with and responses to adults. However, Sigman and Ruskin (1999) compared peer interactions in the playground of 10–12-year-old children with autism, children with DS, and children with developmental delays and reported that the children with autism were less likely than the others to interact socially with other children. Interestingly, those children with autism who shared their playgrounds with TD children engaged in more social interaction. The children with autism also initiated interactions less often, with almost half of the children with autism never initiating interaction. The teachers reported that although 64% of the children with DS had a best friend, this was true of only 27% of the children with autism. Similarly, Attwood et al. (1988) reported that whereas adolescents with DS and TD 4-year-olds interacted with their peers, only around 50% of adolescents with autism did, and those who did, interacted less than the adolescents with DS.

Sigman and Ruskin also explored the relationship between the children's playground behavior and various assessments both at the same age and 6 to 7 years earlier. Not surprisingly, MA and language age were related to social interaction with peers in the children with autism. However, what was more interesting was that children with autism who interacted with their peers at 10–12 years were more likely at 3–6 years to have initiated joint attention and engaged in functional play than those children who did not interact with their peers, even when IQ at 3–6 years was covaried out. In a subsequent paper, Travis, Sigman, and Ruskin (2001) report on the behavior of the most able children and adolescents with autism and with developmental delays studied by Sigman and Ruskin.

The children and adolescents were aged 7–19 years and they all had MAs of 4 years and above. For the children and adolescents with autism, but not those with developmental delays, social interaction with peers in the playground was related to joint attention behavior and empathy shown in a laboratory setting with adults, but not to understanding of false beliefs or emotions, or to response to another's distress.

Another interesting study looked at how children with autism and children with DS interacted with their TD siblings (Knott et al., 1995). Although the children with DS spent more time with their siblings than the children with autism, the children with autism did spend some time with their siblings. However, there were marked differences in the nature of the interaction. Compared with the children with DS, the children with autism seldom initiated interactions and were less likely to respond to initiations from their sibling.

There can be no doubt that children with autism do not have the same understanding of others as TD children or children with LDs and although they show attachment to familiar people they show little evidence of wanting to be involved with others. This raises the question of how children with autism feel about themselves.

What do children with autism feel about themselves?

Children with autism often seem unaware of how odd some of their behavior may be. They may exhibit quite extreme behaviors such as taking off all their clothes in the street or making rather loud embarrassing remarks about other people. Unlike TD children, who might behave like this on the odd occasion, children with autism do not seem to do such things as a way of attracting other people's attention. The purpose seems not to be the effect on others and, given their problems in appreciating how other people feel, it seems unlikely that this could explain this aspect of their behavior.

However, their inability to understand what is in the minds of others, and their ability to remember certain things as they first happened in great detail, can lead them to show distress in certain situations. One of the characteristics of autism is a dislike of change, for example in routines or the arrangement of objects in a room. Children with autism may get extremely agitated at a slight change, such as the order of books on a shelf, and yet ignore other changes. What seems to be happening is that children with autism remember certain things in great detail. Because they seem to focus on sensations from the environment, any alteration to the things which provide these is noticed. This causes disturbances because things are not as they are remembered. Often the distress of children with autism persists until the original order or routine is reestablished. In this sense the nature of their disability can cause extreme upset in children with autism.

Compared with other children, children with autism do not seem to have as much fun when playing (e.g., Dewey, Lord, & Magill, 1988), their reactions are much flatter (Yirmiya, Kasari, Sigman, & Mundy, 1989), and they often appear to be unhappy children. They may cry and be very miserable for no apparent reason. On other occasions, the source of their distress can be identified, for example, a change in their environment. They also become distressed through frustration and failure. This suggests that they may have greater awareness of how they differ from other people than is indicated by many of their other behaviors. For example, the reports of the two adults mentioned in the previous section do indicate that more able adults with autism may be very aware of some of the problems that their difficulties cause them in social encounters (Bemporad, 1979; Rutter, 1983).

Given their limited social contacts, it is relevant to consider whether children with autism experience loneliness. Bauminger and Kasari (2000) asked 8–15-year-olds with autism and IQs between 80 and 140 about loneliness and they reported greater feelings of loneliness than TD individuals matched for CA and IQ. This is interesting given that in their follow-up study of boys with autism when they were in their 20s, Howlin et al. (2000) reported that parents indicated that despite their adult sons' limited or non-existent social contacts few expressed feelings of loneliness. Thus, relatively able individuals with autism may express concern about the consequences of their disability, even though this is not perceived by those around them.

chapter seven

Practical implications

Introduction

The previous five chapters have examined the ways in which certain disabilities can affect development. In this chapter I want to consider some practical implications of the studies discussed in these chapters for research and for how parents and teachers can support the development of children with disabilities. I shall restrict myself to implications which arise from the studies discussed in this book and will use illustrations from the disabilities covered. Although a particular point may be illustrated with reference to one disability only, many of the implications will be relevant to children with other disabilities. Some of the suggestions I shall be making for supporting development are already in operation, although even when this is the case, they are often not available everywhere, and even when they are available they are not always as effective as they could be. Because of this, I have not attempted to indicate which suggestions are in practice, and which are not.

A critical time for all parents who have a child with a disability is when they are first told of their child's disability. Help at this time can be beneficial to both the parents and the child. Parents who receive sensitive support are more likely to accept their children and as a result are more likely to be less distressed and more attentive and positive towards their children than parents who are not helped through the early days.

No two families will react in exactly the same way to the news that their child has a disability. However, a study by Sloper and Turner (1993) of 107 families with children with motor disabilities, including 50 with CP and 17 with SB, identified certain factors which influenced how parents felt about how they were told. The children were aged between 6 months and 13 years and 37% of the parents reported that they were satisfied or very satisfied with how they had been told. However, over 50% of these parents were dissatisfied or very dissatisfied. The parents who reported most satisfaction were also likely to report the following: any early concerns they had before the diagnosis were taken seriously; the person who told them was a good communicator and was sympathetic, understanding, direct, and approachable; they were given enough information which was easy to understand and remember; they had the opportunity to ask questions when first told and subsequently. These findings have clear implications for breaking the news of a disability to parents.

As well as being aware that families differ in their reactions and behavior to their child with a disability, it is also important that every child is considered as an individual, and not just as a member of a group with a particular disability. Stereotypes must be avoided and each child's strengths and weaknesses identified and assessed, rather than relying on assumed characteristics of particular disabilities. Children who superficially have the same disability will be quite different from one another, and the environments in which they grow up will also differ. In order to be able to help individual children, it is essential that their particular needs are considered (e.g., Millar, 1994; Tobin, Bozic, Douglas, Greaney, & Ross, 1997). As Harris et al. (1996) suggested when writing about the relationship between early interactions between mothers and their children with DS and the children's subsequent language development, it is important to identify the sort of guidance that particular families need. Guidance needs to be tailored to individual children and their families, as does educational placement.

How can parents and teachers aid the development of children with disabilities?

Blind children

Parents expect babies to look at them and things around them, smile at familiar faces, turn towards sounds, babble in response to conversation, reach towards interesting objects, pick up toys and objects, and so on. The parents of a blind baby may need help to understand that the absence of many of these behaviors in their baby does not indicate disinterest and passivity. Rather, she shows her interest in what is going on around her in different ways from a sighted child and needs to be helped to access the environment. Parents can be directed towards their baby's hands and body movements, and towards understanding the reasons why she may drop her head and go quiet. Parents need to appreciate the experiences that their child has, the noises she hears, the things she feels and smells, and be helped to adjust their behavior so that it is appropriate to their child's experience, rather than focusing on the visual nature of their own experience. In other words, parents need to be helped to get inside their child, to think about how she experiences the world, and the sense she is likely to make of this experience.

In the first few months, parents can be helped to think about how their blind baby recognizes them, and encouraged to provide opportunities for recognition: for example, talking to her, using varied intonation, keeping in close physical contact, and encouraging her to explore their faces with her hands. Preisler (1997) argues strongly that facilitating social relationships between blind children and their parents and other family members and later on with peers should be a crucial focus for intervention.

Vision provides the sighted child with a great deal of information about her immediate environment. With a single glance a sighted child can locate other people and toys and, if the environment is unfamiliar, can gain a general impression of the layout of the room or space. Without vision this information will be much harder for the child to obtain. However, adults can help the blind child by creating order and routine within her environment so that the child can reliably anticipate where things are and what is going to happen. The order should not be restricted to the physical arrangement of the room and the location of different objects and toys but should extend to activities and social interaction. However, a balance needs to be struck. While the parent needs to create order and consistency in the blind child's environment, the parent must follow and build on the child's interests and activities as much as possible, rather than imposing ideas and suggestions on the child.

Millar (1994, 1997c) has proposed that blind children need inputs from different sources which converge and overlap with information that they already have so that there is consistency and redundancy in the information available to them. If parents are aware of this then they can be encouraged to provide their child with complementary information from different sources, rather than feeling the need to try to select the most relevant information in order to avoid overloading their child. Tobin et al. (1997) provided a couple of case studies showing how blind children may benefit from braille reading books which also provide auditory recordings of the various activities in which the story characters are engaged. This auditory information can be seen as replacing the pictures which are found in young sighted children's reading books. Even if the child, whether or blind or sighted, is unable to read the text, in braille or print, the sounds or pictures respectively can enable them to access aspects of the story's meaning. This additional information, which overlaps with their parent reading the text and them reading the text, may be very important in helping the child to begin to make sense of the braille or print herself.

During the first couple of years, rhymes and routines can provide a particularly useful way of increasing the blind child's understanding of her environment and fostering her social relationships with other people. Parents need to be encouraged to look out for opportunities to develop things the baby does into a routine, such as Tobin (1992) observed develop spontaneously between a 12-month-old and her mother. These routines can help the young blind baby to begin to appreciate that her behavior can influence what other people do and that her actions have consequences. Urwin (1978) also observed a routine which developed between an older blind child and his father. The boy stood on a table and when his dad said, "Ready, steady, go," Jerry hurled himself towards his father. This delighted them both and probably helped Jerry realize that sounds have sources and that there are objects and people beyond his reach. After all, the safe outcome of his leap depended on this understanding. This game is likely to have helped his mobility even though presumably it did not develop with that in mind.

After the first 6 months or so, parents should begin to incorporate objects into routines and rhymes. They need to know that touch, rather than sound, may be a more valuable sense to the blind child early on for finding out about objects and the environment and that blind babies may take more notice of texture than shape or size. They need to watch for signs that their baby has noticed that they have lost contact with an object, and incorporate this into a routine. Games such as give and take are valuable in helping the blind child discover that objects and people continue to exist even when she is not touching them. Some of these routines will be introduced by the parents. However, the most valuable ones in terms of fostering development in the blind child are likely to be those that begin with something that the child does which the parent picks up on and develops into a routinized activity.

We all expect young children to play. However, this is something which may be particularly difficult for blind children because play opportunities often have little structure. Children are given toys and expected to play. But the blind child will be unable to see all that is available and cannot observe what others are doing. Many toys will have little meaning for her. The doll will not feel or smell or sound like a baby; the toy car will not sound or feel or smell like the cars she has experienced. Toys will need to be selected which have meaning for the blind child. She will need to be told what toys and materials are available and, if there are other children around, will need an adult to provide information about what they are doing. However, while it might be tempting to provide the blind child with many toys and materials, it will be easier for her if a few carefully selected toys and materials which can be used together are available at any one time and if she has a regular playmate. Parents could make up a number of sets of related toys and play materials and give the child one set at a time. As the child gets older, the parent could ask the child which set she would like. As in other areas, the blind child will benefit from order and routine in the play opportunities which are provided. But if the parent can build on the interest that the child shows in particular toys and materials this will maximize the child's involvement and enjoyment and help to develop her sense of how she can influence her environment.

Once parents become sensitive to how their young child may interpret things going on around her, and the possible misinterpretations she may make, they will be in a far better position to help their child develop a realistic understanding of the environment. It is very easy for us to take our knowledge for granted and to fail to consider alternatives. For example, we know that cups must be put down on a flat surface for safety, but a blind child, who always gets handed a cup, may drop the cup when she has finished, thinking that she is putting it onto an invisible shelf, or because she thinks that cups only exist when they are in her hand and cease to exist when she lets go. If her parents have an awareness of these possibilities, they can adjust their behavior appropriately: for example, rather than handing their child a cup and taking it when she has finished, they can encourage her to pick up the cup and put it down herself, even if initially they need to guide her hand to the table top and help her feel for the cup. All of this can be accompanied by appropriate conversation, talking to her about what she experiences. For example, when juice is poured into her cup and the cup put on the table, her parent might say, "Hear that, I'm pouring your juice into your cup and now I'm putting it on the table in front of you," rather than just saying, "Here's your juice." Of course, many parents will pick up on their baby's signals and show sensitivity to her experiences without any help. But for some parents this will be difficult, and they may be much encouraged to learn that their baby is interested in the people and objects around her and to appreciate how she shows this.

For all parents, an awareness of the potential problem areas can be useful since this may help them spot problems at an early stage and think about ways of overcoming them. For example, we saw how Toni lay passively on the floor before she became mobile, and how this behavior disappeared once she started to move. Most blind children show one or more stereotyped behaviors and these may get in the way of them interacting with their environment. Tröster, Brambring, and Beelmann (1991c) suggest that stereotyped behaviors may be decreased by involving the blind child in physical activities, although if the behaviors arise because of too much stimulation, the stimulation itself will need to be reduced.

Parents can be made aware of the problems of mobility that their blind child may experience and encouraged and helped to think how mobility can be developed. Parents may not realize that their child's lack of mobility is related to the fact that she does not yet understand that there are objects and people beyond her reach and, without direction, may not see how encouraging her to reach out, and to discover the control she can have of her environment, will aid her mobility. From a very early age parents can draw their child's attention to her hands and feet, perhaps putting little bells on her ankles and wrists, or by encouraging her to use both hands to hold a bottle or cup. Toys which make a noise when touched and which do not roll away are useful, such as rattles which can be stuck to the side of the cot or wobbly toys which sit on the floor or table. These sorts of experience will provide opportunities for the blind child to discover that there is an environment beyond her, and that she can act on it.

As she gets older, one way of encouraging mobility is by providing auditory incentives for movement. For example, the parent can crouch in front of the child who can stand, and talk to her, and as soon as she makes a movement forward she can give her a big hug. Gradually, greater movement can be demanded. It is interesting that Toni's mobility first came by her use of a baby walker. Fraiberg made it clear that she would not recommend this sort of equipment as she feels that it prevents independence. For the same reason, she did not favor playpens. The blind child needs to be helped to discover that there is an environment around her, and one interesting suggestion is that introducing blind infants to water may facilitate their appreciation of the external environment and the effect they can have on it (Ross & Tobin, 1997; Tobin et al., 1997). Once the blind child begins to realize this, her experiences will widen as she moves around, finding new things to play with and places to explore.

The mobility of the older blind child can be helped in a number of ways. She should be encouraged to use the variation in the sounds of echoes to help her walk in a straight line and it may be helpful to point out to her that not all sounds are helpful but may actually cause her to deviate off a straight path. She must learn to ignore irrelevant sounds and to make maximum use of her spatial hearing. She may need to be helped to develop a more mature gait.

One of the most important developments for the blind child and her parents, as for any child, is the beginning of language. However, the blind child is less likely to initiate conversations. She will not point towards something she wants and grunt appealingly at her parent. Although this obvious requesting behavior is absent, the blind baby may make requests.

She may make a slight movement of her hands towards the noise of an object or towards an object which has slipped from her grasp, and parents must be alerted to the significance of this sort of behavior which may otherwise go unnoticed and disappear. It is important that parents talk about aspects of the environment which their child can experience as in "Hear that, I'm pouring the juice into your cup." Names should be provided for things the child hears, smells, and feels. However, it is also important that adults give the child information about the attributes and functions of objects, and not just labels. Information should be provided about things in which the child is already showing an interest. Particularly with children who are just beginning to talk, adults should try to avoid questions such as "What's that?" and instead talk to the child about what she is doing or showing an interest in. As the child gets older, adults should ask the child what she is thinking and feeling and wants rather than testing her knowledge all the time. In addition, adults should tell the blind child what they are feeling and thinking rather than always providing facts and information. But in all this it is crucial that adults do not do too much of the talking and give the blind child plenty of opportunity to respond.

As soon as the blind child has some language she should be encouraged to use it. Many parents feel a need to protect their blind child, and they may try to compensate for her disability by not demanding too much of her. For example, they may interpret what it is their child wants, rather than insisting that she asks for it. The child should be given the opportunity to make decisions. This could be done by asking the child which of two things she wants. This may also reduce the echolalia sometimes heard in blind children. After all, if you are asked, "Would you like a sandwich or a biscuit?" it makes no sense to reply, "You would like a sandwich or a biscuit." Language can be used to promote the child's exploration of her environment. For example, rather than passing the child a biscuit when she asks for it, the parent could say, "Fetch one yourself, they are on a plate in the middle of the table by the window." At times this may seem hard. I remember vividly as a teenager thinking how unhelpful the mother of a blind friend of mine was, when she said, "For goodness sake, Christopher, don't just stand there holding your empty glass, find a table and put it down." And that was in a house he did not know particularly well. But now that I know more about the problems facing the blind child I can see that this parent's attitude probably played a major role in Christopher's realistic understanding of his environment and in his independence.

Many of the implications discussed so far in this section are relevant for teachers working with blind children, as well as for parents. As soon as blindness is diagnosed a peripatetic teacher should be assigned to the family and should visit regularly. As has been seen, there are many ways in which the parents can help their blind child develop, and help from trained and experienced people should be available to all families. For the blind child to derive the maximum from her intact senses, and to be able to achieve independence and satisfaction as she gets older, there must be support and advice available to her parents from the beginning. Such provision should help to minimize the numbers of blind children who run into developmental difficulties later.

Beginning nursery school or playgroup or a new school may be very traumatic for young blind children. How can they be helped? Webster and Roe (1998) make a number of suggestions based on Roe's (1997) observations of young blind children at school. It is vital that blind children are given plenty of time to explore the physical environment so that they can orient themselves. They need to discover where different toys and materials are kept, how the room is laid out, how it relates to other facilities they are likely to use, and so on. This is probably best done by the child and her parent visiting the school on a number of occasions during the school holidays. A simple miniature version of the classroom and the school which they can explore may be helpful and will also introduce them to using models and maps. If a model is used they need to be encouraged to relate the different elements within the model to the overall framework, rather than simply feeling each element in turn.

As well as helping blind children become familiar with the physical layout of their classroom and school, they will also need help to make sense of the social environment. In much the same way that blind children are helped if the physical arrangement of their environment is consistent, consistencies need to be provided in their social environment. This can be done by establishing particular play partnerships, so that two or three children play regularly together. If a blind child is integrated with sighted children, the adults in the classroom will need to point out to the sighted children how they can help the blind child as well as providing information for the blind child about what the other children are doing. Adults should seek out toys, materials, and activities which will encourage the children to do things together. Adults need to foster interaction between children but, once established, be prepared to stand back and let the children interact together. The adults' aim should be to widen the blind child's experiences and opportunities, not to restrict her.

The organization of activities within a playgroup or nursery class will also need careful planning, to ensure that the blind child is aware of what is going on. A routine of different activities needs to be established, with the blind child being actively involved when there is a change to a different activity (e.g., Zanandrea, 1998).

There are also implications for how and what blind children should be taught. Each child should be encouraged to make as much use as possible of any residual vision. Since it is more difficult for a blind child to learn to read braille than for a sighted child to learn to read print, there is a need for more research into how braille can best be taught, for example, whether the use of enlarged braille in the early stages is beneficial (e.g., Harris & Barlow-Brown, 1997) and whether the blind child should initially learn the relationship between a braille character and the phoneme it represents or should also learn the word that the braille cell stands for as a contracted form (e.g., Millar, 1997a, 1997c). Once a blind child is able to read braille she should be made aware of different strategies blind children use when reading as this may help her read more quickly and efficiently (e.g., Millar, 1997a, 1997b).

In other areas of education as well, the blind child needs to be considered from her perspective rather than from the perspective of a sighted child. Parallels should be drawn with sighted children with great caution. For example, most sighted children use their fingers when counting whereas blind children do not. Some researchers suggest that blind children should be encouraged to use their fingers (e.g., Liedtke, 1998), whereas others suggest this is an inappropriate strategy (e.g., Ahlberg & Csocsán, 1999). However, it is crucial that blind children are given the opportunity to experience number through touching small and large collections of objects and listening to groups of objects being dropped so they can learn to estimate how many objects there are without necessarily counting them all. This is just one example, but illustrates that teachers must think carefully about how to approach each topic they teach to ensure that they draw on the blind child's own experience and make available information about different strategies which the child could use, for example, when counting.

It is important to remember that blind children without any other disability can achieve just as much as sighted children. Sighted people are often hampered by their own view of the world and their own ways of doing things, and the main implication for education is the need for a greater awareness of other ways of achieving the educational goals set for sighted children. Educators must think differently, rather than expect blind pupils to think like sighted pupils.

Deaf children

The population of deaf children is extremely heterogeneous and perhaps not surprisingly there are many different approaches to their assessment and treatment (e.g., Roberts & Hindley, 1999). Nevertheless, communication is one of the main issues to arise when considering deaf children. In chapter 3 I examined a number of studies which demonstrate that effective communication in a deaf child, through sign language, can have many positive benefits for development. This is not surprising since sign language is the natural language of deaf people. Children who learn to sign from an early age obviously have a huge advantage in terms of their ability to communicate easily and effortlessly with other signing adults and children compared to those who are exposed only to spoken language. However, the benefits go further than communication. Aspects of cognitive development are advantaged, such as academic achievement, reading and problem solving. Social interaction with other signing children and adults proceeds more smoothly and more sophisticated forms of play are observed. Signing deaf children demonstrate a more advanced understanding of other people in certain empirical tasks and fewer psychiatric problems as they get older.

Many deaf children who learn to sign from an early age will also have deaf parents and this brings added benefits, particularly in terms of early interaction. However, through their parents such children will also be part of a deaf community or culture, and this may be very important in terms of how they perceive being deaf and feel about themselves. Obviously hearing parents who have a deaf child will not be part of such a culture unless, for example, close relations are, such as their own parents. In this sense there is an inevitable difference between deaf children born to deaf parents and those born to hearing parents which cannot be changed. However, although deaf children born to deaf parents will be advantaged from the outset in that their parents may already be fluent native signers and will have effective ways of interacting with deaf people, hearing parents who have a deaf child should be helped and supported so that they can provide their child with an environment which optimizes their development.

Many hearing parents suspect that their child is deaf for some time before deafness is confirmed. Given that we now know that deaf parents interact with their young deaf infants rather differently from how hearing parents interact with hearing and deaf infants, it is important that a diagnosis of deafness is confirmed as soon as possible so that hearing parents can be supported from as early as possible. Lack of babbling by 10 months may be an important indicator of deafness as well as other disorders (e.g., Oller, Eilers, Neal, & Schwartz, 1999).

Hearing parents need information. They need to know that the repetitive arm and hand movements of deaf infants are not an indication of hyperactivity, but may be a precursor of the infant finding gestural ways to communicate. They need to be informed about support groups and put in touch with organizations for deaf children. They need information about different ways into communication and up-to-date evaluations of the alternatives. They need help to perceive deafness positively, rather than as a deficit. But perhaps in the earliest months what they need most is guidance about how to interact with their deaf baby. As we saw in chapter 3, some hearing mothers behave very like deaf mothers anyway. However, many will need help and suggestions. How should this be done?

Research has identified a number of strategies that deaf parents use when interacting with their young deaf children, such as waiting for the child to look back to the parent before making a comment, signing where the child can see both the sign and the object to which it refers, using exaggerated hand movements, pointing to an object then signing its name and finally pointing back to the object, and so on. Even if hearing parents decide not to learn a sign language, many of the strategies that deaf parents use to develop joint attention with their deaf infant can be used alongside oral language and parents should be made aware of them. This could be done by showing parents videos of deaf parents interacting with their young deaf children and discussing the different strategies. Hearing parents could be videoed while interacting with their deaf children and these videos used, with the sound turned off, to discuss the nature of their interaction and possible ways in which they could adapt their approach to their child. The parents could then be videoed trying out different strategies. Obviously this will have to be planned very carefully and carried out with great care and sensitivity over a period of time, taking into account the individuality of different parents.

Although the different strategies adopted by deaf parents are now well documented, we do not know yet how easily hearing parents can adjust their own ways of interacting and whether this will have any impact on the development of their young deaf children. This must be a priority area for research and evaluation projects are under way in Canada and Australia. Nevertheless, the fact that some hearing parents naturally behave more like deaf parents than other hearing parents and that this has an impact on their children's development should give us cause for optimism.

The most significant decision that hearing parents will have to make is whether or not to learn a sign language to use with their deaf children. From the evidence reviewed in chapter 3 it is clear that early access to sign language has many benefits. However, what is more compelling is the evidence that children who learn to sign early on may also acquire more effective spoken language at a later age than children who only experience spoken language. What seems to be crucial is that the child learns a first language as early as possible. The evidence that spoken language presents young deaf children with so many difficulties is a strong argument in favor of all deaf children being given the opportunity to learn sign language. This has a number of implications.

Hearing parents are unlikely to know any sign language and they will need support and help in order to learn. Obviously the more family members who can learn some sign language the better. This will widen the number of people with whom the deaf children will be able to communicate and will be an enormous support for their parents. Parents need to be put in touch with deaf people, and obviously if there are deaf parents with a deaf child nearby this would be particularly helpful. Again this needs to be done sensitively since many parents may find it very difficult to accept that their child is deaf and meeting other deaf people requires some acceptance. However, attitudes are gradually changing and within the general population in the UK and other developed countries, increasing numbers of hearing people are attending sign language classes and there is much greater acceptance of deafness than in the past. This also means that deaf people have much greater access to the hearing community through the use of interpreters.

Very few hearing people who learn to sign as adults become fluent signers and most of them are likely to use a sign system which follows the grammatical rules of their own spoken language, such as Signed Exact English. However, Spencer (1993b) found that even if hearing parents use a sign system rather than a sign language and even if their signing is not very accurate this does not adversely affect their interaction with their 9–18-month-old deaf children and some of the deaf children produced as many signs as hearing infants produce words. In addition, if at all possible, deaf children should have the opportunity to learn the sign language of their country, such as BSL or ASL. This means that deaf children need to mix with native signers who are likely to be deaf themselves. It may be very difficult for parents to accept that others need to teach their child a language. However, if they are able to accept this and learn alongside their child, this will benefit the child enormously. In addition, contact with deaf signing people will hopefully enable parents and the child to begin to see deafness more positively and contact with other deaf people will provide the child with access to a community of deaf children and adults which may become increasingly important as she gets older.

Many children in the Western world attend playgroups and nurseries. These provide an important opportunity for young children to meet and play with other children and to begin to develop independence from their parents and close family members. Such experiences are as important for deaf children as they are for hearing children. However, care needs to be taken in how such groups are organized if deaf children are to benefit as much as possible. Ideally the numbers of deaf and hearing children should be approximately the same. There should also be a similar number of deaf and hearing adults and, in order to encourage interaction regardless of hearing status, the hearing children and adults should be encouraged to learn some signs.

One of the most crucial decisions that parents have to make concerns their choice of school. For parents of deaf children this is a particularly significant decision. If the child is fully integrated into a mainstream school the curriculum will be delivered orally and the child will need an interpreter if they use sign language or a helper if they rely mainly on spoken language. Alternatively, they may attend a hearing impaired unit attached to a mainstream school. Such units normally provide specialist teaching within the unit and support the child when she is integrated into mainstream classes. Finally, deaf children may attend a special school, catering either for deaf children or for children with a range of disabilities, including deafness. It is crucial that parents are informed about what is available and have enough information to make an informed choice, based on their child's needs and abilities.

Given the evidence that deaf children who initially learn a sign language often subsequently acquire more proficient spoken language than deaf children who only experience oral language, there is growing interest in bilingual education for deaf children (e.g., Pickersgill, 1997). Sign bilingualism involves deaf children, from as young an age as possible, learning the sign language of the country, for example BSL or ASL and, once proficient in sign, they are then introduced to the spoken and written language of the same country. However, the adoption of sign bilingualism raises many practical difficulties, such as deaf children needing to be fairly fluent in sign language when they arrive at school, hearing and deaf teachers being fluent in both languages, and questions surround how different areas of the curriculum should be taught, and whether deaf children from hearing families belonging to an ethnic minority group should be learning the spoken language of the majority group or the main language their family uses, and so on. Nevertheless, it is an exciting development and one which needs to be considered very seriously, primarily because it formally acknowledges the status of sign language and its value as the main communication system of the deaf. However, if bilingualism is to be adopted, much will have to change within the education system.

Most deaf children with hearing parents will continue to experience spoken language, primarily through lip-reading and any residual hearing. If parents are involved in any early intervention this is likely to include guidance on how to adjust the way they interact with their child to take account of her deafness plus sign language teaching for themselves and their child. However, in addition to this, and particularly if the parents choose oral language as the principle means of communication for their child, it is important that they consider using cued speech to supplement the information available from lip-reading. It is also important that deaf children are introduced to written language at an early age, perhaps playing games linking the written name of an object to the actual object.

From the evidence cited in chapter 3 it is clear that sign language is far easier for deaf children to acquire than spoken language. This is not to deny that some deaf children do become proficient oral language users. However, these children are in the minority and as yet we have no way of identifying early on which children will succeed with spoken language and which ones will not. Given that acquiring a sign language does not impede acquisition of spoken language, and indeed may facilitate it, it seems essential that deaf children experience and learn sign language from as early an age as possible.

Child with motor disabilities

In chapter 4 I considered the psychological impact on development of SB, CP, and DCD. Children with these different disabilities vary a great deal in the extent and severity of their motor problems and many of them have additional disabilities. As a result, even within the three types of motor disability, the children will differ in the nature and extent of their individual problems. For this reason the relevance of any particular practical suggestion will depend on each child's particular circumstances. Therefore, it is crucial that each child's strengths and weaknesses are examined in detail before suggesting how their development can best be helped. Nevertheless, the studies reviewed in chapter 4 do lead to some suggestions for ways in which the development of children with SB, CP, and DCD can be supported.

In this section I shall consider first some general implications for children with motor problems which severely restrict their movements. I shall then consider some implications for children with SB, CP, and DCD in turn. Finally I shall consider ways of facilitating social and emotional development in children with motor disabilities.

Children who have severe motor disabilities can develop cognitively, and can have an understanding of objects and of people, provided that they have some means of acting on the environment. These children may not be able to interact with objects and people in a conventional way, but they may still reach a level of understanding similar to a child without a disability, albeit by an alternative route. Mulderij (2000) argued that it is important to treat the child as a whole, rather than just focusing on the motor problems. The motor development of these children may differ in many ways from that of TD children but this does not mean that they cannot develop motor skills. What is crucial is that ways are found by which they can act on the environment, rather than them being helped to act in the same ways as TD children.

If the child has no way of interacting, or opportunities are not provided, then these developments may be delayed or even absent. It seems clear that ways and means must be found to provide these sorts of experience for the child who, if left alone, would have no way of interacting. The child who cannot sit up unsupported needs to be provided with a special chair so that her head and body are supported and her hands are free to manipulate toys. If she cannot use her hands in this way then some other way must be found of enabling her to act on her environment. For example, if she can only move her head from side to side then a way should be devised so that this action can alter something in her environment: perhaps some arrangement so that she can move her head against a board which triggers the carousel on a projector to advance a slide. She would then be able to have a direct effect on her environment by changing what is projected on a screen in front of her. Obviously, the more meaningful and useful to her that her interaction with the environment can be made to be, the better.

Children with very severe motor disabilities will be dependent on others to provide many, if not all, of their experiences. Other people will have control over what and how they experience the environment. Parents of TD children, who are sensitive to their development, get ideas from their children about appropriate ways of interacting with them. These parents do not need to be taught about the different developments which follow one another. But the situation may be very different for the parents of children with motor disabilities. These parents may unwittingly restrict the experiences of their children, for example, by underestimating their abilities, by not being aware of subsequent stages of development, by being embarrassed to take them out to public places or by being overprotective and fearful of them coming to harm if they let them explore potentially dangerous situations like climbing the stairs. These parents may need help in choosing appropriate things to do with their children, and advice about ways of compensating for their children's particular problems. Parents must be encouraged to widen the experiences of their children, and given the necessary support, whether financial or emotional, to do this. Importantly, Woolfson (1999) reported that involving preschool children with motor impairments and their parents in an intervention program not only led to advances in the children's development and provided the parents with new parenting skills but also resulted in changes in the parents' perceptions and expectations of their children.

Children with SB experience a wide range of difficulties, especially if they also have hydrocephalus. Many children with SB have higher verbal than nonverbal IQs, which may also be evident physiologically (Ito et al., 1997). Such a discrepancy needs to be taken into account when deciding what material and activities to use with the children and how to present the tasks, since the discrepancy is likely to affect how the children process the material (e.g., Landry, Jordan, & Fletcher, 1994). Conversely, if this discrepancy is not evident in a particular child or is reversed, then appropriate adjustments will have to be made.

When assessing the verbal and nonverbal abilities of children with SB it is important to take into account that children with SB may produce fluent, syntactically correct, fairly complex language which bears little relationship to what others are saying or doing. Thus, as well as assessing vocabulary and syntax it is also important to include a measure of their discourse skills (e.g., Dennis & Barnes, 1993).

The discrepancy between the structure and relevance of the language of children with SB needs to be taken into account when talking with them. Parents and teachers may be misled into thinking that children with SB are more competent language users than they are and, as a result, talk to them at an inappropriate level. It is important to talk to children with SB at a level which is appropriate given their discourse skills. As the children's language skills increase, parents and teachers can increase the complexity of their language to the children. Thus, when children are able to talk about concrete events, more abstract language can be introduced and so on (e.g., Culatta & Young, 1992).

Children with SB often have attentional and planning difficulties and because of this it is important that parents and teachers provide a clear structure for their activities in order to ensure that tasks are completed (Landry et al., 1990). However, as well as providing a clear structure, it is important that children with SB are not left on their own to complete a task. They may need frequent prompting and cueing in order to keep them on task (e.g., Snow, 1999).

The range of difficulties experienced by children with CP is enormous. Some may have few difficulties which interfere little with their everyday lives, whereas others may be very severely disabled and rely on assistance with almost everything. In order to determine their competence it is important that children with motor disabilities, including children with CP, are assessed regularly and in a variety of different situations. Some children may demonstrate greater competence in structured situations than in unstructured situations and on one occasion than on another (e.g., Kennedy et al., 1991).

Children with CP will need help developing their motor skills. Sugden and Utley (1995b) pointed to the importance of identifying motor actions which the children find difficult and working on these. They also suggested that if one hand is more impaired than the other, then the former hand may benefit from using both hands (Utley & Sugden, 1998) although Wann et al. (1998a) questioned this strategy. Complex motor tasks will need to be broken down and the children's skill at each component assessed and developed. Children with CP may also need more time to plan their motor movements (Van Mier et al., 1994).

Interaction between children with CP, particularly those with severe disabilities, and adults can be very one-sided, as can interactions with other children. Both adults and children, even if younger, tend to dominate the interaction. In order to reduce this dominance Pennington and McConachie (1999) suggested that parents should be encouraged to develop their child's conversational skills by asking more open and real questions. Thus, closed questions simply requiring a "Yes" or "No" answer should be avoided, as should questions which simply test the child's knowledge. Asking children questions of the form "Would you like to do a jigsaw or read a book?" requires more from the child than simply asking "Would you like to do a jigsaw?" In addition, the parents should be discouraged from intervening unless the child requests help. It is also important that parents help their children to talk about their ideas and feelings, rather than just focusing on what is going on around them.

Children with CP who have little or no expressive language will need to have an alternative system for communication, such as symbol charts or speech synthesizers. However, it is important that parents and teachers are helped to facilitate the children's communication using such systems, as otherwise the children's communication will not develop and the adults will continue to dominate the interaction (e.g., McConachie & Pennington, 1997). Importantly, use of an alternative communication system by non-speaking children with CP may benefit their reading skills (Smith, 1989).

Studies of children DCD show that they have a number of difficulties as a consequence of their poor motor skills. However, the difficulties these children experience may not be recognized formally and may lead to secondary problems, notably academic and social difficulties, which it might be possible to avert if the disability is recognized early (e.g., Henderson et al., 1991; Smyth, 1992). Parents' early reports of motor difficulties need to be heeded and formal assessments carried out. Schools need to record motor difficulties that children experience systematically and request a formal assessment if necessary. It is important that the extent of the children's difficulties is assessed, as well as whether they have greater problems in some areas than in others. For example, if children have problems with balance and coordination rather than with planning and sequencing motor actions (Dewey & Kaplan, 1994), this will have different implications for how they are helped.

Once a diagnosis of DCD has been obtained, there are a number of ways in which schools can ameliorate the difficulties facing children with DCD, although obviously these will vary depending on the precise difficulties that each child experiences. Thus, Johnstone and Garcia (1994) suggested that given the problems that many children with DCD have holding and manipulating writing instruments, ways should be found to circumvent these. The amount of writing, drawing, or copying required should be minimized. Instead, written class notes should be provided and the children should be encouraged and supported in using computers to write notes and assignments. Tests can be modified in a number of different ways: multiple choice questions can be used which require minimal writing; answers can be given verbally or on a computer. In addition, children with DCD should be allowed extra time to complete assignments.

Children with DCD need additional help to develop and improve their motor skills (e.g., Schoemaker & Kalverboer, 1994). Although practice may improve some of their motor skills, children with DCD are unlikely to overcome them completely. It is therefore important that they are encouraged to take part in activities at which they can succeed, rather than repeatedly being put in situations in which they fail. This will help them gain the respect of their peers for their successes rather than repeatedly being seen as failing.

Given that social isolation is a particular problem for children with motor disabilities, it is important to encourage interaction with other children, both TD children and children with disabilities and including siblings. For children with severe disabilities such as SB or CP it is not sufficient just to put children with motor disabilities and other children together (Martlew, 1989). Parents and teachers need to think carefully about how to facilitate their interaction. Mulderij (1996) made a number of suggestions for children with a range of motor disabilities. Parents should try to develop peer relationships early on, perhaps inviting one to two other children to play regularly with their child at home. The parents should leave the children to get on together as much as possible, rather than intervening and directing.

Mixing with other children at a nursery or playgroup is also important. However, at nursery as well as at home, teachers and parents need to create contexts which will facilitate interaction between the children. Activities need to be provided which are interesting to both children and which are within the competence of the child with motor disabilities but also appropriate for the TD children.

If children with motor disabilities are in mainstream education teachers need to emphasize their skills and talents, rather than focusing on their difficulties. It may even be appropriate to teach the children with motor disabilities a particular skill that perhaps they can excel at. The TD children, particularly when older, need to be encouraged to adjust their behavior to give the child with motor disabilities the space to respond and initiate. They may need to be given examples of open and real questions which will help the child with motor disabilities to join in and questions to avoid. For some children with severe motor problems interaction with TD children may be very difficult. For such children the opportunity to interact with children with other motor disabilities may be very important and reduce their isolation (e.g., Lord et al., 1990).

As they get older, children with motor disabilities can be helped to develop strategies for being included in interactions. Mulderij (1996) identified four strategies used by the children with motor disabilities that she observed: compensation; initiating; acceptance; and creativity. Compensation referred to the children developing a valued skill to a level which matched or was better than that of the TD children; initiating was a strategy whereby the children did not ask if they could play but announced that they were joining in some group activity; acceptance described occasions when the children with motor disabilities offered bribes in return for being included in the interaction, perhaps by providing sweets or rides on their wheelchair; the strategy of creativity involved the children devising ways to make it possible for them to join in, such as requiring that the TD children only walked when playing tag so that the child in a wheelchair could keep up.

Motor disabilities create many different problems, both primary and secondary, for individual children and their families. It is essential that the needs and wishes of the children are taken into account and that any intervention focuses on the whole child, rather than just on the motor problems.

Children with Down's syndrome

Many of the studies discussed in chapter 5 indicate that the development of young children with DS differs in a number of ways from that of TD children. This raises important questions about how to support and facilitate their development. Many intervention programs with young children with disabilities, such as Portage (e.g., Daly, Addington, Kerfoot, & Sigston, 1985), are based on our understanding of the development of TD children. However, if our current theories of development cannot accommodate the different sequences of development observed in children with DS, it is unlikely that theories of development based on TD children are appropriate for guiding intervention with children with DS (e.g., Wishart, 1993). Support for this view comes from findings that although children with DS involved in early intervention programs may show short-term cognitive gains over children who do not experience the intervention (e.g., Champion, 1987), these cognitive gains are not maintained in the long term (e.g., Cunningham, 1986). As Wishart (1998) points out, effective intervention will only become possible when we understand clearly the exact nature of the LDs associated with DS. But for now, what advice and support should be given to parents with young babies with DS? In the absence of theoretical understanding of the processes underlying the development of children with DS, any advice needs to be based on our current understanding of the development of children with DS.

Parents need to be encouraged to interact and play with their baby with DS from the beginning. The baby may appear undemanding and easy, crying less often and less intensely than a TD baby and making fewer vocalizations. But to leave the baby alone at this time is to miss opportunities which could be spent giving the baby attention and stimulation and parents should be encouraged to respond to her weaker signals even though the noises she makes may not feel as demanding as those of TD babies. At this early stage the parents will be coming to terms with the disability and careful, sensitive support is crucial. The parents need to be shown that their baby is developing and, more importantly, they need to be alerted to ways in which they could adjust their behavior in relation what is known about how children with DS develop. It is also important that the additional problems commonly associated with DS are checked regularly, such as eyesight (e.g., Mon-Williams, Jobling, & Wann, 2000; Woodhouse et al., 1997; J. M. Woodhouse et al., 1996) and hearing.

Babies and young children with DS take longer to process information than TD babies and children and they do not remember as much information. Therefore, objects and toys should be presented slowly and children with DS should be given time to look at people and objects and to listen to different sounds and voices. In other words, babies and children with DS need more time than TD babies and children to take in information and respond before new things are introduced or the parent or any other person makes a comment. Parents and others should wait and fit their behavior around the baby's behavior to a greater extent than is necessary with the TD baby. Parents should be encouraged to make their behavior contingent on the baby's behavior, so that the baby is the one who is controlling the speed with which things happen.

In the first year of life babies with DS may show more interest in people than in objects and parents need to find ways of involving objects in the interaction. It may be difficult for the parent to establish interaction between themselves, their child with DS, and an object or something going on in the environment. When interacting with a child with DS, the parent should talk about what the child is doing or showing an interest in, rather than trying to redirect her attention to something different (e.g., Landry & Chapieski, 1989). If the parent tries to redirect the child's attention the child may become disinterested and opportunities for communication and interaction lost. Thus, if parents are interacting with their baby and the baby's attention shifts to a toy or something going on in the environment, the parent should let the baby look at the toy and wait until the baby looks back before making any comment. Any comment that the parent makes should relate to the child's focus of attention. It is also important that if the parent asks the child to do something the request should be for something that the parent knows the child can do, rather than being outside of her ability range, otherwise the child is likely to disengage from the interaction (e.g., Mahoney & Neville-Smith, 1996).

For many parents, adjusting their behavior in these sorts of ways may be very difficult, although some may do it naturally. As Berger (1990) points out, many parents of children with DS are likely to perceive interacting with their young child as synonymous with teaching. This naturally leads them to be more directive, intense, and intrusive. Such parents will need a great deal of support to reduce their level of input to their child in order to give their child the time to take in information and the opportunity to respond. It may be helpful to use videos of the parent interacting with the child to demonstrate the effect of the parent interacting less intensely.

Unlike the TD child, the child with DS in her second year is not so attracted to the sound of her mother's voice. Parents and others such as siblings and other family members need to talk clearly and slowly to the child with DS, repeating phrases and leaving longer gaps between utterances than they might otherwise do (e.g., Glenn & Cunningham, 1983; Summers et al., 1997) to give the child time to take in the information and to vocalize. Glenn and Cunningham also suggest that, because children with DS seem to be especially attracted to nursery rhymes, the possibility of using rhymes to teach words should be explored.

As we saw in chapter 5, children with DS have greater problems in the area of language than would be expected given their development in other areas. This seems to be related to their relatively poor short-term memory for auditory material and poor long-term memory for both verbal and spatial information. This has a number of implications for how parents and teachers should approach language learning with children with DS (e.g., Buckley, 1999). Because of their relatively good visual–spatial short-term memories children with DS who do not show any indication of learning to speak should be introduced to a sign system (e.g., Jenkins, 1993). They should also be introduced to written language even if they have little or no spoken language (e.g., Buckley & Bird, 1993). Both sign language and written language may help their subsequent acquisition of spoken language by capitalizing on their relatively spared short-term visual–spatial memories (e.g., Jarrold et al., 1999b).

Children with DS who have some spoken language are likely to understand more language than they express and although they may have relatively good vocabularies they may produce short, ungrammatical sentences which may be unintelligible. These findings have a number of implications. It is important when talking with children with DS to try to use language which is appropriate to their comprehension, rather than using language which more closely matches their expressive language (e.g., Tingley et al., 1994). This is likely to be quite difficult for parents and teachers since in everyday conversation we often judge the language competence of an individual in terms of their language production and adjust our own language accordingly. Nevertheless, parents and teachers should not be afraid of using more complicated sentence structures than the child herself produces, adjusting their own language more in line with the vocabulary that the child with DS uses rather than the grammatical structure of her sentences.

Children with DS who have relatively large vocabularies but produce short, often ungrammatical, sentences will need help with sentence production (e.g., Hart, 1996). They often omit verbs from their utterances, which increases the likelihood that what they say will be ungrammatical. Therefore one aspect of speech production to target is verb usage, encouraging the children to use verbs that they already have in their vocabularies in appropriate contexts (e.g., Hesketh & Chapman, 1998). Support for developing the complexity of their sentence construction should continue into adolescence and reliance on auditory short-term memory should be minimized throughout. Thus, providing new examples of grammatical constructions by reading new stories to children with DS is probably not particularly useful. Rather, it would be better to read repeatedly the children's favorite stories (e.g., Chapman, 1998). Although, as Jarrold et al. (2000a) point out, the technique of repeating particular sentence constructions is unlikely to be beneficial since rehearsal is not used by TD children until the age of about 7 years and children with DS rarely reach this developmental level.

The poor intelligibility of the language of many children with DS is also another area where parents and teachers can help the child. There may be physical reasons for the poor intelligibility of the language of children with DS; however, the fact that children with DS tend to pronounce words differently on different occasions suggests that they can alter how they pronounce words. Parents and teachers should try to improve the intelligibility of the speech of children with DS by only accepting the correct pronunciation for each word.

A further problem for the child with DS seems to be in relating separate pieces of information together. For example, there is evidence from Morss's (1983, 1985) and Wishart's (e.g., 1993) studies that the child with DS does not build on her previous experience, in that on one occasion she may understand particular things about objects and yet, on a later occasion, she may appear to have forgotten this knowledge. Just because TD children seem to build on what they have previously learned, it cannot be assumed that this will be the case with the child with DS. Tasks need to be repeated and, if a new skill relies on several skills that the child has previously demonstrated, she may need to be reminded of these earlier skills. Similarly, because of their known memory difficulties, all information necessary for a particular task should be made available to the child at the time of doing the task if at all possible, rather than relying on the child remembering information given on a previous occasion. Situations which are fairly open ended, such as pretend play, may present particular difficulties for children with DS. It may be better to have one or two sets of props which support pretend play and to develop relatively set play routines with the child, than to try to engage the child in many different pretend scenarios. The child with DS will learn more from regularly engaging in a few familiar routines than if parents or teachers try to engage her in many different activities.

The difficulties that children with DS have in linking, remembering, and consolidating different bits of information also have implications for assessment. The child with DS should be assessed on more than one occasion, since her performance at any one time may be unreliable. If possible she should also be assessed in different places such as at home as well as in a clinical or educational setting since her motivation to respond may vary in different settings (e.g., Hasan & Messer, 1997). Hasan and Messer also suggest that whenever possible those carrying out assessments should follow the child's interests and adjust the testing accordingly. The problem with this suggestion is that if standardized tests are used the results will be invalidated if the assessment does not follow the specified test procedures. However, as Wishart and Duffy (1990) point out, the fact that children with DS seem to develop differently from TD children indicates that it is inappropriate to rely on test procedures which have been standardized on TD children. One implication of this is that assessment tests need to be developed specifically for children with DS and standardized on them. Such tools could then indicate the extent to which the development of a child with DS is similar to or different from that of other children with DS. Nevertheless, if children with DS are administered tests which have been standardized on TD children, the results need to be interpreted with great caution.

Nursery or playgroup opportunities are important for children with DS. There should be the choice of attending groups organized for children without disabilities as well as specialist groups. The range of ability among children with DS is large and, because of this, it is crucial that each child's preschool or school placement is decided on the basis of her particular capabilities. Educational placement must not be based on the stereotyped view of DS. The abilities of children with DS have been underestimated in the past, and their ultimate potential is not yet known. These children are not necessarily best placed in special schools for children with learning difficulties. Many will benefit from attending mainstream schools and this should be encouraged. Only when it is felt that the needs of both the child with DS and the mainstream children would be better met if the child with DS attended a special school should such a transfer be arranged. Before implementing such a transfer, the possibility of modifying the mainstream school should be explored fully.

Many of the implications discussed above with parents in mind are also relevant to teachers. Teachers must be aware that children with DS may take longer to make sense of particular tasks. Also, they must be aware of the possibility that children with DS do not incorporate old skills into new skills in the same way as TD children. Children with DS must be given more opportunities to rehearse skills which are prerequisite for later ones, and to experience the relationship between different pieces of information. Uecker et al. (1993) recommend the use of simple learning materials and focusing on expanding the intact abilities of children with DS rather than teaching new skills. Like parents, teachers should build on the relatively good visual–spatial memories of children with DS, for example, teaching reading by look and say methods rather than teaching the sounds of individual letters. It is also clear that adolescents and young adults with DS continue to acquire new skills and it is important that they have the opportunity to further their academic skills beyond the usual school leaving age.

Above all, it must not be assumed that children with DS are as incapable as has been believed in the past. Such expectations can be self-fulfilling and detrimental to the children and their families.

Children with autism

Identifying practical implications from studies of children with autism is problematic because although their difficulties are well established, the primary cause of their difficulties is unclear despite extensive research. Unlike, for example, blind children where the initial problem, assuming they have no other disability, is impaired vision, we do not know what underlies the problems experienced by children with autism. Different researchers have argued for different primary problems, including difficulties engaging in social interaction, inability to understand minds, executive dysfunction, weak central coherence. Of course it is possible that autism results from some combination of these or from some as yet unidentified difficulty. As a result it is only possible to identify a range of implications which arise from the different primary problems which have been implicated in autism.

Children with autism cover a wide range of ability, from those with severe learning difficulties which persist into adulthood to a minority who succeed in Higher Education (Howlin et al., 2000). As a result the practical implications which arise from the studies discussed in chapter 6 may be more relevant to some children than to others, depending on their level of ability and particular problems. Nevertheless, even able children with autism will still experience some difficulties, for example, when behavior is dependent on an understanding of other people's minds. However, they may be able to develop or be taught strategies for overcoming at least some of these difficulties. Although they will still not understand the minds of others in the same way that TD children do, they may be able to learn how to adjust their behavior to that of others around them. On the other hand, many children with autism will not be able to make use of such strategies. For such children it may be necessary to make adjustments to their environment in order to minimize their difficulties. Most children with autism will have behaviors which are unacceptable in certain situations and parents, teachers, and professionals will need to work together to identify these behaviors and ways in which they can be altered so that they are more acceptable. Howlin (1998) outlines some of the ways in which this can be approached.

Many parents will come across accounts of claims that autism can be "cured" by following certain regimes and programs. Howlin (1998) reviews a number of these interventions and argues that autism cannot be "cured" despite the claims. She points out that these interventions may lead to short-term improvements but there is no evidence that they have long-lasting effects. A number of them, such as the approach taken by Lovaas (e.g., 1996), are very demanding, and parents need to be given information and support when considering if the possible benefits will outweigh the financial and personal costs involved. Although Howlin does not advocate any of the specific programs, she argues that the development of children with autism can benefit from intervention. Drawing on evidence of our understanding of their development and the effectiveness of different approaches, she describes a number of ways in which communicative and social skills can be developed and repetitive, stereotyped behaviors reduced. In a review of studies which have focused on social skills, Rogers (2000) concludes that the social behavior of children with autism can be altered and indicates the value of involving TD peers.

One of the points made by Howlin and others is that intervention should start as early as possible. Obviously this is dependent upon a diagnosis of autism being made and this may not happen until around the age of 6 years (e.g., Howlin & Moore, 1997). The development of the Checklist for Autism in Toddlers (CHAT, Baron-Cohen et al., 1992) has made it possible for children to be screened for autism at 18 months by health visitors or other health professionals (Baird et al., 2000). While the CHAT will not identify all children who are diagnosed subsequently with autism, a proportion will be identified and can be involved in intervention from a much earlier age than would otherwise be possible. Given that the checklist only takes a few minutes to administer, it should be administered routinely to all children at about 18 months. Any children identified as being at risk of having autism on the basis of the CHAT should then be referred to experienced clinicians for further assessments.

Once a diagnosis of autism is confirmed, parents need to be given advice about the difficulties which their child is likely to experience. Similar advice needs to made available for those involved with the child when she starts any preschool provision and later when she begins school, particularly if she attends a mainstream school where the staff will have less experience of autism than in a school catering specifically for children with autism. Parents and teachers need to be made aware that although much is known about the problems facing children with autism we are still some way from understanding the underlying cause or causes. They should be informed about the main contenders of difficulty understanding minds, executive dysfunction, and weak central coherence as awareness of these will help them appreciate why the child is behaving in a particular way and indicate ways in which changes to their own behavior or the environment may help the child behave more appropriately.

For example, children with autism seldom initiate interaction or pay attention to what others are doing. Despite this, parents and teachers should interact with these children and should encourage them to take part in shared activities. Others should initiate activities and conversations. For children who fail to acquire any useful language, alternative means of communication should be encouraged, such as signing or picture boards. If the children develop some language then adults should try not to be too controlling in order to encourage the children to take some initiative (Rydell & Mirenda, 1994). If children with autism mainly repeat things that have been said to them it is important to clarify whether this echolalic speech is just repetition for its own sake or whether it serves a purpose such as helping the children make sense of what others are saying, or indicating that they are anxious about something. Obviously if the speech serves some purpose for particular children then it would be inappropriate to try to reduce it.

Given the difficulties that children with autism have understanding minds, parents and others need to use simple sentences in which their intended meaning is clear, direct and literal. Thus, metaphor, irony, and jokes should be avoided and questions should indicate exactly what is required. Howlin (1998) gives a number of examples such as saying "Please give me the bread" rather than "Can you pass the bread?" since the child might correctly respond "yes" to the latter question but not actually pass the bread.

Parents and teachers need to understand the difficulties that children with autism may experience in understanding emotions, especially those which stem from beliefs. Some able children with autism will be able to learn the sorts of behaviors which others show when they are experiencing certain emotions and how to behave appropriately. Similarly, they may be able to learn strategies for using pronouns appropriately. However, it needs to be remembered that although some children with autism can be taught how to respond in one situation, they may fail to generalize their learning to a different situation. As a result they may have to be taught the same strategy in different situations.

Some children can be helped to understand minds by describing thoughts as pictures in the head (e.g., Swettenham, 2000). This may enable them to gain some understanding of what others are thinking, although as yet there are very few studies exploring the extent to which such a technique generalizes to different situations (e.g., McGregor, Whiten, & Blackburn, 1998). The use of visual strategies may also help in other areas which involve thinking (e.g., Harris & Leevers, 2000). They cite the example of Temple Grandin, an able and articulate adult with autism, who described her mind as a series of visual images (Grandin, 1996). Harris and Leevers suggest that rather than using verbal approaches to help children with autism understand the process of thinking, approaches involving pictorial material may be more appropriate. Thus, thinking can be explained by giving the child a doll, explaining that the doll is thinking about an object, giving the child a photograph of the object which the child inserts into the doll's head.

One way to minimize the difficulties which children with autism have planning actions in order to achieve particular goals is for adults to take over some of the planning by structuring situations (e.g., Hughes et al, 1997). This can be done by parents and teachers breaking down tasks into separate steps and sequencing activities so that the adults provide the organization which the child with autism finds so difficult. As with behaviors which draw on an understanding of minds, some children with autism will benefit from being taught how to monitor their own behavior, for example, by using feedback from any mistakes they make. But for many children with autism it will be necessary for adults to impose structure and organization.

As we have seen, a small minority of children with autism have exceptional abilities such as in the field of art. Pring et al. (1995) argue that it is important that these individuals are given the opportunity to develop their skills in the same way that a TD child with such an ability would be encouraged. Even though their skills may stand out as very unusual given their difficulties in other areas, it is important that these children are not revered for their special skill but that they are allowed to develop that skill as far as possible.

At the beginning of this section I pointed out that a problem for identifying practical implications from studies of children with autism is that the underlying problem is not yet agreed. However, one way to test whether or not a particular explanation of autism has any validity is to evaluate the effectiveness of interventions which are based on it, not just for the behavior which is targeted by the intervention but also other aspects of the disability (e.g., Bishop, 1997).

Implications for research

In chapter 1 I identified a number of difficulties which arise when carrying out research with children with disabilities. The studies which I have examined in the intervening chapters have illustrated many of these problems but in some cases they have pointed to possible solutions or additional factors which need to be considered. In this section I want to consider the implications of some of the studies for research. Although I have given examples from children with particular disabilities, many of them are also relevant to the study of children with different disabilities, including disabilities not covered in this book.

One of the problems concerns grouping children together because they present with the same disability. Some children with disabilities may be grouped together because they have the same genetic disorder. Thus, most children with DS share a pattern of chromosomes which is specific to DS and different from that of TD children. However, despite this chromosomal similarity there is great variability in terms of the effect that the additional chromosome has on their development. For example, although on average children with DS do not develop to the same level as TD children, individual children with DS vary in the levels of development achieved. In addition, certain areas of development are better preserved in children with DS than other areas of development, although there are individual differences in the extent of this.

In other disabilities children may be grouped together because of similar behaviors. For example, children with DCD all perform poorly on tests of motor skill. However, their difficulties may result from a number of different causes and the motor problems of children with DCD due to different causes may have different origins. This means that although the motor difficulties may appear similar, the underlying reasons for the problems may differ.

The problems which arise when children with particular disabilities are grouped together have important implications for how the development of children with disabilities should be studied. A key question is whether it is appropriate to group children with a particular disability together, based either on a shared cause or similar behavior, given that such an approach will mask individual differences. An alternative is to study individual children. It is clear that much can be learned from individual case studies. However, as Pérez-Pereira and Conti-Ramsden (1999) point out with respect to blind children, if small numbers of children are studied, it is important that they are studied in depth and sufficient data are collected and analyzed both quantitatively and qualitatively to justify any conclusions.

It seems likely that much will be learned about the processes underlying the development of children with a disability by focusing on how individual children progress. As Mervis and Robinson (1999) point out for children with DS, study of those who show more advanced development than expected may be particularly informative and help to address the link between different processes. To illustrate this, they cite the finding that individuals with DS who have good language skills also have good auditory memories and vice versa (Vallar & Papagno, 1993). Similarly, longitudinal studies would help to clarify the relationship between DCD and later social and emotional problems (Schoemaker & Kalverboer, 1994), the question of whether children with DCD have difficulties controlling certain motor actions because of a delay or difference in development (Hill & Wing, 1998), and the nature of language development in children with SB (Morrow & Wachs, 1992).

Longitudinal studies of children with disabilities which are relatively infrequent may also be particularly valuable, especially when there are marked individual differences, as in blind children. Thus, the detailed longitudinal studies of blind children's language by Pérez-Pereira (1994, 1997) and his colleagues (e.g., 1992, 1997; see also 1999) have contributed a great deal to our understanding.

While longitudinal studies may have many advantages, they are costly and time-consuming. It seems likely therefore that many researchers will continue to make group comparisons. In this case it is important that careful thought is given to the basis on which children with a particular disability are included and how different groups of children are matched.

As I have already argued, children who have the same disability often differ greatly from one another in developmental terms. It is therefore crucial that if a group of children are studied the group is as homogeneous as possible. Research with children with DCD illustrates this issue well. Although all children with DCD have motor problems, there is no agreed consensus about the level of performance on standardized tests of motor skill such as the Movement ABC which is required for a diagnosis of DCD. Thus, different studies have included children whose scores fall below the 5th, 10th, 15th, and even 20th percentile. Until the cut-off point for DCD is agreed among researchers and adhered to, it will remain difficult to compare findings across studies which have included children with different degrees of motor problems.

In addition, as Dewey and Kaplan (1994) and Sigmundsson (e.g., 1999) have suggested, some children with DCD may have greater problems in one area than in another. It is important that researchers distinguish children with different sorts of DCD in order to increase the likelihood of identifying specific processes underlying the development of different groups of children. Further, studying the relationship between different types of DCD should help clarify the problems facing children with these motor difficulties (Miyahara & Möbs, 1995). It is also important to distinguish between children with DCD who have additional problems and those who do not. Thus, Gillberg and colleagues' research (e.g., Gillberg et al., 1982; Gillberg & Gillberg, 1983, 1989; Hellgren, Gillberg, Gillberg, & Enerskog, 1993; Hellgren et al., 1994) distinguishing children with DCD and attention difficulties from those with DCD but no attention problems has helped identify problems specific to DCD. Similarly, studying children with autism with IQs in the normal range has contributed to our understanding of how autism affects development, separate from any effects of learning difficulties due to low IQs.

It is also important that as much relevant detail as possible is provided of the children's physical and psychological characteristics. For example, Wills et al. (1990) pointed out that for children with SB it is important that details of the physical characteristics of the children as well as their medical histories are provided in order that the effects of these different factors can be examined. A number of indicators of the severity of SB such as lesion level and the presence or absence of hydrocephalus are quite commonly reported. In addition, Holmbeck and Faier-Routman (1995) argued that the severity of hydrocephalus should be quantified, rather than just using the simple dichotomy of whether or not the child has a shunt. The value of this was seen in the study by Ito et al. (1997) who demonstrated a relationship between measurements of the lateral ventricles and the discrepancy between verbal and nonverbal IQ.

Matching groups of children is not straightforward and two particular difficulties are illustrated well when children with DS are considered. The first is that assessments on developmental scales, such as the Bayley Scales, early in infancy are not correlated with later cognitive development (e.g., Wagner et al., 1990). This raises questions about the meaningfulness of matching infants for developmental age given that the rationale for such matching is that the groups will be of similar cognitive ability. However, the second problem is of greater concern. In chapter 5 we saw that children with DS may achieve a particular overall score on a developmental test by a different combination of passed and failed items than normally seen in TD children. In other words, the profile of items passed and failed may differ between the children, although the same number of items overall is passed. Thus, if children with DS are matched with TD children or children with some other disability on overall developmental score, it is unlikely that they will be matched item by item. The same point is made for children with autism by Hobson (1991). But does this matter?

Most developmental scales employed with young children assess a range of different abilities, including cognitive, perceptual, motor, language, and social skills. To take a specific example, children with DS have particular difficulties in the area of language and consequently they are more likely to fail language items than, say, items assessing social development. Therefore, if a child with DS is matched with a TD child for overall performance on a developmental scale, the child with DS is likely to do relatively well on social items and less well on language items whereas the TD child is more likely to perform at a similar level on both language and social items. Thus, although the children have been matched overall, the matching procedure itself hides underlying differences. This becomes a problem if the research question to be addressed in a study assumes that the children have been matched for particular skills. Ideally the children should be matched on specific aspects of development which are relevant to the research questions being addressed. For example, if expressive and receptive language abilities of children with DS and TD children are being examined, it would make more sense to match the children on expressive language and to compare their receptive language abilities than to match the children for overall developmental age and examine both expressive and receptive language.

A similar problem can be seen when matching children with motor disabilities and TD children. Given the motor problems associated with SB, CP and DCD it is important that when they are matched with TD children for intelligence, the matching relies on items or tests which do not have a motor component. However, it is also important that if verbal items are used these do not result in an overestimation of the children's intellectual ability, such as might occur if verbal tests assessing expressive language are employed with children with SB.

Research focusing on group comparisons raises the question of the composition of the comparison group. Mervis and Robinson (1999) suggest that for DS the most informative comparison is children who only differ from the child with DS in terms of not having DS, that is, monozygotic twins discordant for DS. However, such an approach is hardly realistic for any disability, although Pérez-Pereira has demonstrated clearly the value of studying twins discordant for blindness, though in this case the twins were dizygotic (e.g., 1994, 1999; Pérez-Pereira & Castro, 1992).

In most studies unrelated TD children will make up the comparison group and such comparisons can be informative provided that some of the issues identified above are addressed. Comparisons of children with DS with children with other disabilities can also be informative, provided that the basis for the group selected is sound theoretically (Dykens & Hodapp, 2001). Thus, comparing aspects of social development in children with autism and children with DS may not contribute to our understanding of the social development of children with DS, whereas comparisons with children with other learning difficulties but not DS may help indicate the extent to which a characteristic is unique to children with DS, rather than resulting from learning difficulties. Other comparisons may also help inform our understanding of particular developmental processes. Thus, Jarrold et al. (1999a) argued for dissociable auditory and visual–spatial components of short-term memory on the basis of evidence that adolescents with DS do poorly on auditory memory tasks, in contrast to adolescents with Williams syndrome who do poorly on visual-spatial memory tasks.

It is also important that great care is taken to design tasks which assess the specific process under consideration. Unless this is achieved any differences could be due to something other than the process which was supposedly being examined. This difficulty has been illustrated well for studies of emotion understanding in children with autism by Hobson (1991) and is also particularly evident when studies of blind children and deaf children are examined. For example, Norgate (1998) pointed out that blind children may fail to group objects into categories simply because in the absence of vision it is difficult for them to keep track of the objects. Such a method is therefore inappropriate for studying object categorization in blind children. For children with motor disabilities it is obviously crucial that tasks which are assessing processes other than motor skills do not have a motor component (e.g., Wilson & McKenzie, 1998). In line with this, Fletcher et al. (1996) suggested using tasks presented on computer for children with SB rather than paper and pencil tasks.

If research does rely on group comparisons then it is crucial that particular attention is paid to what data are collected and how the results are examined. For example, it is often difficult to make comparisons across studies because data have been collected and coded in different ways. In terms of results it is important to know whether or not the range of scores of two groups overlap, rather than just that the means are significantly different. In other words, do all the children with a disability behave in the same way as the group means suggest? This is important, as whether or not there is overlap between the behavior of different groups can address questions of universality (a characteristic is shown by all children with the disability) and uniqueness (a characteristic occurs only in children with the disability).

A further implication for research concerns how behavior is interpreted. The behavior of children with and without a disability may look the same but the processes underlying the behavior may differ. For example, in the case of DS, Wright (1998) has shown that the performance of children with DS on object permanence tasks may simply reflect their ability to imitate the hiding action, rather than reflect an underlying representation of the hidden object. It is important that similarities in behavior are not taken to mean that the processes underlying the behavior are necessarily the same. In a related way it is also important that care is taken when interpreting failures on particular tasks. Again drawing on studies with children with DS, children with DS are reported to be more likely than TD children to avoid certain tasks. While such avoidance may reflect an underlying inability, it may also be due to other problems such as inattention or lack of motivation. Researchers, and practitioners, need to be aware of this and to ensure, as far as possible, that such alternative explanations cannot account for the behavior observed. One way around this particular problem is to repeat tasks in different settings and on different occasions. If the child succeeds on some occasions but not on others, it is unlikely that the failures reflect a lack of the ability being tested.

chapter eight
Theoretical implications

Introduction

This chapter considers the implications of the development of children with disabilities for our understanding of development in general. The aim is not to present a new theory of development but rather to point to some factors which any complete account of development must be able to explain. The study of the development of children with disabilities provides an important way of examining our general understanding of development and of indicating inadequacies and limitations of existing theoretical accounts of developmental processes.

How may the development of children with disabilities relate to the development of TD children? Five types of relationships were outlined by Walker and Crawley (1983): delayed; abnormal; compensatory; absent; and normal. Delayed development is simply slower development than in the TD child, but the same stages are passed through and the same processes involved, although the child with a disability may ultimately reach a less advanced stage. By abnormal development, Walker and Crawley are referring to situations when the process of development is different from that seen in TD children and the resulting behaviors or developments are not seen in TD children. In compensatory development, development takes a different route from that taken by TD children, although the end point is the same. When a development is absent, the child with a disability fails to develop in this particular area. Finally, aspects of the development of a child with a disability may be similar to that seen in TD children, and develop within the range of variation reported for TD children. The compensatory type of development is of particular interest from a theoretical point of view, since it may question existing assumptions about how a development comes about. Of course, within any disability any or all of the five relationships to typical development may occur, since the disability may affect different areas of development in different ways.

I shall now consider some of the theoretical implications which arise from each disability considered in this book. It is important to bear in mind that if a child with a disability develops differently from a TD child, it is very likely that the difference is due to the disability. However, it may not be a direct consequence of the disability. It may be caused by some other consequence of the disability, for example, some restriction in the child's environment which is brought about by the disability but which is not inevitable. Alternatively it may be that, for some reason unrelated to the disability, an alternative route to a particular development is not available. All these possibilities need to be considered when examining the theoretical implications of the studies. The aim of any account of development should be to accommodate all of the findings.

Blind children

Most of us know of blind people who have excelled in particular spheres. For example, the musician Stevie Wonder, the broadcaster Peter White, the politician David Blunkett. These examples demonstrate that blindness does not preclude development. And yet the studies reviewed in chapter 2 indicate that the development of blind children differs from that of TD children in many ways. This makes the study of blind children of particular significance for theories of development. If our explanations of development in TD children draw heavily on their ability to see, then studies of blind children indicate that these developments must be able to occur by alternative routes which are not reliant on vision. The identification of alternative routes is perhaps the most important theoretical implication to arise from studies of blind children.

However, there are at least two further important implications. The first arises from studies of blind children who experience many difficulties and do not become competent adolescents and adults. In some cases their difficulties may result from brain damage additional to their blindness. However, some blind children who experience difficulties do not appear to have brain damage, although, of course, we can never completely rule out this possibility. Nevertheless, if we assume that at least some of these children do not have brain damage then it seems likely that the difference between the development of blind children who succeed and those who experience difficulties reflect environmental differences. Any theoretical account of development must be able to account for these environmental influences. The third theoretical implication to arise from studies of blind children concerns our understanding of how different behaviors and developments are related, in particular whether certain behaviors are dependent on the same underlying mechanism or not. I shall consider each of these implications in turn.

The very fact that some children with little or no sight experience relatively few developmental problems clearly demonstrates that development can occur in the absence of visual input. A number of authors have pointed to the important role that language may play as a source of information to the child both in terms of making sense of language itself and for the information that language can provide the child about the environment (e.g., Landau, 1997; Landau & Gleitman, 1985; Pérez-Pereira & Conti-Ramsden, 1999). I shall consider these in a moment. However, it is important to consider the process by which the blind child develops in the first couple of years before she can make much use of language.

During this period the child is discovering a great deal about the environment, for example, that objects and people are entities in their own right and that she can influence her environment. For the sighted child much of this knowledge will be acquired as a result of her observing what is going on around her and the consequences of her own and others' actions. However, visual information is not the only information available. Consider the child's ability to differentiate her mother and a stranger. There are many different ways in which the discrimination could be made by blind children: on the basis of the adults' voices, their characteristic smells, the feel of their faces, the sound of their footsteps, how they hold and react to the child, and so on. Obviously there may be advantages of vision. The sighted child may recognize her mother as she comes through the door even though her mother does not speak. The blind child may not show any recognition until her mother says something. But basically a great deal of information is available through the intact senses of the blind child and this is the information that she uses. Of course, the sighted child may also make use of this information, but for her in most situations, the visual route is likely to be the sense she relies on. Thus, the blind child is drawing on different information from the sighted child, but because the information comes from the same source, the blind child can still obtain a very similar level of understanding to the sighted child.

This idea of the blind child making use of information from different sources which is congruent in some sense with information available to the sighted child has been incorporated into a theory proposed by Millar to explain blind children's spatial understanding (e.g., 1994, 1997c). Millar suggests that spatial development in blind children depends on "convergent active processing in interrelated networks." In other words, the blind child needs to receive inputs from different sources and modalities which converge and overlap with her existing knowledge in order to build up an understanding of space. Millar argues that it is important that there is redundancy in the information from different sources. Although Millar has not extended her theory to other areas of development, it is possible to see how this would work. For example, in the case of the blind child learning to recognize her mother, she will receive information through her intact senses which, because they come from the same source, her mother, will be congruent and overlapping and the blind child will be able to construct an image of her mother from the different bits of information which are available.

Of course, this may sometimes lead the blind child to misunderstand certain aspects of the environment. For example, in chapter 2 we saw how young blind children's understanding of what sighted people can see may be influenced by the fact that they perceive touch and vision as being comparable in some way (e.g., Bigelow, 1988, 1991b). Thus, because they cannot touch objects which are beyond a certain distance, they generalize this to vision. Clearly this misunderstanding may be resolved with experience, and particularly through language, and I shall consider this shortly.

First, I want to consider how blind children make sense of language. As for sighted children, adults will label objects and people that blind children experience through touch, sound, and taste. However, Landau (Landau, 1997; Landau & Gleitman, 1985) and Pérez-Pereira and Conti-Ramsden (1999) argue that blind children can learn a great deal about language through the syntax or the structure of language itself. For example, Landau points out that once children know that nouns are preceded by certain other words, such as definite or indefinite articles or quantifiers, they can recognize words they have never heard before as nouns. Landau and Gleitman demonstrated the understanding that a blind girl had of the verbs "look" and "see," arguing that if such visual terms were dependent on visual experience this would not have been possible. In this way, blind children can begin to make sense of words they hear through how the words fit within the very structure of the language they hear.

I now want to look at language as a source of information available to the blind child. Clearly the acquisition of language by blind children provides them with access to much information about the environment. Through communication with others, blind children can discover a great deal about the people and objects which surround them (e.g., Pérez-Pereira & Conti-Ramsden, 1999). Some of this may be direct, as when they are told something that they did not previously know. But blind children may also learn a great deal about their physical and social environment just by listening to conversations between other people. Blind children, like sighted children, may make use of this linguistic information to confirm things they already know, to raise questions about something they thought they knew but which is inconsistent with what is now being said, or to learn something completely new. As such, language can be an invaluable source of information for blind children.

Thus, there are many different routes to development, and while those involving the visual modality are inaccessible to children with no sight, other routes are available. This leads to the question of why, if there are alternative routes to development, some blind children, who as far as we can tell do not have additional brain damage, experience problems. This question leads to the second theoretical implication of studies of blind children which I want to consider. One possible explanation for some blind children experiencing problems is that for some reason these children are unable to make use of the alternative routes. How could this come about? Millar's theory of "convergent active processing in interrelated networks" could, I believe, explain why some blind children experience more difficulties than others. For example, one could argue that those children experiencing difficulties have not been provided with a range of appropriate inputs. Put another way, information from which they could build up an understanding of their environment has not been made available to them, either in sufficient quantity, quality, or variety to allow for convergence and redundancy. In addition, this sort of account could also explain the individual differences observed among blind children.

Millar has only proposed her theory with respect to blind children's understanding of spatial concepts, including braille, although she does include aspects of language. It is important that the theory is extended to other areas. It is also important that the suggestion that some blind children may fail because of a limitation in the information they receive is examined. However, there are some existing findings which are compatible with Millar's proposal. For example, Norgate et al.'s (1998) study reporting a relationship between differences in the early rhymes and routines engaged in by parents and their blind children and the children's development several years later; Peterson et al.'s (2000) suggestion that conversational differences within the family may account for differences in the development of theory of mind in blind children; Webster and Roe's (1998) view that the contextual information blind children are provided with is a major determinant of their behavior and play. Of course, all these findings could be explained by some difficulty inherent within those children who do less well, rather than resorting to an explanation involving the nature of the information they receive from the environment. However, the attraction of Millar's theory is that specific proposals are made about the nature of the input necessary for development in blind children, in terms of providing converging information from different sources along with a degree of redundancy. This account also has practical implications, as mentioned in chapter 7.

I shall now consider the third theoretical implication arising from studies of blind children. One of the most influential accounts of development has been Piaget's (e.g., 1983). Of particular interest from the point of view of studies of blind children is Piaget's account of development in the first 2 years of life, the sensori-motor period. Piaget outlined six stages through which sighted children pass between birth and about 2 years of age, from simple reflexive responses to the environment to being able to form internal mental representations. The different stages within the sensori-motor period are characterized by distinct behaviors in a range of areas, including reaction to a parent's departure and to the approach of strangers, behavior towards hidden objects, language, understanding of causality, and play. Piaget argued that all these behaviors reflect the children's underlying ability to represent the environment, and that therefore their emergence will necessarily be related. However, some of these relationships are not observed in blind children. For example, Rogers and Puchalski (1988) failed to find a relationship between object permanence and either symbolic play, anxiety when separated from a parent, or fear of strangers in the blind children they studied.

How might we explain these findings? There are several possibilities. For example, it may be that an understanding of object permanence is dependent on more than mental representation. Thus, Rogers and Puchalski (1988) point to the role of spatial memory. If the development of spatial memory has a different time course from the development of mental representation in blind children, this could explain the lack of relationship between object permanence and other behaviors in blind children, assuming that these latter behaviors are not just dependent on mental representation. If spatial memory is also involved in sighted children's understanding of object permanence, then we would have to propose that spatial memory and mental representation develop in parallel in sighted children. Alternatively, it might be that spatial memory is not involved in sighted children's ability to find hidden objects, whereas it is in blind children.

Currently we have no way of distinguishing between these possibilities but they could be tested fairly easily. However, what is important is that findings such as these raise questions about theories of development based on observations of sighted children and suggest different accounts which can then be explored. Interestingly, Bigelow (1992a) reported a relationship between locomotor skills and object permanence which provides some support for object permanence being linked to spatial relationships in blind children, given that mobile children are more likely to have a better grasp of how different objects are related in space than children who are not yet moving around independently.

A further finding which is relevant to Piaget's account of development is the absence of a relationship between object permanence and early language in blind children (Bigelow, 1990). Piaget argued that language development, like object permanence, reflected the child's ability to mentally represent the environment and other cognitive developments. Therefore, if blind children experience difficulties in certain areas of cognitive development, notably their understanding of the permanence of objects, their language development should be delayed. However, the language development of many blind children is more similar to that of sighted children than might be expected given their early cognitive development. This supports the view outlined earlier that blind children may learn a great deal about language through how it is structured. However, there are differences and also marked individual differences. What are the theoretical implications of these findings?

A number of researchers have interpreted the differences seen in the language of blind children as reflecting their delayed cognitive development. However, an alternative is that the language differences reflect differences in how they experience their environment (e.g., Landau & Gleitman, 1985). In other words, blind children talk about what they understand and if the absence of vision leads to rather different understanding from that of sighted children, then their language will also be different. Of course, this implies that there is a relationship between cognition and language in blind children. If this is the case, why did Bigelow fail to find such a relationship? If an explanation based on the different experiences of blind and sighted children is correct, then Bigelow's finding is likely to reflect the fact that the behaviors observed were based on the cognitive and linguistic development of sighted children and such measures would be inappropriate for blind children. Once again, we see the need for more research to evaluate this explanation.

Deaf children

Studies of deaf children are of particular significance theoretically because they demonstrate on the one hand that the environment influences behavior and on the other that certain characteristics of human behavior appear to be pre-programmed. The significant role of the environment and experience is apparent in studies of deaf children's perceptual abilities and how they process information, their problem-solving strategies, the different ways in which deaf and hearing parents interact with their young deaf children, and the effects of shared communication on development. Evidence for certain abilities being pre-programmed is seen in the language-like properties of the gestural systems observed in deaf children with hearing parents and the emergence of Nicaraguan Sign Language. The studies of deaf children also point to there being different routes to development. This is illustrated by studies of deaf parents interacting with their deaf children, deaf children's rhyming judgments, and the development of reading. Studies of deaf children can also elucidate some of the processes underlying development, such as the relationship between language and symbolic play, the influence of modality on language acquisition, the processes involved in linguistic and non-linguistic communication, and the critical period hypothesis. I shall look at each of these in the rest of this section.

The theoretical implication of the effect of deafness on perception is twofold. In the first place, there are findings which demonstrate that deaf children, without the experience of sound, react more slowly to stimuli and make more errors in visual attention tasks than hearing children. Although the faster motor responses of hearing children could be explained by them having additional auditory cues which are not available to deaf children, this cannot explain the visual attention errors. This suggests that experience of hearing a sound and attending to whatever made the sound increases sensitivity and speed of responding to visual information in general.

The second area of evidence pointing to the effect of experience on perception is that if deaf children learn a sign language, this seems to heighten their visual–spatial abilities and they may show a preference for coding information spatially rather than temporally. Thus, not surprisingly, the experience of learning a manual language which capitalizes on visual–spatial information fosters the development of visual–spatial skills. However, these findings are not just restricted to deaf children learning a sign language. Deaf children, as a result of their limited exposure to the sequential structure of spoken language, generally seem to favor non-sequential visual–spatial coding (e.g., Todman & Seedhouse, 1994).

The findings that deaf children are less likely than hearing children to utilize appropriate strategies when trying to solve problems is further evidence of the effect of experience. What is particularly revealing is that what may be crucial is the experience that the young child has early on. Jamieson and Pedersen's (1993) study provides some indication that parents who are responsive to their child's attempts at a task, rather than trying to help regardless of whether the child is succeeding or not, may support the development of problem-solving skills in the child more effectively. What is most significant about this finding was, however, that the least responsive parents were those who could hear and had a deaf child. Thus, communication may have an important role to play in the development of cognitive strategies. Jamieson (e.g., 1994a) argues that these findings support a Vygotskian perspective, emphasizing the importance of social interaction with a more experienced communicator who can scaffold the child's development effectively.

The evidence that the majority of deaf parents adopt particular strategies when interacting with their young deaf infants, strategies which are not adopted by most hearing parents, provides further evidence of how experience can influence behavior. The effect of these strategies is to make the interaction between deaf infants and their deaf parents flow more easily. Clearly, the fact that deaf parents, but not hearing parents, adopt these strategies, indicates that it is not simply the experience of interacting with a young deaf child that leads to these changes in behavior, rather, extensive experience with other deaf people is necessary. It would be interesting to know at what point deaf signing children demonstrate these strategies when communicating with other deaf infants. Certainly, the evidence indicates that by 4 years deaf children modify their signs when communicating with younger deaf children, but whether or not by this age they are using the strategies for establishing joint attention seen in their deaf parents is not yet known.

It is well established that children living in supportive, caring environments are more likely to develop to their full potential than children living in deprived environments. However, it is very difficult to isolate which features of a deprived environment may be critical. The study of deaf children can make a contribution here. A number of studies have pointed to the developmental advantages for deaf children of having deaf parents. In contrast, deaf children born to hearing parents may experience a number of developmental difficulties, often apparent from the first year and extending throughout childhood and into adulthood and evident in many developmental domains. This is despite the fact that many of these children will be living in caring, supportive families who have other children with no developmental problems. The crucial differences between deaf and hearing parents of deaf children is that the former are already likely to be native signers and thus have a communication system which their young child can acquire easily. Thus, the critical differences between deaf and hearing families with a deaf child is that the former have a shared communication system while the latter do not.

The experience of being able to communicate effectively and easily with others has been shown to have a marked effect in a number developmental areas. For example, deaf children with deaf parents, compared to deaf children with hearing parents, understand that their parents are communicative partners earlier, produce more sophisticated play at 18 months, are more efficient problem solvers, realize at younger ages that other people have beliefs and thoughts which are different from their own, communicate proficiently with others, and are more likely to develop age-appropriate reading skills. In other words, a communication system which is shared by the child and her parents, as well as others, can have a profound effect on developmental outcome. Of course, hearing children with hearing parents living in deprived environments share a communication system and therefore this cannot explain why some of them may show poor developmental outcome. However, the evidence from the studies of deaf children suggest that the nature of the communication, particularly the sensitivity and responsivity of the child's communicative partners, may be a crucial factor in poor developmental outcome where there is no other explanation of the child's difficulties.

The area of language acquisition of deaf children has had the most significant theoretical implications for our understanding of developmental processes and in particular for there being some pre-programming of certain developments. Although the gestural systems of only a small number of deaf children with hearing parents in two cultures have been studied, the level of detail of the analyses provide convincing evidence that if children are deprived of access to language they will nevertheless develop ways of communicating with others which share many of the properties of native languages. Thus, deaf children with hearing parents adopting an oral approach develop gestures which are fairly stable in structure over time, are produced in reliable orders, are composed of distinct components combined in various ways, reflect grammatical categories, are used to refer to things which are not present, are used for metalinguistic purposes and in much the same way as inner speech. This is clear evidence for the resilience of language since in the absence of any sophisticated input, the deaf child develops a way of communicating.

What is particularly significant is that the language-like properties of these gestural systems appear to be generated by the child herself, rather than being modeled on gestures used by her parent. In other words, these data provide strong evidence for the view that the developing child has an innate predisposition to generate a system which bears some resemblance to formal languages in the absence of anyone else modeling a language (e.g., Goldin-Meadow, 1997). Goldin-Meadow et al. (1996) argue that because of a basic desire to communicate with others, the deaf child develops gestures which refer to distinct objects and, because of a need to communicate how different things relate, the deaf child produces combinations of gestures. Thus, they argue that these language-like features are not dependent upon language but reflect the need to engage in symbolic human communication.

Although the language-like properties of these gestural systems seem to reside in the child, the evidence from children raised in severely impoverished settings indicates that certain environmental conditions are necessary for the child to generate such systems. Thus, it is necessary for the child to have someone else with whom to communicate, to have something to communicate about, and for no other communication system to be readily available. This last prerequisite is supported by the evidence that the gestures used by the parents, while demonstrating some of the same characteristics as their children's gestures, show fewer language characteristics and, in general, the development of the parents' gestures lagged behind those of their children. The difference is that these adults already have a native language with which they can communicate effectively, albeit not with their own child.

However, it is also clear that deaf children without access to language do not develop gestural systems with as sophisticated language structure as children with access to language, whether it is spoken or sign language. Nevertheless, the emergence of Nicaraguan Sign Language over two decades indicates that a sophisticated language can be developed among individuals deprived of access to an existing language, but that this process takes several decades.

Studies of children with a disability which prevents them from processing or experiencing information in a particular way are of particular interest if theories suggest that a development is reliant on certain sorts of processing or experience. If children with a disability cannot process or experience certain sorts of information and yet still exhibit the behavior for which this sort of processing or experience is argued to be a prerequisite, there are at least two possibilities. Either the original explanation is incorrect or there is more than one route by which to acquire the skill or ability.

Joint attention is a very significant development for the young child, enabling her and her parent to share interests and experiences and providing the opportunity for parents to name objects and things going on around the child. Studies which have focused on hearing children have emphasized the importance of parents talking about what their infants are doing for subsequent language development. Contingency is emphasized and obviously if the name of an object is heard while the infant is looking at or manipulating the object, the relationship between name and object will be easier to establish. Interestingly, deaf parents relocate their signs so that the sign and its referent can be perceived simultaneously, which has parallels with hearing parents talking about what their hearing child is doing. However, other strategies used by deaf parents, such as waiting for the infant to look away from something of interest and towards the parent before her parent signs anything, suggest that there are different routes to language development, given that the acquisition of sign language by deaf children of deaf signing parents follows a similar timescale to the acquisition of spoken language by hearing children.

Study of deaf children can also elucidate the role of auditory information and auditory processing in development. Of particular interest is the deaf child's ability to process phonological information. In chapter 3 I discussed several studies showing that although deaf children do not spontaneously store the names of objects phonologically, they are able to do this if required and, more interestingly, if they use cued speech, which provides information about phonemes which cannot be seen from lip movements, this helps. This demonstrates that phonological information, which we think of as auditory, can also be represented visually (e.g., Dodd et al., 1998), although Leybaert and Charlier (1996) suggest that the knowledge which enables rhyme judgments may not necessarily be visual but may take some abstract form.

Similarly, deaf children seem to use the so-called articulatory rehearsal loop, in that, like hearing children, their recall of pictures is reduced the longer the names of the pictures and, if the deaf children use cued speech, their recall is impaired if the words to be recalled rhyme. Again, these findings suggest that the articulatory rehearsal loop can utilize visual information in place of auditory information.

Awareness of the sounds of language, or phonological awareness, in hearing children who are not yet reading has been linked to later reading ability (e.g., Goswami & Bryant, 1990). A similar relationship has also been shown for deaf children, indicating that a visual representation of phonological information may contribute just as much as an auditory representation. However, what is particularly interesting from a theoretical point of view is that some deaf children show poor phonological awareness and yet become good readers. Harris and Beech (1998) describe two such children and both of them had deaf parents and the children were presumably learning sign language. This and other evidence discussed in chapter 3 supports Harris and Beech's view that there may be more than one route to reading: a route involving phonological processing and a second route involving visual processing.

Studies of deaf children can also clarify the nature of certain processes underlying development. For example, as in other groups of children, deaf children's ability to play symbolically is correlated with their expressive language skills in either speech or sign. However, what is more interesting is that there is some evidence that symbolic play may occur despite poor language skills, although the converse was not reported. In other words, if children have good language skills they play symbolically. This suggests that symbolic ability, presumed to underlie both language and symbolic play, can be evident in children with poor communication skills. Thus, language itself is not necessary for the expression of these skills. This is clear evidence that the symbolic skills themselves are primary and may develop with little or no language. However, the evidence from studies of deaf children has also demonstrated that more sophisticated play skills develop in situations where the child is able to communicate with others effectively (Spencer, 1996). Thus, language and interaction can support the further development of symbolic play skills.

Studies of deaf children born to deaf parents and exposed to a sign language from an early age have a number of implications for our understanding of the process of language acquisition. The evidence on manual babbling, the emergence of early signs and hand preference point strongly to there being some amodal language capacity located in the left hemisphere. Deaf infants are innately predisposed to attend to and discriminate the components of the signs of their deaf parents in much the same way as hearing infants have been shown to discriminate the different sounds within spoken language (e.g., Petitto & Marentette, 1991). However, the studies of deaf children with deaf parents also indicate that language can develop with relatively little input, given that deaf parents sign less to their deaf infants than hearing parents talk to their hearing infants and yet the language development of both groups of infants is similar, albeit in a different modality.

The evidence on the emergence of pronouns and negation in ASL is particularly interesting, indicating that the development of linguistic communication is independent of any non-linguistic means of communication that the child might have developed. Such independence cannot be demonstrated in hearing children learning to talk since preverbal communication and spoken language normally involve different modalities. The observation that deaf children may use a gesture correctly at one age and subsequently, when it is used as part of sign language, use it incorrectly is particularly strong evidence for the independence of these two systems. This independence is evidence against accounts, based on Piaget's theorizing, arguing that language emerges out of non-linguistic knowledge and experience. In contrast, the independence of linguistic and non-linguistic communication in deaf children supports accounts, following Chomsky's view, arguing that language emerges from knowledge structures specific to language (Petitto, 1987; Piattelli-Palmarini, 1994).

The ease with which deaf children acquire sign language if they are exposed to it from an early age in comparison to the difficulties that deaf children have acquiring sign language later, particularly if they have failed to acquire any spoken language, supports the view of there being a critical period for language acquisition, although the age range is not clearly specified. Thus, Bishop and Mogford (1993) suggest it is over the age of 5 years, while Grimshaw et al. (1998) suggest it is probably under 15 years.

Children with motor disabilities

The theoretical impetus for studying children with motor disabilities is to illuminate the role of motor activity in psychological development.

However, there are a number of reasons why this is difficult to examine in practice. First, most children with motor disabilities, even if their motor problems are very severe, can act on the environment in some way. Second, there is great variability in the nature of the motor difficulties experienced by children with supposedly the same disability. Third, many children with motor disabilities have additional disabilities which may, independently of any motor difficulties, lead to problems in development. Nevertheless, it is possible to identify several implications of the studies considered in chapter 4. In particular the studies demonstrate: that development can occur even when there is a severe motor disability; that the nature of the environment influences development; and that development in one area is not independent of development in other areas. I shall consider these in turn in the rest of this section.

Some children with motor disabilities are of average intelligence, including some children with CP, in particular those with athetoid CP, children with SB who do not have hydrocephalus, and children with DCD. These different groups of children have very different motor problems, in terms of both the nature and the severity of their difficulties. These differences will affect the opportunities they have for acting on their environment and for the ways in which they can act. Nevertheless, the fact that some of these children achieve average or above average levels of intelligence points to the conclusion that motor disability alone does not prevent intellectual development. However, stronger evidence for this claim comes from those studies which have failed to find a relationship between development and severity of motor disability. Thus, a number of studies have reported no clear relationship between severity of motor disability in children with SB and intelligence (e.g., Wills et al., 1990) and understanding of objects (Morrow & Wachs, 1992). No relationship has been reported between reading and severity of motor difficulties for children with DCD (Fletcher-Flinn et al., 1997), and normal reading levels have been reported in a few children with severe motor difficulties, including being unable to speak, as a result of CP (Smith, 1989).

What are the implications of this evidence for theory? Piaget's theory of cognitive development stresses the role of action. The evidence certainly does not negate the role of action, although it is quite clear that cognitive development can occur when the child has relatively few ways of acting on the environment. On the other hand, the evidence does not disprove the converse, that cognitive development cannot occur in the absence of action. It seems likely that in order to develop cognitively children need to be able to act on their environment in some way, although the extent of the action may turn out to be minimal.

However, there is some evidence which indicates that motor activity may influence certain aspects of development. For example, children with

CP have been shown to remember the spatial relationships between different locations more effectively if they move themselves to the locations in their wheelchairs than if someone else pushes them (McComas et al., 1997). Such findings are important and more research examining the relationship between how children with motor disabilities can act on their environment and specific developments would make a valuable contribution to our understanding of the role of motor action in development.

Despite evidence indicating that children with motor disabilities can have average or near average cognitive development, many children with motor disabilities are of below average intelligence. How can this evidence be reconciled with the findings that some are of average ability? In some children it seems likely that brain damage accounts for their difficulties. As was evident in chapter 4, many children with CP and children with SB and hydrocephalus are of below average intelligence. In addition, children with SB and hydrocephalus were found to have problems of attention and planning and both these children and children with CP have poor long-term memories for visual and auditory information (e.g., Loss et al., 1998; Scott et al., 1998; Smith, 1989). Thus, brain damage may account for these children's difficulties rather than any problems that they might have acting on their environment as a result of their motor difficulties.

However, there may be another factor influencing development, namely the nature of the child's environment. For example, the understanding of objects that young children with SB have has been shown to be related to aspects of their home environment (Morrow & Wachs, 1992), and it has been suggested that the nature of their play is influenced by the opportunities that they have for play (Landry et al., 1990). Relationships have also been reported between the self-esteem of children with SB and aspects of their parents' behavior, notably how supportive the children felt their parents to be and whether their parents treated them appropriately for their age (Appleton et al., 1997; Wolman & Basco, 1994). This evidence is important because it demonstrates once again that the environment has a role to play in developmental processes. The effect of the environment may be particularly important for children with severe motor disabilities who are dependent on others to bring their environment to them and to provide them with opportunities to interact with their environment.

Interestingly, studies of children with motor disabilities also provide evidence of how adults and young TD children adjust their behavior depending on the behavior of others. Thus, several studies reported in chapter 4 indicated that TD children and adults are more directive when interacting with children with CP and, importantly, this was evident even when the TD children were younger than the children with CP (Dallas et al., 1993a, 1993b; Pennington & McConachie, 1999).

The third implication of studies of children with motor disabilities for our understanding of development is that they illustrate how different areas of development are related. For example, children with CP exhibit the same parallel developments in early language and symbolic play that are seen in TD children (Kennedy et al., 1991). Further, studies of children with DCD illustrate how motor difficulties may influence social and cognitive development. Thus, it appears that as a consequences of their motor difficulties children with DCD have difficulties engaging with their peers in certain sorts of physical activities and this leads to their isolation, feelings of loneliness, and problems developing friendships (e.g., Schoemaker & Kalverboer, 1994; Smyth & Anderson, 2000). In other words, there is a relationship between motor and social development. In addition, it seems quite likely that the poor academic achievements of many children with DCD may arise because they often have low self-esteem as a consequence of their motor and social difficulties. A similar explanation has also been proposed to explain some of the academic, social, and behavior problems of children with SB (Hommeyer et al., 1999).

Conversely, some studies cited in chapter 4 illustrate how certain aspects of development can progress in the absence of other developments. Thus, children with CP demonstrate that receptive language can develop in the absence of expressive language (e.g., Jones et al., 1999). Studies of language in children with SB and hydrocephalus show the relative independence of syntactic and pragmatic skills, in that these children may have relatively good syntactic skills but the content of their language may have little relevance to what others are saying or doing (e.g., Dennis & Barnes, 1993).

Thus, while many studies of children with motor disabilities do not throw a great deal of light on the question of the role of motor activity in psychological development, they do illustrate how complex development is and raise many more theoretical questions than they answer.

Children with Down's syndrome

One of the main reasons for examining the development of children with DS has been to answer the question of whether their development is like that of TD children, but slowed down, or whether they actually develop differently via different processes. Support for either position would be of value theoretically. If development is delayed, then children with DS would provide a way of looking at developmental processes in slow motion. If their development follows a different course, then any adequate theory of development must accommodate the differences. Unfortunately, despite a large number of research studies, there is no consensus about whether or not the development of children with DS is delayed or different. Indeed, as I mentioned at the beginning of chapter 5, some researchers have argued that focusing on the question of delay versus difference may not be particularly helpful. What is more relevant is to examine how different areas of development are related in children with DS (Kamhi & Masterson, 1989). Such evidence can help to elucidate the processes underlying development, perhaps pointing to processes which are common to both TD children and children with DS and to processes which are different between the two groups of children.

Several studies raise questions about the relationships between a number of developments which normally occur in TD children within the first 2 years of life. For example, Piaget (e.g., 1962) argued that imitating a behavior after a delay, referred to as deferred imitation, and finding an object following a series of invisible displacements both occurred at around the age of 18 months in TD infants because both are dependent on the infant being able to store and retrieve a representation of something which is no longer present. However, Rast and Meltzoff (1995) found some children with DS could imitate a previously seen behavior but failed to find objects after a series of invisible hidings. There are several ways in which to account for these findings. One is that the two behaviors may depend on different processes which happen to emerge at the same time in TD children, but emerge at different times in children with DS. An alternative is that both behaviors depend on the ability to represent something which is no longer present plus some other processes which are different for the two behaviors. The additional processes, which could, for example, involve aspects of memory, again might develop at the same age as the representational process in TD children, but at different ages in children with DS. Both these alternatives could account for the findings reported by Rast and Meltzoff and both have implications for how we account for developments seen in TD children. Clearly further research is necessary to clarify the processes underlying these behaviors in both TD children and children with DS.

Interestingly, Wright's (1998) finding that children with DS may retrieve a hidden object by imitating the actions of the researcher when hiding the object suggest that children with DS and TD children may represent what is going on around them in rather different ways. It may be that TD children and children with DS can both form representations of objects and actions, but that representations of objects are dominant in TD children, whereas representations of actions are more likely to guide the search behavior of children with DS. The earlier studies of children with DS searching for objects hidden in different ways by Morss (1983, 1985) and Wishart (e.g., 1987, 1990, 1993) also suggest that the process by which children with DS come to understand that objects continue to exist when out of sight is rather different from the processes thought to underlie the search behaviors of TD children. Children with DS, unlike TD children, do not progress through the same sequence of development in terms of their understanding of objects.

Further questions are raised about Piaget's account of cognitive development by studies examining the relationships between language development and various cognitive abilities, notably the ability to find hidden objects and symbolic play. According to Piaget, the ability to find hidden objects, the emergence of symbolic play, and the onset of language at around the age of 18 months in TD children all reflect the ability to mentally represent objects and actions. However, Messer and Hasan (1994) did not find any clear relationship between, for example, children with DS using words to talk about things disappearing and their ability to find hidden objects. The presence of such relationships in TD children has been used to argue for the same process underlying both developments. This is clearly questioned by studies of children with DS.

Similarly, studies of children with DS suggest that linguistic and symbolic ability may depend on different processes. For example, although Beeghly et al. (1990) found a weak relationship between language and symbolic play, they also found that when the children with DS and TD children were matched for MLU the symbolic play of the children with DS was ahead of that of the TD children. Further, Sigman and Ruskin (1999) reported that the symbolic play of children with DS did not predict language a year later. Taken together, these findings suggest once again that either different processes underlie the ability to play symbolically and language or that both abilities involve several processes, some of which are similar in both children with DS and TD children while some are different.

Further studies indicate that different processes may underlie the development of language in TD children and children with DS. For example, in TD children, there is a relationship between language and the ability to relate objects and people, whereas in children with DS the relationship is between language and the child's interest in objects.

Studies of children with DS also point to there being alternative routes to development and that if one process is impaired another process may take over. For example, despite children with DS having poor phonological awareness, some do learn to read. Clearly they are unlikely to be using a phonological route which is the main route by which TD children learn to read. It seems likely that children with DS, because of their poor auditory short-term memories but relatively good visual–spatial short-term memories, are making a direct link between print and meaning.

So far in this section I have outlined a number of very specific implications for theoretical accounts of development which arise from studies of children with DS. However, many of the studies I discussed in chapter 5 point to more general issues which need to be accommodated within any theory. Two issues stand out in particular. The first concerns the role of the environment. For example, studies of children with DS have shown that in general children brought up in institutions do less well than children brought up at home and that parental expectations and sensitivity can influence developmental outcome. Any theory of development needs to be able to explain the influence of these and other environmental factors.

The second issue is individual differences. While DS may be associated with particular physical and psychological characteristics, there is great variability in the expression of these characteristics. If an extra chromosome has so many effects on behavior, why is it that some children who also have this extra chromosome do not show the effects to the same extent? Understanding the process by which one individual exhibits a particular characteristic whereas another individual does not must be the key to explaining development.

Children with autism

A number of different explanations have been proposed to account for the behaviors which characterize autism, including problems understanding minds, executive dysfunction, weak central coherence, impaired social relationships. Each account is able to explain certain aspects of autism but none meets the three criteria argued to be necessary for an adequate theoretical account, namely that the problem is found in all individuals with autism, that it distinguishes individuals with autism from individuals with other disabilities, and that it precedes the onset of behaviors which characterize autism. As a result the theoretical implications of studies of children with autism are rather different from those of studies of children with other disabilities included in this book. For example, differences between the development of children with profound visual impairments and the development of TD children with sight can point to the role of vision in development. However, because the primary difficulty or difficulties underlying autism are not yet determined, differences between their development and the development of TD children cannot help to clarify the contribution of any particular process. Nevertheless, studies of children with autism do have a number of theoretical implications.

Perhaps the most striking implication of studies of children with autism is that they demonstrate the complexity of human development. Many studies have pointed to ways in which the main impairments of social relations, communication, and stereotyped behaviors may influence one another. They have suggested a number of different prerequisites for these behaviors and influences on later development.

The studies also demonstrate the extent of our ignorance of the processes underlying TD development and any prerequisites for their development. In particular, they show how little is known, despite thousands of studies of both TD children and children with disabilities, about the foundations of human behavior, the complex interactions between different aspects of behavior, and the relationship between brain and behavior. Nevertheless, despite this, the studies do have a contribution to make to our understanding of developmental processes.

In particular, studies of children with autism point to the need for any account of development to have a modular basis, with different modules being responsible for specific developments. Anderson's theory of the Minimal Cognitive Architecture (1992) provides such a theory. Two independent components are proposed, speed of information processing and specific modules. Evidence indicates that speed of processing in children with autism may be unimpaired, whereas certain modules are impaired. The advantage of such a modular account is that it can explain the uneven developmental profile observed in individuals with autism. For example, the visual–spatial skills of children with autism are usually relatively spared and in some children are exceptional. Similarly, aspects of reasoning, memory and recognition may not differ from TD children, whereas many other aspects notably in communicative and social behaviors, are impaired. Further, a modular account can accommodate the specificity of some of the findings, for example, that children with autism have difficulty understanding other people's emotions but can attribute emotions to melodies.

A modular account also fits with the lack of consensus in how to account for autism. It may be that modules associated with understanding minds, executive functions, coherence, and interacting socially are damaged in children with autism but that the extent of damage varies both between and within children. Given that ultimately any developmental account must have some neurological basis, the modular account is also consistent with multi-causal neurological accounts such as proposed by Waterhouse, Fein, and Modahl (1996) who argue that a number of neural mechanisms are dysfunctional in autism. The modular account is also consistent with the likely involvement of a number of genes in autism, in that individuals with autism may vary in the number of contributory genes they carry and consequently vary in the nature and extent of the problems they experience.

The studies also have implications for how we interpret behavior. For example, studies of children with autism have made clear that behaviors which appear to be the same can be explained in a number of different ways. Perhaps the clearest illustration is the different accounts of the difficulties which many children with autism experience with theory of mind tasks. It has been argued by some that this reflects a difficulty in understanding minds, whereas others have suggested that it is due to an inability to disengage from reality. And it may turn out that there is some other explanation. Conversely, is the success of some children with autism on theory of mind tasks because they understand minds or because they are using a different strategy which gives the appearance of understanding? Another example comes from the finding that children with autism perform well on embedded figures tests. Is this due to weak central coherence or because they do not have a preference for global processing, the hierarchization deficit? These examples show how the same behavior can be interpreted in different ways.

The implication for theory is that because performance on particular tasks can only ever indirectly reflect the processes we are attempting to understand, we can only ever hypothesize about the processes. It is important to entertain alternatives and wherever possible eliminate them by careful task design. Further, it seems likely that advances in techniques by which brain activity can be examined and related to different task performance will facilitate closer inspection of underlying processes.

Sometimes the behavior of children with autism indicates that they are processing information in a different way from TD children. This can be seen in some of the studies which have examined how children with autism recognize people. Such findings also have implications for theory in that any theory needs to be able to account for different routes to the same outcome.

A further implication of studies of children with autism concerns how different behaviors are valued. For example, echolalia has been seen as a relatively limited behavior assumed to have no particular developmental role. However, Rydell and Mirenda's (1994) study demonstrates that the use of echolalic utterances by children with autism may reflect understanding and have some linguistic purpose such as providing information or regulating behavior. Similar suggestions have been made by Pérez-Pereira (e.g., 1994) for blind children. Any theory of development must be sufficiently broad to encompass such behaviors. Theories of development must not be restricted simply to behaviors evident among TD children.

Conclusions

Studies of children with disabilities have contributed a tremendous amount to our understanding of development. While we do not have a developmental account which can encompass all the findings, the studies provide some clear pointers which need to be accommodated. Thus, the studies examined in this book have pointed to the complexity and range of behaviors to be explained, the relationships between different behaviors and between behaviors and underlying processes, alternative routes to development, the role of the environment, individual differences, and uneven patterns of development. It is only by studying the development of both children with disabilities and TD children that a complete theory of development can be constructed. This is a task for the future but it is clear that studies of children with disabilities have had a huge impact on our understanding over the past few decades and it seems likely that future research and theorizing will clarify our understanding further. If theory does take account of the development of children with disabilities then not only will the development of TD children be better understood, but practitioners working with children with disabilities will have a much sounder base from which to begin.

References

Aaron, P. G., Keetay, V., Boyd, M., Palmatier, S., & Wacks, J. (1998). Spelling without phonology: A study of deaf and hearing children. *Reading and Writing: An Interdisciplinary Journal*, *10*, 1–22.

Abercrombie, M. L. J. (1964). *Perceptual and Visuo-Motor Disorders in Cerebral Palsy*. Little Club Clinics in Developmental Medicine No. 11. London: Spastics Society and Heinemann.

Abramovitch, R., Stanhope, L., Pepler, D., & Corter, C. (1987). The influence of Down's Syndrome on sibling interaction. *Journal of Child Psychology and Psychiatry*, *28*, 865–879.

Achenbach, T. M. (1991). *Manual for the Child Behavior Checklist/4–18 and 1991 Profile*. Burlington, Vermont: University of Vermont Department of Psychiatry.

Adamson, L. B., & Romski, M. A. (eds) (1997). *Communication and Language Acquisition: Discoveries from Atypical Development*. Baltimore, Maryland: Paul H. Brookes Publishing Co.

Adelson, E., & Fraiberg, S. (1974). Gross motor development in infants blind from birth. *Child Development*, *45*, 114–126.

Ahlberg, A. (2000). *The Sensuous and Simultaneous Experience of Numbers*. Göteborg: Göteborg University.

Ahlberg, A., & Csocsán, E. (1999). How children who are blind experience numbers. *Journal of Visual Impairment and Blindness*, *93*, 549–560.

Ainsworth, M. D. S., & Wittig, B. A. (1969). Attachment and exploratory behavior of one-year-olds in a strange situation. In B. M. Foss (ed.), *Determinants of Infant Behavior*, 4. London: Methuen.

Aitken, S., & Bower, T. G. R. (1982). Intersensory substitution in the blind. *Journal of Experimental Child Psychology*, *33*, 309–323.

Alegria, J., Charlier, B. L., & Mattys, S. (1999). The role of lip-reading and cued speech in the processing of phonological information in French-educated deaf children. *European Journal of Cognitive Psychology, 11*, 451–472.

American Psychiatric Association (1987). *Diagnostic and Statistical Manual of Mental Disorders*. 3rd edition revised. Washington, DC: APA Press.

American Psychiatric Association (1994). *Diagnostic and Statistical Manual of Mental Disorders*. 4th edition. Washington, DC: APA Press.

Ammerman, R. T., Kane, V. R., Slomka, G. T., Reigel, D. H., Franzen, M. D., & Gadow, K. D. (1998). Psychiatric symptomatology and family functioning in children and adolescents with spina bifida. *Journal of Clinical Psychology in Medical Settings, 5*, 449–465.

Anderson, D. E., & Reilly, J. S. (1997). The puzzle of negation: How children move from communicative to grammatical negation in ASL. *Applied Psycholinguistics, 18*, 411–429.

Anderson, E. M. & Spain, B. (1977). *The Child with Spina Bifida*. London: Methuen.

Andersen, E. S., Dunlea, A., & Kekelis, L. S. (1984). Blind children's language: Resolving some differences. *Journal of Child Language, 11*, 645–664.

Andersen, E. S., Dunlea, A., & Kekelis, L. S. (1993). The impact of input: Language acquisition in the visually impaired. *First Language, 13*, 23–49.

Anderson, M. (1992). *Intelligence and Development: A Cognitive Theory*. Oxford: Blackwell.

Anderson, M. (2001). Annotation: Conceptions of intelligence. *Journal of Child Psychology and Psychiatry, 42*, 287–298.

Appleton, P. L., Ellis, N. C., Minchom, P. E., Lawson, V., Böll, V., & Jones, P. (1997). Depressive symptoms and self-concept in young people with spina bifida. *Journal of Pediatric Psychology, 22*, 707–722.

Appleton, P. L., Minchom, P. E., Ellis, N. C., Elliott, C. E., Böll, V., & Jones, P. (1994). The self-concept of young people with spina bifida: A population-based study. *Developmental Medicine and Child Neurology, 36*, 198–215.

Arnold, P., & Mills, M. (2001). Memory for faces, shoes, and objects by deaf and hearing signers and hearing nonsigners. *Journal of Psycholinguistic Research, 30*, 185–195.

Arnold, P., & Murray, C. (1998). Memory for faces and objects by deaf and hearing signers and hearing nonsigners. *Journal of Psycholinguistic Research, 27*, 481–497.

Ashmead, D. H., Wall, R. S., Eaton, S. B., Ebinger, K. A., Snook-Hill, M.-M., Guth, D. A., & Yang, X. (1998a). Echolocation reconsidered: Using spatial variations in the ambient sound field to guide locomotion. *Journal of Visual Impairment and Blindness, 92*, 615–632.

Ashmead, D. H., Wall, R. S., Ebinger, K. A., Eaton, S. B., Snook-Hill, M.-M., & Yang, X. (1998b). Spatial hearing in children with visual disabilities. *Perception, 27*, 105–122.

Atkinson, L., Chisholm, V. C., Scott, B., Goldberg, S., Vaughn, B. E., & Blackwell, J. (1999). Maternal sensitivity, child functional level, and attachment in Down syndrome. *Monographs of the Society for Research in Child Development, 64*, 45–66.

Attwood, A., Frith, U., and Hermelin, B. (1988). The understanding and use of interpersonal gestures by autistic and Down's syndrome children. *Journal of Autism and Developmental Disorders, 18,* 241–257.

Baddeley, A. (1986). *Working Memory.* Oxford: Oxford University Press.

Bailey, A., Luthert, P., Dean, A., Harding, B., Janota, I., & Montgomery, M. (1998a). A clinicopathological study of autism. *Brain, 121,* 889–905.

Bailey, A., Palferman, S., Heavey, L., & Le Couteur, A. (1998b). Autism: The phenotype in relatives. *Journal of Autism and Developmental Disorders, 28,* 369–392.

Bailey, A., Phillips, W., and Rutter, M. (1996). Autism: Towards an integration of clinical, genetic, neuropsychological, and neurobiological perspectives. *Journal of Child Psychology and Psychiatry, 37,* 89–126.

Bailey, A., Le Couteur, A., Gottesman, I., Bolton, P., Simonoff, E., & Yuzda, E. (1995). Autism as a strongly genetic disorder: Evidence from a British twin study. *Psychological Medicine, 25,* 63–77.

Baird, G., Charman, T., Baron-Cohen, S., Cox, A., Swettenham, J., & Wheelwright, S. (2000). A screening instrument for autism at 18 months of age: A 6-year follow-up study. *Journal of the American Academy of Child and Adolescent Psychiatry, 39,* 694–702.

Barlow-Brown, F. (1996). "Early developmental strategies used by blind children learning to read braille." Unpublished Ph.D. thesis, University of London.

Barnett, A., & Henderson, S. E. (1992). Some observations on the figure drawings of clumsy children. *British Journal of Educational Psychology, 62,* 341–355.

Baron-Cohen, S. (1987). Autism and symbolic play. *British Journal of Developmental Psychology, 5,* 139–148.

Baron-Cohen, S. (1988). Social and pragmatic deficits in autism: Cognitive or affective? *Journal of Autism and Developmental Disorders, 18,* 379–402.

Baron-Cohen, S. (1989a). The autistic child's theory of mind: A case of specific developmental delay. *Journal of Child Psychology and Psychiatry, 30,* 285–298.

Baron-Cohen, S. (1989b). Perceptual role taking and protodeclarative pointing in autism. *British Journal of Developmental Psychology, 7,* 113–128.

Baron-Cohen, S. (1992). The theory of mind hypothesis of autism: History and prospects of the idea. *The Psychologist, 5,* 9–12.

Baron-Cohen, S. (1993). From attention-goal psychology to belief-desire psychology: The development of a theory of mind, and its dysfunction. In S. Baron-Cohen, H. Tager-Flusberg, & D. J. Cohen (eds), *Understanding Other Minds: Perspectives from Autism.* Oxford: Oxford University Press.

Baron-Cohen, S. (2000). Theory of mind and autism: A fifteen year review. In S. Baron-Cohen, H. Tager-Flusberg, & D. J. Cohen (eds), *Understanding Other Minds: Perspectives from Autism.* 2nd edition. Oxford: Oxford University Press.

Baron-Cohen, S., & Hammer, J. (1997). Parents of children with Asperger syndrome: What is the cognitive phenotype? *Journal of Cognitive Neuroscience, 9,* 548–554.

Baron-Cohen, S., Allen, J., & Gillberg, C. (1992). Can autism be detected at 18 months? The needle, the haystack, and the CHAT. *British Journal of Psychiatry, 161,* 839–843.

Baron-Cohen, S., Campbell, R., Karmiloff-Smith, A., Grant, J., & Walker, J. (1995). Are children with autism blind to the mentalistic significance of the eyes? *British Journal of Developmental Psychology, 13*, 379–398.

Baron-Cohen, S., Leslie, A. M., & Frith, U. (1985). Does the autistic child have a theory of mind? *Cognition, 21*, 37–46.

Baron-Cohen, S., Mortimore, C., Moriarty, J., Izaguirre, J., & Robertson, M. (1999a). The prevalence of Gilles de la Tourette's syndrome in children and adolescents with autism. *Journal of Child Psychology and Psychiatry, 40*, 213–218.

Baron-Cohen, S., Ring, H. A., Wheelwright, S., Bullmore, E. T., Brammer, M. J., & Simmons, A. (1999b). Social intelligence in the normal and autistic brain: An fMRI study. *European Journal of Neuroscience, 11*, 1891–1898.

Baron-Cohen, S., Spitz, A., & Cross, P. (1993). Do children with autism recognise surprise? A research note. *Cognition and Emotion, 7*, 507–516.

Barraga, N. (ed.) (1970). *Visual Efficiency Scale*. Louisville, Kentucky: American Printing House for the Blind.

Barrett, M., & Eames, K. (1996). Sequential developments in children's human figure drawing. *British Journal of Developmental Psychology, 14*, 219–236.

Bartak, L., Rutter, M., & Cox, A. (1975). A comparative study of infantile autism and specific developmental receptive language disorder. 1. The children. *British Journal of Psychiatry, 126*, 127–145.

Bates, E., Bretherton, I., & Snyder, L. (1988). *From First Words to Grammar*. New York: Cambridge University Press.

Bates, E., Camaioni, L., & Volterra, V. (1975). The acquisition of performatives prior to speech. *Merrill-Palmer Quarterly, 21*, 205–226.

Bauminger, N., & Kasari, C. (2000). Loneliness and friendship in high-functioning children with autism. *Child Development, 71*, 447–456.

Bax, M. C. O. (1964). Terminology and classification of cerebral palsy. *Developmental Medicine and Child Neurology, 6*, 295–297.

Bayley, N. (1969). *Bayley Scales of Infant Development*. New York: Psychological Corporation.

Bayley, N., Rhodes, L., & Gooch, B. (1966). A comparison of the growth and development of institutionalized and home-reared mongoloids: A follow-up study. *California Mental Health Research Digest, 4*, 104–5.

Bebko, J. M. (1984). Memory and rehearsal characteristics of profoundly deaf children. *Journal of Experimental Child Psychology, 38*, 415–428.

Bebko, J. M., & McKinnon, E. E. (1990). The language experience of deaf children: Its relation to spontaneous rehearsal in a memory task. *Child Development, 61*, 1744–1752.

Bebko, J. M., Bell, M. A., Metcalfe-Haggert, A., & McKinnon, E. (1998). Language proficiency and the prediction of spontaneous rehearsal in children who are deaf. *Journal of Experimental Child Psychology, 68*, 51–69.

Beech, J. R., & Harris, M. (1997). The prelingually deaf young reader: A case of reliance on direct lexical access? *Journal of Research in Reading, 20*, 105–121.

Beeghly, M. (1998). Emergence of symbolic play: Perspectives from typical and atypical development. In J. A. Burack, R. M. Hodapp, & E. Zigler (eds), *Handbook of Mental Retardation and Development*. Cambridge: Cambridge University Press.

Beeghly, M. (1999). Temperament in children with Down syndrome. In J. A. Rondal, J. Perera, & L. Nadel (eds), *Down Syndrome: A Review of Current Knowledge*. London: Whurr Publishers Ltd.

Beeghly, M., & Cicchetti, D. (1997). Talking about self and other: Emergence of an internal state lexicon in young children with Down syndrome. *Development and Psychopathology*, 9, 729–748.

Beeghly, M., Weiss-Perry, B., & Cicchetti, D. (1990). Beyond sensorimotor functioning: Early communicative and play development of children with Down syndrome. In D. Cicchetti & M. Beeghly (eds), *Children with Down syndrome: A Developmental Perspective*. Cambridge: Cambridge University Press.

Behl, D. D., Akers, J. F., Boyce, G. C., & Taylor, M. J. (1996). Do mothers interact differently with children who are visually impaired? *Journal of Visual Impairment and Blindness*, 90, 501–511.

Bellugi, U. (1980). Clues from the similarities between signed and spoken language. In U. Bellugi & M. Studdert-Kennedy (eds), *Signed and Spoken Language: Biological Constraints on Linguistic Form*. Berlin: Verlag Chemie.

Bellugi, U., & Klima, E. S. (1972). The roots of language in the sign talk of the deaf. *Psychology Today*, 6, 61–76.

Bellugi, U., O'Grady, L., Lillo-Martin, D., O'Grady-Hynes, M., Van-Hoek, K., & Corina, D. (1990). Enhancement of spatial cognition in deaf children. In V. Volterra & L. Erting (eds), *From Gesture to Language in Hearing and Deaf Children* New York: Springer-Verlag.

Bemporad, J. R. (1979). Adult recollections of a formerly autistic child. *Journal of Autism and Developmental Disorders*, 9, 179–198.

Berger, J. (1990). Interactions between parents and their infants with Down syndrome. In D. Cicchetti & M. Beeghly (eds), *Children with Down syndrome: A Developmental Perspective*. Cambridge: Cambridge University Press.

Berger, J., & Cunningham, C. C. (1981). Early development of social interactions in Down's syndrome and non-handicapped infants. In A. Teirikko, R. Vihavainen, & T. Nenonen (eds), *Finland Speaks. Report of the European Association for Special Education Conference: Communication and Handicap*. Helsinki, Finland: The Finish Association for Special Education.

Berger, J., & Cunningham, C. C. (1983). Development of early vocal behaviors and interactions in Down's syndrome and nonhandicapped infant-mother pairs. *Developmental Psychology*, 19, 322–331.

Berry, P., Gunn, P., & Andrews, R. (1980). Behavior of Down syndrome infants in a strange situation. *American Journal of Mental Deficiency*, 85, 213–218.

Bertenthal, B. I., & Fischer, K. W. (1978). Development of self-recognition in the infant. *Developmental Psychology*, 14, 44–50.

Bieberich, A. A., & Morgan, S. B. (1998). Brief report: Affective expression in children with autism or Down syndrome. *Journal of Autism and Developmental Disorders*, 28, 333–338.

Bigelow, A. E. (1983). Development of the use of sound in the search behavior of infants. *Developmental Psychology*, 19, 317–321.

Bigelow, A. E. (1986). The development of reaching in blind children. *British Journal of Developmental Psychology*, 4, 355–366.

Bigelow, A. E. (1987). Early words of blind children. *Journal of Child Language*, *14*, 47–56.

Bigelow, A. E. (1988). Blind children's concepts of how people see. *Journal of Visual Impairment and Blindness, 82*, 65–68.

Bigelow, A. E. (1990). Relationship between the development of language and thought in young blind children. *Journal of Visual Impairment and Blindness, 84*, 414–418.

Bigelow, A. E. (1991a). Spatial mapping of familiar locations in blind children. *Journal of Visual Impairment and Blindness, 85*, 113–117.

Bigelow, A. E. (1991b). Hiding in blind and sighted children. *Development and Psychopathology, 3*, 301–310.

Bigelow, A. E. (1991c). The effects of distance and intervening obstacles on visual inference in blind and sighted children. *International Journal of Behavioral Development, 14*, 273–283.

Bigelow, A. E. (1992a). Locomotion and search behavior in blind infants. *Infant Behavior and Development, 15*, 179–189.

Bigelow, A. E. (1992b). Blind children's ability to predict what another sees. *Journal of Visual Impairment and Blindness, 86*, 181–184.

Bigelow, A. E. (1996). Blind and sighted children's spatial knowledge of their home environments. *International Journal of Behavioral Development, 19*, 797–816.

Bishop, D. V. M. (1983). Comprehension of English syntax by profoundly deaf children. *Journal of Child Psychology and Psychiatry, 24*, 415–434.

Bishop, D. V. M. (1997). Cognitive neuropsychology and developmental disorders: Uncomfortable bedfellows. *Quarterly Journal of Experimental Psychology, 50*, 899–923.

Bishop, D. V. M., & Mogford, K. (eds) (1993). *Language Development in Exceptional Circumstances*. 2nd edition. Hove, Sussex: Erlbaum.

Block, M. E. (1991). Motor development in children with Down syndrome: A review of the literature. *Adapted Physical Activity Quarterly, 8*, 179–209.

Bolton, P., Macdonald, H., Pickles, A., Rios, P., Goode, S., & Crowson, M. (1994). A case-control family history study of autism. *Journal of Child Psychology and Psychiatry, 35*, 877–900.

Bonvillian, J. D. (1999). Sign language development. In M. Barrett (ed.), *The Development of Language*. Hove, East Sussex: Psychology Press Ltd.

Bonvillian, J. D., Orlansky, M. D., & Novak, L. L. (1983). Early sign language acquisition and its relation to cognition and motor development. In J. G. Kyle, & B. Woll (eds), *Language in Sign: An International Perspective on Sign Language* London: Croom Helm.

Bonvillian, J. D., Richards, H. C., & Dooley, T. T. (1997). Early sign language acquisition and the development of hand preference in young children. *Brain and Language, 58*, 1–22.

Börjeson, M.-C., & Lagergren, J. (1990). Life conditions of adolescents with myelomeningocele. *Developmental Medicine and Child Neurology, 32*, 698–706.

Bormann-Kischkel, C., Vilsmeier, M., & Baude, B. (1995). The development of emotional concepts in autism. *Journal of Child Psychology and Psychiatry, 36*, 1243–1260.

Boucher, J. (1978). Echoic memory capacity in autistic children. *Journal of Child Psychology and Psychiatry, 19*, 161–166.

Boucher, J. (1981). Immediate free recall in early childhood autism: Another point of similarity with the amnesic syndrome. *British Journal of Psychology, 72*, 211–215.

Boucher, J. (1988). Word fluency in high-functioning autistic children. *Journal of Autism and Developmental Disorders, 18*, 637–645.

Boucher, J. (1998). SPD as a distinct diagnostic entity: Logical considerations and directions for future research. *International Journal of Language and Communication Disorders, 33*, 71–81.

Boucher, J., & Lewis, V. (1989). Memory impairments and communication in relatively able autistic children. *Journal of Child Psychology and Psychiatry, 30*, 99–122.

Boucher, J., & Lewis, V. (1990). Guessing or creating? A reply to Baron-Cohen. *British Journal of Developmental Psychology, 8*, 205–206.

Boucher, J., & Lewis, V. (1992). Unfamiliar face recognition in relatively able autistic children. *Journal of Child Psychology and Psychiatry, 33*, 843–859.

Boucher, J., & Warrington, E. K. (1976). Memory deficits in early infantile autism: Some similarities to the amnesic syndrome. *British Journal of Psychology, 67*, 73–87.

Boucher, J., Lewis, V., & Collis, G. (1998). Familiar face and voice matching and recognition in children with autism. *Journal of Child Psychology and Psychiatry, 39*, 171–181.

Boucher, J., Lewis, V., & Collis, G. M. (2000). Voice processing abilities in children with autism, children with specific language impairments, and young typically developing children. *Journal of Child Psychology and Psychiatry, 41*, 847–857.

Bower, T. G. R. (1977). Blind babies see with their ears. *New Scientist, 73*, 255–257.

Bower, T. G. R., & Wishart, J. G. (1979). Toward a unitary theory of development. In E. B. Thoman (ed.), *Origins of the Infant's Social Responsiveness*. Hillsdale, New Jersey: Erlbaum.

Bowler, D. M. (1992). "Theory of mind" in Asperger's syndrome. *Journal of Child Psychology and Psychiatry, 33*, 877–893.

Bowler, D. M., & Briskman, J. A. (2000). Photographic cues do not always facilitate performance on false belief tasks in children with autism. *Journal of Autism and Developmental Disorders, 30*, 305–316.

Bowler, D. M., Gardiner, J. M., & Grice, S. J. (2000). Episodic memory and remembering in adults with Asperger syndrome. *Journal of Autism and Developmental Disorders, 30*, 295–304.

Bowler, D. M., Matthews, N. J., & Gardiner, J. M. (1997). Asperger's syndrome and memory: Similarity to autism but not amnesia. *Neuropsychologia, 35*, 65–70.

Bowman, R. M., McLone, D. G., Grant, J. A., Tomita, T., & Ito, J. A. (2001). Spina bifida outcome: A 25-year prospective. *Pediatric Neurosurgery, 34*, 114–120.

Boyle, C. A., Decouflé, P., & Yeargin-Allsopp, M. (1994). Prevalence and health impact of developmental disabilities in US children. *Pediatrics*, *93*, 399–403.

Brambring, M., & Tröster, H. (1992). On the stability of stereotyped behaviors in blind infants and preschoolers. *Journal of Visual Impairment and Blindness*, *86*, 105–110.

Brandt, B. R. (1996). Impaired tactual perception in children with Down's syndrome. *Scandinavian Journal of Psychology*, *37*, 312–316.

Brandt, B. R., & Rosén, I. (1995), Impaired peripheral somatosensory function in children with Down syndrome. *Neuropediatrics*, *26*, 310–312.

Braverman, M., Fein, D., Lucci, D., & Waterhouse, L. (1989). Affect comprehension in children with pervasive developmental disorders. *Journal of Autism and Developmental Disorders*, *19*, 301–316.

Brian, J. A., & Bryson, S. E. (1996). Disembedding performance and recognition memory in autism/PDD. *Journal of Child Psychology and Psychiatry*, *37*, 865–872.

Brinkworth, R. (1975). The unfinished child: Early treatment and training for the infant with Down's syndrome. *Royal Society of Health Journal*, *95*, 73–78.

Brinton, J. (2001). Measuring language development in deaf children with cochlear implants. *International Journal of Language and Communication Disorders*, *36*, 121–125.

Briskman, J., Happé, F. G. E., & Frith, U. (2001). Exploring the cognitive phenotype of autism: Weak "central coherence" in parents and siblings of children with autism: II. Real-life skills and preferences. *Journal of Child Psychology and Psychiatry*, *42*, 309–316.

Brookshire, B. L., Fletcher, J. M., Bohan, T. P., Landry, S. H., Davidson, K. C., & Francis, D. J. (1995). Specific language deficiencies in children with early onset hydrocephalus. *Child Neuropsychology*, *1*, 106–117.

Brown, R., Hobson, R. P., Lee, A., & Stevenson, J. (1997) Are there "autistic-like" features in congenitally blind children? *Journal of Child Psychology and Psychiatry*, *38*, 693–703.

Brown-Sweeney, S. G., & Smith, B. L. (1997). The development of speech production abilities in children with Down syndrome. *Clinical Linguistics and Phonetics*, *11*, 345–362.

Buckhalt, J. A., Rutherford, R. B., & Goldberg, K. E. (1978). Verbal and nonverbal interaction of mothers with their Down's syndrome and nonretarded infants. *American Journal of Mental Deficiency*, *82*, 337–343.

Buckley, S. (1985). Attaining basic educational skills: Reading, writing and number. In D. Lane, & B. Stratford (eds), *Current Approaches to Down's Syndrome*. London: Holt, Rinehart and Winston.

Buckley, S. (1993). Language development in children with Down's syndrome. *Down's Syndrome: Research and Practice*, *1*, 3–9.

Buckley, S. (1999). Promoting the cognitive development of children with Down syndrome: The practical implications of recent psychological research. In J. A. Rondal, J. Perera, & L. Nadel (eds), *Down Syndrome: A Review of Current Knowledge*. London: Whurr Publishers Ltd.

Buckley, S., & Bird, G. (1993). Teaching children with Down's syndrome to read. *Down's Syndrome: Research and Practice*, *1*, 34–39.

Buium, N., Rynders, J., & Turnure, J. (1974). Early maternal linguistic environment of normal and Down's syndrome language-learning children. *American Journal of Mental Deficiency*, 79, 52–58.

Burack, J. A., Charman, T., Yirmiya, N., & Zelazo, P. R. (2001). Development and autism: Messages from developmental psychopathology. In J. A. Burack, T. Charman, N. Yirmiya, & P. R. Zelazo (eds), *The Development of Autism: Perspectives from Theory and Research*. London: Erlbaum.

Burden, V., & Campbell, R. (1994). The development of word-coding skills in the born deaf: An experimental study of deaf school-leavers. *British Journal of Developmental Psychology*, 12, 331–349.

Burlingham, D. (1979). To be blind in a sighted world. *Psychoanalytic Study of the Child*, 34, 5–30.

Butcher, C., Mylander, C., & Goldin-Meadow, S. (1991). Displaced communication in a self-styled gesture system: Pointing at the nonpresent. *Cognitive Development*, 6, 315–342.

Butterfield, E. C. (1961). A provocative case of overachievement by a mongoloid. *American Journal of Mental Deficiency*, 66, 444–448.

Butterworth, G., & Cicchetti, D. (1978). Visual calibration of posture in normal and motor retarded Down's syndrome infants. *Perception*, 7, 513–525.

Byrne, K., Abbeduto, L., & Brooks, P. (1990). The language of children with spina bifida and hydrocephalus: Meeting task demands and mastering syntax. *Journal of Speech and Hearing Disorders*, 55, 118–123.

Campbell, R., & Wright, H. (1990). Deafness and immediate memory for pictures: Dissociations between "inner speech" and the "inner ear"? *Journal of Experimental Child Psychology*, 50, 259–286.

Cantell, M. H., Smyth, M. M., & Ahonen, T. P. (1994). Clumsiness in adolescence: Educational, motor, and social outcomes of motor delay detected at 5 years. *Adapted Physical Activity Quarterly*, 11, 115–129.

Cantor, G. N., & Girardeau, F. L. (1959). Rhythmic discrimination ability in mongoloid and normal children. *American Journal of Mental Deficiency*, 63, 621–625.

Capps, L., Yirmiya, N., & Sigman, M. (1992). Understanding of simple and complex emotions in nonretarded children with autism. *Journal of Child Psychology and Psychiatry*, 33, 1169–1182.

Carlesimo, G. A., Marotta, L., & Vicari, S. (1997). Long-term memory in mental retardation: Evidence for a specific impairment in subjects with Down's syndrome. *Neuropsychologia*, 35, 71–79.

Carr, J. (1970). Mental and motor development in young mongol children. *Journal of Mental Deficiency Research*, 14, 205–220.

Carr, J. (1975). *Young Children with Down's Syndrome*. London: Butterworth.

Carr, J. (1988). Six weeks to twenty-one years old: A longitudinal study of children with Down's syndrome and their families. *Journal of Child Psychology and Psychiatry*, 29, 407–431.

Carr, J. (1992). Longitudinal research in Down Syndrome. *International Review of Research in Mental Retardation*, 18, 197–223.

Carr, J. (1994). Long term outcome for people with Down's syndrome. *Journal of Child Psychology and Psychiatry*, 35, 425–439.

Carroll, J. B. (ed.) (1956). *Language, Thought and Reality: Selected Writings of*

Benjamin Lee Whorf. Cambridge, Massachusetts: MIT Press.

Carter, C. O. (1974). Clues to the aetiology of neural tube malformations. *Developmental Medicine and Child Neurology*, Supplement 32, 3–15.

Carvajal, F., & Iglesias, J. (1997). Mother and infant smiling exchanges during face-to-face interactions in infants with and without Down syndrome. *Developmental Psychobiology*, 31, 277–286.

Carvajal, F., & Iglesias, J. (2000). Looking behavior and smiling in Down syndrome infants. *Journal of Nonverbal Behavior*, 24, 225–236.

Casari, E. F., & Fantino, A. G. (1998). A longitudinal study of cognitive abilities and achievement status of children with myelomeningocele and their relationship with clinical types. *European Journal of Pediatric Surgery*, 8, 52–54.

Caselli, M. C., Vicari, S., Longobardi, E., Lami, L., Pizzoli, C., & Stella, G. (1998). Gestures and words in early development of children with Down syndrome. *Journal of Speech, Language, and Hearing Research*, 41, 1125–1135.

Cass, H. D., Sonksen, P. M., & McConachie, H. R. (1994). Developmental setback in severe visual impairment. *Archives of Disease in Childhood*, 70, 192–196.

Catherwood, D., Drew, L., Hein, B., & Grainger, H. (1998). Haptic recognition in two infants with low vision assessed by a familiarization procedure. *Journal of Visual Impairment and Blindness*, 92, 212–215.

Caycho, L., Gunn, P., & Siegal, M. (1991). Counting in children with Down syndrome. *American Journal on Mental Retardation*, 95, 575–584.

Celani, G., Battacchi, M. W., & Arcidiacono, L. (1999). The understanding of the emotional meaning of facial expressions in people with autism. *Journal of Autism and Developmental Disorders*, 29, 57–66.

Chakrabarti, S., & Fombonne, E. (2001). Pervasive developmental disorders in preschool children. *Journal of the American Medical Association*, 285, 3093–3099.

Champion, P. (1987). An investigation of the sensorimotor development of Down's syndrome infants involved in an ecologically based early intervention programme: A longitudinal study. *British Journal of Mental Subnormality*, 33, 88–99.

Chapman, R. S. (1998). Language development in children and adolescents with Down syndrome. In J. F. Miller, M. Leddy, & L. A. Leavitt (eds), *Improving the Communication of People with Down Syndrome*. Baltimore: Paul H. Brookes.

Chapman, R. S., Schwartz, S. E., & Kay-Raining Bird, E. (1991). Language skills of children and adolescents with Down syndrome: I. Comprehension. *Journal of Speech and Hearing Research*, 34, 1106–1120.

Chapman, R. S., Seung, H.-Y., Schwartz, S. E., & Kay-Raining Bird, E. (1998). Language skills of children and adolescents with Down syndrome: II. Production deficits. *Journal of Speech, Language, and Hearing Research*, 41, 861–873.

Charlier, B. L., & Leybaert, J. (2000). The rhyming skills of deaf children educated with phonetically augmented speechreading. *Quarterly Journal of Experimental Psychology*, 53, 349–375.

Charlton, J. L., Ihsen, E., & Lavelle, B. M. (2000). Control of manual skills in children with Down syndrome. In D. Weeks, R. Chua, & D. Elliott (eds), *Per-*

ceptual-Motor Behavior in Down Syndrome. Champaign, IL: Human Kinetics.

Charlton, J. L., Ihsen, E., & Oxley, J. (1996). Kinematic characteristics of reaching in children with Down Syndrome. *Human Movement Science*, *15*, 727–743.

Charman, T. (1997). The relationship between joint attention and pretend play in autism. *Development and Psychopathology*, *9*, 1–16.

Charman, T., & Baron-Cohen, S. (1993). Drawing development in autism: The intellectual to visual realism shift. *British Journal of Developmental Psychology*, *11*, 171–185.

Charman, T., & Baron-Cohen, S. (1994). Another look at imitation in autism. *Development and Psychopathology*, *6*, 403–413.

Charman, T., & Lynggaard, H. (1998). Does a photographic cue facilitate false belief performance in subjects with autism? *Journal of Autism and Developmental Disorders*, *28*, 33–42.

Charman, T., Swettenham, J., Baron-Cohen, S., Cox, A., Baird, G., & Drew, A. (1997). Infants with autism: An investigation of empathy, pretend play, joint attention, and imitation. *Developmental Psychology*, *33*, 781–789.

Chen, D. (1996). Parent-infant communication: Early intervention for very young children with visual impairment or hearing loss. *Infants and Young Children*, *9*, 1–12.

Chomsky, N. (1975). *Reflections on Language*. New York: Pantheon Books.

Christiansen, A. S. (2000). Persisting motor control problems in 11- to 12-year-old boys previously diagnosed with deficits in attention, motor control and perception (DAMP). *Developmental Medicine and Child Neurology*, *42*, 4–7.

Cicchetti, D., & Beeghly, M. (1990). *Children with Down syndrome: A Developmental Perspective*. Cambridge: Cambridge University Press.

Cicchetti, D., & Pogge-Hesse, P. (1982). Possible contributions of the study of organically retarded persons to developmental theory. In E. Zigler and D. Balla (eds), *Mental Retardation: The Development-Difference Controversy*. Hillsdale, New Jersey: Erlbaum.

Cicchetti, D., & Schneider-Rosen, K. (1983). Theoretical and empirical considerations in the investigation of the relationship between affect and cognition in atypical populations of infants. In C. Izard, J. Kagan, & R. Zajonc (eds), *Emotions, Cognition and Behaviour*. New York: Cambridge University Press.

Cicchetti, D., & Serafica, F. C. (1981). Interplay among behavioral systems: Illustrations from the study of attachment, affiliation, and wariness in young children with Down's syndrome. *Developmental Psychology*, *17*, 36–49.

Cicchetti, D., & Stroufe, L. A. (1976). The relationship between affective and cognitive development in Down's syndrome infants. *Child Development*, *47*, 920–929.

Cicchetti, D., & Stroufe, L. A. (1978). An organization view of affect: Illustration from the study of Down's syndrome infants. In M. Lewis & L. A. Rosenblum (eds), *The Development of Affect*. New York: Plenum.

Cielinski, K. L., Vaughn, B. E., Seifer, R., & Contreras, J. (1995). Relations among sustained engagement during play, quality of play, and mother-child interaction in samples of children with Down syndrome and normally developing toddlers. *Infant Behavior and Development*, *18*, 163–176.

Clark, P., & Rutter, M. (1981). Autistic children's responses to structure and to interpersonal demands. *Journal of Autism and Developmental Disorders, 11*, 201–217.

Clements, W., & Barrett, M. (1994). The drawings of children and young people with Down's syndrome: A case of delay or difference? *British Journal of Educational Psychology, 64*, 441–452.

Clifton, R. K., Muir, D. W., Ashmead, D. H., & Clarkson, M. G. (1993). Is visually guided reaching in early infancy a myth? *Child Development, 64*, 1099–1110.

Cobo-Lewis, A. B., Oller, D. K., Lynch, M. P., & Levine, S. L. (1996). Relations of motor and vocal milestones in typically developing infants and infants with Down syndrome. *American Journal on Mental Retardation, 100*, 456–467.

Coe, D. A., Matson, J. L., Russell, D. W., Slifer, K. J., Capone, G. T., & Baglio, C. (1999). Behavior problems of children with Down syndrome and life events. *Journal of Autism and Developmental Disorders, 29*, 149–156.

Cole, M., & Scribner, S. (1974). *Culture and Thought.* New York: Wiley.

Conrad, R. (1979). *The Deaf School Child: Language and Cognitive Function.* London: Harper and Row.

Conti-Ramsden, G., & Pérez-Pereira, M. (1999). Conversational interactions between mothers and their infants who are congenitally blind, have low vision, or are sighted. *Journal of Visual Impairment and Blindness, 93*, 691–703.

Corona, R., Dissanayake, C., Arbelle, S., Wellington, P., & Sigman, M. (1998). Is affect aversive to young children with autism? Behavioral and cardiac responses to experimenter distress. *Child Development, 69*, 1494–1502.

Corter, C., Pepler, D., Stanhope, L., & Abramovitch, R. (1992). Home observations of mothers and sibling dyads comprised of Down's syndrome and nonhandicapped children. *Canadian Journal of Behavioural Science, 24*, 1–13.

Cossu, G., Rossini, F., & Marshall, J. C. (1993). When reading is acquired but phonemic awareness is not: A study of literacy in Down's syndrome. *Cognition, 46*, 129–138.

Courchesne, E. (1988). Physioanatomical considerations in Down syndrome. In L. Nadel (ed.), *The Psychobiology of Down syndrome.* London: MIT Press.

Courchesne, E., Karns, C. M., Davis, H. R., Ziccardi, R., Carper, R. A., & Tigue, Z. D. (2001). Unusual brain growth patterns in early life in patients with autistic disorder: An MRI study. *Neurology, 57*, 245–254.

Courchesne, E., Townsend, J., Akshoomoff, N. A., Saitoh, O., Yeung-Courchesne, R., & Lincoln, A. J. (1994). Impairment in shifting attention in autistic and cerebellar patients. *Behavioral Neuroscience, 108*, 848–865.

Courtin, C., & Melot, A.-M. (1998). Development of theories of mind in deaf children. In M. Marschark & M. D. Clark (eds), *Psychological Perspectives on Deafness*, 2. London: Erlbaum.

Cowie, V. A. (1970). *A Study of the Early Development of Mongols.* Oxford: Pergamon.

Cox, A., Klein, K., Charman, T., Baird, G., Baron-Cohen, S., & Swettenham, J. (1999). Autism spectrum disorders at 20 and 42 months of age: Stability of clinical and ADI-R diagnosis. *Journal of Child Psychology and Psychiatry, 40*, 719–732.

Cox, M. V., & Maynard, S. (1998). The human figure drawings of children with Down syndrome. *British Journal of Developmental Psychology*, 16, 133–137.

Crawley, S. B., & Spiker, D. (1983). Mother-child interactions involving two-year-olds with Down's syndrome: A look at individual differences. *Child Development*, 54, 1312–1323.

Critchley, H. D., Daly, E. M., Bullmore, E. T., Williams, S. C. R., van Amelsvoort, T., & Robertson, D. M. (2000). The functional neuroanatomy of social behaviour: Changes in cerebral blood flow when people with autistic disorder process facial expressions. *Brain*, 123, 2203–2212.

Crnic, K. A. (1990). Families of children with Down syndrome: Ecological contexts and characteristics. In D. Cicchetti & M. Beeghly (eds), *Children with Down syndrome: A Developmental Perspective*. Cambridge: Cambridge University Press.

Cromer, R. F. (1973). Conservation by the congenitally blind. *British Journal of Psychology*, 64, 241–250.

Cromer, R. F. (1974). The development of language and cognition: The cognition hypothesis. In B. M. Foss (ed.), *New Perspectives in Child Development*. Harmondsworth: Penguin Books.

Cruickshank, W. M. (1964). The multiple-handicapped child and courageous action. *International Journal for the Education of the Blind*, 14, 65–75.

Cruickshank, W. M. (ed.) (1976). *Cerebral Palsy, a Developmental Disability*. New York: Syracuse University Press.

Culatta, B., & Young, C. (1992). Linguistic performance as a function of abstract task demands in children with spina bifida. *Developmental Medicine and Child Neurology*, 34, 434–440.

Cunningham, C. C. (1979). "Aspects of Early Development in Down Syndrome Infants." Unpublished Ph.D. thesis, University of Manchester.

Cunningham, C. C. (1982). *Down Syndrome: Introduction for Parents*. London: Souvenir Press.

Cunningham, C. C. (1986). Early intervention: Some findings from the Manchester cohort of children with Down's syndrome. In M. Bishop, M. Copley, & J. Porter (eds), *Portage: More than a Teaching Programme?* Windsor: NFER/Nelson.

Cunningham, C. C. (1987). Early intervention in Down's syndrome. In G. Hoskin & G. Murphy (eds), *Prevention of Mental Handicap: A World View*. London: Royal Society of Medicine.

Cunningham, C. C., & McArthur, K. (1981). Hearing loss and treatment in young Down's Syndrome children. *Child: Care, Health and Development*, 7, 357–374.

Cunningham, C. C., & Sloper, P. (1976). *Down's Syndrome Infants: A Positive Approach to Parent and Professional Collaboration*. Manchester: Hester Adrian Research Centre, University of Manchester.

Cunningham, C. C., Morgan, P., & McGucken, R. B. (1984). Down's syndrome: Is dissatisfaction with disclosure of diagnosis inevitable? *Developmental Medicine and Child Neurology*, 26, 33–39.

Cunningham, C. C., Turner, S., Sloper, P., & Knussen, C. (1991). Is the appearance of children with Down syndrome associated with their development and social functioning? *Developmental Medicine and Child Neurology, 33,* 285–295.

D'Angiulli, A., Kennedy, J. M., & Heller, M. A. (1998). Blind children recognizing tactile pictures respond like sighted children given guidance in exploration. *Scandinavian Journal of Psychology, 39,* 187–190.

Dahlgren Sandberg, A., & Hjelmquist, E. (1997). Language and literacy in nonvocal children with cerebral palsy. *Reading and Writing: An Interdisciplinary Journal, 9,* 107–133.

Dahlgren, S., & Trillingsgaard, A. (1996): Theory of mind in non-retarded children with autism and Asperger's Syndrome. A research note. *Journal of Child Psychology and Psychiatry, 37,* 759–763.

Dallas, E., Stevenson, J., & McGurk, H. (1993a). Cerebral-palsied children's interactions with siblings – I. Influence of severity of disability, age and birth order. *Journal of Child Psychology and Psychiatry, 34,* 621–647.

Dallas, E., Stevenson, J., & McGurk, H. (1993b). Cerebral-palsied children's interactions with siblings – II. Interactional structure. *Journal of Child Psychology and Psychiatry, 34,* 649–671.

Daly, B., Addington, J., Kerfoot, S., & Sigston, A. (1985). *Portage: The Importance of Parents.* Windsor: NFER/Nelson.

Das, J. P., & Ojile, E. (1995). Cognitive processing of students with and without hearing loss. *Journal of Special Education, 29,* 323–336.

Davies, S., Bishop, D., Manstead, A. S. R., & Tantam, D. (1994). Face perception in children with autism and Asperger's syndrome. *Journal of Child Psychology and Psychiatry, 35,* 1033–1058.

Davis, A., Wood, S., Healy, R., Webb, H., & Rowe, S. (1995). Risk factors for hearing disorders: Epidemiologic evidence of change over time in the U. K. *Journal of the American Academy of Audiology, 6,* 365–370.

Dawson, G., Meltzoff, A. N., Osterling, J., & Rinaldi, J. (1998b). Neuropsychological correlates of early symptoms of autism. *Child Development, 69,* 1276–1285.

Dawson, G., Meltzoff, A. N., Osterling, J., Rinaldi, J., & Brown, E. (1998a). Children with autism fail to orient to naturally occurring social stimuli. *Journal of Autism and Developmental Disorders, 28,* 479–485.

de Gelder, B., Vroomen, J., & van der Heide, L. (1991). Face recognition and lip-reading in autism. *European Journal of Cognitive Psychology, 3,* 69–86.

Deb, S., & Thompson, B. (1998). Neuroimaging in autism. *British Journal of Psychiatry, 173,* 299–302.

Dekker, R. (1993). Visually impaired children and haptic intelligence test scores: Intelligence test for visually impaired children (ITVIC). *Developmental Medicine and Child Neurology, 35,* 478–489.

Denhoff, E., & Holden, R. H. (1951). Pediatric aspects of cerebral palsy. *Journal of Pediatrics, 39,* 363–373.

Denmark, J. C., Rodda, M., Abel, R. A., Skelton, U., Eldridge, R. W., & Warren, F. (1979). *A Word in Deaf Ears: A Study of Communication and Behaviour in a Sample of 75 Deaf Adolescents.* London: Royal National Institute for the Deaf.

Dennis, M., & Barnes, M. A. (1993). Oral discourse after early-onset hydrocephalus: Linguistic ambiguity, figurative language, speech acts, and script-based inferences. *Journal of Pediatric Psychology, 18*, 639–652.

Dennis, M., Jacennik, B., & Barnes, M. A. (1994). The content of narrative discourse in children and adolescents after early-onset hydrocephalus and in normally developing age peers. *Brain and Language, 46*, 129–165.

Dennis, M., Lazenby, A. L., & Lockyer, L. (2001). Inferential language in high-functioning children with autism. *Journal of Autism and Developmental Disorders, 31*, 47–54.

Dennis, M., Rogers, T., & Barnes, M. A. (2001). Children with spina bifida perceive visual illusions but not multistable figures. *Brain and Cognition, 46*, 108–113.

Dewart, H., & Summers, S. V. (1988). *The Pragmatics Profile of Early Communication Skills*. Windsor: NFER/Nelson.

Dewey, D. (1991). Praxis and sequencing skills in children with sensorimotor dysfunction. *Developmental Neuropsychology, 7*, 197–206.

Dewey, D., & Kaplan, B. J. (1994). Subtyping of developmental motor deficits. *Developmental Neuropsychology, 10*, 265–284.

Dewey, D., Lord, C., & Magill, J. (1988). Qualitative assessment of the effect of play materials in dyadic peer interaction of children with autism. *Canadian Journal of Psychology, 42*, 242–260.

Diamond, A., Prevor, M. B., Callender, G., & Druin, D. P. (1997). Prefontal cortex cognitive deficits in children treated early and continuously for PKU. *Monographs of the Society for Research in Child Development, 62*, 1–206.

Dimcovic, N., & Tobin, M. J. (1995). The use of language in simple classification tasks by children who are blind. *Journal of Visual Impairment and Blindness, 89*, 448–459.

Dissanayake, C., & Crossley, S. A. (1996). Proximity and sociable behaviours in autism: Evidence for attachment. *Journal of Child Psychology and Psychiatry, 37*, 149–156.

Dissanayake, C., & Crossley, S. A. (1997). Autistic children's responses to separation and reunion with their mothers. *Journal of Autism and Developmental Disorders, 27*, 219–308.

Dissanayake, C., Sigman, M., & Kasari, C. (1996). Long-term stability of individual differences in the emotional responsiveness of children with autism. *Journal of Child Psychology and Psychiatry, 37*, 461–467.

Dodd, B. (1976). A comparison of the phonological systems of mental age matched normal, severely subnormal and Down's syndrome children. *British Journal of Disorders of Communication, 11*, 27–42.

Dodd, B., & Leahy, J. (1989). Phonological disorders and mental handicap. In M. Beveridge, G. Conti-Ramsden, & I. Leudar (eds), *Language and Communication in Mentally Handicapped People*. London: Chapman and Hall.

Dodd, B., McIntosh, B., & Woodhouse, L. (1998). Early lipreading ability and speech and language development of hearing-impaired pre-schoolers. In R. Campbell, B. Dodd, & D. Burnham (eds), *Hearing by Eye II: Advances in the Psychology of Speechreading and Auditory-visual Speech*. Hove, East Sussex: Psychology Press Ltd.

Dolk, H., De Wals, P., Gillerot, Y., Lechat, M. F., Aymé, S., & Beckers, R. (1990).

The prevalence at birth of Down syndrome in 19 regions of Europe 1980–6. In W. I. Fraser (ed.), *Key Issues in Mental Retardation Research*. London: Routledge.

Dote-Kwan, J. (1995). Impact of mothers' interactions on the development of their young visually impaired children. *Journal of Visual Impairment and Blindness*, *89*, 46–58.

Dote-Kwan, J., & Hughes, M. (1994). The home environment of young blind children. *Journal of Visual Impairment and Blindness*, *88*, 31–42.

Dote-Kwan, J., Hughes, M., & Taylor, S. L. (1997). Impact of early experiences on the development of young children with visual impairments: Revisited. *Journal of Visual Impairment and Blindness*, *91*, 131–144.

Down, J. Langdon H. (1866). Observations on an ethnic classification of idiots. *Clinical Lectures and Reports by the Medical and Surgical Staff of the London Hospital*, *3*, 259–262.

Drotar, D., Baskiewicz, A., Irvin, N., Kennell, J., & Klaus, M. (1975). The adaptation of parents to the birth of an infant with a congenital malformation: A hypothetical model. *Pediatrics*, *56*, 710–717.

Duffen, L. (1976). Teaching reading to children with little or no language. *Remedial Education*, *11*, 139.

Dunlea, A. (1984). The relation between concept formation and semantic roles: Some evidence from the blind. In L. Feagans, C. Garvey, & R. Golinkoff (eds), *The Origins and Growth of Communication*. Norwood, New Jersey: Ablex Publishing Corporation.

Dunlea, A. (1989). *Vision and the Emergence of Meaning*. Cambridge: Cambridge University Press.

Dwyer, C., & McKenzie, B. E. (1994). Impairment of visual memory in children who are clumsy. *Adaptive Physical Activity Quarterly*, *11*, 179–189.

Dykens, E. M., & Hodapp, R. M. (2001). Research in mental retardation: Toward an etiologic approach. *Journal of Child Psychology and Psychiatry*, *42*, 49–71.

Dykens, E. M., & Kasari, C. (1997). Maladaptive behavior in children with Prader-Willi syndrome, Down syndrome, and non-specific mental retardation. *American Journal on Mental Retardation*, *102*, 228–237.

Dykens, E. M., Hodapp, R. M., & Evans, D. W. (1994). Profiles and development of adaptive behavior in children with Down syndrome. *American Journal on Mental Retardation*, *98*, 580–587.

Eames, K., & Cox, M. V. (1994). Visual realism in the drawings of autistic, Down's syndrome and normal children. *British Journal of Developmental Psychology*, *12*, 235–239.

Eatough, M. (1995). BATOD survey 1994 – England. *Journal of the British Association of Teachers of the Deaf*, *19*, 142–160.

Edwards, R., Ungar, S., & Blades, M. (1998). Route descriptions by visually impaired and sighted children from memory and from maps. *Journal of Visual Impairment and Blindness*, *92*, 512–521.

Edwards-Beckett, J. (1995). Parental expectations and child's self-concept in spina bifida. *Children's Health Care*, *24*, 257–267.

Eilers, R. E., & Oller, D. K. (1994). Infant vocalizations and the early diagnosis of severe hearing impairment. *Journal of Pediatrics, 124,* 199–203.

Eisenberg, L., & Kanner, L. (1956). Early infantile autism, 1943–1955. *American Journal of Orthopsychiatry, 26,* 556–566.

Eisenmajer, R., & Prior, M. (1991). Cognitive linguistic correlates of "theory of mind" ability in autistic children. *British Journal of Developmental Psychology, 9,* 351–364.

Elgar, K., & Campbell, R. (2001). Annotation: The cognitive neuroscience of face recognition: Implications for developmental disorders. *Journal of Child Psychology and Psychiatry, 42,* 705–717.

Eliasson, A.-C., & Gordon, A. M. (2000). Impaired force coordination during object release in children with hemiplegic cerebral palsy. *Developmental Medicine and Child Neurology, 42,* 228–234.

Eliasson, A.-C., Gordon, A. M., & Forssberg, H. (1991). Basic co-ordination of manipulative forces of children with cerebral palsy. *Developmental Medicine and Child Neurology, 33,* 661–670.

Eliasson, A.-C., Gordon, A. M., & Forssberg, H. (1992). Impaired anticipatory control of isometric forces during grasping by children with cerebral palsy. *Developmental Medicine and Child Neurology, 34,* 216–225.

Eliasson, A.-C., Gordon, A. M., & Forssberg, H. (1995). Tactile control of isometric fingertip forces during grasping in children with cerebral palsy. *Developmental Medicine and Child Neurology, 37,* 72–84.

Eliez, S., & Reiss, A. L. (2000). Annotation: MRI neuroimaging of childhood psychiatric disorders: A selective review. *Journal of Child Psychology and Psychiatry, 41,* 679–694.

Emmorey, K., Kosslyn, S. M., & Bellugi, U. (1993). Visual imagery and visual-spatial language: Enhanced imagery abilities in deaf and hearing ASL signers. *Cognition, 46,* 139–181.

Epstein, C. J. (1999). The future of biological research on Down syndrome. In J. A. Rondal, J. Perera, & L. Nadel (eds), *Down Syndrome: A Review of Current Knowledge.* London: Whurr Publishers Ltd.

Erin, J. N. (1986). Frequencies and types of questions in the language of visually-impaired children. *Journal of Visual Impairment and Blindness, 80,* 670–674.

Esquirol, J. E. D. (1838). *Des maladies mentales considérées sous rapports hygiénique et médico-légal.* Paris: Bailliere.

Fabbretti, D., Pizzuto, E., Vicari, S., & Volterra, V. (1997). A story description task in children with Down's syndrome: Lexical and morphosyntactic abilities. *Journal of Intellectual Disability Research, 41,* 165–179.

Fantz, R. L., Fagan, J. F., & Miranda, S. B. (1975). Early visual selectivity: As a function of pattern variables, previous exposure, age from birth and conception, and expected cognitive deficit. In L. B. Cohen & P. Salapatek (eds), *Infant Perception: From Sensation to Cognition. Vol.1. Basic Visual Processes.* New York: Academic Press.

Farrant, A., Blades, M., & Boucher, J. (1998). Source monitoring by children with autism. *Journal of Autism and Developmental Disorders, 28,* 43–50.

Fazzi, E., Lanners, J., Danova, S., Ferrarri-Ginevra, O., Gheza, C., & Luparia, A. (1999). Stereotyped behaviours in blind children. *Brain and Development, 21,* 522–528.

Feldman, H. M., Janosky, J. E., Scher, M. S., & Wareham, N. L. (1994). Language abilities following prematurity, periventricular brain injury, and cerebral palsy. *Journal of Communication Disorders, 27*, 71–90.

Fenson, L., Dale, P. S., Reznick, J. S., Thal, D., Bates, E., & Hartung, J. P. (1991). *Technical Manual for the MacArthur Communicative Development Inventories.* San Diego, CA: San Diego State University.

Ferguson, R., & Buultjens, M. (1995). The play behaviour of young blind children and its relationship to developmental stages. *British Journal of Visual Impairment, 13*, 100–107.

Ferrari, M., & Matthews, W. S. (1983). Self-recognition deficits in autism: Syndrome-specific or general developmental delay? *Journal of Autism and Developmental Disorders, 13*, 317–324.

Fewell, R. R., Ogura, T., Notari-Syverson, A., & Wheeden, C. A. (1997). The relationship between play and communication skills in young children with Down syndrome. *Topics in Early Childhood Special Education, 17*, 103–118.

Fidler, D. J., & Hodapp, R. M. (1999). Craniofacial maturity and perceived personality in children with Down syndrome. *American Journal on Mental Retardation, 104*, 410–421.

Fidler, D. J., Bailey, J. N., & Smalley, S. L. (2000). Macrocephaly in autism and other pervasive developmental disorders. *Developmental Medicine and Child Neurology, 42*, 737–740.

Filipek, P. A. (1999). Neuroimaging in the developmental disorders: The state of the science. *Journal of Child Psychology and Psychiatry, 40*, 113–128.

Fishler, K., & Koch, R. (1991). Mental development in Down syndrome mosaicism. *American Journal on Mental Retardation, 96*, 345–351.

Fisichelli, V. R., & Karelitz, S. (1966). Frequency spectra of the cries of normal infants and those with Down's syndrome. *Psychonomic Science, 6*, 195–196.

Fisichelli, V. R., Haber, A., Davis, J., & Karelitz, S. (1966). Audible characteristics of the cries of normal infants and those with Down's syndrome. *Perceptual and Motor Skills, 23*, 744–746.

Fletcher, J. M., Brookshire, B. L., Landry, S. H., Bohan, T. P., Davidson, K. C., & Francis, D. J. (1996). Attentional skills and executive functions in children with early hydrocephalus. *Developmental Neuropsychology, 12*, 53–76.

Fletcher, J. M., Brookshire, B. L., Landry, S. H., Bohan, T. P., Davidson, K. C., & Francis, D. J. (1995). Behavioral adjustment of children with hydrocephalus: Relationships with etiology, neurological, and family status. *Journal of Pediatric Psychology, 20*, 109–125.

Fletcher, J. M., Francis, D. J., Thompson, N. M., Brookshire, B. L., Bohan, T. P., & Landry, S. H. (1992). Verbal and nonverbal skill discrepancies in hydrocephalic children. *Journal of Clinical and Experimental Neuropsychology, 14*, 593–609.

Fletcher-Flinn, C., Elmes, H., & Strugnell, D. (1997). Visual-perceptual and phonological factors in the acquisition of literacy among children with congenital developmental coordination disorder. *Developmental Medicine and Child Neurology, 39*, 158–166.

Folstein, S., & Rutter, M. (1977). Infantile autism: A genetic study of 21 twin pairs. *Journal of Child Psychology and Psychiatry, 18*, 297–321.

Folstein, S. E., Bisson, E., Santangelo, S. L., & Piven, J. (1998). Finding specific genes that cause autism: A combination of approaches will be needed to maximize power. *Journal of Autism and Developmental Disorders, 28,* 439–445.

Folstein, S. E., Santangelo, S. L., Gilman, S. E., Piven, J., Landa, R., & Lainhart, J. (1999). Predictors of cognitive test patterns in autism families. *Journal of Child Psychology and Psychiatry, 40,* 1117–1128.

Fombonne, E. (1999). The epidemiology of autism: A review. *Psychological Medicine, 29,* 769–786.

Fombonne, E. (2001). Is there an epidemic of autism? *Pediatrics, 107,* 411–413.

Fombonne, E., Bolton, P., Prior, J., Jordan, H., & Rutter, M. (1997). A family study of autism: Cognitive patterns and levels in parents and siblings. *Journal of Child Psychology and Psychiatry, 38,* 667–684.

Fombonne, E., Roge, B., Claverie, J., Courty, S., & Fremolle, J. (1999). Microcephaly and macrocephaly in autism. *Journal of Autism and Developmental Disorders, 29,* 113–119.

Foreman, N., Orencas, C., Nicholas, E., Morton, P., & Gell, M. (1989). Spatial awareness in seven to 11-year-old physically handicapped children in mainstream schools. *European Journal of Special Needs Education, 4,* 171–179.

Fortuny, A. (1999). Prenatal diagnosis of Down syndrome: From surprise to certainty. In J. A. Rondal, J. Perera, & L. Nadel (eds), *Down Syndrome: A Review of Current Knowledge.* London: Whurr Publishers Ltd.

Fowler, A. E. (1990). Language abilities in children with Down syndrome: Evidence for a specific syntactic delay. In D. Cicchetti & M. Beeghly (eds), *Children with Down syndrome: A Developmental Perspective.* Cambridge: Cambridge University Press.

Fraiberg, S. (1968). Parallel and divergent patterns in blind and sighted infants. *Psychoanalytic Study of the Child, 23,* 264–300.

Fraiberg, S. (1977). *Insights from the Blind.* London: Souvenir Press.

Fraiberg, S., & Adelson, E. (1973). Self-representation in language and play: Observations of blind children. *Psychoanalytic Quarterly, 42,* 539–561.

Fraiberg, S., & Adelson, E. (1975). Self-representation in language and play: Observations of blind children. In R. Lenneberg & E. Lenneberg (eds), *The Foundations of Language Development: Multi-disciplinary Approach. Vol. 2.* New York: Academic Press.

Fraiberg, S., Siegel, B. L., & Gibson, R. (1966). The role of sound in the search behavior of a blind infant. *Psychoanalytic Study of the Child, 21,* 327–357.

Franco, F., & Wishart, J. G. (1995). Use of pointing and other gestures by young children with Down syndrome. *American Journal on Mental Retardation, 100,* 160–182.

Fraser, J., & Mitchell, A. (1876). Kalmuck idiocy: Report of a case with autopsy, by J. Fraser, MB, with notes on sixty-two cases by Dr. A. Mitchell, Commissioner in Lunacy. *Journal of Mental Science, 22,* 161–179.

Freeman, B. J., Del'Homme, M., Guthrie, D., & Zhang, F. (1999). Vineland Adaptive Behavior Scale scores as a function of age and initial IQ in 210 autistic children. *Journal of Autism and Developmental Disorders, 29,* 379–384.

Freudenberg, R. P., Driscoll, J. W., & Stern, G. S. (1978). Reactions of adult humans to cries of normal and abnormal infants. *Infant Behavior and Develop-*

ment, 1, 224–227.

Frid, C., Drott, P., Lundell, B., Rasmussen, F., & Anneren, G. (1999). Mortality in Down's syndrome in relation to congenital malformations. *Journal of Intellectual Disability Research, 43,* 234–241.

Frith, U. (1989). *Autism: Explaining the Enigma.* Oxford: Basil Blackwell.

Frith, U., & Frith, C. D. (1974). Specific motor disabilities in Down's syndrome. *Journal of Child Psychology and Psychiatry, 15,* 293–301.

Frith, U., & Happé, F. G. E. (1994). Autism: Beyond "theory of mind". *Cognition, 50,* 115–132.

Furth, H. G. (1973). *Deafness and Learning: A Psychological Approach.* Belmont, California: Wadsworth.

Gadow, K. D., & Sprafkin, J. (1987). *Child Symptom Inventory.* Stony Brook, NY: Checkmate Plus.

Gaines, R., & Halpern-Felsher, B. L. (1995). Language preference and communication development of a hearing and deaf twin pair. *American Annals of the Deaf, 140,* 47–55.

Galati, D., Miceli, R., & Sini, B. (2001). Judging and coding facial expression of emotions in congenitally blind children. *International Journal of Behavioral Development, 25,* 268–278.

Ganiban, J., Wagner, S., & Cicchetti, D. (1990). Temperament and Down syndrome. In D. Cicchetti & M. Beeghly (eds), *Children with Down syndrome: A Developmental Perspective.* Cambridge: Cambridge University Press.

Gath, A. (1974). Sibling reactions to mental handicap: A comparison of the brothers and sisters of mongol children. *Journal of Child Psychology and Psychiatry, 15,* 187–198.

Gath, A. (1985). Parental reactions to loss and disappointment: The diagnosis of Down's syndrome. *Developmental Medicine and Child Neurology, 27,* 392–400.

Gath, A., & Gumley, D. (1986). Behaviour problems in retarded children with special reference to Down's syndrome. *British Journal of Psychiatry, 149,* 156–161.

Gathercole, S. E. (1998). The development of memory. *Journal of Child Psychology and Psychiatry, 39,* 3–27.

Gathercole, S. E., & Badderley, A. D. (1989). Evaluation of the role of phonological short-term memory in the development of vocabulary in children: A longitudinal study. *Journal of Memory and Language, 28,* 200–213.

Geers, A., & Moog, J. (1994). Spoken language results: Vocabulary, syntax, and communication. *Volta Review, 96,* 131–148.

Gepner, B., Deruelle, C., & Grynfeltt, S. (2001). Motion and emotion: A novel approach to the study of face processing by young autistic children. *Journal of Autism and Developmental Disorders, 31,* 37–45.

Gepner, B., Mestre, D., Masson, G., & de Schonen, S. (1995). Postural effects of motion vision in young autistic children. *NeuroReport, 6,* 1211–1214.

Gerhardt, J. B. (1982). The development of object play and classificatory skills in a blind child. *Journal of Visual Impairment and Blindness, 76,* 219–223.

Geuze, R. H., & van Dellen, T. (1990). Auditory precue processing during a movement sequence in clumsy children. *Journal of Human Movement Studies, 19,*

11–24.

Geuze, R. H., Jongmans, M. J., Schoemaker, M. M., & Smits-Engelsman, B. C. M. (2001). Clinical and research diagnostic criteria for developmental coordination disorder: A review and discussion. *Human Movement Science, 20,* 7–47.

Gibbs, M. V., & Thorpe, J. G. (1983). Personality stereotype of noninstitutionalized Down syndrome children. *American Journal of Mental Deficiency, 87,* 601–605.

Gibbs, N. (1981). Reflections on visually handicapped children I have known. *The British Psychological Society Division of Educational and Child Psychology Occasional Papers, 5,* 48–50.

Gibson, D., & Harris, A. (1988). Aggregated early intervention effects: Patterning and longevity of benefits. *Journal of Mental Deficiency Research, 32,* 1–17.

Gilchrist, A., Green, J., Cox, A., Burton, D., Rutter, M., & Le Couteur, A. (2001). Development and current functioning in adolescents with Asperger syndrome: A comparative study. *Journal of Child Psychology and Psychiatry, 42,* 227–240.

Gillberg, C. (1991). Debate and argument: Is autism a pervasive developmental disorder? *Journal of Child Psychology and Psychiatry, 32,* 1169–1170.

Gillberg, C. (1998). Chromosomal disorders and autism. *Journal of Autism and Developmental Disorders, 28,* 415–425.

Gillberg, C., Rasmussen, P., Carlström, G., Svenson, B., & Waldenström, E. (1982). Perceptual, motor and attentional deficits in six-year old children. Epidemiological aspects. *Journal of Child Psychology and Psychiatry, 23,* 131–144.

Gillberg, I. C., & Gillberg, C. (1983). Three year follow-up at age 10 of children with minor neurodevelopmental disorders: Behavioural problems. *Developmental Medicine and Child Neurology, 25,* 438–449.

Gillberg, I. C., & Gillberg, C. (1989). Children with preschool minor neurodevelopmental disorders: Behaviour and school achievement at age 13. *Developmental Medicine and Child Neurology, 31,* 3–13.

Glenn, S. M., & Cunningham, C. C. (1982). Recognition of the familiar words of nursery rhymes by handicapped and nonhandicapped infants. *Journal of Child Psychology and Psychiatry, 23,* 319–327.

Glenn, S. M., & Cunningham, C. C. (1983). What do babies listen to most? A developmental study of auditory preferences in nonhandicapped infants and infants with Down's syndrome. *Developmental Psychology, 19,* 332–337.

Glenn, S. M., Cunningham, C. C., & Joyce, P. F. (1981). A study of auditory preferences in non-handicapped infants and infants with Down's syndrome. *Child Development, 52,* 1303–1307.

Goldin-Meadow, S. (1997). The resilience of language in humans. In C. T. Snowdon & M. Hausberger (eds), *Social Influences on Vocal Development.* Cambridge: Cambridge University Press.

Goldin-Meadow, S., & Mylander, C. (1983). Gestural communication in deaf children: Noneffect of parental input on language development. *Science, 221,* 372–374.

Goldin-Meadow, S., & Mylander, C. (1998). Spontaneous sign systems created by deaf children in two cultures. *Nature, 391,* 279–281.

Goldin-Meadow, S., Butcher, C., Mylander, C., & Dodge, M. (1994). Nouns and verbs in a self-styled gesture system: What's in a name? *Cognitive Psychology*, 27, 259–319.

Goldin-Meadow, S., McNeill, D., & Singleton, J. (1996). Silence is liberating: Removing the handcuffs on grammatical expression in the manual modality. *Psychological Review*, 103, 34–55.

Goldin-Meadow, S., Mylander, C., & Butcher, C. (1995). The resilience of combinatorial structure at the word level: Morphology in self-styled gesture systems. *Cognition*, 56, 195–262.

Goswami, U., & Bryant, P. (1990). *Phonological Skills and Learning to Read*. Hove, Sussex: Erlbaum.

Gottesman, M. (1973). Conservation development in blind children. *Child Development*, 44, 824–827.

Goueffic, S., Vallencien, B., & Leroy-Boisivon, A. (1967). La voix des mongoliens. *Journal Français d'Oto-Rhino-Laryngologie, Audio-Phonologie et Chirurgie Maxillo-Faciale*, 16, 139–141.

Gouin Décarie, T. (1969). A study of the mental and emotional development of the thalidomide child. In B. M. Foss (ed.), *Determinants of Infant Behaviour, 4*. London: Methuen.

Graham, E. E., & Shapiro, E. (1953). Use of the performance scale of the WISC with the deaf child. *Journal of Consulting Psychology*, 17, 396–398.

Grandin, T. (1996). *Thinking in Pictures*. New York: Vintage.

Grant, A. C., Thiagarajah, M. C., & Sathian, K. (2000). Tactile perception in blind Braille readers: A psychophysical study of acuity and hyperacuity using gratings and dot patterns. *Perception and Psychophysics*, 62, 301–312.

Greaney, J., & Reason, R. (1999). Phonological processing in braille. *Dyslexia*, 5, 215–226.

Greaney, J., Tobin, M., & Hill, E. (1999). *Braille Version of the Neale Analysis of Reading Abilities*. London: RNIB.

Green, R. (1999). Audiological assessment. In J. Stokes (ed.), *Hearing Impaired Infants: Support in the First Eighteen Months*. London: Whurr Publishers Ltd.

Green, W. W. (1981). Hearing disorders. In A. E. Blackhurst & W. H. Berdine (eds), *An Introduction to Special Education*. Boston, Massachusetts: Little, Brown.

Greenwald, C., & Leonard, L. (1979). Communicative and sensorimotor development of Down's syndrome children. *American Journal of Mental Deficiency*, 84, 296–303.

Gregory, S. (1976). *The Deaf Child and his Family*. London: George Allen and Unwin.

Gregory, S., & Mogford, K. (1981). Early language development in deaf children. In B. Woll, J. G. Kyle, & M. Deuchar (eds), *Perspectives on BSL and Deafness*. London: Croom Helm.

Gregory, S., Bishop, J., & Sheldon, L. (1995). *Deaf Young People and their Families: Developing Understanding*. Cambridge: Cambridge University Press.

Gregory, S., Smith, S., & Wells, A. (1997). Language and identity in sign bilingual deaf children. *Deafness and Education*, 21, 31–38.

Gresham, F. M., & Elliott, S. N. (1990). *Social Skills Rating System Manual*. Circle Pines, MN: American Guidance Service.

Griffith, E. M., Pennington, B. F., Wehner, E. A., & Rogers, S. J. (1999). Executive functions in young children with autism. *Child Development, 70,* 817–832.

Grimshaw, G. M., Adelstein, A., Bryden, M. P., & MacKinnon, G. E. (1998). First-language acquisition in adolescence: Evidence for a critical period for verbal language development. *Brain and Language, 63,* 237–255.

Gunn, P., Berry, P., & Andrews, R. J. (1982). Looking behavior of Down syndrome infants. *American Journal of Mental Deficiency, 87,* 344–347.

Hadwin, J., Baron-Cohen, S., Howlin, P., & Hill, K. (1997). Does teaching theory of mind have an effect on the ability to develop conversation in children with autism. *Journal of Autism and Developmental Disorders, 27,* 519–537.

Happé, F. G. E. (1993). Communicative competence and theory of mind in autism: A test of relevance theory. *Cognition, 48,* 101–119.

Happé, F. G. E. (1994a). Annotation: Current psychological theories of autism: The "Theory of Mind" account and rival theories. *Journal of Child Psychology and Psychiatry, 35,* 215–229.

Happé, F. G. E. (1994b). *Autism: An Introduction to Psychological Theory.* London: UCL Press.

Happé, F. G. E. (1994c). Wechsler IQ profile and theory of mind in autism: A research note. *Journal of Child Psychology and Psychiatry, 35,* 1461–1472.

Happé, F. G. E. (1994d) An advanced test of theory of mind: Understanding of story characters' thoughts and feelings by able autistic, mentally handicapped and normal children and adults. *Journal of Autism and Developmental Disorders, 24,* 129–154.

Happé, F. G. E. (1995). The role of age and verbal ability in the theory of mind task performance of subjects with autism. *Child Development, 66,* 843–855.

Happé, F. G. E. (1996). Studying weak central coherence at low levels: Children with autism do not succumb to visual illusions. A research note. *Journal of Child Psychology and Psychiatry, 37,* 873–877.

Happé, F. G. E. (1997). Central coherence and theory of mind in autism: Reading homographs in context. *British Journal of Developmental Psychology, 15,* 1–12.

Happé, F. G. E. (1999). Autism: Cognitive deficit or cognitive style? *Trends in Cognitive Science, 3,* 216–222.

Happé, F. G. E. (2000). Parts and wholes, meaning and minds: Central coherence and its relation to theory of mind. In S. Baron-Cohen, H. Tager-Flusberg, & D. J. Cohen (eds), *Understanding Other Minds: Perspectives from Autism.* 2nd edition. Oxford: Oxford University Press.

Happé, F. G. E., & Frith, U. (1991). Debate and argument: How useful is the "PDD" label? *Journal of Child Psychology and Psychiatry, 32,* 1167–1168.

Happé, F. G. E., Briskman, J., & Frith, U. (2001). Exploring the cognitive phenotype of autism: Weak "central coherence" in parents and siblings of children with autism: I. Experimental tests. *Journal of Child Psychology and Psychiatry, 42,* 299–307.

Happé, F. G. E., Ehlers, S., Fletcher, P. C., Frith, U., Johansson, M., & Gillberg, C. (1996). "Theory of mind" in the brain: Evidence from a PET scan study of Asperger syndrome. *NeuroReport, 8,* 197–201.

Harris, D. B. (1963). *Goodenough-Harris Drawing Test.* New York: Harcourt Brace Jovanovich.

Harris, L., Humphrey, G. K., Muir, D. M., & Dodwell, P. C. (1989). Use of the Canterbury child's aid in infancy and early childhood: A case study. *Journal of Visual Impairment and Blindness, 79,* 4–11.

Harris, M. (1992). *Language Experience and Early Language Development: From Input to Uptake.* Hove, East Sussex: Erlbaum.

Harris, M., & Barlow-Brown, F. (1997). Learning to read in blind and sighted children. In V. Lewis & G. Collis (eds), *Blindness and Psychological Development in Young Children.* Leicester: BPS Books.

Harris, M., & Beech, J. R. (1998). Implicit phonological awareness and early reading development in prelingually deaf children. *Journal of Deaf Studies and Deaf Education, 3,* 205–216.

Harris, M., & Mohay, H. (1997). Learning to look in the right place: A comparison of attentional behavior in deaf children with deaf and hearing mothers. *Journal of Deaf Studies and Deaf Education, 2,* 95–103.

Harris, M., Clibbens, J., Chasin, J., & Tibbitts, R. (1989). The social context of early sign language development. *First Language, 9,* 81–97.

Harris, M., Jones, D., Brookes, S., & Grant, J. (1986). Relations between the nonverbal context of maternal speech and rate of language development. *British Journal of Developmental Psychology, 4,* 261–8.

Harris, N. G. S., Bellugi, U., Bates, E., Jones, W., & Rossen, M. (1997). Contrasting profiles of language development in children with Williams and Down syndromes. *Developmental Neuropsychology, 13,* 345–370.

Harris, N. S., Courchesne, E., Townsend, J., Carper, R. A., & Lord, C. (1999). Neuroanatomic contributions to slowed orienting of attention in children with autism. *Cognitive Brain Research, 8,* 61–71.

Harris, P. L., & Leevers, H. J. (2000). Pretending, imagery, and self-awareness in autism. In S. Baron-Cohen, H. Tager-Flusberg, & D. J. Cohen (eds), *Understanding Other Minds: Perspectives from Autism.* 2nd edition. Oxford: Oxford University Press.

Harris, S., Kasari, C., & Sigman, M. D. (1996). Joint attention and language gains in children with Down syndrome. *American Journal on Mental Retardation, 100,* 608–619.

Harrison, R. V., Panesar, J., El-Hakim, H., Abdolell, M., Mount, R. J., & Papsin, B. (2001). The effects of age of cochlear implantation on speech perception outcomes in prelingually deaf children. *Scandinavian Audiology, 30,* 73–78.

Hart, B. (1996). The initial growth of expressive vocabulary among children with Down syndrome. *Journal of Early Intervention, 20,* 211–221.

Harter, S. (1985). *Manual for the Self-Perception Profile for Children.* Denver: University of Denver Press.

Hasan, P. J., & Messer, D. J. (1997). Stability or instability in early cognitive abilities in children with Down's syndrome? *British Journal of Developmental Disabilities, 43,* 93–107.

Hatton, D. D., Bailey, D. B., Burchinal, M. R., & Ferrell, K. A. (1997). Developmental growth curves of preschool children with vision impairments. *Child Development, 68,* 788–806.

Hattori, M., Fujiyama, A., Taylor, T. D. et al. (2000). The DNA sequence of human chromosome 21. *Nature, 405*, 311–3(19.

Hatwell, Y. (1966). *Privation Sensorielle et Intelligence*. Paris: Presses Universitaires de France.

Hauser-Cram, P., Warfield, M. E., Shonkoff, J. P., Krauss, M. W., Upshur, C. C., & Sayer, A. (1999). Family influences on adaptive development in young children with Down syndrome. *Child Development, 70*, 979–989.

Heaton, P., Hermelin, B., & Pring, L. (1998). Autism and pitch processing: A precursor for savant musical ability? *Music Perception, 15*, 291–305.

Heaton, P., Hermelin, B., & Pring, L. (1999b). Can children with autistic spectrum disorders perceive affect in music? An experimental investigation. *Psychological Medicine, 29*, 1405–1410.

Heaton, P., Pring, L., & Hermelin, B. (1999a). A pseudo-savant: A case of exceptional musical splinter skills. *Neurocase, 5*, 503–509.

Heimann, M., & Ullstadius, E. (1999). Neonatal imitation and imitation among children with autism and Down's syndrome. In J. Nadel & G. Butterworth (eds), *Imitation in Infancy*. Cambridge: Cambridge University Press.

Heimann, M., Ullstadius, E., & Swerlander, A. (1998). Imitation in eight young infants with Down's syndrome. *Pediatric Research, 44*, 780–784.

Hellgren, L., Gillberg, C., Gillberg, I. C., & Enerskog, I. (1993). Children with deficits in attention, motor control and perception (DAMP) almost grown up: General health at 16 years. *Developmental Medicine and Child Neurology, 35*, 881–892.

Hellgren, L., Gillberg, I. C., Bågenholm, A., & Gillberg, C. (1994). Children with deficits in attention, motor control and perception (DAMP) almost grown up: Psychiatric and personality disorders at age 16 years. *Journal of Child Psychology and Psychiatry, 35*, 1255–1271.

Henderson, L., Rose, P., & Henderson, S. E. (1992). Reaction time and movement time in children with a developmental coordination disorder. *Journal of Child Psychology and Psychiatry, 33*, 895–905.

Henderson, S. E. (1985). Motor skill development. In D. Lane & B. Stratford (eds), *Current Approaches to Down's Syndrome*. London: Holt, Rinehart and Winston.

Henderson, S. E. (1986). Some aspects of the development of motor control in Down's syndrome. In H. T. A. Whiting & M. G. Wade (eds), *Themes in Motor Development*. Dordrecht: Martinus Nijhoff Publishers.

Henderson, S. E., & Barnett, A. L. (1998). The classification of specific motor coordination disorders in children: Some problems to be solved. *Human Movement Science, 17*, 449–469.

Henderson, S. E., & Hall, D. (1982). Concomitants of clumsiness in young school children. *Developmental Medicine and Child Neurology, 24*, 448–460.

Henderson, S. E., & Sugden, D. A. (1992). *Movement Assessment Battery for Children*. London: Harcourt Brace Jovanovitch.

Henderson, S. E., Barnett, A., & Henderson, L. (1994). Visuospatial difficulties and clumsiness: On the interpretation of conjoined deficits. *Journal of Child Psychology and Psychiatry, 35*, 961–969.

Henderson, S. E., Knight, E., Losse, A., & Jongmans, M. (1991). The clumsy child in school – are we doing enough? *British Journal of Physical Education*, *9*, 2–8.

Hermelin, B. (2001). *Bright Splinters of the Mind: A Personal Story of Research with Autistic Savants*. Philadelphia: Jessica Kingsley.

Hermelin, B., & Pring, L., with Buhler, M., Wolff, S., & Heaton, P. (1999). A visually impaired savant artist: Interacting perceptual and memory representations. *Journal of Child Psychology and Psychiatry*, *40*, 1129–1139.

Hesketh, L. J., & Chapman, R. S. (1998). Verb use by individuals with Down syndrome. *American Journal on Mental Retardation*, *103*, 288–304.

Hetherington, R., & Dennis, M. (1999). Motor function profile in children with early onset hydrocephalus. *Developmental Neuropsychology*, *15*, 25–51.

Hewett, S. (1970). *The Family and the Handicapped Child: A Study of Cerebral Palsied Children in their Homes*. London: Allen and Unwin.

Hill, E. L. (1998). A dyspraxic deficit in specific language impairment and developmental coordination disorder? Evidence from hand and arm movements. *Developmental Medicine and Child Neurology*, *40*, 388–395.

Hill, E. L., & Bishop, D. V. M. (1998). A reaching test reveals weak hand preference in specific language impairment and developmental co-ordination disorder. *Laterality*, *3*, 295–310.

Hill, E. L., & Wing, A. M. (1998). Developmental disorders and the use of grip force to compensate for inertial forces during voluntary movement. In K. J. Connolly (ed.), *The Psychobiology of the Hand*. London: Mac Keith Press.

Hill, E. L., & Wing, A. M. (1999). Coordination of grip force and load force in developmental coordination disorder: A case study. *Neurocase*, *5*, 537–544.

Hill, E. L., Bishop, D. V. M., & Nimmo-Smith, I. (1998). Representational gestures in developmental coordination disorder and specific language impairment: Error-types and the reliability of ratings. *Human Movement Science*, *17*, 655–678.

Hindley, P. (1997). Psychiatric aspects of hearing impairments. *Journal of Child Psychology and Psychiatry*, *38*, 101–117.

Hindley, P. A., Hill, P. D., McGuigan, S., & Kitson, N. (1994). Psychiatric disorder in deaf and hearing impaired children and young people: A prevalence study. *Journal of Child Psychology and Psychiatry*, *35*, 917–934.

Hobson, R. P. (1984). Early childhood autism and the question of egocentrism. *Journal of Autism and Developmental Disorders*, *14*, 85–104.

Hobson, R. P. (1990a). On acquiring knowledge about people and the capacity to pretend: Response to Leslie (1987): *Psychological Review*, *97*, 114–121.

Hobson, R. P. (1990b). On the origins of self and the case of autism. *Development and Psychopathology*, *2*, 163–181.

Hobson, R. P. (1991). Methodological issues for experiments on autistic individuals' perception and understanding of emotion. *Journal of Child Psychology and Psychiatry*, *32*, 1135–1158.

Hobson, R. P. (1993). *Autism and the Development of Mind*. Hove, East Sussex: Erlbaum.

Hobson, R. P., & Lee, A. (1998). Hello and goodbye: A study of social engagement in autism. *Journal of Autism and Developmental Disorders*, *28*, 117–127.

Hobson, R. P., & Lee, A. (1999). Imitation and identification in autism. *Journal of Child Psychology and Psychiatry, 40*, 649–659.

Hobson, R. P., Lee, A., & Brown, R. (1999). Autism and congenital blindness. *Journal of Autism and Developmental Disorders, 29*, 45–56.

Hobson, R. P., Ouston, J., & Lee, A. (1988). What's in a face? The case of autism. *British Journal of Psychology, 79*, 441–453.

Hobson, R. P., Ouston, J., & Lee, A. (1989). Naming emotion in faces and voices: Abilities and disabilities in autism and mental retardation. *British Journal of Developmental Psychology, 7*, 237–250.

Hodapp, R. M., & Zigler, E. (1990). Applying the developmental perspective to individuals with Down syndrome. In D. Cicchetti & M. Beeghly (eds), *Children with Down syndrome: A Developmental Perspective*. Cambridge: Cambridge University Press.

Hodapp, R. M., Evans, D. W., & Gray, F. L. (1999). Intellectual development in children with Down syndrome. In J. A. Rondal, J. Perera, & L. Nadel (eds), *Down Syndrome: A Review of Current Knowledge*. London: Whurr Publishers Ltd.

Hogg, J., & Moss, S. C. (1983). Prehensile development in Down's syndrome and nonhandicapped preschool children. *British Journal of Developmental Psychology, 1*, 189–204.

Holler, K. A., Fennell, E. B., Crosson, B., Boggs, S. R., & Mickle, J. P. (1995). Neuropsychological and adaptive functioning in younger versus older children shunted for early hydrocephalus. *Child Neuropsychology, 1*, 63–73.

Holmbeck, G. N., & Faier-Routman, J. (1995). Spinal lesion level, shunt status, family relationships, and psychosocial adjustment in children and adolescents with spina bifida myelomeningocele. *Journal of Pediatric Psychology, 20*, 817–832.

Holmes-Siedle, M., Lindenbaum, R. H., & Galliard, A. (1982). Vitamin supplements and neural tube defects. *Lancet, 1*, 276.

Holt, K. G., Fonseca, S. T., & LaFiandra, M. E. (2000). The dynamics of gait in children with spastic hemiplegic cerebral palsy: Theoretical and clinical implications. *Human Movement Science, 19*, 375–405.

Hommeyer, J. S., Holmbeck, G. N., Wills, K. E., & Coers, S. (1999). Condition severity and psychosocial functioning in pre-adolescents with spina bifida: Disentangling proximal functional status and distal adjustment outcomes. *Journal of Pediatric Psychology, 24*, 499–509.

Horn, D. G., Lorch, E. P., Lorch, R. F. Jr., & Culatta, B. (1985). Distractibility and vocabulary deficits in children with spina bifida and hydrocephalus. *Developmental Medicine and Child Neurology, 27*, 713–720.

Hosie, J. A., Gray, C. D., Russell, P. A., Scott, C., & Hunter, N. (1998). The matching of facial expressions by deaf and hearing children and their production and comprehension of emotion labels. *Motivation and Emotion, 22*, 293–313.

Hosie, J. A., Russell, P. A., Gray, C. D., Scott, C., Hunter, N., & Banks, J. S. (2000). Knowledge of display rules in prelingually deaf and hearing children. *Journal of Child Psychology and Psychiatry, 41*, 389–398.

Howard, M. A., Cowell, P. E., Boucher, J., Broks, P., Mayes, A., & Farrant, A. (2000). Convergent neuroanatomical and behavioural evidence of an amygdala hypothesis of autism. *NeuroReport, 11,* 2931–2935.

Howlin, P. (1998). Practitioner review: Psychological and educational treatments for autism. *Journal of Child Psychology and Psychiatry, 39,* 307–322.

Howlin, P., & Moore, A. (1997). Diagnosis in autism: A survey of over 1200 patients in the UK. *Autism, 1,* 135–162.

Howlin, P., Mawhood, L., & Rutter, M. (2000). Autism and developmental receptive language disorder – a comparative follow-up in early adult life. II: Social, behavioural, and psychiatric outcomes. *Journal of Child Psychology and Psychiatry, 41,* 561–578.

Hughes, C., & Russell, J. (1993). Autistic children's difficulty with mental disengagement from an object: Its implications for theories of autism. *Developmental Psychology, 29,* 498–510.

Hughes, C., Leboyer, M., & Bouvard, M. (1997). Executive function in parents of children with autism. *Psychological Medicine, 27,* 209–220.

Hughes, C., Plumet, M.-H., & Leboyer, M. (1999). Towards a cognitive phenotype for autism: Increased prevalence of executive dysfunction and superior spatial span amongst siblings of children with autism. *Journal of Child Psychology and Psychiatry, 40,* 705–718.

Hughes, C., Russell, J., & Robbins, T. W. (1994). Evidence for executive dysfunction in autism. *Neuropsychologia, 32,* 477–492.

Hughes, M., Dote-Kwan, J., & Dolendo, J. (1998). A close look at the cognitive play of preschoolers with visual impairments in the home. *Exceptional Children, 64,* 451–462.

Hughes, M., Dote-Kwan, J., & Dolendo, J. (1999). Characteristics of maternal directiveness and responsiveness with young children with visual impairments. *Child: Care, Health and Development, 25,* 285–298.

Huh, J., Williams, H. G., & Burke, J. R. (1998). Development of bilateral motor control in children with developmental coordination disorders. *Developmental Medicine and Child Neurology, 40,* 474–484.

Hull, T., & Mason, H. (1995). Performance of blind children on digit-span tests. *Journal of Visual Impairment and Blindness, 89,* 166–169.

Hulme, C., & MacKenzie, S. (1992). *Working Memory and Severe Learning Difficulties.* Hove, Sussex: Laurence Ehrlbaum.

Hulme, C., Biggerstaff, A., Moran, G., & McKinlay, I. (1982). Visual, kinaesthetic and cross-modal judgements of length by normal and clumsy children. *Developmental Medicine and Child Neurology, 24,* 461–471.

Hunt, G. M. (1990). Open spina bifida: Outcome for a complete cohort treated unselectively and followed into adulthood. *Developmental Medicine and Child Neurology, 32,* 108–118.

Huntington, G. S., & Simeonsson, R. J. (1993). Temperament and adaptation in infants and young children with disabilities. *Infant Mental Health Journal, 14,* 49–60.

Hur, J., & Cochrane, R. (1995). A note on problems and difficulties in administering psychometric tests to young children with cerebral palsy. *British Journal of Developmental Disabilities, 41,* 67–69.

Huurre, T. M., & Aro, H. M. (1998). Psychosocial development among adolescents with visual impairment. *European Child and Adolescent Psychiatry, 7,*

73–78.

Huurre, T. M., Komulainen, E. J., & Aro, H. M. (1999). Social support and self-esteem among adolescents with visual impairments. *Journal of Visual Impairment and Blindness*, *93*, 26–37.

Hyde, M. B., & Power, D. J. (1996). Teachers' ratings of the communication abilities of their deaf students. *American Annals of the Deaf*, *141*, 5–10.

Illingworth, R. S. (1958). *Recent Advances in Cerebral Palsy*. London: J. & A. Churchill, Ltd.

Itard, J. M. G. (1801/1807). Mémoire et rapport sur Victor de l'Aveyron. In L. Malson (1964). *Les Enfants Sauvages*. Paris: Union Générale d'Editions.

Ito, J., Saijo, H., Araki, A., Tanaka, H., Tasaki, T., & Cho, K. (1996). Assessment of visuoperceptual disturbance in children with spastic diplegia using measurements of the lateral ventricles on cerebral MRI. *Developmental Medicine and Child Neurology*, *38*, 496–502.

Ito, J., Saijo, H., Araki, A., Tanaka, H., Tasaki, T., & Cho, K. (1997). Neuroradiological assessment of visuoperceptual disturbance in children with spina bifida and hydrocephalus. *Developmental Medicine and Child Neurology*, *39*, 385–392.

Ittyerah, M., & Samarapungavan, A. (1989). The performance of congenitally blind children in cognitive developmental tasks. *British Journal of Developmental Psychology*, *7*, 129–139.

Ittyerah, M., & Sharma, R. (1997). The performance of hearing-impaired children on handedness and perceptual motor tasks. *Genetic, Social, and General Psychology Monographs*, *123*, 285–302.

Iverson, J. M. (1999). How to get to the cafeteria: Gesture and speech in blind and sighted children's spatial descriptions. *Developmental Psychology*, *35*, 1132–1142.

Iverson, J. M., & Goldin-Meadow, S. (1997). What's communication got to do with it? Gesture in children blind from birth. *Developmental Psychology*, *33*, 453–467.

Jackson, A. L. (2001). Language facility and theory of mind development in deaf children. *Journal of Deaf Studies and Deaf Education*, *6*, 161–176.

Jacobs, P. A., Baikie, A. G., Court Brown, W. M., & Strong, J. A. (1959). The somatic chromosomes in mongolism. *Lancet*, *1*, 710.

Jamieson, J. R. (1994a). Instructional discourse strategies: Differences between hearing and deaf mothers of deaf children. *First Language*, *14*, 153–171.

Jamieson, J. R. (1994b). Teaching as transaction: Vygotskian perspectives on deafness and mother-child interaction. *Exceptional Children*, *60*, 434–449.

Jamieson, J. R. (1995). A signed form of private speech: Observations of two deaf children of deaf parents in a mathematics class. *Exceptionality Education Canada*, *5*, 19–36.

Jamieson, J. R. (1997). The value of "deaf eyes": Early interventions with young deaf children and their families. *Exceptionality Education Canada*, *7*, 51–68.

Jamieson, J. R., & Pedersen, E. D. (1993). Deafness and mother-child interaction: Scaffolded instruction and the learning of problem-solving skills. *Early Development and Parenting*, *2*, 229–242.

Jarrold, C., Baddeley, A. D., & Hewes, A. K. (1999a). Genetically dissociated components of working memory: Evidence from Down's and Williams syndrome. *Neuropsychologia, 37,* 637–651.

Jarrold, C., Baddeley, A. D., & Hewes, A. K. (2000a). Verbal short-term memory deficits in Down syndrome: A consequence of problems in rehearsal? *Journal of Child Psychology and Psychiatry, 40,* 233–244.

Jarrold, C., Baddeley, A. D., & Phillips, C. (1999b) Down syndrome and the phonological loop: The evidence for, and importance of, a specific verbal short-term memory deficit. *Down Syndrome: Research and Practice, 6,* 61–75.

Jarrold, C., Boucher, J., & Smith, P. K. (1994a). Executive function deficits and the pretend play of children with autism: A research note. *Journal of Child Psychology and Psychiatry, 35,* 1473–1482.

Jarrold, C., Boucher, J., & Smith, P. K. (1996). Generativity deficits in pretend play in autism. *British Journal of Developmental Psychology, 14,* 275–300.

Jarrold, C., Butler, D. W., Cottington, E. M., & Jimenez, F. (2000b). Linking theory of mind and central coherence bias in autism and in the general population. *Developmental Psychology, 36,* 126–138.

Jarrold, C., Smith, P., Boucher, J., & Harris, P. (1994b). Comprehension of pretense in children with autism. *Journal of Autism and Developmental Disorders, 24,* 433–455.

Jenkins, C. (1993). Expressive language delay in children with Down's syndrome: A specific cause for concern. *Down's Syndrome: Research and Practice, 1,* 10–14.

Jobling, A. (1999). Attainment of motor proficiency in school-aged children with Down syndrome. *Adapted Physical Activity Quarterly, 16,* 344–361.

Jobling, A., & Mon-Williams, M. (2000). Motor development in Down syndrome: A longitudinal perspective. In D. Weeks, R. Chua, & D. Elliott (eds), *Perceptual-Motor Behavior in Down Syndrome.* Champaign, IL: Human Kinetics.

Johnston, F., & Stansfield, J. (1997). Expressive pragmatic skills in pre-school children with and without Down's syndrome: Parental perceptions. *Journal of Intellectual Disability Research, 41,* 19–29.

Johnstone, B., & Garcia, L. (1994). Neuropsychological evaluation and academic implications for developmental coordination disorder: A case study. *Developmental Neuropsychology, 10,* 369–375.

Jolliffe, T., & Baron-Cohen, S. (1997). Are people with autism and Asperger syndrome faster than normal on the embedded figure test? *Journal of Child Psychology and Psychiatry, 38,* 527–534.

Jones, H. A., Horn, E. M., & Warren, S. F. (1999). The effects of motor skill acquisition on the development of intentional communication. *Journal of Early Intervention, 22,* 25–37.

Jones, O. (1977). Mother-child interaction with pre-linguistic Down's syndrome and normal infants. In H. R. Schaffer (ed.), *Studies in Mother-Infant Interaction.* London: Academic Press.

Jongmans, M. J., Mercuri, E., Dubowitz, L. M. S., & Henderson, S. E. (1998). Perceptual-motor difficulties and their concomitants in six-year-old children born prematurely. *Human Movement Science, 17,* 629–653.

Kadesjö, B., & Gillberg, C. (1998). Attention deficits and clumsiness in Swedish 7-year-old children. *Developmental Medicine and Child Neurology, 40,* 796–

804.

Kadesjö, B., & Gillberg, C. (1999). Developmental coordination disorder in Swedish 7-year-old children. *Journal of the American Academy of Child and Adolescent Psychiatry, 38,* 820–828.

Kamhi, A. G., & Masterson, J. J. (1989). Language and cognition in mentally handicapped people: Last rites for the difference-delay controversy. In M. Beveridge, G. Conti-Ramsden, & I. Leudar (eds), *Language and Communication in Mentally Handicapped People.* London: Chapman and Hall.

Kanner, L. (1943). Autistic disturbances of affective contact. *Nervous Child, 2,* 217–250.

Kaplan, B. J., Wilson, B. N., Dewey, D., & Crawford, S. G. (1998). DCD may not be a discrete disorder. *Human Movement Science, 17,* 471–490.

Karrer, J. H., Karrer, R., Bloom, D., Chaney, D., & Davis, R. (1998). Event-related brain potentials during an extended visual recognition memory task depict delayed development of cerebral inhibitory processes among 6-month-old infants with Down syndrome. *International Journal of Psychophysiology, 29,* 167–200.

Kasari, C., Freeman, S. F. N., & Hughes, M. A. (2001). Emotion recognition by children with Down syndrome. *American Journal on Mental Retardation, 106,* 59–72.

Kasari, C., Freeman, S., Mundy, P., & Sigman, M. D. (1995). Attention regulation by children with Down syndrome: Coordinated joint attention and social referencing looks. *American Journal on Mental Retardation, 100,* 128–136.

Kasari, C., Sigman, M., & Yirmiya, N. (1993a) Focused and social attention of autistic children in interactions with familiar and unfamiliar adults: A comparison of autistic, mentally retarded, and normal children. *Development and Psychopathology, 5,* 403–414.

Kasari, C., Sigman, M., Baumgartner, P., & Stipek, D. J. (1993b). Pride and mastery in children with autism. *Journal of Child Psychology and Psychiatry, 34,* 353–362.

Kawashima, R., Sugiura, M., Kato, T., Nakamura, A., Hatano, K., & Ito, K. (1999). The human amygdala plays an important role in gaze monitoring: A PET study. *Brain, 122,* 779–783.

Kay, L., & Strelow, E. (1977). Blind babies need specially designed aids. *New Scientist, 74,* 709–712.

Kay-Raining Bird, E., Cleave, P. L., & McConnell, L. (2000). Reading and phonological awareness in children with Down syndrome: A longitudinal study. *American Journal of Speech-Language Pathology, 9,* 319–330.

Kaye, J. A., Melero-Montes, M. D., & Jick, H. (2001). Mumps, measles, and rubella vaccine and the incidence of autism recorded by general practitioners: A time trend analysis. *British Medical Journal, 322,* 460–463.

Kazak, S., Collis, G. M., & Lewis, V. (1997). Can young people with autism refer to knowledge states? Evidence from their understanding of "know" and "guess". *Journal of Child Psychology and Psychiatry, 38,* 1001–1010.

Keeler, W. R. (1958). Autistic patterns and defective communication in blind children with retrolental fibroplasia. In P. H. Hoch & J. Zubin (eds), *Psychopathology of Communication.* New York: Grune and Stratton.

Kef, S., Hox, J. J., & Habekothé, H. T. (2000). Social networks of visually impaired and blind adolescents: Structure and effect on well-being. *Social Networks, 22*, 73–91.

Kehoe, L. (1978). Poor hearing exacerbates Down's syndrome. *New Scientist, 80*, 341.

Kekelis, M. A., & Andersen, E. S. (1984). Family communication styles and language development. *Journal of Visual Impairment and Blindness, 78*, 54–64.

Kekelis, M. A., & Prinz, P. M. (1996). Blind and sighted children with their mothers: The development of discourse skills. *Journal of Visual Impairment and Blindness, 90*, 423–436.

Kelly, L. P. (1995). Processing of bottom-up and top-down information by skilled and average deaf readers and implications for whole language instruction. *Exceptional Children, 61*, 318–334.

Kennedy, M. D., Sheridan, M. K., Radlinski, S. H., & Beeghly, M. (1991). Play-language relationships in young children with developmental delays: Implications for assessment. *Journal of Speech and Hearing Research, 34*, 112–122.

Kephart, J. G., Kephart, C. P., & Schwarz, G. C. (1974). A journey into the world of the blind child. *Exceptional Children, 40*, 421–427.

Klein, B. P., & Mervis, C. B. (1999). Contrasting patterns of cognitive abilities of 9- and 10-year olds with Williams syndrome or Down syndrome. *Developmental Neuropsychology, 16*, 177–196.

Klin, A. (2000). Attributing social meaning to ambiguous visual stimuli in higher-functioning autism and Asperger syndrome: The Social Attribution Task. *Journal of Child Psychology and Psychiatry, 41*, 831–846.

Klin, A., Lang, J., Cicchetti, D. V., & Volkmar, F. R. (2000). Brief report: Interrater reliability of clinical diagnosis and DSM-IV criteria for autistic disorder: Results of the DSM-IV autism field trial. *Journal of Autism and Developmental Disorders, 30*, 163–167.

Klin, A., Volkmar, F. R., & Sparrow, S. S. (1992). Autistic social dysfunction: Some limitations of the theory of mind hypothesis. *Journal of Child Psychology and Psychiatry, 33*, 861–876.

Knieps, L. J., Walden, T. A., & Baxter, A. (1994). Affective expressions of toddlers with and without Down syndrome in a social referencing context. *American Journal on Mental Retardation, 99*, 301–312.

Knott, F., Lewis, C., & Williams, T. (1995). Sibling interaction of children with learning disabilities: A comparison of autism and Down's syndrome. *Journal of Child Psychology and Psychiatry, 36*, 965–976.

Knox, M. (1983). Changes in the frequency of language use by Down's syndrome children interacting with non-retarded peers. *Education and Training of the Mentally Retarded, 18*, 185–190.

Koegel, R. L., & Wilhelm, H. (1973). Selective responding to the components of multiple visual cues by autistic children. *Journal of Experimental Child Psychology, 15*, 442–453.

Koester, L. S. (1995). Face-to-face interactions between hearing mothers and their deaf or hearing infants. *Infant Behavior and Development, 18*, 145–153.

Koester, L. S., Brooks, L. R., & Karkowski, A. M. (1998b). A comparison of the vocal patterns of deaf and hearing mother-infant dyads during face-to-face interactions. *Journal of Deaf Studies and Deaf Education, 3*, 290–301.

Koester, L. S., Karkowski, A. M., & Traci, M. A. (1998a). How do deaf and hearing mothers regain eye contact when their infants look away? *American Annals of the Deaf, 143*, 5–13.

Koester, L. S., Papoušek, H., & Smith-Gray, S. (2000). Intuitive parenting, communication, and interaction with deaf infants. In P. E. Spencer, C. J. Erting, & M. Marschark (eds), *The Deaf Child in the Family and at School*. Mahwah, N.J.: Erlbaum.

Kokubun, M. (1999). Are children with Down syndrome less careful in performing a tray-carrying task than children with other types of mental retardation? *Perceptual and Motor Skills, 88*, 1173–1176.

Kokubun, M., & Koike, T. (1995). Problems in balance performance in mental retardation. *Medicine and Sport Science, 40*, 191–197.

Kokubun, M., Haishi, K., Okuzumi, H., & Hosobuchi, T. (1995). Factors affecting age of walking by children with mental retardation. *Perceptual and Motor Skills, 80*, 547–552.

Kokubun, M., Shinmyo, T., Ogita, M., Morita, K., Furuta, M., & Haishi, K. (1997). Comparison of postural control of children with Down syndrome and those with other forms of mental retardation. *Perceptual and Motor Skills, 84*, 499–504.

Kolk, C. J. V. (1977). Intelligence testing for visually impaired persons. *Journal of Visual Impairment and Blindness, 71*, 158–163.

Kopp, C. B., & Shaperman, J. (1973). Cognitive development in the absence of object manipulation during infancy. Extended report. Brief report published in *Developmental Psychology, 9*, 430.

Kraijer, D. (2000). Review of adaptive behavior studies in mentally retarded persons with autism/pervasive developmental disorder. *Journal of Autism and Developmental Disorders, 30*, 39–47.

Krakow, J., & Koop, C. (1982). Sustained attention in young Down syndrome children. *Topics in Early Childhood Special Education, 2*, 32–42.

Kučera, J. (1969). Age at walking, at eruption of deciduous teeth and response to ephedrine in children with Down's syndrome. *Journal of Mental Deficiency Research, 13*, 143–148.

Kuhtz-Buschbeck, J. P., Sundholm, L. K., Eliasson, A.-C., & Forssberg, H. (2000). Quantitative assessment of mirror movements in children and adolescents with hemiplegic cerebral palsy. *Developmental Medicine and Child Neurology, 42*, 728–736.

Kumin, L. (1994). Intelligibility of speech in children with Down syndrome in natural settings: Parents' perspective. *Perceptual and Motor Skills, 78*, 307–313.

Kumin, L., Councill, C., & Goodman, M. (1994). A longitudinal study of the emergence of phonemes in children with Down syndrome. *Journal of Communication Disorders, 27*, 292–303.

Kyle, J. G. (1981). Reading development in deaf children. *Journal of Research in Reading, 3*, 86–97.

Kyle, J. G., & Allsop, L. (1982). Communicating with young deaf people. *Teacher of the Deaf, 6*, 89–95.

Kyle, J. G., & Woll, B. (1985). *Sign Language. The Study of Deaf People and their Language*. London: Cambridge University Press.

Landau, B. (1991a). Spatial representation of objects in the young blind child. *Cognition, 38*, 145–178.

Landau, B. (1991b) Knowledge and its expression in the blind child. In D. P. Keating & H. Rosen (eds), *Constructivist Perspectives on Developmental Psychopathology and Atypical Development*. London: Erlbaum.

Landau, B. (1997). Language and experience in blind children: Retrospective and prospective. In V. Lewis & G. M. Collis (eds), *Blindness and Psychological Development in Young Children*. Leicester: The British Psychological Society.

Landau, B., & Gleitman, L. R. (1985). *Language and Experience: Evidence from the Blind Child*. Cambridge, Massachusetts: Harvard University Press.

Landau, B., Spelke, E., & Gleitman, H. (1984). Spatial knowledge in a young blind child. *Cognition, 16*, 225–260.

Landgren, M., Kjellman, B., & Gillberg, C. (1998). Attention deficit disorder with developmental coordination disorders. *Archives of Disease in Childhood, 79*, 207–212.

Landry, S. H., & Chapieski, M. L. (1989). Joint attention and infant toy exploration: Effects of Down syndrome and prematurity. *Child Development, 60*, 103–118.

Landry, S. H., & Loveland, K. A. (1988). Communication behaviors in autism and developmental language delay. *Journal of Child Psychology and Psychiatry, 29*, 621–634.

Landry, S. H., Copeland, D., Lee, A., & Robinson, S. (1990). Goal-directed behavior in children with spina bifida. *Journal of Developmental and Behavioral Pediatrics, 11*, 306–311.

Landry, S. H., Garner, P. W., Pirie, D., & Swank, P. R. (1994). Effects of social context and mothers' requesting strategies on Down's syndrome children's social responsiveness. *Developmental Psychology, 30*, 293–302.

Landry, S. H., Jordan, T., & Fletcher, J. M. (1994). Developmental outcomes for children with spina bifida and hydrocephalus. In M. G. Tramontana & S. R. Hooper (eds), *Advances in Child Neuropsychology*. New York: Springer-Verlag.

Landry, S. H., Robinson, S. S., Copeland, D., & Garner, P. W. (1993). Goal-directed behavior and perception of self competence in children with spina bifida. *Journal of Pediatric Psychology, 18*, 389–396.

Lane, H., & Bahan, B. (1998). Ethics of cochlear implantation in young children: A review and reply from a Deaf-World perspective. *Otolaryngology-Head and Neck Surgery, 119*, 297–313.

Langaas, T., Mon-Williams, M., Wann, J. P., Pascal, E., & Thompson, C. (1998). Eye movements, prematurity and developmental co-ordination disorder. *Vision Research, 38*, 1817–1826.

Langdell, T. (1978). Recognition of faces: An approach to the study of autism. *Journal of Child Psychology and Psychiatry, 19*, 255–268.

Langdon-Down, R. L. (1906). Some observations on the mongolian type of imbecility. *Journal of Mental Science, 52*, 187–190.

Lartz, M. N., & Lestina, L. J. (1995). Strategies deaf mothers use when reading to young deaf or hard of hearing children. *American Annals of the Deaf*,

140, 358–362.

Lauritsen, M., Mors, O., Mortensen, P. B., & Ewald, H. (1999). Infantile autism and associated autosomal chromosome abnormalities: A register-based study and a literature survey. *Journal of Child Psychology and Psychiatry, 40*, 335–345.

Laws, G. (1998). The use of nonword repetition as a test of phonological memory in children with Down syndrome. *Journal of Child Psychology and Psychiatry, 39*, 1119–1130.

Laws, G., & Lawrence, L. (2001). Spatial representation in the drawings of children with Down's syndrome and its relationship to language and motor development: A preliminary investigation. *British Journal of Developmental Psychology, 19*, 453–473.

Le Couteur, A., Bailey, A., Goode, S., Pickles, A., Robertson, S., & Gottesman, I. (1996). A broader phenotype of autism: The clinical spectrum in twins. *Journal of Child Psychology and Psychiatry, 37*, 785–801.

Le Couteur, A., Rutter, M., Lord, C., Rios, P., Robertson, S., & Holdgrafer, M. (1989). Autism Diagnostic Interview-Revised. *Journal of Autism and Developmental Disorders, 19*, 363–389.

Leboyer, M., Plumet, M.-H., Goldblum, M.-C., Perez-Diaz, F., & Marchaland, C. (1995). Verbal versus visuospatial abilities in relatives of autistic girls. *Developmental Neuropsychology, 11*, 139–154.

Lederberg, A. R. (1984). Interaction between deaf preschoolers and unfamiliar hearing adults. *Child Development, 55*, 598–606.

Lederberg, A. R. (1991). Social interaction among deaf preschoolers: The effects of language ability and age. *American Annals of the Deaf, 136*, 53–59.

Lederberg, A. R., & Mobley, C. E. (1990). The effect of hearing impairment on the quality of attachment and mother-toddler interaction. *Child Development, 61*, 1596–1604.

Lederberg, A. R., & Prezbindowski, A. K. (2000). Impact of child deafness on mother-toddler interaction: Strengths and weaknesses. In P. E. Spencer, C. J. Erting, & M. Marschark (eds), *The Deaf Child in the Family and at School.* Mahwah, N.J.: Erlbaum.

Lederberg, A. R., Ryan, H. B., & Robbins, B. L. (1986). Peer interaction in young deaf children: The effect of partner hearing status and familiarity. *Developmental Psychology, 22*, 691–700.

Lee, A., & Hobson, R. P. (1998). On developing self-concepts: A controlled study of children and adolescents with autism. *Journal of Child Psychology and Psychiatry, 39*, 1131–1144.

Lee, A., Hobson, R. P., & Chiat, S. (1994). I, you, me, and autism: An experimental study. *Journal of Autism and Developmental Disorders, 24*, 155–176.

Leekam, S. R., & Perner, J. (1991). Does the autistic child have a metarepresentational deficit? *Cognition, 40*, 203–218.

Leekam, S. R., & Prior, M. (1994). Can autistic children distinguish lies from jokes? A second look at second-order belief attribution. *Journal of Child Psychology and Psychiatry, 35*, 901–915.

Leekam, S. R., Hunnisett, E., & Moore, C. (1998). Targets and cues: Gaze-following in children with autism. *Journal of Child Psychology and Psychiatry*,

39, 951–962.

Leekam, S. R., López, B., & Moore, C. (2000). Attention and joint attention in preschool children with autism. *Developmental Psychology*, *36*, 261–273.

Leekam, S., Baron-Cohen, S., Perrett, D., Milders, M., & Brown, S. (1997). Eye-direction detection: A dissociation between geometric and joint attention skills in autism. *British Journal of Developmental Psychology*, *15*, 77–95.

Leevers, H. J., & Harris, P. L. (1998). Drawing impossible entities: A measure of the imagination in children with autism, children with learning disabilities, and normal 4-year-olds. *Journal of Child Psychology and Psychiatry*, *39*, 399–410.

Lefebvre, C., & Reid, G. (1998). Prediction in ball catching by children with and without a developmental coordination disorder. *Adapted Physical Activity Quarterly*, *15*, 299–315.

Legerstee, M., & Weintraub, J. (1997). The integration of person and object attention in infants with and without Down syndrome. *Infant Behavior and Development*, *20*, 71–82.

Leifer, J., & Lewis, M. (1984). Acquisition of conversational response skills by young Down syndrome and non-retarded children. *American Journal of Mental Deficiency*, *88*, 610–618.

Lemanek, K. L., Jones, M. L., & Lieberman, B. (2000). Mothers of children with spina bifida: Adaptational and stress processing. *Children's Health Care*, *29*, 19–35.

Leonard, S., Bower, C., Petterson, B., & Leonard, H. (1999). Medical aspects of school-aged children with Down syndrome. *Developmental Medicine and Child Neurology*, *41*, 683–688.

Leslie, A. M. (1987). Pretense and representation: The origins of "theory of mind". *Psychological Review*, *94*, 412–426.

Leslie, A. M., & Frith, U. (1990). Prospects for a cognitive neuropsychology of autism: Hobson's choice. *Psychological Review*, *97*, 122–131.

Leslie, A. M., & Thaiss, L. (1992). Domain specificity in conceptual development: Neuropsychological evidence from autism. *Cognition*, *43*, 225–251.

Levine, L. M., & Antia, S. D. (1997). The effect of partner hearing status on social and cognitive play. *Journal of Early Intervention*, *21*, 21–35.

Levtzion-Korach, O., Tennenbaum, A., Schnitzer, R., & Ornoy, A. (2000). Early motor development of blind children. *Journal of Paediatrics and Child Health*, *36*, 226–229.

Lewis, C., & Mitchell, P. (eds) (1994). *Children's Early Understanding of Mind: Origins and Development*. Hillsdale, New Jersey: Erlbaum.

Lewis, V. A., & Bryant, P. E. (1982). Touch and vision in normal and Down's syndrome babies. *Perception*, *11*, 691–701.

Lewis, V., & Boucher, J. (1988). Spontaneous, instructed and elicited play in relatively able autistic children. *British Journal of Developmental Psychology*, *6*, 325–339.

Lewis, V., & Boucher, J. (1991). Skill, content and generative strategies in autistic children's drawings. *British Journal of Developmental Psychology*, *9*, 393–416.

Lewis, V., & Boucher, J. (1995). Generativity in the play of young people with autism. *Journal of Autism and Developmental Disorders*, *25*, 105–121.

Lewis, V., & Boucher, J. (1997). *The Test of Pretend Play*. London: Harcourt

Brace Jovanovich.

Lewis, V., & Collis, G. M. (1997). Methodological and theoretical issues associated with the study of children with visual impairments. In V. Lewis & G. M. Collis (eds), *Blindness and Psychological Development in Young Children*. Leicester: The British Psychological Society.

Lewis, V., Boucher, J., Lupton, L., & Watson, S. (2000b). Relationships between symbolic play, functional play, verbal and non-verbal ability in young children. *International Journal of Language and Communication Disorders*, 35, 117–127.

Lewis, V., Collis, G., Shadlock, R., Potts, M., & Norgate, S. (2002). New methods for studying blind children's understanding of familiar space. *British Journal of Visual Impairment*, 20, 17–23.

Lewis, V., Norgate, S., Collis, G., & Reynolds, R. (2000a). The consequences of visual impairment for children's symbolic and functional play. *British Journal of Developmental Psychology*, 18, 449–464.

Leybaert, J. (1998). Phonological representations in deaf children: The importance of early linguistic experience. *Scandinavian Journal of Psychology*, 39, 169–173.

Leybaert, J. (2000). Phonology acquired through the eyes and spelling in deaf children. *Journal of Experimental Child Psychology*, 75, 291–318.

Leybaert, J., & Alegria, J. (1993). Is word processing involuntary in deaf children? *British Journal of Developmental Psychology*, 11, 1–29.

Leybaert, J., & Alegria, J. (1995). Spelling development in deaf and hearing children: Evidence for use of morpho-phonological regularities in French. *Reading and Writing*, 7, 89–109.

Leybaert, J., & Charlier, B. (1996). Visual speech in the head: The effect of cued-speech on rhyming, remembering, and spelling. *Journal of Deaf Studies and Deaf Education*, 1, 234–248.

Liao, H.-F., Jeng, S.-F., Lai, J.-S., Cheng, C.-K., & Hu, M.-H. (1997). The relation between standing balance and walking function in children with spastic diplegic cerebral palsy. *Developmental Medicine and Child Neurology*, 39, 106–112.

Libby, S., Powell, S., Messer, D., & Jordan, R. (1997). Imitation of pretend play acts by children with autism and Down syndrome. *Journal of Autism and Developmental Disorders*, 27, 365–383.

Libby, S., Powell, S., Messer, D., & Jordan, R. (1998). Spontaneous play in children with autism: A reappraisal. *Journal of Autism and Developmental Disorders*, 28, 487–497.

Lie, H. R., Lagergren, J., Rasmussen, F., Lagerkvist, B., Hagelsteen, J., & Börjeson, M.-C. (1991). Bowel and bladder control of children with myelomeningocele: A Nordic study. *Developmental Medicine and Child Neurology*, 33, 1053–1061.

Liedtke, W. (1998). Fostering the development of number sense in young children who are blind. *Journal of Visual Impairment and Blindness*, 92, 346–349.

Lillard, A. S. (1997). Other folks' theories of mind and behaviour. *Psychological Science*, 8, 268–274.

Lind, J., Vuorenkoski, V., Rosberg, G., Partanen, T. J., & Wasz-Höckert, O. (1970). Spectographic analysis of vocal responses to pain stimuli in infants with Down's syndrome. *Developmental Medicine and Child Neurology, 12*, 478–486.

Lindsten, J., Marsk, L., Berglund, K., Iselius, L., Ryman, N., & Annerén, G. (1981). Incidence of Down's syndrome in Sweden during the years 1968–1977. In G. R. Burgio, M. Fraccaro, L. Tiepolo, & U. Wolf (eds), *Trisomy 21: An International Symposium, Italy, 1979*. Berlin: Springer-Verlag.

Linn, M. I., Goodman, J. F., & Lender, W. L. (2000). Played out? Passive behavior by children with Down syndrome during unstructured play. *Journal of Early Intervention, 23*, 264–278.

Liss, M., Fein, D., Allen, D., Dunn, M., Feinstein, C., & Morris, R. (2001a). Executive functioning in high-functioning children with autism. *Journal of Child Psychology and Psychiatry, 42*, 261–270.

Liss, M., Harel, B., Fein, D., Allen, D., Dunn, M., & Feinstein, C. (2001b). Predictors and correlates of adaptive functioning in children with developmental disorders. *Journal of Autism and Developmental Disorders, 31*, 219–230.

Lockyer, L., & Rutter, M. (1969). A five to fifteen year follow up study of infantile psychosis: III Psychological aspects. *British Journal of Psychiatry, 115*, 865–882.

Lord, C. (1995). Follow-up of two-year-olds referred for possible autism. *Journal of Child Psychology and Psychiatry, 36*, 1365–1382.

Lord, C., Pickles, A., McLennan, J., Rutter, M., Bregman, J., & Folstein, S. (1997). Diagnosing autism: Analyses of data from the Autism Diagnostic Interview. *Journal of Autism and Developmental Disorders, 27*, 501–517.

Lord, C., Risi, S., Lambrecht, L., Cook, E. H. Jr., Leventhal, B. L., & DiLavore, P. C. (2000). The Autism Diagnostic Observation Schedule-Generic: A standard measure of social and communication deficits associated with the spectrum of autism. *Journal of Autism and Developmental Disorders, 30*, 205–223.

Lord, C., Rutter, M., Goode, S., Heemsbergen, J., Jordan, H., & Mawood, L. (1989). Autism Diagnostic Observation Schedule: A standardized observation of communicative and social behaviour. *Journal of Autism and Developmental Disorders, 19*, 185–212.

Lord, J., Varzos, N., Behrman, B., Wicks, J., & Wicks, D. (1990). Implications of mainstream classrooms for adolescents with spina bifida. *Developmental Medicine and Child Neurology, 32*, 20–29.

Lord, R., & Hulme, C. (1987). Perceptual judgements of normal and clumsy children. *Developmental Medicine and Child Neurology, 29*, 250–257.

Lord, R., & Hulme, C. (1988a). Visual perception and drawing ability in clumsy and normal children. *British Journal of Developmental Psychology, 6*, 1–9.

Lord, R., & Hulme, C. (1988b). Patterns of rotary pursuit performance in clumsy and normal children. *Journal of Child Psychology and Psychiatry, 29*, 691–701.

‾imer, J., & Tobin, M. J. (1980). Modified Braille codes, reading rates and ‾ace saving. *New Beacon, 64*, 281–284.

‾e, G. (1990). Sensorimotor and action development in autistic children from ‾ncy to early childhood. *Journal of Child Psychology and Psychiatry, 31*, ‾761.

‾, Yeates, K. O., & Enrile, B. G. (1998). Attention in children with my-‾ingocele. *Child Neuropsychology, 4*, 7–20.

Losse, A., Henderson, S. E., Elliman, D., Hall, D., Knight, E., & Jongmans, M. (1991). Clumsiness in children – do they grow out of it? A 10-year follow-up study. *Developmental Medicine and Child Neurology, 33*, 55–68.

Lotter, V. (1966). Epidemiology of autistic conditions in young children: I Prevalence. *Social Psychiatry, 1*, 124–137.

Lotter, V. (1967a). "The Prevalence of the Autistic Syndrome in Children." Unpublished Ph.D. thesis, University of London.

Lotter, V. (1967b). Epidemiology of autistic conditions in young children: II Some characteristics of the parents and children. *Social Psychiatry, 1*, 163–173.

Lotter, V. (1974). Factors related to outcome in autistic children. *Journal of Autism and Childhood Schizophrenia, 4*, 263–277.

Lovaas, O. I. (1996). The UCLA young autism model of service delivery. In C. Maurice (ed.), *Behavioral Intervention for Young Children with Autism*. Austin, Texas: Pro-Ed.

Loveland, K. A. (1987). Behavior of young children with Down syndrome before the mirror: Exploration. *Child Development, 58*, 768–778.

Loveland, K. A., & Kelley, M. L. (1991). Development of adaptive behavior in preschoolers with autism or Down syndrome. *American Journal on Mental Retardation, 96*, 13–20.

Loveland, K. A., & Tunali, B. (1991). Social scripts for conversational interactions in autism and Down syndrome. *Journal of Autism and Developmental Disorders, 21*, 177–186.

Loveland, K. A., McEvoy, R. E., Tunali, B., & Kelley, M. L. (1990). Narrative story telling in autism and Down's syndrome. *British Journal of Developmental Psychology, 8*, 9–24.

Loveland, K. A., Tunali-Kotoski, B., Chen, R., Brelsford, K. A., Ortegon, J., & Pearson, D. A. (1995). Intermodal perception of affect in persons with autism or Down syndrome. *Development and Psychopathology, 7*, 409–418.

Loveland, K. A., Tunali-Kotoski, B., Pearson, D. A., Brelsford, K. A., Ortegon, J., & Chen, R. (1994). Imitation and expression of facial affect in autism. *Development and Psychopathology, 6*, 433–444.

Lowenfeld, B. (1948). Effects of blindness on the cognitive functions of children. *Nervous Child, 7*, 45–54.

Lupton, L., & Lewis, V. (1997). Changes in parent-child interaction in response to intervention. *European Journal of Psychology of Education, 12*, 385–400.

Lyle, J. G. (1960). The effect of an institution environment upon the verbal development of imbecile children. III The Brooklands Residential Family Unit. *Journal of Mental Deficiency Research, 4*, 14–23.

Lynas, W. (1994). Choosing between communication options in the education of deaf children. *Journal of the British Association of Teachers of the Deaf, 18*, 141–153.

Lynas, W. (1999). Communication options. In J. Stokes (ed.), *Hearing Impaired Infants: Support in the First Eighteen Months*. London: Whurr Publishers Ltd.

Lynch, M. P., Oller, D. K., Steffens, M. L., & Buder, E. H. (1995a). Phrasing in prelinguistic vocalizations. *Developmental Psychobiology, 28*, 3–25.

Lynch, M. P., Oller, D. K., Steffens, M. L., Levine, S. L., Basinger, D. L., & Umbel, V. (1995b). Onset of speech-like vocalizations in infants with Down syndrome. *American Journal on Mental Retardation, 100*, 68–86.

Lyon, M. E. (1997). Symbolic play and language development in young deaf children. *Deafness and Education, 21*, 10–20.

MacTurk, R., Vietze, P., McCarthy, M., McQuiston, S., & Yarrow, L. (1985). The organization of exploratory behavior in Down syndrome and non-delayed infants. *Child Development, 56*, 573–587.

Maeland, A. F. (1992). Handwriting and perceptual-motor skills in clumsy, dysgraphic, and "normal" children. *Perceptual and Motor Skills, 75*, 1207–1217.

Mahoney, G., & Neville-Smith, A. (1996). The effects of directive communications on children's interactive engagement: Implications for language intervention. *Topics in Early Childhood Special Education, 16*, 236–250.

Mahoney, G., Fors, S., & Wood, S. (1990). Maternal directive behavior revisited. *American Journal on Mental Retardation, 94*, 398–406.

Mahoney, W. J., Szatmari, P., MacLean, J. E., Bryson, S. E., Bartolucci, G., & Walter, S. D. (1998). Reliability and accuracy of differentiating pervasive developmental disorder subgroups. *Journal of the American Academy of Child and Adolescent Psychiatry, 37*, 278–285.

Maller, S. J., & Braden, J. P. (1993). The construct and criterion-related validity of the WISC-III with deaf adolescents. *Journal of Psychoeducational Assessment, 11*, 105–113.

Mandal, M. K., Asthana, H. S., Dwivedi, C. B., & Bryden, M. P. (1999). Hand preference in the deaf. *Journal of Developmental and Physical Disabilities, 11*, 265–273.

Mandelbaum, D. G. (ed.) (1958). *Selected Writings of Edward Sapir in Language, Culture and Personality*. Berkeley and Los Angeles: University of California Press.

Manjiviona, J., & Prior, M. (1995). Comparison of Asperger syndrome and high-functioning autistic children on a test of motor impairment. *Journal of Autism and Developmental Disorders, 25*, 23–39.

Mans, L., Cicchetti, D., & Stroufe, L. A. (1978). Mirror reactions of Down's syndrome infants and toddlers: Cognitive underpinnings of self recognition. *Child Development, 49*, 1247–1250.

Markoulis, D. (1988). Moral and cognitive reasoning features in congenitally blind children: Comparisons with the sighted. *British Journal of Developmental Psychology, 6*, 59–69.

Marschark, M. (1993). *Psychological Development of Deaf Children*. Oxford: Oxford University Press.

Marschark, M., & Everhart, V. S. (1999). Problem-solving by deaf and hearing students: Twenty Questions. *Deafness and Education International, 1*, 65–82.

Marschark, M., & Mayer, T. S. (1998). Mental representation and memory in deaf adults and children. In M. Marschark & M. D. Clark (eds), *Psychological Perspectives on Deafness, 2*. London: Erlbaum.

Marschark, M., Green, V., Hindmarsh, G., & Walker, S. (2000). Understanding theory of mind in children who are deaf. *Journal of Child Psychology and Psychiatry, 41*, 1067–1073.

Marschark, M., Mouradian, V., & Halas, M. (1994). Discourse rules in the language productions of deaf and hearing children. *Journal of Experimental Child Psychology, 57,* 89–107.

Martinez, M., & Silvestre, N. (1995). Self-concept in profoundly deaf adolescent pupils. *International Journal of Psychology, 30,* 305–316.

Martini, R., Heath, N., & Missiuna, C. (1999). A North American analysis of the relationship between definitions of learning disability and developmental coordination disorder. *International Journal of Special Education, 14,* 46–58.

Martlew, M. (1989). Observations on a child with cerebral palsy and her twin sister made in an integrated nursery and at home. *Child: Care, Health and Development, 15,* 175–194.

Marvin, C., & Kasal, K. R. (1996). A semantic analysis of signed communication in an activity-based classroom for preschool children who are deaf. *Language, Speech, and Hearing Services in Schools, 27,* 57–67.

Masataka, N. (1995). Absence of mirror-reversal tendency in cutaneous pattern perception and acquisition of a signed language in deaf children. *British Journal of Developmental Psychology, 13,* 97–106.

Mawhood, L., Howlin, P., & Rutter, M. (2000). Autism and developmental receptive language disorder – a comparative follow-up in early adult life. I: Cognitive and language outcomes. *Journal of Child Psychology and Psychiatry, 41,* 547–559.

Mayberry, R. I., & Eichen, E. B. (1991). The long-lasting advantage of learning sign language in childhood: Another look at the critical period for language acquisition. *Journal of Memory and Language, 30,* 486–512.

McAlpine, L. M., & Moore, C. L. (1995). The development of social understanding in children with visual impairments. *Journal of Visual Impairment and Blindness, 89,* 349–358.

McComas, J., Dulberg, C., & Latter, J. (1997). Children's memory for locations visited: Importance of movement and choice. *Journal of Motor Behavior, 29,* 223–229.

McConachie, H. (1990). Early language development and severe visual impairment. *Child: Care, Health and Development, 16,* 55–61.

McConachie, H., & Pennington, L. (1997). In-service training for schools on augmentative and alternative communication. *European Journal of Disorders of Communication, 32,* 277–288.

McConachie, H. R., & Moore, V. (1994). Early expressive language of severely visually impaired children. *Developmental Medicine and Child Neurology, 36,* 230–240.

McConkey, R. (1985). Play. In D. Lane & B. Stratford (eds), *Current Approaches to Down's Syndrome.* London: Holt, Rinehart and Winston.

McCune, L. (1995). A normative study of representational play at the transition to language. *Developmental Psychology, 31,* 198–206.

McDermott, S., Coker, A. L., Mani, S., Krishnaswami, S., Nagle, R. J., & Barnett-Queen, L. L. (1996). A population-based analysis of behavior problems in children with cerebral palsy. *Journal of Pediatric Psychology, 21,* 447–463.

McEvoy, R. E., Rogers, S. J., & Pennington, B. F. (1993). Executive function and social communication deficits in young autistic children. *Journal of Child Psychology and Psychiatry, 34,* 563–578.

McGregor, E., Whiten, A., & Blackburn, P. (1998). Teaching theory of mind by highlighting intention and illustrating thoughts: A comparison of their effectiveness with 3–year-olds and autistic individuals. *British Journal of Developmental Psychology, 16,* 281–300.

McHale, S. M., Simeonsson, R. J., Marcus, L. M., & Olley, J. G. (1980). The social and symbolic quality of autistic children's communication. *Journal of Autism and Developmental Disorders, 10,* 299–310.

McHugh, E., & Pyfer, J. (1999). The development of rocking among children who are blind. *Journal of Visual Impairment and Blindness, 93,* 82–95.

McManus, I. C., Sik, G., Cole, D. R., Melton, A. F., Wong, J., & Kloss, J. (1988). The development of handedness in children. *British Journal of Developmental Psychology, 6,* 257–273.

Meadow, K. P. (1980). *Deafness and Child Development.* London: Edward Arnold.

Meadow-Orlans, K. P. (1997). Effects of mother and infant hearing status on interactions at twelve and eighteen months. *Journal of Deaf Studies and Deaf Education, 2,* 27–36.

Meadow-Orlans, K. P., & Spencer, P. E. (1996). Maternal sensitivity and the visual attentiveness of children who are deaf. *Early Development and Parenting, 5,* 213–223.

Meadow-Orlans, K. P., & Steinberg, A. G. (1993). Effects of infant hearing loss and maternal support on mother-infant interactions at 18 months. *Journal of Applied Developmental Psychology, 14,* 407–426.

Meier, R. P., & Willerman, R. (1995). Prelinguistic gesture in deaf and hearing infants. In K. Emmorey & J. S. Reilly (eds), *Language, Gesture, and Space.* Hove, Sussex: Erlbaum.

Meline, T. (1997). Description of phonological patterns for nineteen elementary-age children with hearing losses. *Perceptual and Motor Skills, 85,* 643–653.

Merrills, J. D., Underwood, G., & Wood, D. J. (1994). The word recognition skills of profoundly, prelingually deaf children. *British Journal of Developmental Psychology, 12,* 365–384.

Mervis, C. B., & Robinson, B. F. (1999). Methodological issues in cross-syndrome comparisons: Matching procedures, sensitivity (Se), and specificity (Sp). *Monographs of the Society for Research in Child Development, 64,* 115–130.

Messer, D. J., & Hasan, P. J. (1994). Early communication and cognition in children with Down's syndrome. *Down's syndrome: Research and Practice, 2,* 3–10.

Miles, J. H., Hadden, L. L., Takahashi, T. N., & Hillman, R. E. (2000). Head circumference is an independent clinical finding associated with autism. *American Journal of Medical Genetics, 95,* 339–350.

Miletic, G. (1994). Vibrotactile perception: Perspective taking by children who are visually impaired. *Journal of Visual Impairment and Blindness, 88,* 550–563.

Miletic, G. (1995). Perspective taking: Knowledge of level 1 and level 2 rules by congenitally blind, low vision, and sighted children. *Journal of Visual Impairment and Blindness, 89,* 514–523.

Millar, S. (1994). *Understanding and Representing Space: Theory and Evidence from Studies with Blind and Sighted Children.* Oxford: Clarendon Press.

Millar, S. (1997a). *Reading by Touch*. London: Routledge.

Millar, S. (1997b). Reading without vision. In V. Lewis & G. Collis (eds), *Blindness and Psychological Development in Young Children*. Leicester: BPS Books.

Millar, S. (1997c). Theory, experiment and practical application in research on visual impairment. *European Journal of Psychology of Education*, 12, 415–430.

Millar, S. (1999). Veering re-visited: Noise and posture cues in walking without sight. *Perception*, 28, 765–780.

Millar, S., & Ittyerah, M. (1991). Movement imagery in young and congenitally blind children: Mental practice without visuo-spatial information. *International Journal of Behavioral Development*, 15, 125–146.

Miller, C. K. (1969). Conservation in blind children. *Education of the Visually Handicapped*, 1, 101–105.

Miller, G. (1989). Minor congenital anomalies and ataxic cerebral palsy. *Archives of Disease in Childhood*, 64, 557–562.

Miller, J., Seeley, A., Miolo, G., Rosin, M., & Murray-Branch, J. (1992). "Vocabulary acquisition in young children with Down's syndrome: Speech and Sign." Paper presented at the *9th World Congress of the International Association for the Scientific Study of Mental Deficiency*, Queensland, Australia.

Mills, A. (1988). Visual handicap. In D. Bishop & K. Mogford (eds), *Language Development in Exceptional Circumstances*. London: Churchill Livingston.

Mills, A. E. (1987). The development of phonology in the blind child. In B. Dodd & R. Campbell (eds), *Hearing by Eye: The Psychology of Lip-reading*. London: Erlbaum.

Millward, C., Powell, S., Messer, D., & Jordan, R. (2000). Recall for self and other in autism: Children's memory for events experienced by themselves and their peers. *Journal of Autism and Developmental Disorders*, 30, 15–28.

Minchom, P. E., Ellis, N. C., Appleton, P. L., Lawson, V., Böll, V., & Jones, P. (1995). Impact of functional severity on self concept in young people with spina bifida. *Archives of Disease in Childhood*, 73, 48–52.

Minnett, A., Clark, K., & Wilson, G. (1994). Play behaviour and communication between deaf and hard of hearing children and their hearing peers in an integrated preschool. *American Annals of the Deaf*, 139, 420–429.

Minter, M. E., Hobson, R. P., & Pring, L. (1991). Recognition of vocally expressed emotion by congenitally blind children. *Journal of Visual Impairment and Blindness*, 85, 411–415.

Minter, M., Hobson, R. P., & Bishop, M. (1998). Congenital visual impairment and "theory of mind." *British Journal of Developmental Psychology*, 16, 183–196.

Miranda, S. B. (1976). Visual attention in defective and high-risk infants. *Merrill-Palmer Quarterly*, 22, 201–228.

Miranda, S. B., & Fantz, R. L. (1973). Visual preferences of Down's syndrome and normal infants. *Child Development*, 44, 555–561.

Miranda, S. B., & Fantz, R. L. (1974). Recognition memory in Down's syndrome and normal infants. *Child Development*, 45, 651–660.

Missiuna, C., & Polatajko, H. (1995). Developmental dyspraxia by any other name: Are they all just clumsy children? *The American Journal of Occupa-*

tional Therapy, 49, 619–627.

Mitchell, P., & Isaacs, J. E. (1994). Understanding of verbal representation in children with autism: The case of referential opacity. *British Journal of Developmental Psychology, 12,* 439–454.

Mitchell, P., Saltmarsh, R., & Russell, H. (1997). Overly literal interpretations of speech in autism: Understanding that messages arise from minds. *Journal of Child Psychology and Psychiatry, 38,* 685–692.

Mitchell, R. W. (1993). Mental models of self recognition: Two theories. *New Ideas in Psychology, 11,* 295–325.

Mittwoch, U. (1952). The chromosome complement in a mongolian imbecile. *Annals of Eugenics, 17,* 37.

Miyahara, M., & Möbs, I. (1995). Developmental dyspraxia and developmental coordination disorder. *Neuropsychology Review, 5,* 245–268.

Miyamoto, R. T., Kirk, K. I., Svirsky, M. A., & Sehgal, S. T. (1999). Communication skills in pediatric cochlear implant recipients. *Acta Oto-Laryngologica, 119,* 219–224.

Mohay, H. (2000). Language in sight: Mothers' strategies for making language visually accessible to deaf children. In P. E. Spencer, C. J. Erting, & M. Marschark (eds), *The Deaf Child in the Family and at School.* Mahwah, New Jersey: Erlbaum.

Molfese, D. L., Freeman, R. B. J., & Palermo, D. S. (1975). The ontogeny of brain lateralization for speech and nonspeech sounds. *Brain and Language, 2,* 356–368.

Mon-Williams, M. A., Wann, J. P., & Pascal, E. (1994). Opthalmic factors in developmental coordination disorder. *Adapted Physical Activity Quarterly, 11,* 170–178.

Mon-Williams, M. A., Wann, J. P., & Pascal, E. (1999). Visual-proprioceptive mapping in children with developmental coordination disorder. *Developmental Medicine and Child Neurology, 41,* 247–254.

Mon-Williams, M., Jobling, A., & Wann, J. P. (2000). Opthalmic factors in Down syndrome: A motoric perspective. In D. Weeks, R. Chua & D. Elliott (eds), *Perceptual-Motor Behavior in Down Syndrome.* Champaign, IL: Human Kinetics.

Montague, J. C., Brown, W. S., & Hollien, H. (1974). Vocal fundamental frequency characteristics of institutionalized Down's syndrome children. *American Journal of Mental Deficiency, 78,* 414–418.

Moore, D. G., Hobson, R. P., & Lee, A. (1997). Components of person perception: An investigation with autistic, non-autistic retarded and typically developing children and adolescents. *British Journal of Developmental Psychology, 15,* 401–424.

Moore, M. K., Clark, D., Mael, M., Rajotte, P., & Stoel-Gammon, C. (1977). "The relationship between language and object permanence development." Paper presented at the meeting of the *Society for Research in Child Development,* March, New Orleans, Louisiana.

Moore, V., & McConachie, H. (1994). Communication between blind and severely visually impaired children and their parents. *British Journal of Developmental Psychology, 12,* 491–502.

Morford, J. P., & Goldin-Meadow, S. (1997). From here and now to there and then: The development of displaced reference in homesign and English. *Child Development*, *68*, 420–435.

Morrongiello, B. A., Humphrey, G. K., Timney, B., Choi, J., & Rocca, P. T. (1994). Tactual object exploration and recognition in blind and sighted children. *Perception*, *23*, 833–848.

Morrongiello, B. A., Timney, B., Humphrey, G. K., Anderson, S., & Skory, C. (1995). Spatial knowledge in blind and sighted children. *Journal of Experimental Child Psychology*, *59*, 211–233.

Morrow, J. D., & Wachs, T. D. (1992). Infants with myelomeningocele: Visual recognition memory and sensorimotor abilities. *Developmental Medicine and Child Neurology*, *34*, 488–498.

Morss, J. R. (1983). Cognitive development in the Down's syndrome infant: Slow or different? *British Journal of Educational Psychology*, *53*, 40–47.

Morss, J. R. (1985). Early cognitive development: Difference or delay. In D. Lane & B. Stratford (eds), *Current Approaches to Down's Syndrome*. London: Holt, Rinehart and Winston.

Moss, S., & Hogg, J. (1987). The integration of manipulative movements in children with Down's syndrome and their non-handicapped peers. *Human Movement Science*, *6*, 67–99.

Mottron, L., & Belleville, S. (1993). A study of perceptual analysis in a high-level autistic subject with exceptional graphic abilities. *Brain and Cognition*, *23*, 279–309.

Mottron, L., Belleville, S., & Ménard, E. (1999b). Local bias in autistic subjects as evidenced by graphic tasks: Perceptual hierarchization or working memory deficit? *Journal of Child Psychology and Psychiatry*, *40*, 743–755.

Mottron, L., Burack, J. A., Stauder, J. E. A., & Robaey, P. (1999a). Perceptual processing among high-functioning persons with autism. *Journal of Child Psychology and Psychiatry*, *40*, 203–211.

Mottron, L., Morasse, K., & Belleville, S. (2001). A study of memory functioning in individuals with autism. *Journal of Child Psychology and Psychiatry*, *42*, 253–260.

Mottron, L., Peretz, I., & Ménard, E. (2000). Local and global processing of music in high-functioning persons with autism: Beyond central coherence? *Journal of Child Psychology and Psychiatry*, *41*, 1057–1065.

Mulderij, K. J. (1996). Research into the lifeworld of physically disabled children. *Child: Care, Health and Development*, *22*, 311–322.

Mulderij, K. J. (1997). Peer relations and friendship in physically disabled children. *Child: Care, Health and Development*, *23*, 379–389.

Mulderij, K. J. (2000). Dualistic notions about children with motor disabilities: Hands to lean on or to reach out? *Qualitative Health Research*, *10*, 39–50.

Mulford, R. (1988). First words of the blind child. In M. D. Smith & J. L. Locke (eds), *The Emergent Lexicon: The Child's Development of a Linguistic Vocabulary*. London: Academic Press.

Mundy, P., Kasari, C., Sigman, M., & Ruskin, E. (1995). Nonverbal communication and early language acquisition in children with Down syndrome and in normally developing children. *Journal of Speech and Hearing Research*, *38*,

157–167.

Mundy, P., Sigman, M., & Kasari, C. (1990). A longitudinal study of joint attention and language development in autistic children. *Journal of Autism and Developmental Disorders*, 20, 115–128.

Mundy, P., Sigman, M., & Kasari, C. (1993). The theory of mind and joint-attention deficits in autism. In S. Baron-Cohen, H. Tager-Flusberg, & D. J. Cohen (eds), *Understanding Other Minds: Perspectives from Autism*. Oxford: Oxford University Press.

Mundy, P., Sigman, M., & Kasari, C. (1994). Joint attention, developmental level, and symptom presentation in autism. *Development and Psychopathology*, 6, 389–401.

Murphy, M. A., & Vogel, J. B. (1985). Looking out from the isolator: David's perception of the world. *Developmental and Behavioral Pediatrics*, 6, 118–121.

Murphy, M., Bolton, P. F., Pickles, A., Fombonne, E., Piven, J., & Rutter, M. (2000). Personality traits of the relatives of autistic probands. *Psychological Medicine*, 30, 1411–1424.

Nadel, L. (1999). Learning and memory in Down syndrome. In J. A. Rondal, J. Perera, & L. Nadel (eds), *Down Syndrome: A Review of Current Knowledge*. London: Whurr Publishers Ltd.

Nagera, H., & Colonna, A. B. (1965). Aspects of the contribution of sight to ego and drive development. *Psychoanalytic Study of the Child*, 20, 267–287.

Nassau, J. H., & Drotar, D. (1997). Social competence among children with central nervous system-related chronic health conditions: A review. *Journal of Pediatric Psychology*, 22, 771–793.

Naveen, K. V., Srinivas, R. S., Nirmala, K. S., Nagendra, H. R., & Telles, S. (1997). Middle latency auditory evoked potentials in congenitally blind and normal sighted subjects. *International Journal of Neuroscience*, 90, 105–111.

Naveen, K. V., Srinivas, R., Nirmala, K. S., Nagarathna, R., Nagendra, H. R., & Telles, S. (1998). Differences between congenitally blind and normally sighted subjects in the P1 component of middle latency auditory evoked potentials. *Perceptual and Motor Skills*, 86, 1192–1194.

Navon, D. (1977). Forest before trees: The precedence of global features in visual perception. *Cognitive Psychology*, 9, 353–383.

Neale, M. D. (1989). *Neale Analysis of Reading Ability*. Windsor: NFER/Nelson.

Nelson, K. B., & Ellenberg, J. H. (1986). Antecedents of cerebral palsy: Multivariate analysis of risk. *New England Journal of Medicine*, 315, 81–86.

Newnham, C., & McKenzie, B. E. (1993). Cross-modal transfer of sequential visual and haptic shape information by clumsy children. *Perception*, 22, 1061–1073.

Norgate, S. H. (1998). Research methods for studying the language of blind children. In N. Hornberger & D. Corson (eds), *The Encyclopedia of Language and Education*, 8. The Netherlands: Kluwer Academic Publishers.

Norgate, S., Collis, G. M., & Lewis, V. (1998). The developmental role of rhymes and routines for congenitally blind children. *Cahiers de Psychologie Cognitive/Current Psychology of Cognition*, 17, 451–477.

Norris, M., Spaulding, P. J., & Brodie, F. H. (1957). *Blindness in Children*. Chicago: University of Chicago Press.

Notoya, M., Suzuki, S., & Furukawa, M. (1994). Effects of early manual instruction on the oral-language development of two deaf children. *American Annals of the Deaf, 139*, 348–351.

O'Connor, N., & Hermelin, B. (1992). Do young calendrical calculators improve with age? *Journal of Child Psychology and Psychiatry, 33*, 907–912.

Ochaita, E., & Huertas, J. A. (1993). Spatial representation by persons who are blind: A study of the effects of learning and development. *Journal of Visual Impairment and Blindness, 87*, 37–41.

Ohnishi, T., Matsuda, H., Hashimoto, T., Kunihiro, T., Nishikawa, M., & Uema, T. (2000). Abnormal regional cerebral blood flow in childhood autism. *Brain, 123*, 1838–1844.

Ohr, P. S., & Fagen, J. W. (1991). Conditioning and long-term memory in three-month-old infants with Down syndrome. *American Journal on Mental Retardation, 96*, 151–162.

Oller, D. K., & Eilers, R. E. (1988). The role of audition in infant babbling. *Child Development, 59*, 441–466.

Oller, D. K., Eilers, R. E., Neal, A. R., & Schwartz, H. K. (1999). Precursors to speech in infancy: The prediction of speech and language disorders. *Journal of Communication Disorders, 32*, 223–245.

Øster, J., Mikkelsen, M., & Nielsen, A. (1975). Mortality and lifetable in Down's syndrome. *Acta Paediatrica Scandinavica, 64*, 322–326.

Osterling, J., & Dawson, G. (1994). Early recognition of children with autism: A study of first birthday home video tapes. *Journal of Autism and Developmental Disorders, 24*, 247–257.

Ozonoff, S., & Jensen, J. (1999). Brief report: Specific executive function profiles in three neurodevelopmental disorders. *Journal of Autism and Developmental Disorders, 29*, 171–177.

Ozonoff, S., & McEvoy, R. E. (1994). A longitudinal study of executive function and theory of mind development in autism. *Development and Psychopathology, 6*, 415–431.

Ozonoff, S., Pennington, B. F., & Rogers, S. J. (1990). Are there emotion perception deficits in young autistic children? *Journal of Child Psychology and Psychiatry, 31*, 343–361.

Ozonoff, S., Pennington, B. F., & Rogers, S. J. (1991a). Executive function deficits in high-functioning autistic individuals: Relationship to theory of mind. *Journal of Child Psychology and Psychiatry, 32*, 1081–1105.

Ozonoff, S., Rogers, S. J., & Pennington, B. F. (1991b). Asperger's syndrome: Evidence of an empirical distinction from high-functioning autism. *Journal of Child Psychology and Psychiatry, 32*, 1107–1122.

Ozonoff, S., Rogers, S. J., Farnham, J. M., & Pennington, B. F. (1993). Can standard measures identify subclinical markers of autism? *Journal of Autism and Developmental Disorders, 23*, 429–441.

Ozonoff, S., Strayer, D. L., McMahon, W. M., & Filloux, F. (1994). Executive function abilities in autism and Tourette Syndrome: An information processing approach. *Journal of Child Psychology and Psychiatry, 35*, 1015–1032.

Palferman, S., Matthews, N., Turner, M. et al. (2001). A genomewide screen for autism: Strong evidence for linkage to chromosomes 2q, 7q, and 16p. *American Journal of Human Genetics*, 69, 570–581.

Parush, S., Yochman, A., Cohen, D., & Gershon, E. (1998). Relation of visual perception and visual-motor integration for clumsy children. *Perceptual and Motor Skills*, 86, 291–295.

Pathak, K., & Pring, L. (1989). Tactual picture recognition in congenitally blind and sighted children. *Applied Cognitive Psychology*, 3, 337–350.

Pennington, B. F., & Ozonoff, S. (1996). Executive functions and developmental psychopathology. *Journal of Child Psychology and Psychiatry*, 37, 51–87.

Pennington, L., & McConachie, H. (1999). Mother-child interaction revisited: Communication with non-speaking physically disabled children. *International Journal of Language and Communication Disorders*, 34, 391–416.

Pennington, L., & McConachie, H. (2001a). Interaction between children with cerebral palsy and their mothers: The effects of speech intelligibility. *International Journal of Language and Communication Disorders*, 36, 371–393.

Pennington, L., & McConachie, H. (2001b). Predicting patterns of interaction between children with cerebral palsy and their mothers. *Developmental Medicine and Child Neurology*, 43, 83–90.

Pereira, H. S., Landgren, M., Gillberg, C., & Forssberg, H. (2001). Parametric control of fingertip forces during precision grip lifts in children with DCD (developmental coordination disorder) and DAMP (deficits in attention motor control and perception). *Neuropsychologia*, 39, 478–488.

Pérez-Pereira, M. (1994). Imitations, repetitions, routines, and the child's analysis of language: Insights from the blind. *Journal of Child Language*, 21, 317–337.

Pérez-Pereira, M. (1999). Deixis, personal reference, and the use of pronouns by blind children. *Journal of Child Language*, 26, 655–680.

Pérez-Pereira, M., & Castro, J. (1992). Pragmatic functions of blind and sighted children's language: A twin case study. *First Language*, 12, 17–37.

Pérez-Pereira, M., & Castro, J. (1997). Language acquisition and the compensation of visual deficit: New comparative data on a controversial topic. *British Journal of Developmental Psychology*, 15, 439–459.

Pérez-Pereira, M., & Conti-Ramsden, G. (1999). *Language Development and Social Interaction in Blind Children*. Hove, Sussex: Psychology Press Ltd.

Pérez-Pereira, M., & Conti-Ramsden, G. (2001). The use of directives in verbal interactions between blind children and their mothers. *Journal of Visual Impairment and Blindness*, 95, 133–149.

Peters, A. M. (1994). The interdependence of social, cognitive and linguistic development: Evidence from a visually impaired child. In H. Tager-Flusberg (ed.), *Constraints on Language Acquisition: Studies of Atypical Children*. Hove, Sussex: Erlbaum.

Peterson, C. C., & Siegal, M. (1995). Deafness, conversation and theory of mind. *Journal of Child Psychology and Psychiatry*, 36, 459–474.

Peterson, C. C., & Siegal, M. (1998). Changing focus on the representational mind: Deaf, autistic and normal children's concepts of false photos, false drawings and false beliefs. *British Journal of Developmental Psychology*, 16, 301–320.

Peterson, C. C., & Siegal, M. (1999). Representing inner worlds: Theory of mind in autistic, deaf, and normal hearing children. *Psychological Science, 10,* 126–129.

Peterson, C. C., Peterson, J. L., & Webb, J. (2000). Factors influencing the development of a theory of mind in blind children. *British Journal of Developmental Psychology, 18,* 431–447.

Petitto, L. A. (1987). On the autonomy of language and gesture: Evidence from the acquisition of personal pronouns in American Sign Language. *Cognition, 27,* 1–52.

Petitto, L. A., & Marentette, P. F. (1991). Babbling in the manual mode: Evidence for the ontogeny of language. *Science, 251,* 1493–1496.

Philippe, A., Martinez, M., Guilloud-Bataille, M., Gillberg, C., Råstam, M., & Sponheim, E. (1999). Genome-wide scan for autism susceptibility genes. *Human Molecular Genetics, 8,* 805–812.

Phillips, W., Gómez, J. C., Baron-Cohen, S., Laá, V., & Rivière, A. (1995). Treating people as objects, agents, or "subjects": How young children with and without autism make requests. *Journal of Child Psychology and Psychiatry, 36,* 1383–1398.

Piaget, J. (1953). *The Origin of Intelligence in the Child.* London: Routledge and Kegan Paul. First published 1936.

Piaget, J. (1962). *Play, Dreams and Imitation in Childhood.* New York: Norton.

Piaget, J. (1967). *Biologie et Connaissance.* Paris: Gallimard.

Piaget, J. (1983). Piaget's theory. In P. H. Mussen (ed.), *Handbook of Child Psychology.* 4th edition. New York: Wiley.

Piaget, J., & Inhelder, B. (1969). *The Psychology of the Child.* London: Routledge and Kegan Paul.

Piattelli-Palmarini, M. (1994). Ever since language and learning: Afterthoughts on the Piaget-Chomsky debate. *Cognition, 50,* 315–346.

Pickersgill, M. (1997). Towards a model of bilingual education for deaf children. *Deafness and Education, 21,* 10–19.

Piek, J. P., & Edwards, K. (1997). The identification of children with developmental coordination disorder by class and physical education teachers. *British Journal of Educational Psychology, 67,* 55–67.

Piek, J. P., & Skinner, R. A. (1999). Timing and force control during a sequential tapping task in children with and without motor coordination problems. *Journal of the International Neuropsychological Society, 5,* 320–329.

Piek, J. P., Dworcan, M., Barrett, N. C., & Coleman, R. (2000). Determinants of self worth in children with and without developmental coordination disorder. *International Journal of Disability, Development and Education, 47,* 259–272.

Piek, J. P., Pitcher, T. M., & Hay, D. A. (1999). Motor coordination and kinaesthesis in boys with attention deficit-hyperactivity disorder. *Developmental Medicine and Child Neurology, 41,* 159–165.

Pierce, K., & Courchesne, E. (2001). Evidence for a cerebellar role in reduced exploration and stereotyped behavior in autism. *Biological Psychiatry, 49,* 655–664.

Pilowsky, T., Yirmiya, N., Shulman, C., & Dover, R. (1998). The Autism Diagnostic Interview-Revised and the Childhood Autism Rating Scale: Differences between diagnostic systems and comparison between genders. *Journal of Au-*

tism and Developmental Disorders, 28, 143–151.

Pitcairn, T. K., & Wishart, J. G. (1994). Reactions of young children with Down's syndrome to an impossible task. *British Journal of Developmental Psychology, 12,* 485–489.

Pitcairn, T. K., & Wishart, J. G. (2000). Face processing in children with Down syndrome. In D. J. Weeks, R. Chua, & D. Elliott (eds), *Perceptual-Motor Behavior in Down Syndrome.* Champaign, IL: Human Kinetics.

Piven, J., & Palmer, P. (1997). Cognitive deficits in parents from multiple-incidence autism families. *Journal of Child Psychology and Psychiatry, 38,* 1011–1022.

Piven, J., Palmer, P., Landa, R., Santangelo, S., Jacobi, D., & Childress, D. (1997). Personality and language characteristics in parents from multiple-incidence autism families. *American Journal of Medical Genetics, 74,* 398–411.

Plaisted, K., O'Riordan, M., & Baron-Cohen, S. (1998). Enhanced visual search for a conjunctive target in autism: A research note. *Journal of Child Psychology and Psychiatry, 39,* 777–783.

Plaisted, K., Swettenham, J., & Rees, L. (1999). Children with autism show local precedence in a divided attention task and global precedence in a selective attention task. *Journal of Child Psychology and Psychiatry, 40,* 733–742.

Polatajko, H. J., Fox, A. M., & Missiuna, C. (1995). An international consensus on children with developmental coordination disorder. *Canadian Journal of Occupational Therapy, 62,* 3–6.

Powell, J. E., Edwards, A., Edwards, M., Pandit, B. S., Sungum-Paliwal, S. R., & Whitehouse, W. (2000). Changes in the incidence of childhood autism and other autistic spectrum disorders in preschool children from two areas of the West Midlands, UK. *Developmental Medicine and Child Neurology, 42,* 624–628.

Powell, R. P., & Bishop, D. V. M. (1992). Clumsiness and perceptual problems in children with specific language impairment. *Developmental Medicine and Child Neurology, 34,* 755–765.

Power, D. J., & Hyde, M. B. (1997). Multisensory and unisensory approaches to communicating with deaf children. *European Journal of Psychology of Education, 12,* 449–464.

Power, D. J., Wood, D. J., Wood, H. A., & MacDougall, J. (1990). Maternal control over conversations with hearing and deaf infants and young children. *First Language, 10,* 19–35.

Powers, S. (1996). Deaf pupils' achievements in ordinary schools. *Journal of the British Association of Teachers of the Deaf, 20,* 111–123.

Powers, S. (1998). An analysis of deaf pupils' examination results in ordinary schools in 1996. *Deafness and Education, 22,* 30–36.

Preisler, G. M. (1981). Modification of communication by a small deaf child. *American Annals of the Deaf, 126,* 411–416.

Preisler, G. M. (1983). *Deaf Children in Communication: A Study of Communication Strategies used by Deaf Children in Social Interactions.* Laholm: Trydells Tryckeri.

Preisler, G. M. (1991). Early patterns of interaction between blind infants and their sighted mothers. *Child: Care, Health and Development, 17,* 65–90.

Preisler, G. M. (1993). A descriptive study of blind children in nurseries with sighted children. *Child: Care, Health and Development, 19,* 295–315.

Preisler, G. M. (1995). The development of communication in blind and in deaf infants: Similarities and differences. *Child: Care, Health and Development, 21,* 79–110.

Preisler, G. M. (1997). Social and emotional development of blind children: A longitudinal study. In V. Lewis & G. Collis (eds), *Blindness and Psychological Development in Young Children.* Leicester: BPS Books.

Preisler, G. M., & Ahlström, M. (1997). Sign language for hard of hearing children: A hindrance or a benefit for their development? *European Journal of Psychology of Education, 12,* 465–477.

Preisler, G. M., Ahlström, M., & Tvingstedt, A.-L. (1997). The development of communication and language in deaf preschool children with cochlear implants. *International Journal of Pediatric Otorhinolaryngology, 41,* 263–272.

Pring, L. (1988). The "reverse-generation" effect: A comparison of memory performance between blind and sighted children. *British Journal of Psychology, 79,* 387–400.

Pring, L. (1994). Touch and go: Learning to read braille. *Reading Research Quarterly, 29,* 67–74.

Pring, L., & Hermelin, B., with Buhler, M., & Walker, I. (1997). Native savant talent and acquired skill. *Autism, 1,* 199–214.

Pring, L., & Mulkern, K. (1992). Memory in blind and sighted children. *European Review of Applied Psychology, 42,* 243–248.

Pring, L., Dewart, H., & Brockbank, M. (1998). Social cognition in children with visual impairments. *Journal of Visual Impairment and Blindness, 92,* 754–768.

Pring, L., Hermelin, B., & Heavey, H. (1995). Savants, segments, art and autism. *Journal of Child Psychology and Psychiatry, 36,* 1065–1076.

Prior, M., & Hoffmann, W. (1990). Neuropsychological testing of autistic children through an exploration with frontal lobe tests. *Journal of Autism and Developmental Disorders, 20,* 581–590.

Prior, M., Eisenmajer, R., Leekam, S., Wing, L., Gould, J., & Ong, B. (1998). Are there subgroups within the autistic spectrum? A cluster analysis of a group of children with autistic spectrum disorders. *Journal of Child Psychology and Psychiatry, 39,* 893–902.

Pueschel, S. M., Bernier, J. C., & Pezzullo, J. C. (1991). Behavioural observations in children with Down's syndrome. *Journal of Mental Deficiency Research, 35,* 502–511.

Quittner, A. L., Smith, L. B., Osberger, M. J., Mitchell, T. V., & Katz, D. B. (1994). The impact of audition on the development of visual attention. *Psychological Science, 5,* 347–353.

Rast, M., & Meltzoff, A. N. (1995). Memory and representation in young children with Down syndrome: Exploring deferred imitation and object permanence. *Development and Psychopathology, 7,* 393–407.

Recchia, S. L. (1997). Social communication and response to ambiguous stimuli in toddlers with visual impairments. *Journal of Applied Developmental Psychology, 18,* 297–316.

Recchia, S. L. (1998). Response to ambiguous stimuli by three toddlers who are blind as a measure of mother-child communication. *Journal of Visual Impair-*

ment and Blindness, 92, 581–592.

Reilly, J. S., & Bellugi, U. (1996). Competition on the face: Affect and language in ASL motherese. *Journal of Child Language, 23,* 219–239.

Reimer, A. M., Smits-Engelsman, B. C. M., & Siemonsma-Boom, M. (1999). Development of an instrument to measure manual dexterity in children with visual impairments aged 6–12. *Journal of Visual Impairment and Blindness, 93,* 643–658.

Renner, P., Klinger, L. G., & Klinger, M. R. (2000). Implicit and explicit memory in autism: Is autism an amnesic disorder? *Journal of Autism and Developmental Disorders, 30,* 3–14.

Reynell, J. (1978). Developmental patterns of visually handicapped children. *Child: Care, Health and Development, 4,* 291–303.

Reynell, J. (1979). *Manual for the Reynell-Zinkin Scales.* Windsor: NFER/Nelson.

Ricks, D. M. (1975). Vocal communication in pre-verbal normal and autistic children. In N. O'Connor (ed.), *Language, Cognitive Deficits, and Retardation.* London: Butterworths.

Rieffe, C., & Meerum Terwogt, M. (2000). Deaf children's understanding of emotions: Desires take precedence. *Journal of Child Psychology and Psychiatry, 41,* 601–608.

Rinehart, N. J., Bradshaw, J. L., Moss, S. A., Brereton, A. V., & Tonge, B. J. (2000). A typical interference of local detail on global processing in high-functioning autism and Asperger's syndrome. *Journal of Child Psychology and Psychiatry, 41,* 769–778.

Ring, H. A., Baron-Cohen, S., Wheelwright, S., Williams, S. C., Brammer, M., & Andrew, C. (1999). Cerebral correlates of preserved cognitive skills in autism: A functional MRI study of Embedded Figures Task performance. *Brain, 122,* 1305–1315.

Ritvo, E. R., Freeman, B. J., Mason-Brothers, A., Mo, A., & Ritvo, A. M. (1985). Concordance for the syndrome of autism in 40 pairs of affected twins. *American Journal of Psychiatry, 142,* 74–77.

Roach, M. A., Barratt, M. S., Miller, J. F., & Leavitt, L. A. (1998). The structure of mother-child play: Young children with Down syndrome and typically developing children. *Developmental Psychology, 34,* 77–87.

Roberts, C., & Hindley, P. (1999). Practitioner review: The assessment and treatment of deaf children with psychiatric disorders. *Journal of Child Psychology and Psychiatry, 40,* 151–167.

Rodrigue, J. R., Morgan, S. B., & Geffken, G. R. (1991). A comparative evaluation of adaptive behavior in children and adolescents with autism, Down syndrome, and normal development. *Journal of Autism and Developmental Disorders, 21,* 187–196.

Rodriguez, M. S., & Lana, E. T. (1996). Dyadic interactions between deaf children and their communication partners. *American Annals of the Deaf, 141,* 245–251.

Roe, J. (1997). "Peer relationships, play and language of visually impaired children." Unpublished Ph.D. thesis, University of Bristol.

Rogers, S. C., & Weatherall, J. A. C. (1976). Anencephalus, spina bifida and congenital hydrocephalus. England and Wales, 1964–1972. *Studies on Medical and Population Subjects, 32.* London: HMSO.

Rogers, S. J. (2000). Interventions that facilitate socialization in children with autism. *Journal of Autism and Developmental Disorders, 30,* 399–409.

Rogers, S. J., & Newhart-Larson, S. (1989). Characteristics of infantile autism in five children with Leber's congenital amaurosis. *Developmental Medicine and Child Neurology, 31,* 598–608.

Rogers, S. J., & Pennington, B. F. (1991). A theoretical approach to the deficits in infantile autism. *Development and Psychopathology, 3,* 137–162.

Rogers, S. J., & Puchalski, C. B. (1984). Development of symbolic play in visually impaired young children. *Topics in Early Childhood Special Education, 3,* 57–63.

Rogers, S. J., & Puchalski, C. B. (1986). Social smiles of visually impaired infants. *Journal of Visual Impairment and Blindness, 80,* 863–865.

Rogers, S. J., & Puchalski, C. B. (1988). Development of object permanence in visually impaired infants. *Journal of Visual Impairment and Blindness, 82,* 137–142.

Rogers-Warren, A. (1980). *Playing and Learning Together.* Lawrence: University of Kansas, Early Childhood Institute. (ERIC Document Reproduction Service No ED 231 104).

Rollin, H. R. (1946). Personality in mongolism with special reference to the incidence of catatonic psychosis. *American Journal of Mental Deficiency, 51,* 219–237.

Ropar, D., & Mitchell, P. (1999). Are individuals with autism and Asperger's syndrome susceptible to visual illusions? *Journal of Child Psychology and Psychiatry, 40,* 1283–1293.

Ropar, D., & Mitchell, P. (2001). Susceptibility to illusions and performance on visuospatial tasks in individuals with autism. *Journal of Child Psychology and Psychiatry, 42,* 539–549.

Rosenbluth, R., Grossman, E. S., & Kaitz, M. (2000). Performance of early-blind and sighted children on olfactory tasks. *Perception, 29,* 101–110.

Rosenthal, J., Massie, H., & Wulff, K. (1980). A comparison of cognitive development in normal and psychotic children in the first two years of life from home movies. *Journal of Autism and Developmental Disorders, 10,* 433–444.

Ross, S., & Tobin, M. J. (1997). Object permanence, reaching, and locomotion in infants who are blind. *Journal of Visual Impairment and Blindness, 91,* 25–32.

Ruff, H. A., Saltarelli, L. M., Capozoli, M., & Dubiner, K. (1992). The differentiation of activity in infants' exploration of objects. *Developmental Psychology, 28,* 851–861.

Rumsey, J. M. (1985). Conceptual problem-solving in highly verbal, nonretarded autistic men. *Journal of Autism and Developmental Disorders, 15,* 23–36.

Rumsey, J. M., & Ernst, M. (2000). Functional neuroimaging of autistic disorders. *Mental Retardation and Developmental Disabilities Research Reviews, 6,* 171–179.

Rumsey, J. M., & Hamburger, S. D. (1988). Neuropsychological findings in high-functioning autistic men with infantile autism, residual state. *Journal of Clinical and Experimental Neuropsychology, 10,* 201–221.

Rumsey, J. M., & Hamburger, S. D. (1990). Neuropsychological divergence of high-level autism and severe dyslexia. *Journal of Autism and Developmental Disorders, 20*, 155–168.

Ruskin, E. M., Kasari, C., Mundy, P., & Sigman, M. (1994b). Attention to people and toys during social and object mastery in children with Down syndrome. *American Journal on Mental Retardation, 99*, 103–111.

Ruskin, E. M., Mundy, P., Kasari, C., & Sigman, M. (1994a) Object mastery motivation of children with Down syndrome. *American Journal on Mental Retardation, 98*, 499–509.

Russell, J. (ed.) (1997). *Autism as an Executive Disorder.* Oxford: Oxford University Press.

Russell, J., & Hill, E. L. (2001). Action-monitoring and intention reporting in children with autism. *Journal of Child Psychology and Psychiatry, 42*, 317–328.

Russell, J., Jarrold, C., & Henry, L. (1996). Working memory in children with autism and with moderate learning difficulties. *Journal of Child Psychology and Psychiatry, 37*, 673–686.

Russell, J., Mauthner, N., Sharpe, S., & Tidswell, T. (1991). The "windows task" as a measure of strategic deception in preschoolers and autistic subjects. *British Journal of Developmental Psychology, 9*, 331–350.

Russell, J., Saltmarsh, R., & Hill, E. (1999). What do executive factors contribute to the failure on false belief tasks by children with autism? *Journal of Child Psychology and Psychiatry, 40*, 859–868.

Russell, P. A., Hosie, J. A., Gray, C. D., Scott, C., Hunter, N., & Banks, J. S. (1998). The development of theory of mind in deaf children. *Journal of Child Psychology and Psychiatry, 39*, 903–910.

Rutter, M. (1978). Diagnosis and definition. In M. Rutter & E. Schopler (eds), *Autism: A Reappraisal of Concepts and Treatments.* New York: Plenum.

Rutter, M. (1983). Cognitive deficits in the pathogenesis of autism. *Journal of Child Psychology and Psychiatry, 24*, 513–531.

Rutter, M. (1999). The Emanuel Miller Memorial Lecture (1998). Autism: Two-way interplay between research and clinical work. *Journal of Child Psychology and Psychiatry, 40*, 169–188.

Rutter, M., Bartak, L., & Newman, S. (1971). Autism – a central disorder of cognition and language? In M. Rutter (ed.), *Infantile Autism: Concepts, Characteristics and Treatment.* Edinburgh: Churchill Livingstone.

Rutter, M., Graham, P., Chadwick, O. F. D., & Yule, W. (1976). Adolescent turmoil: Fact or fiction? *Journal of Child Psychology and Psychiatry, 17*, 35–56.

Rutter, M., Greenfeld, D., & Lockyer, L. (1967). A five to fifteen year follow-up study of infantile psychosis: II Social and behavioural outcome. *British Journal of Psychiatry, 113*, 1183–1199.

Rydell, P. J., & Mirenda, P. (1991). The effects of two levels of linguistic constraint on echolalia and generative language production in children with autism. *Journal of Autism and Developmental Disorders, 21*, 131–157.

Rydell, P. J., & Mirenda, P. (1994). Effects of high and low constraint utterances on the production of immediate and delayed echolalia in young children with autism. *Journal of Autism and Developmental Disorders*, 24, 719–735.

Rynders, J. E. (1999). Promoting the educational competence of students with Down syndrome. In J. A. Rondal, J. Perera, & L. Nadel (eds), *Down Syndrome: A Review of Current Knowledge*. London: Whurr Publishers Ltd.

Rynders, J. E., Spiker, D., & Horrobin, J. M. (1978). Underestimating the educability of Down's syndrome children: Examination of methodological problems in recent literature. *American Journal of Mental Deficiency*, 82, 440–448.

Sadetzki, S., Chetrit, A., Akstein, E., Luxenburg, O., Keinan, L., & Litvak, I. (1999). Risk factors for infant mortality in Down's syndrome: A nationwide study. *Paediatric and Perinatal Epidemiology*, 13, 442–451.

Sampaio, E. (1989). Is there a critical age for using the sonicguide with blind infants? *Journal of Visual Impairment and Blindness*, 83, 105–108.

Sampaio, E., Bril, B., & Brenière, Y. (1989). La vision est-elle nécessaire pour apprendre à marcher? Etude préliminaire et approche méthodologique. *Psychologie Française*, 34, 71–78.

Sapir, E. (1912). Language and environment. *American Anthropologist*, n.s., 226–242.

Savelsbergh, G. J. P., Netelenbos, J. B., & Davids, K. (1989). Motor abilities of deaf children. *Physical Education Review*, 12, 31–35.

Savelsbergh, G. J. P., Netelenbos, J. B., & Whiting, H. T. A. (1991). Auditory perception and the control of spatially coordinated action of deaf and hearing children. *Journal of Child Psychology and Psychiatry*, 32, 489–500.

Schellingerhout, R., Smitsman, A. W., & van Galen, G. P. (1997). Exploration of surface-texture in congenitally blind infants. *Child: Care, Health and Development*, 23, 247–264.

Schellingerhout, R., Smitsman, A. W., & van Galen, G. P. (1998). Haptic object exploration in congenitally blind infants. *Journal of Visual Impairment and Blindness*, 92, 674–678.

Scheuffgen, K., Happé, F. G. E., Anderson, M., & Frith, U. (2000). High "intelligence", low "IQ"? Speed of processing and measured IQ in children with autism. *Development and Psychopathology*, 12, 83–90.

Schlesinger, H., & Meadow, K. (1972). *Sound and Sign: Childhood Deafness and Mental Health*. Berkeley: University of California Press.

Schneekloth, L. H. (1989). Play environments for visually impaired children. *Journal of Visual Impairment and Blindness*, 83, 196–201.

Schoemaker, M. M., & Kalverboer, A. F. (1994). Social and affective problems of children who are clumsy: How early do they begin? *Adapted Physical Activity Quarterly*, 11, 130–140.

Schopler, E., Reichler, R. J., & Rocher-Renner, B. (1988). *The Childhood Autism Rating Scale (CARS)*. Los Angeles: Western Psychological Services.

Schultz, R. T., Gauthier, I., Klin, A., Fulbright, R., Anderson, A. W., & Volkmar, F. (2000). Abnormal ventral temporal cortical activity among individuals with autism and Asperger syndrome during face discrimination. *Archives of General Psychiatry*, 37, 331–340.

Scott, F. J., & Baron-Cohen, S. (1996a). Imagining real and unreal things: Evidence of a dissociation in autism. *Journal of Cognitive Neuroscience*, 8, 371–382.

Scott, F. J., & Baron-Cohen, S. (1996b). Logical, analogical and psychological reasoning in autism: A test of the Cosmides theory. *Development and Psychopathology*, *8*, 235–245.

Scott, F. J., Baron-Cohen, S., & Leslie, A. (1999). "If pigs could fly": A test of counterfactual reasoning and pretence in children with autism. *British Journal of Developmental Psychology*, *17*, 349–362.

Scott, M. A., Fletcher, J. M., Brookshire, B. L., Davidson, K. C., Landry, S. H., & Bohan, T. C. (1998). Memory functions in children with early hydrocephalus. *Neuropsychology*, *12*, 578–589.

Scully, C. (1973). Down's syndrome. *British Journal of Hospital Medicine*, *10*, 89–98.

Seefeldt, T. A., Holmbeck, G. N., Belvedere, M. C., Gorey-Ferguson, L., Hommeyer, J. S., & Hudson, T. (1997). Socioeconomic status and democratic parenting in families of preadolescents with spina bifida. *Psi Chi Journal of Undergraduate Research*, *2*, 5–12.

Séguin, E. (1846). *Le traitement moral, l'hygiène et l'éducation des idiots*. Paris: J. B. Baillière.

Selfe, L. (1977). *Nadia: A Case of Extraordinary Drawing Ability in an Autistic Child*. London: Academic Press.

Selfe, L. (1983). *Normal and Anomalous Representational Drawing Ability in Children*. London: Academic Press.

Serafica, F. C. (1990). Peer relations of children with Down syndrome. In D. Cicchetti & M. Beeghly (eds), *Children with Down syndrome: A Developmental Perspective*. Cambridge: Cambridge University Press.

Serafica, F. C., & Cicchetti, D. (1976). Down's syndrome children in a strange situation: Attachment and exploratory behaviors. *Merrill-Palmer Quarterly*, *22*, 137–150.

Shah, A., & Frith, U. (1983). An islet of ability in autistic children: A research note. *Journal of Child Psychology and Psychiatry*, *24*, 613–620.

Shah, A., & Frith, U. (1993). Why do autistic individuals show superior performance on the Block Design task? *Journal of Child Psychology and Psychiatry*, *34*, 1351–1364.

Shaw, J., & Jamieson, J. (1995). Interactions of an integrated deaf child with his hearing partners: A Vygotskian perspective. *ACEHI Journal*, *21*, 4–29.

Shaw, J., & Jamieson, J. (1997). Patterns of classroom discourse in an integrated, interpreted elementary school setting. *American Annals of the Deaf*, *142*, 40–47.

Sheinkopf, S. J., Mundy, P., Oller, D. K., & Steffens, M. (2000). Vocal atypicalities of preverbal autistic children. *Journal of Autism and Developmental Disorders*, *30*, 345–354.

Shepperdson, B. (1995). Two longitudinal studies of the abilities of people with Down's syndrome. *Journal of Intellectual Disability Research*, *39*, 419–431.

Shipe, D., & Shotwell, A. M. (1965). Effect of out-of-home care on mongoloid children: A continuation study. *American Journal of Mental Deficiency*, *69*, 649–652.

Shumway-Cook, A., & Woollacott, M. H. (1985). Dynamics of postural control in the child with Down syndrome. *Physical Therapy*, *65*, 1315–1322.

Shurtleff, D. B., & Lemire, R. J. (1995). Epidemiology, etiologic factors, and pre-natal diagnosis of open spinal dysraphism. *Neurosurgery Clinics of North America*, 6, 183–194.

Shuttleworth, G. E. (1883). Physical features of idiocy in relation to classification and prognosis. *Liverpool Medico-Chirurgical Journal*, 3, 282–301.

Shuttleworth, G. E. (1900). *Mentally-deficient Children: Their Treatment and Training*. London: P. Blakiston's.

Siegel, D. J., Minshew, N. J., & Goldstein, G. (1996). Wechsler IQ profiles in diagnosis of high-functioning autism. *Journal of Autism and Developmental Disorders*, 26, 389–406.

Sigman, M., & Mundy, P. (1989). The development of social attachments in children with autism. *Journal of the American Academy of Child and Adolescent Psychiatry*, 28, 74–81.

Sigman, M., & Ruskin, E. (1999). Continuity and change in the social competence of children with autism, Down syndrome, and developmental delays. *Monographs of the Society for Research in Child Development*, 64, 1–114.

Sigman, M., Kasari, C., Kwon, J., & Yirmiya, N. (1992). Responses to the negative emotions of others by autistic, mentally retarded and normal children. *Child Development*, 63, 796–807.

Sigmundsson, H. (1999). Inter-modal matching and bimanual co-ordination in children with hand-eye co-ordination problems. *Nordisk Fysioterapi*, 3, 55–64.

Sigmundsson, H., Ingvaldsen, R. P., & Whiting, H. T. A. (1997a). Inter- and intra-sensory modality matching in children with hand-eye coordination problems. *Experimental Brain Research*, 114, 492–499.

Sigmundsson, H., Ingvaldsen, R. P., & Whiting, H. T. A. (1997b). Inter- and intrasensory modality matching in children with hand-eye coordination problems: Exploring the developmental lag hypothesis. *Developmental Medicine and Child Neurology*, 39, 790–796.

Sigmundsson, H., Whiting, H. T. A., & Ingvaldsen, R. P. (1999). "Putting your foot in it!" A window into clumsy behaviour. *Behavioural Brain Research*, 102, 129–136.

Simmons, F. B. (1977). Automated screening test for newborns. The Crib-o-gram. In B. F. Joffe (ed.), *Hearing Loss in Children*. London: University Park Press.

Sinet, P.-M. (1999). Towards the identification of the genes involved in the pathogenesis of Down syndrome. In J. A. Rondal, J. Perera, & L. Nadel (eds), *Down Syndrome: A Review of Current Knowledge*. London: Whurr Publishers Ltd.

Sinkkonen, J. (1994). *Hearing Impairment: Communication and Personality Development*. Helsink: Department of Child Psychiatry, University of Helsinki.

Sinson, J. C., & Wetherick, N. E. (1981). The behavior of children with Down syndrome in normal playgroups. *Journal of Mental Deficiency Research*, 25, 113–120.

Sinson, J. C., & Wetherick, N. E. (1982). Mutual gaze in preschool Down and normal children. *Journal of Mental Health Deficiency Research*, 26, 123–129.

Sisco, F. H., & Anderson, R. J. (1980). Deaf children's performance on the WISC-R relative to hearing status of parents and child-rearing experiences. *American Annals of the Deaf*, 125, 923–930.

Skellenger, A. C., Rosenblum, L. P., & Jager, B. K. (1997). Behaviors of preschoolers with visual impairments in indoor play settings. *Journal of Visual Impairment and Blindness, 91*, 519–530.

Skorji, V., & McKenzie, B. (1997). How do children who are clumsy remember modelled movements? *Developmental Medicine and Child Neurology, 39*, 404–408.

Skuse, D. H. (1993). Extreme deprivation in early childhood. In D. V. M. Bishop & K. Mogford (eds), *Language Development in Exceptional Circumstances.* Hove, Sussex: Erlbaum.

Sloper, P., & Turner, S. (1993). Determinants of parental satisfaction with disclosure of disability. *Developmental Medicine and Child Neurology, 35*, 816–825.

Sloper, P., Cunningham, C. C., Turner, S., & Knussen, C. (1990a). Factors related to the academic attainments of children with Down's syndrome. *British Journal of Educational Psychology, 60*, 284–298.

Sloper, P., Turner, S., Knussen, C., & Cunningham, C. C. (1990b). Social life of school children with Down's syndrome. *Child: Care, Health and Development, 16*, 235–251.

Smith, B. L., & Stoel-Gammon, C. (1996). A quantitative analysis of reduplicated and variegated babbling in vocalizations by Down syndrome infants. *Clinical Linguistics and Phonetics, 10*, 119–129.

Smith, I. M., & Bryson, S. E. (1994). Imitation and action in autism: A critical review. *Psychological Bulletin, 116*, 259–273.

Smith, M. M. (1989). Reading without speech: A study of children with cerebral palsy. *The Irish Journal of Psychology, 10*, 601–614.

Smithells, R. W., Sheppard, S., Schorah, C. J., Sellar, M. J., Nevin, N. C., & Harris, R. (1981). Vitamin supplementation and neural tube defects. *Lancet, 2*, 1424–1425.

Smyth, M. M., & Anderson, H. I. (2000). Coping with clumsiness in the school playground: Social and physical play in children with coordination impairments. *British Journal of Developmental Psychology, 18*, 389–413.

Smyth, M. M., & Mason, U. C. (1997). Planning and execution of action in children with and without developmental coordination disorder. *Journal of Child Psychology and Psychiatry, 38*, 1023–1037.

Smyth, M. M., & Mason, U. C. (1998). Direction of response in aiming to visual and proprioceptive targets in children with and without developmental coordination disorder. *Human Movement Science, 17*, 515–539.

Smyth, T. R. (1991). Abnormal clumsiness in children: A defect of motor programming? *Child: Care, Health and Development, 17*, 283–294.

Smyth, T. R. (1992). Impaired motor skill (clumsiness) in otherwise normal children: A review. *Child: Care, Health and Development, 18*, 283–300.

Smyth, T. R. (1994). Clumsiness in children: A defect of kinaesthetic perception? *Child: Care, Health and Development, 20*, 27–36.

Smyth, T. R. (1996). Clumsiness: Kinaesthetic perception and translation. *Child: Care, Health and Development, 22*, 1–9.

Snow, J. H. (1999). Executive processes for children with spina bifida. *Children's Health Care, 28*, 241–253.

Snow, J. H., Prince, M., Souheaver, G., Ashcraft, E., Stefans, V., & Edmonds, J.

(1994). Neuropsychological patterns of adolescents and young adults with spina bifida. *Archives of Clinical Neuropsychology, 9,* 277–287.

So, L. K. H., & Dodd, B. J. (1994). Down's syndrome and the acquisition of phonology by Cantonese-speaking children. *Journal of Intellectual Disability Research, 38,* 501–517.

Sparrow, S. S., Balla, D., & Cicchetti, D. (1984). *Vineland Adaptive Behavior Scales (Survey Form).* Circle Pines, MN: American Guidance Service.

Spencer, P. (1993a). Communication behaviors of infants with hearing loss and their hearing mothers. *Journal of Speech and Hearing Research, 36,* 311–321.

Spencer, P. E. (1993b). The expressive communication of hearing mothers and deaf infants. *American Annals of the Deaf, 138,* 275–283.

Spencer, P. E. (1996). The association between language and symbolic play at two years: Evidence from deaf toddlers. *Child Development, 67,* 867–876.

Spencer, P. E., & Deyo, D. A. (1993). Cognitive and social aspects of deaf children's play. In M. Marschark & M. D. Clark (eds), *Psychological Perspectives on Deafness.* Hillsdale, New Jersey: Erlbaum.

Spencer, P. E., & Lederberg, A. R. (1997). Different modes, different models: Communication and language of young deaf children and their mothers. In L. B. Adamson & M. A. Romski (eds), *Communication and Language Acquisition: Discoveries from Atypical Development.* Baltimore, Maryland: Paul H. Brookes Publishing Co.

Spencer, P. E., & Meadow-Orlans, K. P. (1996). Play, language, and maternal responsiveness: A longitudinal study of deaf and hearing infants. *Child Development, 67,* 3176–3191.

Spencer, P. E., Bodner-Johnson, B. A., & Gutfreund, M. K. (1992). Interacting with infants with a hearing loss: What can we learn from mothers who are deaf? *Journal of Early Intervention, 16,* 64–78.

Spencer, P. E., Koester, L. S., & Meadow-Orlans, K. P. (1994). Communicative interactions of deaf and hearing children in a day care centre. *American Annals of the Deaf, 139,* 512–518.

Spiker, D., & Ricks, M. (1984). Visual self-recognition in autistic children: Developmental relationships. *Child Development, 55,* 214–225.

St. James, P. J., & Tager-Flusberg, H. (1994). An observational study of humor in autism and Down syndrome. *Journal of Autism and Developmental Disorders, 24,* 603–617.

Steffenburg, S., Gillberg, C., Hellgren, L., Anderson, L., Gillberg, I., & Jakobsson, G. (1989). A twin study of autism in Denmark, Finland, Iceland, Norway, and Sweden. *Journal of Child Psychology and Psychiatry, 30,* 405–416.

Sterne, A., & Goswami, U. (2000). Phonological awareness of syllables, rhymes, and phonemes in deaf children. *Journal of Child Psychology and Psychiatry, 41,* 609–625.

Stith, L. E., & Fishbein, H. D. (1996). Basic money-counting skills of children with mental retardation. *Research in Developmental Disabilities, 17,* 185–201.

Stoel-Gammon, C. (1997). Phonological development in Down syndrome. *Mental Retardation and Developmental Disabilities Research Reviews, 3,* 300–306.

Stone, V. E. (2000). The role of the frontal lobes and the amygdala in theory of mind. In S. Baron-Cohen, H. Tager-Flusberg, & D. J. Cohen (eds), *Understand-*

ing Other Minds: Perspectives from Autism. 2nd edition. Oxford: Oxford University Press.

Stone, W. L., Lee, E. B., Ashford, L., Brissie, J., Hepburn, S. L., & Coonrod, E. E. (1999a). Can autism be diagnosed accurately in children under 3 years? *Journal of Child Psychology and Psychiatry, 40,* 219–226.

Stone, W. L., Ousley, O. P., Hepburn, S. L., Hogan, K. L., & Brown, C. S. (1999b). Patterns of adaptive behavior in very young children with autism. *American Journal on Mental Retardation, 104,* 187–199.

Stone, W. L., Ousley, O. Y., Yoder, P. J., Hogan, K. L., & Hepburn, S. L. (1997). Nonverbal communication in two- and three-year-old children with autism. *Journal of Autism and Developmental Disorders, 27,* 677–696.

Stores, R. (1993). A preliminary study of sleep disorders and daytime behaviour problems in children with Down's syndrome. *Down's Syndrome: Research and Practice, 1,* 29–33.

Stratford, B., & Ching, E. Y.-Y. (1983). Rhythm and time in the perception of Down's syndrome children. *Journal of Mental Deficiency Research, 27,* 23–38.

Stratford, B., & Ching, E. Y.-Y. (1989). Responses to music and movement in the development of children with Down's syndrome. *Journal of Mental Deficiency Research, 33,* 13–24.

Sugden, D., & Utley, A. (1995a). Interlimb coupling in children with hemiplegic cerebral palsy. *Developmental Medicine and Child Neurology, 37,* 293–309.

Sugden, D., & Utley, A. (1995b). Vocabulary of grips in children with hemiplegic cerebral palsy. *Physiotherapy Theory and Practice, 11,* 67–79.

Summers, M., Hahs, J., & Summers, C. R. (1997). Conversational patterns of children with disabled and nondisabled siblings. *Applied Psycholinguistics, 18,* 277–291.

Sutherland, G. A. (1899). Mongolian imbecility in infants. *Practitioner, 63,* 632–642.

Svirsky, M. A., Robbins, A. M., Kirk, K. I., Pisoni, D. B., & Miyamoto, R. T. (2000). Language development in profoundly deaf children with cochlear implants. *Psychological Science, 11,* 153–158.

Swettenham, J. (1996). Can children with autism be taught to understand false belief using computers? *Journal of Child Psychology and Psychiatry, 37,* 157–165.

Swettenham, J. (2000). Teaching theory of mind to individuals with autism. In S. Baron-Cohen, H. Tager-Flusberg, & D. J. Cohen (eds), *Understanding Other Minds: Perspectives from Autism.* 2nd edition. Oxford: Oxford University Press.

Swettenham, J., Baron-Cohen, S., Charman, T., Cox, A., Baird, G., & Drew, A. (1998). The frequency and distribution of spontaneous attention shifts between social and nonsocial stimuli in autistic, typically developing, and nonautistic developmentally delayed infants. *Journal of Child Psychology and Psychiatry, 39,* 747–754.

Szatmari, P., Jones, M. B., Zwaigenbaum, L., & MacLean, J. E. (1998). Genetics of autism: Overview and new directions. *Journal of Autism and Developmental Disorders, 28,* 351–368.

Tager-Flusberg, H. (1992). Autistic children's talk about psychological states: Deficits in the early acquisition of a theory of mind. *Child Development, 63,*

161–172.

Tager-Flusberg, H. (1993). What language reveals about the understanding of minds in children with autism. In S. Baron-Cohen, H. Tager-Flusberg, & D. J. Cohen (eds), *Understanding Other Minds: Perspectives from Autism*. Oxford: Oxford University Press.

Tager-Flusberg, H. (1995). "Once upon a ribbit": Stories narrated by autistic children. *British Journal of Developmental Psychology*, 13, 45–59.

Tager-Flusberg, H. (2000). Language and understanding minds: Connections in autism. In S. Baron-Cohen, H. Tager-Flusberg, & D. J. Cohen (eds), *Understanding Other Minds: Perspectives from Autism*. 2nd edition. Oxford: Oxford University Press.

Tager-Flusberg, H. (2001). A reexamination of the theory of mind hypothesis of autism. In J. A. Burack, T. Charman, N. Yirmiya, & P. R. Zelazo (eds), *The Development of Autism: Perspectives from Theory and Research*. London: Erlbaum.

Tager-Flusberg, H., & Anderson, M. (1991). The development of contingent discourse ability in autistic children. *Journal of Child Psychology and Psychiatry*, 32, 1123–1134.

Tager-Flusberg, H., & Sullivan, K. (1994). Predicting and explaining behavior: A comparison of autistic, mentally retarded and normal children. *Journal of Child Psychology and Psychiatry*, 35, 1059–1076.

Tait, P. (1972). Behavior of young blind children in a controlled play session. *Perception and Motor Skills*, 34, 963–969.

Tantam, D., Monaghan, L., Nicholson, H., & Stirling, J. (1989). Autistic children's ability to interpret faces: A research note. *Journal of Child Psychology and Psychiatry*, 30, 623–630.

Taylor, B., Miller, E., Farrington, C. P., Petropoulos, M. C., Favot-Mayaud, I., & Li, J. (1999). Autism and measles, mumps, and rubella vaccine: No epidemiological evidence for a causal association. *Lancet*, 353, 2026–2029.

Teplin, S. W. (1995). Visual impairment in infants and young children. *Infants and Young Children*, 8, 18–51.

Tew, B. (1979). The "cocktail party syndrome" in children with hydrocephalus and spina bifida. *Journal of Disorders of Communication*, 14, 89–101.

Tew, B. J., & Laurence, K. M. (1972). The ability and attainment of spina bifida patients born in South Wales between 1956–1962. *Developmental Medicine and Child Neurology, Supplement 27*, 124–131.

Thompson, R., Cicchetti, D., Lamb, M., & Malkin, K. (1985). The emotional responses of Down syndrome and normal infants in the strange situation: The organisation of affective behavior in infants. *Developmental Psychology*, 21, 828–841.

Tillman, M. H. (1967a). The performance of blind and sighted children on the Wechsler Intelligence Scale for Children: Study I. *International Journal for the Education of the Blind*, 16, 65–74.

Tillman, M. H. (1967b). The performance of blind and sighted children on the Wechsler Intelligence Scale for Children: Study II. *International Journal for the Education of the Blind*, 16, 106–112.

Tillman, M. H. (1973). Intelligence scales for the blind: A review with implications for research. *Journal of School Psychology, 11*, 80–87.

Tingley, E. C., Gleason, J. B., & Hooshyar, N. (1994). Mothers' lexicon of internal state words in speech to children with Down syndrome and to nonhandicapped children at mealtime. *Journal of Communication Disorders, 27*, 135–155.

Tirosh, E., Schnitzer, M. R., Atar, S., & Jaffe, M. (1992). Severe visual deficits in infancy in Northern Israel: An epidemiological perspective. *Journal of Pediatric Ophthalmology and Strabismus, 29*, 366–369.

Tirosh, E., Schnitzer, M. R., Davidovitch, M., & Cohen, A. (1998). Behavioural problems among visually impaired between 6 months and 5 years. *International Journal of Rehabilitation Research, 21*, 63–70.

Tizard, J. (1960). The residential care of mentally handicapped children. *Proceedings of London Conference on the Scientific Aspects of Mental Deficiency, 2*, 659–666.

Tjio, J. H., & Levan, A. (1956). The chromosome number in man. *Hereditas, 42*, 1–6.

Tobin, M. J. (1972). Conservation of substance in the blind and partially sighted. *British Journal of Educational Psychology, 42*, 192–197.

Tobin, M. J. (1992). The language of blind children: Communication, words, and meanings. *Language and Education: An International Journal, 6*, 177–182.

Tobin, M. J. (1994). *Assessing Visually Handicapped People: An Introduction to Test Procedures*. London: David Fulton Publishers.

Tobin, M. J., Bozic, N., Douglas, G., Greaney, J., & Ross, S. (1997). Visually impaired children: Development and implications for education. *European Journal of Psychology of Education, 12*, 431–447.

Tobin, M. J., Tooze, F. H. G., Chapman, E. K., & Moss, S. C. (1978). *Look and Think: A Handbook on Visual Perception Training for Severely Visually Handicapped Children*. London: Schools Council.

Todman, J., & Seedhouse, E. (1994). Visual-action code processing by deaf and hearing children. *Language and Cognitive Processes, 9*, 129–141.

Tomblin, J. B., Spencer, L., Flock, S., Tyler, R., & Gantz, B. (1999). A comparison of language achievement in children with cochlear implants and children using hearing aids. *Journal of Speech, Language, and Hearing Research, 42*, 497–511.

Torfs, C. P., & Christianson, R. E. (1998). Anomalies in Down syndrome individuals in a large population-based registry. *American Journal of Medical Genetics, 77*, 431–438.

Travis, L., Sigman, M., & Ruskin, E. (2001). Links between social understanding and social behavior in verbally able children with autism. *Journal of Autism and Developmental Disorders, 31*, 119–130.

Tredgold, A. F. (1908). *Mental Deficiency (Amentia)*. London: Baillière, Tindall and Cox.

Tröster, H., & Brambring, M. (1992). Early social-emotional development in blind infants. *Child: Care, Health and Development, 18*, 207–227.

Tröster, H., & Brambring, M. (1994). The play behavior and play materials of blind and sighted infants and preschoolers. *Journal of Visual Impairment and Blindness, 88*, 421–432.

Tröster, H., Brambring, M., & Beelmann, A. (1991a). Prevalence and situational causes of stereotyped behaviors in blind infants and preschoolers. *Journal of Abnormal Child Psychology, 19, 569–590.*

Tröster, H., Brambring, M., & Beelmann, A. (1991b). The age dependence of stereotyped behaviours in blind infants and preschoolers. *Child: Care, Health and Development, 17, 137–157.*

Tröster, H., Brambring, M., & Beelmann, A. (1991c). Prevalence and situational causes of stereotyped behaviors in blind infants and preschoolers. *Journal of Abnormal Child Psychology, 19, 569–590.*

Turner, M. A. (1999a). Annotation: Repetitive behaviour in autism: A review of psychological research. *Journal of Child Psychology and Psychiatry, 40, 839–849.*

Turner, M. A. (1999b). Generating novel ideas: Fluency performance in high-functioning and learning disabled individuals with autism. *Journal of Child Psychology and Psychiatry, 40, 189–201.*

Turner, S., & Sloper, P. (1996). Behaviour problems among children with Down's syndrome: Prevalence, persistence and parental appraisal. *Journal of Applied Research in Intellectual Disabilities, 9, 129–144.*

Turner, S., Sloper, P., Knussen, C., & Cunningham, C. C. (1991). Factors relating to self-sufficiency in children with Down's syndrome. *Journal of Mental Deficiency Research, 35, 13–24.*

Uecker, A., Mangan, P. A., Obrzut, J. E., & Nadel, L. (1993). Down syndrome in neurobiological perspective: An emphasis on spatial cognition. *Journal of Clinical Child Psychology, 22, 266–276.*

Ungar, S., Blades, M., & Spencer, C. (1995a). Mental rotation of a tactile layout by young visually impaired children. *Perception, 24, 891–900.*

Ungar, S., Blades, M., & Spencer, C. (1995b). Visually impaired children's strategies for memorizing a map. *British Journal of Visual Impairment, 13, 27–32.*

Ungar, S., Blades, M., & Spencer, C. (1996). The ability of visually impaired children to locate themselves on a tactile map. *Journal of Visual Impairment and Blindness, 90, 526–535.*

Ungar, S., Blades, M., & Spencer, C. (1997). Teaching visually impaired children to make distance judgments from a tactile map. *Journal of Visual Impairment and Blindness, 91, 163–174.*

Urwin, C. (1978). "The Development of Communication between Blind Infants and their Parents: Some Ways into Language." Unpublished Ph.D. thesis, University of Cambridge.

Urwin, C. (1981). Early language development in blind children. *The British Psychological Society Division of Educational and Child Psychology Occasional Papers, 5, 78–93.*

Urwin, C. (1983). Dialogue and cognitive functioning in the early language development of three blind children. In A. E. Mills (ed.), *Language Acquisition in the Blind Child.* London: Croom Helm.

Utley, A., & Sugden, D. (1998). Interlimb coupling in children with hemiplegic cerebral palsy during reaching and grasping at speed. *Developmental Medicine and Child Neurology, 40, 396–404.*

Vallar, G., & Papagno, C. (1993). Preserved vocabulary acquisition in Down's syndrome: The role of phonological short-term memory. *Cortex, 29,* 467–483.

Van Borsel, J. (1996). Articulation in Down's syndrome adolescents and adults. *European Journal of Disorders of Communication, 31,* 415–444.

van der Meulen, J. H. P., Denier van der Gon, J. J., Gielen, C. C. A. M., Gooskens, R. H. J. M., & Willemse, J. (1991a). Visuomotor performance of normal and clumsy children. I: Fast goal-directed arm-movements with and without visual feedback. *Developmental Medicine and Child Neurology, 33,* 40–54.

van der Meulen, J. H. P., Denier van der Gon, J. J., Gielen, C. C. A. M., Gooskens, R. H. J. M., & Willemse, J. (1991b). Visuomotor performance of normal and clumsy children. II: Arm-tracking with and without visual feedback. *Developmental Medicine and Child Neurology, 33,* 118–129.

Van Mier, H., Hulstijn, W., & Meulenbroek, R. G. J. (1994). Movement planning in children with motor disorders: Diagnostic implications of pattern complexity and previewing in copying. *Developmental Neuropsychology, 10,* 231–254.

Vaughn, B. E., Goldberg, S., Atkinson, L., Marcovitch, S., MacGregor, D., & Seifer, R. (1994). Quality of toddler-mother attachment in children with Down syndrome: Limits to interpretation of strange situation behavior. *Child Development, 65,* 95–108.

Vernon, McC. (1967). Relationship of language to the thinking process. *Archives of General Psychiatry, 16,* 325–333.

Vettel, J. K., & Windsor, J. (1997). Maternal wait time after questions for children with and without Down syndrome. *Research in Developmental Disabilities, 18,* 93–100.

Vicari, S., Bellucci, S., & Carlesimo, G. A. (2000a). Implicit and explicit memory: A functional dissociation in persons with Down syndrome. *Neuropsychologia, 38,* 240–251.

Vicari, S., Caselli, M. C., & Tonucci, F. (2000b). Asynchrony of lexical and morphosyntactic development in children with Down syndrome. *Neuropsychologia, 38,* 634–644.

Vietze, P., McCarthy, M., McQuiston, S., MacTurk, R., & Yarrow, L. (1983). Attention and exploratory behavior in infants with Down syndrome. In T. Field & A. Sostek (eds), *Infants Born at Risk: Perceptual and Physical Processes.* New York: Grune and Stratton.

Visser, J., Geuze, R. H., & Kalverboer, A. F. (1998). The relationship between physical growth, the level of activity and the development of motor skills in adolescence: Differences between children with DCD and controls. *Human Movement Science, 17,* 573–608.

Volkmar, F. R., & Cohen, D. J. (1991). Debate and Argument: The utility of the term pervasive developmental disorder. *Journal of Child Psychology and Psychiatry, 32,* 1171–1172.

Volkmar, F. R., Szatmari, P., & Sparrow, S. S. (1993). Sex differences in Pervasive Developmental Disorders. *Journal of Autism and Developmental Disorders, 23,* 579–591.

Vostanis, P., Hayes, M., & Du Feu, M. (1997a). Behavioural and emotional problems in hearing impaired children: A preliminary study of teacher and parent ratings. *European Journal of Special Needs Education, 12,* 239–246.

Vostanis, P., Hayes, M., Du Feu, M., & Warren, J. (1997b). Detection of behavioural and emotional problems in deaf children and adolescents: Comparison of two rating scales. *Child: Care, Health and Development, 23*, 233–246.

Vygotsky, L. S. (1962). *Thought and Language.* Cambridge, Massachusetts: MIT Press.

Waardenburg, P. J. (1932). *Das menschliche Auge und seine Erbanlagen.* The Hague: Martinus Nijhoff.

Wade, M. G., Van Emmerik, R., & Kernozek, T. W. (2000). Atypical dynamics of motor behavior in Down syndrome. In D. Weeks, R. Chua, & D. Elliott (eds), *Perceptual-Motor Behavior in Down Syndrome.* Champaign, IL: Human Kinetics.

Wagner, S., Ganiban, J., & Cicchetti, D. (1990). Attention, memory, and perception in infants with Down syndrome: A review and commentary. In D. Cicchetti & M. Beeghly (eds), *Children with Down syndrome: A Developmental Perspective.* Cambridge: Cambridge University Press.

Walden, T. A., & Ogan, T. A. (1988). The development of social referencing. *Child Development, 59*, 1230–1240.

Walker, E. C., Tobin, M. J., & McKennell, A. C. (1992). *Blind and Partially-sighted Children in Britain: The RNIB Survey, 2.* London: HMSO.

Walker, J. A., & Crawley, S. B. (1983). Conceptual and methodological issues in studying the handicapped infant. In S. Gray Garwood & R. R. Fewell (eds), *Educating Handicapped Infants: Issues in Development and Intervention.* Rockville, Maryland: Aspen Systems Corporation.

Wallander, J. L., Feldman, W. S., & Varni, J. W. (1989a). Physical status and psychosocial adjustment in children with spina bifida. *Journal of Pediatric Psychology, 14*, 89–102.

Wallander, J. L., Hubert, N. C., & Varni, J. W. (1988). Child and maternal temperament characteristics, goodness of fit, and adjustment in physically handicapped children. *Journal of Clinical Child Psychology, 17*, 336–344.

Wallander, J. L., Varni, J. W., Babani, L., Banis, H. T., DeHaan, C. B., & Wilcox, K. T. (1989b). Disability parameters, chronic strain, and adaptation of physically handicapped children and their mothers. *Journal of Pediatric Psychology, 14*, 23–42.

Wann, J. P. (1991). The integrity of visual-proprioceptive mapping in cerebral palsy. *Neuropsychologia, 29*, 1095–1106.

Wann, J. P., Mon-Williams, M., & Carson, R. G. (1998a). Assessing manual control in children with coordination difficulties. In K. J. Connolly (ed.), *The Psychobiology of the Hand.* London: Mac Keith Press.

Wann, J. P., Mon-Williams, M., & Rushton, K. (1998b). Postural control and coordination disorders: The swinging room revisited. *Human Movement Science, 17*, 491–513.

Warren, D. H. (1977). *Blindness and Early Childhood Development.* New York: American Foundation for the Blind.

Warren, D. H. (1984). *Blindness and Early Child Development.* 2nd edition. New York: American Foundation for the Blind.

Waterhouse, L., Fein, D., & Modahl, C. (1996). Neurofunctional mechanisms in autism. *Psychological Review, 103*, 457–489.

Watson, J. B. (1913). Psychology as the behaviorist views it. *Psychological Review*, 20, 158–177.

Watson, L. R. (1998). Following the child's lead: Mothers' interactions with children with autism. *Journal of Autism and Developmental Disorders*, 28, 51–59.

Webster, A., & Roe, J. (1998). *Children with Visual Impairments: Social Interaction, Language and Learning*. London: Routledge.

Wechsler, D. (1974). *Manual for the Intelligence Scale for Children*. Revised edition. New York: The Psychological Corporation.

Weinberg, B., & Zlatin, M. (1970). Speaking fundamental frequency characteristics of five- and six-year-old children with mongolism. *Journal of Speech and Hearing Research*, 13, 418–425.

Werner, E., Dawson, G., Osterling, J., & Dinno, N. (2000). Brief report: Recognition of autism spectrum disorder before one year of age: A retrospective study based on home videotapes. *Journal of Autism and Developmental Disorders*, 30, 157–162.

Whorf, B. L. (1940). Science and linguistics. *Technology Review*, 42, 227–231, 247–248.

Wiegersma, P. H., & Van der Velde, A. (1983). Motor development of deaf children. *Journal of Child Psychology and Psychiatry*, 24, 103–111.

Wilbur, R. B. (1987). *American Sign Language: Linguistic and Applied Dimensions*. 2nd edition. Boston: College Hill.

Williams, E., Reddy, V., & Costall, A. (2001). Taking a closer look at functional play in children with autism. *Journal of Autism and Developmental Disorders*, 31, 67–77.

Williams, H. G., Woollacott, M. H., & Ivry, R. (1992). Timing and motor control in clumsy children. *Journal of Motor Behavior*, 24, 165–172.

Williams, M. (1956). *Intelligence Test for Children with Defective Vision*. Birmingham: University of Birmingham.

Williams, M. (1968). Superior intelligence of children blinded from retinoblastoma. *Archives of Diseases of Childhood*, 43, 204–210.

Williams, M. (1971). Braille reading. *The Teacher of the Blind*, 59, 103–116.

Wills, D. M. (1970). Vulnerable periods in the early development of blind children. *Psychoanalytic Study of the Child*, 25, 461–480.

Wills, D. M. (1981). Entry into boarding school and after. *The British Psychological Society Division of Educational and Child Psychology Occasional Papers*, 5, 42–47.

Wills, K. E. (1993). Neuropsychological functioning in children with spina bifida and/or hydrocephalus. *Journal of Clinical Child Psychology*, 22, 247–265.

Wills, K. E., Holmbeck, G. N., Dillon, K., & McLone, D. G. (1990). Intelligence and achievement in children with myelomeningocele. *Journal of Pediatric Psychology*, 15, 161–176.

Wilson, M., & Emmorey, K. (1998). A "word length effect" for sign language: Further evidence for the role of language in structuring working memory. *Memory and Cognition*, 26, 584–590.

Wilson, M. M. (1970). Children with cerebral palsy. *Education Survey*, No 7. London: H.M.S.O.

Wilson, P. H., & Maruff, P. (1999). Deficits in the endogenous control of covert visuospatial attention in children with developmental coordination disorder. *Human Movement Science, 18*, 421–442.

Wilson, P. H., & McKenzie, B. E. (1998). Information processing deficits associated with developmental coordination disorder: A meta-analysis of research findings. *Journal of Child Psychology and Psychiatry, 39*, 829–840.

Wilson, P. H., Maruff, P., & McKenzie, B. E. (1997). Covert orienting of visuospatial attention in children with developmental coordination disorder. *Developmental Medicine and Child Neurology, 39*, 736–745.

Wilson, T., & Hyde, M. (1997). The use of signed English pictures to facilitate reading comprehension by deaf students. *American Annals of the Deaf, 142*, 333–341.

Wiltshire, S. (1987). *Drawings*. London: J. M. Dent.

Wimpory, D. C., Hobson, R. P., Williams, J. M. G., & Nash, S. (2000). Are infants with autism socially engaged? A study of recent retrospective parental reports. *Journal of Autism and Developmental Disorders, 30*, 525–536.

Wing, L. (1969). The handicaps of autistic children – a comparative study. *Journal of Child Psychology and Psychiatry, 10*, 1–40.

Wing, L. (ed.) (1976). *Early Childhood Autism*. 2nd edition. Oxford: Pergamon Press.

Wing, L. (1988). The continuum of autistic characteristics. In E. Schopler & G. Mesibov (eds), *Diagnosis and Assessment in Autism*. New York: Plenum Press.

Wing, L. (1997). The autistic spectrum. *Lancet, 350*, 1761–1766.

Wishart, J. G. (1987). Performance of young non-retarded children and children with Down syndrome on Piagetian infant search tasks. *American Journal of Mental Deficiency, 92*, 169–177.

Wishart, J. G. (1988). Early learning in infants and young children with Down syndrome. In L. Nadel (ed.), *The Psychobiology of Down syndrome*. London: MIT Press.

Wishart, J. G. (1990). Learning to learn: The difficulties faced by infants and young children with Down's syndrome. In W. I. Fraser (ed.), *Key Issues in Mental Retardation Research*. London: Routledge.

Wishart, J. G. (1991). Taking the initiative in learning: A developmental investigation of infants with Down syndrome. *International Journal of Disability, Development and Education, 38*, 27–44.

Wishart, J. G. (1993). The development of learning difficulties in children with Down's syndrome. *Journal of Intellectual Disability Research, 37*, 389–403.

Wishart, J. G. (1998). Development in children with Down syndrome: Facts, findings, the future. *International Journal of Disability, Development and Education, 45*, 343–363.

Wishart, J. G., & Duffy, L. (1990). Instability of performance on cognitive tests in infants and young children with Down's syndrome. *British Journal of Educational Psychology, 60*, 10–22.

Witkin, H. A., Oltman, P. K., Chase, J. B., & Friedman, F. (1971). Cognitive patterning in the blind. In J. Hellmuth (ed.), *Cognitive Studies, 2*. New York: Bruner/Mazel.

Wode, H. (1983). Precursors and the study of the impaired language learner. In A. E. Mills (ed.), *Language Acquisition in the Blind Child: Normal and Defi-*

cient. London: Croom Helm.

Wolchik, S. A. (1983). Language patterns of parents of young autistic and normal children. *Journal of Autism and Developmental Disorders*, *13*, 167–180.

Wolman, C., & Basco, D. E. (1994). Factors influencing self-esteem and self-consciousness in adolescents with spina bifida. *Journal of Adolescent Health*, *15*, 543–548.

Wood, D. (1981). Some developmental aspects of prelingual deafness. In B. Woll, J. G. Kyle, & M. Deuchar (eds), *Perspectives on BSL and Deafness*. London: Croom Helm.

Wood, D. J., & Middleton, D. J. (1975). A study of assisted problem solving. *British Journal of Psychology*, *66*, 181–191.

Wood, D., Wood, H., Griffiths, A., & Howarth, I. (1986). *Teaching and Talking with Deaf Children*. Chichester: Wiley.

Woodhouse, J. M., Cregg, M., Gunter, H. L., Sanders, D. P., Saunders, K. J., & Pakeman, V. H. (unpublished). The effect of age, size of target and cognitive factors on accommodative responses of children with Down syndrome.

Woodhouse, J. M., Pakeman, V. H., Cregg, M., Saunders, K. J., Parker, M., & Fraser, W. I. (1997). Refractive errors in young children with Down syndrome. *Optometry and Vision Science*, *74*, 844–851.

Woodhouse, J. M., Pakeman, V. H., Saunders, K. J., Parker, M., Fraser, W. I., & Lobo, S. (1996). Visual acuity and accommodation in infants and young children with Down's syndrome. *Journal of Intellectual Disability Research*, *40*, 49–55.

Woodhouse, W., Bailey, A., Rutter, M., Bolton, P., Baird, G., & Le Couteur, A. (1996). Head circumference in autism and other pervasive developmental disorders. *Journal of Child Psychology and Psychiatry*, *37*, 665–672.

Woolfson, L. H. (1999). Using a model of transactional developmental regulation to evaluate the effectiveness of an early intervention programme for pre-school children with motor impairments. *Child: Care, Health and Development*, *25*, 55–79.

Workman, S. H. (1986). Teachers' verbalizations and the social interaction of blind preschoolers. *Journal of Visual Impairment and Blindness*, *80*, 532–534.

World Health Organization (1980). *International Classification of Impairments, Disabilities, and Handicaps: A Manual of Classification*. Geneva.

World Health Organization (1993). *The ICD-10 Classification of Mental and Behavioural Disorders: Clinical Descriptions and Diagnostic Guidelines*. Geneva.

World Health Organization (2001). *International Classification of Functioning, Disability and Health: Final Draft*. Geneva.

Wright, I. (1998). "The development of representation in children with Down's syndrome." Unpublished Ph.D. thesis, University of Warwick.

Wyver, S. R., & Markham, R. (1998). Do children with visual impairments demonstrate superior short-term memory, memory strategies, and metamemory? *Journal of Visual Impairment and Blindness*, *92*, 799–811.

Yirmiya, N., Erel, O., Shaked, M., & Solomonica-Levi, D. (1998). Meta-analyses comparing theory of mind abilities of individuals with autism, individuals with mental retardation, and normally developing individuals. *Psychological Bulle-*

tin, 124, 283–307.

Yirmiya, N., Kasari, C., Sigman, M., & Mundy, P. (1989). Facial expressions of affect in autistic, mentally retarded and normal children. *Journal of Child Psychology and Psychiatry, 30,* 725–735.

Yirmiya, N., Pilowsky, T., Solomonica-Levi, D., & Shulman, C. (1999). Brief report: Gaze behaviour and theory of mind abilities in individuals with autism, Down syndrome, and mental retardation of unknown etiology. *Journal of Autism and Developmental Disorders, 29,* 333–341.

Yirmiya, N., Solomonica-Levi, D., Shulman, C., & Pilowsky, T. (1996). Theory of mind abilities in individuals with autism, Down syndrome, and mental retardation of unknown etiology: The role of age and intelligence. *Journal of Child Psychology and Psychiatry, 37,* 1003–1014.

Yoder, P. J., Hooshyar, N., Klee, T., & Schaffer, M. (1996). Comparison of the types of child utterances mothers expand in children with language delays and with Down's syndrome. *Journal of Intellectual Disability Research, 40,* 557–567.

Yoshinaga-Itano, C., & Downey, D. M. (1996). The effect of hearing loss on the development of metacognitive strategies in written language. *Volta Review, 98,* 97–143.

Zanandrea, M. (1998). Play, social interaction, and motor development: Practical activities for preschoolers with visual impairments. *Journal of Visual Impairment and Blindness, 92,* 176–188.

Zelazo, P. D., Burack, J. A., Benedetto, E., & Frye, D. (1996). Theory of mind and rule use in individuals with Down's syndrome: A test of the uniqueness and specificity claims. *Journal of Child Psychology and Psychiatry, 37,* 479–484.

Ziatas, K., Durkin, K., & Pratt, C. (1998). Belief term development in children with autism, Asperger syndrome, specific language impairment, and normal development: Links to theory of mind development. *Journal of Child Psychology and Psychiatry, 39,* 755–763.

Zigler, E. (1967). Familial mental retardation: A continuing dilemma. *Science, 155,* 292–298.

Zurmöhle, U.-M., Homann, T., Schroeter, C., Rothgerber, H., Hommel, G., & Ermert, J. A. (1998). Psychosocial adjustment of children with spina bifida. *Journal of Child Neurology, 13,* 64–70.

Subject Index

Name Index